Fractional Calculus: Theory and Applications—Volume I

Fractional Calculus: Theory and Applications—Volume I

Editors

António Lopes
Alireza Alfi
Liping Chen
Sergio Adriani David

MDPI Basel • Beijing • Wuhan • Barcelona • Belgrade • Novi Sad • Cluj • Manchester

Editors
António Lopes
University of Porto
Porto
Portugal

Alireza Alfi
Shahrood University of Technology
Shahrood
Iran

Liping Chen
Hefei University of Technology
Hefei
China

Sergio Adriani David
University of São Paulo
Pirassununga
Brazil

Editorial Office
MDPI
St. Alban-Anlage 66
4052 Basel, Switzerland

This is a reprint of articles from the Topic published online in the open access journals *Fractal and Fractional* (ISSN 2504-3110), *Axioms* (ISSN 2075-1680), *Mathematical and Computational Applications* (ISSN 2297-8747), *Mathematics* (ISSN 2227-7390), and *Symmetry* (ISSN 2073-8994) (available at: https://www.mdpi.com/topics/Fractional_Calculus).

For citation purposes, cite each article independently as indicated on the article page online and as indicated below:

Lastname, A.A.; Lastname, B.B. Article Title. *Journal Name* **Year**, *Volume Number*, Page Range.

Volume I
ISBN 978-3-7258-1145-8 (Hbk)
ISBN 978-3-7258-1146-5 (PDF)
doi.org/10.3390/books978-3-7258-1146-5

Set
ISBN 978-3-7258-1143-4 (Hbk)
ISBN 978-3-7258-1144-1 (PDF)

Contents

Preface

Fractional calculus (FC) generalizes the operations of differentiation and integration to non-integer orders. FC has emerged as an important tool for the study of dynamical systems since fractional order operators are non-local and capture the history of dynamics. Moreover, FC and fractional processes have become one of the most useful approaches to dealing with the particular properties of (long) memory effects in a myriad of applied sciences. Linear, nonlinear, and complex dynamical systems have attracted researchers from many areas of science and technology, involved in systems modelling and control, with applications to real-world problems. Despite the extraordinary advances in FC, addressing both systems' modelling and control, new theoretical developments and applications are still needed in order to accurately describe or control many systems and signals characterized by chaos, bifurcations, criticality, symmetry, memory, scale invariance, fractality, fractionality, and other rich features. This reprint focuses on new and original research results on fractional calculus in science and engineering. Manuscripts address fractional calculus theory, methods for fractional differential and integral equations, nonlinear dynamical systems, advanced control systems, fractals and chaos, complex dynamics, and other topics of interest within FC.

António Lopes, Alireza Alfi, Liping Chen, and Sergio Adriani David
Editors

mathematics

Article

Recursive Identification for MIMO Fractional-Order Hammerstein Model Based on AIAGS

Qibing Jin, Bin Wang * and Zeyu Wang

Institute of Automation, Beijing University of Chemical Technology, Beijing 100020, China; jinqb@mail.buct.edu.cn (Q.J.); wangzeyu@buct.edu.cn (Z.W.)
* Correspondence: 2019210478@buct.edu.cn

Abstract: In this paper, adaptive immune algorithm based on a global search strategy (AIAGS) and auxiliary model recursive least square method (AMRLS) are used to identify the multiple-input multiple-output fractional-order Hammerstein model. The model's nonlinear parameters, linear parameters, and fractional order are unknown. The identification step is to use AIAGS to find the initial values of model coefficients and order at first, then bring the initial values into AMRLS to identify the coefficients and order of the model in turn. The expression of the linear block is the transfer function of the differential equation. By changing the stimulation function of the original algorithm, adopting the global search strategy before the local search strategy in the mutation operation, and adopting the parallel mechanism, AIAGS further strengthens the original algorithm's optimization ability. The experimental results show that the proposed method is effective.

Keywords: adaptive immune algorithm; multiple-input multiple-output; fractional-order model; Hammerstein model; system identification

Citation: Jin, Q.; Wang, B.; Wang, Z. Recursive Identification for MIMO Fractional-Order Hammerstein Model Based on AIAGS. *Mathematics* **2022**, *10*, 212. https://doi.org/10.3390/math10020212

Academic Editors: António M. Lopes, Alireza Alfi, Liping Chen and Sergio A. David

Received: 30 November 2021
Accepted: 9 January 2022
Published: 11 January 2022

1. Introduction

In recent years, with the rapid economic and social development, the complexity of industry has been increasing. In order to understand and control these industrial processes more accurately, it is necessary to study system identification. However, in real life, nonlinear processes are inevitable and widespread. Nowadays, there is no definite characterization for nonlinear processes. A block-oriented model is a description of nonlinear model, which is the result of the interaction between the dynamic linear module and static nonlinear module. These model components can be connected in series, parallel, or feedback [1]. Hammerstein model is a typical block-oriented model that consists of a static nonlinear block in cascade with a dynamic linear block [2]. Because the dynamic behavior of the model is only included in the linear block, and the nonlinear block is static, this feature is conducive to identifying and controlling the nonlinear system constructed by the Hammerstein model [3]. Hammerstein model is extensively used to identify nonlinear systems [4–7]. As the model is widely used, the identification methods are also intensively discussed. These methods include neural networks [8,9], piecewise linear model [6], least square method [10], support vector machine [11], combined prior information [12], and so on.

In real life, it is evident that the dynamic linear block based on integer order cannot fully simulate the real model [13]. The fractional-order model extends the order of the model from the integer level to the fractional level. Therefore, the study of the fractional-order nonlinear model is essential [14]. At present, fractional-order models have been discussed in many fields, such as molecular materials [15,16], the voltage and current of the drive end impedance [17], industrial battery [18–20], and so on.

With the wide application of the fractional-order model, the problem of model identification has also been intensively discussed. However, the current methods have some limitations. The particle swarm optimization algorithm can be used to identify the parameters of the fractional Hammerstein model [21]. This method excessively depends on the optimization ability of the algorithm and does not consider the internal relationship between system parameters. Once the optimization algorithm has problems, it will significantly impact the identification results. The Levenberg–Marquardt algorithm developed by combining the two decomposition principles [22] can only be applied to the theoretical environment. Once the system is affected by noise, the model's parameters will not be identified exactly. Reference [23] also requires an ideal environment. Some scholars pay attention to the fractional-order Hammerstein model with single-input single-output [24–28]. Some pay attention to the fractional-order Hammerstein model with multiple-input multiple-output, but most use the state space equation as the linear block of the model [29,30]. However, fractional-order calculus is a whole concept [31]. Using the transfer function of differential equation to construct the linear block of the Hammerstein model can better integrate the two concepts.

Based on the above background, this paper discusses a new method to identify the nonlinear coefficients, linear coefficients, and fractional order of the MIMO fractional Hammerstein model. In this method, AIAGS greatly improves the optimization ability by improving the immune algorithm's stimulation function and search strategy. Then, the algorithm estimates the initial values of all MIMO fractional Hammerstein model parameters, including fractional order. The estimated result provides relatively accurate initial values for the subsequent algorithm. It solves the problem that the two-step method [28], which identifies coefficient and order, depends on the initial values. Then, using AMRLS, a method for accurate parameter identification of the MIMO fractional-order model is proposed. Finally, the effectiveness of the proposed method is verified by numerical simulation.

The main contribution of this paper is to propose an adaptive immune algorithm with a global search strategy to accurately identify the initial parameters of the fractional Hammerstein system. Secondly, a new recursive identification method for coefficients and fractional order of MIMO fractional-order nonlinear system with differential equation transfer function as linear block model is derived using an auxiliary model. Due to the different ways of selecting the optimal solution, the AIAGS algorithm proposed in this paper has higher reliability than the classical immune algorithm. Based on the auxiliary model, the recursive identification algorithm for the MIMO fractional Hammerstein model is given using the recursive least square method. The method in this paper solves the initial value problem of previous methods and provides more accurate initial values. This initial value cooperates with AMRLS, making the result of parameters identification of multi-input and multi-output fractional Hammerstein model closer to reality.

In this paper, an improved immune algorithm is proposed in Section 2. In Section 3, a new recursive identification method for MIMO fractional-order Hammerstein model with differential equation transfer function as linear block model is derived by using auxiliary model is discussed. In Section 4, numerical simulations show the effectiveness of the proposed method. Finally, Section 5 gives some conclusions.

2. Adaptive Immune Algorithm Based on Global Search Strategy

2.1. Review of Immune Algorithms

The immune algorithm is an adaptive intelligent system inspired by immunology and simulates the functions and principles of the biological immune system to solve complex problems. It retains several characteristics of the biological immune system, including global search capability, diversity maintenance mechanism, strong robustness, and parallel distributed search mechanism. The immune algorithm automatically generates the initial population by uniform probability distribution. After initialization, the population evolves and improves by the following steps: calculation of stimulation, selection, cloning, mutation, clonal inhibition, etc. [32].

2.2. AIAGS

2.2.1. Stimulation Improvement

Individual stimulation is the evaluation result of individual quality, which needs to be comprehensively considered individual affinity and concentration. The individual stimulation can usually be obtained by a simple mathematical calculation based on the evaluation results of individual affinity and concentration. In the traditional immune algorithm [33], the stimulation is expressed as

$$f_{sim}(x_i) = a \cdot f_{aff}(x_i) - b \cdot f_{den}(x_i) \quad (1)$$

where x_i means the ith individual of the population; $f_{aff}(x_i)$ is affinity, which represents the Euclidean distance between the current individual and the optimal individual; $f_{den}(x_i)$ is the concentration, indicating the number of other individuals whose Euclidean distance between the current individual and other individuals is within a certain threshold; $f_{sim}(x_i)$ is the stimulation; a and b is the calculation parameter. The algorithm will sort the individuals according to the stimulation and make the next choice.

This paper made the following changes to the coefficients of affinity and concentration. Firstly, the minus sign of Equation (1) is changed on the plus sign. Because the concentration represents the quality of population diversity, and too high concentration means that there are many very similar individuals in the population, the key point of the immune algorithm is to suppress the individuals with a high concentration to achieve global optimization. However, in both the original algorithm and various improved immune algorithms today, the coefficient b is non-negative, which leads to a minor incentive for individuals with low affinity and high concentration [34–38]. This improvement conforms to the core concept of the algorithm.

Secondly, this paper designs a parameter β related to the current population's maximum, minimum, and individual affinity values. In the original algorithm, the a and b are constants. In various improved algorithms [34–38], the adaptive coefficients are only related to the number of current iterations. Because the comparison of stimulations between individuals is carried out in the population of the current iteration, these adaptive coefficients are not different from constants. They will not affect the stimulation ranking of the population. In this paper, because β is quadratic when selecting individuals based on stimulations, individuals with low affinity and individuals with high affinity will be considered, increasing the global searchability. The parameter is expressed as

$$\beta = \left(\frac{f_{aff}(x_i) - f_{aff_a}}{f_{aff_{max}} - f_{aff_a}} \right)^2 \quad (2)$$

where f_{aff_a} is the average of $f_{aff_{max}}$ and $f_{aff_{min}}$.

Finally, after a certain number of iterations, the population will move closer to the optimal global individual. If the concentration problem is also considered, it may give up the found optimal range and select the new random individual when selecting the individuals. Therefore, a monotone decreasing adaptive operator is designed in this paper. In the middle and later iteration stages, the concentration effect is negligible.

To sum up, the stimulation for this paper is expressed as

$$f_{sim}(x_i) = (1-\beta) \cdot f_{aff}(x_i) + [1 - \sqrt{\frac{2gen}{G} - \left(\frac{gen}{G}\right)^2}] \cdot 0.5\beta \cdot f_{den}(x_i) \quad (3)$$

where gen means the current number of iterations and G is the total number of iterations.

After improvement, the approximate trend of individual stimulations is shown in Figure 1a. The approximate trend of the stimulations of the original or other improved immune algorithm is shown in Figure 1b. The x-axis is 100 individuals sorted from smallest to largest according to affinity, and the y-axis is individual stimulation. It can be seen from Figure 1 that the original algorithm and other improved algorithms generally only select individuals with low affinity. In contrast, the algorithm in this paper can consider individuals with high affinity.

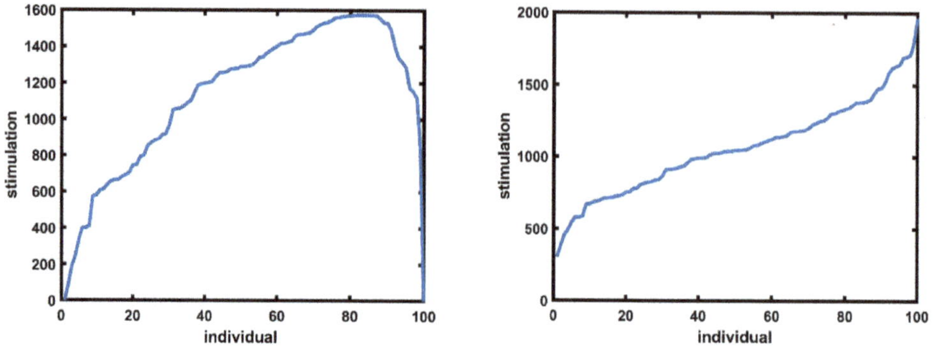

(a) **(b)**

Figure 1. Comparison of stimulations. (**a**) The stimulations of AIAGS. (**b**) The stimulations of other algorithms.

2.2.2. Mutation Strategy Improvement

The original algorithm has a single strategy in the mutation stage. The algorithm improved by others will enrich the mutation strategy and improve the probability of all individuals for mutation. However, the mutation strategy is selected only by random numbers, which makes the algorithm not flexible [38].

The algorithm of this paper has two minor changes in the mutation stage. First, an adaptive operator pm that changes from algebra is designed, and its value decreases monotonically between 0 and 0.8. The parameter can be expressed as

$$pm = 0.8 \cdot \left(1 - \frac{gen}{G}\right) \tag{4}$$

Secondly, when setting the global optimization step, a variable sv is added based on adaptation, gradually changing the mutation step. The optimal individual is selected for retention of the individuals after several mutations, which greatly enhances the global search ability.

To sum up, the mutation strategy for this paper can be expressed as

$$x_{i,j} = \begin{cases} x_{best,j} + pm \cdot (x_{r1,j} - x_{r2,j}), & rand > pm \\ x_{r1,j} + (pm + sv) \cdot (x_{r2,j} - x_{r3,j}), & otherwise \end{cases} \tag{5}$$

where i means the sequence of individuals in the population; j denotes the sequence of dimensions in the individual; x_{r1}, x_{r2}, and x_{r3} are different individuals randomly selected from the population except for the x_i.

Obviously, in the early stage of the iteration, the mutation strategy will mostly choose the second mutation strategy, edge mutation strategy, which will enhance the global optimization ability of the algorithm. In the middle and later stages of the iteration, the first mutation strategy, the optimal individual mutation strategy, will be selected for local search.

2.2.3. Simulated Annealing Strategy

The simulated annealing algorithm mimics the annealing process in metallurgy and is classified as a single-based solution method. After comparing the current optimal solution with the previous optimal solution, if the fitness of the current optimal solution is greater than that of the previous one, it may abandon the current result and choose the previous result [39].

At the end of the improved algorithm, simulated annealing is added to avoid the algorithm falling into the local optimum. Some people have done similar work, but both the initial algorithm and others' improved algorithm use stimulus to evaluate the optimal solution [33]. This paper uses affinity to evaluate the optimal solution at the end. However, the stimulation of the optimal individual of the previous generation may be slightly big, resulting in not being selected during mutation selection, so the affinity of the optimal individual of the current generation may be greater than that of the previous generation. At this time, the effect of simulated annealing will likely jump back to the result to optimize further. The replacement for such a case depends on the probability p as defined as

$$p = e^{-\Delta F} \Delta F = \frac{f_{aff}(x_i')}{f_{aff}(x_i)} - 1 \quad (6)$$

where x_i' is the current optimal solution; x_i denotes the previous optimal solution. This part will replace the solution if $p < rand(0,1)$.

2.2.4. Pseudo Code of AIAGS

To sum up, there are some innovations of this paper on the existing immune algorithms. The pseudo code of AIAGS is explained in detail in Algorithm 1. The flowchart of AIAGS is explained in detail in Figure 2.

Algorithm 1: AIAGS	
Step.1	Define the objective function $F(x)$;
Step.2	Initialize population X;
Step.3	Evaluate all the individuals x_i by the objective function $F(x)$;
Step.4	Calculate the affinity $f_{aff}(x_i)$ and concentration $f_{den}(x_i)$ of each individual;
Step.5	Initialize the number of iteration $m = 1$;
Step.6	While m < max number of iterations M;
Step.7	Calculate the stimulation $f_{sim}(x_i)$ of each individual by the Equation (3);
Step.8	Select the individuals in the population by stimulation and clone the individuals;
Step.9	Mutate the cloned individuals by the Equation (5);
Step.10	If the generated mutation vector exceeds the boundary, a new mutation vector is generated randomly until it is within the boundary;
Step.11	Inhibit cloning and calculate the affinity of each new individual;
Step.12	Generate optimal individual by Simulated Annealing by the Equation (6);
Step.13	End;
Step.14	$m = m + 1$;
Step.15	End while;
Step.16	Return the best solution.

2.3. *Benchmark Function*

Due to the limitations of intelligent optimization algorithms, unlike the traditional algorithm, which has a mathematical theoretical basis, it is not strict. After improving the optimization algorithm, most people use the classical benchmark function to test the algorithm's effectiveness. This article uses eight classical and four CEC2017 benchmark functions to evaluate AIAGS. The $u()$ of F6 and F7 is expressed as

$$u(x_i, a, k, m) = \begin{cases} K(x_i - a)^m, & \text{if } x_i > a \\ 0, & -a \leqslant x_i \geqslant a \\ K(-x_i - a)^m, & -a \leqslant x_i \end{cases} \quad (7)$$

These classical functions are divided into three groups: unimodal (F1–F4), multimodal (F5–F7), and fixed-dimension multimodal (F8). The unimodal benchmark function has only one optimal solution, which can verify the development and convergence. The multimodal benchmark function has many optimal solutions. However, there is only one global optimal solution, and the rest are local optimal solutions. The fixed dimensional multimodal functions can define the desired number of design variables and could provide a different search space. Therefore, the multimodal functions are responsible for testing exploration and avoiding the entrapment in the optimal local solution. Hybrid and composition functions can reflect some problems that are closer to reality [40]. In Table 1, the corresponding properties of these functions are listed, where dim represents the dimensions of the functions and range indicates the scope of the search space.

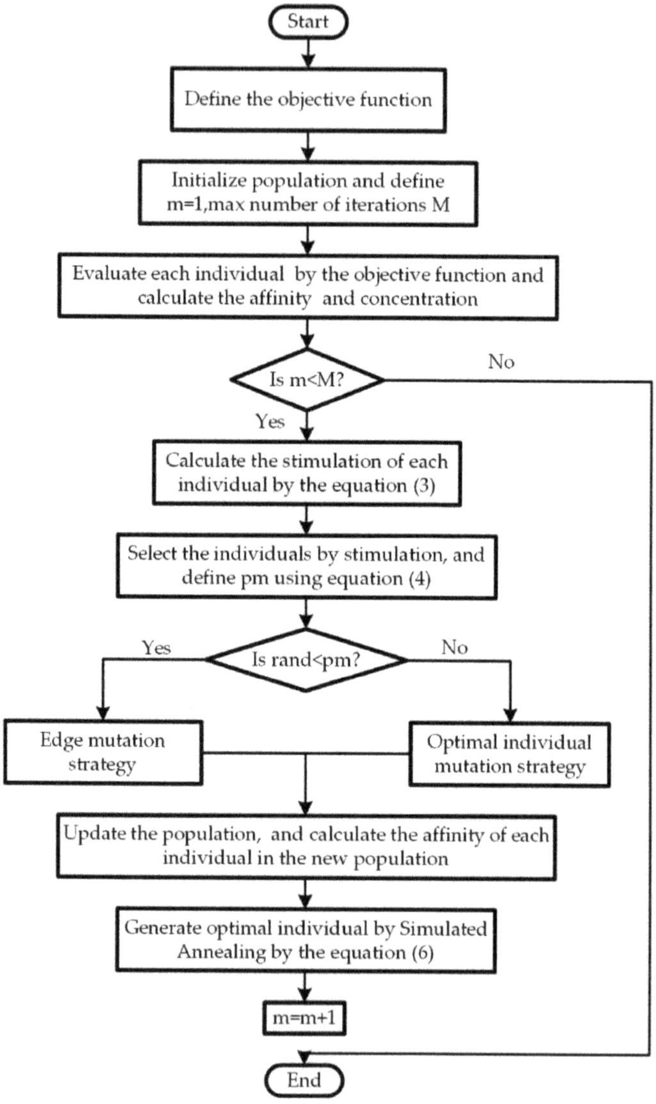

Figure 2. AIAGS.

Table 1. Benchmark functions.

Name	Formula	Range	f_{min}
Sphere	$F1(x) = \sum_{i=1}^{D} x_i^2$	[−20, 20]	0
Schwefel 1.2	$F2(x) = \sum_{i=1}^{D}\left(\sum_{j=1}^{i} x_j\right)^2$	[−100, 100]	0
Rosenbrock	$F3(x) = \sum_{i=1}^{D-1}[100\cdot\left(x_i^2 - x_{i+1}\right)^2 + (x_i - 1)^2]$	[−30, 30]	0
Step	$F4(x) = \sum_{i=1}^{D}(x_i + 0.5)^2$	[−100, 100]	0
Ackley	$F5(x) = -20\exp\left(-0.2\sqrt{\frac{1}{n}\sum_{i=1}^{D} x_i^2}\right) - \exp\left[\frac{1}{D}\sum_{i=1}^{D}\cos(2\pi x_i)\right] + 20 + e$	[−40, 40]	0
Generalized penalized 1	$F6(x) = \frac{\pi}{n}[10\sin(\pi y_1)] + \sum_{i=1}^{D-1}(y_i - 1)^2[1 + 10\sin^2(\pi y_{i+1}) + \sum_{i=1}^{D} u(x_i, 10, 100, 4)], y_i = 1 + \frac{x_i+1}{4}$	[−50, 50]	0
Generalized penalized 2	$F7(x) = 0.1\{\sin^2(3\pi x_1) + \sum_{i=1}^{D}(x_i - 1)^2[1 + \sin^2(3\pi x_i + 1)] + (x_D - 1)^2 1 + \sin^2(2\pi x_D)\} + \sum_{i=1}^{n} u(x_i, 5, 100, 4)$	[−50, 50]	0
Shekel's Foxholes	$F8(x) = \left[\frac{1}{500} + \sum_{j=1}^{25}\frac{1}{j+\sum_{i=1}^{2}}\left(x_i - a_{ij}\right)\right]^{-1}$	[−70, 70]	1
Hybrid function 4 (N = 4)	$F9(x)$	[−100, 100]	1400
Hybrid function 7 (N = 5)	$F10(x)$	[−100, 100]	1700
Composition function 1 (N = 3)	$F11(x)$	[−100, 100]	2100
Composition function 4 (N = 4)	$F12(x)$	[−100, 100]	2400

2.3.1. Comparison of AIAGS with Other Algorithms

In order to reflect the improvement effect of the immune algorithm in this paper, this section compares AIAGS with the original immune algorithm two improved immune algorithms: improved artificial immune algorithm (IAIA) [28] and modified artificial immune algorithm (MAIA) [29], and two new algorithms: Harris hawks optimization (HHO) [41] and Aquila optimizer (AO) [42]. The parameter settings of the counterparts' algorithms are given in Table 2. The comparison results are shown in Table 3. However, intelligent algorithms are highly accidental. After several tests, this paper calculates the average value and standard deviation of each test result to avoid misleading the experimental results and the practical application of the algorithm.

Table 2. Parameter settings.

Algorithm	Parameter Settings
AIAGS	δ = 0.1, sv = 0.2
AO	α = 0.5, δ = 0.5
IA	α = 2, β = 1, δ = 0.2, pm = 0.7
IAIA	α = 2, β = 1, δ = 0.613, pm = 0.7
MAIA	δ = 0.8, pm = 0.8, cr = 0.8
HHO	α = 0.5, δ = 0.5

Table 3. Comparison of results obtained for the benchmark functions.

	AIAGS	AO	IA	IAIA	MAIA	HHO
F1						
worst	0	2.86×10^{-71}	0.000124	0.000145	0.030882	1.98×10^{-46}
best	0	7.37×10^{-76}	7.65×10^{-5}	3.54×10^{-5}	0.001683	2.62×10^{-58}
Avg	0	5.74×10^{-72}	9.86×10^{-5}	7.71×10^{-5}	0.012509	1.99×10^{-47}
Std	0	1×10^{-71}	1.46×10^{-5}	3.28×10^{-5}	0.009914	5.95×10^{-47}
F2						
worst	0	2.82×10^{-56}	0.006578	0.022761	16.07011	1.71×10^{-42}
best	0	1.72×10^{-73}	0.002606	0.013182	0.812125	1.15×10^{-51}

Table 3. *Cont.*

	AIAGS	AO	IA	IAIA	MAIA	HHO
Avg	0	2.82×10^{-57}	0.003962	0.017273	4.565824	3.78×10^{-43}
Std	0	8.93×10^{-57}	0.001401	0.003087	4.947259	6.69×10^{-43}
F3						
worst	6.39×10^{-7}	0.001305	433.5283	696.2436	83.41411	0.008889
Best	5.5×10^{-9}	5×10^{-6}	0.99727	0.762353	4.4702	2.1×10^{-5}
Avg	9.99×10^{-8}	0.000319	80.76008	143.8289	29.75245	0.002238
Std	1.83×10^{-7}	0.000424	143.8194	240.8117	30.68641	0.002581
F4						
worst	0	6.97×10^{-5}	0.004139	0.00329	0.00329	9.33×10^{-5}
Best	0	2.3×10^{-7}	0.001612	0.00174	0.00174	7.93×10^{-10}
Avg	0	1.87×10^{-5}	0.003066	0.002567	0.002567	2.05×10^{-5}
Std	0	2.32×10^{-5}	0.00077	0.00053	0.00053	2.64×10^{-5}
F5						
worst	8.88×10^{-16}	8.88×10^{-16}	4.663342	3.223428	1.019824	8.88×10^{-16}
Best	8.88×10^{-16}	8.88×10^{-16}	0.017455	0.019081	0.137416	8.88×10^{-16}
Avg	8.88×10^{-16}	8.88×10^{-16}	1.139553	0.342006	0.437464	8.88×10^{-16}
Std	0	0	1.617355	1.012431	0.323219	0
F6						
worst	4.71×10^{-32}	3.84×10^{-5}	4.772913	6.250579	0.005788	2.07×10^{-5}
Best	4.71×10^{-32}	7.83×10^{-8}	1.16×10^{-5}	0.335882	0.000107	1.56×10^{-7}
Avg	4.71×10^{-32}	7.48×10^{-6}	1.984778	3.781554	0.001743	6.34×10^{-6}
Std	0	1.16×10^{-5}	1.830602	2.512286	0.002048	6.86×10^{-6}
F7						
worst	1.35×10^{-32}	0.000281	0.000101	8.19×10^{-5}	0.039677	0.000501
best	1.35×10^{-32}	1.31×10^{-6}	5.21×10^{-5}	3.87×10^{-5}	0.002672	1.18×10^{-7}
Avg	1.35×10^{-32}	4.25×10^{-5}	8.01×10^{-5}	5.89×10^{-5}	0.017996	8.5×10^{-5}
Std	2.88×10^{-48}	8.69×10^{-5}	1.55×10^{-5}	1.58×10^{-5}	0.01293	0.000143
F8						
worst	0.998004	2.982105	1.992031	0.998004	0.999027	1.992031
best	0.998004	0.998004	0.998004	0.998004	0.998004	0.998004
Avg	0.998004	1.593234	1.166875	0.998004	0.998107	1.196819
Std	2.34×10^{-16}	0.958412	0.362935	2.01×10^{-15}	0.000323	0.397606
F9						
worst	1528.366	5142.015	2215.496	2302.871	5755.439	4349.2
best	1472.889	1557.776	1443.205	1428.962	1488.148	1450.039
Avg	1503.786	2462.484	1580.193	1655.434	2510.73	1833.8
Std	19.26844	978.4552	223.2629	287.2931	1264.939	843.7423
F10						
worst	1794.68	1838.131	1763.443	1782.14	2200.955	1840.59
Best	1744.138	1731.296	1722.813	1725.397	1766.414	1744.772
Avg	1774.579	1781.842	1738.947	1748.674	1898.936	1781.998
Std	17.10128	32.03933	10.8574	22.15373	122.3724	30.2191
F11						
worst	2260.104	2338.993	2264.487	2288.434	2319.733	2388.341
Best	2209.787	2204.09	2200.005	2200.003	2201.822	2205.34
Avg	2236.802	2272.26	2211.444	2211.249	2265.511	2272.888
Std	18.17673	56.04231	18.0651	25.8142	44.29724	71.44948
F12						
worst	2717.367	2778.692	2772.984	2762.261	2824.593	2857.503
Best	2521.748	2746.416	2500.074	2500.073	2505.906	2770.847
Avg	2626.946	2767.838	2669.676	2629.372	2710.07	2799.953
Std	61.88762	9.524766	114.739	111.2591	104.6337	28.32715

2.3.2. Convergence

Convergence is the ability of the algorithm to search and converge to an acceptable solution in a certain time. Convergence is an important index to evaluate the performance of the algorithm. An algorithm has high convergence, which means fast optimization speed and high precision. Generally, the convergence speed can be measured by the number of iterations, and the convergence value can measure the accuracy.

The convergence curves of AIAGS and the other five algorithms in 12 benchmark functions are shown in Figure 3. It can be seen from Table 2 and Figure 3 that the convergence speed and optimization ability of AIAGS are not the strongest in individual benchmark functions. On the whole, AIAGS is far better than other immune algorithms in terms of convergence speed and optimization ability, and it is also better than the other two algorithms.

2.4. *Summary*

In this chapter, the immune algorithm's stimulation function and mutation strategy are improved, and simulated annealing is added to the final step to select the optimal solution. The core idea of these improvements is to avoid finding the optimal local solution. After improving the algorithm, 12 different types of benchmark functions are used to evaluate the algorithm's performance. Experiments show that the development and exploration ability of AIAGS is significantly improved compared with the previous immune algorithm. These conclusions provide substantial proof for the following system identification work.

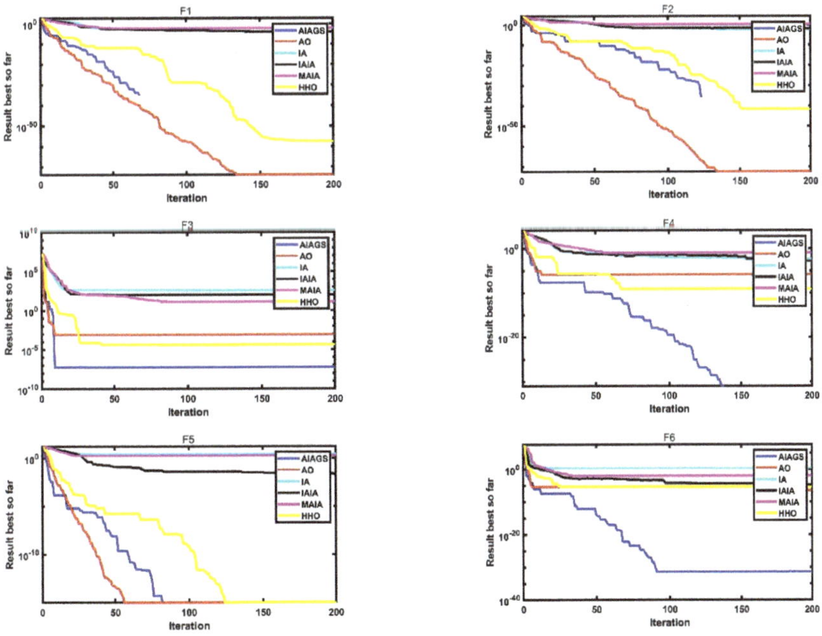

Figure 3. *Cont.*

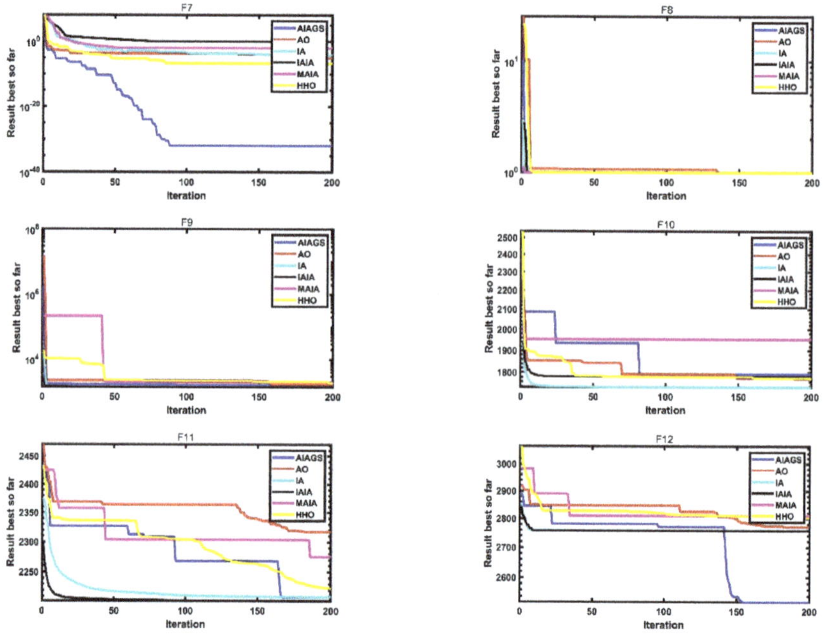

Figure 3. The convergence curves of AIAGS and other six algorithms.

3. Identification Method of MIMO Fractional Order Hammerstein Model

3.1. MIMO Fractional Order Hammerstein Model

3.1.1. Fractional Order Differentiation

At present, there are three definitions widely used in the field of fractional calculus: Grünwald–Letnikov (GL), Riemann–Liouville (RL), and Caputo definitions. Because the GL is easy to program [43], this paper considers it the research object. The definition of fractional order calculus can be expressed as

$$D_t^{\alpha} f(t) = \lim_{h \to 0} \frac{1}{h^{\alpha}} \sum_{j=0}^{\left[\frac{t-t_0}{h}\right]} (-1)^j \begin{pmatrix} \alpha \\ j \end{pmatrix} f(t - jh) \tag{8}$$

where α is the fractional order. Because this paper explores differential equations, $\alpha > 0$. h is the sampling time; [] means that the integer part is reserved; $(-1)^j \begin{pmatrix} \alpha \\ j \end{pmatrix}$ is the binomials of $(1-z)^{\alpha}$. By denoting w_j^{α} to replace the binomials, so w_j^{α} can be expressed as

$$w_j^{\alpha} = (-1)^j \begin{pmatrix} \alpha \\ j \end{pmatrix} = \frac{(-1)^j \Gamma(\alpha + 1)}{\Gamma(j+1)\Gamma(\alpha - j + 1)} \tag{9}$$

Finally, when $t_0 = 0$, the definition of fractional order calculus can be expressed as

$$D_t^{\alpha} f(t) = \frac{1}{h^{\alpha}} \sum_{j=0}^{\left[\frac{t-a}{h}\right]} w_j^{\alpha} f(t - jh) \tag{10}$$

3.1.2. MIMO Fractional-Order Hammerstein System

The MIMO Hammerstein model of this paper can be schematically represented in Figure 4. Hammerstein model is a typical nonlinear model composed of static nonlinear block and dynamic linear block. the dynamic linear block can be expressed as

$$\begin{bmatrix} y_1(t) \\ y_2(t) \\ \vdots \\ y_N(t) \end{bmatrix} = \begin{bmatrix} G_{1,1} & G_{1,2} & \dots & G_{1,M} \\ G_{2,1} & G_{2,2} & \dots & G_{2,M} \\ \vdots & & & \\ G_{N,1} & G_{N,2} & \dots & G_{N,M} \end{bmatrix} \begin{bmatrix} u_1'(t) \\ u_2'(t) \\ \vdots \\ u_M'(t) \end{bmatrix} \tag{11}$$

where $y_k(t)$ is the kth system output; $u_l'(t)$ is generated by the lth system input $u_l(t)$ through the nonlinear block, which can be expressed as

$$\begin{aligned} u_l'(t) &= c_{l,1}\cdot f_{l,1}(u_l(t)) + c_{l,2}\cdot f_{l,2}(u_l(t)) + \ldots + c_{l,n_{lc}}\cdot f_{l,n_{lc}}(u_l(t)) \\ &= \textstyle\sum_{m=1}^{n_{lc}} c_{l,m}\cdot f_{l,m}(u_l(t)) \end{aligned} \tag{12}$$

where $c_{l,\cdot}$ are coefficients to be identified; $f_{l,\cdot}()$ are a series of basic functions. $G_{k,l}$ is a fractional-order transfer function, which can reflect the relationship between $u_l'(t)$ and $y_k(t)$; it is defined as

$$G_{k,l}(s) = \frac{b_{k,l,m}s^{m\alpha} + b_{k,l,m-1}s^{(m-1)\alpha} + \cdots + b_{k,l,0}}{a_{k,l,n}s^{n\alpha} + a_{k,l,n-1}s^{(n-1)\alpha} + \cdots + a_{k,l,0}} \tag{13}$$

where $a_{k,l,\cdot}$ and $b_{k,l,\cdot}$ are coefficients to be identified; α is the fractional order to be identified. For the convenience of calculation and programming, in this paper $a_{k,l,0}$ is assumed to be 1. According to Equations (11) and (13), the kth system output can be expressed as

$$\begin{aligned} y_k &= G_{k,1}u_1' + G_{k,2}u_2' + \cdots + G_{k,M}u_M' \\ &= \frac{b_{k,1,m}s^{m\alpha}+b_{k,1,m-1}s^{(m-1)\alpha}+\dots+b_{k,1,0}}{a_{k,1,n}s^{n\alpha}+a_{k,1,n-1}s^{(n-1)\alpha}+\dots+a_{k,1,1}s^{\alpha}+1}u_1' \\ &+ \frac{b_{k,2,m}s^{m\alpha}+b_{k,2,m-1}s^{(m-1)\alpha}+\dots+b_{k,2,0}}{a_{k,2,n}s^{n\alpha}+a_{k,2,n-1}s^{(n-1)\alpha}+\dots+a_{k,2,1}s^{\alpha}+1}u_2' \\ &+ \cdots + \frac{b_{k,M,m}s^{m\alpha}+b_{k,M,m-1}s^{(m-1)\alpha}+\dots+b_{k,M,0}}{a_{k,M,n}s^{n\alpha}+a_{k,M,n-1}s^{(n-1)\alpha}+\dots+a_{k,M,1}s^{\alpha}+1}u_M' \end{aligned} \tag{14}$$

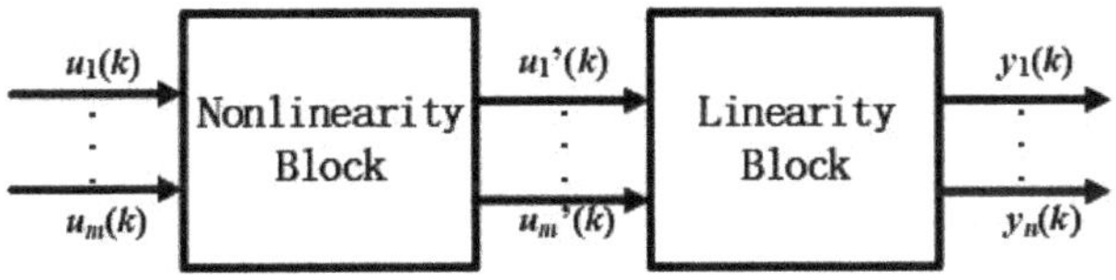

Figure 4. MIMO Hammerstein model.

By reduction of fractions to a common denominator and simplifying Equation (14), we can get an equation described as

$$\begin{aligned} &\left(A_{k,N_A}s^{N_A\alpha} + A_{k,N_{A-1}}s^{(N_A-1)\alpha} + \cdots + A_{k,1}s^{\alpha} + 1\right)y_k \\ = &\left(B_{k,1,N_B}s^{N_B\alpha} + B_{k,1,N_B-1}s^{(N_B-1)\alpha} + \cdots + B_{k,1,0}\right)u_1' + \\ &\left(B_{k,2,N_B}s^{N_B\alpha} + B_{k,2,N_B-1}s^{(N_B-1)\alpha} + \cdots + B_{k,2,0}\right)u_2' + \cdots + \\ &\left(B_{k,M,N_B}s^{N_B\alpha} + B_{k,M,N_B-1}s^{(N_B-1)\alpha} + \cdots + B_{k,M,0}\right)u_M' \end{aligned} \tag{15}$$

where A is the polynomial containing a; B is the polynomial containing a and b; the coefficient of fractional order $N_A = M * n$, $N_B = (M-1) * n + m$. To sum up, the MIMO fractional-order Hammerstein system discussed in this paper can be expressed as

$$\begin{cases} y_k(t) + \sum_{i=1}^{n_A} A_{k,i} D^{i\alpha} y_k(t) = \sum_{l=0}^{M} \sum_{j=0}^{n_B} B_{k,l,j} D^{j\alpha} u_l'(t) \\ y_k'(t) = y_k(t) + v(t) \end{cases} \tag{16}$$

where $v(t)$ is the Gaussian white noise; $y_k'(t)$ is the measured output containing noise. According to Equations (10) and (16), the MIMO fractional-order Hammerstein system can be expressed as

$$\begin{aligned} y_k'(t) = \frac{1}{\left(1+\sum_{i=1}^{n_A} A_i/h^{i\alpha}\right)} \cdot \Bigg[& \sum_{l=0}^{M} \sum_{i=0}^{n_B} \sum_{m=1}^{n_{lc}} \frac{B_{k,l,i}}{h^{i\alpha}} c_{l,m} \cdot \sum_{j=0}^{[t/h]} w_j^{i\alpha} f_{l,m}(u_l(t-jh)) \\ & - \sum_{i=1}^{n_A} \frac{A_i}{h^{i\alpha}} \sum_{j=1}^{[t/h]} w_j^{i\alpha} y_k(t-jh) \Bigg] + v(t) \end{aligned} \tag{17}$$

3.2. Parameter Identification Based on Auxiliary Model Recursive Least Square Method

In the MIMO fractional-order Hammerstein model, all the coefficients and the fractional order are needed to be identified. Previous articles usually considered only part of coefficients or for the SISO system. The work of this paper is rarely concerned before. The identification work is divided into coefficient identification and order identification. However, the two results affect each other, which cannot identify coefficients precisely without a precise fractional order. This paper will first use a series of input and output data to obtain the initial values of coefficients and the fractional order by the AIAGS algorithm mentioned above. The initial value is a little precise. Then, the initial value will be used to get the parameter identification result of the fractional-order Hammerstein model through the auxiliary model recursive least squares (AMRLS) algorithm.

3.2.1. Coefficient Identification

According to the basic knowledge of system identification, the input–output relations can be expressed as

$$y_k'(t) = y_k(t) + v(t) = \varnothing_k(t) \cdot \theta_k^{\,T} + v(t) \tag{18}$$

where $\varnothing_k(t)$ is the variable vector including input–output data, which is expressed as

$$\begin{aligned} \varnothing_k(t) &= \left[\varnothing_{k,A}(t), \varnothing_{B_{k,1,0}}(t), \varnothing_{B_{k,1,1}}(t), \ldots, \varnothing_{B_{k,1,n_B}}(t), \ldots, \varnothing_{B_{k,M,0}}(t), \varnothing_{B_{k,M,1}}(t), \ldots, \varnothing_{B_{k,M,n_B}}(t)\right] \\ \varnothing_{k,A}(t) &= \left[-\sum_{j=1}^{[t/h]} w_j^{\alpha} y_k(t-jh), \ldots, -\sum_{j=1}^{[t/h]} w_j^{n_A\alpha} y_k(t-jh)\right] \\ \varnothing_{B_{k,l,i}}(t) &= \left[\sum_{j=0}^{[t/h]} w_j^{i\alpha} f_{l,1}(u_l(t-jh)), \ldots, \sum_{j=0}^{[t/h]} w_j^{i\alpha} f_{l,M}(u_l(t-jh))\right] \end{aligned} \tag{19}$$

According to Equations (16) and (17), the vector θ_k is found and expressed as

$$\begin{aligned} \theta_k &= \left[\theta_{k,A}, \theta_{B_{k,1,0}}, \ldots, \theta_{B_{k,1,n_B}}, \ldots, \theta_{B_{k,M,0}}, \ldots, \theta_{B_{k,M,n_B}}\right] \\ \theta_{k,A} &= \left[Q_{k,1}, Q_{k,2}, \ldots, Q_{k,n_A}\right] \\ \theta_{B_{k,l,i}} &= \left[W_{k,1,i} c_{1,1}, \ldots, W_{k,1,i} c_{1,n_{lc}}, \ldots, W_{k,M,i} c_{M,1}, \ldots, W_{k,M,i} c_{M,n_{lc}}\right] \end{aligned} \tag{20}$$

where

$$\begin{aligned} Q_{k,i} &= \frac{\frac{A_{k,i}}{h^{i\alpha}}}{1+\sum_{i=1}^{n_A} \frac{A_{k,i}}{h^{i\alpha}}} \\ W_{k,l,j} &= \frac{\frac{B_{k,l,j}}{h^{j\alpha}}}{1+\sum_{i=1}^{n_A} \frac{A_{k,i}}{h^{i\alpha}}} \end{aligned} \tag{21}$$

It can be clearly seen that θ_k contains coefficients that need to be identified. It is worth mentioning that $y_k(t-jh)$ is unknown so that $\theta_{k,A}$ cannot be identified directly by $\varnothing_{k,A}(t)$. According to references [44], an auxiliary model is used to estimate the unknown variable $y_k(t-jh)$. The auxiliary model of this paper can be schematically represented in Figure 5. The main idea of the auxiliary model is that the real output of the system $y_k{}'(t)$ is replaced by the output of the auxiliary model $y_{amk}(t)$. Then, the identification problem has changed from the relationship between $y_k{}'(t)$ and u_l to the relationship between $y_{amk}(t)$ and u_l.

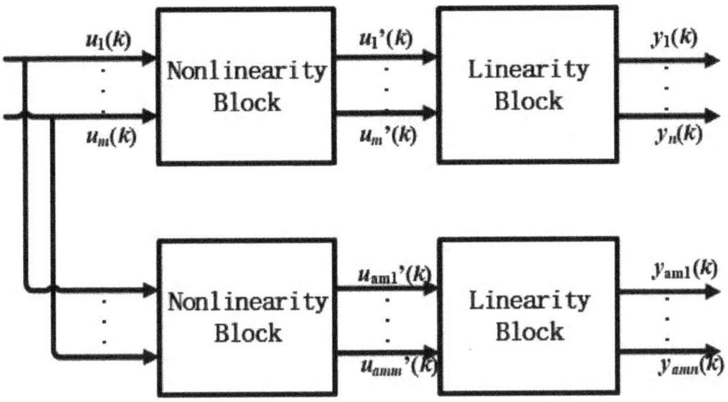

Figure 5. The MIMO Hammerstein model based on the auxiliary model.

According to Figure 5, the input–output relations of the auxiliary model can be written as

$$y_{amk}(t) = \varnothing_{amk}(t) \cdot \theta_{amk}{}^{T} \tag{22}$$

where

$$\begin{gathered}\varnothing_{amk}(t) = \left[\varnothing_{amk,A}(t), \varnothing_{B_{k,1,0}}(t), \varnothing_{B_{k,1,2}}(t), \ldots, \varnothing_{B_{k,1,n_B}}(t), \ldots, \varnothing_{B_{k,M,0}}(t), \varnothing_{B_{k,M,2}}(t), \ldots, \varnothing_{B_{k,M,n_B}}(t)\right] \\ \varnothing_{amk,A}(t) = \left[-\sum_{j=1}^{[t/h]} w_j^{\alpha} y_{amk}(t-jh), \ldots, -\sum_{j=1}^{[t/h]} w_j^{n_A\alpha} y_{amk}(t-jh)\right]\theta_{amk} = \hat{\theta_k}\end{gathered} \tag{23}$$

The estimate of $\varnothing_k(t)$ can be used as the value of the auxiliary model information vector $\varnothing_{amk}(t)$ and the parameter identification of θ_k can be used as the value of the auxiliary model parameter vector θ_{amk}. Define the criterion function as

$$J\left(\hat{\theta_k}^{T}\right) = \frac{1}{2}\sum_{i=1}^{t}\left[y_k{}'(i) - \varnothing_{amk}(i)\hat{\theta_k}^{T}\right]^2 \tag{24}$$

By finding the minimum value of the criterion function, the value of $\varnothing_{amk}(i)\hat{\theta_k}^{T}$ can approach the value of $y_k{}'(i)$ to identify $\hat{\theta_k}$. The minimum value can be obtained by the following equation.

$$\frac{\partial J\left(\hat{\theta_k}^{T}\right)}{\partial \hat{\theta_k}^{T}} = -\sum_{i=1}^{t} \varnothing_{amk}{}^{T}(i) \cdot [y_k{}'(i) - \varnothing_{amk}(i)\hat{\theta_k}^{T}] = 0 \tag{25}$$

When $\sum_{i=1}^{t} \varnothing_{amk}{}^{T}(i-1) \cdot \varnothing_{amk}(i-1)$ can be inversed, the value of $\hat{\theta_k}$ can be identified by the recursive least squares as follows:

$$\begin{aligned}\hat{\theta_k}^T(t) &= \left[\sum_{i=1}^{t} \varnothing_{amk}{}^T(i-1)\cdot\varnothing_{amk}(i-1)\right]^{-1}\cdot \sum_{i=1}^{t} \varnothing_{amk}{}^T(i) y_k{}'(i) \\ \hat{\theta_k}^T(t) &= \hat{\theta_k}^T(t-1) + L(t)\left[y_k{}'(t) - \varnothing_{amk}(t)\hat{\theta_k}^T(t-1)\right] \\ L(t) &= P(t-1)\varnothing_{amk}{}^T(t)\left[1+\varnothing_{amk}(t)P(t-1)\varnothing_{amk}{}^T(t)\right]^{-1} \\ P(t) &= [I - L(t)\varnothing_{amk}(t)]P(t-1)\end{aligned} \tag{26}$$

where $P(0)$ is a diagonal matrix in which the main diagonal elements are huge and equal.

According to the above equations, the elements of $\hat{\theta_k}$ are all identified. Without losing generality, assuming $c_{l,1}$ as 1 can facilitate calculation and ensure the uniqueness of the final parameters. Then, the unique values of $W_{k,l,j}$ and $c_{l,m}$ are calculated; they can be expressed as

$$\begin{aligned} W_{k,l,j} &= \theta_{B_{k,l,i}}\left[(l-1) * n_{lc} + 1\right] \\ c_{l,m} &= \sum_{i=0}^{n_{lc}} \frac{\theta_{B_{k,l,i}}(k)}{W_{k,l,j}}\end{aligned} \tag{27}$$

So far, the estimates of A, B, and c have been obtained.

3.2.2. Order Identification

In the previous section, this paper discusses the identification of coefficients. Substituting the accurate estimated value of the coefficients into Equation (17) can identify the order accurately. Define the criterion function as

$$J(\alpha) = \frac{1}{2}\sum_{i=1}^{t}\left[y_k{}'(i) - \hat{y_k}(i)\right]^2 \tag{28}$$

By finding the minimum value of the criterion function, the value of $\hat{y_k}(i)$ can approach the value of $y_k{}'(i)$. The minimum value can be obtained by the following equation:

$$\frac{\partial J(\alpha)}{\partial \alpha} = -\sum_{i=1}^{t} \frac{\partial \hat{y_k}(i)}{\partial \alpha}\cdot\left[y_k{}'(i) - \hat{y_k}(i)\right] = 0 \tag{29}$$

where

$$\begin{aligned}\frac{\partial \hat{y_k}(t)}{\partial \alpha} &= -\frac{\partial}{\partial \alpha}\left(\hat{G_{k,1}}(s^\alpha)u_1'(t) + \hat{G_{k,2}}(s^\alpha)u_2'(t) + \cdots + \hat{G_{k,M}}(s^\alpha)u_M'(t)\right) \\ &= \sum_{l=0}^{M}\left[\left(\frac{B_{k,l,N_B}s^{N_B\alpha}+\cdots+B_{k,l,0}}{\left(A_{k,N_A}s^{N_A\alpha}+\cdots+1\right)^2}\right)\right. \\ &\left.\cdot\left(N_A\cdot A_{k,N_A}s^{N_A\alpha} + \cdots + A_{k,1}s^\alpha\right) - \frac{N_B\cdot B_{k,l,N_B}s^{N_B\alpha}+\cdots+B_{k,l,1}s^\alpha}{A_{k,N_A}s^{N_A^\alpha}+\cdots+1}\right]\cdot\ln(s)\cdot u_l'(t)\end{aligned} \tag{30}$$

According to references [24], $\ln(s)\cdot u_l'(t)$ can be replaced by $s^\alpha\cdot(\ln(s)/s^\alpha)\cdot u_l'(t)$. The inverse Laplace transform of $\ln(s)/s^\alpha$ is a digamma function can be expressed as

$$L^{-1}\left(\frac{\ln(s)}{s^\alpha}\right) = \frac{t^{\alpha-1}}{\Gamma(\alpha)}\left[\frac{1}{\Gamma(\alpha)}\frac{d\Gamma(\alpha)}{d\alpha} - \ln(t)\right] \tag{31}$$

Then, $\ln(s)\cdot u_l'(t)$ can be expressed as

$$D^\alpha\left[\frac{1}{\Gamma(\alpha)}\frac{d\Gamma(\alpha)}{d\alpha}D^\alpha u_l'(t) - \frac{1}{\Gamma(\alpha)}\int_0^t (t-\tau)^{\alpha-1}\ln(t-\tau)u_l'(t)d\tau\right] \tag{32}$$

It's easy to see that α can be calculated by Equations (28)–(32).

3.3. Summary

So far, the estimates of A, B, c, and α have been obtained. Because A are polynomials about a, B are polynomials about a and b, it is feasible to estimate the value of n_A a by the value of n_A A. Then, it is feasible to estimate the value of b by the value of a and B. To sum up, all estimates work has been completed.

4. Experimental Results

In this section, two numerical examples will demonstrate the validity of the proposed method.

4.1. Example 1

Consider the following model, which is expressed as

$$\begin{bmatrix} y_1(t) \\ y_2(t) \end{bmatrix} = \begin{bmatrix} G_{1,1} & G_{1,2} \\ G_{2,1} & G_{2,2} \end{bmatrix} \begin{bmatrix} u_1'(t) \\ u_2'(t) \end{bmatrix} y'(\mathrm{t}) = y(\mathrm{t}) + v(\mathrm{t}) \tag{33}$$

where

$$\begin{aligned} G_{1,1} &= \tfrac{4}{5s^{0.3}+1},\ G_{1,2} = \tfrac{3}{3s^{0.3}+1}, \\ G_{2,1} &= \tfrac{4}{6s^{0.3}+1},\ G_{2,2} = \tfrac{5}{2s^{0.3}+1}. \\ u_1'(t) &= u_1(t) + 0.5{u_1}^2(t) + 0.3{u_1}^3(t) + 0.1{u_1}^4(t) \\ u_2'(t) &= u_2(t) + 0.4{u_2}^2(t) + 0.2{u_2}^3(t) + 0.1{u_2}^4(t) \end{aligned} \tag{34}$$

The inputs u_1 and u_2 are persistent excitation signal sequences with unit variance and zero mean. $v(\mathrm{t})$ is the stochastic Gaussian noise with zero mean and variance is 0.005. Then, the outputs $y(\mathrm{t})$ are generated by their respective transfer functions of the MIMO fractional-order Hammerstein model.

According to the model, the θ to be identified are

$$\begin{aligned} \theta &= [a_{1,1,1}, a_{1,2,1}, b_{1,1,0}, b_{1,2,0}, a_{2,1,1}, a_{2,2,1}, b_{2,1,0}, b_{2,2,0}, c_{1,1}, c_{1,2}, c_{1,3}, c_{2,1}, c_{2,2}, c_{2,3}, \alpha] \\ &= [5,\ 3,\ 4,\ 3,\ 6,\ 2,\ 4,\ 5,\ 0.5,\ 0.3,\ 0.1,\ 0.4,\ 0.2,\ 0.1,\ 0.3] \end{aligned} \tag{35}$$

The identification steps are described in Section 3. At first, the intelligent optimization algorithm identifies the initial value of the model. Then, using AMRLS to identify the model coefficients, and at this time regarding the initial value of fractional order as the model's actual value. When the coefficients are estimated, the estimated values of the coefficients are considered to be the true value to identify the fractional order. Finally, identifying coefficients and order is repeated until the iteration's end or satisfactory results are obtained. The pseudo-code of the identification process is explained in detail in Algorithm 2.

Algorithm 2: Identification process	
Step.1	Collect the dates of all inputs, outputs;
Step.2	Obtain the initial of unknown parameters by using intelligent optimization algorithm;
Step.3	**While** m < max number of iterations M;
Step.4	Estimate the value of model coefficients according to Equation (25);
Step.5	Estimate the value of fractional order according to Equation (29);
Step.6	If the two criterion function values J within the actual accuracy requirements;
Step.7	Break;
Step.8	End;
Step.9	$m = m + 1$;
Step.10	**End while;**
Step.11	Return the best solution.

In order to reflect the importance of the initial value of fractional order, in this section, the initial value is identified by three different optimization algorithms: AIAGS, HHO, and AO. The next identification work is carried out under four initial values. This section evaluates the final identification results from two aspects: RQE and MSE. They can be expressed as

$$\begin{aligned} \text{RQE} &= \sqrt{\frac{(\hat{\theta}-\theta)^2}{\theta^2}} \\ \text{MSE} &= \frac{\sum_{n}^{i=1}(y_i-\hat{y}_i)^2}{n} \end{aligned} \tag{36}$$

where $\hat{\theta}$ and $\hat{y}_i$ are estimated values; θ and y_i are true values.

The final identification results obtained by Algorithm 2 are shown in Table 4, and the RQE and MSE of the results are shown in Table 5. The outputs of the real model and the outputs of the model obtained through identification are shown in Figures 6 and 7. Figure 8 shows the estimated fractional-order convergence curve.

Table 4. The final identification results.

Method (and AMRLS)	$a_{1,1,1}$	$a_{1,2,1}$	$b_{1,1,0}$	$b_{1,2,0}$	$a_{2,1,1}$	$a_{2,2,1}$	$b_{2,1,0}$	$b_{2,2,0}$	$c_{1,1}$	$c_{1,2}$	$c_{1,3}$	$c_{2,1}$	$c_{2,2}$	$c_{2,3}$	α	α_0
AIAGS	5.127	3.120	3.976	2.959	6.118	2.017	3.996	4.970	0.501	0.289	0.095	0.400	0.200	0.100	0.299	0.333
AO	4.619	3.325	3.887	3.465	5.377	1.760	4.196	5.272	0.509	0.297	0.098	0.404	0.198	0.098	0.275	0.391
HHO	4.641	3.329	3.882	3.448	5.289	1.757	4.152	5.283	0.508	0.296	0.097	0.404	0.198	0.099	0.278	0.382

Table 5. The RQE and MSE of the results.

Method (and AMRLS)	AIAGS	AO	HHO
RQE	0.1360	0.2931	0.2987
MSE	0.0144	0.0944	0.1019

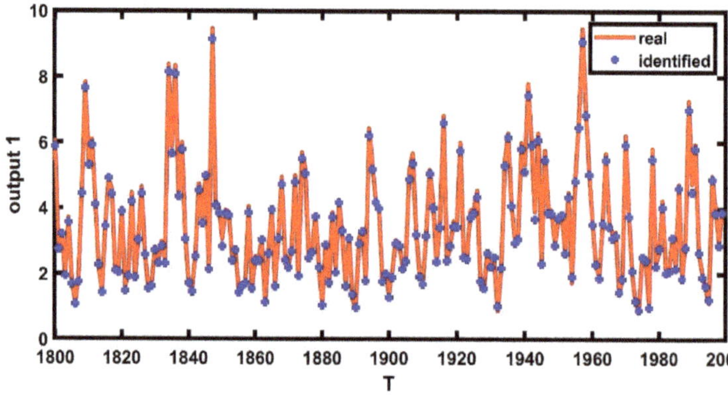

Figure 6. The real output 1 and the identified output 1.

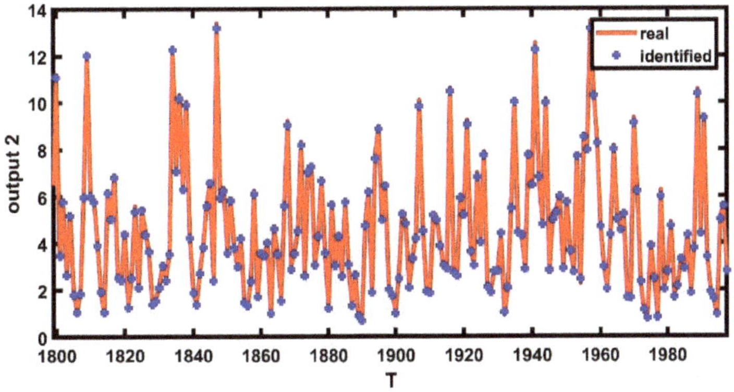

Figure 7. The real output 2 and the identified output 2.

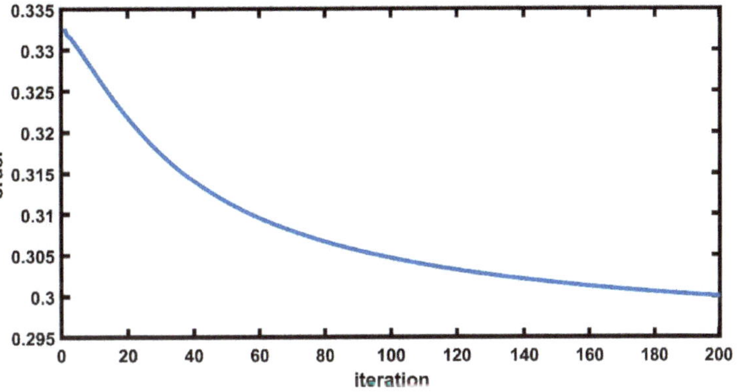

Figure 8. The estimated fractional-order convergence curve.

4.2. Example 2

Consider the following model, which is expressed as

$$\begin{bmatrix} y_1(t) \\ y_2(t) \end{bmatrix} = \begin{bmatrix} G_{1,1} & G_{1,2} \\ G_{2,1} & G_{2,2} \end{bmatrix} \begin{bmatrix} u_1'(t) \\ u_2'(t) \end{bmatrix} \quad (37)$$
$$y'(\mathrm{t}) = y(\mathrm{t}) + v(\mathrm{t})$$

where

$$\begin{gathered} G_{1,1} = \frac{5}{2s^{0.7}+1},\ G_{1,2} = \frac{1.7s^{0.7}+1.9}{1.5s^{1.4}+1.3s^{0.7}+1}, \\ G_{2,1} = \frac{1.8s^{\alpha}+1.5}{2.2s^{1.4}+2.1s^{0.7}+1},\ G_{2,2} = \frac{1}{1.6s^{0.7}+1}. \\ u_1'(t) = u_1(t) + 0.5{u_1}^2(t) + 0.2{u_1}^3(t) + 0.1{u_1}^4(t) \\ u_2'(t) = u_2(t) + 0.4{u_2}^2(t) + 0.3{u_2}^3(t) + 0.1{u_2}^4(t) \end{gathered} \quad (38)$$

The parameter meanings are similar to that of Example 1, so θ can be expressed as

$$\begin{aligned} \theta &= [a_{1,1,1}, a_{1,2,2}, a_{1,2,1}, b_{1,1,0}, b_{1,2,1}, b_{1,2,0}, a_{2,1,2}, a_{2,1,1}, a_{2,2,1}, b_{2,1,1}, b_{2,1,0}, b_{2,2,0}, c_{1,1}, c_{1,2}, c_{1,3}, c_{2,1}, c_{2,2}, c_{2,3}, \alpha] \\ &= [2, 1.5, 1.3, 5, 1.7, 1.9, 2.2, 2.1, 1.6, 1.8, 1.5, 1,\ 0.5,\ 0.2,\ 0.1,\ 0.4,\ 0.3,\ 0.1,\ 0.7] \end{aligned} \quad (39)$$

By repeating the identification process similar to Example 1, the final identification results are shown in Table 6, and the RQE and MSE of the results are shown in Table 7. The outputs of the real model and the outputs of the model obtained through identification are shown in Figures 9 and 10. Figure 11 shows the estimated fractional-order convergence curve.

Table 6. The final identification results.

Method (and AMRLS)	$a_{1,1,1}$	$a_{1,2,2}$	$a_{1,2,1}$	$b_{1,1,0}$	$b_{1,2,1}$	$b_{1,2,0}$	$a_{2,1,2}$	$a_{2,1,1}$	$a_{2,2,1}$	$b_{2,1,1}$	$b_{2,1,0}$	$b_{2,2,0}$	$c_{1,1}$	$c_{1,2}$	$c_{1,3}$	$c_{2,1}$	$c_{2,2}$	$c_{2,3}$	α
AIAGS	2.002	1.501	1.297	5.033	1.703	1.915	2.164	2.215	1.766	1.675	1.564	1.029	0.504	0.191	0.095	0.385	0.293	0.101	0.700
AO	2.946	1.453	1.174	5.642	1.127	1.832	2.459	2.544	0.733	4.680	1.626	1.122	0.483	0.188	0.100	0.347	0.290	0.106	0.582
HHO	3.182	1.42	1.197	5.697	1.004	1.808	2.463	2.605	0.691	4.962	1.631	1.132	0.482	0.188	0.100	0.344	0.288	0.106	0.570

Table 7. The RQE and MSE of the results.

Method (and AMRLS)	AIAGS	AO	HHO
RQE	0.1819	0.6579	0.6935
MSE	0.0351	0.5133	0.6626

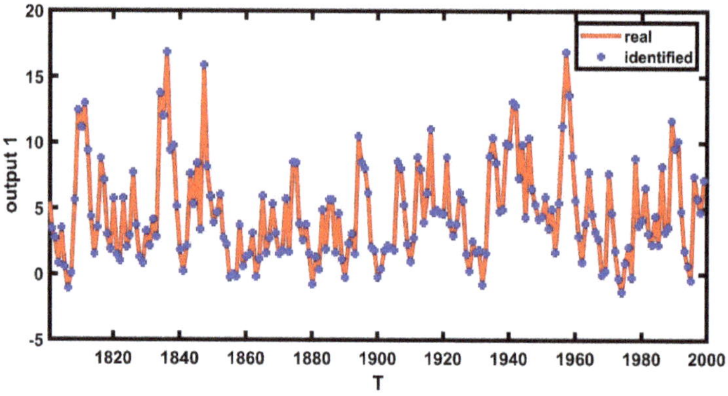

Figure 9. The real output 1 and the identified output 1.

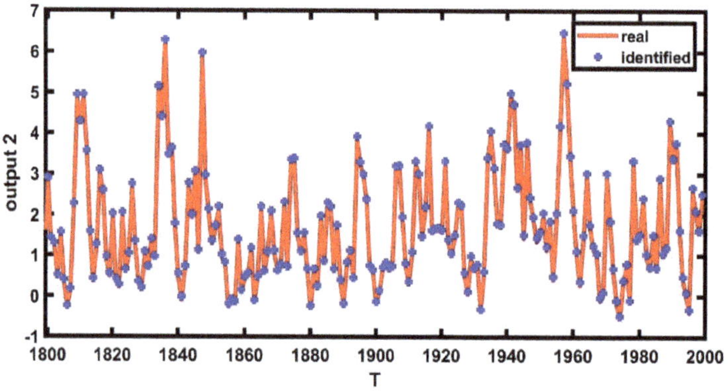

Figure 10. The real output 2 and the identified output 2.

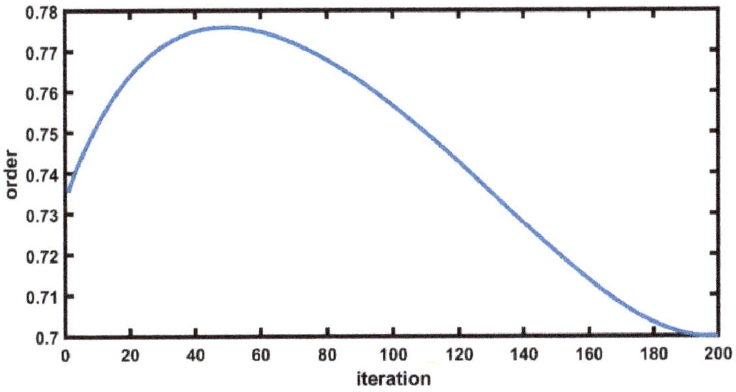

Figure 11. The estimated fractional-order convergence curve.

5. Conclusions

This paper discusses a new identification method for MIMO fractional-order Hammerstein models. In order to improve the accuracy of identification results, the identification process needs a heuristic algorithm to provide the initial value. Because the immune algorithm is prone to premature convergence, this paper improves the immune algorithm and proposes AIAGS. In AIAGS, the immune algorithm's stimulation function and mutation strategy are improved, and simulated annealing is added to the final step to select the optimal solution. The core idea of these improvements is to avoid finding the optimal local solution. Then, through the obtained initial value, the auxiliary model recursive least squares method is used to accurately identify all the MIMO fractional-order Hammerstein model parameters. The experimental results show the effectiveness of the proposed algorithm. The proposed methods in this paper can be applied to other literature [45–47], such as parameter identification problems of different systems, engineering applications, fault diagnosis, and so on.

Author Contributions: Conceptualization, Q.J. and B.W.; methodology, Q.J.; software, B.W.; validation, Q.J., B.W. and Z.W.; formal analysis, B.W.; investigation, B.W.; resources, Q.J.; data curation, Q.J. and B.W.; writing—original draft preparation, B.W.; writing—review and editing, Q.J., B.W. and Z.W.; visualization, Q.J.; supervision, Q.J. All authors have read and agreed to the published version of the manuscript.

Funding: This research received no external funding.

Institutional Review Board Statement: Not applicable.

Informed Consent Statement: Not applicable.

Data Availability Statement: In the paper, all the data generation information has been given in detail in the related chapter.

Conflicts of Interest: The authors declare no conflict of interest.

References

1. Billings, S.A.; Fakhouri, S.Y. Identification of systems containing linear dynamic and static nonlinear element. *Automatica* **1982**, *18*, 15–26. [CrossRef]
2. Narendra, K.S.; Gallman, P.G. An Iterative Method for the Identification of Nonlinear Systems using the Hammerstein Model. *IEEE Trans. Autom. Control* **1966**, *AC11*, 546–550. [CrossRef]
3. Moghaddam, M.J.; Mojallali, H.; Teshnehlab, M. Recursive identification of multiple-input single-output fractional-order Hammerstein model with time delay. *Appl. Soft Comput.* **2018**, *70*, 486–500. [CrossRef]
4. Chen, H.F. Strong consistency of recursive identification for Hammerstein systems with discontinuous piecewise-linear memoryless block. *IEEE Trans. Autom. Control AC* **2005**, *50*, 1612–1617. [CrossRef]

5. Sznaier, M. Computational complexity analysis of set membership identification of Hammerstein and Wiener systems. *Automatica* **2009**, *45*, 701–705. [CrossRef]
6. Kung, M.C.; Womack, B. Discrete time adaptive control of linear dynamic systems with a two-segment piecewise-linear asymmetric nonlinearity. *IEEE Trans. Autom. Control* **2003**, *29*, 170–172. [CrossRef]
7. Mccannon, T.E.; Gallagher, N.C.; Minoo-Hamedani, D.; Wise, J.L. On the design of nonlinear discrete-time predictors. *IEEE Trans. Inf. Theory* **1982**, *28*, 366–371. [CrossRef]
8. Jin, Q.; Wang, H.; Su, Q. A novel optimization algorithm for MIMO Hammerstein model identification under heavy-tailed noise. *ISA Trans.* **2018**, *72*, 77–91. [CrossRef] [PubMed]
9. Jin, Q.; Xu, Z.; Cai, W. An Improved Whale Optimization Algorithm with Random Evolution and Special Reinforcement Dual-Operation Strategy Collaboration. *Symmetry* **2021**, *13*, 238. [CrossRef]
10. Dong, S.; Yu, L.; Zhang, W.A. Robust extended recursive least squyares identification algorithm for Hammerstein systems with dynamic disturbances. *Digit. Signal Process.* **2020**, *101*, 102716. [CrossRef]
11. Dhaifallah, M.A.; Westwick, D.T. Support Vector Machine Identification of Output Error Hammerstein Models. *IFAC Proc. Vol.* **2011**, *44*, 13948–13953. [CrossRef]
12. Schlegel, M.; Čech, M. Fractal System Identification for Robust Control—The Moment Approach. In Proceedings of the 5th International Carpathian Control Conference, Zakopane, Poland, 25–28 May 2004.
13. Torvik, P.J.; Bagley, R.L. On the Appearance of the Fractional Derivative in the Behavior of Real Materials. *J. Appl. Mech.* **1984**, *51*, 725–728. [CrossRef]
14. Zhao, C.; Dingy, X. Closed-form solutions to fractional-order linear differential equations. *Front. Electr. Electr. Eng. China* **2008**, *3*, 214–217. [CrossRef]
15. Chen, S.; Liu, F.; Turner, I. Numerical inversion of the fractional derivative index and surface thermal flux for an anomalous heat conduction model in a multi-layer medium. *Appl. Math. Model.* **2018**, *59*, 514–526. [CrossRef]
16. Deng, J. Higher-order stochastic averaging for a SDOF fractional viscoelastic system under bounded noise excitation. *J. Frankl. Inst.* **2017**, *354*, 7917–7945. [CrossRef]
17. Das, S. *Functional Fractional Calculus*; Springer: Berlin/Heidelberg, Germany, 2011; pp. 110–122.
18. Table, M.A.; Béthoux, O.; Godoyb, E. Identification of a PEMFC fractional order model. *Int. J. Hydrogen Energy* **2017**, *42*, 1499–1509.
19. Kumar, S.; Ghosh, A. Identification of fractional order model for a voltammetric E-tongue system. *Measurement* **2019**, *150*, 107064. [CrossRef]
20. Zhang, Q.; Shang, Y.; Li, Y. A novel fractional variable-order equivalent circuit model and parameter identification of electric vehicle Li-ion batteries. *ISA Trans.* **2019**, *97*, 448–457. [CrossRef]
21. Hammar, K.; Djamah, T.; Bettayeb, M. Fractional hammerstein system identification using particle swarm optimization. In Proceedings of the 2015 7th International Conference on Modelling, Identification and Control (ICMIC) 2015, Sousse, Tunisia, 18–20 December 2015; pp. 1–6.
22. Hammar, K.; Djamah, T.; Bettayeb, M. Fractional Hammerstein system identification based on two decomposition principles. *IFAC-PapersOnLine* **2019**, *52*, 206–210. [CrossRef]
23. Chetoui, M.; Aoun, m. Instrumental variables based methods for linear systems identification with fractional models in the EIV context. In Proceedings of the 2019 16th International Multi-Conference on Systems, Signals & Devices (SSD) 2019, Istanbul, Turkey, 21–24 March 2019; pp. 90–95.
24. Wang, J.; Wei, Y.; Liu, T. Fully parametric identification for continuous time fractional order Hammerstein systems. *J. Frankl. Inst.* **2020**, *357*, 651–666. [CrossRef]
25. Cui, R.; Wei, Y.; Chen, Y. An innovative parameter estimation for fractional-order systems in the presence of outliers. *Nonlinear Dyn.* **2017**, *89*, 453–463. [CrossRef]
26. Tang, Y.; Liu, H.; Wang, W. Parameter identification of fractional order systems using block pulse functions. *Signal Process.* **2015**, *107*, 272–281. [CrossRef]
27. Cui, R.; Wei, Y.; Cheng, S. An innovative parameter estimation for fractional order systems with impulse noise. *Isa Trans.* **2017**, 120–129. [CrossRef] [PubMed]
28. Zhao, Y.; Yan, L.; Chen, Y. Complete parametric identification of fractional order Hammerstein systems. In Proceedings of the ICFDA'14 International Conference on Fractional Differentiation and Its Applications 2014, Catania, Italy, 23–25 June 2014; pp. 1–6.
29. Zeng, L.; Zhu, Z.; Shu, L. Subspace identification for fractional order Hammerstein systems based on instrumental variables. *Int. J. Control Autom. Syst.* **2012**, *10*, 947–953.
30. Khanra, M.; Pal, J. Reduced Order Approximation of MIMO Fractional Order Systems. *IEEE J. Emerg. Sel. Top. Circuits Syst.* **2013**, *3*, 451–458. [CrossRef]
31. Lakshmikantham, V.; Vatsala, A.S. Basic theory of fractional differential equations. *Nonlinear Anal. Theory Methods Appl.* **2008**, *69*, 2677–2682. [CrossRef]
32. Chun, J.S.; Jung, H.K.; Hahn, S.Y. A study on comparison of optimization performances between immune algorithm and other heuristic algorithms. *IEEE Trans Magn.* **1998**, *34*, 297222975.
33. Castro, L.N.; Castro, D.L.; Timmis, J. *Artificial Immune Systems: A New Computational Intelligence Approach*; Springer Science & Business Media: London, UK, 2002.

34. Chen, X.L.; Li, J.Q.; Han, Y.Y. Improved artificial immune algorithm for the flexible job shop problem with transportation time. *Meas. Control* **2020**, *53*, 2111–2128. [CrossRef]
35. Lu, L.; Guo, Z.; Wang, Z. Parameter Estimation for a Capacitive Coupling Communication Channel Within a Metal Cabinet Based on a Modified Artificial Immune Algorithm. *IEEE Access* **2021**, 75683–75698. [CrossRef]
36. Samigulina, G.; Samigulina, Z. Diagnostics of industrial equipment and faults prediction based on modified algorithms of artificial immune systems. *J. Intell. Manuf.* **2021**. [CrossRef]
37. Yu, T.; Xie, M.; Li, X. Quantitative method of damage degree of power system network attack based on improved artificial immune algorithm. In Proceedings of the ICAIIS 2021: 2021 2nd International Conference on Artificial Intelligence and Information Systems, Chongqing, China, 28–30 May 2021.
38. Xu, Y.; Zhang, J. Regional Integrated Energy Site Layout Optimization Based on Improved Artificial Immune Algorithm. *Energies* **2020**, *13*, 4381. [CrossRef]
39. Eker, E.; Kayri, M.; Ekinci, S. A New Fusion of ASO with SA Algorithm and Its Applications to MLP Training and DC Motor Speed Control. *Arab. J. Sci. Eng.* **2021**, *46*, 3889–3911. [CrossRef]
40. Wu, G.; Mallipeddi, R.; Suganthan, P.N. *Problem Definitions and Evaluation Criteria for the CEC 2017 Competition and Special Session on Constrained Single Objective Real-Parameter Optimization*; Technical Report; Nanyang Technological University: Singapore, 2016.
41. Heidari, A.A.; Mirjalili, S.; Faris, H.; Aljarah, H. Harris hawks optimization: Algorithm and applications. *Future Gener. Comput. Syst.* **2019**, *97*, 849–872. [CrossRef]
42. Abualigah, L.; Yousri, D.; Elaziz, M.A. Matlab Code of Aquila Optimizer: A novel meta-heuristic optimization algorithm. *Comput. Ind. Eng.* **2021**, *157*, 107250. [CrossRef]
43. Dzieliński, A.; Sierociuk, D. Stability of discrete fractional order state-space systems. *IFAC Proc. Vol.* **2006**, *39*, 505–510. [CrossRef]
44. Ding, F.; Chen, H.; Li, M. Multi-innovation least squares identification methods based on the auxiliary model for MISO systems. *Appl. Math. Comput.* **2007**, *187*, 658–668. [CrossRef]
45. Zhao, X.; Lin, Z.; Bo, F. Research on Automatic Generation Control with Wind Power Participation Based on Predictive Optimal 2-Degree-of-Freedom PID Strategy for Multi-area Interconnected Power System. *Energies* **2018**, *11*, 3325. [CrossRef]
46. Ding, J.; Chen, J.; Lin, J. Particle filtering based parameter estimation for systems with output-error type model structures. *J. Frankl. Inst.* **2019**, *356*, 5521–5540. [CrossRef]
47. Wang, L.; Liu, H.; Dai, L. Novel Method for Identifying Fault Location of Mixed Lines. *Energies* **2018**, *11*, 1529. [CrossRef]

mathematics

Article

Non-Instantaneous Impulsive BVPs Involving Generalized Liouville–Caputo Derivative

Ahmed Salem * and Sanaa Abdullah

Department of Mathematics, Faculty of Science, King Abdulaziz University, P.O. Box 80203, Jeddah 21589, Saudi Arabia; samalotebi@kau.edu.sa
* Correspondence: asaalshreef@kau.edu.sa

Abstract: This manuscript investigates the existence, uniqueness and Ulam–Hyers stability (UH) of solution to fractional differential equations with non-instantaneous impulses on an arbitrary domain. Using the modern tools of functional analysis, we achieve the required conditions. Finally, we provide an example of how our results can be applied.

Keywords: non-instantaneous impulses; Generalized Liouville–Caputo derivative; Leray–Schauder alternative theorem

MSC: 34A08; 34A12; 47H08; 47H10; 46B45

Citation: Salem, A.; Abdullah, S. Non-Instantaneous Impulsive BVPs Involving Generalized Liouville–Caputo Derivative. *Mathematics* **2022**, *10*, 291. https://doi.org/10.3390/math10030291

Academic Editors: António M. Lopes, Alireza Alfi, Liping Chen and Sergio A. David

Received: 13 December 2021
Accepted: 13 January 2022
Published: 18 January 2022

1. Introduction

The study of differential equations with fractional order has become increasingly popular in recent decades. The reasons behind it are fractional order derivatives provide powerful tools for describing inherited or defined properties in a wide range of science and engineering fields [1–8].

There are several approaches of fractional derivatives, Riemann–Liouville, Caputo, Hadamard, Hilfer, etc. It is important to cite that the Caputo derivative is useful to affront problems where initial conditions are done in the function and in the respective derivatives of integer order. Due to the importance of the Caputo version, there are many versions established as generalization of it, such as Caputo–Katugampola, Caputo–Hadamard, Caputo–Fabrizio, etc. Furthermore, it is drown attention of huge number of contributors to study physical and mathematical modelings contain it and its related versions, see [9–13] and references cited therein.

Finding exact solutions to the differential equations, whether they are ordinary, partial, or fractional, is a extremely difficult and complex issue, and that is why mathematicians have resorted to studying the properties of solutions such as existence, uniqueness, stability, invariant, controllability and others. The most important of these properties are existence and uniqueness which attracted the attention of many contributors to their study [14–20]. Furthermore, Ulam–Hyers stability analysis that is necessary for nonlinear problems in terms of optimization and numerical solutions and plays a key role in numerical solutions where exact solutions are difficult to get.

The fractional differential equations (FDEs) with instantaneous impulses are increasingly being used to analyze abrupt shifts in the evolution pace of dynamical systems, such as those brought about by shocks, disturbances, and natural disasters [21,22]. The duration of instantaneous impulses is relatively short in comparison to the duration of the overall process. However, certain dynamics of evolution processes have been observed to be inexplicable by instantaneous impulsive dynamic systems. As an instance, the injection and absorption of drugs in the blood is a gradual and continuous process. Here, each spontaneous, the action begins in an arbitrary fixed position and lasts for a finite amount of time. This type of system is known as a non-instantaneous impulsive system, which are more suitable for investigating the dynamics of evolutionary processes [23–25] and the references cited therein. Hernandaz and O'Regan [26] discussed the evolution equations involving non-instantaneous impulses of the form:

$$\begin{cases} x' = Ax(t) + f(t, x(t)), & t \in (s_k, t_{k+1}], k = 0, 1, \cdots, m, \\ y(t) = g_k(t, x(t)), & t \in (t_k, s_k], k = 1, 2, \cdots, m, \\ x(0) = x_0. \end{cases}$$

Liu et al. [27] explored generalized Ulam–Hyers–Rassias stability for the following fractional differential equation:

$$\begin{cases} {}^cD^v_{0,w} z(w) = f(w, z(w)), & w \in (w_k, s_k],\ k = 0, 1, \cdots, m,\ 0 < v < 1, \\ z(w) = g_k(w, z(w)), & w \in (s_{k-1}, w_k],\ k = 1, \cdots, m \end{cases}$$

where ${}^cD^v_{0,w}$ is a Caputo derivative of fractional order $0 < v < 1$ with the lower limit 0. Ho and Ngo [28] analyzed generalized Ulam–Hyers–Rassias stability for the following fractional differential equation:

$$\begin{cases} {}^cD^{\alpha,\rho}_{a^+} x(t) = f(t, x(t)), & t \in (t_k, s_k],\ k = 0, 1, \cdots, m,\ 0 < \alpha < 1, \\ x(t) = I_k(t, x(t)), & t \in (s_{k-1}, t_k],\ k = 1, \cdots, m, \\ x(a^+) = x_0 \end{cases}$$

where ${}^cD^{\alpha,\rho}_{a^+}$ is a Caputo–Katugampola derivative of fractional order $0 < \alpha < 1$. Recently, Abbas [29] has studied non-instantaneous impulsive fractional integro-differential equations with proportional fractional derivatives with respect to another function by using the nonlinear alternative Leray–Schauder type and the Banach contraction mapping principle

$$\begin{cases} {}_aD^{\alpha,\rho,g} y(t) = f(t, y(t), {}_aI^{\beta,\rho,g} y(t)), & t \in (s_k, t_{k+1}], k = 0, 1, \cdots, m, \\ y(t) = \Psi_k(t, y(t_k^+)), & t \in (t_k, s_k], k = 1, 2, \cdots, m, \\ {}_aI^{\beta,\rho,g} y(u) = y_0, & y_0 \in \mathbb{R} \end{cases}$$

where $0 < \alpha \leq 1, \beta, \rho > 0, {}_aD^{\alpha,\rho,g}$ is the proportional fractional derivative of order α with respect to another function g.

It is remarkable that the most of contributions focus on the case when the order of fractional derivative lies in the unit interval $(0, 1)$. This observation encourages us to study these equations when the order of fractional derivative lies in the unit interval $(1, 2)$. Furthermore, although the Generalized Liouville–Caputo fractional derivative is considered a generalization of Caputo and Hadamard fractional derivatives, there is a rareness of the studies with this approach.

Inspire of the above, we investigate the existence of solutions for non-instantaneous impulsive fractional boundary value problems in this paper. Specifically, we consider the following problem:

$$\begin{cases} {}^cD^{\beta,\rho}_{0^+} y(\tau) = h(\tau, y(\tau), \tau^{1-\rho} y'(\tau)), & \tau \in (s_r, \tau_{r+1}], r = 0, 1, \cdots, k, \\ y(\tau) = \Phi_r(\tau, y(\tau), y(\tau_r - 0), & \tau \in (\tau_r, s_r], r = 1, 2, \cdots, k, \\ y'(\tau) = \tau^{\rho-1} \Psi_r(\tau, y(\tau), y(\tau_r - 0), & \tau \in (\tau_r, s_r], r = 1, 2, \cdots, k, \\ y(0) = y_0, \quad \lim_{\tau \to 0} \tau^{1-\rho} y'(\tau) = y_1, & y_0, y_1 \in \mathbb{R} \end{cases} \tag{1}$$

where all intervals are subset of $J = [0, T]$, ${}^cD^{\beta,\rho}$ is a generalized Caputo–Liouville (Katugampola) derivative of order $1 < \beta \leq 2$ and type $0 < \rho \leq 1$ and $h : J \times \mathbb{R} \times \mathbb{R} \to \mathbb{R}$ is a given continuous function. Here, $0 = s_0 < \tau_1 < s_1 < \cdots < \tau_k < s_k < \tau_{k+1} = T, k \in \mathbb{N}$ are fixed real numbers and Φ_r and $\Psi_r : (\tau_r, s_r) \to \mathbb{R}, r = 1, \cdots, k$ are non-instantaneous impulses.

The main objectives of our work are to develope the existence theory and Ulam–Hyers stability of non-instantaneous impulsive BVPs involving Generalized Liouville–Caputo derivatives. This work is based on modern functional analysis techniques. Three basic results introduce: the first two deal with the existence and uniqueness of solutions by applying a nonlinear Leray–Schauder alternative theorem and the Banach fixed point theorem, respectively. While the third concerns the Ulam–Hyers stability analysis of solutions for the given problem by establishing a criterion for ensuring various types of Ulam–Hyers stability.

For the rest of the paper, it is arranged as follows: Section 2 provides some preliminary concepts about our work and a key lemma that deals with the linear variant of the given problem, along with giving a formula for converting the given problem into a fixed point problem.Using the Banach contraction mapping principle and the Leray–Schauder nonlinear alternative, the existence and uniqueness of problem (1) are presented in Section 3.

Remark 1. *For fractional differential equation for non-instantaneous impulsive (1).The intervals* $(\tau_r, s_r], r = 1, \cdots, k$ *are known as non-instantaneous impulse intervals, and the functions* $\Phi_r(\tau, y(\tau), y(\tau_r - 0)), r = 1, \cdots, k$ *are known as non-instantaneous impulsive functions. The fractional differential equation with non-instantaneous impulses (1) is reduced to a fractional differential equation with instantaneous impulses if* $\tau_r = s_{r-1}, r = 1, \cdots, k$.

2. Preliminaries

Let the space of continuous real-valued functions on J be denoted by $C(J, \mathbb{R})$. Consider the space

$$\mathcal{P}C(J, \mathbb{R}) = \{y : J \to \mathbb{R} : y \in C((\tau_k, \tau_{k+1}], \mathbb{R})\}$$

and there exist $y(\tau_k^-)$ and $y(\tau_k^+), k = 1, \cdots, r$ with $y(\tau_k^-) = y(\tau_k)$.

Furthermore, consider the space:

$$\mathcal{P}C^1_\delta(J, \mathbb{R}) = \{y : J \to \mathbb{R} : \delta y \in PC(J, \mathbb{R})\}$$

such that $\delta y(\tau_k^+)$ and $\delta y(\tau_k^-)$ exist and δy is left continuous at τ_k for $k = 1, \cdots, r$ and $\delta = \tau^{1-\rho} d/d\tau$. The space $\mathcal{P}C^1_\delta(J, \mathbb{R})$ equipped with the norm:

$$||y|| = \sup_{\tau \in J}\{|y(\tau)|_{\mathcal{P}C} + |\delta y(\tau)|_{\mathcal{P}C^1_\delta}\} = ||y(\tau)||_{\mathcal{P}C} + ||\delta y(\tau)||_{\mathcal{P}C^1_\delta}.$$

Furthermore, we recall that:

$$\mathcal{A}C^n(J, \mathbb{R}) = \{h : J \to \mathbb{R} : h, h', ..., h^{n-1} \in C(J, R)\}$$

and $h^{(n-1)}$ is absolutely continuous.

For $0 \leq \varepsilon < 1$, we define the space:

$$C_{\varepsilon,\rho}(J, \mathbb{R}) = \{f : J \to \mathbb{R} : (\tau^\rho - a^\rho)^\varepsilon f(\tau) \in C(J, \mathbb{R})\}$$

endowed with the norm

$$||f||_{C_{\varepsilon,\rho}} = ||(\tau^\rho - a^\rho)^\varepsilon f(\tau)||_C.$$

Furthermore, we define a class of functions f that is absolutely continuous $\delta^{n-1}, n \in \mathbb{N}$ derivative, denoted by $\mathcal{A}C^n_\delta(J, \mathbb{R})$ as follows:

$$\mathcal{A}C^n_\delta(J, \mathbb{R}) = \left\{f : J \to \mathbb{R} : \delta^k f \in \mathcal{A}C(J, \mathbb{R}), \delta = \tau^{1-\rho}\frac{d}{d\tau}, k = 0, 1, \cdots, n-1\right\}$$

Equipped with the norm

$$||f||_{C^n_\delta} = \sum_{k=0}^{n-1} ||\delta^k f||_C.$$

Generally, a space of functions that is endowed with the norm

$$||f||_{C^n_{\delta,\varepsilon}} = \sum_{k=0}^{n-1} ||\delta^k f||_C + ||\delta^n f||_{C_{\varepsilon,\rho}}$$

is defined by

$$C^n_{\delta,\varepsilon}(J,\mathbb{R}) = \{f : J \to \mathbb{R} : f \in \mathcal{AC}^n_\delta(J,\mathbb{R}), \delta^n f \in C_{\varepsilon,\rho}(J,\mathbb{R})\}.$$

Note that $C^n_{\delta,0} = C^n_\delta$.

Definition 1 ([30]). *The left-sided and right-sided generalized fractional integrals of order $\alpha > 0$ and type $0 < \rho \leq 1$ are defined, respectively, by:*

$$I^{\alpha,\rho}_{a^+} f(x) = \frac{\rho^{1-\alpha}}{\Gamma(\alpha)} \int_a^x (x^\rho - t^\rho)^{\alpha-1} t^{\rho-1} f(t)dt,$$
$$I^{\alpha,\rho}_{b^-} f(x) = \frac{\rho^{1-\alpha}}{\Gamma(\alpha)} \int_x^b (x^\rho - t^\rho)^{\alpha-1} t^{\rho-1} f(t)dt.$$

Definition 2 ([31]). *Let $n = [\alpha] + 1$, $n \in \mathbb{N}$, $0 \leq a < b < \infty$ and $f \in \mathcal{AC}^n_\delta[a,b]$. The left-sided and right-sided Generalized Liouville–Caputo-type (Katugampola) fractional derivatives of order $\alpha > 0$ and type $0 < \rho \leq 1$ are defined via the above generalized integrals, respectively, as*

$$({}^cD^{\alpha,\rho}_{a^+} f)(x) = \left(I^{n-\alpha,\rho}_{a^+} \left(x^{1-\rho} \frac{d}{dx} \right)^n f \right)(x) = \frac{\rho^{1-n+\alpha}}{\Gamma(n-\alpha)} \int_a^x \frac{t^{\rho-1}}{(x^\rho - t^\rho)^{1-n+\alpha}} \left(t^{1-\rho} \frac{d}{dt} \right)^n f(t)dt,$$
$$({}^cD^{\alpha,\rho}_{b^-} f)(x) = \left(I^{n-\alpha,\rho}_{b^-} \left(-x^{1-\rho} \frac{d}{dx} \right)^n f \right)(x) = \frac{\rho^{1-n+\alpha}}{\Gamma(n-\alpha)} \int_x^b \frac{t^{\rho-1}}{(x^\rho - t^\rho)^{1-n+\alpha}} \left(-t^{1-\rho} \frac{d}{dt} \right)^n f(t)dt.$$

Lemma 1 ([31]). *Let $n - 1 < \alpha \leq n$; $n \in \mathbb{N}$ and $f \in \mathcal{AC}^n_\delta[a,b]$ or $f \in C^n_\delta[a,b]$. Then,*

$$I^{\alpha,\rho}_{a^+} {}^cD^{\alpha,\rho}_{a^+} f(x) = f(x) - \sum_{k=0}^{n-1} \frac{\delta^k f(a)}{k!} \left(\frac{t^\rho - a^\rho}{\rho} \right)^k,$$
$$I^{\alpha,\rho}_{b^-} {}^cD^{\alpha,\rho}_{b^-} f(x) = f(x) - \sum_{k=0}^{n-1} \frac{(-1)^k \delta^k f(b)}{k!} \left(\frac{b^\rho - t^\rho}{\rho} \right)^k.$$

In particular, for $1 < \alpha \leq 2$, we have:

$$I^{\alpha,\rho}_{a^+} {}^cD^{\alpha,\rho}_{a^+} f(x) = f(x) - f(a) - \frac{t^\rho - a^\rho}{\rho} \delta f(a),$$
$$I^{\alpha,\rho}_{b^-} {}^cD^{\alpha,\rho}_{b^-} f(x) = f(x) - f(b) + \frac{b^\rho - t^\rho}{\rho} \delta f(b).$$

Lemma 2. *Let $1 < \beta < 2$ and $v : J \to \mathbb{R}$ be an integrable function. Then, there is a solution to the linear problem:*

$$\begin{aligned}
{}^cD^{\beta,\rho}_{s_r} y(\tau) &= v(\tau) & \tau &\in (s_r, \tau_{r+1}], r = 0,1,\cdots,k \\
y(\tau) &= \Phi_r(\tau, y(\tau), y(\tau_r - 0)), & \tau &\in (\tau_r, s_r], r = 1,2,\cdots,k \\
\tau^{1-\rho} y'(\tau) &= \Psi_r(\tau, y(\tau), y(\tau_r - 0)), & \tau &\in (\tau_r, s_r], r = 1,2,\cdots,k \\
y(0) &= y_0, \quad \lim_{\tau \to 0} \tau^{1-\rho} y'(\tau) = y_1, & y_0, y_1 &\in \mathbb{R}
\end{aligned} \tag{2}$$

given by:

$$y(\tau)=\begin{cases}\frac{\rho^{1-\beta}}{\Gamma(\beta)}\int_0^{\tau} t^{\rho-1}(\tau^\rho-t^\rho)^{\beta-1}v(t)dt+y_0+\frac{y_1}{\rho}\tau^\rho, & \tau\in[0,\tau_1],\\ \Phi_r(\tau,y(\tau),y(\tau_r-0)), & \tau\in(\tau_r,s_r],\\ \frac{\rho^{1-\beta}}{\Gamma(\beta)}\int_{s_r}^{\tau} t^{\rho-1}(\tau^\rho-t^\rho)^{\beta-1}h(t)dt+\Phi_r(s_r,y(s_r),y(\tau_r-0)) & \\ +\frac{\tau^\rho-s_r^\rho}{\rho}\Psi_r(s_r,y(s_r),y(\tau_r-0)), & \tau\in(s_r,\tau_{r+1}].\end{cases}\tag{3}$$

Proof. Applying the operator $I_{s_r}^{\beta,\rho}$ to fractional differential equation in (2) and using Lemma 1, we have:

$$y(\tau)=I_{s_r}^{\beta,\rho}v(\tau)+c_{1,r}+c_{2,r}\frac{\tau^\rho-s_r^\rho}{\rho}\quad\text{and}\quad\tau^{1-\rho}y'(\tau)=I_{s_r}^{\beta-1,\rho}v(\tau)+c_{2,r}$$

where $c_{1,r},c_{2,r}\in\mathbb{R}$, $r=0,1,\cdots,k$ are constants to be determined.

- For $\tau\in[0,\tau_1]$, we obtain:

$$y(\tau)=I_0^{\beta,\rho}v(\tau)+c_{1,0}+c_{2,0}\frac{\tau^\rho}{\rho}\quad\text{and}\quad\tau^{1-\rho}y'(\tau)=I_0^{\beta-1,\rho}v(\tau)+c_{2,0}.$$

  Applying the initial conditions $y(0)=y_0$ and $\lim_{\tau\to0}\tau^{\rho-1}y'(\tau)=y_1$ give $c_{1,0}=y_0$ and $c_{2,0}=y_1$ which imply that:

$$y(\tau)=I_0^{\beta,\rho}v(\tau)+y_0+y_1\frac{\tau^\rho}{\rho}\quad\text{and}\quad\tau^{1-\rho}y'(\tau)=I_0^{\beta-1,\rho}v(\tau)+y_1.$$

- For $\tau\in(\tau_1,s_1]$. Then,

$$y(\tau)=\Phi_1(\tau,y(\tau),y(\tau_1-0))\quad\text{and}\quad y'(\tau)=\tau^{\rho-1}\Psi_1(\tau,y(\tau),y(\tau_1-0)).$$

- For $\tau\in(s_1,\tau_2]$. Then,

$$y(\tau)=I_{s_1}^{\beta,\rho}v(\tau)+c_{1,1}+c_{2,1}\frac{\tau^\rho-s_1^\rho}{\rho}\quad\text{and}\quad\tau^{1-\rho}y'(\tau)=I_{s_1}^{\beta-1,\rho}v(\tau)+c_{2,1}.$$

  Due to the previous impulsive conditions, we get

$$c_{1,1}=\Phi_1(s_1,y(s_1),y(\tau_1-0))\quad\text{and}\quad c_{2,1}=\Psi_1(s_1,y(s_1),y(\tau_1-0))$$

  which imply that

$$y(\tau)=I_{s_1}^{\beta,\rho}v(\tau)+\Phi_1(s_1,y(s_1),y(\tau_1-0))+\Psi_1(s_1,y(s_1),y(\tau_1-0))\frac{\tau^\rho-s_1^\rho}{\rho},$$
$$\tau^{1-\rho}y'(\tau)=I_{s_1}^{\beta-1,\rho}v(\tau)+\Psi_1(s_1,y(s_1),y(\tau_1-0)).$$

- By similar process. For $\tau\in(s_r,\tau_{r+1}]$. Then,

$$y(\tau)=I_{s_r}^{\beta,\rho}v(\tau)+\Phi_r(s_r,y(s_r),y(\tau_r-0))+\frac{\tau^\rho-s_r^\rho}{\rho}\Psi_r(s_r,y(s_r),y(\tau_r-0)).$$

Hence, from the previous, we obtain the solution (3). By direct computation, the converse follows. The proof is complete. □

Next, we present the concept of Ulam stability for problem (1). First, consider $\mathcal{E} = \mathcal{PC}^1_\delta(J,\mathbb{R}) \cap \mathcal{AC}^2_\delta(J,\mathbb{R})$ with $y \in \mathcal{E}$ and $\epsilon > 0$. Let us introduce the following inequality

$$\begin{cases} \|{}^cD^{\beta,\rho}_{s_r} y(\tau) - h(\tau)\| & \leq \epsilon, \qquad \tau \in (s_r, \tau_{r+1}], r = 0,1,\cdots,k \\ \|y(\tau) - \Phi_r\| & \leq \epsilon, \qquad \tau \in (\tau_r, s_r], r = 1,\cdots,k \\ \|\tau^{1-\rho} y'(\tau) - \Psi_r\| & \leq \epsilon, \qquad \tau \in (\tau_r, s_r], r = 1,\cdots,k \end{cases} \tag{4}$$

Definition 3 ([32]). *If there is a constant $\Lambda > 0$ and $\epsilon > 0$ such that for any solution $\widetilde{y} \in \mathcal{E}$ of the inequality (4), there is a unique solution $y \in \mathcal{E}$ to the problem (1) fulfilling*

$$\|\widetilde{y}(\tau) - y(\tau)\| \leq \Lambda\epsilon.$$

Then the problem (1) is said to be UH stable.

Definition 4 ([32]). *If there is a function $\mu \in (\mathbb{R}^+, \mathbb{R}^+), \mu(0) = 0$, for $\epsilon > 0$ such that for any solution $\widetilde{y} \in \mathcal{E}$ of the inequality (4), there is a unique solution $y \in \mathcal{E}$ to the problem (1) fulfilling*

$$\|\widetilde{y}(\tau) - y(\tau)\| \leq \mu(\epsilon).$$

Then the problem (1) is said to be GUH stable.

Remark 2. *If one has a function $\varrho \in \mathcal{E}$ together with a sequences $\varrho_r, r = 0,\cdots,r$ dependent on y. Then $y \in \mathcal{E}$ is called a solution of the inequality (4) such that:*

$$\begin{array}{lll} (a) & |\varrho(\tau)| \leq \epsilon, |\varrho_r| \leq \epsilon, & \tau \in J, r = 0,\cdots,k \\ (b) & {}^cD^{\beta,\rho}_{s_r}\widetilde{y}(\tau) = \widetilde{h}(\tau) + \varrho(\tau), & \tau \in (s_r, \tau_{r+1}], r = 0,1,\cdots,k \\ (c) & \widetilde{y}(\tau) = \Phi_r(\tau, \widetilde{y}(\tau), \widetilde{y}(\tau_r - 0)) + \varrho_r, & \tau \in (\tau_r, s_r], r = 1,2,\cdots,k \\ (d) & \tau^{1-\rho}\widetilde{y}'(\tau) = \Psi_r(\tau, \widetilde{y}(\tau), \widetilde{y}(\tau_r - 0)) + \varrho_r, & \tau \in (\tau_r, s_r], r = 1,2,\cdots,k. \end{array}$$

3. Existence and Uniqueness Results

Our results for uniqueness and existence for problem (1) are presented in this section. By using Lemma 2, we convert the non-instantaneous fractional differential Equation (1) into a fixed point problem. define the operator $\mathcal{G} : \mathcal{E} \to \mathcal{E}$ by:

$$\mathcal{G}y(\tau) = \begin{cases} \dfrac{\rho^{1-\beta}}{\Gamma(\beta)} \displaystyle\int_0^\tau t^{\rho-1}(\tau^\rho - t^\rho)^{\beta-1} h(t)dt + y_0 + \frac{y_1}{\rho}\tau^\rho, & \tau \in [0,\tau_1], \\ \Phi_r(\tau, y(\tau), y(\tau_r - 0)), & \tau \in (\tau_r, s_r], \\ \dfrac{\rho^{1-\beta}}{\Gamma(\beta)} \displaystyle\int_{s_r}^\tau t^{\rho-1}(\tau^\rho - t^\rho)^{\beta-1} h(t)dt + \Phi_r(s_r, y(s_r), y(\tau_r - 0)) & \\ + \dfrac{\tau^\rho - s_r^\rho}{\rho}\Psi_r(s_r, y(s_r), y(\tau_r - 0)), & \tau \in (s_r, \tau_{r+1}]. \end{cases} \tag{5}$$

where $h(\tau) = h(\tau, y(\tau), \tau^{1-\rho}y'(\tau))$.

To explain and prove our main results, we first introduce these hypotheses. Consider the following

($\mathfrak{H}_1$) The function $h : [0,T] \times \mathbb{R} \times \mathbb{R} \to \mathbb{R}$ is continuous and $\Phi_r, \Psi_r : [\tau_r, s_r] \times \mathbb{R} \times \mathbb{R} \to \mathbb{R}$ are continuous functions $\forall r = 1,\cdots,k$ and $k \in \mathbb{N}$.

($\mathfrak{H}_2$) $|\widehat{h}(\tau)| = |h(\tau, y, \tau^{1-\rho}y')| \leq q(\tau)v(|y|)$, where $q \in C([0,T], \mathbb{R}^+)$ and $v : \mathbb{R}^+ \to \mathbb{R}^+$ is a nondecreasing function.

($\mathfrak{H}_3$) There exist constants $\vartheta_r > 0, \vartheta_r^* > 0,\ r = 1,\cdots,k; k \in \mathbb{N}$ such that

$$|\Phi_r(\tau, y, v)| \leq \vartheta_r, \qquad \text{and} \qquad |\Psi_r(\tau, y, v)| \leq \vartheta_r^*$$

$\forall \tau \in [\tau_r, s_r]\ ,\ y, v \in \mathbb{R}$.

($\mathfrak{H}_4$) There exist $\mathcal{A} > 0$ satisfies $||y||_{\mathcal{E}} \neq \mathcal{A}$ for some $y \in \mathcal{E}$.

($\mathfrak{H}_5$) There exist positive constants $\kappa_{1r}, \kappa_{2r}, \kappa_{1r}^*$ and κ_{2r}^*, $r = 1, \cdots, k; k \in \mathbb{N}$ such that:

$$\begin{aligned}
|\Phi_r(\tau, y_1, v_1) - \Phi_r(\tau, y_2, v_2)| &\leq \kappa_{1r}|y_1 - y_2| + \kappa_{2r}|v_1 - v_2|, \\
|\Psi_r(\tau, y_1, v_1) - \Psi_r(\tau, y_2, v_2)| &\leq \kappa_{1r}^*|y_1 - y_2| + \kappa_{2r}^*|v_1 - v_2|
\end{aligned}$$

for each $\tau \in [\tau_r, s_r]$ and $y_1, y_2, v_1, v_2 \in \mathbb{R}$.

($\mathfrak{H}_6$) There exists $\mathcal{L} > 0$ satisfies

$$|h(\tau, y, \delta y) - h(\tau, u, \delta u)| \leq \mathcal{L}(|y - u| + \delta|y - u|)$$

$\forall \tau \in [0, T]$ and $y, u \in \mathbb{R}$.

Below are the short constants that we will use later to simplify handling:

$$\Omega = \Omega(\beta) + \Omega(\beta - 1) \tag{6}$$

$$\Omega_r = \Omega_r(\beta) + \Omega_r(\beta - 1), \tag{7}$$

$$\mathcal{Q} = \frac{\mathcal{A}}{\Omega||q||v(\mathcal{A}) + |y_0| + \frac{|y_1|}{\rho}(\rho + \tau_1^{\rho})}, \tag{8}$$

$$\mathcal{Q}_{1r} = \frac{\mathcal{A}}{\vartheta_r + \vartheta_r^*}, \tag{9}$$

$$\mathcal{Q}_{2r} = \frac{\mathcal{A}}{\Omega_r||q||v(\mathcal{A}) + \vartheta_r + \frac{\vartheta_r^*}{\rho}(\rho + T^{\rho} - s_r^{\rho})} \tag{10}$$

where $r = 1, 2, \cdots, k; k \in \mathbb{N}$,

$$\Omega(\beta) = \frac{\tau_1^{\rho\beta}}{\rho^{\beta}\Gamma(\beta + 1)} \quad \text{and} \quad \Omega_r(\beta) = \frac{(T^{\rho} - s_r^{\rho})^{\beta}}{\rho^{\beta}\Gamma(\beta + 1)}.$$

Lemma 3 ([33,34]). *(Leray–Schauder nonlinear alternative) Assume that $\mathbb{E}$ is a Banach space, B is a convex closed subset of $\mathbb{E}$, and $Y \subset B$ is an open subset and $0 \in Y$. If $\mathcal{F} : \overline{Y} \to B$ is continuous and compact, then either*

- *In $\overline{Y}$, $\mathcal{F}$ has a fixed point; or*
- *For some $\lambda \in (0, 1)$, there exists $y \in \partial Y$ and $y = \lambda\mathcal{F}y$.*

Theorem 1. *Consider Hypotheses ($\mathfrak{H}_1$)–($\mathfrak{H}_4$) satisfied. If*

$$\max_r\{\mathcal{Q}, \mathcal{Q}_{1r}, \mathcal{Q}_{2r}\} > 1$$

where $\mathcal{Q}$, $\mathcal{Q}_{1r}$ and $\mathcal{Q}_{2r}$ are given by Equations (8), (9) and (10), respectively. Then, the problem in Equation (1) has at least one solution in $[0, T]$.

Proof. Verifying the hypotheses of Leray–Schauder nonlinear alternative involves a number of steps. The first step is to demonstrate that the operator $\mathcal{G} : \mathcal{E} \to \mathcal{E}$ defined by Equation (5) maps bounded sets into bounded sets in $\mathcal{E}$. In other word, we show that for a positive number ω, there exists a positive constant $\mathcal{I}$ such that $||\mathcal{G}y||_{\mathcal{E}} \leq \mathcal{I}$ for any $y \in B_{\omega}$ where B_{ω} is a closed bounded set defined as

$$B_{\omega} = \left\{(y, \delta y) : y \in \mathcal{E} \wedge ||y||_{\mathcal{E}} = ||y||_{\mathcal{PC}} + ||\delta y||_{\mathcal{PC}_{\delta}^1} \leqslant \omega\right\}$$

with the radius:

$$\omega \geqslant \max\left\{\Omega||q||v(\omega) + |y_0| + \frac{|y_1|}{\rho}(\rho + \tau_1^{\rho}), \vartheta_r + \vartheta_r^*, \Omega_r||q||v(\omega) + \vartheta_r + \frac{\vartheta_r^*}{\rho}(\rho + T^{\rho} - s_r^{\rho})\right\}.$$

Then, in light of $(\mathfrak{H}_2)$ and $(\mathfrak{H}_3)$, we have

- **Case I.** For each $\tau \in [0, \tau_1]$ and $(y, \delta y) \in B_\omega$. Using (6), we have

$$\|\mathcal{G}y\|_{\mathcal{PC}} \leq \sup_{\tau \in [0,\tau_1]} I_{0^+}^{\beta,\rho}|\widehat{h}(t)| + |y_0| + |\frac{y_1}{\rho}\tau^\rho| \leq \Omega(\beta)\|q\|v(\omega) + |y_0| + \frac{|y_1|}{\rho}\tau_1^\rho.$$

Similarly, one can establish that

$$\|\delta\mathcal{G}y\|_{\mathcal{PC}_\delta^1} \leq \sup_{\tau \in [0,\tau_1]} I_{0^+}^{\beta-1,\rho}|\widehat{h}(t)| + |y_1| \leq \Omega(\beta-1)\|q\|v(\omega) + |y_1|.$$

Consequently, we have

$$\|\mathcal{G}y\|_{\mathcal{E}} \leq \Omega\|q\|v(\omega) + |y_0| + \frac{|y_1|}{\rho}(\rho + \tau_1^\rho) := \mathcal{I}_1.$$

- **Case II.** For each $\tau \in (\tau_r, s_r]$, $r = 1, 2, \cdots, k$ and $(y, \delta y) \in B_\omega$, we get

$$\|\mathcal{G}y\|_{\mathcal{E}} = \|\mathcal{G}y\|_{\mathcal{PC}} + \|\delta\mathcal{G}\|_{\mathcal{PC}_\delta^1} \leq \vartheta_r + \vartheta_r^* := \mathcal{I}_{2r}.$$

- **Case III.** For each $\tau \in (s_r, \tau_{r+1}]$, $r = 1, 2, \cdots, k$ and $(y, \delta y) \in B_\omega$. Using (7), we have

$$\begin{aligned}\|\mathcal{G}y\|_{\mathcal{PC}} \leq &\sup_{\tau \in (s_r,\tau_{r+1}]} I_{s_r}^{\beta,\rho}|\widehat{h}(t)| + |\Phi_r(s_r, y(s_r), y(\tau_r - 0))| + |\frac{\tau^\rho - s_r^\rho}{\rho}\Psi_r(s_r, y(s_r), y(\tau_r - 0))| \\ &\leq \Omega_r(\beta)\|q\|v(\omega) + \vartheta_r + \frac{\vartheta_r^*}{\rho}(T^\rho - s_r^\rho).\end{aligned}$$

In a similar manner, one can obtain:

$$\|\delta\mathcal{G}y\|_{\mathcal{PC}_\delta^1} \leq \Omega_r(\beta-1)\|q\|v(\omega) + \vartheta_r^*.$$

Hence, we deduce that:

$$\|\mathcal{G}y\|_{\mathcal{E}} \leq \Omega_r\|q\|v(\omega) + \vartheta_r + \frac{\vartheta_r^*}{\rho}(\rho + T^\rho - s_r^\rho) := \mathcal{I}_{3r}.$$

From the above three inequalities, we can conclude that $\|\mathcal{G}y\|_{\mathcal{E}} \leq \mathcal{I}$ where $\mathcal{I} = \max_r\{\mathcal{I}_1, \mathcal{I}_{2r}, \mathcal{I}_{3r}\}$. Thus, the operator $\mathcal{G}$ maps bounded sets into bounded sets of the space $\mathcal{E}$.

In the next step, we check that the operator $\mathcal{G}$ maps bounded sets into equicontinuous sets in $\mathcal{E}$.Considering the condition $(\mathfrak{H}_1)$, $\mathcal{G}$ is continuous.

- **Case I.** For each $0 \leqslant \zeta_1 < \zeta_2 \leqslant \tau_1$ and $(y, \delta y) \in B_\omega$, we obtain that

$$\begin{aligned}|(\mathcal{G}y)(\zeta_2) - (\mathcal{G}y)(\zeta_1)| &\leq \frac{\rho^{1-\beta}}{\Gamma(\beta)}\int_0^{\zeta_1} t^{\rho-1}\Big[(\zeta_2^\rho - t^\rho)^{\beta-1} - (\zeta_1^\rho - t^\rho)^{\beta-1}\Big]|\widehat{h}(t)|dt \\ &+ \frac{\rho^{1-\beta}}{\Gamma(\beta)}\int_{\zeta_1}^{\zeta_2} t^{\rho-1}(\zeta_2^\rho - t^\rho)^{\beta-1}|\widehat{h}(t)|dt + \frac{|y_1|}{\rho}\Big(\zeta_2^\rho - \zeta_1^\rho\Big) \\ &\leq \|q\|v(|y|)\frac{1}{\rho^\beta\Gamma(\beta+1)}\Big(\zeta_2^{\rho\beta} - \zeta_1^{\rho\beta}\Big) + \frac{|y_1|}{\rho}\Big(\zeta_2^\rho - \zeta_1^\rho\Big) \\ &\Rightarrow 0 \quad \text{as} \quad \zeta_2 \to \zeta_1.\end{aligned}$$

Similarly, one can establish that:

$$
\begin{aligned}
&|(\delta\mathcal{G}y)(\zeta_2)-(\delta\mathcal{G}y)(\zeta_1)|\\
&\leq \|q\|v(|y|)\frac{\rho^{2-\beta}}{\Gamma(\beta-1)}\left(\int_0^{\zeta_1} t^{\rho-1}\Big[(\zeta_1^\rho-t^\rho)^{\beta-2}-(\zeta_2^\rho-t^\rho)^{\beta-2}\Big]dt+\int_{\zeta_1}^{\zeta_2} t^{\rho-1}(\zeta_2^\rho-t^\rho)^{\beta-2}dt\right)\\
&\leq 2\|q\|v(|y|)\frac{1}{\rho^{\beta-1}\Gamma(\beta)}\left(\zeta_2^\rho-\zeta_1^\rho\right)^{\beta-1}\\
&\Rightarrow 0 \quad \text{as} \quad \zeta_2\to\zeta_1.
\end{aligned}
$$

- **Case II.** For each$\tau_r \leqslant \zeta_1 < \zeta_2 < s_r, r = 1,2,\cdots,k$ and $(y,\delta y)\in B_\omega$, we have

$$
\begin{aligned}
|(\mathcal{G}y)(\zeta_2)-(\mathcal{G}y)(\zeta_1)| &\leq |\Phi_r(\zeta_2,y(\zeta_2),y(\tau_r-0))|-|\Phi_r(\zeta_1,y(\zeta_1),y(\tau_r-0))|\\
|(\delta\mathcal{G}y)(\zeta_2)-(\delta\mathcal{G}y)(\zeta_1)| &\leq |\Psi_r(\zeta_2,y(\zeta_2),y(\tau_r-0))|-|\Psi_r(\zeta_1,y(\zeta_1),y(\tau_r-0))|.
\end{aligned}
$$

Due to the continuity of both functions. It is clear that the above inequality approaches zero when letting $\zeta_2\to\zeta_1$.

- **Case III.** For each $s_r \leqslant \zeta_1 < \zeta_2 < \tau_{r+1}, r = 1,2,\cdots,k$, and $(y,\delta y)\in B_\omega$, we get

$$
\begin{aligned}
&|(\mathcal{G}y)(\zeta_2)-(\mathcal{G}y)(\zeta_1)| \leq \frac{\rho^{1-\beta}}{\Gamma(\beta)}\int_{s_r}^{\zeta_1} t^{\rho-1}\Big[(\zeta_2^\rho-t^\rho)^{\beta-1}-(\zeta_1^\rho-t^\rho)^{\beta-1}\Big]\Big|\widehat{h}(t)\Big|dt\\
&+\frac{\rho^{1-\beta}}{\Gamma(\beta)}\int_{\zeta_1}^{\zeta_2} t^{\rho-1}(\zeta_2^\rho-t^\rho)^{\beta-1}\Big|\widehat{h}(t)\Big|dt+\frac{\zeta_2^\rho-\zeta_1^\rho}{\rho}|\Psi_r(s_r,y(s_r),y(\tau_r-0))|\\
&\leq \|q\|v(|y|)\frac{1}{\rho^\beta\Gamma(\beta+1)}\left[\left(\zeta_2^\rho-s_r^\rho\right)^\beta-\left(\zeta_1^\rho-s_r^\rho\right)^\beta\right]+\frac{\zeta_2^\rho-\zeta_1^\rho}{\rho}|\Psi_r(s_r,y(s_r),y(\tau_r-0))|\\
&\Rightarrow 0 \quad \text{as} \quad \zeta_2\to\zeta_1.
\end{aligned}
$$

Moreover, we have:

$$
\begin{aligned}
&|(\delta\mathcal{G}y)(\zeta_2)-(\delta\mathcal{G}y)(\zeta_1)|\\
&\leq \|q\|v(|y|)\frac{\rho^{2-\beta}}{\Gamma(\beta-1)}\left(\int_{s_r}^{\zeta_1} t^{\rho-1}\Big[(\zeta_1^\rho-t^\rho)^{\beta-2}-(\zeta_2^\rho-t^\rho)^{\beta-2}\Big]dt+\int_{\zeta_1}^{\zeta_2} t^{\rho-1}(\zeta_2^\rho-t^\rho)^{\beta-2}dt\right)\\
&\leq \|q\|v(|y|)\frac{1}{\rho^{\beta-1}\Gamma(\beta)}\Big[2(\zeta_2^\rho-\zeta_1^\rho)^{\beta-1}+(\zeta_1^\rho-s_r^\rho)^{\beta-1}-(\zeta_2^\rho-s_r^\rho)^{\beta-1}\Big]\\
&\Rightarrow 0 \quad \text{as} \quad \zeta_2\to\zeta_1.
\end{aligned}
$$

As a result of the three inequalities above, we conclude that $\|(\mathcal{G}y)(\zeta_2)-(\mathcal{G}y)(\zeta_1)\|_\mathcal{E}\to 0$ independently of $(y,\delta y)\in B_\omega$ as $\zeta_2\to\zeta_1$. Using the preceding arguments and the Arzela-Ascoli theorem, the operator $\mathcal{G}:\mathcal{E}\to\mathcal{E}$ is completely continuous.

Finally, we show that there exist an open set $Y\subset\mathcal{E}$ with $y\neq\lambda\mathcal{G}y$ for $\lambda\in(0,1)$ and $y\in\partial Y$. Consider the equation $y=\lambda\mathcal{G}y$ for $\lambda\in(0,1)$. Then based on **Step 1**, we have the following cases:

- **Case I.** For each $\tau\in[0,\tau_1]$, one has

$$
\|y(\tau)\| = \|\lambda(\mathcal{G}y)(\tau)\| \leq \Omega\|q\|v(\|y\|)+|y_0|+\frac{|y_1|}{\rho}(\rho+\tau_1^\rho)
$$

which implies that:

$$
\frac{\|y\|_\mathcal{E}}{\Omega\|q\|v(\|y\|_\mathcal{E})+|y_0|+\frac{|y_1|}{\rho}(\rho+\tau_1^\rho)}\leq 1. \tag{11}
$$

- **Case II.** For each $\tau \in (\tau_r, s_r], r = 1, 2, \cdots, k$, one has

$$\|y(\tau)\| = \|\lambda(\mathcal{G}y)(\tau)\| \leq \vartheta_r + \vartheta_r^*$$

which implies that:

$$\frac{\|y\|_{\mathcal{E}}}{\vartheta_r + \vartheta_r^*} \leq 1. \tag{12}$$

- **Case III.** For each $\tau \in (s_r, \tau_{r+1}], r = 1, \cdots, k$, we obtain:

$$\|y(\tau)\| = \|\lambda(\mathcal{G}y)(\tau)\| \leq \Omega_r \|q\| v(\|y\|) + \vartheta_r + \frac{\vartheta_r^*}{\rho}(\rho + T^\rho - s_r^\rho)$$

which implies that:

$$\frac{\|y\|_{\mathcal{E}}}{\Omega_r \|q\| v(\|y\|_{\mathcal{E}}) + \vartheta_r + \frac{\vartheta_r^*}{\rho}(\rho + T^\rho - s_r^\rho)} \leq 1. \tag{13}$$

If (11)–(13) are combined with $(\mathfrak{H}_4)$ and given condition $\max_r\{\mathcal{Q}, \mathcal{Q}_{1r}, \mathcal{Q}_{2r}\} > 1$. A positive number $\mathcal{A}$ such that $\|y\|_{\mathcal{E}} \neq \mathcal{A}$ can be found. Create a set $Y = \{y \in \mathcal{E} : \|y\|_{\mathcal{E}} < \mathcal{A}\}$ with the operator $\mathcal{G} : \overline{Y} \to \mathcal{E}$ being continuous and completely continuous. In light of the choice of Y, there is no $y \in \partial Y$ satisfying $y = \lambda \mathcal{G} y$ for $\lambda \in (0, 1)$. Thus, it follows from the nonlinear alternative of Leray–Schauder, the operator $\mathcal{G}$ has a fixed point $y \in \overline{Y}$ that corresponds to a solution to Equation (1). □

Using the contraction mapping principle, we ensure the uniqueness of solution to problem (1).

Theorem 2. *Suppose that Hypotheses* ($\mathfrak{H}_1, \mathfrak{H}_3, \mathfrak{H}_5$ *and* $\mathfrak{H}_6$) *are satisfied. If*

$$\Delta = \max_r \left\{ \mathcal{L}\Omega, \mathcal{K}_r + \mathcal{K}_r^*, \mathcal{L}\Omega_r + \mathcal{K}_r + \tfrac{\mathcal{K}_r^*}{\rho}(\rho + T^\rho - s_r^\rho) \right\} < 1 \tag{14}$$

where $\mathcal{K}_r = \kappa_{1r} + \kappa_{2r}$ *and* $\mathcal{K}_r^* = \kappa_{1r}^* + \kappa_{2r}^*$. *Thus, the non-instantaneous impulsive fractional differential Equation (1) has a unique solution on* J.

Proof. Let us consider a set:

$$B_r = \left\{ (y, \delta y) : y \in \mathcal{E} \wedge \|y\|_{\mathcal{E}} = \|y(\tau)\|_{\mathcal{PC}} + \|\delta y(\tau)\|_{\mathcal{PC}_\delta^1} \leqslant r \right\}$$

with radius

$$r \geq \max_r \left\{ \frac{\Omega \mathrm{N} + |y_0| + \frac{|y_1|}{\rho}(\rho + \tau_1^\rho)}{1 - \mathcal{L}\Omega}, \vartheta_r + \vartheta_r^*, \frac{\Omega_r \mathrm{N} + \vartheta_r + \frac{\vartheta_r^*}{\rho}(\rho + T^\rho - s_r^\rho)}{1 - \mathcal{L}\Omega_r} \right\}$$

where $\sup_{\tau \in [0,T]} |h(\tau, 0, 0)| = \mathrm{N}$. Clearly, $\mathcal{G}$ is well defined and $\mathcal{G}y \in \mathcal{E}$ for all $y \in \mathcal{E}$. All that remains is to demonstrate that $\mathcal{G}$ is a contraction mapping. Thus, three cases are considered:

- **Case I.** For each $\tau \in [0, \tau_1]$ and $(y, \delta y), (v, \delta v) \in \mathcal{E}$. Using (6), we get

$$\begin{aligned}
\|\mathcal{G}y - \mathcal{G}v\|_{\mathcal{PC}} &\leq \sup_{\tau \in [0, \tau_1]} \frac{\rho^{1-\beta}}{\Gamma(\beta)} \int_0^\tau t^{\rho-1}(\tau^\rho - t^\rho)^{\beta-1} \left| h(t, y, t^{1-\rho} y') - h(t, v, t^{1-\rho} v') \right| dt \\
&\leq \mathcal{L}\Omega(\beta) \|y - v\|.
\end{aligned}$$

Similarly, we can obtain:

$$\|\delta\mathcal{G}y-\delta\mathcal{G}v\|_{\mathcal{PC}^1_\delta}\leq\mathcal{L}\Omega(\beta-1)\|y-v\|$$

which implies that:

$$\|\mathcal{G}y-\mathcal{G}v\|_{\mathcal{E}}\leq\mathcal{L}\Omega\|y-v\|.$$

- **Case II.** For each $\tau\in(\tau_r,s_r], r=1,2,\cdots,k$ and $(y,\delta y),(v,\delta v)\in\mathcal{E}$, we have:

$$\|\mathcal{G}y-\mathcal{G}v\|_{\mathcal{PC}}\leq(\kappa_{1r}+\kappa_{2r})\|y-v\|.$$

In addition:

$$\|\delta\mathcal{G}y-\delta\mathcal{G}v\|_{\mathcal{PC}^1_\delta}\leq(\kappa^*_{1r}+\kappa^*_{2r})\|y-v\|.$$

Consequently, we have:

$$\|\mathcal{G}y-\mathcal{G}v\|_{\mathcal{E}}\leq(\mathcal{K}_r+\mathcal{K}^*_r)\|y-v\|.$$

- **Case III.** For each $\tau\in(s_r,\tau_{r+1}], r=1,2,\cdots,k$ and $(y,\delta y),(v,\delta v)\in\mathcal{E}$. Using (7), we obtain:

$$\begin{aligned}
&\|\mathcal{G}y-\mathcal{G}v\|_{\mathcal{PC}}\\
&\leq\sup_{\tau\in(s_r,\tau_{r+1}]}\frac{\rho^{1-\beta}}{\Gamma(\beta)}\int_{s_r}^{\tau}t^{\rho-1}(\tau^\rho-t^\rho)^{\beta-1}\left|h(t,y,t^{1-\rho}y')-h(t,v,t^{1-\rho}v')\right|dt\\
&+|\Phi_r(s_r,y(s_r),y(\tau_r-0))-\Phi_r(s_r,v(s_r),v(\tau_r-0))|\\
&+\left|\frac{\tau^\rho-s_r^\rho}{\rho}(\Psi_r(s_r,y(s_r),y(\tau_r-0))-\Psi_r(s_r,v(s_r),v(\tau_r-0)))\right|\\
&\leq\left[\mathcal{L}\Omega_r(\beta)+\mathcal{K}_r+\frac{\mathcal{K}^*_r}{\rho}(T^\rho-s_r^\rho)\right]\|y-v\|.
\end{aligned}$$

In a similar manner, it can be shown that:

$$\|\delta\mathcal{G}y-\delta\mathcal{G}v\|_{\mathcal{PC}^1_\delta}\leq[\mathcal{L}\Omega_r(\beta-1)+\mathcal{K}^*_r]\|y-v\|$$

which leads to:

$$\|\mathcal{G}y-\mathcal{G}v\|_{\mathcal{E}}\leq\left[\mathcal{L}\Omega_r+\mathcal{K}_r+\frac{\mathcal{K}^*_r}{\rho}(\rho+T^\rho-s_r^\rho)\right]\|y-v\|.$$

From the above, we obtain: $\|\mathcal{G}y-\mathcal{G}v\|_{\mathcal{E}}\leq\Delta\|y-v\|$ which, in view of the given condition $\Delta<1$, shows that the operator $\mathcal{G}$ is a contraction. This implies that the problem in Equation (1) has a unique solution on$[0,T]$, according to the Banach contraction mapping principle. □

4. Stability Analysis

We present results regarding the Ulam–Hyers stability of our problem (1) in this section.

Theorem 3. *Suppose that Hypotheses $(\mathfrak{H}_1)$, $(\mathfrak{H}_5$ and $(\mathfrak{H}_6)$ are satisfied. Then, the non-instantaneous impulsive fractional differential Equation (1) is Ulam–Hyers stable and Generalized Ulam–Hyers stable if $\Delta<1$ where Δ is defined as (14).*

Proof. Assuming a unique solution $y \in \mathcal{E}$ to the problem (1) corresponds to any solution $\widetilde{y} \in \mathcal{E}$ of the inequality (4). Then, in light of Lemma 2, we have:

$$y(\tau) = \begin{cases} \frac{\rho^{1-\beta}}{\Gamma(\beta)} \int_0^\tau t^{\rho-1}(\tau^\rho - t^\rho)^{\beta-1} v(t)dt + y_0 + \frac{y_1}{\rho}\tau^\rho, & \tau \in [0, \tau_1], \\ \Phi_r(\tau, y(\tau), y(\tau_r - 0)), & \tau \in (\tau_r, s_r], \\ \frac{\rho^{1-\beta}}{\Gamma(\beta)} \int_{s_r}^\tau t^{\rho-1}(\tau^\rho - t^\rho)^{\beta-1} h(t)dt + \Phi_r(s_r, y(s_r), y(\tau_r - 0)) & \\ + \frac{\tau^\rho - s_r^\rho}{\rho} \Psi_r(s_r, y(s_r), y(\tau_r - 0)), & \tau \in (s_r, \tau_{r+1}]. \end{cases}$$

Further, if $\widetilde{y}$ is the solution of inequality (4) and using Remark 2, we get:

$$\begin{aligned} {}^cD_{s_r}^{\beta,\rho}\widetilde{y}(\tau) &= \widetilde{h}(\tau) + \varrho(\tau) & \tau \in (s_r, \tau_{r+1}], r = 0, 1, \cdots, k \\ \widetilde{y}(\tau) &= \Phi_r(\tau, \widetilde{y}(\tau), \widetilde{y}(\tau_r - 0) + \varrho_r, & r = 1, 2, \cdots, k \\ \tau^{1-\rho}\widetilde{y}'(\tau) &= \Psi_r(\tau, \widetilde{y}(\tau), \widetilde{y}(\tau_r - 0) + \varrho_r, & r = 1, 2, \cdots, k \end{aligned}$$

where $\widetilde{h}(\tau) = h(\tau, \widetilde{y}(\tau), \tau^{1-\rho}\widetilde{y}'(\tau))$ and

$$\widetilde{y}(\tau) = \begin{cases} I_0^{\beta,\rho}\widetilde{h}(\tau) + I_0^{\beta,\rho}\varrho(\tau) + y_0 + \frac{y_1}{\rho}\tau^\rho, & \tau \in [0, \tau_1], \\ \Phi_r(\tau, \widetilde{y}(\tau), \widetilde{y}(\tau_r - 0)) + \varrho_r, & \tau \in (\tau_r, s_r], \\ I_{s_r}^{\beta,\rho}\widetilde{h}(\tau) + I_{s_r}^{\beta,\rho}\varrho(\tau) + \Phi_r(s_r, \widetilde{y}(s_r), \widetilde{y}(\tau_r - 0)) & \\ + \frac{\tau^\rho - s_r^\rho}{\rho} \Psi_r(s_r, \widetilde{y}(s_r), \widetilde{y}(\tau_r - 0)) + \frac{\varrho_r}{\rho}(\rho + \tau^\rho - s_r^\rho), & \tau \in (s_r, \tau_{r+1}]. \end{cases}$$

For each $\tau \in [0, \tau_1]$, we consider:

$$\begin{aligned} \|\widetilde{y}(\tau) - y(\tau)\|_{\mathcal{PC}} &\leq \frac{\rho^{1-\beta}}{\Gamma(\beta)} \int_0^\tau t^{\rho-1}(\tau^\rho - t^\rho)^{\beta-1} \left|\widetilde{h}(t) - h(t)\right| dt + \frac{\rho^{1-\beta}}{\Gamma(\beta)} \int_0^\tau t^{\rho-1}(\tau^\rho - t^\rho)^{\beta-1} |\varrho(t)| dt \\ &\leq \mathcal{L}\Omega(\beta)\|\widetilde{y} - y\|_{\mathcal{E}} + \epsilon\Omega(\beta). \end{aligned}$$

Similarly, we can obtain:

$$\|\delta\widetilde{y}(\tau) - \delta y(\tau)\|_{\mathcal{PC}_\delta^1} \leq \mathcal{L}\Omega(\beta - 1)\|\widetilde{y} - y\|_{\mathcal{E}} + \epsilon\Omega(\beta - 1)$$

which implies that:

$$\|\widetilde{y}(\tau) - y(\tau)\|_{\mathcal{E}} \leq \mathcal{L}\Omega\|\widetilde{y} - y\|_{\mathcal{E}} + \epsilon\Omega.$$

Or, equivalently,

$$\|\widetilde{y} - y\|_{\mathcal{E}} \leq \frac{\epsilon\Omega}{1 - \mathcal{L}\Omega}, \qquad \mathcal{L}\Omega < 1.$$

For each $\tau \in (\tau_r, s_r], r = 1, 2, \cdots, k$, we consider:

$$\begin{aligned} \|\widetilde{y}(\tau) - y(\tau)\|_{\mathcal{PC}} &\leq |\Phi_r(\tau, \widetilde{y}(\tau), \widetilde{y}(\tau_r - 0)) - \Phi_r(\tau, y(\tau), y(\tau_r - 0))| + |\varrho_r|, \\ &\leq (\kappa_{1r} + \kappa_{2r})\|\widetilde{y} - y\| + \epsilon. \end{aligned}$$

In addition:

$$\|\delta\widetilde{y}(\tau) - \delta y(\tau)\|_{\mathcal{PC}_\delta^1} \leq (\kappa_{1r}^* + \kappa_{2r}^*)\|\widetilde{y} - y\|_{\mathcal{E}} + \epsilon.$$

Consequently, we have:

$$\|\widetilde{y}-y\|_{\mathcal{E}} \leq (\mathcal{K}_r+\mathcal{K}_r^*)\|\widetilde{y}-y\|_{\mathcal{E}}+2\epsilon.$$

Or, equivalently:

$$\|\widetilde{y}-y\|_{\mathcal{E}} \leq \frac{2\epsilon}{1-(\mathcal{K}_r+\mathcal{K}_r^*)}, \qquad \mathcal{K}_r+\mathcal{K}_r^*<1.$$

For each $\tau \in (s_r, \tau_{r+1}], r = 1, 2, \cdots, k$, we consider:

$$\begin{aligned}\|\widetilde{y}(\tau)-y(\tau)\|_{\mathcal{PC}} \leq& \frac{\rho^{1-\beta}}{\Gamma(\beta)}\int_{s_r}^{\tau} t^{\rho-1}(\tau^\rho-t^\rho)^{\beta-1}\left|\widetilde{h}(t)-h(t)\right|dt+\frac{\rho^{1-\beta}}{\Gamma(\beta)}\int_{s_r}^{\tau} t^{\rho-1}(\tau^\rho-t^\rho)^{\beta-1}|\varrho(t)|dt\\ &+|\Phi_r(\tau,\widetilde{y}(\tau),\widetilde{y}(\tau_r-0))-\Phi_r(\tau,y(\tau),y(\tau_r-0))|+|\varrho_r|\\ &+\left|\frac{\tau^\rho-s_r^\rho}{\rho}\right||\Psi_r(\tau,\widetilde{y}(\tau),\widetilde{y}(\tau_r-0))-\Psi_r(\tau,y(\tau),y(\tau_r-0))|+\left|\frac{\tau^\rho-s_r^\rho}{\rho}\varrho_r\right|\\ \leq& \left[\mathcal{L}\Omega_r(\beta)+\mathcal{K}_r+\frac{\mathcal{K}_r^*}{\rho}(T^\rho-s_r^\rho)\right]\|\widetilde{y}-y\|_{\mathcal{E}}+\epsilon\left(1+\frac{T^\rho-s_r^\rho}{\rho}\right).\end{aligned}$$

In a similar manner, it can be shown that:

$$\|\delta\widetilde{y}(\tau)-\delta y(\tau)\|_{\mathcal{PC}_\delta^1} \leq [\mathcal{L}\Omega_r(\beta-1)+\mathcal{K}_r^*]\|\widetilde{y}-y\|_{\mathcal{E}}+\epsilon$$

which leads to:

$$\|\widetilde{y}(\tau)-y(\tau)\|_{\mathcal{E}} \leq \frac{(2\rho+T^\rho-s_r^\rho)\varepsilon}{\rho\left(1-\mathcal{L}\Omega_r-\mathcal{K}_r-\frac{\mathcal{K}_r^*}{\rho}(\rho+T^\rho-s_r^\rho)\right)}, \quad \mathcal{L}\Omega_r+\mathcal{K}_r+\frac{\mathcal{K}_r^*}{\rho}(\rho+T^\rho-s_r^\rho)<1.$$

Then, for each $\tau \in J$, we obtain:

$$\|\widetilde{y}(\tau)-y(\tau)\|_{\mathcal{E}} \leq \Lambda\epsilon.$$

where $\Lambda = \max_r\left\{\frac{\Omega}{1-\mathcal{L}\Omega}, \frac{2}{1-(\mathcal{K}_r+\mathcal{K}_r^*)}, \frac{2\rho+T^\rho-s_r^\rho}{\rho\left(1-\mathcal{L}\Omega_r-\mathcal{K}_r-\frac{\mathcal{K}_r^*}{\rho}(\rho+T^\rho-s_r^\rho)\right)}\right\}$. □

Thus, the solution of (1) is UH stable if $\Delta < 1$. Additionally, by setting $\mu(\epsilon) = \Lambda$ and $\mu(0) = 0$. Then, the solution of (1) becomes GUH stable.

5. Applications

In this section, we describe an application of our main results to demonstrate how they can be applied.

Example 1. *Consider the following non-instantaneous impulsive fractional differential equations:*

$$\begin{aligned}&{}^cD_{s_r}^{\beta,\rho}y(\tau)=h(\tau,y(\tau),\delta y(\tau)) && \tau\in(0,\tfrac{1}{3}]\cup(\tfrac{2}{3},1],\\ &y(\tau)=\frac{3}{4}\tau^2+\frac{1}{12}\sin y(\tau)+\frac{1}{8}\cos y(\tau_r-0), && \tau\in(\tfrac{1}{3},\tfrac{2}{3}],\\ &\delta y(\tau)=\frac{3}{2}\tau+\frac{1}{14}\cos y(\tau)+\frac{1}{10}\sin y(\tau_r-0), && \tau\in(\tfrac{1}{3},\tfrac{2}{3}],\\ &y(0)=0, \qquad \lim_{\tau\to 0}\delta y(\tau)=1\end{aligned} \tag{15}$$

where $J = [0,1], 0 = s_0 < \tau_1 = \frac{1}{3} < s_1 = \frac{2}{3} < \tau_2 = 1, \rho = \frac{1}{2}, \beta = \frac{5}{4}$ *and* $h(\tau, y(\tau), \delta y(\tau))$ *will be determined later. Using the given data, we can find that*

$$\begin{aligned} &\Omega(\beta) \approx 1.05646621, && \Omega(\beta-1) \approx 1.14365822, && \Omega \approx 2.20012444, \\ &\Omega_r(\beta) \approx 0.25212249, && \Omega_r(\beta-1) \approx 0.85871184, && \Omega_r \approx 1.11083434. \end{aligned}$$

In our example, we take

$$\begin{aligned} \Phi_1(\tau, y, v) &= \frac{3}{4}\tau^2 + \frac{1}{12}\sin y + \frac{1}{8}\cos v, \\ \Psi_1(\tau, y, v) &= \frac{3}{2}\tau + \frac{1}{14}\cos y + \frac{1}{10}\sin v. \end{aligned}$$

It is clear that they are continuous on the interval $(\frac{1}{3}, \frac{2}{3}]$ *which meets the first assumption and satisfy*

$$\begin{aligned} |\Phi_1(\tau, y, v)| &\le \left|\frac{3}{4}\tau^2\right| + \left|\frac{1}{12}\sin y\right| + \left|\frac{1}{8}\cos v\right| \le \frac{3}{4}\left(\frac{2}{3}\right)^2 + \frac{1}{12} + \frac{1}{8} = \frac{13}{24}, \\ |\Psi_1(\tau, y, v)| &\le \left|\frac{3}{2}\tau\right| + \left|\frac{1}{14}\cos y\right| + \left|\frac{1}{10}\sin v\right| \le 1 + \frac{1}{14} + \frac{1}{10} = \frac{82}{70} \end{aligned}$$

for all $\tau \in (\frac{1}{3}, \frac{2}{3}]$ *and* $y, v \in \mathbb{R}$. *These lead to the third assumption is verified with* $\vartheta_1 = 13/24$ *and* $\vartheta_1^* = 82/70$.

Theorem 4 (Application to Theorem 1). *The Leray–Schauder nonlinear alternative theorem has been applied in Theorem 1 with the assumptions* $(\mathfrak{H}_1)$*–*$(\mathfrak{H}_3)$. *To illustrate our investigation, let us take*

$$h(\tau, y(\tau), \delta y(\tau)) = \frac{1}{2\sqrt{5-\tau}}\left[\frac{1}{15\pi}\sin(5\pi y) + \frac{3|\delta y(\tau)|}{4(|\delta y(\tau)| + 1)}\right].$$

It is obvious that the function h is continuous which meets the first assumption and satisfies

$$|\widehat{h}(\tau)| = |h(\tau, y, \delta y)| \le \frac{1}{2\sqrt{5-\tau}}\left(\frac{1}{3}\|y\| + \frac{3}{4}\right) := q(\tau)v(\|y\|)$$

where

$$q(\tau) = \frac{1}{2\sqrt{5-\tau}} \qquad \text{and} \qquad v(\|y\|) = \frac{1}{3}\|y\| + \frac{3}{4}.$$

for all $\tau \in (0, \frac{1}{3}] \cup (\frac{2}{3}, 1]$. *It is obvious that the function* $q(\tau)$ *is nondecreasing function which admits the hypothesis* $(\mathfrak{H}_2)$ *with* $||q|| \le q(1) = 1/4$. *The condition* $(\mathfrak{H}_4)$ *and (11)–(13) imply that*

$$\mathcal{A} > \max_r \left\{ \frac{\frac{3\|q\|}{4}\Omega + \frac{1}{\rho}(\rho + \tau_1^\rho)}{1 - \frac{\|q\|}{3}\Omega}, \vartheta_r + \vartheta_r^*, \frac{\frac{3\|q\|}{4}\Omega_r + \vartheta_r + \frac{\vartheta_r^*}{\rho}(\rho + T^\rho - s_r^\rho)}{1 - \frac{\|q\|}{3}\Omega_r} \right\}$$

$$\mathcal{A} > \max\{3.018702359, 1.713095238, 2.539578874\}$$

$$\mathcal{A} > 3.018702359.$$

Therefore, the conditions of Theorem (1) are satisfied, and consequently,on $[0,1]$ *there exists at least one solution to the boundary value problem (15).*

Theorem 5 (Application to Theorem 2). *To demonstrate Theorem 2, which is based on the Banach fixed point theorem, we take*

$$h(\tau, y(\tau), \delta y(\tau)) = \frac{e^{-2\tau}(|y(\tau)| + |\delta y(\tau)|)}{(1+9e^{\tau})(1+|y(\tau)|+|\delta y(\tau)|)}$$

It is clear that the function $h : [0,1] \times \mathbb{R} \times \mathbb{R} \to \mathbb{R}$ *is continuous and that it fulfills the hypothesis* $(\mathfrak{H}_2)$

$$\begin{aligned}|h(\tau, y, \delta y) - h(\tau, u, \delta u)| &\leq \frac{e^{-2\tau}|(|y| + |\delta y|) - (|u| + |\delta u|)|}{(1+9e^{\tau})|(1+|y|+|\delta y|)(1+|u|+|\delta u|)|} \\ &\leq \frac{1}{10}\Big||y| - |u|\Big| + \Big||\delta y| - |\delta u|\Big| \\ &\leq \frac{1}{10}(|y-u| + |\delta y - \delta u|).\end{aligned}$$

with $\mathcal{L} = 1/10$. *For all* $\tau \in (\frac{1}{3}, \frac{2}{3}]$ *and* $y_1, y_2, v_1, v_2 \in \mathbb{R}$, *we get*

$$\begin{aligned}|\Phi_1(\tau, y_1, v_1) - \Phi_1(\tau, y_2, v_2)| &\leq \frac{1}{12}|y_1 - y_2| + \frac{1}{8}|v_1 - v_2|, \\ |\Psi_1(\tau, y_1, v_1) - \Psi_1(\tau, y_2, v_2)| &\leq \frac{1}{14}|y_1 - y_2| + \frac{1}{10}|v_1 - v_2|.\end{aligned}$$

Thus, the condition $(\mathfrak{H}_5)$ *of Theorem 2 is satisfied with*

$$\begin{aligned}\kappa_{11} &= \frac{1}{12}, & \kappa_{21} &\frac{1}{8}, & \mathcal{K}_1 &\approx 0.20833333, \\ \kappa_{11}^* &= \frac{1}{14}, & \kappa_{22}^* &= \frac{1}{10}, & \mathcal{K}_1^* &\approx 0.17142857.\end{aligned}$$

In conclusion, we have

$$\begin{aligned}\Delta &= \max_r \left\{\mathcal{L}\Omega, \mathcal{K}_r + \mathcal{K}_r^*, \mathcal{L}\Omega_r + \mathcal{K}_r + \tfrac{\mathcal{K}_r^*}{\rho}(\rho + T^{\rho} - s_r^{\rho})\right\} \\ &= \max\{0.22001244, 0.37976190, 0.55376046\} = 0.55376046 < 1.\end{aligned}$$

Hence, the problem in Equations (15) has a unique solution on $[0,1]$ *by Theorem 2.*

Theorem 6 (Application to Theorem 3). *To demonstrate Theorem 3, we take*

$$h(\tau, y(\tau), \delta y(\tau)) = \frac{|y(\tau)|}{2(\tau+8)(1+|y(\tau)|)} + \frac{|\delta y(\tau)|}{(\tau+16)}$$

It is clear that the function $h : [0,1] \times \mathbb{R} \times \mathbb{R} \to \mathbb{R}$ *is continuous and that it fulfills the hypothesis* $(\mathfrak{H}_6)$

$$\begin{aligned}|h(\tau, y, \delta y) - h(\tau, u, \delta u)| &\leq \frac{|(|y| - |u|)|}{2(\tau+8)|(1+|y|)(1+|u|)|} + \frac{|(|\delta y| - |\delta u|)|}{(\tau+16)} \\ &\leq \frac{1}{16}\Big||y| - |u|\Big| + \Big||\delta y| - |\delta u|\Big| \\ &\leq \frac{1}{16}(|y-u| + |\delta y - \delta u|).\end{aligned}$$

Clearly the assumptions of Theorem 3 are fulfilled with

$$\mathcal{L} = \frac{1}{16}, \qquad \mathcal{K}_1 \approx 0.20833333, \qquad \mathcal{K}_1^* \approx 0.17142857.$$

$$\Delta = \max\{0.137507777, 0.37976190, 0.55376046\} = 0.51210450 < 1.$$

In conclusion, we have:

$$\|\widetilde{y} - y\| \leq \Lambda\epsilon, \qquad \tau \in J,$$

where ϵ is any positive real constant, and

$$\Lambda = \max\left\{\frac{\Omega}{1-\mathcal{L}\Omega}, \frac{2}{1-(\mathcal{K}_r+\mathcal{K}_r^*)}, \frac{2\rho + T^\rho - s_r^\rho}{\rho\left(1-\mathcal{L}\Omega_r - \mathcal{K}_r - \frac{\mathcal{K}_r^*}{\rho}(\rho + T^\rho - s_r^\rho)\right)}\right\},$$

$$\Lambda = \max\{2.55089191, 3.22456811, 0.24394774\},$$

$$\Lambda = 3.22456811 > 0.$$

Consequently,

$$\|\widetilde{y} - y\| \leq (3.22456811)\epsilon,$$

Thus, problem (15) is UH stable.

Moreover, by putting $\mu(\epsilon) = (3.22456811)\epsilon$ with $\mu(0) = 0$, problem (15) becomes GUH stable.

6. Conclusions

Our work involved the development of the existence theory and Ulam–Hyers stability of non-instantaneous impulsive BVPs involving Generalized Liouville–Caputo derivatives. This work is based on modern functional analysis techniques. Three conclusions have been obtained: the first two deal with the existence and uniqueness of solutions, while the third concerns the stability analysis of solutions for the given problem. The first existence result is based on a nonlinear Leray–Schauder alternative, while the second is based on the Banach fixed point theorem. The third conclusion establishes a criterion for ensuring various types of Ulam–Hyers stability, that is necessary for nonlinear problems in terms of optimization and numerical solutions and plays a key role in numerical solutions where exact solutions are difficult to get.

Author Contributions: Formal analysis, A.S. and S.A.; Investigation, A.S. and S.A.; Methodology, S.A.; Resources, A.S.; Software, S.A.; Supervision, A.S.; Writing—original draft, S.A. All authors have read and agreed to the published version of the manuscript.

Funding: This project was funded by the Deanship of Scientific Research (DSR), King Abdulaziz University, Jeddah, under grant No. (D-310-130-1443). The authors, therefore, gratefully acknowledge DSR technical and financial support.

Institutional Review Board Statement: Not applicable.

Informed Consent Statement: Not applicable.

Data Availability Statement: Not applicable.

Acknowledgments: Our deep appreciation goes out to anonymous referees for their helpful suggestions and valuable advice.

Conflicts of Interest: The authors declare that they do not have any competing interests.

References

1. Podlubny, I. *Fractional Differential Equations*; Academic Press: San Diego, CA, USA, 1999.
2. Kilbas, A.; Srivastava, H.; Trujillo, J. *Theory and Applications of Fractional Differential Equations*; Elsevier: Amsterdam, The Netherlands, 2006.
3. Lakshmikantham, V.; Vatsala, A. Basic theory of fractional differential equations. *Nonlinear Anal. TMA* **2008**, *69*, 2677–2682. [CrossRef]
4. Fallahgoul, H.; Focardi, S.; Fabozzi, F. *Fractional Calculus and Fractional Processes with Applications to Financial Economics: Theory and Application*; Elsevier: London, UK; Academic Press: London, UK, 2017.
5. Salem, A.; Mshary, N. On the Existence and Uniqueness of Solution to Fractional-Order Langevin Equation. *Adv. Math. Phys.* **2020**, *2020*, 8890575. [CrossRef]
6. Salem, A.; Al-Dosari, A. Positive Solvability for Conjugate Fractional Differential Inclusion of $(k, n-k)$ Type without Continuity and Compactness. *Axioms* **2021**, *10*, 170. [CrossRef]
7. Salem, A.; Alnegga, M. Measure of Noncompactness for Hybrid Langevin Fractional Differential Equations. *Axioms* **2020**, *9*, 59. [CrossRef]
8. Salem, A.; Alghamdi, B. Multi-Strip and Multi-Point Boundary Conditions for Fractional Langevin Equation. *Fractal Fract.* **2020**, *4*, 18. [CrossRef]
9. Ganesh, A.; Deepa, S.; Baleanu, D.; Santra, S.S.; Moaaz, O.; Govindan, V.; Ali, R. Hyers-Ulam-Mittag–Leffler stability of fractional differential equations with two caputo derivative using fractional fourier transform. *AIMS Math.* **2022**, *7*, 1791–1810. [CrossRef]
10. He, B.-B.; Zhou, H.-C. Caputo-Hadamard fractional Halanay inequality. *Appl. Math. Lett.* **2022**, *125*, 107723. [CrossRef]
11. Dehestani, H.; Ordokhani, Y. An efficient approach based on Legendre–Gauss–Lobatto quadrature and discrete shifted Hahn polynomials for solving Caputo–Fabrizio fractional Volterra partial integro-differential equations. *J. Comput. Appl. Math.* **2022**, *403*, 113851. [CrossRef]
12. Salem, A.; Mshary, N.; El-Shahed, M.; Alzahran, F. Compact and Noncompact Solutions to Generalized Sturm–Liouville and Langevin Equation with Caputo-Hadamard Fractional Derivative. *Math. Probl. Eng.* **2021**, *2021*, 9995969. [CrossRef]
13. Salem, A.; Almaghamsi, L. Existence Solution for Coupled System of Langevin Fractional Differential Equations of Caputo Type with Riemann-Stieltjes Integral Boundary Conditions. *Symmetry* **2021**, *13*, 2123. [CrossRef]
14. Adjabi, Y.; Samei, M.E.; Matar, M.M.; Alzabut, J. Langevin differential equation in frame of ordinary and Hadamard fractional derivatives under three point boundary conditions. *AIMS Math.* **2021**, *6*, 2796–2843. [CrossRef]
15. Boutiara, A.; Abdo, M.S.; Alqudah, M.A.; Abdeljawad, T. On a class of Langevin equations in the frame of Caputo function-dependent-kernel fractional derivatives with antiperiodic boundary conditions. *AIMS Math.* **2021**, *6*, 5518–5534. [CrossRef]
16. Hilal, K.; Ibnelazyz, L.; Guida, K.; Melliani, S. Fractional Langevin Equations with Nonseparated Integral Boundary Conditions. *Adv. Math. Phys.* **2020**, *2020*, 3173764. [CrossRef]
17. Salem, A.; Al-Dosari, A. Existence results of solution for fractional Sturm–Liouville inclusion involving composition with multi-maps. *J. Taibah Univ. Sci.* **2020**, *14*, 721–733. [CrossRef]
18. Salem, A.; Alghamdi, B. Multi-Point and Anti-Periodic Conditions for Generalized Langevin Equation with Two Fractional Orders. *Fractal Fract.* **2019**, *3*, 51. [CrossRef]
19. Salem, A. Existence results of solutions for ant-periodic fractional Langevin equation. *J. Appl. Anal. Comput.* **2020**, *10*, 2557–2574. [CrossRef]
20. Salem, A.; Alshehri, H.M.; Almaghamsi, L. Measure of noncompactness for an infinite system of fractional Langevin equation in a sequence space. *Adv. Differ. Equ.* **2021**, *2021*, 132. [CrossRef]
21. Benchohra, M.; Henderson, J.; Ntouyas, S.K. *Impulsive Differential Equations and Inclusions*; Hindawi: New York, NY, USA, 2006.
22. Agarwal, R.; Hristova, S.; O'Regan, D. Iterative techniques for the initial value problem for Caputo fractional differential equations with non-instantaneous impulses. *Appl. Math. Comput.* **2018**, *334*, 407–421. [CrossRef]
23. Luo, D.; Luo, Z. Existence of solutions for fractional differential inclusions with initial value condition and non-instantaneous impulses. *Filomat* **2019**, *33*, 5499–5510. [CrossRef]
24. Wang, J.; Feckan, M.; Zhou, Y. A survey on impulsive fractional differential equations. *Fract. Calc. Appl. Anal.* **2016**, *19*, 806–831. [CrossRef]
25. Liu, S.; Wang, J.; Zhou, Y. Optimal control of non-instantaneous impulsive differential equations. *J. Frankl. Inst.* **2017**, *354*, 7668–7698. [CrossRef]
26. Hernandaz, E.; O'Regan, D. On a new class of abstract impulsive differential equation. *Proc. Am. Math. Soc.* **2013**, *141*, 1641–1649. [CrossRef]
27. Wang, J.; Zhou, Y.; Lin, Z. On a new class of impulsive fractional differential equations. *Appl. Math. Comput.* **2014**, *242*, 649–657. [CrossRef]
28. Ho, V.; Ngo, V.H. Non-instantaneous impulses interval-valued fractional differential equations with Caputo-Katugampola fractional derivative concept. *Fuzzy Sets Syst.* **2021**, *404*, 111–141. [CrossRef]
29. Abbas, M.I. Non-instantaneous impulsive fractional integro-differential equations with proportional fractional derivatives with respect to another function. *Math. Methods Appl. Sci.* **2021**, *44*, 10432–10447. [CrossRef]
30. Katugampola, U.N. New approach to a generalized fractional integral. *Appl. Math. Comput.* **2011**, *218*, 860–865. [CrossRef]

31. Jarad, F.; Abdeljawadb, T.; Baleanu, D. On the generalized fractional derivatives and their Caputo modification. *J. Nonlinear Sci. Appl.* **2017**, *10*, 2607–2619. [CrossRef]
32. Rus, I.A. Ulam stabilities of ordinary differential equations in a Banach space. *Carpath. J. Math.* **2010**, *26*, 103–107.
33. Kiryakova, V. *Generalized Fractional Calculus and Applications*; Longman Scientific & Technical; Wiley: New York, NY, USA, 1994.
34. Granas, A.; Dugundji, J. *Fixed Point Theory*; Springer: New York, NY, USA, 2003.

mathematics

Article

Adopting Feynman–Kac Formula in Stochastic Differential Equations with (Sub-)Fractional Brownian Motion

Bodo Herzog [1,2,3]

[1] Economics Department, ESB Business School, Reutlingen University, 72762 Reutlingen, Germany; Bodo.Herzog@Reutlingen-University.de
[2] Reutlingen Research Institute (RRI), 72762 Reutlingen, Germany
[3] Institute of Finance and Economics (IFE), Reutlingen University, 72762 Reutlingen, Germany

Abstract: The aim of this work is to establish and generalize a relationship between fractional partial differential equations (fPDEs) and stochastic differential equations (SDEs) to a wider class of stochastic processes, including fractional Brownian motions $\{B_t^H, t \geq 0\}$ and sub-fractional Brownian motions $\{\xi_t^H, t \geq 0\}$ with Hurst parameter $H \in (\frac{1}{2}, 1)$. We start by establishing the connection between a fPDE and SDE via the Feynman–Kac Theorem, which provides a stochastic representation of a general Cauchy problem. In hindsight, we extend this connection by assuming SDEs with fractional- and sub-fractional Brownian motions and prove the generalized Feynman–Kac formulas under a (sub-)fractional Brownian motion. An application of the theorem demonstrates, as a by-product, the solution of a fractional integral, which has relevance in probability theory.

Keywords: Cauchy problem; fractional-PDE; SDE; fractional Brownian motion; sub-fractional processes; Feynman–Kac formula; fractional calculus

Citation: Herzog, B. Adopting Feynman–Kac Formula in Stochastic Differential Equations with (Sub-)Fractional Brownian Motion. *Mathematics* **2022**, *10*, 340. https://doi.org/10.3390/math10030340

Academic Editors: António M. Lopes, Alireza Alfi, Liping Chen and Sergio A. David

Received: 28 December 2021
Accepted: 21 January 2022
Published: 23 January 2022

1. Introduction

Consider the Cauchy problem [1] of the following parabolic partial differential equation (PDE) on $\mathbb{R}^d$

$$\begin{aligned} \frac{\partial}{\partial t}u(x,t) &= \kappa\frac{\partial^2}{\partial x^2}u(x,t) + \eta B^H(t), \qquad t \geq 0, x \in \mathbb{R}^d, \\ u(x,0) &= u_0(x), \end{aligned} \tag{1}$$

where $u(x,t) \in C^{2,1}$, $u_0(x)$ is a bounded measurable function and $B^H(t)$ is a fractional Brownian motion (cf. Section 2). Without loss of generality, we assume that the parameter κ is constant. This second-order PDE has a stochastic representation for $\eta = 0$, according to the Feynman–Kac formula [2,3]. Indeed, we obtain

$$u(x_t,t) = \mathbb{E}_{x,t}[u_T(x)], \tag{2}$$

if x_t satisfies Equation (3) and the function $\sigma(x_t,t)$ is sufficiently integrable

$$dx_t = \mu(x_t,t)dt + \sigma(x_t,t)dB_t^H, \tag{3}$$

where B_t^H is a Brownian motion (BM) if the Hurst parameter is of $H = \frac{1}{2}$ [4–6]. Additionally, the problem of (1) has an intimate relationship to the fractional partial differential equation (fPDE) [7]:

$$\frac{\partial^{1/2}}{\partial t^{1/2}}u(x,t) = -\frac{\partial}{\partial x}u(x,t). \tag{4}$$

Note that this equation contains a fractional derivative in general or a semi-derivative in respect of time in special [8–13].

There is a large amount of the literature devoted to each issue of the Cauchy problem [6,14]. This research closes a gap by considering the linking relationships of (sub-)fractional Brownian motions as well as fPDEs. The Feynman–Kac formula (2) provides a unique weak solution to Equation (1). Different versions of the Feynman–Kac formula have been discovered for a variety of problems [15,16]. Some generalizations of the Feynman–Kac formula are discovered by Querdiane and Silva [17] and Hu et al. [18,19]. A Feynman–Kac formula also exists for Lévy processes by Nualart and Schoutens [20].

Advancements in stochastic differential equations and fractional partial differential equations to analyse complex systems are related to our research [21–24]. Furthermore, recent developments in fractional calculus contributed to a better understanding and further studies of the relationships between fractional PDEs and stochastic calculus [25–31]. However, we are concerned about the linkage of the Cauchy problem and the representation by a fPDE, as well as the Feynman–Kac formula. For the Cauchy problem, we generalize the stochastic representation of Feynman–Kac by utilizing fractional Brownian motion (fBM) with Hurst parameter $H > 1/2$.

In addition, the more recent literature looks at the idea of sub-fractional Brownian motion (sub-fBM). A sub-fBM is an intermediate between a Brownian motion and fractional Brownian motion. The existence and properties, such as long-range dependence, self-similarity and non-stationarity were introduced by Bojdecki et al. [32] and Tudor et al. [33,34]. Since the sub-fractional Brownian motion is not a martingale, methods of stochastic analysis are more sophisticated. However, several authors developed stochastic calculus and integration concepts for an fBM [25] and sub-fBM [35–37]. Recently, for a sub-fractional Brownian motion with Hurst parameters $H > \frac{1}{2}$, a maximal inequality was established according to the Burkholder–Davis–Gundy inequality for fractional Brownian motion [38]. It turns out that fBM and sub-fBM are adequate stochastic processes in scientific applications [13,39].

In this paper, our purpose is to construct and prove a general link of the Cauchy problem with the Feynman–Kac equation via Itô's formula for fBM and sub-fBM. Consequently, this paper links the solution of $u(x,t)$ defined by Equation (1) with the stochastic Feynman–Kac representation to a fractional Brownian motion $\{B_t^H\}$ and sub-fBM $\{\xi_t^H\}$. We prove the result and show the properties of (sub-)fractional processes in stochastic analysis. Note that, throughout this paper, we frequently assume $\frac{1}{2} < H < 1$.

The paper is organized as follows. Section 2 contains preliminaries on fractional calculus, particularly fractional Brownian motion. Thereafter, we examine sub-fractional stochastic processes and integration rules in Section 3. Here, we list the definitions and assumptions for the remainder of the article. In Section 4, we link the Cauchy problem to the Feynman–Kac formula with stochastic differential equations driven by fractional and sub-fractional Brownian motions. We state our theorems and prove our statements. In Section 5, we examine the Cauchy problem and the relationship to fractional partial differential equations (fPDE). Furthermore, we find a new fractional derivative and integral with relevance in probability theory. The conclusion is in Section 6.

2. Preliminaries

In the following section, we define preliminary concepts on fractional stochastic processes and fractional calculus.

2.1. Fractional Calculus

Since we deal with the Hurst parameter H, we need to know fractional calculus. Let $a, b \in \mathbb{R}$, $a < b$. Let $f \in L^1(a,b)$ and $\alpha > 0$. The left- and right-sided fractional integral of f of order α are defined for $x \in (a,b)$, respectively, as

$$ {}_aD_x^{-\alpha} f(x) = {}_aI_x^{\alpha} f(x) = \frac{1}{\Gamma(\alpha)} \int_a^x (x-u)^{\alpha-1} f(u)du \qquad -\infty \le a \le x, $$

and

$$ {}_xD_b^{-\alpha}f(x) = {}_xI_b^{\alpha}f(x) = \frac{1}{\Gamma(\alpha)}\int_x^b (u-x)^{\alpha-1}f(u)du \qquad -\infty \le x \le b. $$

This is the fractional integral of Riemann–Liouville type. Similarly, the fractional left- and right-sided derivative, for $f \in I_a^{\alpha}(L^p)$ and $0 < \alpha < 1$, are defined by

$$ {}_aI_x^{-\alpha}f(x) = {}_aD_x^{\alpha}f(x) = \frac{1}{\Gamma(1-\alpha)}\left(\frac{d}{dx}\right)\int_a^x (x-u)^{-\alpha}f(u)du \tag{5} $$

and

$$ {}_xI_b^{-\alpha}f(x) = {}_xD_b^{\alpha}f(x) = \frac{-1}{\Gamma(1-\alpha)}\left(\frac{d}{dx}\right)\int_x^b (u-x)^{-\alpha}f(u)du, \tag{6} $$

for all $x \in (a,b)$ and $I_a^{\alpha}(L^p)$ is the image of $L^p(a,b)$. It is easy to see that if $f \in I_a^1(L^1)$,

$$ {}_aD_{x\,a}^{\alpha}D_x^{1-\alpha}f(x) = Df(x), \qquad {}_bD_{x\,b}^{\alpha}D_x^{1-\alpha}f(x) = Df(x). \tag{7} $$

Note $D^{\alpha}f(x)$ exists for all $f \in C^{\beta}([a,b])$ if $\alpha < \beta$.

2.2. Fractional Stochastic Process

Mandelbrot and van Ness defined a fractional Brownian Motion (fBM), B_t^H, as a Brownian motion, $B(t)$, together with a Hurst parameter (or Hurst index) $H \in (0,1)$ in 1968 [8]. The new feature of fBM's is that the increments are interdependent. The latter property is defined as self-similarity. A self-similar process has invariance with respect to changes in timescale (scaling-invariance). Almost all other stochastic processes, such as the standard Brownian Motion or Lévy processes, likely have independent increments. They create the famous class of Markov processes. Empirically, there is ubiquitous evidence in science that fractional stochastic processes, for instance, spectral densities with a sharp peak, are related to the phenomena of long-range interdependence over time. Indeed, the observable presence of interdependence in many real-world applications calls for fractional stochastic processes.

Definition 1. *Let H be $0 < H < 1$ and B_0 an arbitrary real number. We call $B^H(t,\omega)$ a fractional Brownian Motion (fBM) with Hurst parameter H and starting value B_0 at time 0, such as*

(1) $B^H(0,\omega) = B_0$, *and;*

(2) $B^H(t,\omega) - B^H(0,\omega) = \frac{1}{\Gamma(H+\frac{1}{2})}\left[\int_{-\infty}^0 [(t-s)^{H-\frac{1}{2}} - (-s)^{H-\frac{1}{2}}]dB(s,\omega) + \int_0^t (t-s)^{H-\frac{1}{2}} dB(s,\omega)\right]$ *[Wyle fractional integral];*

(3) *[Or equivalently by the Riemann-Liouville fractional integral:* $B^H(t,\omega) - B^H(0,\omega) = \frac{1}{\Gamma(H+\frac{1}{2})}\int_0^t (t-s)^{H-\frac{1}{2}}dB(s,\omega)$*].*

We immediately obtain the corollary.

Corollary 1. *For $H = \frac{1}{2}$ and $B_0 = 0$, we obtain a Brownian Motion $B(t,\omega) = B^{\frac{1}{2}}(t,\omega)$.*

Proof. If $H = \frac{1}{2}$, we obtain $B^{\frac{1}{2}}(t,\omega) - B^{\frac{1}{2}}(0,\omega) = \frac{1}{\Gamma(1)}\int_0^t dB(s,\omega) = B(t,\omega)$. □

For values of H, such as $0 < H < \frac{1}{2}$ or $\frac{1}{2} < H < 1$ the fBM $B^H(t,\omega)$ has different properties. If $0 < H < \frac{1}{2}$, we say that it has the property of short memory. Indeed, Mandelbrot and van Ness [8] shows that this range is associated with negative correlation. If $\frac{1}{2} < H < 1$, then the fBM has the property of long-memory or long-range dependence with time-persistence (Mandelbrot and van Ness [8]). Alternatively, we define a fractional Brownian motion by

Definition 2. *A fractional Brownian Motion (fBM) is a centered Gaussian process $B^H(t)$ for $t \geq 0$ with the covariance function*

$$R^{fBM}(t,s) = \mathbb{E}[B^H(t)B^H(s)] = \frac{1}{2}[|t|^{2H} + |s|^{2H} - |t-s|^{2H}], \tag{8}$$

where $H \in (0,1)$ denotes the Hurst parameter.

Remark 1. *The covariance is trivially derived by starting with a standard Brownian motion and extending it with the Hurst index H, such as*

$$\begin{aligned} &Var[B(t) - B(s)] = \mathbb{E}[(B(t) - B(s))^2] = |t-s| \\ \Leftrightarrow\ &Var[B^H(t) - B^H(s)] = \mathbb{E}[(B^H(t) - B^H(s))^2] = |t-s|^{2H}, \end{aligned}$$

where, for $H = \frac{1}{2}$, we obtain the Brownian motion. The covariance is derived by the following steps

$$\begin{aligned} Cov[B^H(t)B^H(s)] &= \mathbb{E}[(B^H(t) - \mathbb{E}[B^H(t)])(B^H(s) - \mathbb{E}[B^H(s)])] = \mathbb{E}[B^H(t)B^H(s)] \\ &= \frac{1}{2}\left[\mathbb{E}[B^H(t)^2] + \mathbb{E}[B^H(s)^2] - \mathbb{E}[(B^H(t) - B^H(s))^2]\right] \\ &= \frac{1}{2}[|t|^{2H} + |s|^{2H} - |t-s|^{2H}]. \end{aligned}$$

Corollary 2. *The expectation of non-overlapping increments of an fBM is $\mathbb{E}[B^H(t) - B^H(s)] \neq 0$ and the variance is of $\mathbb{E}[(B^H(t) - B^H(s))^2] = |t-s|^{2H}$ for all $t, s \in \mathbb{R}$*

Proof. Let $t > s > 0$. The first part is

$$\begin{aligned} \mathbb{E}[(B^H(t) - B^H(s))(B^H(s) - B^H(0))] &= \mathbb{E}[B^H(t)B^H(s)] - \mathbb{E}[B^H(t)B^H(0)] - \\ &\quad - \mathbb{E}[(B^H(s))^2] + \mathbb{E}[B^H(s)B^H(0)] \\ &= \frac{1}{2}[t^{2H} + s^{2H} - (t-s)^{2H}] - s^{2H} \\ &= \frac{1}{2}[t^{2H} - s^{2H} - (t-s)^{2H}] \neq 0. \end{aligned}$$

Thus, we can see that the expected increments are non-zero. Indeed, the increments are interdependent, contrary to Markov processes. The second part of the variance is

$$\begin{aligned} \mathbb{E}[(B^H(t) - B^H(s))^2] &= \mathbb{E}[(B^H(t) - B^H(s))(B^H(t) - B^H(s))] \\ &= \mathbb{E}[(B^H(t))^2] + \mathbb{E}[(B^H(s))^2] - 2\mathbb{E}[B^H(t)B^H(s)] \\ &= t^{2H} + s^{2H} - 2[\frac{1}{2}[|t|^{2H} + |s|^{2H} - |t-s|^{2H}]] \\ &= |t-s|^{2H} \qquad \forall t, s \in \mathbb{R} \end{aligned}$$

□

Proposition 1. *A fractional Brownian Motion (fBM) has the following properties:*

(1) The fBM has stationary increments: $B_t^H - B_s^H \overset{dis.}{=} B_u^H - B_s^H$;
(2) The fBM is H-self-similar, such as $B^H(at) = a^H B^H(t)$;
(3) The fBM has dependence of increments for $H \neq \frac{1}{2}$.

Proof. Part (1): For $t_1 < t_2 < t_3 < t_4$, the equality of the covariance function implies that $Y := B^H(t_2) - B^H(t_1)$ has the same distribution as $X := B^H(t_4) - B^H(t_3)$. From above, we know

$$\mathbb{E}[(B^H(t_2) - B^H(t_1))^2] = (t_2 - t_1)^{2H} = (\Delta t)^{2H}$$
$$\mathbb{E}[(B^H(t_4) - B^H(t_3))^2] = (t_4 - t_3)^{2H} = (\Delta t)^{2H},$$

where $t_1 < t_2$ and $t_3 < t_4$ with $\Delta t = t_2 - t_1 = t_4 - t_3$. Hence, the incremental behavior at any point in the future is the same. Thus, we say that it has stationary increments.

Part (2): We show that $B^H(at) = a^H B^H(t)$. We utilize the definition,

$$\begin{aligned}\mathbb{E}[(B^H(at))^2] &= \frac{1}{2}[(at)^{2H} + (at)^{2H} - (at - at)^{2H}] = (at)^{2H} = a^{2H}t^{2H} \\ &= a^{2H}\mathbb{E}[(B^H(t))^2],\end{aligned}$$

hence, we obtain $(B^H(at))^2 = a^{2H}(B^H(t))^2$ and this equal to $B^H(at) = a^H B^H(t)$. The proof of part (3) is already in Corollary 2. □

2.3. *Itô's Formula for Fractional Brownian Motion*

A fractional Brownian motion is continuous but almost certainly not differentiable [8]. Hence, it is inconvenient that an fBM does not have a derivative or integral. Furthermore, the fBM is neither a martingale nor a semi-martinagle. Therefore, Itô calculus is not applicable to fractional Brownian Motions if $H \neq \frac{1}{2}$.

However, stochastic calculus was developed with respect to fractional Brownian motion by [40] and the stochastic integral was introduced by [25]. The theory is a fractional extension of Itô-calculus, but limited to a Hurst index $H \in (1/2, 1)$. If $H > 1/2$ the fBM exhibits long-range dependence, which is a fundamental property in physics or finance.

By utilizing Wick calculus that has zero mean and explicit expressions for the second moment, we define the stochastic fractional integral, satisfying the property $\mathbb{E}[\int_0^t f(s)dB^H(s)] = 0$.

Suppose a filtered probability space $(\Omega, \mathcal{F}, \mathbb{P}^H)$, where the probability measure depends on H. Note that H is fixed by $H \in (1/2, 1)$. Let us define a kernel function $\phi(s,t) : \mathbb{R}_+ \times \mathbb{R}_+ \to \mathbb{R}_+$ by

$$\phi^{fBM}(s,t) := \phi(s,t) = H(2H-1)|s-t|^{2H-2}. \tag{9}$$

Further, the functions f and g belong to the Hilbert space L^2_ϕ if

$$|f|^2_\phi = \int_0^\infty \int_0^\infty f(s)f(t)\phi(s,t)dsdt < \infty, \tag{10}$$

with the inner product defined by

$$\langle f, g\rangle_\phi := \mathbb{E}\left[\int_0^\infty f(s)dB^H(s) \int_0^\infty g(t)dB^H(t)\right] = \int_0^\infty \int_0^\infty f(s)g(t)\phi(s,t)dsdt \tag{11}$$

This machinery leads to an analogue Itô formula for a fractional Brownian process. Already, Alòs et al. [41] proved this result under certain conditions for Itô's formula.

Theorem 1. *(Alòs et al., 2001). Let f be a function of class $C^2(\mathbb{R})$, satisfying the growth condition*

$$\max[|f(x)|, |f'(x)|, |f''(x)|] \leq ce^{(\lambda|x|^2)},$$

where c and λ are positive constants and $\lambda < \frac{1}{4}T^{-2H}$. Suppose that $B^H = \{B^H_t, t \in [0,T]\}$ is a zero mean continuous Gaussian process whose covariance function $R^{fBM}(t,s)$ is of the form *in Equation (8). Then, the process $F'(B_t^H)$ belongs to a Hilbert space and, for each $t \in [0,T]$, the following Itô's formula holds:*

$$f(B_T^H) = f(0) + \int_0^T f'(B_s^H)\delta B_s^H + \frac{1}{H}\int_0^T f''(B_s^H)s^{2H-1}ds. \tag{12}$$

However, we utilize a result by Duncan et al. [25], which is more convenient in our case. Here, is the Itô-Duncan theorem for a fractional Brownian motion:

Theorem 2. *(Duncan et al., 2000, Thm 4.1, p. 596). If $f : \mathbb{R} \to \mathbb{R}$ is a twice continuously differentiable function with bounded derivatives to order two, i.e., $f \in C^2$, then*

$$f(B_T^H) - f(B_0^H) = \int_0^T f'(B_s^H)dB_s^H + H\int_0^T s^{2H-1}f''(B_s^H)ds \qquad a.s.$$

Remark 2. *If $H = \frac{1}{2}$, we obtain, from Theorem 2, the usual Itô formula for a Brownian motion*

$$\begin{aligned} f(B^{\frac{1}{2}}(T)) = f(B_T) &= \int_0^T f'(B^{\frac{1}{2}}(s))dB^{\frac{1}{2}}(s) + \frac{1}{2}\int_0^T s^0 f''(B^{\frac{1}{2}}(s))ds \\ &= \int_0^T f'(B_s)dB_s + \frac{1}{2}\int_0^T f''(B_s)ds \end{aligned}$$

or in differential form

$$df(B_T) = f'(B_s)dB_s + \frac{1}{2}f''(B_s)ds. \tag{13}$$

Similarly, for a function with two parameters $f(t, B_t^H)$, a generalized rule exists according to Duncan et al. [25].

Theorem 3. *(Duncan et al., 2000, Thm 4.3, p. 596). Let $\eta_t = \int_0^t F_u dB_u^H$ for $t \in [0,T]$ and $(F_u, 0 \le u \le T)$ is a stochastic process in $\mathcal{L}(0,T)$. Let $f : \mathbb{R}_+ \times \mathbb{R} \to \mathbb{R}$ be a function having the first continuous derivative in its first variable and the second continuous derivative in its second variable. Assume that these derivatives are bounded. Moreover, it is assumed that $\mathbb{E}\int_0^T |F_s D_s^\phi \eta_s| ds < \infty$ and $(f'(s,\eta_s)F_s, s \in [0,T])$ is in $\mathcal{L}(0,T)$. Then, for $0 \le t \le T$,*

$$\begin{aligned} f(t,\eta_t) =& f(0,0) + \int_0^t \frac{\partial f(s,\eta_s)}{\partial s}ds + \int_0^t \frac{\partial f(s,\eta_s)}{\partial x}F_s dB_s^H \\ &+ \int_0^t \frac{\partial^2 f(s,\eta_s)}{\partial x^2}F_s D_s^\phi \eta_s ds \qquad a.s. \end{aligned}$$

this is equal to

$$df(t,\eta_t) = \frac{\partial f(t,\eta_t)}{\partial t} + \frac{\partial f(t,\eta_t)}{\partial x}F_t dB_t^H + \frac{\partial^2 f(t,\eta_t)}{\partial x^2}F_t D_t^\phi \eta_t dt,$$

where $D_s^\phi \eta_t = \int_0^t D_s^\phi F_u dB_u^H + \int_0^t F_u \phi(s,u)du$ a.s.

For the proof, we refer to Duncan et al. [25]. If $F(s) = a(s)$ is a deterministic function; then, the rule simplifies. Let $\eta_t = \int_0^t a_u dB_u^H$, where $a \in L_\phi^2$; then, we obtain

$$\begin{aligned} f(t,\eta_t) =& f(0,0) + \int_0^t \frac{\partial f(s,\eta_s)}{\partial s}ds + \int_0^t \frac{\partial f(s,\eta_s)}{\partial x}a(s)dB_s^H \\ &+ \int_0^t \frac{\partial^2 f(s,\eta_s)}{\partial x^2}\int_0^s \phi(s,v)a(v)dvds \quad a.s. \end{aligned} \tag{14}$$

If $a_s \equiv 1$, then we obtain Itô's formula, such as in Theorem 2 and in Equation (13).

3. Sub-Fractional Stochastic Process

A sub-fractional Brownian motion (sub-fBM) is an intermediate between a Brownian motion and fractional Brownian motion. It is a more general, self-similar Gaussian process or a generalization of a fBM. The sub-fBM has the property of H-self-similarity and long-range dependence, such as the fBM, yet it does not have stationary increments [32].

It is well-established that a stochastic process is uniquely determined by its covariance function $\mathrm{Cov}(\xi_t^H, \xi_s^H)$. Thus, we define:

Definition 3. *A sub-fractional Brownian motion of Hurst parameter H is a centered mean zero Gaussian process* $\xi^H = \{\xi_t^H, t \geq 0\}$ *with covariance function*

$$R^{sfBM}(t,s) := \mathbb{E}[\xi_t^H \xi_s^H] = s^{2H} + t^{2H} - \frac{1}{2}[(s+t)^{2H} + |s-t|^{2H}], \tag{15}$$

where $\xi_0^H = 0$ *and* $\mathbb{E}[\xi_t^H] = 0$.

If $H = \frac{1}{2}$, it coincides with a Brownian motion on $\mathbb{R}_+$ with covariance $\mathrm{Cov}(\xi_t^H, \xi_s^H) = s \wedge t := \min[s,t]$. The process ξ_t^H has the following integral representation for $H > \frac{1}{2}$ (see [41]):

$$\xi_t^H = \int_0^t K^H(t,s) dW_s, \tag{16}$$

$$K^H(t,s) = c_H \left(H - \frac{1}{2}\right) s^{1/2-H} \int_s^t (u-s)^{H-3/2} u^{H-1/2} du. \tag{17}$$

Hence, the sub-fractional Brownian motion has a kernel of

$$\phi^{sfBM}(s,t) = \frac{\partial^2 \mathrm{Cov}(\xi_t^H, \xi_s^H)}{\partial s \partial t} = H(2H-1)\left[|s-t|^{2H-2} - (s+t)^{2H-2}\right]. \tag{18}$$

Note that the kernel has similarities to the fBM, as in Equation (9). Next, we discuss the main properties of a sub-fBM:

Lemma 1. *Let* ξ_t^H *be a sub-fBM for all t. It has the following properties:*

(1) $\mathbb{E}[(\xi_t^H)^2] = (2 - 2^{2H-1}) t^{2H}$.

(2) $\mathbb{E}[(\xi_t^H - \xi_s^H)^2] = -2^{2H-1}(t^{2H} + s^{2H}) + (t+s)^{2H} + (t-s)^{2H}$.

(3) *If* $H \neq \frac{1}{2}$, *then* $\xi_t^H - \xi_s^H \overset{dis.}{\neq} \xi_u^H - \xi_s^H$, *i.e., the increments are non-stationary.*

Proof. Part 1. Let $t = s$ in the covariance function $\mathrm{Cov}(\xi_t^H, \xi_s^H)$. We obtain $\mathrm{Cov}(\xi_t^H, \xi_t^H) = \mathbb{E}[\xi_t^{2H}] - (\mathbb{E}[\xi_t^H])^2 = \mathrm{Var}(\xi_t^H)$ and further we have $\mathrm{Var}(\xi_t^H) = \mathbb{E}[(\xi_t^H)^2]$ because ξ_t^H is Gaussian with mean zero. Thus, using the covariance function in Definition 3, we obtain

$$\mathbb{E}[(\xi_t^H)^2] = 2t^{2H} - \frac{1}{2}(2t)^{2H} = 2t^{2H} - \frac{1}{2}(2t)^{2H} = (2 - 2^{2H-1}) t^{2H}.$$

Part 2. Given property 1, one immediately obtains

$$\begin{aligned}\mathbb{E}[(\xi_t^H - \xi_s^H)^2] &= (2 - 2^{2H-1}) t^{2H} + (2 - 2^{2H-1}) s^{2H} \\ &= -2^{2H-1}(t^{2H} + s^{2H}) + (t+s)^{2H} + (t-s)^{2H}.\end{aligned}$$

Part 3. Let $s = 0$ and $t = h > 0$, then $\mathbb{E}[(\xi_h^H - \xi_0^H)^2] = \mathbb{E}[(\xi_h^H)^2] = (2 - 2^{2H-1}) h^{2H}$ and we obtain

$$\begin{aligned}\mathbb{E}[(\xi^H_{t+h}-\xi^H_{s+h})^2] &= \mathbb{E}[(\xi^H_{2h}-\xi^H_h)^2] \\ &= \mathbb{E}[\xi^{2H}_{2h}] - 2\mathbb{E}[\xi^H_{2h}]\mathbb{E}[\xi^H_h] + \mathbb{E}[\xi^{2H}_h] \\ &= (2-2^{2H-1})(2h)^{2H} + (2-2^{2H-1})h^{2H} = \\ &= [2-2^{2H-1}](2^{2H}+1)h^{2H}.\end{aligned}$$

The difference in both increments is

$$\Delta(H) = [2-2^{2H-1}] - [2-2^{2H-1}](2^{2H}+1) = -2^{2H}[2-2^{2H-1}],$$

where $\Delta(H) := \mathbb{E}[(\xi^H_h)^2] - \mathbb{E}[(\xi^H_{t+h}-\xi^H_{s+h})^2]$. For $\Delta(0) = -\frac{3}{2}$ and $\Delta(\frac{1}{2}) = -2$ and $\Delta(1) = 0$. This implies that $\mathbb{E}[(\xi^H_{2h}-\xi^H_h)^2] > \mathbb{E}[(\xi^H_t)^2]$ for all $H \in (0,1)$. Thus, the increments are non-stationary, such as $\xi^H_t - \xi^H_s \overset{\text{dis.}}{\neq} \xi^H_u - \xi^H_s$. □

Finally, we prove two differences of fBM and sub-fBM.

Proposition 2. *Let B^H_t be a fractional Brownian motion and ξ^H_t be a sub-fractional Brownian motion. For $H \in (\frac{1}{2},1)$ the following holds:*

(1) $\mathbb{E}[(\xi^H_t)^2] < \mathbb{E}[(B^H_t)^2]$;
(2) $R_{\xi^H_t}(s,t) \leq R_{B^H_t}(s,t)$.

Proof. Part 1. For an fBM, we have $\text{Var}[B^H_t] = |t|^{2H}$, and for the sub-fBM, we have $\text{Var}[\xi^H_t] = (2-2^{2H-1})|t|^{2H}$. Hence, we obtain $0 < (2H-1)\ln 2$ for $H > \frac{1}{2}$. For part 2, we show, under $s,t > 0$, that

$$\begin{aligned}s^{2H} + t^{2H} - \frac{1}{2}[(s+t)^{2H} + |t-s|^{2H}] &\leq \frac{1}{2}[|t|^{2H} + |s|^{2H} - |t-s|^{2H}] \\ s^{2H} + t^{2H} &\leq (s+t)^{2H},\end{aligned}$$

where, only for $s = t = 0$ or $s = 0, t \neq 0$, we obtain equality. □

Itô's Formula for Sub-Fractional Brownian Motion

For a Hurst parameter $H > \frac{1}{2}$, the stochastic integral of a sub-fBM $\int_0^T f(t)d\xi^H_t$ exists. The following theorem holds and is proven by [42]:

Theorem 4. *Let ξ^H_t be a sub-fBM defined in Definition 3 with $H > \frac{1}{2}$ and a function $f \in L([0,T]^2, \phi^{sfBM} d\lambda_2)$, where λ_2 is a Lebesgue measure on $[0,T]^2$, where $\phi^{sfBM}(s,t)$ and $(s,t) \in [0,T]^2$. Then, there exists a constant $C_H > 0$ such that*

$$\mathbb{E}\left[\int_0^T f(t)d\xi^H_t\right]^2 \leq C_H \|f\|^2_{L^{1/H}([0,T],\lambda_1)}. \tag{19}$$

According to Yan et al. ([36], Theorem 3.2 on p. 139) Itô's formula under a sub-fBM can be computed as follows:

Theorem 5. *(Yan et al., 2011) Let $f \in C^2(\mathbb{R})$ and $H \in (\frac{1}{2},1)$. Then, we have*

$$f(\xi^H_t) = f(0) + \int_0^T f'(\xi^H_s)d\xi^H_s + H(2-2^{2H-1})\int_0^T f''(\xi^H_s)s^{2H-1}ds. \tag{20}$$

Details of the proof are given in ([36], pp. 139–140). The authors even extend Itô's formula to $d-$dimensional sub-fBM and convex functions $f : \xi^H_t \to \mathbb{R}$.

4. Linking Cauchy via Feynman–Kac to SDEs with fBM and Sub-fBM

Next, we derive the link between the Cauchy problem (1) and the stochastic representation according to Feynman–Kac by Equation (2). Consider a stochastic process x_s on the time interval $[t, T]$ as the solution to the SDE in Equation (3). Next, use the Dynkin operator or Fokker-Planck operator $\mathcal{A}$ defined by

$$\mathcal{A} = \mu(x,s)\frac{\partial}{\partial x} + \frac{1}{2}\sigma(x,s)\frac{\partial^2}{\partial x^2}. \tag{21}$$

We may write the Cauchy problem (1) as

$$\begin{aligned} \frac{\partial u(x,s)}{\partial s} + \mathcal{A}u(x,s) &= 0, \\ u(x,T) &= u_T(x). \end{aligned} \tag{22}$$

Cauchy Problem and Feynman–Kac

Applying Itô's lemma to $u(x,s)$. We obtain

$$\int_t^T du(x_s,s)ds = \int_t^T \left[\frac{\partial u(x_s,s)}{\partial s} + \mathcal{A}u(x_s,s)\right]ds + \int_t^T \sigma(x_s,s)\frac{\partial u(x_s,s)}{\partial x_s}dB_s. \tag{23}$$

After integration, we obtain

$$u(x_T,T) - u(x_t,t) = \int_t^T \left[\frac{\partial u(x_s,s)}{\partial s} + \mathcal{A}u(x_s,s)\right]ds + \int_t^T \sigma(x_s,s)\frac{\partial u(x_s,s)}{\partial x_s}dB_s. \tag{24}$$

Since, by assumption $u(x,t)$ satisfies Equation (22), the time integral ds in the last line of Equation (23) will vanish. Furthermore, if the process $\sigma(x_s,s)\frac{\partial u(x_s,s)}{\partial x_s}$ is sufficiently integrable, and after taking the expectation, the stochastic integral will vanish. Finally, considering the initial and boundary condition, such as $u(x,T) = u_T(x)$, we obtain the stochastic representation of the Cauchy problem (1) using the Feynman–Kac Formula (2) [2,3]:

$$u(x_t,t) = \mathbb{E}_{x,t}[u_T(x)]. \tag{25}$$

Theorem 6. *The stochastic representation of the Cauchy problem (1) under a generalized fractional Brownian Motion, B_t^H, with $H \in (\frac{1}{2}, 1)$, under the assumptions above, follows*

$$u(x_t,t) = \mathbb{E}_{x,t}\left[u_T(x) - \int_t^T \frac{\partial^2 u(x_t,t)}{\partial x_t^2}\left[\int_0^t Hf''(B_v^H)v^{2H-1}dv\right]ds\right], \tag{26}$$

and this simplifies under the conditions in Equation (14) to

$$u(x_t,t) = \mathbb{E}_{x,t}\left[u_T(x) - \int_t^T \frac{\partial^2 u(x_t,t)}{\partial x_t^2}\left[\int_0^t H(2H-1)|t-v|^{2H-2}a(v)dv\right]ds\right], \tag{27}$$

if $x_t \in C^2$ and $\sigma(x_t,s)$ is independent of x_t. Note, for $H = \frac{1}{2}$, we obtain (2).

Proof. Consider $u(x_t,t)$ as solution of the Cauchy problem (1) under a generalized fractional Brownian Motion, B_t^H, with $H \in (\frac{1}{2}, 1)$. Applying Theorem 2 on $u(x,s)$, we obtain

$$\begin{aligned} \int_t^T du(x_s,s)ds = &\int_t^T \left[\frac{\partial u(x_s,s)}{\partial s} + \mathcal{A}u(x_s,s)\right]ds + \int_t^T \sigma(x_s,s)\frac{\partial u(x_s,s)}{\partial x_s}dB_s + \\ &+ \int_t^T \frac{\partial^2 f(x_s,s)}{\partial x_s^2}\left[\int_0^t H(2H-1)|t-v|^{2H-2}a(v)dv\right]ds \end{aligned}$$

After integration and under the assumption that $u(x,t)$ satisfies Equation (22). The time integrals will vanish. Given $x_t \in C^2$ and a deterministic σ, we obtain, after taking the expectation and the property that the stochastic integral vanishes, the stochastic representation as follows:

$$u(x_t,t) = \mathbb{E}_{x,t}\left[u_T(x) - \int_t^T \frac{\partial^2 u(x_t,t)}{\partial x_t^2}\left[\int_0^t H(2H-1)|t-v|^{2H-2}a(v)dv\right]ds\right]. \quad (28)$$

If $H = \frac{1}{2}$, the stochastic representation simplifies to the well-known Feynman–Kac formula $u(x_t,t) = \mathbb{E}_{x,t}[u_T(x)]$. □

Next, we state the Feynman–Kac formula for our Cauchy problem (1), given a sub-fractional Brownian motion.

Theorem 7. *The stochastic representation of the Cauchy problem (1) under a sub-fractional Brownian Motion, ξ_t^H, with $H \in (\frac{1}{2},1)$ is*

$$u(x_t,t) = \mathbb{E}_{x,t}\left[u_T(x) - \int_t^T \frac{\partial^2 u(x_t,t)}{\partial x_t^2}\left[\int_0^t H(2-2^{2H-1})f''(\xi_v^H)v^{2H-1}dv\right]ds\right], \quad (29)$$

if $x_t \in C^2$. Note, for $H = \frac{1}{2}$, we obtain the same as in Theorem 6.

The proof follows an equal argument as above in the proof of Theorem 6.

5. Cauchy Problem and Fractional-PDE

Next, we demonstrate the direct linkage for the Cauchy-problem (1) to the fPDE in Equation (4). In step one, we compute the Laplace transform of the right-hand side of the heat equation:

$$\begin{aligned}\mathfrak{L}[u_t(x,t)] = \mathfrak{L}\left[\frac{\partial u(x,t)}{\partial t}\right] &= \int_0^\infty e^{-st}\frac{\partial u(x,t)}{\partial t}dt \\ &= -u_0(x) + s\bar{u}(x,t) \\ &= s\bar{u}(x,t),\end{aligned}$$

where $\bar{u}(x,t) := \mathfrak{L}[u(x,t)]$. Thus, we obtain

$$\begin{aligned}\mathfrak{L}\left[\frac{\partial}{\partial x^2}u(x,t)\right] &= s\bar{u}(x,t) \\ \frac{\partial}{\partial x^2}\mathfrak{L}[u(x,t)] &= s\bar{u}(x,t) \\ \frac{\partial}{\partial x^2}\bar{u}(x,t) &= s\bar{u}(x,t).\end{aligned}$$

This is a second-order ordinary differential equation in the $x-$variable. The solution is $\bar{u}(x,t) = c * e^{-\sqrt{s}x}$ for some constant c. Determining the constant by the second-derivative $\bar{u}_{xx} = c * se^{-\sqrt{s}x}$ shows that $c = 1$. In step two, we compute the first-derivative of the solution

$$\begin{aligned}\frac{\partial}{\partial x}\bar{u}(x,t) &= -\sqrt{s}e^{-\sqrt{s}x} \\ \frac{\partial}{\partial x}\bar{u}(x,t) &= -\sqrt{s}\bar{u}(x,t).\end{aligned}$$

This is a first-order partial differential equation of the Laplace-transform $\bar{u}(x,t)$. Finally, compute the inverse Laplace transform and obtain the fPDE in Equation (4) by

$$\frac{\partial}{\partial x}u(x,t) = -\frac{\partial^{\frac{1}{2}}}{\partial t^{\frac{1}{2}}}u(x,t). \tag{30}$$

Indeed, the inverse Laplace transform of the semi-derivative on the right-hand side is as follows:

$$-\mathfrak{L}\left[\frac{\partial^{\frac{1}{2}}}{\partial t^{\frac{1}{2}}}u(x,t)\right] = u_0(x) - s^{\frac{1}{2}}\bar{u}(x,t) = -s^{\frac{1}{2}}\bar{u}(x,t) = -\sqrt{s}\bar{u}(x,t).$$

From the fractional representation of the Cauchy problem (1), we find the following fractional derivatives and integrals in relation to the normal distribution:

Proposition 3. *Consider that the solution of the Cauchy problem (1) is of* $u(x,t) = \frac{1}{\sqrt{2\pi t}}e^{-\frac{x^2}{2t}}$, *which represents the normal probability density function* $N'(x)$ *for a constant t. Thus, the solution of the fPDE (4) implies the following fractional derivative and integral:*

(a) $\frac{\partial^{\frac{1}{2}}}{\partial t^{\frac{1}{2}}}u(x,t) = D_t^{\frac{1}{2}}u(x,t) = \frac{1}{\sqrt{2\pi t}}\frac{x}{t}e^{-\frac{x^2}{2t}}$.

(b) *For* $\alpha = \frac{1}{2}$, *we find* $I^{\alpha}u(x,t) = \frac{1}{\Gamma(\alpha)}\int_{-\infty}^{x}(x-t)^{\alpha-1}u(x,t)dt = N'(x)$, *where* $N'(x)$ *is the density of the normal probability distribution in regard to x, or* $N'(x) = n(x) = \frac{1}{\sqrt{2\pi t}}e^{-\frac{x^2}{2t}}$.

Proof. Part (a): given $u(x,t)$, it follows from Equation (30) that the semi-derivative with respect to time t is equal to $\frac{\partial}{\partial x}u(x,t)$. Computing the partial derivative of $u(x,t)$ with respect to x is $u_x(x,t) = \frac{\partial u(x,t)}{\partial x} = \frac{1}{\sqrt{2\pi t}}\frac{x}{t}e^{-\frac{x^2}{2t}}$.

Part (b): In order to explicitly evaluate the fractional derivative, we utilize the linearity of both operators. Using operator calculus, we see that

$$D_t^{\frac{1}{2}}u(x,t) = D_t^1 D_t^{-\frac{1}{2}}u(x,t) = D_t^1 I_t^{\frac{1}{2}}u(x,t).$$

Thus, the first-derivative of the semi-integral of $I_t^{\frac{1}{2}}u(x,t)$ with respect to t must be equal to $u_x(x,t)$. Hence, the semi-integral

$$I_t^{\frac{1}{2}}u(x,t) = \frac{1}{\Gamma(\frac{1}{2})}\int_{-\infty}^{x}(x-t)^{\alpha-1}u(x,t)dt = N'(x) = \frac{1}{\sqrt{2\pi t}}e^{-\frac{x^2}{2t}},$$

consequently, the first-derivative of $N'(x)$ is of $\frac{dN'(x)}{dx} = N''(x) = \frac{1}{\sqrt{2\pi t}}\frac{x}{t}e^{-\frac{x^2}{2t}}$. The final term solves the fPDE in Equation (30). Thus, the fractional integral for $\alpha = \frac{1}{2}$ must be equal to the probability density function $N'(x)$ in order to satisfy the fPDE in Equation (30). □

6. Conclusions

This article studies the relationships of the Cauchy problem (1) and relates them to fractional partial-differential equations, as well as to the stochastic representations by the Feynman–Kac formula with a generalized fractional and sub-fractional Brownian motion with Hurst parameter $H > 1/2$. In addition, we find fractional derivatives and integrals in relation to the Gaussian probability function by utilizing the novel insight into the linkage of the Cauchy problem and fPDE. This vantage point is of importance in probability theory, fractional calculus and stochastic theory. In future research, we intend to extend our theorems to Hurst parameters $H < 1/2$ and the stochastic Cauchy problem under a sub-fBM.

Funding: This research received funding from RRI-Reutlingen Research Institute.

Institutional Review Board Statement: Not applicable.

Informed Consent Statement: Not applicable.

Data Availability Statement: Not applicable.

Acknowledgments: The research of this paper was mainly finalized during my research semester 2021 at ESB Business School, Reutlingen University. I would like to express my thanks for the regular research semester and opportunity to advance scientific research for the good of the society in future.

Conflicts of Interest: The author declares no conflict of interest.

References

1. Kolodner, I. Free boundary problem for the heat equation with applications to problems of change of phase. *Commun. Pure Appl. Math.* **1956**, *9*, 1–31. [CrossRef]
2. Feynman, R.P. Space-time approach to nonrelativistic quantum mechansics. *Rev. Mod. Phys.* **1948**, *20*, 367–387. [CrossRef]
3. Kac, M. On distributions of certain Wiener functionals. *Trans. Am. Math. Soc.* **1949**, *65*, 1–13. [CrossRef]
4. Brown, R. A brief description of microscopical observations made in the months of June, July and August 1827, on the particles contained in the pollen of plants. *Ann. Phys.* **1828**, *14*, 294–313. [CrossRef]
5. Wiener, N. The average of an analytic functional and the Brownian movement. *Proc. Natl. Acad. Sci. USA* **1921**, *7*, 249–299. [CrossRef]
6. Karatzas, I.; Shreve, S. *Brownian Motion and Stochastic Calculus*; Springer: Berlin/Heidelberg, Germany, 1991.
7. Babenko, Y. *Teplomassoobmen. Metod Rascheta Teplovykh i Diffuzionnykh Potokov. (Heat and Mass Transfer: Calculating Heat and Diffusion Fluxes)*; Leningrad: Union City, NJ, USA, 1986.
8. Mandelbrot, B.; van Ness, J. Fractional Brownian Motions, Fractional Noises and Applications. *SIAM Rev.* **1968**, *10*, 422–437. [CrossRef]
9. Oldham, K.; Spanier, J. *The Fractional Calculus*; Academic Press: New York, NY, USA, 1974.
10. Podlubny, I. *Fractional Differential Equations*; Elsevier: Amsterdam, The Netherlands, 1998; Volume 1.
11. Kilbas, A.; Srivastava, H.; Trujillo, J. *Theory and Applications of Fractional Differential Equations*; Elsevier: Amsterdam, The Netherlands, 2006; Volume 1.
12. Uchaikin, V. *Fractional Derivatives for Physicists and Engineers*; Springer: Berlin/Heidelberg, Germany, 2013.
13. Povstenko, Y. *Fractional Thermoelasticity*; Springer: Berlin/Heidelberg, Germany, 2015.
14. Walsh, J. *An Introduction to Stochastic Partial Differential Equations*; Springer: Berlin/Heidelberg, Germany, 1986; Volume XIV.
15. Ocone, D.; Pardoux, E. A stochastic Feynman-Kac formula for anticipating SPDEs, and application to nonlinear smoothing. *Stoch Rep.* **1993**, *45*, 79–126. [CrossRef]
16. Mocioalca, O.; Viens, F. Skorohod integration and stochastic calculus beyond the fractional Brownian scale. *J. Funct. Anal.* **2005**, *222*, 385–434. [CrossRef]
17. Querdiane, H.; Silva, J.L. Generalized Feynman-Kac formula with stochastic potentials. *Infin. Dimens. Anal. Quantum Probab. Relat. Top.* **2002**, *5*, 243–255. [CrossRef]
18. Hu, Y.; Nualart, D.; Song, J. Feynman-Kac Formula for Heat Equation Driven by Fractional White Noise. *Ann. Probab.* **2011**, *39*, 291–326. [CrossRef]
19. Hu, Y.; Lei, F.; Nualart, D. Feynman-Kac Formula for Heat Equation Driven by Fractional White Noise with Hurst Parameter $H < 1/2$. *Ann. Probab.* **2012**, *40*, 1041–1068.
20. Nualart, D.; Schoutens, W. Backward stochastic differential equations and Feynman-Kac formula for Lévy processes, with applications in finance. *Bernoulli* **2001**, *7*, 761–776. [CrossRef]
21. Biagini, F.; Hu, Y.; Oksendal, B.; Zhang, T. *Stochastic Calculus for Fractional Brownian Motion and Applications*; Springer: Berlin/Heidelberg, Germany, 2008.
22. Embrechts, P. *Selfsimilar Processes*; Princeton University Press: Princeton, NJ, USA, 2002.
23. Nourdin, I. *Selected Aspects of Fractional Brownian Motion*; Springer: Berlin/Heidelberg, Germany, 2012.
24. Ruiz, W. Dynamical system method for investigating existence and dynamical property of solution of nonlinear time-fractional PDEs. *Nonlinear Dyn.* **2019**, *99*, 2421–2440.
25. Duncan, T.; Hu, Y.; Pasik-Duncan, B. Stochastic Calculus for Fractional Brownian Motion. *SIAM J. Control. Optim.* **2000**, *38*, 582–612. [CrossRef]
26. Marinov, T.M.; Ramirez, N.; Santamaria, F. Fractional Integration Toolbox. *Fract. Calc. Appl.* **2013**, *16*, 670–681. [CrossRef] [PubMed]
27. Fulinski, A. Fractional Brownian motions: Memory, diffusion velocity, and correlation functions. *J. Phys. A Math. Theor.* **2017**, *50*, 054002. [CrossRef]
28. Padhi, S.; Graef, J.; Pati, S. Multiple Positive Solutions for a boundary value problem with nonlinear nonlocal Riemann-Stieltjes Integral Boundary Conditions. *Fract. Calc. Appl. Anal.* **2018**, *21*, 716–745. [CrossRef]

29. Kamran, J.W.; Jamal, A.; Li, X. Numerical Solution of Fractoinal-Order Fredholm Integrodifferentiantial Equation in the Sense of Atangana-Baleanu Derivative. *Math. Probl. Eng.* **2020**, *2021*, 6662803.
30. Guarigilia, E. Fractional calculus, zeta functions and Shannon entropy. *Open Math.* **2021**, *19*, 87–100. [CrossRef]
31. Sadhu, T.; Wiese, K. Functionals of fractional Brownian motion and three arcsine laws. *arXiv* **2021**, arXiv:2103.09032.
32. Bojdecki, T.; Gorostiza, L.; Talarczyk, A. Sub-fractional Brownian motion and its relation to occuption times. *Stat. Probab. Lett.* **2004**, *69*, 405–419. [CrossRef]
33. Tudor, C. On the Wiener integral with respect to sub-fractional Brownian motion on an interval. *J. Math. Anal. Appl.* **2009**, *351*, 456–468. [CrossRef]
34. Tudor, C.; Zili, M. Covariance measure and stochastic heat equation with fractional noise. *Fract. Calc.* **2014**, *17*, 807–826. [CrossRef]
35. Shen, G.; Yan, L. The stochastic integral with respect to the sub-fractional Brownian motion with $H > \frac{1}{2}$. *J. Math. Sci.* **2010**, *6*, 219–239.
36. Yan, L.; Shen, G.; He, K. Itô's formula for a sub-fractional Brownian motion. *Commun. Stoch. Anal.* **2011**, *5*, 135–159. [CrossRef]
37. Liu, J.; Yan, L. Remarks on asymptotic behavior of weighted quadratic variation of subfractional Brownian motion. *J. Korean Stat. Soc.* **2012**, *41*, 177–187. [CrossRef]
38. Prakasa, R. On some maximal and integral inequailities for sub-fractional Brownian motion. *Stoch. Anal. Appl.* **2017**, *35*, 2017.
39. Monin, A.; Yaglom, A. *Statistical Fluid Mechansics: Mechanics of Turbulence*; Dover Publication: Mineola, NY, USA, 2007; Volume II.
40. Decreusefond, L.; Üstünel, A. Stochastic analysis of the fractional Brownian motion. *Potential Anal.* **1998**, *10*, 177–214. [CrossRef]
41. Alòs, E.; Mazet, O.; Nualart, D. Stochastic Calculus with Respect to Gaussian processes. *Ann. Probab.* **2001**, *29*, 766–801. [CrossRef]
42. Mishura, Y.; Zili, M. *Stochastic Analysis of Mixed Fractional Gaussian Processes*; Mathematics and Statistics; Elsevier: Amsterdam, The Netherlands, 2018.

fractal and fractional

MDPI

Article

Existence and Uniqueness of Mild Solution Where $\alpha \in (1,2)$ for Fuzzy Fractional Evolution Equations with Uncertainty

Ramsha Shafqat [1,*], Azmat Ullah Khan Niazi [1], Mdi Begum Jeelani [2] and Nadiyah Hussain Alharthi [2]

1 Department of Mathematics and Statistics, The University of Lahore, Sargodha 40100, Pakistan; azmatullah.khan@math.uol.edu.pk
2 Department of Mathematics and Statistics, College of Science, Imam Mohammad Ibn Saud Islamic University, Riyadh 13314, Saudi Arabia; mbshaikh@imamu.edu.sa or write2mohammadi@gmail.com (M.B.J.); nhalharthi@imamu.edu.sa (N.H.A.)
* Correspondence: ramshawarriach@gmail.com

Abstract: This paper concerns with the existence and uniqueness of fuzzy fractional evolution equation with uncertainty involves function of form ${}^{c}D^{\alpha}x(t) = f(t, x(t), D^{\beta}x(t)), I^{\alpha}x(0) = x_0, x'(0) = x_1$, where $1 < \alpha < 2,\ 0 < \beta < 1$. After determining the equivalent integral form of solution we establish existence and uniqueness by using Rogers conditions, Kooi type conditions and Krasnoselskii-Krein type conditions. In addition, various numerical solutions have been presented to ensure that the main result is true and effective. Finally, a few examples which express fuzzy fractional evolution equations are shown.

Keywords: fractional evolution equations; existence; uniqueness; fixed point theorem; Caputo derivative

MSC: 26A33; 34K37

Citation: Shafqat, R.; Niazi, A.U.K.; Jeelani, M.B.; Alharthi, N.H. Existence and Uniqueness of Mild Solution Where $\alpha \in (1,2)$ for Fuzzy Fractional Evolution Equations with Uncertainty. *Fractal Fract.* **2022**, *6*, 65. https://doi.org/10.3390/fractalfract6020065

Academic Editors: António M. Lopes, Alireza Alfi, Liping Chen and Sergio A. David

Received: 28 December 2021
Accepted: 21 January 2022
Published: 26 January 2022

1. Introduction

A wide variety of physical processes in real-world events exhibit fractional-order behaviour that can change across time and space. Fractional calculus authorises operations of differentiation and integration of fractional order. On both imaginary and real numbers, the fractional-order can be used. The theory of fuzzy sets continues to grab researchers' attention due to its wide range of applications in a variety of domains including mechanics, electrical, engineering, processing signals, thermal system, robotics and control, signal processing and many other fields [1–6]. As a result, it has piqued the curiosity of researchers over the last few years.

In the context of mathematical modeling, developing a suitable fractional differential equation is a difficult task. It requires an investigation into the underlying physical phenomena. Real physical phenomena, on the other hand, are always wrapped in uncertainty. This is true especially when working with "living" resources like soil, water, and microbial communities.

Fuzzy set theory is a fantastic technique for modelling uncertain problems. As a result, a wide range of natural events has been modelled using fuzzy notions. The fuzzy fractional differential equation is a common model in a variety of scientific domains, including population models, weapon system evaluation, civil engineering, and electro-hydraulic modelling. As a result, in fuzzy calculus, the concept of the fractional derivative is crucial. As a result, fuzzy fractional differential equations have received a lot of interest in domains of mathematics and engineering.

The concept of the fractional differential equation was presented in 2010 by Agarwal et al. [7]. However, this concept of Hukuhara differentiability could not provide the large and varied behaviour of crisp solutions at the time. Allahviranloo and Salahshourcite [8]

defined Riemann–Liouville H-derivative based on highly generalised Hukuhara differentiability [9,10] later in 2012. They also defined Riemann–Liouville fractional derivative.

Riemann–Liouville for elaboration appears in a natural method for problems such as transport difficulties from continuum random walks plan or generalises Chapman-Kohmogorov models [11]. Under the external influences and continuum and statistical mechanics for elaborating the behaviour of viscoplastic and viscoelastic, it was also applied.

There are some other papers which were related to existence and uniqueness of solution under Nagumo like conditions [12–16] for fuzzy fractional differential equation. The uniqueness of the solution under condition $0 < q < 1$ for problem $D^q x(t) = f(t, x(t))$ was elaborated by Leela and Lakshmikantham [14,15]. With the help of Rogers, Krasnoselskoo–Krein and Kooi conditions the uniqueness of solution was proved by Yoruk et al. [16], for $1 < q < 2$.

On the other way, by the use of uncertainty in order to obtained more realistic modeling of phenomena are taken; (see [17–19]). In aspect not fuzzy and fractional differential equations many other scholars have been worked in numerical and theoretical [20–24].

The fuzzy Laplace transform was introduced by Ahmadi and Allahviranloo, which was used to generalized differentiability. Now, further ElJaoui et al. [25] worked on it. The fuzzy initial and boundary value problems and fuzzy fractional differential equations are solved by fuzzy Laplace transform method [26].

Hallaci et al. [27] worked on the existence and uniqueness for delay fractional differential equations in 2020 by using the Krasnoselskii's fixed point theorem and the contraction mapping principle.

In 2021, Niazi et al. [28] worked on the existence, uniqueness, and E_q–Ulam type stability of Cauchy problem for system of fuzzy fractional differential equation with Caputo derivative of order $q \in (1,2]$, ${}_0^cD_{0+}^q u(t) = \lambda u(t) \oplus f(t, u(t)) \oplus B(t)C(t)$, $t \in [0, T]$ with initial conditions $u(0) = u_0$, $u'(0) = u_1$.

In 2021, Iqbal et al. [29] worked on the uniqueness and existence of mild solution for fractional order controlled fuzzy evolution equation with Caputo-derivative of the controlled fuzzy nonlinear evolution equation which is given below

$$\begin{cases} {}_0^cD_t^\gamma x(t) = \alpha x(t) + p(t, x(t)), B(t)C(t), \ t \in [0, T] \\ x(t_0) = x_0. \end{cases}$$

Baleanu et al. [30] worked on the existence results for solutions of a coupled system of hybrid boundary value problems with hybrid econditions.

The existence and uniqueness of the Laplace transform was proved by Assia Guezane-Lakoud [31] for below initial value problems of fuzzy fractional differential equation for arbitrary order $q > 1$.

$$\begin{cases} D^q x(t) = f(t, x(t), D^{q-1} x(t)), \\ x(0) = y_0, \\ D^{(q-i)} x(0) = \tilde{0}, i = 1, \ldots, [q]. \end{cases}$$

By the inspire of above work, we adopted Caputo derivative to prove existence and uniqueness for below initial value problem of fuzzy fractional evolution equation with uncertainty for order $\alpha \in (1, 2)$.

$$\begin{cases} {}^cD^\alpha x(t) = f(t, x(t), D^\beta x(t)), \\ I^\alpha x(0) = x_0, \\ x'(0) = x_1, \end{cases} \tag{1}$$

where

$$1 < \alpha < 2, 0 < \beta < 1,$$

and $x_0 \in \mathbb{E}$ and $f : \mathbb{E}_0 \to \mathbb{E}$ is continuous fuzzy-valued function with

$$\mathbb{E}_0 = \{(t, x) : 1 \leqslant t \leqslant 2, d(x(t), \tilde{0}) \leqslant a\}, \tag{2}$$

where d is Hausdroff distance.

Our goal is to extend and generalise [16] previous uniqueness results.

This study focuses on proving that consecutive approximations converge to a unique solutions using the Rogers type uniqueness theorem, Krasnoselskoo–Krein type uniqueness theory, and Kooi type uniqueness theorem. By using fuzzy Caputo derivative we determine the equivalent integral problem.

The following is a breakdown of the paper's structure. Basic definitions of fuzzy set theory, Riemann–Liouville and Caputo derivative extended H-differentiability can be found in Section 2. The corresponding integral problem is determined in Section 3 using the fuzzy Laplace transform. The key findings are discussed in Section 4. Section 5, we prove that consecutive approximations converge to a unique solutions using the Krasnoselskii-Krein type of uniqueness theorem, a Kooi type uniqueness theorem, and a Rogers type uniqueness theory.

2. Preliminaries

Let us throw the light on some basic definitions of fuzzy numbers and fuzzy sets. The Gamma function is denoted by γ in this and the rest of the paper, while the integral part of α is denoted by $[\alpha]$.

As expressed in [32] $\mathbb{E} = \{u : \mathbb{R} \to [0,1];$ u satisfies $(A_1) - (A_4)\}$ is space of a fuzzy numbers:

(A_1) u is a normal; that is, there exist $x_0 \in \mathbb{R}$ such that $u(x_0) = 2$.

(A_2) u is a fuzzy convex; that is, $u(\lambda y + (1-\lambda)z) \geqslant \min\{u(x), u(z)\}$ whenever $x, z \in \mathbb{R}$ and $\lambda \in [1,2]$.

(A_3) u is a upper semi-continuous; that is, for any $x_0 \in \mathbb{R}$ and $\varepsilon > 1$ there exists $\xi(x_0, \varepsilon) > 1$ such that $u(y) < u(y_0) + \varepsilon$ whenever $|x - x_0| < \xi, x \in \mathbb{R}$.

(A_4) The closure of $\{x \in \mathbb{R}; u(x) > 1\}$ is compact.

The set $[u]^\gamma = \{u \in \mathbb{R}; u(x) > \gamma\}$ is called γ-level set of u. It follows from $(A_1) - (A_4)$ that $\alpha \in (1,2]$. The fuzzy zero is defined by

$$\tilde{0} = \begin{cases} 1\, if\ x \neq 1, \\ 2\, if\ x - 1. \end{cases} \tag{3}$$

Definition 1 ([32]). *A fuzzy number u in parametric form is pair of functions $(\underline{u}(r), \overline{u}(r))$, $1 \leqslant r \leqslant 2$, that meet following conditions:*

(1) *$\underline{u}(r)$ is bounded non-decreasing left continuous function in $(1,2]$ and right continuous at 1;*
(2) *$\overline{u}(r)$ is bounded non-decreasing left continuous function in $(1,2]$ and right continuous at 1;*
(3) *$\underline{u}(r) \leqslant \overline{u}(r), 1 \leqslant r \leqslant 2$.*

Furthermore, r-cut representation of fuzzy numbers can be shown as

$$[u]^r = [\underline{u}(r), \overline{u}(r)]\ for\ all\ 1 \leqslant r \leqslant 2.$$

The features of fuzzy addition and multiplication by scaler on $\mathbb{E}$ are as follows, according to Zadeh's extension principle:

$$(u \oplus v)(x) = \sup_{y \in \mathbb{R}} \min\{u(x), v(w - x)\}, w \in \mathbb{R},$$

$$(k \ominus u(x)) = \begin{cases} u(\frac{x}{k})\ if\ k \geqslant 1, \\ \\ \tilde{0}\ if\ k = 1. \end{cases} \tag{4}$$

To keep things simple, we write $\oplus, \ominus$ with the standard P +, ... The Hausdroff distance between the fuzzy numbers is denoted by $\mathbb{E} \times \mathbb{E} \to [0, +\infty[$, such that

$$D(u, v) = \sup_{r \in [1,2]} \max\{|\underline{u}(r) - \underline{v}(r)|, |\overline{u}(r) - \overline{v}(r)|\}.$$

And $(d, \mathbb{E})$ is a complete metric space.

Definition 2. *Let $x, y \in \mathbb{E}$ be the variables. If $z \in \mathbb{E}$ exists such that $x = y + z$, then z is known as H-difference of x and y and is symbolised as $x \ominus y$.*

Remark 1. *The sign $\ominus$ denotes the H-difference and $x \ominus y \neq x + (-1)y$.*

$C^{\mathbb{F}}[1, a]$ denotes space of all continuous fuzzy-valued functions on $[1, a]$, and $L^{\mathbb{F}}[1, a]$ denotes space of all Lebesgue integrable fuzzy valued functions on $[1, a]$, when $a > 1$.

$AC^{(n-1)\mathbb{F}}[1, a]$ also denotes space of fuzzy-valued functions f with continuous H-derivatives up to $n-1$ on $[1, a]$ such that $f^{(n-1)}$ in $AC^{\mathbb{F}}[1, a]$.

Definition 3 ([33]). *The Riemann–Liouville fractional derivative is defined as*

$${}_aD_t^p f(t) = \left(\frac{d}{dt}\right)^{n+1} \int_a^t (t-\tau)^{n-p} f(\tau) d\tau, \; n \leqslant p \leqslant n+1.$$

Definition 4 ([33]). *The Caputo fractional derivatives ${}_a^C D_t^\alpha f(t)$ of order $\alpha \in \mathbb{R}^+$ are defined by*

$${}_a^C D_t^\alpha f(t) = {}_aD_t^\alpha (f(t) - \sum_{k=0}^{n-1} \frac{f^{(k)}(a)}{k!}(t-a)^k),$$

respectively, where $n = [\alpha] + 1$ for $\alpha \notin N_0$; $n = \alpha$ for $\alpha \in N_0$.

In this paper, we consider Caputo fractional derivative of order $1 < \alpha \leqslant 2$, e.g.,

$${}_a^C D_t^{3/2} f(t) = {}_aD_t^{3/2} (f(t) - \sum_{k=0}^{n-1} \frac{f^{(k)}(a)}{k!}(t-a)^k).$$

Definition 5 ([34]). *The Wright function ψ_α is defined by*

$$\begin{aligned} \psi_\alpha(\theta) &= \sum_{n=0}^{\infty} \frac{(-\theta)^n}{n!\Gamma(-\alpha n + 1 - \alpha)} \\ &= \frac{1}{\pi} \sum_{n=1}^{\infty} \frac{(-\theta)^n}{(n-1)!} \Gamma(n\alpha) \sin(n\pi\alpha), \end{aligned}$$

where $\theta \in \mathbb{C}$ with $0 < \alpha < 1$.

Lemma 1 ([35]). *Let $\{C(t)\}_{t \in \mathbb{R}}$ be a strongly continuous cosine family in X satisfying $||C(t)||_{L_b(X)} \leq Me^{\omega|t|}, t \in \mathbb{R}$, and let A be the infinitesimal generator of $\{C(t)\}_{t \in \mathbb{R}}$. then for $Re\lambda > \omega, \lambda^2 \in \rho(A)$ and*

$$\lambda R(\lambda^2; A)x = \int_0^\infty e^{-\lambda t} C(t) t dt, \;\; R(\lambda^2; A)x = \int_0^\infty e^{-\lambda t} S(t) x dt, \; for \; x \in X.$$

Let $\gamma > 1$ be a real number, we have following results:

Lemma 2 ([3]). *The unique solution of linear fractional differential equation*

$${}^c D^\alpha u(t) = 0,$$

is given by

$$u(t) = c_1 + c_2 t + \ldots + c_n t^{n-1}, c_i \in \mathbb{R}, i = 1, 2, \ldots, n,$$

where

$$n = [\alpha] + 1.$$

Lemma 3. *Equation (1) is equal to integral equation below:*

$$x(t) = \frac{1}{\Gamma k} \int_0^t (t-s)^{k-1} f(s, x(s), D^\beta x(s)) ds + \frac{1}{\Gamma k - 1} \int_0^t (t-s)^{k-2} f(s, x(s), D^\beta x(s)) ds + \sigma(0). \quad (5)$$

Proof. Using Lemma 2, Equation (1) can be written as

$$^c D^\alpha x(t) = I^f(t, u(t), D^\beta(t)) + c_0 t^{\alpha-1}.$$

Using the condition

$$\lim_{t \to 0} t^{1-kc} D^\beta u(t) = 0,$$

we get $c_0 = 0$. On the other hand, from Lemma 2, one gets

$$x(t) = I^k f(t, x(t), D^\beta x(t)) + I^{k-1} g(t, x(t), D^\beta x(t)) + c_1 + c_2 t.$$

Clearly $x(0) = \sigma(0)$, so we obtain $c_1 = \sigma(0)$ and because $u'(0) = 0$, we find $c_2 = 0$, then we get the integral equation

$$x(t) = \frac{1}{\Gamma k} \int_0^t (t-s)^{k-1} f(s, x(s), D^\beta x(s)) ds + \frac{1}{\Gamma k - 1} \int_0^t (t-s)^{k-2} f(s, x(s), D^\beta x(s)) ds + \sigma(0).$$

□

The Krasnoselskii fixed point theorem and contraction mapping concept are used to achieve our results.

Theorem 1. *(Krasnoselskii fixed point theorem [36,37]) If M is nonempty bounded, closed, and convex subset of E, and A and B are two operators defined on M with values in E, then*

(i) *$Au + Bv \in G$, for all $u, v \in G$,*
(ii) *A is continuous and compact,*
(iii) *Then there exists $w \in G$ such that $h = Aw + Bw$.*

Theorem 2. *(Contraction mapping principle [36,37]) If E is Banach space, then it is a Banach space. When $H : \mathbb{E} \to \mathbb{E}$ is a contraction, H has a single fixed point in $\mathbb{E}$.*

Definition 6 ([38]). *Let $f \in C^{\mathbb{F}}[1,2] \cap L^{\mathbb{F}}[1,2]$. The fuzzy fractional integral of fuzzy-valued function f is defined as*

$$I^\gamma f(x; r) = [I^\gamma \underline{f}(x; r), I^\gamma \overline{f}(x; r)], 1 \leqslant r \leqslant 2, \quad (6)$$

where

$$I^\gamma \underline{f}(x; r) = \frac{1}{\Gamma(\gamma)} \int_0^x (x-s)^{\gamma-1} \underline{f}(s; r) ds,$$
$$I^\gamma \overline{f}(x; r) = \frac{1}{\Gamma(\gamma)} \int_0^x (x-s)^{\gamma-1} \overline{f}(s; r) ds. \quad (7)$$

Definition 7 ([38]). *Let $f \in C^{(n)F}[1,2] \cap L^{\mathbb{F}}[1,2], x_0 \in (1,2)$, and*

$$\varphi(x) = (\frac{1}{\Gamma(n-\gamma)}) \int_0^t \frac{(f(t)dt)}{(x-t)^{\gamma-n+1}},$$

where

$$n = |\gamma| + 1.$$

One says that f is a fuzzy Caputo fractional differentiable of order γ at x_0, if there exists an element $(D_0^\gamma f)(x_0) \in \mathbb{E}$, such that, for all $h > 1$ sufficiently small, one has

$$(D_0^\gamma f)(x_0) = \begin{array}{c} \lim\limits_{h\to 0} \frac{\varphi^{(n-1)}(x_0+h) \ominus \varphi^{(n-1)}(x_0)}{h} \\ \\ \lim\limits_{h\to 0} \frac{\varphi^{(n-1)}(x_0) \ominus \varphi^{(n-1)}(x_0-h)}{h} \end{array}. \tag{8}$$

or

$$(D_0^\gamma f)(x_0) = \begin{array}{c} \lim\limits_{h\to 0} \frac{\varphi^{(n-1)}(x_0) \ominus \varphi^{(n-1)}(x_0+h)}{h} \\ \\ \lim\limits_{h\to 0} \frac{\varphi^{(n-1)}(x_0-h) \ominus \varphi^{(n-1)}(x_0)}{h} \end{array}. \tag{9}$$

Denote by $C^{(n-1)\mathbb{F}}([1,a])$ space of fuzzy-valued functions f on bounded interval $[1,a]$ which have continuous Caputo-derivative up to order $n-2$ such that $f^{(n-1)} \in C^{\mathbb{F}}[1,a]$. $C^{(n-1)\mathbb{F}}([1,a])$ is a complete metric space endowed by metric D such that for every $g, h \in C^{(n-1)\mathbb{F}}([1,a])$

$$D(g,h) = \sum_{i=0}^{n-1} \sup_{t\in[1,a]} d(g^{(i)}(t), h^{(i)}(t)). \tag{10}$$

We say fuzzy-valued function f is ${}^c[(i)\text{-}\gamma]$-differentiable if it is differentiable as in definition case (i) and ${}^c[(ii)\text{-}\gamma]$-differentiable if it is differentiable as in definition case (ii) in the rest of the article.

Definition 8 ([38]). *Let $f \in C^{(n)\mathbb{F}} \cap L^{\mathbb{F}}[1,2], x_0 \in (1,2)$, and*

$$\varphi(x) = \left(\frac{1}{\Gamma(\beta-n)}\right) \int_0^x \left(f(t)\frac{dt}{(x-t)^{\beta-n+1}}\right),$$

where $n = \gamma + 2$ such that $1 \leqslant r \leqslant 2$; then

(i) *if f is ${}^c[(i)\text{-}\gamma]$-differentiable fuzzy-valued function, then*

$$(D_0^\gamma f)(x_0;r) = [(D_0^\gamma \underline{f})(x_0;r), (D_0^\gamma \overline{f})(x_0;r)], \tag{11}$$

or

(ii) *if f is ${}^c[(i)\text{-}\gamma]$-differentiable fuzzy-valued function, then*

$$(D_0^\gamma f)(x_0;r) = [(D_0^\gamma \overline{f})(x_0;r), (D_0^\gamma \underline{f})(x_0;r)], \tag{12}$$

where

$$\begin{array}{l} (D_0^\gamma \underline{f})(x_0;r) = \left[\frac{1}{\Gamma(n-\gamma)} \int_0^t (x-t)^{n-\gamma-1} \underline{f}(t;r)dt\right]_{x=x_0} \\ (D_0^\gamma \overline{f})(x_0;r) = \left[\frac{1}{\Gamma(n-\gamma)} \int_0^t (x-t)^{n-\gamma-1} \overline{f}(t;r)dt\right]_{x=x_0} \end{array}. \tag{13}$$

The fuzzy Laplace transforms L of Caputo-derivative for fuzzy-valued functions is proved by the following theorem.

Theorem 3. *Let $f \in C^{(n)\mathbb{F}}[1,\infty) \cap L^{\mathbb{F}}[1,\infty)$; has the below:*

(i) *if f is ${}^c[(i)\text{-}\gamma]$-differentiable fuzzy-valued function,*

$$L\left[(D_0^\gamma f)(x_0)\right] = p^\gamma L[f(t)] \ominus \left(\sum_{k=0}^{n-1} p^{\gamma-k-1} D^k\right)(1), \tag{14}$$

or

(ii) *if f is ${}^{c}[(i)\text{-}\gamma]$-differentiable fuzzy-valued function,*

$$L\Big[(D_0^{\gamma}f)(x_0)\Big] = -\Big(\sum_{k=0}^{n-1} p^{\gamma-k-1}D^k\Big)(1) \ominus \Big(-p^{\gamma}L[f(t)]\Big) \tag{15}$$

3. Fuzzy Fractional Integral Equation

Using well-known fuzzy Laplace transform, we investigate the relationship between Equation (1) and fuzzy integral form in this section.

In fact, by applying the Laplace transform to both sides of the equation, get a better result.

$$D^{\alpha}x(t) = f\Big(t, x(t), D^{\beta}x(t)\Big) \triangleq g(t,x), \tag{16}$$

we obtain

$$L[D^{\alpha}x(t)] = L\Big[f\Big(t, x(t), D^{\beta}x(t)\Big)\Big]. \tag{17}$$

We get two situations depending on the nature of Caputo-differentiability.

Case 1.

If $D^{\alpha}x$ is fuzzy-valued function that is ${}^{c}[(i)\text{-}\alpha]$-differentiable,

$$Lr(t,x) = -\Big(\sum_{k=0}^{n-1} p^{\beta-k-1}D^k\Big)(1) \ominus p^{\alpha}L[x(t)], \tag{18}$$

and the above equation becomes dependent on the lower and higher functions of $D^{\alpha}x$,

$$\begin{cases} L[\underline{r}(t,x,r)] = p^{\alpha}L[\underline{x}(t;r)] - \sum_{k=0}^{n-1} p^{\gamma-k-1}D^k\underline{x}(1;r), \\ L[\overline{r}(t,x,r)] = p^{\alpha}L[\overline{x}(t;r)] - \sum_{k=0}^{n-1} p^{\gamma-k-1}D^k\overline{x}(1;r), \end{cases} \tag{19}$$

where

$$\begin{cases} L[r(t,x,r)] = \min\{r(t,u)|u \in [\underline{x}(t;r), \overline{x}(t;r)]\}, 1 \leqslant r \leqslant 2, \\ L[\overline{r}(t,x,r)] = \max\{r(t,u)|u \in [\underline{x}(t;r), \overline{x}(t;r)]\}, 1 \leqslant r \leqslant 2, \end{cases} \tag{20}$$

For the purpose of simplicity, we will assume that in order to solve system (19),

$$\begin{cases} L[\underline{x}(t;r)] = H_1(p;r), \\ L[\overline{x}(t;r)] = K_1(p;r). \end{cases} \tag{21}$$

$H_1(p:r)$ and $K_1(p;r)$ are solutions of the previous system (19); it produces

$$\begin{cases} \underline{x}(t;r) = L^{-1}[H_1(p;r)], \\ \overline{x}(t;r) = L^{-1}[K_1(p;r)]. \end{cases} \tag{22}$$

Case 2.

If $D^{\alpha}x$ is fuzzy-valued function that is ${}^{c}[(ii)\text{-}\alpha]$-differentiable,

$$Lr(t,x) = p^{\alpha}L[x(t)] \ominus \Big(\sum_{k=0}^{n-1} p^{\beta-k-1}D^k\Big)(1), \tag{23}$$

and the above equation becomes dependent on the lower and higher functions of $D^{\alpha}x$,

$$\begin{cases} L[\underline{r}(t,x,r)] = p^{\alpha}L[\underline{x}(t;r)] - \sum_{k=0}^{n-1} p^{\beta-k-1}D^{k}\underline{x}(1;r), \\ L[\overline{r}(t,x,r)] = p^{\alpha}L[\overline{x}(t;r)] - \sum_{k=0}^{n-1} p^{\beta-k-1}D^{k}\overline{x}(1;r), \end{cases} \tag{24}$$

where

$$\begin{cases} L[\underline{r}(t,x,r)] = \min\{r(t,u)|u \in [\underline{x}(t;r),\overline{x}(t;r)]\}, 1 \leqslant r \leqslant 2, \\ L[\overline{r}(t,x,r)] = \max\{r(t,u)|u \in [\underline{x}(t;r),\overline{x}(t;r)]\}, 1 \leqslant r \leqslant 2. \end{cases} \tag{25}$$

For the purpose of simplicity, we will assume that in order to solve system (24),

$$\begin{cases} L[\underline{x}(t;r)] = H_2(\alpha;r), \\ L[\overline{x}(t;r)] = K_2(\alpha;r), \end{cases} \tag{26}$$

where $H_2(p;r)$ and $K_2(p;r)$ are solutions of the previous system (24). After that, we get

$$\begin{cases} \underline{x}(t;r) = L^{-1}[H_2(\alpha;r)], \\ \overline{x}(t;r) = L^{-1}[K_2(\alpha;r)]. \end{cases} \tag{27}$$

We derive the following for both instances, taking into account the beginning value and initial conditions of Equation (1), using linearity of inverse Laplace transform on systems (21) and (27).

If and only if x is solution for following integral equation, x is a solution for Equation (1):

$$x(t) = C_q(t)x_0 \oplus K_q(t)x_1 \oplus \frac{1}{\Gamma\alpha}\int_0^t (t-s)^{k-1}f(s,x(s),D^{\beta}x(s))ds \tag{28}$$

in respect to ^{c}[(i)-α]-differentiability, and

$$\hat{x}(t) = C_q(t)x_0(-1) \ominus K_q(t)x_1 \ominus (-1)\frac{1}{\Gamma\alpha}\int_0^t (t-s)^{k-1}f(s,x(s),D^{\beta}x(s))ds \tag{29}$$

in respect to ^{c}[(ii)-α]-differentiability.

4. Main Results

Now, stated Kransnoselskii-Krein type conditions for fuzzy fractional differential Equation (1).

Theorem 4. *Suppose $f \in C(\mathbb{E}_0, \mathbb{E})$ satisfy Kransnoselskii-Krein type requirements as follows:*

(H_1) $d((f,x,y), f(t,\overline{x},\overline{y})) \leqslant \min\{\Gamma(\alpha),2\}(\frac{(k+\gamma(\alpha-[\alpha]))}{2t^{1-\gamma(\alpha-[\alpha])}})[d(x,\overline{x}) + d(y,\overline{y})], t \neq 1$ *and* $1 < \alpha < 2$,

(H_2) $d(f(t,x,y), f(t,\overline{x},\overline{y})) \leqslant \zeta d(f(t,x,y), f(t,\overline{x},\overline{y}) \leqslant \zeta d(x,\overline{x})^{\gamma} + t^{\gamma(\alpha-[\alpha])}d(y,\overline{y})^{\gamma}$,

where ζ and k are positive constants and

$$k(2-\gamma) < 2 + \gamma(\alpha - [\alpha]);$$

then in the sense of ^{c}[(i)-γ]-differentiability, solution x is a unique and in sense of ^{c}[(i)-γ]-differentiability, solution x is a unique on $[1,\kappa]$, where

$$\kappa = \min\left\{2, \left(\frac{b\Gamma(2+\alpha)}{G}\right)^{\frac{1}{\alpha}}, \frac{d}{G}\right\},$$

and G is bound for f on $\mathbb{E}_0$ *that is,*

$$d(f,\tilde{0}) \leqslant G.$$

Proof. To begin, let us assume that x and y are any two solutions of (1) in ^{c}[(i)-γ]-differentiability and assume

$$\varphi(t) = d(x(t), y(t))$$

and

$$\sigma(t) = d(D^\beta x(t), D^\beta y(t)).$$

Note that

$$\varphi(1) = \sigma(1) = 1.$$

We define

$$R(t) = \int_0^t [\varphi^\gamma(s) + s^{\gamma(\alpha-[\alpha])}\sigma^\gamma(s)]ds;$$

clearly R(1) = 1.

Using Equation (28) and condition (H_2),

$$\begin{aligned} \varphi(t) &\leqslant \zeta \int_0^t (t-s)^{q-1}[\varphi^\gamma(s) + s^{\gamma(\alpha-[\alpha])}\sigma^\gamma(s)]ds \\ &\leqslant \zeta t^{q-1} R(t) \qquad (30) \\ \sigma(t) &\leqslant \int_0^t \zeta\varphi\varphi^\gamma(s) + t^{\gamma(\alpha-[\alpha])}\sigma(s)^\gamma ds \\ &\leqslant \zeta R(t). \qquad (31) \end{aligned}$$

We use the same symbol C to represent all of the other constants that appear in the rest of the proof for the purpose of simplicity.

We have

$$\begin{aligned} R'(t) &= \varphi(t) + t^{\gamma(\alpha-[\alpha])}\sigma^\gamma(s) \\ &\leqslant C[t^{\gamma\beta} + t^\gamma(\alpha - [\alpha])]R^\gamma(t). \end{aligned} \qquad (32)$$

Since $R(t) > 1$ for $t > 0$, multiplying both sides of (32) by $(1-\gamma)R^{-\gamma}(t)$ and then integrate

$$R(t) < C\left(t^{\left((\frac{\gamma}{(1-\gamma)})\alpha+1\right)} + t^{\left(\frac{\gamma}{(1-\gamma)}\right)\alpha+\left(\frac{(1-\gamma[\gamma])}{(1-\gamma)}\right)}\right) \qquad (33)$$

Making use of the fact that

$$(a+b)t^{(1-\gamma)} \leqslant \frac{1}{2^{1-\gamma}-1}(a^{(1-\gamma)} + b^{(1-\gamma)}) \qquad (34)$$

for every $a, b \in (1,2)$, Equation (33) becomes

$$R(t) < C\left(t^{\left(\frac{\gamma\alpha}{1-\gamma}+1\right)} + t^{\left(\frac{\gamma\alpha}{1-\gamma}+\frac{1-\gamma[\gamma]}{1-\gamma}\right)}\right). \qquad (35)$$

For $t \in [0,\mu]$, this yields the following estimates for φ and σ:

$$\begin{aligned}\varphi(t) &\leqslant C\left(t^{\left(\frac{\alpha}{1-\gamma}\right)} + t^{\left(\frac{\alpha}{1-\gamma}+\frac{\gamma(1-[\alpha])}{1-\gamma}\right)}\right),\\ \sigma(t) &\leqslant C\left(t^{\left(\frac{\gamma}{1-\gamma}\alpha+1\right)} + t^{\left(\frac{\gamma}{1-\gamma}\alpha+\frac{1-\gamma[\alpha]}{1-\gamma}\right)}\right).\end{aligned} \tag{36}$$

Define function $\eta(t) = t^{-k}\max\varphi(t),\sigma(t)$ for $t \in (1,2]$. When either $t^{-k}\varphi(t)$ or $t^{-k}\sigma(t)$ is maximum,

$$1 \leqslant \eta(t) \leqslant C\left(t^{\left(\frac{\alpha}{1-\gamma}-k\right)} + t^{\left(\frac{\alpha}{1-\gamma}+\frac{\gamma(1-[\alpha])}{(1-\gamma)-k}\right)}\right), \tag{37}$$

or

$$1 \leqslant \eta(t) \leqslant C\left(t^{\left(\frac{\gamma}{1-\gamma}\alpha+1-k\right)} + t^{\left(\frac{\alpha\gamma}{1-\gamma}+\frac{(1-\gamma[\alpha])}{(1-\gamma)-k}\right)}\right). \tag{38}$$

Since

$$k(1-\gamma) < 1+\gamma(\alpha-[\alpha])$$

(by assumption), we have

$$\begin{aligned} &< 1+\gamma(\alpha-[\alpha])\\ &< \alpha\\ (k-1)(1-\gamma) &< \gamma\alpha\\ k(1-\gamma) &< \alpha+\gamma-\gamma[\alpha]\\ &< \gamma\alpha+1-\gamma[\alpha].\end{aligned}$$

In the above inequalities, all of the t exponents are positive. As a result, $\lim\limits_{t\to 0^+}\eta(t) = 0$. As a result, the function η is continuous in $[0,\eta]$ if $\eta(0) = 0$ is defined. In fact, because η is continuous function, if η does not vanish at some points t, i.e., $\eta(t) > 1$ on $[0,\eta]$, then there exists maximum $g > 1$ attained when t is equal to some t_1. $1 \leqslant t_1 \leqslant \eta \leqslant 2$ such that $\eta(s) < g = \eta(t_1)$, for $s \in [0,t_1)$. However, we receive either result from condition (H_1).

$$g = \eta(t_1) = t_1^{-k}\varphi(t_1) \leqslant \min(\Gamma(\alpha),2)g t_1^{\alpha-2+\gamma(\alpha-[\alpha])} < g \tag{39}$$

$$g = \eta(t_1) = t_1^{-k}\sigma(t_1) \leqslant \min(\Gamma(\alpha),2)g t_1^{\gamma(\alpha-[\alpha])} < g \tag{40}$$

which is a contradiction. As a result, the solution's uniqueness is established in terms of ^{c}[(i)-α]-differentiability. We emit the second part of proof because it is nearly identical to ^{c}[(i)-α]-differentiability. □

Theorem 5. *(Kooi's type uniqueness theorem). Suppose f satisfies below conditions:*

(J_1) $d((f,x,y),f(t,\overline{x},\overline{y}) \leqslant \min\{\Gamma(\alpha),2\}\left(\frac{(k+\gamma(\alpha-[\alpha]))}{2t^{1-\gamma(\alpha-[\alpha])}}\right)[d(x,\overline{x}+d(y,\overline{y}],t \neq 1$ *and* $1<\alpha<2$,

(J_2) $t^{\beta}d(f(t,x,y),f(t,\overline{x},\overline{y})) \leqslant c[d(x,\overline{x})^{\gamma} + t^{\gamma(\alpha-[\alpha])}d(y,\overline{y})^{\gamma}$,

where c and k are positive constants and

$$k(2-\gamma) < 2+\gamma(\alpha-[\alpha])-\mu,$$

for $(t,x,y),(t,\overline{x},\overline{y}) \in R_0$; then in the sense of ^{c}[(i)-γ]-differentiability, solution x is a unique and in sense of ^{c}[(i)-γ]-differentiability, solution $\hat{x}$ is a unique.

Lemma 4. *For a real number $a > 1$, consider φ and σ, two non-negative continuous functions on interval $[0, \mu]$. Let*

$$\eta(t) = \int_0^t (\varphi(s) + s^{\alpha-[\alpha]+2})ds.$$

Consider the following:

(i) $\varphi(t) \leqslant t^{\alpha-[\alpha]}\eta(t)$;
(ii) $\sigma(t) \leqslant \eta(t)$;
(iii) $\varphi(t) = o(t^{\alpha-[\alpha]}e^{-\frac{1}{t}})$;
(iv) $\sigma(t) = o(e^{-\frac{1}{t}})$.

Proof. Let

$$\eta(t) = \int_0^t (\varphi(s) + s^{\alpha-[\alpha]+2})ds.$$

After differentiating η and using (ii), we get $t > 0$,

$$\eta'(t) \leqslant (\frac{1}{t^2})\eta(t),$$

so that $e^{\frac{1}{t}}\eta(t)$ is decreasing. Now from (iii) and (iv), if $\epsilon > 0$ then, for small t, we get

$$e^{\frac{1}{t}}\eta(t) \leqslant e^{\frac{1}{t}} \int_0^t \frac{1}{2s^2} 2e^{-\frac{1}{s}} ds = \epsilon. \tag{41}$$

Hence,

$$\lim_{t \to 1} e^{\frac{1}{t}}\eta(t) = 1.$$

This means that $\eta(t) \leqslant 1$. Finally, because of (i), η is nonnegative, and hence $\eta = 1$. □

Theorem 6. *(Roger's type uniqueness theorem). Verify following conditions with function f:*
(K_1) $d((f, x, y), \tilde{0}) \leqslant \min\{\Gamma(\alpha), 2\} o(\frac{e^{\frac{-1}{t}}}{t^2})$, *uniformly for positive and bounded x and y on $\mathbb{E}$,*
(K_2) $d(f(t, x, y), f(t, \overline{x}, \overline{y})) \leqslant \min\{\Gamma(\alpha)(\frac{1}{2t^{\alpha-[\alpha]+2}})[d(x, \overline{x}) + t^{(\alpha-[\alpha])}d(y, \overline{y})]$.
The problem then has only one solution.
This theorem's proof is based mainly on Lemma 4.

Proof. Suppose x and y are any two solutions of (1) in ${}^c[(i)\text{-}\gamma]$-differentiability, assume

$$\varphi(t) = d(x(t), y(t))$$

and

$$\sigma(t) = d(D^\beta x(t), D^\beta y(t));$$

we get for $t \in [0, \mu] \subset [1, 2]$.

$$\begin{aligned}
\varphi(t) &\leqslant \frac{1}{k}\int_0^t (t-s)^{k-1} d[f(s, x(s), D^\beta x(s)), f(s, y(s), D^\beta y(s))]ds \\
&\leqslant \frac{(t-s)^{k-1}}{2s^{\alpha-[\alpha]+2}}[\varphi(s) + s^{\alpha-[\alpha]}\sigma(s)]ds \\
&\leqslant t^{\alpha-1}\int_0^t \frac{1}{2s^{\alpha-[\alpha]+2}}[\varphi(s) + s^\beta\sigma(s)]ds
\end{aligned}$$

$$
\begin{aligned}
&\leqslant t^{\alpha-[\alpha]}\int_0^t \frac{1}{2s^{\alpha-[\alpha]+2}}[\varphi(s)+s^{\beta}\sigma(s)]ds \\
&\leqslant t^{\alpha-[\alpha]}\eta(t) \\
\sigma(t) &\leqslant \int_0^t d[f(s,x(s),D^{\beta}x(s)),f(s,y(s),D^{\beta}y(s))]ds \\
&\leqslant \int_0^t \frac{\min\{\Gamma(\alpha),2\}}{2s^{\alpha-[\alpha]+2}}[\varphi(s)+s^{\alpha-[\alpha]}\sigma(s)]ds \\
&\leqslant \int_0^t \frac{1}{2s^{\alpha-[\alpha]+2}}[\varphi(s)+s^{\alpha-[\alpha]}\sigma(s)]ds \\
&\leqslant \varphi(t),
\end{aligned}
\tag{42}
$$

where φ has the same definition as in Lemma 4.

In addition, if $\epsilon > 1$, we get condition (K_1) for small t,

$$
\begin{aligned}
\varphi(t) &\leqslant \frac{t^{k-1}}{\Gamma(k)}\int_0^t (t-s)^{k-1}d[f(s,x(s),D^{\beta}x(s)),f(s,y(s),D^{\beta}y(s))]ds \\
&\leqslant (t-s)^{k-1}2(\epsilon)\int_0^t \frac{e^{-\frac{1}{s}}}{s^2}ds \\
&\leqslant t^{k-1}e^{-\frac{1}{s}}2\epsilon \\
&\leqslant t^{\alpha-[\alpha]}e^{-\frac{1}{s}}2\epsilon
\end{aligned}
\tag{43}
$$

$$
\begin{aligned}
\sigma(t) &\leqslant \int_0^t (t-s)^{k-1}d[f(s,x(s),D^{\beta}x(s)),f(s,y(s),D^{\beta}y(s))]ds \\
&\leqslant 2\epsilon\min\{2,\Gamma(k)\}\int_0^t \frac{e^{-\frac{1}{s}}}{s^2}ds \\
&\leqslant 2\epsilon e^{-\frac{1}{s}}.
\end{aligned}
$$

We get $d(x(t),y(t)) = 1$ for every $t \in [1,2]$ by applying Lemma 4, proving uniqueness of solution of fuzzy fractional evolution Equation (1) in ^{c}[(i)-γ]-differentiability. We skip the second section of the evidence because it is nearly identical to the first. □

Theorem 7. *Let $f \in C(\mathbb{E}_0,\mathbb{E})$ satisfy above Theorem 4. Then there's series of approximations.*

$$
x_n(t) = C_q(t)x_0 + K_q(t)x_1(t) + \frac{1}{\Gamma\alpha}\int_0^t (t-s)^{k-1}f(s,x(s),D^{\beta}x(s))ds \tag{44}
$$

in sense of ^{c}[(i)-γ]-differentiability or

$$
\hat{x}_n(t) = C_q(t)x_0 \ominus (-1)K_q(t)x_1 \ominus (-1)\frac{1}{\Gamma\alpha}\int_0^t (t-s)^{k-1}f(s,x(s),D^{\beta}x(s))ds \tag{45}
$$

converge to unique solution of fuzzy fractional evolution equation in sense of ^{c}[(ii)-γ]-differentiability (1).

Proof. Using the Ascoli–Arzela Theorem, we show the Theorem 7 for sequence x_n in sense of ^{c}[(i)-γ]-differentiability without losing generality. We omit the sequence $\{\hat{x}_n\}$ because its convergence in terms of ^{c}[(ii)-γ]-differentiability is very comparable.

Step 1: The sequences $\{x_j\}_{j\geqslant 0}$ and $\{D^{q-1}x_j\}_{j\geqslant 0}$ are well defined, continuous and uniformly bounded on $[0,\mu]$;

$$
\begin{cases}
d(x_{j+1}(t),x_0) \leqslant \int_0^t d(f(s,x_j(s),D^{\beta}x_j(s)),\tilde{0})ds \\
d(D^{\beta}x_j(t),x_0) \leqslant \int_0^t d(d(s,x_j(s),D^{\beta}x_j(s)),\tilde{0})ds
\end{cases}
. \tag{46}
$$

For $j = 1$ and $t \in [0, \mu]$, we have

$$\begin{cases} d(x_1(t), x_0) \leqslant \frac{Gt^2}{\Gamma(\alpha+1)} \leqslant a \\ \\ d(D^\beta x_1(t), x_0) \leqslant Gt \leqslant g \end{cases}. \tag{47}$$

Furthermore, for each $i \in 0, \ldots, \beta$;

$$\begin{aligned} d(x_1^{(i)}(t), \tilde{0}) &= d(D^i I^\alpha f(t, x_0(t), D^\beta x_0(t), \tilde{0}) \\ &= d(I^{\alpha-i} f(t, x_0(t), D^\beta x_0(t), \tilde{0}) \\ &= \Gamma(\beta) \\ \int_0^t (t-s)^{\alpha-i-1} d(f(t, x_0(s), D^\beta x_0(s)), \tilde{0}) ds &\leqslant \frac{N}{\Gamma(\alpha-i)} \int_0^t (t-s)^{\alpha-i-1} ds \end{aligned}$$

$$\begin{aligned} &\leqslant \frac{Nt^{\alpha-i}}{(\alpha-i)\Gamma(\alpha-i)} \\ &\leqslant \frac{Nt^{\alpha-1}}{\Gamma(\alpha-i+1)}. \end{aligned}$$

The sequences $\{x_{j+1}(t)\}$ and $\{D^\beta x_{j+1}(t)\}$ are properly defined and uniformly bounded on $[0, \mu]$ by induction.
Step 2: We show that in $[0, \mu]$, the functions x and y are continuous, where x and y are defined by

$$\begin{cases} x(t) = \lim_{j \to \infty} \sup \xi_j^0(t), \\ \\ y(t) = \lim_{j \to \infty} \sup \zeta_j(t), \end{cases} \tag{48}$$

as a result

$$\begin{cases} \xi_j^1(t) = d(x_j(t), x_{j-1}(t)), \\ \\ \zeta_j(t) = d(D^\beta x_j(t), D^\beta x_{j-1}(t)). \end{cases} \tag{49}$$

Take note of the following:

$$g(t) = \sum_{i \leqslant n-1} \lim_{j \to \infty} \xi_j^i(t), \tag{50}$$

where

$$\xi_j^i(t) = d(x_j^{(i)}(t), x_{j-1}^{(i)}(t)). \tag{51}$$

For $0 \leqslant t_1 \leqslant t_2$ and for every $i \in \{0, \ldots, n-1\}$, we obtain

$$\begin{aligned} d(\xi_j^i(t_1) - \xi_j^i(t_2)) &= d(x_{j+1}^{(i)}(t_1), x_j^{(i)}(t_1)) - d(x_{j+1}^{(i)}(t_2), x_j^{(i)}(t_2)) \\ &\leqslant d\bigg[\int_0^{t_1}(t_1-s)^{k-1-i}d(f(s,x_j(s),D^\beta x(s)), f(s,x_{j-1}(s)D_{j-1}^\beta x(s)))ds \\ &\quad - \int_0^{t_2}(t_2-s)^{k-1-i}d(f(s,x_j(s),D^\beta x(s)), f(s,x_{j-1}(s)D_{j-1}^\beta x(s)))\bigg]ds \\ &\leqslant \frac{2N}{\Gamma(k-i)}d\bigg[\int_0^{t-1}(t_1-s)^{k-1-i} - (t_2-s)^{k-1-i}ds - \int_{t_1}^{t_2}(t_2-s)^{k-1-i}ds\bigg] \\ &\leqslant \frac{2N}{(k-i)\Gamma(k-i)}\left[t_1^{k-i} - t_2^{k-i} + 2(t_2-t_1)^{k-i}\right] \\ &\leqslant \frac{4N}{\Gamma(k-i+1)}(t_2-t_1)^{k-i}. \end{aligned} \tag{52}$$

In the above inequalities, right-hand side is at the most $\frac{4N}{\Gamma(k-i+1)}(t_2-t_1)^{k-i}+\epsilon$ for large n if $\epsilon > 0$ provided that

$$d(t_2 - t_1) \leqslant \mu \leqslant \frac{4N}{\Gamma(k-i+1)}(t_2-t_1)^{k-i}, \tag{53}$$

for each $i \leqslant n-1$. ϵ is arbitrary and t_1, t_2 can be interchangeable, we get

$$\begin{aligned} d(n(t_1) - n(t_2)) &\leqslant \sum_{i \leqslant n-1}\left\{\frac{4N}{\Gamma(k-i+1)}(t_2-t_1)^{k-i}\right\} \\ &\leqslant \frac{4N(n-1)}{\Gamma(k+1)}(t_2-t_1)^k. \end{aligned} \tag{54}$$

The same goes for $y(t)$, and we obtain

$$d(y(t_1) - y(t_2)) \leqslant 2Nd(t_2 - t_1). \tag{55}$$

These results indicate that x and y are continuous on $[0, \mu]$.
Step 3: We check that $\{D^\beta j_{n+1}(t)\}$ family is equi-continuous in $C^{\mathbb{E}}([0,\mu],\mathbb{E})$ and that the $\{x_{j+1}(t)\}$ family is equi-continuous in $C^{(n-1)\mathbb{F}}([0,\mu],\mathbb{E})$. Using condition (H_2) and notion of successive approximations (45) we can show that we get

$$\begin{cases} \xi_{j+1}^0(t) \leqslant c\int_0^t (t-s)^{k-1}[\xi_j^0(s)^\gamma + s^{\gamma(\alpha-[\alpha])}\zeta_j(s)^\gamma]ds, \\ \xi_{j+1}^i(t) \leqslant c\int_0^t (t-s)^{k-i-1}[\xi_j^0(s)^\gamma + s^{\gamma(\alpha-[\alpha])}\zeta_j(s)^\gamma]ds. \end{cases} \tag{56}$$

As a consequence, we obtain the following estimation:

$$D(x_{j+1}, x_j) \leqslant \sum_{i \leqslant n-1} c\int_1^2 (1-s)^{k-i-1}[d(x_j(s) - x_{j-1}(s))^\gamma + s^{\gamma(\alpha-[\alpha])}d(D^\beta x_j(s) - D^\beta x_{j-1}(s))^\gamma]ds. \tag{57}$$

There exists a subsequence of integers $\{j_k\}$, according to the Arzela-Ascoli Theorem,

$$\begin{cases} d(x_{j_p}(t), x_{j-1_{p(t)}}) \to y(t) \ as\ j_l \to \infty, \\ d(D^\beta x_{j_p}(t), D^\beta x_{j_{p-1}}(t)) \to y(t) \ as\ j_l \to \infty. \end{cases} \tag{58}$$

Let us note

$$\begin{cases} u^*(t) = \lim_{p\to\infty} \sup d(x_{j_p}(t), x_{j_{p-1}}(t)), \\ v^*(t) = \lim_{p\to\infty} \sup d(D^\beta x_{j_p}(t), D^\beta x_{j_{p-1}}(t)). \end{cases} \tag{59}$$

Further, if $\{d(x_j, x_{j-1})\} \to 0$ and $\{d(D^\beta x_j, D^\beta x_{j-1})\} \to 0$ as $j \to \infty$, limit of any consecutive x_n approximation in solution x of (1), which was demonstrated to be unique in Theorem 4. As a result, a subsequence selection is unnecessary, because entire sequence $\{x_j\}$ converges evenly to $x(t)$. To do so, simply establish that $x = 1$ and $y = 1$, which will result in $u * (t)$ and $v * (t)$ being same.

$$R(t) = \int_0^t [y(s)^\gamma + s^\gamma(\alpha - [\alpha])v(s)^\gamma]ds \tag{60}$$

and by defining

$$\eta * (t) = t^{-p} \max\{x(t), y(t)\}.$$

We demonstrate this as

$$\lim_{t\to 0^+} \eta * (t) = 0.$$

We'll now show that $\eta * (t) = 0$. Assume that $\eta * (t) > 0$ at any point in the range $[0, \mu]$; then t_1 exists that is

$$1 \leqslant \bar{g} = \eta(t_1) = \max_{0\leqslant t\leqslant \mu} \eta * (t).$$

Hence, from condition (H_1), we obtain

$$\bar{g} = \eta(t_1) = t_1^{-p} x(t_1) \leqslant \min(\Gamma(\alpha), 2)\bar{g} t_1^{\beta-\gamma(\alpha-[\alpha])} < \bar{g}, \tag{61}$$

or

$$\bar{g} = \eta(t_1) = t_1^{-p} y(t_1) \leqslant \min(\Gamma(\alpha), 2)\bar{g} t_1^{\gamma(\alpha-[\alpha])} < \bar{g}. \tag{62}$$

We end up with a contradiction in both circumstances. As a result, $\eta * (t) - 0$. As a result, iteration (45), on $[0, \mu]$, converges evenly to the unique solution x of (1). □

5. Examples

Example 1. *Consider the initial value problem:*

$$^cD^{\frac{3}{5}}x = f(t,x) = \begin{cases} Ft^{\frac{3\gamma}{5i-\gamma}}\ 1 \leqslant t \leqslant 2, -\infty \leqslant x \leqslant 1, \\ Ft^{\frac{3\gamma}{5i-\gamma}} \oplus F^{\frac{Fx^2}{t^{\frac{3}{5}}}}\ 1 \leqslant t \leqslant 2, 1 \leqslant xt^{\frac{3}{5}}(1-\gamma)^{-1}, \\ 0,\ 1 \leqslant t \leqslant 2, t^{\frac{3}{5}}(1-\gamma)^{-1} \leqslant x \leqslant \infty, \end{cases} \tag{63}$$

$x(1) = 1$,
where

$$1 \leqslant \alpha \leqslant 2,$$

then

$$F = \Gamma\left(\frac{3}{5}\right)\left(\frac{3}{5}k - \frac{1}{2}\right),\ q = \frac{3}{5},\ c = \frac{F5^{1-\gamma}}{\Gamma(\frac{3}{5})},$$

$k > 2$ *and* $k(1-\gamma) < 2$.

In the strip, function $f(t,x)$ is continuous. $1 \leqslant t \leqslant 2, |x| < \infty$, can be proved in each of the cases.

(i) $1 \leqslant x, \bar{x} \leqslant t^{\frac{3}{5}}(1-\gamma)^{-1}$,

(ii) $t^{\frac{3}{5}}(1-\gamma)^{-1} < x < \infty, -\infty < \bar{x} < 1$,

(iii) $t^{\frac{3}{5}}(1-\gamma)^{-1} < x < \infty, 0 \leqslant \bar{x} \leqslant t^{\frac{3}{5}}(1-\gamma)^{-1}$,

(iv) $0 \leqslant x \leqslant t^{\frac{3}{5}}(1-\gamma)^{-1}, -\infty < \bar{x} < 1$,

that following estimates hold:

$$\begin{aligned} |f(t,x) - f(t,\bar{x}| &\leqslant \frac{F}{t^{\frac{3}{5}}}|x-\bar{x}|, \\ &\leqslant F2^{1-\gamma}|x-\bar{x}|^{\gamma}. \end{aligned}$$

Therefore, initial value problem has unique solution for order $(1,2]$.

Example 2. *If we consider initial value problem with Caputo derivative*

$$\begin{aligned} &{}^{c}D^{\alpha}(x) = f(t, x, {}^{c}D^{\beta}x(t)), \\ &I^{\alpha}x(0) = x_0, \\ &x'(0) = x_1, \\ &{}^{c}D^{\beta}x(0) = 0, \end{aligned} \tag{64}$$

where $1 < \alpha < 2$, then solution of given equation is equal to

$$x(t) = C_q(t)x_0 + K_q(t)x_1 + \frac{1}{\Gamma\alpha}\int_0^t (t-s)^{\alpha-1} f(s, x(s))ds. \tag{65}$$

Let the function f in above equation satisfy following Krasnoselskii-Krein type conditions:
(H_1) $d(f(t,x), f(t,y)) \leqslant \Gamma(q)\frac{\alpha(k-1)+1}{t^{\alpha}}d(x,y), t \neq 0$, *where* $k > 1$.
(H_2) $d(f(t,x), f(t,y)) \leqslant \zeta d(x,y)^{\beta}$, *where ζ is constant,* $0 < \beta < 1$, *and* $k(1-\beta) < 1$, *for* $(t,x),(t,y) \in \mathbb{R}$.

Then approximations are given by

$$x_{n+1}(t) = C_q(t)x_0 + K_q(t)x_1 + \frac{1}{\Gamma\alpha}\int_0^t (t-s)^{\alpha-1} f(s, x_n(s))ds, \tag{66}$$

converges uniformly to a unique solution $x(t)$ of given equations on $\{0, \mu\}$ where

$$\mu = \min\left\{c, \left(\frac{e\Gamma(1+\alpha)}{J}\right)^{\frac{1}{\alpha}}\right\},$$

J is bound for f on $\mathbb{R}$.

6. Conclusions

The existence and uniqueness of the class of high-order fuzzy Krasnoselskii-Krein conditions are investigated in this paper. This is a fruitful field with a wide range of research projects that can lead to various applications and theories. In future projects, we hope to learn more about fuzzy fractional evolution problems. Using the Caputo derivative, we can discover uniqueness and existence with uncertainty. Future work could include expanding on the concept proposed in this mission, including observability, and generalizing other activities. This is an interesting area with a lot of study going on that could lead to a lot of different applications and theories. This is a path to which we want to invest considerable resources.

Author Contributions: R.S., A.U.K.N., M.B.J. and N.H.A. contributed equally to the writing of this paper. All authors have read and agreed to the published version of the manuscript.

Funding: This work is not funded by government or any private agency.

Data Availability Statement: Data is original and references are given where required.

Acknowledgments: The authors would like to acknowledge The University of Lahore, for the provision of the research plate form to complete this research work.

Conflicts of Interest: The authors declare that they have no known competing financial interest or personal relationships that could have appeared to influence the work reported in this paper.

References

1. Ahmad, B.; Nieto, J.J. Existence results for a coupled system of nonlinear fractional differential equations with three-point boundary conditions. *Comput. Math. Appl.* **2009**, *58*, 1838–1843. [CrossRef]
2. Ahmad, B.; Ntouyas, S.K.; Agarwal, R.P.; Alsaedi, A. On fractional differential equations and inclusions with nonlocal and average-valued (integral) boundary conditions. *Adv. Differ. Equ.* **2016**, *2016*, 80. [CrossRef]
3. Kilbas, A.A.; Srivastava, H.M.; Trujillo, J.J. *Theory and Applications of Fractional Differential Equations*; Elsevier: Amsterdam, The Netherlands, 2006; Volume 204.
4. Lakshmikantham, V.; Vatsala, A.S. Basic theory of fractional differential equations. *Nonlinear Anal. Theory Methods Appl.* **2008**, *69*, 2677–2682. [CrossRef]
5. Podlubny, I. *Fractional Differential Equations: An Introduction to Fractional Derivatives, Fractional Differential Equations, to Methods of Their Solution and Some of Their Applications*; Elsevier: Amsterdam, The Netherlands, 1998.
6. Mansouri, S.S.; Gachpazan, M.; Fard, O.S. Existence, uniqueness and stability of fuzzy fractional differential equations with local Lipschitz and linear growth conditions. *Adv. Differ. Equ.* **2017**, *2017*, 240. [CrossRef]
7. Sakulrang, S.; Moore, E.J.; Sungnul, S.; de Gaetano, A. A fractional differential equation model for continuous glucose monitoring data. *Adv. Differ. Equ.* **2017**, *2017*, 150. [CrossRef]
8. Agarwal, R.P.; Lakshmikantham, V.; Nieto, J.J. On the concept of solution for fractional differential equations with uncertainty. *Nonlinear Anal. Theory Methods Appl.* **2010**, *72*, 2859–2862. [CrossRef]
9. Bede, B.; Gal, S.G. Generalizations of the differentiability of fuzzy-number-valued functions with applications to fuzzy differential equations. *Fuzzy Sets Syst.* **2005**, *151*, 581–599. [CrossRef]
10. Allahviranloo, T.; Salahshour, S.; Abbasbandy, S. Explicit solutions of fractional differential equations with uncertainty. *Soft Comput.* **2012**, *16*, 297–302. [CrossRef]
11. Salahshour, S.; Allahviranloo, T.; Abbasbandy, S. Solving fuzzy fractional differential equations by fuzzy Laplace transforms. *Commun. Nonlinear Sci. Numer. Simul.* **2012**, *17*, 1372–1381. [CrossRef]
12. Chidouh, A.; Guezane-Lakoud, A.; Bebbouchi, R. Positive solutions for an oscillator fractional initial value problem. *J. Appl. Math. Comput.* **2017**, *54*, 57–68. [CrossRef]
13. Chidouh, A.; Guezane-Lakoud, A.; Bebbouchi, R. Positive solutions of the fractional relaxation equation using lower and upper solutions. *Vietnam. J. Math.* **2016**, *44*, 739–748. [CrossRef]
14. Lakshmikantham, V.; Leela, S. A Krasnoselskii–Krein-type uniqueness result for fractional differential equations. *Nonlinear Anal. Theory Methods Appl.* **2009**, *71*, 3421–3424. [CrossRef]
15. Lakshmikantham, V.; Leela, S. Nagumo-type uniqueness result for fractional differential equations. *Nonlinear Anal.* **2009**, *71*, 2886–2889. [CrossRef]
16. Yoruk, F.; Bhaskar, T.G.; Agarwal, R.P. New uniqueness results for fractional differential equations. *Appl. Anal.* **2013**, *92*, 259–269. [CrossRef]
17. Ahmadian, A.; Salahshour, S.; Baleanu, D.; Amirkhani, H.; Yunus, R. Tau method for the numerical solution of a fuzzy fractional kinetic model and its application to the oil palm frond as a promising source of xylose. *J. Comput. Phys.* **2015**, *294*, 562–584. [CrossRef]
18. Chalco-Cano, Y.; Rufián-Lizana, A.; Román-Flores, H.; Jiménez-Gamero, M.D. Calculus for interval-valued functions using generalized Hukuhara derivative and applications. *Fuzzy Sets Syst.* **2013**, *219*, 49–67. [CrossRef]
19. Malinowski, M.T. Existence theorems for solutions to random fuzzy differential equations. *Nonlinear Anal. Theory Methods Appl.* **2010**, *73*, 1515–1532. [CrossRef]
20. Alikhani, R.; Bahrami, F.; Jabbari, A. Existence of global solutions to nonlinear fuzzy Volterra integro-differential equations. *Nonlinear Anal. Theory Methods Appl.* **2012**, *75*, 1810–1821. [CrossRef]
21. Li, Y.; Li, J. Stability analysis of fractional order systems based on T–S fuzzy model with the fractional order α: $0 < \alpha < 1$. *Nonlinear Dyn.* **2014**, *78*, 2909–2919.
22. Liu, X.; Zhang, L.; Agarwal, P.; Wang, G. On some new integral inequalities of Gronwall–Bellman–Bihari type with delay for discontinuous functions and their applications. *Indag. Math.* **2016**, *27*, 1–10. [CrossRef]
23. Malinowski, M.T. Random fuzzy fractional integral equations–theoretical foundations. *Fuzzy Sets Syst.* **2015**, *265*, 39–62. [CrossRef]

24. Tariboon, J.; Ntouyas, S.K.; Agarwal, P. New concepts of fractional quantum calculus and applications to impulsive fractional q-difference equations. *Adv. Differ. Equ.* **2015**, *2015*, 18. [CrossRef]
25. ElJaoui, E.; Melliani, S.; Chadli, L.S. Solving second-order fuzzy differential equations by the fuzzy Laplace transform method. *Adv. Differ. Equ.* **2015**, *2015*, 66. [CrossRef]
26. Hoa, N.V.; Phu, N.D. Fuzzy functional integro-differential equations under generalized H-differentiability. *J. Intell. Fuzzy Syst.* **2014**, *26*, 2073–2085. [CrossRef]
27. Hallaci, A.; Boulares, H.; Ardjouni, A. Existence and uniqueness for delay fractional differential equations with mixed fractional derivatives. *Open J. Math. Anal.* **2020**, *4*, 26–31. [CrossRef]
28. Niazi, A.U.K.; He, J.; Shafqat, R.; Ahmed, B. Existence, uniqueness, and Eq–Ulam-type stability of fuzzy fractional differential equation. *Fractal Fract.* **2021**, *5*, 66. [CrossRef]
29. Iqbal, N.; Niazi, A.U.K.; Shafqat, R.; Zaland, S. Existence and Uniqueness of Mild Solution for Fractional-Order Controlled Fuzzy Evolution Equation. *J. Funct. Spaces* **2021**, *8*, 5795065. [CrossRef]
30. Baleanu, D.; Khan, H.; Jafari, H.; Khan, R.A.; Alipour, M. On existence results for solutions of a coupled system of hybrid boundary value problems with hybrid conditions. *Adv. Differ. Equ.* **2015**, *2015*, 318. [CrossRef]
31. Souahi, A.; Guezane-Lakoud, A.; Hitta, A. On the existence and uniqueness for high order fuzzy fractional differential equations with uncertainty. *Adv. Fuzzy Syst.* **2016**, *2016*, 5246430. [CrossRef]
32. Zimmermann, H.J. *Fuzzy Set Theory—And Its Applications*; Springer Science & Business Media: Berlin/Heidelberg, Germany, 2011. [CrossRef]
33. San, D.; Podlubny, I. *Fractional Differential Equations*; Academic Press: Cambridge, MA, USA, 1999.
34. Mainardi, F.; Paradisi, P.; Gorenflo, R. Probability Distributions Generated by Fractional Diffusion Equations. *arXiv* **2007**, arXiv:0704.0320.
35. Travis, C.C.; Webb, G.F. Cosine families and abstract nonlinear second order differential equations. *Acta Math. Hung.* **1978**, *32*, 75–96.
36. Smart, D.R. *Fixed Point Theorems*; Cup Archive; University Press Cambridge: Cambridge, UK, 1980; Volume 66. [CrossRef]
37. Zeidler, E. *Nonlinear Functional Analysis and Its Applications: III: Variational Methods and Optimization*; Springer Science & Business Media: Berlin/Heidelberg, Germany, 2013
38. Allahviranloo, T.; Abbasbandy, S.; Shahryari, M.R.; Salahshour, S.; Baleanu, D. On Solutions of Linear Fractional Differential Equations with Uncertainty. *Abstr. Appl. Anal.* **2013**, *2013*, 178378. Available online: https://www.hindawi.com/journals/aaa/2013/178378/ (accessed on 27 December 2021).

fractal and fractional

MDPI

Article

Overview of One-Dimensional Continuous Functions with Fractional Integral and Applications in Reinforcement Learning

Wang Jun [1,2], Cao Lei [1,*], Wang Bin [2], Gong Hongtao [2] and Tang Wei [1]

[1] College of Command Information System, Army Engineering University of PLA, Nanjing 210001, China; junwang920811@163.com (W.J.); leonheart_tang@163.com (T.W.)
[2] Troops of 78092, Chengdu 610031, China; desperado_24@163.com (W.B.); xiaotaoust@163.com (G.H.)
* Correspondence: caolei.nj@foxmail.com

Abstract: One-dimensional continuous functions are important fundament for studying other complex functions. Many theories and methods applied to study one-dimensional continuous functions can also be accustomed to investigating the properties of multi-dimensional functions. The properties of one-dimensional continuous functions, such as dimensionality, continuity, and boundedness, have been discussed from multiple perspectives. Therefore, the existing conclusions will be systematically sorted out according to the bounded variation, unbounded variation and hölder continuity. At the same time, unbounded variation points are used to analyze continuous functions and construct unbounded variation functions innovatively. Possible applications of fractal and fractal dimension in reinforcement learning are predicted.

Keywords: continuous functions; unbounded variation; fractal dimension; reinforcement learning

Citation: Jun, W.; Lei, C.; Bin, W.; Hongtao, G.; Wei, T. Overview of One-Dimensional Continuous Functions with Fractional Integral and Applications in Reinforcement Learning. *Fractal Fract.* **2022**, *6*, 69. https://doi.org/10.3390/fractalfract6020069

Academic Editor: António M. Lopes

Received: 10 January 2022
Accepted: 22 January 2022
Published: 27 January 2022

1. Introduction

It is a widely held view that dimensionality is an important indicator to describe functions, but different functions have many disparate internal structures and properties. Traditional topological dimension had not dealt with some characteristics of the intricate functions well. In recent years, there is a growing body of literature that recognises the importance of using fractal dimension instead of topological dimension to describe the functions. The fractal dimension is an extension of the topological dimension. The fractal dimension reflects the effectiveness of the space occupied by the complex sets, and it is a measure of the irregularity of the complex sets. It is cross-combined with the chaos theory of dynamical systems and complements each other. It admits that the part of the world may show similarity with the whole in a certain aspect under certain conditions or processes. The value of the fractal dimension can be not only an integer but also a fraction. So fractal dimension can measure complex sets like the Cantor ternary set. From the point of view of the measure theory, the fractal dimension is the jump point that makes the measure of the set change from infinity to zero. Fractal dimension includes the Hausdorff dimension, the Box dimension and the Packing dimension. Each dimension has a special definition and many calculation methods. The tool for studying fractal dimension is no longer just classic calculus, and a full discussion about the properties of continuous functions lies beyond the scope of classical calculus. Fractional calculus (FC) has gradually become the main method [1–3]. Since classical calculus is a special case of fractional calculus [4], many problems that cannot be measured by classical calculus can be solved by fractional calculus, such as studying the properties of continuous functions that are continuous but not differentiable everywhere [5,6]. The most widely used FC is the Riemann-Liuville fractional calculus and the Weyl-Marchaud fractional calculus.

Recent work has established that one-dimensional continuous functions have significant and useful properties [7]. For instance, the Box dimension of bounded variation functions and the functions with Riemann-Liuville fractional calculus are both one. The

Box dimension of continuous functions is not less than one. Fractional integral does not increase the dimensionality of the functions, and this special operator makes the fractal dimension have a special linear relationship.

However, there are still some issues that are worth considering and discussing. For example, is the Hausdorff dimension of a continuous function with bounded variation equal to one? What are the Hausdorff dimension and the Box dimension of functions satisfying the Hölder condition? Is there a one-dimensional unbounded variation function? Can the function of unbounded variation and bounded variation be mutually converted under special prerequisites? Are there other ways to better explore unbounded variation functions effectively? It is these original questions that promote the emergence of new concepts and many new analytical tools. A few years ago, scholars always used the definition of bounded variation to define the unbounded variation function. The definition is not conducive to exploring the nature of the unbounded variation function. As unbounded variation functions defined by the unbounded variation point directly, a new perspective for studying unbounded variation functions was gradually discovered. At the same time, the relevant conclusions about unbounded variation points have also been rigorously proved. For example, the Box dimension of an unbounded variation function with only an unbounded variation point is one. If this function has self-similarity at the same time, its Hausdorff dimension is also one. A more interesting topic is to investigate the changes between some classic functions and the functions after fractional calculus. These changes usually include fractal dimension [8–10], continuity [11,12], boundedness [13,14] and types of fractional calculus [15,16].

After concentrated discussions on some special functions theoretically [17,18], scholars do not have any visual information of the functions [19,20]. The most obvious evidence is the Weierstrass function. Researchers not only know about its functional properties, but also clearly know what its image looks like. Nevertheless, scholars are not very familiar with the image of any one-dimensional continuous functions with an unbounded variation point. Therefore, several attempts have been made to construct the special functions [21], such as one-dimensional continuous functions with finite or infinite unbounded variation points, and unbounded variation functions that satisfy the Hölder condition. The construction process of these special functions mainly uses some compression, translation and symmetric transformations. There are also some special unbounded variation functions that are obtained by special operations on the basis of the devil function [22].

So far, there existed many research angles and conclusions on one-dimensional continuous functions and their fractional calculus [23]. In order to have a comprehensive understanding, this paper will systematically sort out the current research results from the perspectives of bounded variation, unbounded variation and the Hölder condition. A more detailed analysis of unbounded variation functions through the unbounded variation point will also be elaborated. Combined with the very popular reinforcement learning in machine learning, some very interesting practical applications are predicted. For example, the evaluation model based on the fractal dimension and the random search method based on the fractal structure. The advantage of the fractal evaluation model based on the fractal dimension is that the method based on the local information can evaluate the distance between any two states to the equilibrium state. The distance can speed up the calculation process of algorithms. At the same time, evaluating the current state during the training process can also optimize and improve algorithms reasonably. The fractal random search method also makes full use of the self-similarity to reduce the search time as much as possible on the basis of ensuring the probe of the entire space. Finally, the framework to prove the convergence of reinforcement learning algorithms is introduced using fractal attractors.

The main innovations of this manuscript are as follows. First, the existing conclusions about one-dimensional continuous functions are summarized through three different classification methods, which is helpful to study other complex functions. The second is to introduce the concept of the unbounded variation point to directly study unbounded variation functions. The unbounded variation point can effectively grasp the essence of unbounded variation functions. At the same time, some special unbounded variation functions can be constructed based on the unbounded variation point, and the images of these complex unbounded variation functions can be easily obtained. Third, by combining reinforcement learning and fractal theory, some possible application directions are predicted, and a unique fractal evaluation model is proposed. These results can provide some new ideas for other researchers.

Section 2 mainly recalled some basic concepts, such as the definition of fractal dimension, bounded variation functions, unbounded variation points and fractional calculus. Section 3 mainly discussed the bounded variation function and its fractional calculus. Section 4 focused on the correlation between the continuity of Hölder and variation functions. Section 5 primarily explored the unbounded variation function through the unbounded variation point, and gave the construction process of one-dimensional continuous unbounded variation functions. Section 6 forecasted some applications of fractal and fractal functions in reinforcement learning and analyzed the advantages and disadvantages of these methods. The logical structure of this paper is shown in Figure 1.

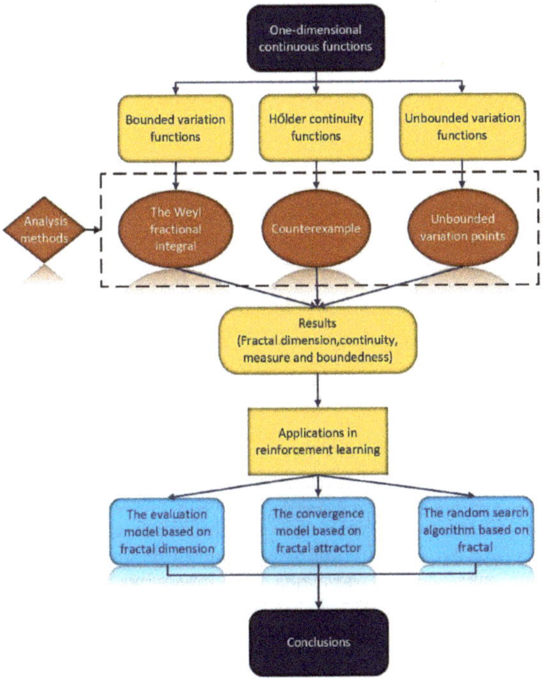

Figure 1. The logical structure of the paper.

2. Basic Concepts

Among fractal dimension, the Box dimension is the most widely used. However, some other dimension is still mentioned in some engineering problems, such as the modified Box dimension and the Packing dimension. At the same time, the relationship between these dimension is often analyzed and compared in theoretical research. Most of the definitions are based on measurement theory, and there are also some interrelationships between various dimension. Typical definitions of fractal dimension are as follows.

Definition 1. ([24,25]) *Let F be a non-empty bounded subset of R^n and $N_\delta(F)$ be the smallest number of sets of diameter at most δ which can cover F. The lower and upper Box dimension of F respectively are defined as*

$$\underline{\dim}_B(F) = \underline{\lim}_{\delta \to 0} \frac{\log N_\delta(F)}{-\log \delta}, \tag{1}$$

and

$$\overline{\dim}_B(F) = \overline{\lim}_{\delta \to 0} \frac{\log N_\delta(F)}{-\log \delta}. \tag{2}$$

If (1) and (2) are equal, the common value is the Box dimension of F:

$$\dim_B(F) = \lim_{\delta \to 0} \frac{\log N_\delta(F)}{-\log \delta}.$$

If F can be decomposed into a countable number of pieces $F_1, F_2, \cdots$ in such a way that the dimension of the largest piece should be as small as possible. This idea leads to the following modified Box-counting dimension,

$$\underline{\dim}_{MB}(F) = \inf\{\sup_i \underline{\dim}_B F_i : F \subset \bigcup_{i=1}^{\infty} F_i\}, \tag{3}$$

$$\overline{\dim}_{MB}(F) = \inf\{\sup_i \overline{\dim}_B F_i : F \subset \bigcup_{i=1}^{\infty} F_i\}. \tag{4}$$

If (3) and (4) are equal, the common value is the modified Box-counting dimension of F. Let

$$\mathscr{P}^s(F) = \inf\{\sum_i \mathscr{P}_0^s(F_i) : F \subset \bigcup_{i=1}^{\infty} F_i\}.$$

It may be shown that $\mathscr{P}^s(F)$ is the s-dimensional Packing measure. The definition of the Packing dimension [26] in the usual way:

$$\dim_P F = \sup\{s : \mathscr{P}^s(F) = \infty\} = \inf\{s : \mathscr{P}^s(F) = 0\}.$$

The above dimension is put forward for some specific problems. In the research process, the appropriate fractal dimension should be selected according to the needs. For example, the measurement of the Hausdorff dimension is more accurate and the calculation of the Box dimension is simpler through programs.

The Jordan decomposition theorem is widely applied in the proof process of various problems, and the core concept of the theorem is the function with bounded variation. The definition of the bounded variation function is shown in Definition 2. The unbounded variation function can be defined by the complementary set of bounded variation functions, but this paper will research unbounded variation functions through the unbounded variation point that can be found in Definition 3.

Definition 2. ([27]) *Let $f(x)$ be defined on $I = [0,1]$. A set of points $P = \{x_0, x_1, \cdots, x_n\}$, satisfying the inequalities $0 = x_0 < x_1 < \cdots < x_{n-1} < x_n = 1$, is called a partition. $P = \{x_0, x_1, \cdots, x_n\}$ is a partition of I and write $\triangle f_k = f(x_k) - f(x_{k-1})$, for $k = 1, 2, \cdots, n$. If there exists a positive number M such that*

$$\sum_{k=1}^{n} |\triangle f_k| \leq M,$$

for all partitions of I, $f(x)$ is said to be of bounded variation on I.

Bounded variation functions have many important properties [28,29]. Such as, a monotonic function is a bounded variation function. The sum, difference, and product of a finite number of bounded variation functions are still the bounded variation function. The absolutely continuous function must be the function of bounded variation.

Definition 3. *(UV point) Let $f(x)$ be a continuous function on I.*

(1) For $p \in (0,1)$. There exists a closed subinterval $Q = [q_1, q_2]$ $(0 \le q_1 < p < q_2 \le 1)$ of I such that the variation of $f(x)$ on Q is finite, then denote $(p, 0)$ as a bounded variation point of $f(x)$, or $(p, 0)$ as an unbounded variation point of $f(x)$.

(2) For $p = 0$ or $p = 1$. There is a closed subinterval $Q = [0, q_1]$ $(0 < x \le 1)$ or $Q = [q_1, 1]$ $(0 \le q_1 < 1)$ of I and the variation of $f(x)$ on Q is finite, then denote $(p, 0)$ is a bounded variation point of $f(x)$, otherwise $(p, 0)$ is an unbounded variation point of $f(x)$.

Due to the complexity of the function structure, the functions of unbounded variation are often non-differentiable functions in the defined interval. The concept of the UV point grasps the essence of unbounded variation functions and transforms the complex structure cleverly. Classical calculus is difficult to analyse the properties of unbounded variation functions, but the properties of some special unbounded variation functions can be investigated by fractional calculus [30,31]. This article mainly utilizes the Riemann-Liouville fractional integral and the Weyl fractional integral [32] to study unbounded variation functions. Their definitions can be found in Definition 4.

Definition 4. *([33,34]) (1) Let $f(x) \in C_I, \nu > 0$. $D^{-\nu} f(0) = 0$ and for $x \in (0,1]$,*

$$D^{-\nu} f(x) = \frac{1}{\Gamma(\nu)} \int_0^x (x-t)^{\nu-1} f(t) dt$$

is the Riemann-Liouville fractional integral of $f(x)$ of order ν.

(2) Let $f(x)$ be a continuous function defined on $(-\infty, +\infty)$ and $0 < \nu < 1$.

$$W^{-\nu} f(x) = \frac{1}{\Gamma(\nu)} \int_x^\infty (t-x)^{\nu-1} f(t) dt$$

is called as the Weyl fractional integral of $f(x)$ of order ν.

The abbreviation C_I and BV_I will be represented for continuous functions and bounded variation functions defined on I respectively. Denote $G(f, I)$ as the image of $f(x)$ on I. Denote bounded variation function and unbounded variation function as BVF and UVF respectively. C_0 is the Cantor set.

3. Bounded Variation Functions and Their Fractional Integral

The structure of the bounded variation function is not complex. Simple calculations show that its Box dimension is one [35,36]. Furthermore, the bounded variation function after the Weyl fractional integral is still a bounded variation function, so its Box dimension is still one. The relationship between them can be shown in Figure 2.

The proof process of the above related conclusions will be given in detail. First of all, a frequently occurring lemma is necessary to be displayed.

Lemma 1. *Given a function $f(x)$ and an interval $[a, b]$, R_f is the maximum range of $f(x)$ over $[a, b]$, i.e.,*

$$R_f[a, b] = \sup_{a < x, y < b} |f(x) - f(y)|.$$

Let $f(x) \in C_I \cap BV_I$. Suppose that $0 < \delta < 1$ and m be the least integer greater than or equal to δ^{-1}. If N_δ is the number of squares of the δ-mesh that intersect $G(f, I)$, then

$$\delta^{-1}\sum_{i=0}^{m-1} R_f[i\delta,(i+1)\delta] \le N_\delta \le 2m+\delta^{-1}\sum_{i=0}^{m-1} R_f[i\delta,(i+1)\delta].$$

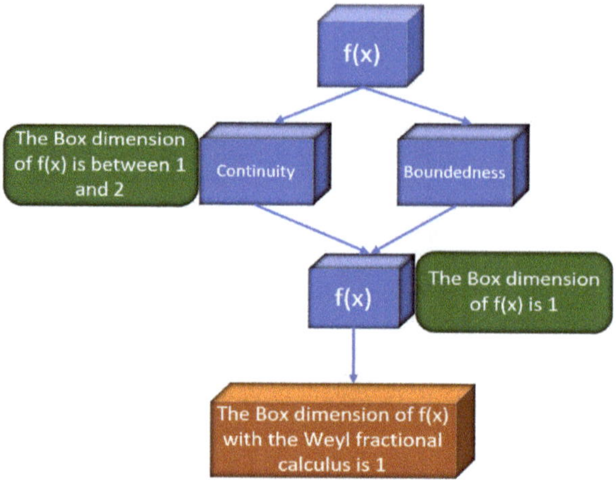

Figure 2. The properties of bounded variation functions.

Proof of Lemma 1. The number of mesh squares of δ in the column above the interval $[i\delta,(i+1)\delta]$ that intersect $G(f,I)$ belongs to $[R_f[i\delta,(i+1)\delta]/\delta, 2+(R_f[i\delta,(i+1)\delta]/\delta)]$. By summing all such intervals together, the lemma can be proved. □

Theorem 1. *(1) If* $\underline{\dim}_B G(f,I)\ge 1$ *and* $f(x)$ *is a continuous function,* $\overline{\dim}_B G(f,I)\le 2$.
(2) If $f(x)\in C_I\bigcap BV_I$, $\dim_B G(f,I)=1$.

Proof of Theorem 1. By using Definition 1,

$$\underline{\dim}_B G(f,I)\ge \underline{\lim}_{\delta\to 0}\frac{\log\frac{C}{\delta}}{-\log\delta}=1,\ \overline{\dim}_B G(f,I)\le \overline{\lim}_{\delta\to 0}\frac{\log\frac{C}{\delta^2}}{-\log\delta}=2.$$

Let $\{x_i\}_{i=1}^n$ be arbitrary points satisfying $0=x_0<x_1<x_2<\cdots<x_n=1$, then

$$\sup_{(x_0,x_1,\cdots,x_n)}\sum_{k=1}^{n}|f(x_k)-f(x_{k-1})|<C.$$

Let m be the least integer greater than or equal to $\frac{1}{\delta}$. N_δ is the number of squares of the $\delta-$mesh that intersect $G(f,I)$. Combining Lemma 1,

$$N_\delta\le 2m+\delta^{-1}\sum_{i=1}^{m} R_f[(i-1)\delta,i\delta].$$

For $1\le i\le m-1$ and $x_{i,\,0}=i\delta$, $x_{i,\,3}=(i+1)\delta$, $x_{i,\,1}$, $x_{i,\,2}\in(i\delta,(i+1)\delta)$,

$$R_f[i\delta,(i+1)\delta]\le \sup_{x_{i,\,0}<x_{i,\,1}<x_{i,\,2}<x_{i,\,3}}\sum_{k=1}^{3}|f(x_i,k)-f(x_i,k-1)|.$$

There exists a positive constant C such that $N_\delta\le C\delta^{-1}$ and

$$\overline{\dim}_B G(f,I)\le 1,\ 0<v<1.$$

Simultaneously, the topolopy dimension of a continuous function $f(x)$ is no less than 1,

$$\underline{\dim}_B G(f,I) \geq 1,\ 0 < v < 1.$$

Thus, $\dim_B G(f,I) = 1$. □

If non-negative constants C and α can be found to formula the following inequation

$$|f(x) - f(y)| \leq C|x-y|^{\alpha},$$

$f(x)$ is a Hölder continuous function [37]. When $\alpha = 1$, $f(x)$ is a Lipschitz continuous function. Throughout this paper, the term $f(x) \in LipC$ means that $f(x)$ is a Lipschitz continuous function on I and the Lipschitz constant is C.

Corollary 1. *If $f(x) \in LipC$, then* $\dim_B G(f,I) = 1$.

Proof of Corollary 1. $f(x) \in LipC, \forall\, x,y \in I,$

$$|\, f(x) - f(y) \,| \leq C \,|\, x - y \,|\,.$$

Let $\{x_i\}_{i=1}^{n}$ be arbitrary points satisfying $0 = x_0 < x_1 < x_2 < \cdots < x_n = 1$. Since

$$\sup_{(x_0,\, x_1, \ldots,\, x_n)} \sum_{k=1}^{n} |f(x_k) - f(x_{k-1})| \leq C \sum_{k=1}^{n} |x_k - x_{k-1}| \leq C,$$

$f(x) \in BV_I$ and $\dim_B G(f,I) = 1$. □

Corollary 1 shows that a function that satisfies the Lipschitz condition must be a BVF. However, a function that satisfies the Hölder condition is not necessarily a BVF [38,39]. The counter-example is as follows:

$$f(x) = \begin{cases} -1/\ln x, & 0 < x \leq 0.5, \\ 0, & x = 0. \end{cases}$$

Obviously, since this function is monotonically increasing in $[0, 0.5]$, it is a BVF. But for any $\alpha > 0$, this function does not satisfy the Hölder condition of order α.

Theorem 2. *If $f(x) \in C_I \bigcap BV_I$,* $\dim_B G(W^{-v}f, I) = 1$.

Proof of Theorem 2. Since $f(x) \in C_I$ and $f(x)$ is of bounded variation on I, $f(x)$ can be replaced with the difference of two monotone increasing and continuous functions $g_1(x)$ and $g_2(x)$ by the Jordan decomposition theorem, $f(x) = g_1(x) - g_2(x)$, where $g_1(x) = h_1(x) - c$, $g_2(x) = h_2(x) - c$, $h_1(x) = h_2(x) = c$ on $[1, +\infty)$. Then $h_1(x)$ and $h_2(x)$ are also monotone increasing and continuous functions.

(1) If $f(0) \geq 0$, let $g_1(0) \geq 0$ and $g_2(0) = 0$. By Definition 4,

$$G_1(x) = W^{-v}g_1(x) = \frac{1}{\Gamma(v)} \int_x^{\infty} \frac{h_1(t) - c}{(t-x)^{1-v}} dt,\ 0 < v < 1,$$

$G_1(x)$ still is a continuous function on I when $g_1(x)$ is a continuous function. Let $0 \leq x_1 \leq x_2 \leq 1$ and $0 < v < 1$,

$$\begin{aligned}
&G_1(x_2) - G_1(x_1) \\
=&\frac{1}{\Gamma(v)} \int_{x_2}^{\infty} (t-x_2)^{v-1}(h_1(t)-c)dt - \frac{1}{\Gamma(v)} \int_{x_1}^{\infty} (t-x_1)^{v-1}(h_1(t)-c)dt \\
=&\frac{1}{\Gamma(v)} \int_{x_2}^{1} (t-x_2)^{v-1}(h_1(t)-c)dt - \frac{1}{\Gamma(v)} \int_{x_1}^{1} (t-x_1)^{v-1}(h_1(t)-c)dt \\
=&\frac{1}{\Gamma(v)}(\int_{x_2}^{1} (t-x_2)^{v-1}h_1(t)dt - \int_{x_1}^{1} (t-x_1)^{v-1}h_1(t)dt) \\
&+ \frac{1}{\Gamma(v)}(\int_{x_1}^{1} (t-x_1)^{v-1}cdt - \int_{x_2}^{1} (t-x_2)^{v-1}cdt) \\
=&\frac{1}{\Gamma(v)} \int_{x_1}^{1-x_2+x_1} (t-x_1)^{v-1}(h_1(t-x_1+x_2) - h_1(t))dt \\
&+ \frac{1}{\Gamma(v)} \int_{1+x_1-x_2}^{1} (t-x_1)^{v-1}(c-h_1(t))dt \\
\geq&0.
\end{aligned}$$

Thus, $G_1(x)$ still is a monotone increasing and continuous function on I. If

$$G_2(x) = W^{-v}g_2(x) = \frac{1}{\Gamma(v)} \int_{x}^{\infty} \frac{h_2(t)-c}{(t-x)^{1-v}}dt,\ 0 < v < 1,$$

$G_2(x)$ is also a monotone increasing and continuous function on I.

(2) If $f(0) < 0$, let $g_1(x) = 0$ and $g_2(x) > 0$. Using a similar way, both $W^{-v}g_1(x)$ and $W^{-v}g_2(x)$ are monotone increasing and continuous functions on I. So $W^{-v}f(x)$ still is a BVF on I and

$$\dim_B G(W^{-v}f, I) = 1.$$

□

4. Unbounded Variation Functions (UVFs)

4.1. A Special UVF

The construction process of the devil stair function $d(x)$ will be elaborated firstly. Then, a peculiar continuous function $D(x)$ of unbounded variation on I will be constructed on the basis of $d(x)$.

If $x \in (\frac{1}{3}, \frac{2}{3})$, $d_1(x) = \frac{1}{2}$. Let $d_1(0) = 0$ and $d_1(1) = 1$. $d_1(x)$ can be exhibited on I by connecting $d_1(0), d_1(\frac{1}{3}), d_1(\frac{2}{3})$ and $d_1(1)$ with line segments.

If $x \in (\frac{1}{9}, \frac{2}{9}), d_2(x) = \frac{1}{4}$. If $x \in (\frac{7}{9}, \frac{8}{9}), d_2(x) = \frac{3}{4}$. Connecting $d_1(0), d_2(\frac{1}{9}), d_2(\frac{2}{9}), d_1(\frac{1}{3})$, $d_1(\frac{2}{3})$, $d_2(\frac{7}{9}), d_2(\frac{8}{9})$ and $d_1(1)$ with line segments to form $d_2(x)$ on I.

By induction, $d_n(x) (n \geq 3)$ can be constructed. Let $d(x) = \lim_{n \to \infty} d_n(x)$.

The construction of $D_1(x)$ is based on $d_1(x)$ with two more line segments whose length are 1. The line segments and the part of $d_1(x)$, $x \in (\frac{1}{3}, \frac{2}{3})$ make up an isosceles triangle. In $D_1(x)$, the triangle is shown without the base line.

The construction of $D_2(x)$ is based on $d_2(x)$ and $D_1(x)$. Simultaneously for $x \in (0, \frac{1}{3})$ or $x \in (\frac{1}{3}, \frac{2}{3})$, using similar ways to construct $D_2(x)$ like as $d_1(x) \to D_1(x)$. However, the length of line segments added is $\frac{1/2}{2^1}$.

The construction of $D_3(x)$ is based on $d_3(x)$ and $D_2(x)$. Simultaneously for $x \in (0, \frac{1}{9})$, $x \in (\frac{2}{9}, \frac{1}{3})$, $x \in (\frac{2}{3}, \frac{7}{9})$, or $x \in (\frac{8}{9}, 1)$, using similar steps to construct $D_3(x)$ like as $d_1(x) \to D_1(x)$. The process of constructing is similar, the only difference is the length of line segments added is $\frac{1/3}{2^2}$.

By induction, the construction of $D_n(x)$ is based on $d_n(x)$ and $D_{n-1}(x)$. The length of line segments is $\frac{1/n}{2^{n-1}}$. Then, $D(x) = \lim_{n\to\infty} D_n(x)$. Images of $d(x)$ and $D(x)$ are given as follows Figure 3.

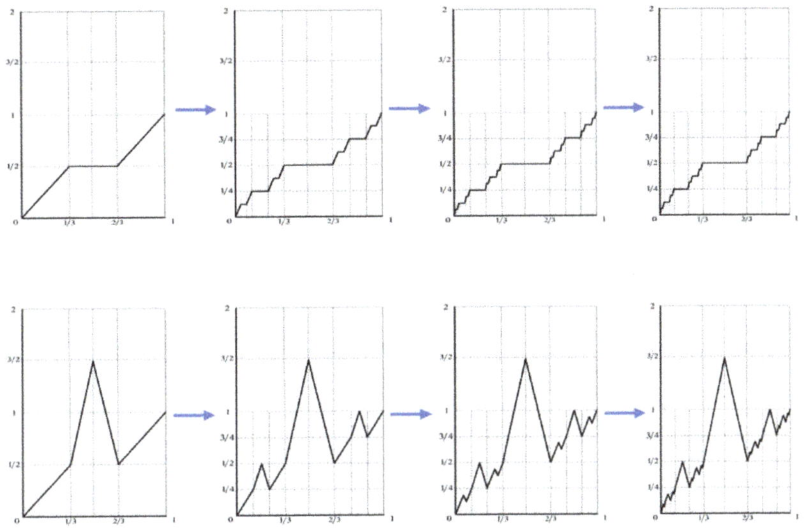

Figure 3. The image of $d(x)$ and $D(x)$.

Combining the construction process of $D(x)$, properties of the function will be investigated.

Property 1. *The length of $G(D, I)$ is infinite on I. The lebesgue measure of differentiable points on I is one.*

Proof of Property 1. Length of $G(D, I)$ is no less than

$$1\cdot 2\cdot 1 + 2\cdot 2\cdot \frac{1/2}{2} + 4\cdot 2\cdot \frac{1/3}{4} + \cdots + 2^{n-1}\cdot 2\cdot \frac{1/n}{2^{n-1}} + \cdots = 2\sum_{n=1}^{\infty}\frac{1}{n} = \infty.$$

Thus, the length of $G(D, I)$ is infinite on I. Let A be the set of differentiable points of $D(x)$ on I.

$$m(A) = \frac{1}{3} + 2\cdot\frac{1}{9} + 4\cdot\frac{1}{27} + \cdots + 2^{n-1}\cdot\frac{1}{3^n} + \cdots = 1.$$

Denote B as the set of non-differentiable points of $D(x)$ on I, then

$$m(B) = 1 - 1 = 0.$$

□

Property 2. *The Box dimension of $D(x)$ is one and $D(x)$ has uncountable unbounded variation points on I.*

Proof of Property 2. Since $D(x)$ is a continuous function, $\underline{\dim}_B G(D, I) \geq 1$. Let $0 < \delta < 1$, $\frac{1}{\delta} \leq n \leq 1 + \frac{1}{\delta}$. The number of squares of the $\delta-$mesh that intersect $G(D, I)$ are less than

$$2n + \frac{1}{\delta}\sum_{i=1}^{n}\frac{1}{i} + 2\frac{1}{\delta}.$$

Thus,

$$\begin{aligned}\overline{\dim}_B G(D,I) &\leq \overline{\lim_{\delta\to 0}} \frac{\log[2n+\frac{1}{\delta}\sum_{i=1}^{n}\frac{1}{i}+2\frac{1}{\delta}]}{-\log\delta} \\ &\leq \overline{\lim_{\delta\to 0}} \frac{\log[2n+2\delta^{-1}(\log(n+1)+1)]}{-\log\delta} \\ &\leq 1.\end{aligned}$$

Further analysis showed that $\dim_B G(D,I) = 1$.

If $\forall\, x \in C_0$, a positive number N_0 will be found such that variation of any subinterval I_x containing x of I is at least

$$\begin{aligned}&\frac{1}{2^{N_0}}\frac{1}{N_0} + 2\frac{1}{2^{N_0+1}}\frac{1}{N_0+1} + 2^2\frac{1}{2^{N_0+2}}\frac{1}{N_0+2} + \cdots \\ =& \frac{1}{2^{N_0}}\sum_{n=1}^{\infty}\frac{1}{N_0+n-1} \\ =& \frac{1}{2^{N_0}}\left(\sum_{n=1}^{\infty}\frac{1}{n} - \sum_{n=1}^{N_0-1}\frac{1}{n}\right) \\ =& \infty.\end{aligned}$$

Thus, $(x,0)$ is an unbounded variation point of $D(x)$ on I. Since the arbitrariness of x, the number of unbounded variation points of $D(x)$ on I is uncountable. □

Now, the construction of $H(x)$ that contains uncountable UV points will be displayed. Divided I into three equal intervals,

$$I_{1,1} = [0,\frac{1}{3}],\ I_{1,2} = [\frac{1}{3},\frac{2}{3}],\ I_{1,3} = [\frac{2}{3},1].$$

Two line segments are added such that constituting an isosceles triangle with $I_{1,2}$ and the length of the segment is 1, Then $I_{1,2}$ will be removed. $I_{1,1}$ and $I_{1,3}$ are divided into three equal intervals respectively,

$$\begin{aligned}I_{1,1} &= I_{2,1}\bigcup I_{2,2}\bigcup I_{2,3}, \\ I_{1,3} &= I_{2,4}\bigcup I_{2,5}\bigcup I_{2,6}.\end{aligned}$$

Four line segments are added such that constituting an isosceles triangle with $I_{2,2}$ and $I_{2,5}$. The length of the segment is $\frac{1}{4}$. Furthermore, delete $I_{2,2}$ and $I_{2,5}$. Similar way can get H_3 and H_4. H_n can be got From H_{n-1}. By dividing

$$I_{n-1,1},\ I_{n-1,3},\ I_{n-1,4},\ I_{n-1,6},\cdots,\ I_{n-1,3\cdot 2^{n-2}-1},\ I_{n-1,3\cdot 2^{n-2}}$$

into three equal intervals respectively,

$$\begin{aligned}I_{n-1,1} &= I_{n,1}\bigcup I_{n,2}\bigcup I_{n,3}, \\ I_{n-1,3\cdot 2^{n-2}} &= I_{n,3\cdot 2^{n-1}-2}\bigcup I_{n,3\cdot 2^{n-1}-1}\bigcup I_{n,3\cdot 2^{n-1}}.\end{aligned}$$

2^n line segments are added such that constituting an isosceles triangle with

$$I_{n-1,2},\ I_{n-1,5},\cdots,\ I_{n-1,3\cdot 2^{n-2}-1}.$$

The length of the segment is $\frac{1}{n\cdot 2^{n-1}}$. Then delete $I_{n,2}, I_{n,5},\cdots, I_{n,3\cdot 2^{n-1}-1}$. The image of $H(x)$ is Figure 4.

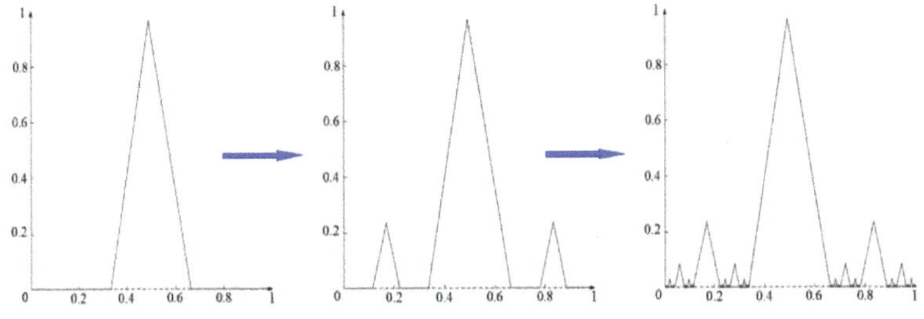

Figure 4. The image of $H(x)$.

Obviously, $H(x)$ is a continuous function. Firstly, the length of $H(x)$ on I is $\sum\limits_{n=1}^{\infty} \frac{1}{n} = \infty$, the variation of $H(x)$ on I is infinite. Secondly, the number of $\delta-$mesh squares that intersect $G(H,I)$ is at most $\delta^{-1} \sum\limits_{n=1}^{\infty} \frac{1}{n} + 2\delta^{-1}$ and

$$\dim_B G(H,I) = \lim_{\delta \to 0} \frac{\log(\delta^{-1} \sum\limits_{n=1}^{\infty} \frac{1}{n} + 2\delta^{-1})}{-\log \delta} = 1.$$

Finally, $\forall x_0 \in C_0 \cup [a,b]$, the variation of $H(x)$ on $[a,b]$ is $\sum\limits_{n=N_0}^{\infty} \frac{1}{N_0 2^{N_0-1}} \frac{1}{n} = \infty$, where N_0 is a positive integer. So $H(x)$ contains uncountable UV points.

The function that satisfies the Lipschitz condition must be a BVF, but the function that satisfies the Hölder condition is not necessarily a BVF [40,41]. The following two special functions are just the best evidence for the above conclusion.

4.2. UVF Satisfying the Hölder Condition of Order $\alpha (0 < \alpha < 1)$

Let $A_n = a_1 + a_2 + \cdots + a_n + \cdots$ be the convergence series of positive terms and any of terms is monotonically decreasing. The sum of A_n is s and the construction process of the function $f_\alpha(x)$ on $[0,s]$ is as follows:

$$f(x) = 0, x \in \{0, a_1, a_1 + a_2, a_1 + a_2 + a_3\};$$
$$f(x) = \frac{1}{n}, x \in \{a_1 + a_2 + \cdots + a_{n-1} + \frac{a_n}{2} (n = 1, 2, \cdots)\};$$
$$f(s) = 0.$$

$f_\alpha(x)$ is linear in the following intervals, such as $[a_1 + \cdots + a_{n-1}, a_1 + \cdots + a_{n-1} + \frac{a_n}{2}]$, $[a_1 + \cdots + a_{n-1} + \frac{a_n}{2}, a_1 + \cdots + a_{n-1} + a_n]$, $n = 1, 2, \cdots$. The specific image of $f_\alpha(x)$ is as follows Figure 5.

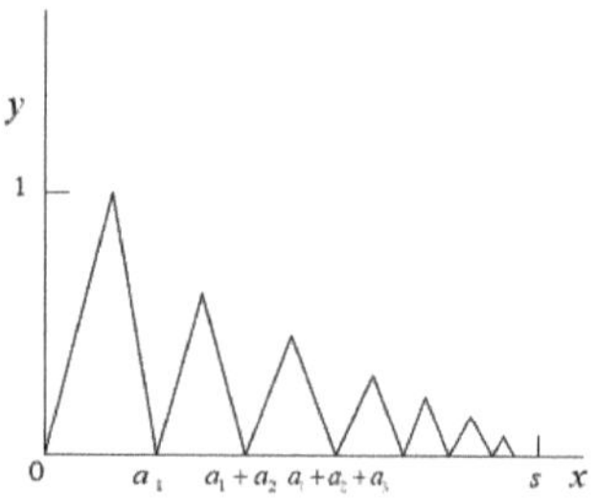

Figure 5. The image of $f_\alpha(x)$.

Theorem 3. *$f_\alpha(x)$ is a continuous function on $[0,s](0 < s \leq 1)$ and the total variation of $f_\alpha(x)$ in the interval $[0,s]$ is infinite.*

Proof of Theorem 3. From the specific construction process of $f_\alpha(x)$, $f_\alpha(x)$ is a continuous function on $[0,s]$ obviously. The proof of its total variation is infinite will be given next. Consider the following partition: $0 < \frac{a_1}{2} < a_1 < a_1 + \frac{a_2}{2} < +a_1 + a_2 < a_1 + a_2 + \frac{a_3}{2} < a_1 + a_2 + a_3 < \cdots < a_1 + a_2 + \cdots + a_k$. Then,

$$\begin{aligned}
V_0^s(f(x)) =& |f(\frac{a_1}{2}) - f(0)| + |f(a_1) - f(\frac{a_1}{2})| + |f(a_1 + \frac{a_1}{2}) - f(a_1)| \\
&+ \cdots + |f(a_1 + a_2 + \cdots + a_k) - f(a_1 + a_2 + \cdots + a_{k-1} + \frac{a_k}{2})| \\
&+ |f(s) - f(a_1 + a_2 + \cdots + a_k)| \\
=& 1 + 1 + \frac{1}{2} + \frac{1}{2} + \cdots + \frac{1}{k} + \frac{1}{k} \\
=& +\infty.
\end{aligned}$$

The conclusion is $\lim\limits_{k \to +\infty} V_0^s(f(x)) = +\infty$. Thus, $f_\alpha(x)$ is an UVF on $[0,s]$. □

Theorem 4. *$f_\alpha(x)$ satisfies the Hölder condition of a given order α $(0 < \alpha < 1)$.*

Proof of Theorem 4. Case one: two points $P_1(x_1, y_1)$, $P_2(x_2, y_2)$ on the interval are selected arbitrarily, but the two points are in the same linear interval, $a_1 + \cdots + a_{n-1} \leq x_1 < x_2 \leq a_1 + \cdots + a_{n-1} + \frac{a_n}{2}$. Then the specific image of Case one is as follows Figure 6.

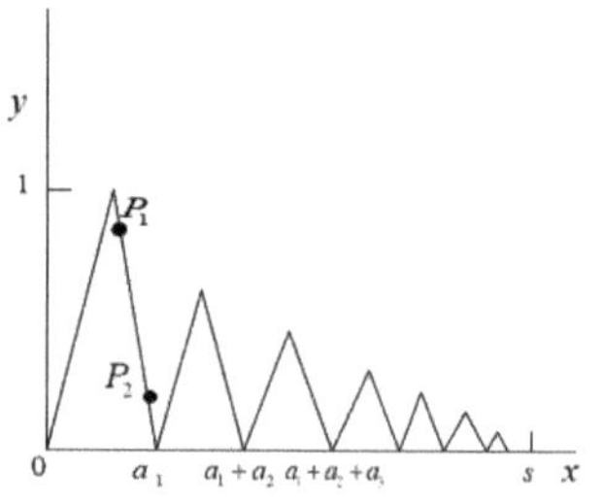

Figure 6. Case one.

$$|y_2 - y_1| = \frac{2}{na_n}|x_2 - x_1| = \frac{2|x_2 - x_1|^{1-\alpha}}{na_n}|x_2 - x_1|^{\alpha}$$
$$< \frac{2a_n^{1-\alpha}}{na_n}|x_2 - x_1|^{\alpha}$$
$$= \frac{2}{na_n^{\alpha}}|x_2 - x_1|^{\alpha}.$$

Therefore, it is significant to select the appropriate sequence a_n to make $\frac{2}{na_n^{\alpha}}$ bounded. a sequence that satisfies the above formula can be found easily, such as $a_n = n^{\frac{-1}{\alpha}}$.

Case two: If the two points $P_1(x_1, y_1)$, $P_2(x_2, y_2)$ are not in the same linear interval, moving P_1 to $P_3(x_3, y_3)$ through translation transformation. Then the specific image of Case two is as follows Figure 7.

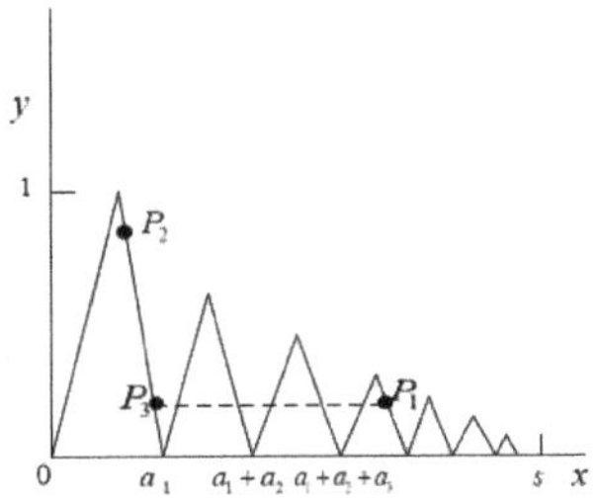

Figure 7. Case two.

Combined with the proof of Case one, $|y_2 - y_1| = |y_2 - y_3| \le C|x_2 - x_3|^{\alpha}$.

□

Since $f_\alpha(x)$ is a continuous function, the lower Box dimension of $f_\alpha(x)$ is greater than or equal to 1. The number of $\delta-$mesh squares that intersect $G(f_\alpha, [0, s])$ is at most $\delta^{-1}\sum_{n=1}^{\infty}\frac{1}{n} + 2\delta^{-1}$,

$$\dim_B G(f_\alpha, [0, s]) = \lim_{\delta \to 0} \frac{\log(\delta^{-1}\sum_{n=1}^{\infty}\frac{1}{n} + 2\delta^{-1})}{-\log\delta} = 1.$$

4.3. *UVF Not Satisfying the Hölder Condition of Any Order α ($\alpha > 0$)*

An UVF $g(x)$ that does not satisfy the Hölder condition of any order α ($\alpha > 0$) on the basis of $f_\alpha(x)$ will be constructed. Since $f_\alpha(x)$ satisfies the Hölder condition of order α ($0 < \alpha < 1$) on $[0, s]$, for $\alpha^* > \alpha$, $x = a_1 + a_2 + \cdots + a_{n-1} + \frac{a_n}{2}$, $y = a_1 + a_2 + \cdots + a_{n-1} + a_n$,

$$\lim_{n \to +\infty} \frac{f(y) - f(x)}{|y - x|^{\alpha^*}} = \frac{\frac{1}{n}}{(\frac{a_n}{2})^{\alpha^*}} = \frac{\frac{1}{n}}{(\frac{1}{2n^{\frac{1}{\alpha}}})^{\alpha^*}} = 2^{\alpha^*} n^{\frac{\alpha^*}{\alpha} - 1} = +\infty.$$

Thus, $f_\alpha(x)$ does not satisfy the Hölder condition of any order $\alpha^*(\alpha^* > \alpha)$ on $[0, s]$. Denote $\sigma_n = \sum_{k=1}^{\infty}\frac{1}{k^n}$ and divide the interval I as follows,

$$0 = \beta_2 < \beta_3 < \beta_4 < \cdots < \beta_n < \cdots (\beta_n \to 1, n \to +\infty).$$

(1) If n is an even number, $g(x)$ can be obtained by compressing $f_{\frac{1}{n}}(x)$ by n times on the ordinate, compressing by $\frac{\sigma_n}{\beta_{n+1}-\beta_n}$ times on the abscissa and moving β_n to the right along the abscissa,

$$g(x) = \frac{1}{n} f_{\frac{1}{n}}[\frac{\sigma_n(x-\beta_n)}{\beta_{n+1}-\beta_n}].$$

(2) If n an is odd number,

$$g(x) = \frac{1}{n} f_{\frac{1}{n}}[\frac{\sigma_n(\beta_{n+1}-x)}{\beta_{n+1}-\beta_n}].$$

In addition to the above construction process, an additional supplementary definition $f(1) = 0$ is reasonable. The specific image of $g(x)$ is as follows Figure 8.

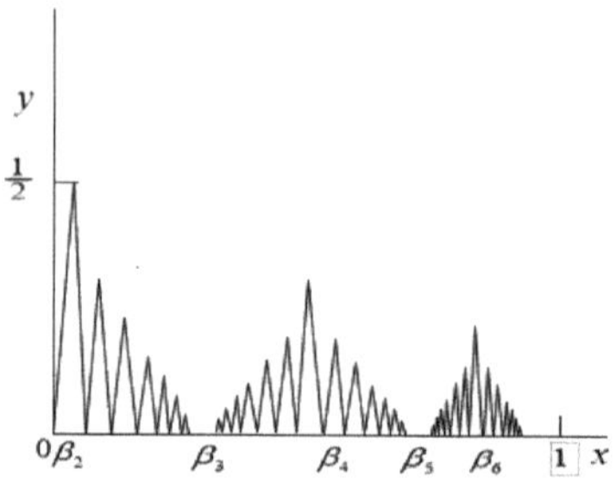

Figure 8. The image of $g(x)$.

From the construction process of $g(x)$, $g(x)$ is defined everywhere on the interval I and $g(x)$ is a continuous function. Through similar calculation, it can be known that the total variation of this function is also infinite. $g(x)$ is also an UVF.

However, for interval $[\beta_n, \beta_{n+1}]$, $g(x)$ satisfies the Hölder condition of order $\frac{1}{n}$ and does not satisfy the Hölder condition of order $\frac{1}{n-1}$. Therefore, the function $g(x)$ does not satisfy the Hölder condition of any order $\alpha(\alpha > 0)$. Since $g(x)$ is a continuous function, the Box dimension of $g(x)$ is more than one.

4.4. UVF Contained Finite UV Points

The introduction of the unbounded variation points gives a new way to study unbounded variation functions [42]. Many conclusions about unbounded variation functions can be obtained by analyzing the number and location of unbounded variation points. At the same time, if the function has self-similarity, some remarkable conclusions can be strictly demonstrated, such as Corollary 2 and Theorem 8.

Lemma 2. ([24]) *If $F \subset R^n$, then $\dim_P F = \overline{\dim}_{MB} F$.*

Researchers have established the following relation for $F \subset R^n$:

$$\dim_H F \leq \underline{\dim}_{MB} F \leq \overline{\dim}_{MB} F = \dim_P F \leq \overline{\dim}_B F.$$

Theorem 5. *If $f(x)$ is a continuous function on I and $(1,0)$ is the only UV point of $f(x)$, then*

$$\dim_H G(f,I) = \dim_P G(f,I) = \dim_{MB} G(f,I) = 1.$$

Proof of Theorem 5. Since $f(x)$ is a continuous function on I,

$$1 \leq \dim_H G(f,I) \leq \underline{\dim}_B G(f,I).$$

$\forall\, \delta > 0, I = (\bigcup_{i=1}^{\infty} E_i) \bigcup [1-\delta, 1]$, where E_i are subsets of I.

$$\dim_H G(f,[1-\delta,1]) \leq \overline{\dim}_B G(f,[1-\delta,1]) \leq \overline{\lim_{\delta \to 0}} \frac{\log \frac{M}{\delta}}{-\log \delta} = 1,$$

where M is a positive constant.

$$\overline{\dim}_{MB} G(f,I) = \inf\{\sup_{\delta} \overline{\dim}_B G(f,(\bigcup_{i=1}^{\infty} E_i) \bigcup [1-\delta,1])\} = 1.$$

Thus,

$$1 \leq \dim_H G(f,I) \leq \overline{\dim}_{MB} G(f,I) = 1.$$

It is already becoming apparent that

$$\dim_H G(f,I) = \dim_P G(f,I) = \dim_{MB} G(f,I) = 1.$$

□

Theorem 6. *If $f(x)$ is a continuous function containing at most finite UV points on I, then*

$$\dim_H G(f,I) = \dim_P G(f,I) = \dim_{MB} G(f,I) = 1.$$

Proof of Theorem 6. Let $x_1 < x_2 < \cdots < x_n$ be UV points of $f(x)$, n disjoint intervals $[a_i, x_i] \subset I$ can be found, where $i = 1, 2, \cdots, n$. Denote $A = \bigcup_{i=1}^{n} [a_i, x_i]$. By Lemma 2,

$$\dim_H G(f,[a_i,x_i]) = \dim_P G(f,[a_i,x_i]) = \dim_{MB} G(f,[a_i,x_i]) = 1.$$

Since the Hausdorff dimension has the property of countable stability,

$$\begin{aligned} \dim_H G(f,I) &= \dim_H G(f, A \bigcup (I \backslash A)) \\ &= \max\{\dim_H G(f,A), \dim_H G(f, I\backslash A)\} \\ &= 1. \end{aligned}$$

Given $\varepsilon = \min_{1 \leq i < j \leq n} |x_i - x_j|$, $C_i = [a_i - \frac{\varepsilon}{2}, a_i + \frac{\varepsilon}{2}]$, $C_{n+1} = I \setminus (\bigcup_{i=1}^{n} C_i)$.

$$\overline{\dim}_B G(f, C_i) = 1,$$

where $i = 1, 2, \cdots, n+1$. Combining the definition of the modified Box-counting dimension,

$$\overline{\dim}_{MB} G(f,I) = \inf\{\sup_i \overline{\dim}_B C_i : I \subset \bigcup_{i=1}^{n+1} C_i\} = 1.$$

It is easy to check that

$$\dim_H G(f,I) = \dim_P G(f,I) = \dim_{MB} G(f,I) = 1.$$

□

Corollary 2. *If a continuous function $f(x)$ has the property of self-similar on I and $(1,0)$ is the only UV point of, then*

$$\dim_H G(f,I) = \dim_B G(f,I) = 1.$$

Proof of Corollary 2. Since $f(x)$ is self-similar on I, $G(f,I)$ is compact and

$$\overline{\dim}_B(G(f,I)\bigcap V) = \overline{\dim}_B G(f,I)$$

for all open sets V those intersect $G(f,I)$ and $\overline{\dim}_B G(f,I) = \overline{\dim}_{MB} G(f,I)$. Thus,

$$\dim_H G(f,I) = \dim_P G(f,I) = \dim_{MB} G(f,I) = \dim_B G(f,I) = 1.$$

□

4.5. UVF Contained Infinite UV Points

Theorem 7. *Let $f(x)$ be a continuous function on I. $f(x)$ has infinite and countable UV points and only one accumulation point, then*

$$\dim_H G(f,I) = 1.$$

Proof of Theorem 7. Since $f(x)$ is a continuous function on I,

$$1 \le \dim_H G(f,I) \le \underline{\dim}_B G(f,I).$$

(1) $(0,0)$ is an accumulation point: denote the above countable UV points as

$$x_1 > x_2 > x_3 > \cdots > x_n > \cdots.$$

$\forall\delta > 0$, $\dim_H G(f,[0,\delta]) = 1$, there is not an accumulation point in other positions, Thus, there exists $E_i \subset I$ and E_i only contains one UV point x_i, $E_i \bigcap E_j = \varnothing$ when $i \neq j$. $f(x)$ only has an UV point on E_i and

$$\dim_H G(f,E_i) = 1.$$

Denote $E = \bigcup\limits_{i=1}^{\infty} E_i$. By the countable stability of the Hausdorff dimension,

$$\begin{aligned}\dim_H G(f,I) &= \dim_H(G(f,E)\bigcup G(f,[0,\delta])) \\ &= \sup\{\dim_H G(f,E), \dim_H G(f,[0,\delta])\} = 1.\end{aligned}$$

Thus,

$$\dim_H G(f,I) = 1.$$

(2) $(1,0)$ is an accumulation point: denote the above countable UV points as

$$x_1 < x_2 < x_3 < \cdots < x_n < \cdots.$$

$\forall\,\delta > 0$, $\dim_H G(f,[1-\delta,1]) = 1$, there is not an accumulation point in other points. There exists $E_i \subset I$ and E_i only contains one UV point x_i, $E_i \bigcap E_j = \varnothing$ when $i \neq j$. $f(x)$ only has an UV point on E_i and

$$\dim_H G(f,E_i) = 1.$$

Denote $E = \bigcup\limits_{i=1}^{\infty} E_i$.

$$\begin{aligned}\dim_H G(f,I) &= \dim_H(G(f,E)\bigcup G(f,[0,\delta])) \\ &= \sup\{\dim_H G(f,E), \dim_H G(f,[0,\delta])\} = 1.\end{aligned}$$

Thus

$$\dim_H G(f,I) = 1.$$

(3) $x_n \in (0,1), (x_n, 0)$ is an accumulation point: $\forall\, \delta > 0, \dim_H G(f, [x_n - \delta, x_n + \delta]) = 1$.
By the above discussions,

$$\dim_H G(f, I) = 1.$$

□

Theorem 8. *Let $f(x)$ be a continuous function containing countable UV points and $f(x)$ only have an accumulation point on I. If $f(x)$ is self-similar, then*

$$\dim_H G(f, I) = \dim_B G(f, I) = 1.$$

Proof. Since $f(x)$ is a continuous function on I,

$$1 \le \dim_H G(f, I) \le \underline{\dim}_B G(f, I).$$

Denote the above uncountable UV points as $x_1, x_2, x_3, \cdots$. There exists $[a_i, x_i]$ and $[a_i, x_i] \bigcap [a_j, x_j] = \emptyset$ when $i \neq j$. Thus, $f(x)$ only have an UV point on $[a_i, x_i]$ and

$$\dim_B G(f, [a_i, x_i]) = 1.$$

Thus,

$$\overline{\dim}_{MB} G(f, E) = \inf\{\sup_i \overline{\dim}_B G(f, [a_i, x_i]) : E = \bigcup_{i=1}^{N-1} [a_i, x_i]\} = 1.$$

Denote $E = \bigcup_{i=1}^{N-1} [a_i, x_i]$, $F = [a_N, 1]$ and $H = \bigcup_{i=1}^{N-1} [x_i, a_{i+1}]$ where $a_1 = 0$. Further inferences show that $f(x)$ is a BVF on H and

$$\dim_H G(f, H) = \dim_B G(f, H) = 1.$$

It can be seen from the similar calculation process that

$$\begin{aligned} \overline{\dim}_{MB} G(f, I) &= \overline{\dim}_{MB} (G(f, E) \bigcup G(f, F) \bigcup G(f, H)) \\ &= \inf\{\sup\{\dim_H G(f, E), \dim_H G(f, F), \dim_H G(f, H)\}\} = 1. \end{aligned}$$

Since $f(x)$ is self-similar on I, $G(f, I)$ is compact and

$$\overline{\dim}_B (G(f, I) \bigcap V) = \overline{\dim}_B G(f, I)$$

for all open sets V that intersect $G(f, I)$. Thus,

$$\overline{\dim}_B G(f, I) = \overline{\dim}_{MB} G(f, I).$$

Notice that the conclusion $\underline{\dim}_B G(f, I) \ge 1$ remains true.

$$\dim_H G(f, I) = \dim_P G(f, I) = \dim_{MB} G(f, I) = \dim_B G(f, I) = 1.$$

□

5. Possible Applications in Reinforcement Learning

Since AlphaGo has shown amazing abilities in Go [43,44], reinforcement learning in machine learning has gradually been paid attention and researched by many scholars [45–48]. The core idea of reinforcement learning is to use the continuous interaction between the agent and the environment to maximize the long-term cumulative return expectation. The agent learns the optimal strategy through the mechanism of trial and error. Taking the expectation of maximizing returns as the goal makes reinforcement learning "foresight", not just focusing on the immediate situation, so the strategies obtained through reinforcement learning are scientific. Since the optimal strategy can be learned by reinforcement learning, Reinforcement learning has become an emerging method of researching decision theory. At the same time, the learning process of the agent in reinforcement learning is dynamic, and the required data is also generated through interaction with the environment, so a large amount of original label data is not required.

With the advent of deep neural networks, deep reinforcement learning can solve many complex problems. The seemingly complex fractal sets also have special regularity (self-similarity). Therefore, can fractals and fractal dimension be used in the learning process of the agent to speed up the learning speed of the agent or improve the search efficiency of algorithms? This section will introduce several possible applications of fractal and fractal dimension in reinforcement learning.

5.1. The Evaluation Model Based on Fractal Dimension

The main basis of the fractal evaluation model is the fractal dimension. Fractal dimension is an important indicator of system stability. The multi-dimensional vector can be formed by utilizing the parameters, such as actions and states of agents. Many multi-dimensional vectors may establish a special set. The fractal dimension of the set can determine the distance between the current state and the equilibrated state. The equilibrium state is that all agents are in a stable state and there is no motivation to change the current strategy. The main operational flows of the fractal evaluation model are as follows.

Step one: data standardization. The number of states and agents are K, N respectively. State $\mathbb{S} = (s_1, s_2, \cdots, s_N, a_1, a_2, \cdots, a_N, r_1, r_2, \cdots, r_N)$. Standardization is to eliminate the differences caused by the species of each data. Standardized data is $\mathbb{S} = (y_{ij})$, $i = 1, 2, \cdots, K \in \mathbb{Z}^+, y = 1, 2, \cdots, 3N \in \mathbb{Z}^+$.

Step two: weight. $w_j = d_j / \sum_{i=1}^{N} d_j$,
where $d_j = \max_{1 \le i,k \le K} \mid y_{ij} - y_{kj} \mid, j = 1, 2, \cdots, N \in \mathbb{Z}^+$.

Step three: calculate $N(r)$. The distance used in the algorithm is unified as Euclidean distance. $3N$ data of each state can be regarded as points on each coordinate axis in the 3n-dimensional space. These points constitute a subset of the $3n$-dimensional Euclidean space E^{3N}. The distance from each point to the origin is d_{ij} and let $R = \max(d_{ij})$, $i = 1, 2, \cdots, K \in \mathbb{Z}^+$, $j = 1, 2, \cdots, 3N \in \mathbb{Z}^+$. For a specific state, $N(r)$ is the number of all points satisfying $d_{ij} < r$ and r is the radius of the hypersphere. Keep adjusting the value of radius r until $r = R$ and $N(r) = N$. When the radius is r, the number of points contained in the hypersphere is $N(r) = \sum_{i=0}^{3N} sgn(r - d_{ij})$ and $sgn(x)$ is a symbolic function,

$$sgn(x) = \begin{cases} 1, & x > 0 \\ 0, & x \le 0 \end{cases}$$

Step four: calculate the fractal dimension. $D = \log N(r) / \log r$.

From the above calculation process, the number of sample points contained in the hypersphere with r will change continuously as the radius alters. At the same time, the graph of the function formed by the above standardized data points is usually non-linear. The fractal dimension D in this step can be fitted by the least square method,

$$D = \frac{3N \sum_{i=1}^{3N} \log N(r_i) \log r_i - \sum_{i=1}^{3N} \log N(r_i) \sum_{i=1}^{3N} \log r_i}{3N \sum_{i=1}^{3N} (\log r_i)^2 - \left(\sum_{i=1}^{3N} \log r_i \right)^2}.$$

At present, most reinforcement learning algorithms are based on global information. However, due to the limitations of communication and observation, the agent cannot obtain all the information in practical. Therefore, the MDP(Markov decision process) model used to solve basic reinforcement learning problems is not applicable. Researchers establish the POMDP(Partially observable markov decision process) model [49,50] to solve partially observable reinforcement learning problems. The main solutions include function approximation, opponent modeling, and graph theory.

Fractal dimension is another new idea to optimize POMDP. The theoretical foundation of using fractal dimension to evaluate stability is mainly based on the Lyapunov stability theory. The larger fractal dimension of the set, the more stable points in the set. Therefore, the set with lager fractal dimension is more stable than the set with small fractal dimension under the same disturbance. The advantage of this method is that the agent does not need to know global information. The strategy selection of agents can be guided by the fractal dimension, and the correct strategy direction can optimize the algorithm. At the same time, for a game where there is no pure strategy Nash equilibrium, it is still possible to compare the distance between any two situations and the equilibrium state by calculating the fractal dimension.

5.2. The Convergence Model Based on Fractal Attractor

At present, the convergence of most reinforcement learning algorithms lacks rigorous proofs. However, due to the powerful fitting ability of multiple neural networks [51–53], the algorithm can converge better in various experimental environments. The convergence obtained in the experiment cannot effectively understand the essence of the problem and optimize the existing algorithm. Obviously, the convergence of an algorithm is the fixed point of a particular function mathematically. Solving the fixed point problem can also be transformed into an attractor in fractal theory. Therefore, the convergence of the algorithm can be verified by calculating the existence of attractors. Surprisingly, the calculation of attractors has theoretical guarantees. Therefore, can the Bellman equation in reinforcement learning be regarded as an iterative function system, and then its solution is the attractor of the iterative function system? The idea of the model is shown in Figure 9.

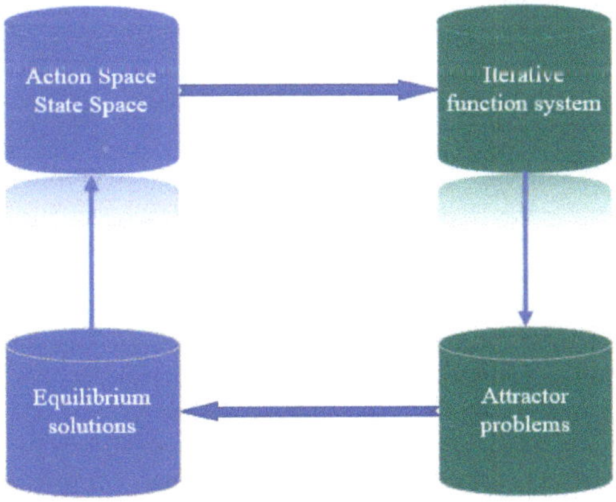

Figure 9. The frame of convergence model.

The advantage of this convergence model lies in its versatility, which can prove the convergence of a class of similar algorithms. The method of theoretical proof is conducive to finding the essence of the problem, so as to provide different ideas for the optimization algorithm.

5.3. The Random Search Algorithm Based on Fractal

Exploration and utilization is one of the important research directions in deep reinforcement learning. The goal of exploration is to find more information about the environment, and the purpose of utilization is to use the known environmental information to maximize rewards. In short, exploration is to try behaviors that have not yet been tried, while utilization is to choose the next action from the knowledge that agents have already mastered. The balance between exploration and utilization is the basic issue of reinforcement learning. In deep reinforcement learning tasks, in order to obtain the best strategy, it is often necessary to collect more information. For solving the problem of exploration and utilization, researchers have proposed many classic methods. The ϵ-greedy method is a commonly used strategy for greedy exploration.

However, the exploratory efficiency of this method is not good. Fractals generally have the following characteristics. One is that both the whole and the part have irregularities, and the other is that the internal structure has self-similarity and unevenness. The search method based on the fractal structure can reduce the search time as much as possible on the basis of ensuring that all spaces are explored. Due to the self-similar structure of the fractal, the algorithm does not always need to repeat the previous training during the training process. Thus the way can reduce a lot of unnecessary training time. Therefore, whether the above-mentioned characteristics of fractal can be used to achieve efficient search is looking forward to follow-up research and discussion. At present, there has been a lot of research on using fractals to improve search efficiency [54–56], but these algorithms can still continue to be optimized.

6. Conclusions

This manuscript systematically sorts out the conclusions about one-dimensional continuous functions. The Box dimension of bounded variation functions and the functions with the Weyl fractional integral are both one. The Box dimension of continuous functions that satisfy the Lipschitz condition is also one. These results also fully show that fractional calculus does not increase the dimensionality of functions. This conclusion seems simple, but no one seems to have carried out a rigorous proof. The structure of unbounded variation function is more complicated. The construction process of several special unbounded variation functions is displayed firstly, and a lot of general conclusions about unbounded variation functions are proved by using UV points. Combined with the self-similarity, the conclusions of the fractal dimension of some special functions are also strictly proved. These conclusions are very helpful for perfecting the theory of unbounded variation. At the same time, in order to increase the practical significance of the above conclusions, some applications of fractal and fractal dimension in reinforcement learning are also introduced. On the one hand, these works can sort out the current results, and on the other hand, some useful ideas and research directions can also be shown to other researchers. The evaluation model based on fractal dimension proposed in this manuscript can effectively accelerate the convergence speed of many reinforcement learning algorithms by using fractal dimension to judge the stability of any state. This model is an important result of the combination of the two theories, and it is believed that more fractal theories will be applied to reinforcement learning.

However, the research on one-dimensional continuous functions is far from over. In particular, what are the necessary and sufficient conditions for the conversion between unbounded variation and bounded variation? Are there other theories and tools that can be used to study one-dimensional continuous functions? Can existing relevant conclusions about one-dimensional continuous functions be extended to multi-dimensional continuous functions? Can the conclusion of the unbounded variation function be used in other fields?

Author Contributions: Conceptualization, W.J., and C.L.; methodology W.J.; Data curation, W.B.; formal analysis, G.H. writing original draft, W.J. and T.W. All authors have read and agreed to the published version of the manuscript.

Funding: Research was funded by National Natural Science Foundation of China (grant number 61806221387 and 12071218).

Institutional Review Board Statement: The study was conducted according to the guidelines of the Declaration of Helsinki, and approved by the Institutional Review Board.

Informed Consent Statement: Informed consent was obtained from all subjects involved in the study.

Data Availability Statement: Not applicable.

Acknowledgments: Research is supported by National Natural Science Foundation of China (61806221 and 12071218).

Conflicts of Interest: The authors declare no conflict of interest.

References

1. Srivastava, H.M.; Kashuri, A.; Mohammed, P.O.; Nonlaopon, K. Certain inequalities pertaining to some new generalized fractional integral operators. *Fractal Fract.* **2021**, *5*, 160. [CrossRef]
2. Khan, M.B.; Noor, M.A.; Abdeljawad, T.; Mousa, A.A.A.; Abdalla, B.; Alghamdi, S.M. LR-preinvex interval-valued functions and Riemann–Liouville fractional integral inequalities. *Fractal Fract.* **2021**, *5*, 243. [CrossRef]
3. Machado, J.T.; Mainardi, F.; Kiryakova, V. Fractional calculus: Quo vadimus? (Where are we going?). *Fract. Calc. Appl. Anal.* **2015**, *18*, 495–526. [CrossRef]
4. Butera, S.; Paola, M.D. A physically based connection between fractional calculus and fractal geometry. *Ann. Phys.* **2014**, *350*, 146–158. [CrossRef]
5. Kolwankar, K.M.; Gangal, A.D. Fractional differentiability of nowhere differentiable functions and dimensions. *Chaos Solitons Fractals* **1996**, *6*, 505–513. [CrossRef]
6. Kolwankar, K.M.; Gangal, A.D. Hölder exponent of irregular signals and local fractional derivatives. *Pramana J. Phys.* **1997**, *48*, 49–68. [CrossRef]
7. Nigmatullin, R.R.; Baleanu, D. Relationships between 1*D* and space fractals and fractional integrals and their applications in physics. In *Applications in Physics, Part A*; De Gruyter: Berlin, Germany, 2019; Volume 4, pp. 183–220 .
8. Tatom, F.B. The relationship between fractional calculus and fractals. *Fractals* **1995**, *3*, 217–229. [CrossRef]
9. Zähle, M.; Ziezold, H. Fractional derivatives of weierstrass-type functions. *J. Comput. Appl. Math.* **1996**, *76*, 265–275. [CrossRef]
10. Liang, Y.S. The relationship between the Box dimension of the Besicovitch functions and the orders of their fractional calculus. *Appl. Math. Comput.* **2008**, *200*, 197–207. [CrossRef]
11. Ruan, H.J.; Su, W.Y.; Yao, K. Box dimension and fractional integral of linear fractal interpolation functions. *J. Approx. Theory* **2009**, *161*, 187–197. [CrossRef]
12. Liang, Y.S. Box dimensions of Riemann-Liouville fractional integrals of continuous functions of bounded variation. *Nonlinear Anal.* **2010**, *72*, 4304–4306. [CrossRef]
13. Liang, Y.S. Fractal dimension of Riemann-Liouville fractional integral of 1-dimensional continuous functions. *Fract. Calc. Appl. Anal.* **2018**, *21*, 1651–1658. [CrossRef]
14. Wu, J.R. On a linearity between fractal dimensions and order of fractional calculus in Hölder space. *Appl. Math. Comput.* **2020**, *385*, 125433. [CrossRef]
15. Verma, S.; Viswanathan, P. A note on Katugampola fractional calculus and fractal dimensions. *Appl. Math. Comput.* **2018**, *339*, 220–230. [CrossRef]
16. Verma, S.; Viswanathan, P. Bivariate functions of bounded variation: Fractal dimension and fractional integral. *Indag. Math.* **2020**, *31*, 294–309. [CrossRef]
17. Bush, K.A. Continuous functions without derivatives. *Am. Math. Mon.* **1952**, *59*, 222–225. [CrossRef]
18. Shen, W.X. Hausdorff dimension of the graphs of the classical Weierstrass functions. *Math. Z.* **2018**, *289*, 223–266. [CrossRef]
19. Su, W.Y. Construction of fractal calculus. *Sci. China Math. Chin. Ser.* **2015**, *45*, 1587–1598. [CrossRef]
20. Xie, T.F.; Zhou, S.P. On a class of fractal functions with graph box dimension 2. *Chaos Solitons Fractals* **2004**, *22*, 135–139. [CrossRef]
21. Liang, Y.S.; Su, W.Y. Von Koch curves and their fractional calculus. *Acta Math. Sin. Chin. Ser.* **2011**, *54*, 227–240.
22. Wang, J.; Yao, K. Construction and analysis of a special one-dimensional continuous functions. *Fractals* **2017**, *25*, 1750020. [CrossRef]
23. Wang, J.; Yao, K.; Liang, Y.S. On the connection between the order of Riemann-Liouvile fractional falculus and Hausdorff dimension of a fractal function. *Anal. Theory Appl.* **2016**, *32*, 283–290. [CrossRef]
24. Falconer, K.J. *Fractal Geometry: Mathematical Foundations and Applications*; John Wiley Sons Inc.: Chicheste, PA , USA, **1990**.
25. Wen, Z.Y. *Mathematical Foundations of Fractal Geometry*; Science Technology Education Publication House: Shanghai, China, 2000. (In Chinese)
26. Hu, T.Y.; Lau, K.S. Fractal dimensions and singularities of the weierstrass type functions. *Trans. Am. Math. Soc.* **1993**, *335*, 649–665. [CrossRef]
27. Zheng, W.X.; Wang, S.W. *Real Function and Functional Analysis*; High Education Publication House: Beijing, China, 1980. (In Chinese)
28. Tian, L. The estimates of Hölder index and the Box dimension for the Hadamard fractional integral. *Fractals* **2021**, *29*, 2150072. [CrossRef]
29. Wang, C.Y. R-L Algorithm: An approximation algorithm for fractal signals based on fractional calculus. *Fractals* **2020**, *24*, 2150243. [CrossRef]

30. Oldham, K.B.; Spanier, J. *The Fractional Calculus*; Academic Press: New York, NY, USA, 1974.
31. Teodoro, G.S.; Machado, J.A.; Oliveira, E.C. A review of definitions of fractional derivatives and other operators. *J. Comput. Phys.* **2019**, *388*, 195–208. [CrossRef]
32. Kiryakova, V.S. *Generalized Fractional Calculus and Applications*; CRC Press: Boca Raton, FL, USA, 1993.
33. Miller, K.S.; Ross, B. *An Introduction to the Fractional Calculus and Fractional Differential Equations*; John Wiley Sons Inc.: New York, NY, USA, 1976.
34. Podlubny, I. Geometric and physical interpretation of fractional integration and fractional differentiation. *Fract. Calc. Appl. Anal.* **2002**, *5*, 367–386.
35. Mu, L.; Yao, K.; Wang, J. Box dimension of weyl fractional integral of continuous functions with bounded variation. *Anal. Theory Appl.* **2016**, *32*, 174–180. [CrossRef]
36. Kilbas, A.A.; Titioura, A.A. Nonlinear differential equations with marchaud-hadamard-type fractional derivative in the weighted sapce of summable functions. *Math. Model. Anal.* **2007**, *12*, 343–356. [CrossRef]
37. Tian, L. Hölder continuity and box dimension for the Weyl fractional integral. *Fractals* **2020**, *28*, 2050032. [CrossRef]
38. Yao, K.; Liang, Y.S.; Su, W.Y.; Yao, Z.Q. Fractal dimension of fractional derivative of self-affine functions. *Acta Math. Sin. Chin. Ser.* **2013**, *56*, 693–698.
39. Xu, Q. Fractional integrals and derivatives to a class of functions. *J. Xuzhou Norm. Univ.* **2006**, *24*, 19–23.
40. Stein, E.M. *Singular Integrals and Differentiability Properties of Functions*; Princeton University Press: Princeton, NJ, USA , 1970.
41. Liang, Y.S.; Su, W.Y. Fractal dimensions of fractional integral of continuous functions. *Acta Math. Sin.* **2016**, 32, 1494–1508. [CrossRef]
42. Liang, Y.S.; Zhang, Q. 1-dimensional continuous functions with uncountable unbounded variation points. *Chin. J. Comtemporary Math.* **2018**, *39*, 129–136.
43. Silver, D.; Schrittwieser, J.; Simonyan, K.; Antonoglou, I.; Huang, A.; Guez, A.; Hubert, T.; Baker, L.; Lai, M.; Bolton, A.; et al. Mastering the game of go without human knowledge. *Nature* **2017**, *550*, 354–359. [CrossRef]
44. Magnani, L. *AlphaGo, Locked Strategies, and Eco-Cognitive Openness*; Eco-Cognitive Computationalism Springer: Cham, Switzerland, 2021; pp. 45–71.
45. Liu, S.; Pan, Z.; Cheng, X. A novel fast fractal image compression method based on distance clustering in high dimensional sphere surface. *Fractals* **2017**, 25, 1740004. [CrossRef]
46. Li, S.; Wu, Y.; Cui, X.; Dong, H.; Fang, F.; Russell, S. Robust multi-agent reinforcement learning via minimax deep deterministic policy gradient. *Proc. Aaai Conf. Artif. Intell.* **2019**, *33*, 4213–4220. [CrossRef]
47. Li, G.; Jiang, B.; Zhu, H.; Che, Z.; Liu, Y. Generative attention networks for multi-agent behavioral modeling. *Proc. Aaai Conf. Artif. Intell.* **2020**, *34*, 7195–7202. [CrossRef]
48. Liu, S.; Wang, S.; Liu, X.Y.; Gandomi, A.H.; Daneshmand, M.; Muhammad, K.; de Albuquerque, V.H.C. Human Memory Update Strategy: A multi-layer template update mechanism for remote visual monitoring. *IEEE Trans. Multimed.* **2021**, *23*, 2188–2198. [CrossRef]
49. Hoerger, M.; Kurniawati, H. An on-line POMDP solver for continuous observation spaces. In Proceedings of the 2021 IEEE International Conference on Robotics and Automation (ICRA), Xi'an, China, 30 May–5 June 2021; pp. 7643–7649.
50. Igl, M.; Zintgraf, L.; Le, T.A.; Wood, F.; Whiteson, S. Deep variational reinforcement learning for POMDPs. *Int. Conf. Mach. Learn.* **2018**, *16*, 2117–2126.
51. Zhou, Z H. Neural Networks . In *Machine Learning*; Springer: Singapore, 2021.
52. Yang, L.; Zhang, R.Y.; Li, L.; Xie, X. Simam: A simple parameter-free attention module for convolutional neural networks. *Int. Conf. Mach. Learn.* **2021**, *26*, 11863–11874.
53. Almatroud, A.O. Extreme multistability of a fractional-order discrete-time neural network. *Fractal Fract.* **2021**, *5*, 202. [CrossRef]
54. Alomoush, M.I. Optimal combined heat and power economic dispatch using stochastic fractal search algorithm. *J. Mod. Power Syst. Clean Energy* **2020**, *8*, 276–286. [CrossRef]
55. Tran, T.T.; Truong, K.H. Stochastic fractal search algorithm for reconfiguration of distribution networks with distributed generations. *Ain Shams Eng. J.* **2020**, *11*, 389–407. [CrossRef]
56. Pham, L.H.; Duong, M.Q.; Phan, V.D.; Nguyen, T.T.; Nguyen, H.N. A high-performance stochastic fractal search algorithm for optimal generation dispatch problem. *Energies* **2019**, *12*, 1796. [CrossRef]

fractal and fractional MDPI

Article

On Transformation Involving Basic Analogue to the Aleph-Function of Two Variables

Dinesh Kumar [1,*], Dumitru Baleanu [2,3], Frédéric Ayant [4,5] and Norbert Südland [6]

1 Department of Applied Sciences, College of Agriculture-Jodhpur, Agriculture University Jodhpur, Jodhpur 342304, India
2 Department of Mathematics, Cankaya University, Ankara 06530, Turkey; dumitru@cankaya.edu.tr
3 Institute of Space Sciences, 077125 Magurele-Bucharest, Romania
4 Collége Jean L'herminier, Allée des Nymphéas, 83500 La Seyne-sur-Mer, France; fredericayant@gmail.com
5 Department VAR, Avenue Joseph Raynaud Le parc Fleuri, 83140 Six-Fours-les-Plages, France
6 Aage GmbH, Röntgenstraße 24, 73431 Aalen, Baden-Württemberg, Germany; norbert.suedland@aage-leichtbauteile.de
* Correspondence: dinesh_dino03@yahoo.com

Abstract: In our work, we derived the fractional order q-integrals and q-derivatives concerning a basic analogue to the Aleph-function of two variables (AFTV). We discussed a related application and the q-extension of the corresponding Leibniz rule. Finally, we presented two corollaries concerning the basic analogue to the I-function of two variables and the basic analogue to the Aleph-function of one variable.

Keywords: Fractional q-integral; q-derivative operators; basic analogue to the Aleph-function; basic analogue to the I-function; q-Leibniz rule

Citation: Kumar, D.; Baleanu, D.; Ayant, F.; Südland, N. On Transformation Involving Basic Analogue to the Aleph-Function of Two Variables. *Fractal Fract.* **2022**, *6*, 71. https://doi.org/10.3390/fractalfract6020071

Academic Editors: António M. Lopes, Alireza Alfi, Liping Chen and Sergio A. David

Received: 12 December 2021
Accepted: 19 January 2022
Published: 28 January 2022

1. Introduction

Fractional calculus represents an important part of mathematical analysis. The concept of fractional calculus was born from a famous correspondence between L'Hopital and Leibniz in 1695. In the last four decades, it has gained significant recognition and found many applications in diverse research fields (see [1–6]). The fractional basic (or $q-$) calculus is the extension of the ordinary fractional calculus in the q-theory (see [7–10]). We recall that basic series and basic polynomials, particularly the basic (or $q-$) hypergeometric functions and basic (or $q-$) hypergeometric polynomials, are particularly applicable in several fields, e.g., Finite Vector Spaces, Lie Theory, Combinatorial Analysis, Particle Physics, Mechanical Engineering, Theory of Heat Conduction, Non-Linear Electric Circuit Theory, Cosmology, Quantum Mechanics, and Statistics. In 1952, Al-Salam introduced the q-analogue to Cauchy's formula [11] (see also [12]). Agarwal [13] studied certain fractional q-integral and q-derivative operators. In addition, various researchers reported image formulas of various q-special functions under fractional q-calculus operators, for example, Kumar et al. [14], Sahni et al. [15], Yadav and Purohit [16], Yadav et al. [17,18], and maybe more. The q-extensions of the Saigo's fractional integral operators were defined by Purohit and Yadav [19]. Several authors utilised such operators to evaluate a general class of q-polynomials, the basic analogue to Fox's H-function, basic analogue to the I-function, fractional q-calculus formulas for various special functions, etc. The readers can see more related new details in [16–18,20] on fractional q-calculus.

The purpose of the present manuscript is to discuss expansion formulas, involving the basic analogue to AFTV [21]. The q-Leibniz formula is also provided.

We recall that q-shifted factorial $(a;q)_n$ has the following form [22,23]

$$(a;q)_n = \begin{cases} 1, & (n=0) \\ \prod_{i=0}^{n-1}(1-aq^i), & (n \in \mathbb{N}\cup\{\infty\}) \end{cases}, \tag{1}$$

such that $a, q \in \mathbb{C}$ and it is assumed that $a \neq q^{-m}$ $(m \in \mathbb{N}_0)$.

The expression of the q-shifted factorial for negative subscript is written by

$$(a;q)_{-n} = \frac{1}{(1-aq^{-1})(1-aq^{-2})\cdots(1-aq^{-n})} \quad (n \in \mathbb{N}_0). \tag{2}$$

Additionally, we have

$$(a;q)_\infty = \prod_{i=0}^{\infty}\left(1-aq^i\right) \quad (a,q \in \mathbb{C};\ |q|<1). \tag{3}$$

Using (1)–(3), we conclude that

$$(a;q)_n = \frac{(a;q)_\infty}{(aq^n;q)_\infty} \qquad (n \in \mathbb{Z}), \tag{4}$$

its extension to $n = \alpha \in \mathbb{C}$ as:

$$(a;q)_\alpha = \frac{(a;q)_\infty}{(aq^\alpha;q)_\infty} \qquad (\alpha \in \mathbb{C};\ |q|<1), \tag{5}$$

such that the principal value of q^α is considered.

We equivalently have a form of (1), given as

$$(a;q)_n = \frac{\Gamma_q(a+n)(1-q)^n}{\Gamma_q(a)} \qquad (a \neq 0,-1,-2,\cdots), \tag{6}$$

where the q-gamma function is expressed as [8]:

$$\Gamma_q(a) = \frac{(q;q)_\infty}{(q^a;q)_\infty(1-q)^{a-1}} = \frac{(q;q)_{a-1}}{(1-q)^{a-1}}, \ (a \neq 0,-1,-2,\cdots). \tag{7}$$

The expression of the q-analogue to the Riemann–Liouville fractional integral operator (RLI) of $f(x)$ has the following expression [12]:

$$I_q^\mu\{f(x)\} = \frac{1}{\Gamma_q(\mu)}\int_0^x (x-tq)_{\mu-1} f(t)\,\mathrm{d}_q t, \tag{8}$$

here, $\Re(\mu) > 0,\ |q| < 1$ and

$$[x-y]_v = x^v \prod_{n=0}^{\infty}\left[\frac{1-(y/x)q^n}{1-(y/x)q^{n+v}}\right] = x^v\left(\frac{y}{x};q\right)_v \quad (x \neq 0). \tag{9}$$

The basic integral [8] is given by

$$\int_0^x f(t)\mathrm{d}_q t = x(1-q)\sum_{k=0}^{\infty} q^k f\left(xq^k\right). \tag{10}$$

Equation (8), in conjunction with (10); then, we have the series representation of (RLI), as follows

$$I_q^\mu f(x) = \frac{x^\mu(1-q)}{\Gamma_q(\mu)}\sum_{k=0}^{\infty} q^k\left[1-q^{k+1}\right]_{\mu-1} f\left(xq^k\right). \tag{11}$$

We mention that for $f(x) = x^{\lambda-1}$, the following can be written [16]

$$I_q^\mu\left(x^{\lambda-1}\right) = \frac{\Gamma_q(\lambda)}{\Gamma_q(\lambda+\mu)}x^{\lambda+\mu-1} \quad (\Re(\lambda+\mu)>0). \tag{12}$$

2. Basic Analogue to Aleph-Function of Two Variables

We recall that AFTV [21] is an extension of the I-function possessing two variables [24]. Here, in the present article, we define a basic analogue to AFTV.

We record

$$G(q^a) = \left[\prod_{n=0}^{\infty}(1 - q^{a+n})\right]^{-1} = \frac{1}{(q^a;q)_\infty}. \tag{13}$$

Next, we have

$$\begin{aligned}
&\aleph(z_1, z_2; q) \\
&= \aleph^{0,n_1;m_2,n_2:m_3,n_3}_{P_i,Q_i,\tau_i;r;P_{i'},Q_{i'},\tau_{i'};r';P_{i''},Q_{i''},\tau_{i''};r''}\left(\begin{array}{c} z_1 \\ ;q \\ z_2 \end{array}\middle| \begin{array}{c} (a_j;\alpha_j,A_j)_{1,n_1}, [\tau_i(a_{ji};\alpha_{ji},A_{ji})]_{n_1+1,P_i}; \\ \\ [\tau_i(b_{ji};\beta_{ji},B_{ji})]_{1,Q_i}; \end{array}\right. \\
&\quad \left.\begin{array}{c} (c_j,\gamma_j)_{1,n_2}, \left[\tau_{i'}\left(c_{ji'},\gamma_{ji'}\right)\right]_{n_2+1,P_{i'}}; (e_j,E_j)_{1,n_3}, \left[\tau_{i''}\left(e_{ji''},\gamma_{ji''}\right)\right]_{n_3+1,P_{i''}} \\ \\ (d_j,\delta_j)_{1,m_2}, \left[\tau_{i'}\left(d_{ji'},\delta_{ji'}\right)\right]_{m_2+1,Q_{i'}}; (f_j,F_j)_{1,m_3}, \left[\tau_{i''}\left(f_{ji''},F_{ji''}\right)\right]_{m_3+1,Q_{i''}} \end{array}\right) \\
&= \frac{1}{(2\pi\omega)^2}\int_{L_1}\int_{L_2}\pi^2\phi(s_1,s_2;q)z_1^{s_1}z_2^{s_2}\,d_qs_1\,d_qs_2,
\end{aligned} \tag{14}$$

where $\omega = \sqrt{-1}$, and

$$\begin{aligned}
\phi(s_1,s_2;q) &= \frac{\prod_{j=1}^{n_1} G\left(q^{1-a_j+\alpha_j s_1+A_j s_2}\right)}{\sum_{i=1}^{r}\tau_i\left\{\prod_{j=1}^{Q_i} G\left(q^{1-b_{ji}+\beta_{ji}s_1+B_{ji}s_2}\right)\prod_{j=n_1+1}^{P_i} G\left(q^{a_{ji}-\alpha_{ji}s_1-A_{ji}s_2}\right)\right\}} \\
&\times \frac{\prod_{j=1}^{m_2} G\left(q^{d_j-\delta_j s_1}\right)\prod_{j=1}^{n_2} G\left(q^{1-c_j+\gamma_j s_1}\right)}{\sum_{i'=1}^{r'}\tau_{i'}\left\{\prod_{j=m_2+1}^{Q_{i'}} G\left(q^{1-d_{ji'}+\delta_{ji'}s_1}\right)\prod_{j=n_2+1}^{P_{i'}} G\left(q^{c_{ji'}-\gamma_{ji'}s_1}\right)\right\}G(q^{1-s_1})\sin\pi s_1} \\
&\times \frac{\prod_{j=1}^{m_3} G\left(q^{f_j-F_j s_2}\right)\prod_{j=1}^{n_3} G\left(q^{1-e_j+E_j s_2}\right)}{\sum_{i''=1}^{r''}\tau_{i''}\left\{\prod_{j=m_3+1}^{Q_{i''}} G\left(q^{1-f_{ji''}+F_{ji''}s_2}\right)\prod_{j=n_3+1}^{P_{i''}} G\left(q^{e_{ji''}-E_{ji''}s_2}\right)\right\}G(q^{1-s_2})\sin\pi s_2},
\end{aligned} \tag{15}$$

where $z_1, z_2 \neq 0$ and are real or complex. An empty product is elucidated as unity, and $P_i, P_{i'}, P_{i''}, Q_i, Q_{i'}, Q_{i''}, m_1, m_2, m_3, n_1, n_2, n_3$ are non-negative integers, such that $Q_i, Q_{i'}, Q_{i''} > 0$; $\tau_i, \tau_{i'}, \tau_{i''} > 0 (i = 1, \cdots, r;\ i' = 1, \cdots, r';\ i'' = 1, \cdots, r'')$. All the As, αs, γs, δs, Es, and Fs are presumed to be positive quantities for standardization intention, the as, bs, cs, ds, es, and fs are complex numbers. The definition of a basic analogue to AFTV will, however, make sense, even if some of these quantities are equal to zero. The contour L_1 is in the s_1-plane and goes from $-\omega\infty$ to $+\omega\infty$, with loops where necessary, to make sure that the poles of $G\left(q^{d_j-\delta_j s_1}\right)$ $(j = 1, \cdots, m_2)$ are to the right-hand side and all the poles of $G\left(q^{1-a_j+\alpha_j s_1+A_j s_2}\right)$ $(j = 1, \cdots, n_1)$, $G\left(q^{1-c_j+\gamma s_1}\right)$ $(j = 1, \cdots, n_2)$ lie to the left-hand side of L_1. The contour L_2 is in the s_2-plane and goes from $-\omega\infty$ to $+\omega\infty$, with loops where necessary, to ensure that the poles of $G\left(q^{f_j-F_j s_2}\right)$ $(j = 1, \cdots, m_3)$ are to the right-hand side and all the poles of $G\left(q^{1-a_j+\alpha_j s_1+A_j s_2}\right)$ $(j = 1, \cdots, n_1)$, $G\left(q^{1-e_j+E_j s_2}\right)$ $(j = 1, \cdots, n_2)$ lie to the left-hand side of L_2. For values of $|s_1|$ and $|s_2|$, the integrals converge, if $\Re(s_1\log(z_1) - \log\sin\pi s_1) < 0$ and $\Re(s_2\log(z_2) - \log\sin\pi s_2) < 0$.

3. Main Formulas

Here, we obtain fractional q-integral and q-derivative formulas concerning the basic analogue to AFTV. Here, we have the following notations:

$$A_1 = \left(a_j;\alpha_j, A_j\right)_{1,n_1}, \left[\tau_i\left(a_{ji};\alpha_{ji}, A_{ji}\right)\right]_{n_1+1,P_i}; \; B_1 = \left[\tau_i\left(b_{ji};\beta_{ji}, B_{ji}\right)\right]_{1,Q_i}. \tag{16}$$

$$C_1 = \left(c_j,\gamma_j\right)_{1,n_2}, \left[\tau_{i'}\left(c_{ji'},\gamma_{ji'}\right)\right]_{n_2+1,P_{i'}}; \left(e_j, E_j\right)_{1,n_3}, \left[\tau_{i''}\left(e_{ji''},\gamma_{ji''}\right)\right]_{n_3+1,P_{i''}}. \tag{17}$$

$$D_1 = \left(d_j,\delta_j\right)_{1,m_2}, \left[\tau_{i'}\left(d_{ji'},\delta_{ji'}\right)\right]_{m_2+1,Q_{i'}}; \left(f_j, F_j\right)_{1,m_3}, \left[\tau_{i''}\left(f_{ji''},F_{ji''}\right)\right]_{m_3+1,Q_{i''}}. \tag{18}$$

Theorem 1. *Let $\Re(\mu) > 0$, $\rho_i \in \mathbb{Z}^+$ $(i=1,2)$, and $|q| < 1$; then, the Riemann–Liouville fractional q-integral of* (14) *exists and is given as*

$$I_q^{\mu}\left\{x^{\lambda-1}\aleph^{0,n_1;m_2,n_2:m_3,n_3}_{P_i,Q_i,\tau_i;r;P_{i'},Q_{i'},\tau_{i'};r';P_{i''},Q_{i''},\tau_{i''};r''}\left(\begin{matrix} z_1x^{\rho_1} \\ \\ z_2x^{\rho_2}\end{matrix} ; q \left| \begin{matrix} A_1;C_1 \\ \\ B_1;D_1\end{matrix}\right.\right)\right\} = (1-q)^{\mu}x^{\lambda+\mu-1}$$
$$\times \aleph^{0,n_1+1;m_2,n_2:m_3,n_3}_{P_i+1,Q_i+1,\tau_i;r;P_{i'},Q_{i'},\tau_{i'};r';P_{i''},Q_{i''},\tau_{i''};r''}\left(\begin{matrix} z_1x^{\rho_1} \\ \\ z_2x^{\rho_2}\end{matrix} ; q \left| \begin{matrix} (1-\lambda;\rho_1,\rho_2), A_1;C_1 \\ \\ B_1,(1-\lambda-\mu;\rho_1,\rho_2);D_1\end{matrix}\right.\right), \tag{19}$$

where $\Re(s_i \log(z_i) - \log\sin \pi s_i) < 0$ $(i=1,2)$.

Proof. We apply the definitions (8) and (14) in the left-hand side of (19), we have (say $\mathcal{I}$)

$$\mathcal{I} = \frac{1}{\Gamma_q(\alpha)}\int_0^x (x-yq)_{\alpha-1}\left\{y^{\lambda-1}\frac{1}{(2\pi\omega)^2}\int_{L_1}\int_{L_2}\pi^2\phi(s_1,s_2;q)\prod_{i=1}^{2}(z_iy^{\rho_i})^{s_i}\mathrm{d}_qs_1\mathrm{d}_qs_2\right\}\mathrm{d}_qy. \tag{20}$$

By using standard calculations, we arrive at

$$\mathcal{I} = \frac{y^{\lambda-1}}{\Gamma_q(\alpha)}\frac{1}{(2\pi\omega)^2}$$
$$\times \int_{L_1}\int_{L_2}\pi^2\phi(s_1,s_2;q)\prod_{i=1}^{2}z_i^{s_i}\left\{\int_0^x (x-yq)_{\alpha-1}y^{\lambda+\sum_{i=1}^{2}\rho_is_i-1}\mathrm{d}_qy\right\}\mathrm{d}_qs_1\,\mathrm{d}_qs_2$$
$$= \frac{1}{(2\pi\omega)^2}\int_{L_1}\int_{L_2}\pi^2\phi(s_1,s_2;q)\prod_{i=1}^{2}z_i^{s_i}I_q^{\mu}\left\{x^{\lambda+\sum_{i=1}^{2}\rho_is_i-1}\right\}\mathrm{d}_qs_1\,\mathrm{d}_qs_2. \tag{21}$$

Next, we apply formula (12) to the equation above; then, we get

$$\mathcal{I} = \frac{1}{(2\pi\omega)^2}\int_{L_1}\int_{L_2}\pi^2\phi(s_1,s_2;q)\prod_{i=1}^{2}z_i^{s_i}\frac{\Gamma_q\left(\lambda+\sum_{i=1}^{2}\rho_is_i\right)}{\Gamma_q\left(\lambda+\mu+\sum_{i=1}^{2}\rho_is_i\right)}x^{\lambda+\mu+\sum_{i=1}^{2}\rho_is_i-1}\mathrm{d}_qs_1\mathrm{d}_qs_2. \tag{22}$$

Considering the above q-Mellin–Barnes double contour integrals in terms of the basic analogue to AFTV, we obtain (19). □

If we use a fractional q-derivative operator without initial values, defined as

$$I_q^{-\mu}\{f(x)\} = D^{\mu}_{x,q}\{f(x)\} = \frac{1}{\Gamma_q(-\mu)}\int_0^x (x-tq)_{-\mu-1}f(t)\,\mathrm{d}_qt, \tag{23}$$

where $\Re(\mu) < 0$; then, we yield the following result:

Theorem 2. *For $\Re(\mu) > 0$, $\rho_i \in \mathbb{Z}^+$ $(i = 1,2)$, and $|q| < 1$, the Riemann–Liouville fractional q-derivative of (14) exists and is given by*

$$D^{\mu}_{x,q}\left\{x^{\lambda-1}\aleph^{0,n_1;m_2,n_2:m_3,n_3}_{P_i,Q_i,\tau_i;r;P_{i'},Q_{i'},\tau_{i'};r';P_{i''},Q_{i''},\tau_{i''};r''}\left(\begin{array}{c} z_1x^{\rho_1} \\ \\ z_2x^{\rho_2}\end{array};q\left|\begin{array}{c} A_1;C_1 \\ \\ B_1;D_1\end{array}\right.\right)\right\} = (1-q)^{-\mu}x^{\lambda-\mu-1}$$
$$\times\ \aleph^{0,n_1+1;m_2,n_2:m_3,n_3}_{P_i+1,Q_i+1,\tau_i;r;P_{i'},Q_{i'},\tau_{i'};r';P_{i''},Q_{i''},\tau_{i''};r''}\left(\begin{array}{c} z_1x^{\rho_1} \\ \\ z_2x^{\rho_2}\end{array};q\left|\begin{array}{c} (1-\lambda;\rho_1,\rho_2),A_1;C_1 \\ \\ B_1,(1-\lambda+\mu;\rho_1,\rho_2);D_1\end{array}\right.\right), \tag{24}$$

where $\Re(s_i\log(z_i) - \log\sin\pi s_i) < 0$ $(i = 1,2)$.

Proof. If we replace μ by $-\mu$ in (19), and follow the proof of Theorem 1, then we can easily obtain (24). □

4. Leibniz's Formula

The q-expression of the Leibniz rule for the fractional q-derivatives [13] is written below

Lemma 1. *For regular functions $U(x)$ and $V(x)$, we have*

$$D^{\alpha}_{x,q}\{U(x)V(x)\} = \sum_{n=0}^{\infty}\frac{(-1)^n q^{\frac{n(n+1)}{2}}[q^{-\mu};q]_n}{(q;q)_n}\, D^{\mu-n}_{x,q}\{U(xq^n)\}D^{n}_{x,q}\{V(x)\}. \tag{25}$$

Next, we have the following formula:

Theorem 3. *For $\Re(\mu) < 0$, $\rho_i \in \mathbb{Z}^+$ $(i = 1,2)$, then the Riemann–Liouville fractional q-derivative of a product of two basic function is written as*

$$\aleph^{0,n_1+1;m_2,n_2:m_3,n_3}_{P_i+1,Q_i+1,\tau_i;r;P_{i'},Q_{i'},\tau_{i'};r';P_{i''},Q_{i''},\tau_{i''};r''}\left(\begin{array}{c} z_1x^{\rho_1} \\ \\ z_2x^{\rho_2}\end{array};q\left|\begin{array}{c} (1-\lambda;\rho_1,\rho_2),A_1;C_1 \\ \\ B_1,(1-\lambda+\mu;\rho_1,\rho_2);D_1\end{array}\right.\right)$$
$$= \sum_{n=0}^{\infty}\frac{(-1)^n q^{n\lambda+\frac{n(n-1)}{2}}[q^{-\mu};q]_n}{(q;q)_n\,(q^{\lambda};q)_{n-\mu}}$$
$$\times\ \aleph^{0,n_1+1;m_2,n_2:m_3,n_3}_{P_i+1,Q_i+1,\tau_i;r;P_{i'},Q_{i'},\tau_{i'};r';P_{i''},Q_{i''},\tau_{i''};r''}\left(\begin{array}{c} z_1x^{\rho_1} \\ \\ z_2x^{\rho_2}\end{array};q\left|\begin{array}{c} (0;\rho_1,\rho_2),A_1;C_1 \\ \\ B_1,(n;\rho_1,\rho_2);D_1\end{array}\right.\right), \tag{26}$$

where $\Re(s_i\log(z_i) - \log\sin\pi s_i) < 0$ $(i = 1,2)$.

Proof. To apply the q-Leibniz rule, we take

$$U(x) = x^{\lambda-1} \text{ and } V(x) = \aleph^{0,n_1;m_2,n_2:m_3,n_3}_{P_i,Q_i,\tau_i;r;P_{i'},Q_{i'},\tau_{i'};r';P_{i''},Q_{i''},\tau_{i''};r''}\left(\begin{array}{c} z_1x^{\rho_1} \\ \\ z_2x^{\rho_2}\end{array};q\left|\begin{array}{c} A_1;C_1 \\ \\ B_1;D_1\end{array}\right.\right).$$

By using Lemma 1, we obtain the following relation:

$$D^{\mu}_{x,q}\left\{x^{\lambda-1}\aleph^{0,n_1;m_2,n_2:m_3,n_3}_{P_i,Q_i,\tau_i;r;P_{i'},Q_{i'},\tau_{i'};r';P_{i''},Q_{i''},\tau_{i''};r''}\left(\begin{array}{c} z_1x^{\rho_1} \\ \\ z_2x^{\rho_2}\end{array};q\left|\begin{array}{c} A_1;C_1 \\ \\ B_1;D_1\end{array}\right.\right)\right\}$$
$$= \sum_{n=0}^{\infty}\frac{(-1)^n q^{\frac{n(n+1)}{2}}[q^{-\mu};q]_n}{(q;q)_n}\, D^{\mu-n}_{x,q}(xq^n)^{\lambda-1}D^{n}_{x,q}\{\aleph(z_1x^{\rho_1},z_2x^{\rho_2};q)\}. \tag{27}$$

Next, by using Theorem 2 and setting $\lambda = 1$, we obtain

$$D^{n}_{x,q}\{\aleph(z_1x^{\rho_1}, z_2x^{\rho_2}; q)\}$$
$$= (1-q)^{-n}x^{-n}\,\aleph^{0,n_1+1;m_2,n_2:m_3,n_3}_{P_i+1,Q_i+1,\tau_i;r;P_{i'},Q_{i'},\tau_{i'};r';P_{i''},Q_{i''},\tau_{i''};r''}\left(\begin{array}{c} z_1x^{\rho_1} \\ \\ z_2x^{\rho_2} \end{array}; q \left| \begin{array}{c} (0;\rho_1,\rho_2), A_1; C_1 \\ \\ B_1, (n;\rho_1,\rho_2); D_1 \end{array}\right.\right). \tag{28}$$

By using the above equation and the following result:

$$D^{\mu}_{x,q}\left\{x^{\lambda-1}\right\} = \frac{\Gamma_q(\lambda)}{\Gamma_q(\lambda-\mu)}x^{\lambda-\mu-1} \quad (\lambda \neq -1,-2,\cdots), \tag{29}$$

We can easily obtain the desired result (26) after several algebraic manipulations. □

5. Particular Cases

By setting $\tau_i, \tau_{i'}, \tau_{i''} \to 1$, the basic analogue to AFTV reduces to the basic analogue to the I-function of two variables [24].

Let

$$A'_1 = (a_j;\alpha_j, A_j)_{1,n_1}, (a_{ji};\alpha_{ji}, A_{ji})_{n_1+1,P_i}; \; B'_1 = (b_{ji};\beta_{ji}, B_{ji})_{1,Q_i}. \tag{30}$$

$$C'_1 = (c_j,\gamma_j)_{1,n_2}, \left(c_{ji'},\gamma_{ji'}\right)_{n_2+1,P_{i'}}; (e_j, E_j)_{1,n_3}, \left(e_{ji''},\gamma_{ji''}\right)_{n_3+1,P_{i''}}. \tag{31}$$

$$D'_1 = (d_j,\delta_j)_{1,m_2}, \left(d_{ji'},\delta_{ji'}\right)_{m_2+1,Q_{i'}}; (f_j, F_j)_{1,m_3}, \left(f_{ji''}, F_{ji''}\right)_{m_3+1,Q_{i''}}. \tag{32}$$

We have the following result:

Corollary 1.

$$I^{0,n_1+1;m_2,n_2:m_3,n_3}_{P_i+1,Q_i+1;r;P_{i'},Q_{i'},;r';P_{i''},Q_{i''},;r''}\left(\begin{array}{c} z_1x^{\rho_1} \\ \\ z_2x^{\rho_2} \end{array}; q \left| \begin{array}{c} (1-\lambda;\rho_1,\rho_2), A'_1; C'_1 \\ \\ B'_1, (1-\lambda+\mu;\rho_1,\rho_2); D'_1 \end{array}\right.\right)$$
$$= \sum_{n=0}^{\infty}\frac{(-1)^n q^{n\lambda+\frac{n(n-1)}{2}}[q^{-\mu};q]_n}{(q;q)_n\,(q^{\lambda};q)_{n-\mu}}$$
$$\times\; I^{0,n_1+1;m_2,n_2:m_3,n_3}_{P_i+1,Q_i+1;r;P_{i'},Q_{i'},;r';P_{i''},Q_{i''};r''}\left(\begin{array}{c} z_1x^{\rho_1} \\ \\ z_2x^{\rho_2} \end{array}; q \left| \begin{array}{c} (0;\rho_1,\rho_2), A'_1; C'_1 \\ \\ B'_1, (n;\rho_1,\rho_2); D'_1 \end{array}\right.\right), \tag{33}$$

where $\Re(s_i\log(z_i) - \log\sin\pi s_i) < 0 \; (i = 1,2)$.

Proof. By setting $\tau_i, \tau_{i'}, \tau_{i''} \to 1$ and following the proof of Theorem 3, we can easily obtain the desired result (33). □

Remark 1. *If the basic analogue to the I-function of two variables reduces to the basic analogue to the H-function of two variables [25], then we can obtain the result due to Yadav et al. [18].*

The basic analogue to AFTV reduces to the basic analogue to AFTV, defined by Ahmad et al. [26].

Let

$$A = (a_j, A_j)_{1,n}, \cdots, \left[\tau_i(a_{ji}, A_{ji})\right]_{n+1,p_i}. \tag{34}$$

$$B = (b_j, B_j)_{1,m}, \cdots, \left[\tau_i(b_{ji}, B_{ji})\right]_{m+1,q_i}. \tag{35}$$

Then, we have following relation:

Corollary 2.

$$\aleph^{m,n+1}_{p_i+1,q_i+1,\tau_i;r}\left(zx^{\rho};q\left|\begin{matrix}(1-\lambda;\rho),A\\B,(1-\lambda+\mu;\rho)\end{matrix}\right.\right)$$
$$=\sum_{n=0}^{\infty}\frac{(-1)^n q^{n\lambda+\frac{n(n-1)}{2}}[q^{-\mu};q]_n}{(q;q)_n\,(q^{\lambda};q)_{n-\mu}}\aleph^{m,n+1}_{p_i+1,q_i+1,\tau_i;r}\left(zx^{\rho};q\left|\begin{matrix}(0;\rho),A\\B,(n;\rho)\end{matrix}\right.\right). \tag{36}$$

If we set $\tau_i \to 1$ in (36), then the basic analogue to AFTV reduces to the basic analogue to the I-function of one variable. We have

Corollary 3.

$$I^{m,n+1}_{p_i+1,q_i+1;r}\left(zx^{\rho};q\left|\begin{matrix}(1-\lambda;\rho),(a_j,A_j)_{1,n},\cdots,(a_{ji},A_{ji})_{n+1,p_i}\\ \\(b_j,B_j)_{1,m},\cdots,(b_{ji},B_{ji})_{m+1,q_i},(1-\lambda+\mu;\rho)\end{matrix}\right.\right)$$
$$=\sum_{n=0}^{\infty}\frac{(-1)^n q^{n\lambda+\frac{n(n-1)}{2}}[q^{-\mu};q]_n}{(q;q)_n}$$
$$\times\; I^{m,n+1}_{p_i+1,q_i+1;r}\left(zx^{\rho};q\left|\begin{matrix}(0;\rho),(a_j,A_j)_{1,n},\cdots,(a_{ji},A_{ji})_{n+1,p_i}\\ \\(b_j,B_j)_{1,m},\cdots,(b_{ji},B_{ji})_{m+1,q_i},(n;\rho)\end{matrix}\right.\right). \tag{37}$$

Remark 2. *If the basic analogue to AFTV reduces to the basic analogue to the H-function of one variable (see [27]), then we can report a similar expression.*

Remark 3. *We can generalize the q-extension of the Leibniz rule for the basic analogue to special multivariable functions; by this, we can obtain similar formulas by using similar methods.*

6. Conclusions

After the famous letter between L'Hopital and Leibniz from 1695, using integral transformations, we obtained a new field in mathematics, called fractional calculus. Among other things, there are fractional derivative and fractional integrals, as well as fractional differential equations. It is also well-known that fractional calculus operators and their basic (or $q-$) analogues have many applications, such as signal processing, bio-medical engineering, control systems, radars, sonars, to solve dual integral and series equations in elasticity, etc. In this article, we have proposed the fractional-order q-integrals and q-derivatives involving a basic analogue to AFTV [11,12,26,28]. Some remarkable applications of these integrals and derivatives have also been discussed. By specializing the various parameters as well as the variables in the basic analogue to AFTV, we can obtain a large number of q-extensions of the Leibniz rule, involving a large set of basic functions, that is, the product of such basic functions, which are describable in terms of the basic analogue to the H-function [25,27], the basic analogue to Meijer's G-function [27], the basic analogue to MacRobert's E-function [29], and the basic analogue to the hypergeometric function [10,16–18].

Author Contributions: Conceptualization, D.K.; Data curation, D.B., F.A. and N.S.; Formal analysis, D.K., D.B., F.A. and N.S.; Funding acquisition, D.B.; Investigation, D.K. and F.A.; Methodology, D.K., D.B. and F.A.; Resources, F.A. and N.S.; Supervision, D.B. and N.S. All authors have read and agreed to the published version of the manuscript.

Funding: This research received no external funding.

Institutional Review Board Statement: Not applicable.

Informed Consent Statement: Not applicable.

Data Availability Statement: Not applicable.

Acknowledgments: The author (D.K.) would like to thank the Agriculture University Jodhpur for supporting and encouraging this work.

Conflicts of Interest: All authors declare that they have no conflict of interest.

References

1. Kumar, D.; Choi, J. Generalized fractional kinetic equations associated with Aleph function. *Proc. Jangjeon Math. Soc.* **2016**, *19*, 145–155.
2. Kumar, D.; Gupta, R.K.; Shaktawat, B.S.; Choi, J. Generalized fractional calculus formulas involving the product of Aleph-function and Srivastava polynomials. *Proc. Jangjeon Math. Soc.* **2017**, *20*, 701–717.
3. Kumar, D.; Ram, J.; Choi, J. Certain generalized integral formulas involving Chebyshev Hermite polynomials, generalized M-series and Aleph-function, and their application in heat conduction. *Int. J. Math. Anal.* **2015**, *9*, 1795–1803. [CrossRef]
4. Ram, J.; Kumar, D. Generalized fractional integration of the ℵ-function. *J. Raj. Acad. Phy. Sci.* **2011**, *10*, 373–382.
5. Samko, G.; Kilbas, A.A.; Marichev, O.I. *Fractional Integrals and Derivatives: Theory and Applications*; Gordon and Breach Science Publishers: New York, NY, USA, 1993.
6. Südland, N.; Volkmann, J.; Kumar, D. Applications to give an analytical solution to the Black Scholes equation. *Integral Transform. Spec. Funct.* **2019**, *30*, 205–230. [CrossRef]
7. Exton, H. q-hypergeometric functions and applications. *Ellis Horwood Series: Mathematics and its Applications*; Ellis Horwood Ltd.: Chichester, UK , 1983; 347p.
8. Gasper, G.; Rahman, M. *Basic Hypergeometric Series*; Cambridge University Press: Cambridge, UK, 1990.
9. Rajkovic, P.M.; Marinkovic, S.D.; Stankovic, M.S. Fractional integrals and derivatives in q-calculus. *Appl. Anal. Discrete Math.* **2007**, *1*, 311–323.
10. Slater, L.J. *Generalized Hypergeometric Functions*; Cambridge University Press: Cambridge, UK, 1966.
11. Al-Salam, W.A. q-analogues of Cauchy's formula. *Proc. Am. Math. Soc.* **1952–1953** , *17*, 182–184.
12. Al-Salam, W.A. Some fractional q-integrals and q-derivatives. *Proc. Edinburgh Math. Soc.* **1966**, *15*, 135–140. [CrossRef]
13. Agarwal, R.P. Certain fractional q-integrals and q-derivatives. *Proc. Camb. Phil. Soc.* **1969**, *66*, 365–370. [CrossRef]
14. Kumar, D.; Ayant, F.Y.; Tariboon, J. On transformation involving basic analogue of multivariable H-function. *J. Funct. Spaces* **2020**, *2020*, 2616043. [CrossRef]
15. Sahni, N.; Kumar, D.; Ayant, F.Y.; Singh, S. A transformation involving basic multivariable I-function of Prathima. *J. Ramanujan Soc. Math. Math. Sci.* **2021**, *8*, 95–108.
16. Yadav, R.K.; Purohit, S.D. On applications of Weyl fractional q-integral operator to generalized basic hypergeometric functions. *Kyungpook Math. J.* **2006**, *46*, 235–245.
17. Yadav, R.K.; Purohit, S.D.; Kalla, S.L.; Vyas, V.K. Certain fractional q-integral formulae for the generalized basic hypergeometric functions of two variables. *J. Inequal. Spec. Funct.* **2010**, *1*, 30–38.
18. Yadav, R.K.; Purohit, S.D.; Vyas, V.K. On transformations involving generalized basic hypergeometric function of two variables. *Rev. Téc. Ing. Univ. Zulia.* **2010**, *33*, 176–182.
19. Purohit, S.D.; Yadav, R.K. On generalized fractional q-integral operators involving the q-gauss hypergeometric function. *Bull. Math. Anal. Appl.* **2010**, *2*, 35–44.
20. Galué, L. Generalized Erdélyi-Kober fractional q-integral operator. *Kuwait J. Sci. Eng.* **2009**, *36*, 21–34.
21. Kumar, D. Generalized fractional differintegral operators of the Aleph-function of two variables. *J. Chem. Biol. Phys. Sci. Sec. C* **2016**, *6*, 1116–1131.
22. Jia, Z.; Khan, B.; Agarwal, P.; Hu, Q.; Wang, X. Two new Bailey Lattices and their applications . *Symmetry* **2021**, *13*, 958. [CrossRef]
23. Jia, Z.; Khan, B.; Hu, Q.; Niu, D. Applications of generalized q-difference equations for general q-polynomials. *Symmetry* **2021**, *13*, 1222. [CrossRef]
24. Sharma, C.K.; Mishra, P.L. On the I-function of two variables and its certain properties. *Acta Ciencia Indica* **1991**, *17*, 1–4.
25. Saxena, R.K.; Modi, G.C.; Kalla, S.L. A basic analogue of H-function of two variable. *Rev. Tec. Ing. Univ. Zulia* **1987**, *10*, 35–39.
26. Ahmad, A.; Jain, R.; Jain, D.K. q-analogue of Aleph-function and its transformation formulae with q-derivative. *J. Stat. Appl. Pro.* **2017**, *6*, 567–575. [CrossRef]
27. Saxena, R.K.; Modi, G.C.; Kalla, S.L. A basic analogue of Fox's H-function. *Rev. Tec. Ing. Univ. Zulia* **1983**, *6*, 139–143.
28. Ayant, F.Y.; Kumar, D. Certain finite double integrals involving the hypergeometric function and Aleph-function. *Int. J. Math. Trends Technol.* **2016**, *35*, 49–55. [CrossRef]
29. Agarwal, R. A basic analogue of MacRobert's E-function. *Glasg. Math. J.* **1961**, *5*, 4–7. [CrossRef]

fractal and fractional

MDPI

Article

Switched Fractional Order Multiagent Systems Containment Control with Event-Triggered Mechanism and Input Quantization

Jiaxin Yuan *,† and Tao Chen †

School of Air Transportation, Shanghai University of Engineering Science, Shanghai 201620, China; chentao960520@163.com
* Correspondence: yuanke2964@sjtu.edu.cn
† These authors contributed equally to this work.

Abstract: This paper studies the containment control problem for a class of fractional order nonlinear multiagent systems in the presence of arbitrary switchings, unmeasured states, and quantized input signals by a hysteresis quantizer. Under the framework of the Lyapunov function theory, this paper proposes an event-triggered adaptive neural network dynamic surface quantized controller, in which dynamic surface control technology can avoid "explosion of complexity" and obtain fractional derivatives for virtual control functions continuously. Radial basis function neural networks (RBFNNs) are used to approximate the unknown nonlinear functions, and an observer is designed to obtain the unmeasured states. The proposed distributed protocol can ensure all the signals remain semi-global uniformly ultimately bounded in the closed-loop system, and all followers can converge to the convex hull spanned by the leaders' trajectory. Utilizing the combination of an event-triggered scheme and quantized control technology, the controller is updated aperiodically only at the event-sampled instants such that transmitting and computational costs are greatly reduced. Simulations compare the event-triggered scheme without quantization control technology with the control method proposed in this paper, and the results show that the event-triggered scheme combined with the quantization mechanism reduces the number of control inputs by 7% to 20%.

Keywords: fractional order multiagent systems; containment control; event-triggered mechanism; input quantization; switched systems; neural network; observer

Citation: Yuan, J.; Chen, T. Switched Fractional Order Multiagent Systems Containment Control with Event-Triggered Mechanism and Input Quantization. *Fractal Fract.* **2022**, *6*, 77. https://doi.org/10.3390/fractalfract6020077

Academic Editors: António M. Lopes, Alireza Alfi, Liping Chen and Sergio A. David

Received: 23 December 2021
Accepted: 28 January 2022
Published: 31 January 2022

1. Introduction

Multiagent systems (MASs) cooperative control technology has been widely used in many fields [1–4]. As the most basic research content of multiagent cooperative control, the consensus problem has made much progress [5–11]. Further study of the cooperative control problem of multiagent systems, extending the consensus control of a single leader, considers multiagent cooperative control in the case of multiple leaders, and designs a controller to make the followers converge to a convex hull composed of multiple leaders, which is called containment control. As a special case of cooperative control, many research results of MASs containment control have been reported in the field of integer order control, such as adaptive control [12,13], feedback control [14,15], linear matrix inequalities (LMIs) [16,17], sliding mode control [18], and so on.

Due to the unique memory properties of fractional calculus and the ability to accurately model the system, fractional calculus is suitable for describing real physical systems with genetics [19,20]. At present, the Caputo fractional differential definition is widely used in engineering, and there have been many achievements on the fractional derivative definition and control research of fractional order nonlinear systems. For example, Ref. [21] studied the numerical approximation for the spread of the SIQR model with a Caputo fractional derivative. Ref. [22] expanded the garden equation to the Caputo derivative and

Atangana-Baleanu fractional derivative in the sense of Caputo. Ref. [23] established the Caputo fractional derivatives for exponential s-convex functions. Some new k-Caputo fractional derivative inequalities were established in [24] by using Hermite-Hadamard-Mercer type inequalities for differentiable mapping. Ref. [25] proposed two fractional derivatives by taking the Caputo fractional derivative and replacing the simple derivative with a proportional type derivative, which can be expressed as a combination of existing fractional operators in several different ways. In order to perform reliable and effective numerical processing of nonlinear singular fractional Lane-Emden differential equations, based on fractional Meyer wavelet artificial neural network optimization, combined with the comprehensive strength of genetic algorithm-assisted active set method, Ref. [26] proposed a stochastic calculation solver fractional Meyer Wavelet Artificial Neural Network Genetic Algorithm and Active Sets. In reference [27], the authors studied variable order fractional order and constant order fractional order systems with uncertain and external disturbance terms and proposed a variable order fractional control method for tracking control.

At present, the research into the multiagent systems containment control problem has made some progress in the field of fractional order systems. In reference [28], the authors applied the matrices singular value decomposition and LMI techniques for obtaining sufficient conditions to solve the containment problem of fractional order multiagent systems (FOMASs). In reference [29], the authors considered the distributed containment control problem for FOMASs with a double-integrator and designed a distributed projection containment controller for each follower. Due to the general approximation theory of the neural network (NN) and fuzzy logic system, it is often used to deal with the uncertainty of nonlinear systems to obtain unknown nonlinear functions [30]. For example, based on the neural network algorithm, reference [31] designed a distributed control algorithm to ensure that the follower converged to the leader signal in FOMASs. For the FOMASs containment control, an adaptive NN containment controller was designed in reference [12], in which RBFNNs were applied for the unknown functions. In most practical applications, it is usually necessary to obtain the unmeasurable state of the system through a state observer. For example, reference [32] designed a state observer to provide an estimate for unmeasured consensus errors and disturbances of FOMASs. Reference [33] designed an observer to obtain the state of the agent for FOMASs containment control. It should be recognized that the abovementioned fractional order nonlinear system is a kind of non-switched system, and the switched system is another more complex system, which is composed of multiple subsystems and is formed by signal switching between the systems. For the switched system, when switching between subsystems, the system parameters will change greatly, and the nonlinear function of its system will become discontinuous, so the performance of the system may be affected or even unstable [34]. Therefore, it is well worth investigating how to obtain conditions that make the switching system stable for all switching signals. Reference [35] studied the stability and robust stabilization of switched fractional order systems and provided two stability theorems for switched fractional order systems under the arbitrary switching. Based on the fractional Lyapunov stability criterion, reference [36] designed an adaptive fuzzy controller for the uncertain fractional-order switched nonlinear systems and ensured that the tracking error converged to a small neighborhood of the origin regardless of arbitrary switching. The switching control method for strictly feedback switched nonlinear systems was studied by using the average dwell time method in references [37,38].

The traditional time sampling mechanism will cause unnecessary waste of communication resources. In modern technology, an event-triggered mechanism and quantized mechanism can reduce the action frequency of the controller, thus overcoming the problem of wasting communication resources [39]. For example, reference [40] solved the problem of event-triggered fuzzy adaptive tracking control for MASs with input quantization and reduced the communication burden by combining an asymmetric hysteresis quantizer and event triggering mechanism. Based on quantized feedback control, Reference [41] studied the problem of adaptive event-triggered tracking for nonlinear systems with external disturbances. In reference [42], the authors designed an adaptive neural control scheme for integer order uncertain nonlinear systems by combining an event-triggered scheme with input quantization technology. For the containment problem of MASs with unmeasured states, reference [43] developed a quantized control scheme based on the event-triggered backstepping control technique. To the best of our knowledge, the containment control problem of switched fractional order multiagent systems (SFOMAS) combining an event-triggered mechanism and input quantization techniques has not been studied, which motivates the research presented in this paper. Furthermore, the combination of the event-triggered mechanism and the input quantification can reduce the operating frequency of the actuation system and thus reduce energy consumption. Therefore, the research in this paper has great value in the practical engineering application of MASs and reducing the fatigue loss in the system.

Based on the previous discussion, this paper designs an observer-based event-triggered adaptive neural network dynamic surface quantized controller to addresses the containment control of SFOMASs. Compared with the previous research work, the main contributions of the control method discussed in this paper are summarized as follows.

(1) Comparison with [34,37,38], an adaptive neural network dynamic surface controller is proposed to address the containment control problem of SFOMASs, in which the controller combines the event-triggered mechanism and input quantization to reduce controller action frequency in this paper.

(2) Compared with references [38,40], the state observer is used to estimate system states, and the RBFNN is developed to estimate uncertain parts. In comparison with references [41,43], fractional order DSC technology is used to avoid the "explosion of complexity" that can occur during traditional backstepping design processes and to obtain fractional derivatives for virtual control continuously.

The rest of the paper is organized as follows. Section 2 introduces basic theory about fractional calculus and SFOMASs. In Section 3, first, we construct an observer to estimate the system state, then a controller is proposed based on the adaptive dynamic surface control method; finally, the stability is proved by the Lyapunov function theory. Section 4 provides the numerical simulations to show the viability and efficiency of the proposed controller. Section 5 offers conclusions.

2. Preliminaries

2.1. Fractional Calculus

The Caputo fractional derivative [44] is defined as

$$ {}_{0}^{C}D_t^{\alpha} f(t) = \frac{1}{\Gamma(n-\alpha)} \int_0^t \frac{f^{(n)}(\tau)}{(t-\tau)^{1+\alpha-n}} d\tau, $$

where $n \in N$ and $n-1 < \alpha \leq n, \Gamma(z) = \int_0^{\infty} t^{z-1} e^{-t} dt$ is the Gamma function.

Lemma 1 ([45]). *For a complex number β and two real numbers α, v satisfying $\alpha \in (0,1)$ and*

$$ \frac{\pi\alpha}{2} < vs. < \min\{\pi, \pi\alpha\} $$

For all integers $n \geq 1$, we can obtain

$$ E_{\alpha,\beta}(\varsigma) = -\sum_{j=1}^{\infty} \frac{1}{\Gamma(\beta-\alpha j)} + o\left(\frac{1}{|\varsigma|^{n+1}}\right) $$

when $|\varsigma| \to \infty, v \leq |\arg(\varsigma)| \leq \pi$.

Lemma 2 ([45]). *If v satisfies the condition of Lemma 1, then the following inequality relation holds*

$$\left|E_{\alpha,\beta}(\varsigma)\right| \leq \frac{\mu}{1+|\varsigma|}$$

where $\alpha \in (0,2)$ and β is an arbitrary real number, $\mu > 0$, $v \leq |\arg(\varsigma)| \leq \pi$, and $|\varsigma| \geq 0$.

Lemma 3 ([46]). *Let $x(t) \in R^l$ be a vector of differentiable function. Then, the following inequality holds*

$$D^{\alpha}\left(x^T(t)Px\right) \leq 2x^T(t)PD^{\alpha}x(t)$$

where $\alpha \in (0,1)$ and P is a positive definite diagonal matrix.

Lemma 4 ([47]). *(Young's inequality) For any $x, y \in R^n$, the following inequality relationship holds*

$$x^T y \leq \frac{c^a}{a}\|x\|^a + \frac{1}{bc^b}\|y\|^b$$

where $a > 1, b > 1, c > 0$, and $(a-1)(b-1) = 1$.

Lemma 5 ([48]). *For $m \in R$ and $n > 0$, the following inequality holds*

$$0 \leq |m| - \frac{m^2}{\sqrt{m^2+n^2}} \leq n$$

Lemma 6 ([44]). *Suppose that the Lyapunov function $V(t,x)$ satisfies $D^{\alpha}V(t,x) \leq -CV(t,x)+D$. Let $0 < \alpha < 1$, $C > 0$ and $D \geq 0$, the following inequality holds*

$$V(t,x) \leq V(0)E_{\alpha}(-Ct^{\alpha}) + \tfrac{D\mu}{C}, \quad t \geq 0$$

Then, $V(t,x)$ is bounded on $[0,t]$ and fractional order systems are stable, where μ is defined in Lemma 2.

2.2. Problem Formulation

In the paper, we consider the following fractional order multiagent system.

$$\begin{cases} D^{\alpha}x_{i,1}(t) = x_{i,2} + f_{i,1}^{\sigma(t)}(x_{i,1}) \\ D^{\alpha}x_{i,l}(t) = x_{i,l+1} + f_{i,l}^{\sigma(t)}(x_{i,1}, x_{i,2}, \ldots, x_{i,l}) \\ D^{\alpha}x_{i,n}(t) = u_i(t) + f_{i,n}^{\sigma(t)}(x_{i,1}, x_{i,2}, \ldots, x_{i,n}) \\ \qquad y_i = x_{i,1} \end{cases} \tag{1}$$

where $l = 2, \ldots, n-1$, $\alpha \in (0,1)$; $X_{i,l} = (x_{i,1}, x_{i,2}, \ldots, x_{i,l})^T \in R^l$ are the system state vectors, and $u_i(t)$ is the control input of the system. It should be noted that the control input in this paper considers the quantization mechanism and the event-triggered technology. y_i is the system output, and $f_{i,l}^{\sigma(t)}(x_{i,1}, x_{i,2}, \ldots, x_{i,l})$ are unknown nonlinear functions. $\sigma(t)$ is a piecewise continuous function that is used to describe the triggering conditions for switching between subsystems. It is called a switching signal, for example, if $\sigma(t) = q$, it means that $q-th$ subsystem is activated.

Rewriting system (1):

$$D^{\alpha}X_i = A_iX_i + K_iy_i + \sum_{l=1}^{n} B_{i,l}\left[f_{i,l}^{q}(X_{i,l})\right] + B_iu_i(t) \tag{2}$$

where $A_i = \begin{bmatrix} -k_{i,1} & & & \\ \vdots & & I_{n-1} & \\ -k_{i,n} & 0 & \cdots & 0 \end{bmatrix}$, $K_i = \begin{bmatrix} k_{i,1} \\ \vdots \\ k_{i,n} \end{bmatrix}$, $B_i = \begin{bmatrix} 0 \\ \vdots \\ 1 \end{bmatrix}$, $B_{i,l} = [0 \ldots 1 \ldots 0]^T$, and given a positive matrix $Q_i^T = Q_i$, there exists a positive matrix $P_i^T = P_i$ satisfying

$$A_i^T P_i + P_i A_i = -2Q_i \tag{3}$$

Control objectives: This paper aims to design an observer-based adaptive neural network dynamic surface controller, so that all the signals remain bounded in the closed-loop system and enable all followers to converge to the leaders' convex hull. Meanwhile, we utilize the combination of an event-triggered scheme and quantized mechanism to reduce the transmission frequency of the control input.

2.3. Hysteresis Quantizer

In this paper, the hysteresis quantizer is used to reduce chattering. The quantizer $q_i(\omega_i(t))$ is shown as the following form [49].

$$q_i(\omega_i(t))=\begin{cases} \omega_{is} sign(\omega_i), & \frac{\omega_{is}}{1+d} < |\omega_i| \leq \frac{\omega_{is}}{1-d} \\ \omega_{is}(1+d) sign(\omega_i), & \omega_{is} < |\omega_i| \leq \frac{\omega_{is}(1+d)}{1-d} \\ 0, & 0 \leq |\omega_i| < \omega_{\min} \end{cases} \tag{4}$$

where $\omega_{is} = n^{1-s}\omega_{\min}(s = 1, 2, \ldots)$ with parameters $\omega_{\min} > 0$ and $0 < n < 1$, $d = \frac{1-n}{1+n}$. Meanwhile, $q_i(\omega_i(t))$ is in the set $U = [0, \pm\omega_{is}, \pm\omega_{is}(1+d)]$, *and* $s = 1, 2, \ldots$. $\omega_{\min}$ determines the magnitude of the dead-zone for $q_i(\omega_i(t))$.

Lemma 7 ([49])**.** *The system inputs $q_i(\omega_i(t))$ can be described as*

$$q_i(\omega_i(t))=H(\omega_i)\omega_i(t) + L_i(t) \tag{5}$$

where $1 - d \leq H(\omega_i) \leq 1 + d, |L(t)| \leq \omega_{\min}$.

2.4. Graph Theory

Suppose that there exist N followers, labeled as agents 1 to N, and M leaders, labeled as agents $N+1$ to $N+M$. The information exchange between followers is represented by a directed graph $G = (w, \varepsilon, \bar{A})$, in which $w = \{n_1, \ldots, n_{N+M}\}$. The set of edge is exhibited as $\varepsilon = \{(n_i, n_j)\} \in w \times w$, which expresses that follower i and follower j can exchange information, and $N_i = \{j | (n_i, n_j) \in \varepsilon\}$ means the neighbor set of followers i. Furthermore, $\bar{A} = \{a_{ij}\} \in R^{(N+M)\times(N+M)}$ is the Adjacency matrix, a_{ij} of $\bar{A}$ is represented as if $(n_i, n_j) \notin \varepsilon$, $a_{ij} = 0$; if not, $a_{ij} = 1$. It is supposed that $a_{ij} = 0$. A directed graph G has a spanning tree if there exists at least one node called a root node, which has a directed path to all the other nodes. Define the Laplacian matrix $L = D - \bar{A} \in R^{(N+M)\times(N+M)}$ and the diagonal matrix $D = diag(d_1, \ldots, d_{N+M})$, in which $d_i = \sum_{j=1}^{N+M} a_{ij}$.

Suppose that leaders $N+1, \ldots, N+M$ do not receive the information from followers and other leaders, and the followers $1, \ldots, N$ have at least one neighbor. Therefore, the Laplacian matrix L related to directed communication graph G is described as follows:

$$L = \begin{bmatrix} L_1 & L_2 \\ 0_{M\times N} & 0_{M\times M} \end{bmatrix}$$

where $L_1 \in R^{N\times N}$ is the matrix related to the communication between the N followers, and $L_2 \in R^{N\times M}$ is the communication from M leaders to N followers. Let $r(t) = [r_{N+1}, r_{N+2}, \ldots, r_{N+M}]^T$, and $Co(r(t)) = \left\{\sum_{j=N+1}^{N+M} \theta_j r_j \middle| r_j \in r(t), \theta_j > 0, \sum_{j=N+1}^{N+M} \theta_j = 1\right\}$. Define the convex hull as $r_d(t) = [r_{d,1}(t), r_{d,2}(t), \ldots, r_{d,M}(t)]^T = -L_1^{-1} L_2 r(t)$. The containment errors are defined as $e_i = y_i - r_{d,i}$. Let $e=[e_1,e_2,\ldots,e_N]^T$, $y=[y_1,y_2,\ldots,y_N]^T$, then $e = y - r_d(t)$.

2.5. Neural Network Approximation

Due to its universal approximation characteristics, neural networks have been widely used in the identification and control of uncertain nonlinear systems [10]. In this paper, we employ an RBFNNs to identify the nonlinear functions. The unknown function $f(Z)$ can be expressed as

$$f_{nn}(Z) = \theta^T \varphi(Z)$$

where θ is the weight vector and $\varphi(Z)$ is the basis function vector. In this paper, due to applying radial basis function neural networks (RBFNNs), Gaussian basis functions are used. For any unknown function $f(Z)$ defined over a compact set U, there exists the neural network $\theta^{*T}\varphi(Z)$ and arbitrary accuracy $\varepsilon(Z)$ such that

$$f(Z) = \theta^{*T}\varphi(Z) + \varepsilon(Z)$$

where θ^* is the vectors of optimal parameters defined by $\theta^* = \arg\min_{\theta\in\Omega}\left[\sup_{Z\in U}\left|f(Z) - \theta^T\varphi(Z)\right|\right]$, and $\varepsilon(Z)$ denotes the minimum approximation error.

Assumption 1. *The optimal approximation errors remain bounded, there exists a positive constant ε_0, satisfying $|\varepsilon(Z)| \le \varepsilon_0$.*

3. Main Results

3.1. Observer Design

Assumption 2. *In this paper, we employ neural networks to identify the nonlinear functions. The unknown functions $f_i(X), i = 1,\ldots,n$ can be expressed as*

$$f_i(X_i|\theta_i)=\theta_i^T\varphi_i(X_i), 1 \le i \le n. \tag{6}$$

Furthermore, we assume that the state variables of system (1) are not available. The state observer is designed as follows:

$$\begin{aligned} D^\alpha \hat{X}_i &= A_i\hat{X}_i + K_i y_i + \sum_{l=1}^{n} B_{i,l}\hat{f}_{i,l}^q(\hat{X}_{i,l}|\theta_{i,l}) + B_i u_i(t) \\ \hat{y}_i &= C_i\hat{X}_i \end{aligned} \tag{7}$$

where $C_i = [1\ldots0\ldots0]$, and $\hat{X}_{i,l} = (\hat{x}_{i,1},\hat{x}_{i,2},\ldots,\hat{x}_{i,l})^T$ are the estimated values of $X_{i,l} = (x_{i,1},x_{i,2},\ldots,x_{i,l})^T$.

We define $e_i = X_i - \hat{X}_i$ as the observation error, and then, according to Equations (2) and (6), one has

$$D^\alpha e_i = A_i e_i + \sum_{l=1}^{n} B_{i,l}\left[f_{i,l}^q(\hat{X}_{i,l}) - \hat{f}_{i,l}^q(\hat{X}_{i,l}|\theta_{i,l}) + \Delta f_{i,l}^q\right] \tag{8}$$

where $\Delta f_{i,l}^q = f_{i,l}^q(X_{i,l}) - f_{i,l}^q(\hat{X}_{i,l})$.

By Assumption 2, we can obtain

$$\hat{f}_{i,l}^q(\hat{X}_{i,l}|\theta_{i,l}) = \theta_{i,l}^T\varphi_{i,l}(\hat{X}_{i,l}). \tag{9}$$

According to the definition of a neural network, the optimal parameter vector is defined as

$$\theta_{i,l}^{*} = \arg\min_{\theta_{i,l}\in\Omega_{i,l}}\left[\sup_{\hat{X}_{i,l}\in U_{i,l}}\left|\hat{f}_{i,l}^{q}(\hat{X}_{i,l}|\theta_{i,l}) - f_{i,l}^{q}(\hat{X}_{i,l})\right|\right]$$

where $1 \le l \le n$, $\Omega_{i,l}$ and $U_{i,l}$ are compact regions for $\theta_{i,l}$, $X_{i,l}$ and $\hat{X}_{i,l}$.
Furthermore, we define that the following equation holds

$$\begin{aligned}
\varepsilon_{i,l}^{q} &= f_{i,l}^{q}(\hat{X}_{i,l}) - \hat{f}_{i,l}^{q}\left(\hat{X}_{i,l}\middle|\theta_{i,l}^{*}\right) \\
\tilde{\theta}_{i,l} &= \theta_{i,l}^{*} - \theta_{i,l}, l = 1,2,\ldots,n
\end{aligned}$$

where $\varepsilon_{i,l}$ is the optimal approximation error, and $\tilde{\theta}_{i,l}$ is the parameters estimation error.

Assumption 3. *The optimal approximation errors remain bounded, there exist positive constants* ε_{i0}, *satisfying* $\left|\varepsilon_{i,l}^{q}\right| \le \varepsilon_{i0}$.

Assumption 4. *The following relationship holds*

$$|f_i(X) - f_i(\hat{X})| \le \gamma_i \|X - \hat{X}\|$$

where γ_i *is a set of known constants.*

By Equations (8) and (9), we have

$$\begin{aligned}
D^{\alpha}e_i &= A_i e_i + \sum_{l=1}^{n} B_{i,l}\left[f_{i,l}^{q}(\hat{X}_{i,l}) - \hat{f}_{i,l}(\hat{X}_{i,l}|\theta_{i,l}) + \Delta f_{i,l}^{q}\right] \\
&= A_i e_i + \sum_{l=1}^{n} B_{i,l}\left[\varepsilon_{i,l}^{q} + \Delta f_{i,l}^{q} + \tilde{\theta}_{i,l}^{T}\varphi_{i,l}(\hat{X}_{i,l})\right] \\
&= A_i e_i + \Delta f_i + \varepsilon_i + \sum_{l=1}^{n} B_{i,l}\left[\tilde{\theta}_{i,l}^{T}\varphi_{i,l}(\hat{X}_{i,l})\right]
\end{aligned} \tag{10}$$

where $\varepsilon_i = \left[\varepsilon_{i,1}^{q},\ldots,\varepsilon_{i,n}^{q}\right]^{T}$, $\Delta f_i = \left[\Delta f_{i,1}^{q},\ldots,\Delta f_{i,n}^{q}\right]^{T}$.

We construct the first Lyapunov function:

$$V_0 = \sum_{i=1}^{N} V_{i,0} = \sum_{i=1}^{N}\frac{1}{2}e_i^{T}P_i e_i. \tag{11}$$

According to Lemma 3, we obtain

$$D^{\alpha}V_{i,0} \le -e_i^{T}Q_i e_i + e_i^{T}P_i(\varepsilon_i + \Delta f_i) + e_i^{T}P_i\sum_{l=1}^{n} B_{i,l}\tilde{\theta}_{i,l}^{T}\varphi_{i,l}(\hat{X}_{i,l}). \tag{12}$$

By Lemma 4 and Assumption 4, we obtain

$$
\begin{aligned}
& e_i^T P_i(\varepsilon_i + \Delta f_i) + e_i^T P_i \sum_{l=1}^{n} B_{i,l}\tilde{\theta}_{i,l}^T \varphi_{i,l}(\hat{X}_{i,l}) \\
& \le \left| e_i^T P_i \varepsilon_i \right| + \left| e_i^T P_i \Delta f_{i,l}^q \right| + \frac{1}{2} e_i^T P_i^T P_i e_i + \frac{1}{2} \sum_{l=1}^{n} \tilde{\theta}_{i,l}^T \varphi_{i,l} \varphi_{i,l}^T \tilde{\theta}_{i,l}^2 \\
& \le \|e_i\|^2 + \frac{1}{2}\|P_i\varepsilon_i\|^2 + \frac{1}{2}\|P_i\|^2 \sum_{l=1}^{n} \left| \Delta f_{i,l}^q \right|^2 + \frac{1}{2}\lambda_{i,\max}^2(P_i)\|e_i\|^2 + \frac{1}{2}\sum_{l=1}^{n} \tilde{\theta}_{i,l}^T \tilde{\theta}_{i,l} \\
& \le \|e_i\|^2 \left(1 + \frac{1}{2}\|P_i\|^2 \sum_{l=1}^{n} \gamma_{i,l}^{q\,2} + \frac{1}{2}\lambda_{i,\max}^2(P_i) \right) + \frac{1}{2}\|P_i\varepsilon_i\|^2 + \frac{1}{2}\sum_{l=1}^{n} \tilde{\theta}_{i,l}^T \tilde{\theta}_{i,l}.
\end{aligned}
\tag{13}
$$

By Equations (12) and (13), one has

$$
D^\alpha V_{i,0} \le -q_{i,0}\|e_i\|^2 + \frac{1}{2}\|P_i\varepsilon_i^*\|^2 + \frac{1}{2}\sum_{l=1}^{n} \tilde{\theta}_{i,l}^T \tilde{\theta}_{i,l} \tag{14}
$$

where $q_{i,0} = -\left(1 + \frac{1}{2}\|P_i\|^2 \sum_{l=1}^{n} \gamma_{i,l}^{q\,2} + \frac{1}{2}\lambda_{i,\max}^2(P_i) \right) + \lambda_{i,\min}(Q_i)$.

Combining (11) and (14), we can obtain

$$
\begin{aligned}
D^\alpha V_0 & \le \sum_{i=1}^{N} \left(-q_{i,0}\|e_i\|^2 + \frac{1}{2}\|P_i\varepsilon_i\|^2 + \frac{1}{2}\sum_{l=1}^{n} \tilde{\theta}_{i,l}^T \tilde{\theta}_{i,l} \right) \\
& \le -q_0\|e\|^2 + \frac{1}{2}\|P\varepsilon\|^2 + \sum_{i=1}^{N}\sum_{l=1}^{n} \frac{1}{2}\tilde{\theta}_{i,l}^T \tilde{\theta}_{i,l}.
\end{aligned}
\tag{15}
$$

3.2. Controller Design

Theorem 1. *For the SFOMASs* (1) *where Assumptions 1-4 hold, we construct a state observer* (7)*, by designing an event-triggered adaptive neural network dynamic surface quantized controller* (86)*, virtual control laws* (28), (46) *and* (62)*, together with the presented designs, which can ensure that all the signals remain bounded, and enables all followers to converge to the leader's convex hull.*

Proof. In this section, under the framework of adaptive backstepping design, based on Lyapunov stability theory, combined with quantized control, event-triggered technology, and neural network technology, we design virtual control laws and control input.

We define the error surfaces as follows:

$$
\begin{aligned}
s_{i,1} &= \sum\nolimits_{j=1}^{N} a_{ij}(y_i - y_j) + \sum\nolimits_{j=N+1}^{N+M} a_{ij}\left(y_i - y_{dj}(t)\right) \\
s_{i,l} &= \hat{x}_{i,l} - v_{i,l} \\
w_{i,l} &= v_{i,l} - \alpha_{i,l-1}, l = 2, \ldots, n-1
\end{aligned}
\tag{16}
$$

where $w_{i,l}$ is the error between $v_{i,l}$ obtained by the fractional order filter, and the virtual control function $\alpha_{i,l-1}$; $s_{i,l}$ denotes error surfaces; $\hat{x}_{i,l}$ is the estimation of $x_{i,l}$; y_i is the system output; and $y_{dj}(t)$ represents the leader signal. □

Step 1. According to Equations (16) and (1), we have

$$
\begin{aligned}
D^\alpha s_{i,1} = & d_i\left(x_{i,2} + \theta_{i,1}^T \varphi(\hat{X}_{i,1}) + \tilde{\theta}_{i,1}^T \varphi(\hat{X}_{i,1}) + \varepsilon_{i,1}^q + \Delta f_{i,1}^q \right) - \sum_{j=N}^{N+M} a_{ij} D^\alpha y_d \\
& - \sum_{j=1}^{N} a_{ij}\left(x_{j,2} + \theta_{j,1}^T \varphi(\hat{X}_{j,1}) + \tilde{\theta}_{j,1}^T \varphi(\hat{X}_{j,1}) + \varepsilon_{j,1}^q + \Delta f_{j,1}^q \right).
\end{aligned}
\tag{17}
$$

Substituting $x_{*,2} = e_{*,2} + \hat{x}_{*,2}$ and (16) into (17), one has

$$\begin{aligned} D^{\alpha}s_{i,1} = & d_i\left(s_{i,2} + w_{i,2} + \alpha_{i,1} + e_{i,2} + \theta_{i,1}^{T}\varphi(\hat{X}_{i,1}) + \tilde{\theta}_{i,1}^{T}\varphi(\hat{X}_{i,1}) + \varepsilon_{i,1}^{q} + \Delta f_{i,1}{}^{q}\right) \\ & - \sum\nolimits_{j=N+1}^{N+M} a_{ij}D^{\alpha}y_{di} - \sum\nolimits_{j=1}^{N} a_{ij}\left(\hat{x}_{j,2} + e_{j,2} + \theta_{j,1}^{T}\varphi(\hat{X}_{j,1}) + \tilde{\theta}_{j,1}^{T}\varphi(\hat{X}_{j,1}) + \varepsilon_{j,1}^{q} + \Delta f_{j,1}^{q}\right) \end{aligned} \tag{18}$$

where $\tilde{\theta}_{*,1} = \theta_{*,1}^{*} - \theta_{*,1}$, $d_i = \sum_{j=1}^{N+M} a_{ij}$, $\theta_{*,1}$ denotes the estimation of θ_{*1}^{*}.

We construct the Lyapunov function:

$$V_1 = V_0 + \sum_{i=1}^{N} V_{i,1} = V_0 + \frac{1}{2}\sum_{i=1}^{N}\left(s_{i,1}^2 + \frac{1}{\sigma_{i,1}}\tilde{\theta}_{i,1}^{T}\tilde{\theta}_{i,1} + \frac{1}{r_{i,1}}\tilde{\delta}_{i,1}^2 + \sum\nolimits_{j=1}^{N} a_{ij}\left(\frac{1}{\sigma_{j,1}}\tilde{\theta}_{j,1}^{T}\tilde{\theta}_{j,1} + \frac{1}{r_{j,1}}\tilde{\delta}_{j,1}^2\right)\right) \tag{19}$$

where $\tilde{\theta}_{*,l} = \theta_{*,l}^{*} - \theta_{*,l}$ are the parameter estimation errors, $\tilde{\delta}_{*,l} = \delta_{*,l}^{*} - \delta_{*,l}$ are the upper bound estimation errors, and $\sigma_{*,l}$ and $r_{*,l}$ denote design constant parameters.

Then, we can obtain

$$\begin{aligned} D^{\alpha}V_1 &= D^{\alpha}\left(V_0 + \sum_{i=1}^{N} V_{i,1}\right) \\ &= D^{\alpha}V_0 + \sum_{i=1}^{N}\left\{s_{i,1}D^{\alpha}s_{i,1} + \frac{1}{\sigma_{i,1}}\tilde{\theta}_{i,1}^{T}D^{\alpha}\tilde{\theta}_{i,1}\right. \\ &\quad \left. + \frac{1}{r_{i,1}}\tilde{\delta}_{i,1}D^{\alpha}\tilde{\delta}_{i,1} + \sum\nolimits_{j=1}^{N} a_{ij}\left(\frac{1}{\sigma_{j,1}}\tilde{\theta}_{j,1}^{T}D^{\alpha}\tilde{\theta}_{j,1} + \frac{1}{r_{j,1}}\tilde{\delta}_{j,1}D^{\alpha}\tilde{\delta}_{j,1}\right)\right\}. \end{aligned} \tag{20}$$

Substituting (18) into (20), we arrive at

$$\begin{aligned} D^{\alpha}V_1 \le & D^{\alpha}V_0 + \sum_{i=1}^{N}\left\{s_{i,1}\left[d_i\left(s_{i,2} + w_{i,2} + \alpha_{i,1} + e_{i,2} + \theta_{i,1}^{T}\varphi(\hat{X}_{i,1}) + \tilde{\theta}_{i,1}^{T}\varphi(\hat{X}_{i,1}) + \varepsilon_{i,1}^{q} + \Delta f_{i,1}^{q}\right)\right.\right. \\ & \left. - \sum\nolimits_{j=N+1}^{N+M} a_{ij}D^{\alpha}y_{dj} - \sum\nolimits_{j=1}^{N} a_{ij}\left(\hat{x}_{j,2} + e_{j,2} + \theta_{j,1}^{T}\varphi(\hat{X}_{j,1}) + \tilde{\theta}_{j,1}^{T}\varphi(\hat{X}_{j,1}) + \varepsilon_{j,1}^{q} + \Delta f_{j,1}^{q}\right)\right] \\ & \left. + \frac{1}{\sigma_{i,1}}\tilde{\theta}_{i,1}^{T}D^{\alpha}\tilde{\theta}_{i,1} + \frac{1}{r_{i,1}}\tilde{\delta}_{i,1}D^{\alpha}\tilde{\delta}_{i,1} + \sum\nolimits_{j=1}^{N} a_{ij}\left(\frac{1}{\sigma_{j,1}}\tilde{\theta}_{j,1}^{T}D^{\alpha}\tilde{\theta}_{j,1} + \frac{1}{r_{j,1}}\tilde{\delta}_{j,1}D^{\alpha}\tilde{\delta}_{j,1}\right)\right\}. \end{aligned} \tag{21}$$

Following Lemma 4, one has

$$s_{i,1}d_i(s_{i,2} + w_{i,2}) \le s_{i,1}^2 + \frac{d_i^2}{2}\left(s_{i,2}^2 + w_{i,2}^2\right) \tag{22}$$

$$s_{i,1}d_ie_{i,2} + s_{i,1}\sum\nolimits_{j=1}^{N} a_{ij}e_{j,2} \le s_{i,1}^2 + \frac{d_i^2}{2}\left(\|e_{i,2}\|^2 + \|e_{j,2}\|^2\right). \tag{23}$$

Denoting $\varepsilon_{*,l}^{q} + \Delta f_{*,l}^{q} = \Delta_{*,l}$ and $|\Delta_{i,l}| \le \delta_{i,l}^{*}$, the following inequalities hold

$$s_{*,1}\Delta_{*,1} \le |s_{*,1}\Delta_{*,1}| \le |s_{*,1}||\Delta_{*,1}| \le |s_{*,1}|\delta_{*,1}^{*} = |s_{*,1}|\left(\tilde{\delta}_{*,1} + \delta_{*,1}\right). \tag{24}$$

Considering (24), one has

$$D^{\alpha}V_1 \leq D^{\alpha}V_0 + \sum_{i=1}^{N}\Big\{s_{i,1}\Big[d_i\Big(\alpha_{i,1} + \theta_{i,1}^T\varphi(\hat{X}_{i,1}) + \tilde{\theta}_{i,1}^T\varphi(\hat{X}_{i,1}) \ +\varepsilon_{i,1}^q + \Delta f_{i,1}^q\Big)$$
$$- \sum\nolimits_{j=N+1}^{N+M} a_{ij}D^{\alpha}y_{dj} - \sum\nolimits_{j=1}^{N} a_{ij}\big(\hat{x}_{j,2} + \theta_{j,1}^T\varphi(\hat{X}_{j,1}) + \tilde{\theta}_{j,1}^T\varphi(\hat{X}_{j,1}) + \varepsilon_{j,1}^q + \Delta f_{j,1}^q\big)\Big]$$
$$+ s_{i,1}d_i(s_{i,2} + w_{i,2}) + s_{i,1}d_ie_{i,2} + s_{i,1}\Big(-\sum\nolimits_{j=1}^{N} a_{ij}e_{j,2}\Big) + \frac{1}{\sigma_{i,1}}\tilde{\theta}_{i,1}^T D^{\alpha}\tilde{\theta}_{i,1} \tag{25}$$
$$+ \frac{1}{r_{i,1}}\tilde{\delta}_{i,1}D^{\alpha}\tilde{\delta}_{i,1} + \sum\nolimits_{j=1}^{N} a_{ij}\left(\frac{1}{\sigma_{j,1}}\tilde{\theta}_{j,1}^T D^{\alpha}\tilde{\theta}_{j,1} + \frac{1}{r_{j,1}}\tilde{\delta}_{j,1}D^{\alpha}\tilde{\delta}_{j,1}\right)\Big\}.$$

Substituting (22) and (23) into (25) produces

$$D^{\alpha}V_1 \leq D^{\alpha}V_0 + \sum_{i=1}^{N}\Big\{s_{i,1}\Big[d_i\Big(\alpha_{i,1} + \theta_{i,1}^T\varphi(\hat{X}_{i,1}) + \tilde{\theta}_{i,1}^T\varphi(\hat{X}_{i,1}) \ +\varepsilon_{i,1}^q + \Delta f_{i,1}^q\Big)$$
$$- \sum\nolimits_{j=N+1}^{N+M} a_{ij}D^{\alpha}y_{dj} - \sum\nolimits_{j=1}^{N} a_{ij}\big(\hat{x}_{j,2} + \theta_{j,1}^T\varphi(\hat{X}_{j,1}) + \tilde{\theta}_{j,1}^T\varphi(\hat{X}_{j,1}) + \varepsilon_{j,1}^q + \Delta f_{j,1}^q\big)\Big]$$
$$+ s_{i,1}^2 + \frac{d_i^2}{2}\left(s_{i,2}^2 + w_{i,2}^2\right) + s_{i,1}^2 + \frac{d_i^2}{2}\left(\|e_{i,2}\|^2 + \|e_{j,2}\|^2\right) \tag{26}$$
$$+ \frac{1}{\sigma_{i,1}}\tilde{\theta}_{i,1}^T D^{\alpha}\tilde{\theta}_{i,1} + \frac{1}{r_{i,1}}\tilde{\delta}_{i,1}D^{\alpha}\tilde{\delta}_{i,1} + \sum\nolimits_{j=1}^{N} a_{ij}\left(\frac{1}{\sigma_{j,1}}\tilde{\theta}_{j,1}^T D^{\alpha}\tilde{\theta}_{j,1} + \frac{1}{r_{j,1}}\tilde{\delta}_{j,1}D^{\alpha}\tilde{\delta}_{j,1}\right)\Big\}.$$

Substituting (15) into (26), one has

$$D^{\alpha}V_1 \leq -q_1\|e\|^2 + \frac{1}{2}\|P\varepsilon\|^2 + \sum_{i=1}^{N}\sum_{l=1}^{n}\frac{1}{2}\tilde{\theta}_{i,l}^T\tilde{\theta}_{i,l} + \sum_{i=1}^{N}\Big\{s_{i,1}\Big[d_i\Big(\alpha_{i,1} + \theta_{i,1}^T\varphi(\hat{X}_{i,1})$$
$$+\varepsilon_{i,1}^q + \Delta f_{i,1}^q\Big) - \sum\nolimits_{j=N+1}^{N+M} a_{ij}D^{\alpha}y_d - \sum\nolimits_{j=1}^{N} a_{ij}\big(\hat{x}_{j,2} + \theta_{j,1}^T\varphi(\hat{X}_{j,1}) + \tilde{\theta}_{j,1}^T\varphi(\hat{X}_{j,1})$$
$$+\varepsilon_{j,1}^q + \Delta f_{j,1}^q\big)\Big] + 2s_{i,1}^2 + \frac{d_i^2}{2}\left(s_{i,2}^2 + w_{i,2}^2\right) - \frac{1}{\sigma_{i,1}}\tilde{\theta}_{i,1}^T D^{\alpha}\theta_{i,1} - \frac{1}{r_{i,1}}\tilde{\delta}_{i,1}D^{\alpha}\delta_{i,1} \tag{27}$$
$$+ \sum\nolimits_{j=1}^{N} a_{ij}\left(-\frac{1}{\sigma_{j,1}}\tilde{\theta}_{j,1}^T D^{\alpha}\theta_{j,1} - \frac{1}{r_{j,1}}\tilde{\delta}_{j,1}D^{\alpha}\delta_{j,1}\right)\Big\}$$

where $q_1 = q_0 - \sum_{i=1}^{N} d_i^2$.

We design the virtual control function $\alpha_{i,1}$ and parameters adaptive laws

$$\alpha_{i,1} = \frac{1}{d_i}\Big(-c_{i1}s_{i,1} - 2s_{i,1} + \sum\nolimits_{j=1}^{N} a_{ij}\big(\hat{x}_{j,2} + \theta_{j,1}^T\varphi_{j,1}\big) + \sum\nolimits_{j=N+1}^{N+M} a_{ij}D^{\alpha}y_{dj}\Big)$$
$$- \theta_{i,1}^T\varphi_{i,1} - sign(s_{i,1})\left(\delta_{i,1} - \sum\nolimits_{j=1}^{N}\frac{a_{ij}}{d_i}\delta_{j,1}\right). \tag{28}$$

$$D^{\alpha}\theta_{i,1} = \sigma_{i,1}d_i\varphi_{i,1}(\hat{X}_{i,1})s_{i,1} - \rho_{i,1}\theta_{i,1} \tag{29}$$

$$D^{\alpha}\theta_{j,1} = -\sigma_{j,1}\varphi_{j,1}(\hat{X}_{j,1})s_{i,1} - \rho_{j,1}\theta_{j,1} \tag{30}$$

$$D^{\alpha}\delta_{i,1} = r_{i,1}d_i|s_{i,1}| - \eta_{i,1}\delta_{i,1} \tag{31}$$

$$D^{\alpha}\delta_{j,1} = -r_{j,1}|s_{i,1}| - \eta_{j,1}\delta_{j,1} \tag{32}$$

Substituting (29)–(32) into (27) produces

$$\begin{aligned}
&D^{\alpha}V_1 \\
&\leq -q_1\|e\|^2 + \frac{1}{2}\|P\varepsilon\|^2 + \sum_{i=1}^{N}\sum_{l=1}^{n}\frac{1}{2}\tilde{\theta}_{i,l}^T\tilde{\theta}_{i,l} + \sum_{i=1}^{N}\Big\{s_{i,1}\Big[d_i\Big(\alpha_{i,1} + \theta_{i,1}^T\varphi(\hat{X}_{i,1}) + \varepsilon_{i,1}^q + \Delta f_{i,1}^q\Big) \\
&-\sum\nolimits_{j=N+1}^{N+M} a_{ij}D^{\alpha}y_{dj} - \sum\nolimits_{j=1}^{N} a_{ij}\Big(\hat{x}_{j,2} + \theta_{j,1}^T\varphi(\hat{X}_{j,1}) + \varepsilon_{j,1}^q + \Delta f_{j,1}^q\Big)\Big] + \frac{\rho_{i,1}}{\sigma_{i,1}}\tilde{\theta}_{i,1}^T\theta_{i,1} - \tilde{\delta}_{i,1}d_i|s_{i,1}| \\
&+\frac{\eta_{i,1}}{r_{i,1}}\tilde{\delta}_{j,1}\delta_{i,1} + \sum\nolimits_{j=1}^{N} a_{ij}\Big(\frac{\rho_{j,1}}{\sigma_{j,1}}\tilde{\theta}_{j,1}^T\theta_{j,1} + \tilde{\delta}_{j,1}|s_{i,1}| + \frac{\eta_{j,1}}{r_{j,1}}\tilde{\delta}_{j,1}\delta_{j,1}\Big) + 2s_{i,1}^2 + \frac{d_i^2}{2}\Big(s_{i,2}^2 + w_{i,2}^2\Big)\Big\}.
\end{aligned} \tag{33}$$

Substituting (28) into (33), we have

$$\begin{aligned}
D^{\alpha}V_1 \leq\ & -q_1\|e\|^2 + \frac{1}{2}\|P\varepsilon\|^2 + \sum_{i=1}^{N}\sum_{l=1}^{n}\frac{1}{2}\tilde{\theta}_{i,l}^T\tilde{\theta}_{i,l} \\
&+\sum_{i=1}^{N}\Big\{s_{i,1}\Big[-c_{i1}s_{i,1} - sign(s_{i,1})\Big(d_i\delta_{i,1} - \sum\nolimits_{j=1}^{N} a_{ij}\delta_{j,1}\Big) + d_i\Big(\varepsilon_{i,1}^q + \Delta f_{i,1}^q\Big)\Big) \\
&-\sum\nolimits_{j=1}^{N} a_{ij}\Big(\varepsilon_{j,1}^q + \Delta f_{j,1}^q\Big)\Big] + \frac{\rho_{i,1}}{\sigma_{i,1}}\tilde{\theta}_{i,1}^T\theta_{i,1} - \tilde{\delta}_{i,1}d_i|s_{i,1}| + \frac{\eta_{i,1}}{r_{i,1}}\tilde{\delta}_{i,1}\delta_{i,1} \\
&+\sum\nolimits_{j=1}^{N} a_{ij}\Big(\frac{\rho_{j,1}}{\sigma_{j,1}}\tilde{\theta}_{j,1}^T\theta_{j,1} + \tilde{\delta}_{j,1}|s_{i,1}| + \frac{\eta_{j,1}}{r_{j,1}}\tilde{\delta}_{j,1}\delta_{j,1}\Big) + \frac{d_i^2}{2}\Big(s_{i,2}^2 + w_{i,2}^2\Big)\Big\}.
\end{aligned} \tag{34}$$

Substituting (24) into (34), we have

$$\begin{aligned}
D^{\alpha}V_1 \leq\ & -q_1\|e\|^2 + \frac{1}{2}\|P\varepsilon\|^2 + \sum_{i=1}^{N}\sum_{l=1}^{n}\frac{1}{2}\tilde{\theta}_{i,l}^T\tilde{\theta}_{i,l} + \sum_{i=1}^{N}\Big\{-c_{i1}s_{i,1}^2 + \frac{\rho_{i,1}}{\sigma_{i,1}}\tilde{\theta}_{i,1}^T\theta_{i,1} + \frac{\eta_{i,1}}{r_{i,1}}\tilde{\delta}_{i,1}\delta_{i,1} \\
&+\sum\nolimits_{j=1}^{N} a_{ij}\Big(\frac{\rho_{j,1}}{\sigma_{j,1}}\tilde{\theta}_{j,1}^T\theta_{j,1} + \frac{\eta_{j,1}}{r_{j,1}}\tilde{\delta}_{j,1}\delta_{j,1}\Big) + \frac{d_i^2}{2}\Big(s_{i,2}^2 + w_{i,2}^2\Big)\Big\}.
\end{aligned} \tag{35}$$

By using the DSC technique, the state variable $v_{i,2}$ can be obtained by the following equation:

$$\lambda_{i,2}D^{\alpha}v_{i,2} + v_{i,2} = \alpha_{i,1}, \quad v_{i,2}(0) = \alpha_{i,1}(0). \tag{36}$$

According to Equations (16) and (36), we have

$$D^{\alpha}w_{i,2} = D^{\alpha}v_{i,2} - D^{\alpha}\alpha_{i,1} = -\frac{v_{i,2} - \alpha_{i,1}}{\lambda_{i,2}} - D^{\alpha}\alpha_{i,1} = -\frac{w_{i,2}}{\lambda_{i,2}} + B_{i,2} \tag{37}$$

where $B_{i,2}$ is a continuous function of variables $s_{i,1}, s_{i,2}, w_{i,2}, \theta_{i,1}, \theta_{j,1}, \delta_{i,1}, \delta_{j,1}, s_{j,3}, w_{j,3}, y_{dj}, D^{\alpha}y_{dj}$, $D^{\alpha}\big(D^{\alpha}y_{dj}\big)$, and there may exist an unknown constant M_{i2} such that $|B_{i2}| \leq M_{i2}$ holds.

Step 2. Defining the second surface error $s_{i,2} = \hat{x}_{i,2} - v_{i,2}$, we have

$$D^{\alpha}s_{i,2} = D^{\alpha}\hat{x}_{i,2} - D^{\alpha}v_{i,2} = \hat{x}_{i,3} + k_{i,2}e_{i,1} + \tilde{\theta}_{i,2}^T\varphi_{i,2} + \theta_{i,2}^T\varphi_{i,2} + \varepsilon_{i,2}^q + \Delta f_{i,2}^q - D^{\alpha}v_{i,2}. \tag{38}$$

According to Equation (16), we can obtain

$$D^{\alpha}s_{i,2} = s_{i,3} + w_{i,3} + \alpha_{i,2} + k_{i,2}e_{i,1} + \tilde{\theta}_{i,2}^T\varphi_{i,2} + \theta_{i,2}^T\varphi_{i,2} + \varepsilon_{i,2}^q + \Delta f_{i,2}^q - D^{\alpha}v_{i,2}. \tag{39}$$

Select the Lyapunov function as follows:

$$V_2 = V_1 + \sum_{i=1}^{N}V_{i,2} = V_1 + \frac{1}{2}\sum_{i=1}^{N}\Big(s_{i,2}^2 + \frac{1}{\sigma_{i,2}}\tilde{\theta}_{i,2}^T\tilde{\theta}_{i,2} + \frac{1}{r_{i,2}}\tilde{\delta}_{i,2}^2 + w_{i,2}^2\Big). \tag{40}$$

Further, we can obtain

$$D^{\alpha}V_2 \leq D^{\alpha}V_1 + \sum_{i=1}^{N}\big(s_{i,2}(s_{i,3} + w_{i,3} + \alpha_{i,2} + k_{i,2}e_{i,1} + \tilde{\theta}_{i,2}^{T}\varphi_{i,2} + \theta_{i,2}^{T}\varphi_{i,2} + \Delta_{i,2} \\ -D^{\alpha}v_{i,2}) + \frac{1}{\sigma_{i,2}}\tilde{\theta}_{i,2}^{T}D^{\alpha}\tilde{\theta}_{i,2} + \frac{1}{r_{i,2}}\tilde{\delta}_{i,2}D^{\alpha}\tilde{\delta}_{i,2} + w_{i,2}D^{\alpha}w_{i,2}\big). \tag{41}$$

Similar to the previous calculation, the following inequalities hold

$$s_{i,2}(s_{i,3} + w_{i,3}) \leq s_{i,2}^2 + \frac{1}{2}\left(s_{i,3}^2 + w_{i,3}^2\right) \tag{42}$$

$$s_{i,2}k_{i,2}e_{i,1} \leq \frac{1}{2}s_{i,2}^2 + \frac{k_{i,2}^2}{2}\|e_{i,1}\|^2 \tag{43}$$

$$s_{i,2}\Delta_{i,2} \leq |s_{i,2}\Delta_{i,2}| \leq |s_{i,2}||\Delta_{i,2}| \leq |s_{i,2}|\delta_{i,2}^{*} = |s_{i,2}|(\tilde{\delta}_{i,2} + \delta_{i,2}). \tag{44}$$

Substituting (42)–(44) into (41), we obtain

$$D^{\alpha}V_2 \leq D^{\alpha}V_1 + \sum_{i=1}^{N}\Big(s_{i,2}\big(\alpha_{i,2} + \tilde{\theta}_{i,2}^{T}\varphi_{i,2} + \theta_{i,2}^{T}\varphi_{i,2} - D^{\alpha}v_{i,2}\big) + |s_{i,2}|(\tilde{\delta}_{i,2} + \delta_{i,2}) \\ + \frac{3}{2}s_{i,2}^2 + \frac{1}{2}\left(s_{i,3}^2 + w_{i,3}^2\right) + \frac{k_{i,2}^2}{2}\|e_{i,1}\|^2 - \frac{1}{\sigma_{i,2}}\tilde{\theta}_{i,2}^{T}D^{\alpha}\theta_{i,2} - \frac{1}{r_{i,2}}\tilde{\delta}_{i,2}D^{\alpha}\delta_{i,2} + w_{i,2}D^{\alpha}w_{i,2}\Big). \tag{45}$$

We select the virtual controller $\alpha_{i,2}$ and the parameters adaptive laws as follows:

$$\alpha_{i,2} = -c_{i,2}s_{i,2} - \frac{3}{2}s_{i,2} - \frac{d_i^2}{2}s_{i,2} - \theta_{i,2}^{T}\varphi_{i,2} + \frac{\alpha_{i,1} - v_{i,2}}{\lambda_{i,2}} - sign(s_{i,2})\delta_{i,2} \tag{46}$$

$$D^{\alpha}\theta_{i,2} = \sigma_{i,2}\varphi_{i,2}(\hat{X}_{i,2})s_{i,2} - \rho_{i,2}\theta_{i,2} \tag{47}$$

$$D^{\alpha}\delta_{i,2} = r_{i,2}|s_{i,2}| - \eta_{i,2}\delta_{i,2}. \tag{48}$$

Substituting (35), (38) and (47)–(48) into (45), we have

$$D^{\alpha}V_2 \leq -q_1\|e\|^2 + \frac{1}{2}\|P\varepsilon\|^2 + \sum_{i=1}^{N}\sum_{l=1}^{n}\frac{1}{2}\tilde{\theta}_{i,l}^{T}\tilde{\theta}_{i,l} + \sum_{i=1}^{N}\Bigg\{-c_{i1}s_{i,1}^2 + \frac{\rho_{i,1}}{\sigma_{i,1}}\tilde{\theta}_{i,1}^{T}\theta_{i,1} + \frac{\eta_{i,1}}{r_{i,1}}\tilde{\delta}_{i,1}\delta_{i,1} \\ + \sum_{j=1}^{N} a_{ij}\left(\frac{\rho_{j,1}}{\sigma_{j,1}}\tilde{\theta}_{j,1}^{T}\theta_{j,1} + \frac{\eta_{j,1}}{r_{j,1}}\tilde{\delta}_{j,1}\delta_{j,1}\right) + \frac{d_i^2}{2}\left(s_{i,2}^2 + w_{i,2}^2\right)\Bigg\} \\ + \sum_{i=1}^{N}\Bigg\{s_{i,2}\Bigg[-c_{i,2}s_{i,2} - \frac{3}{2}s_{i,2} - \frac{d_i^2}{2}s_{i,2} - \theta_{i,2}^{T}\varphi_{i,2} + \frac{\alpha_{i,1} - v_{i,2}}{\lambda_{i,2}} - sign(s_{i,2})\delta_{i,2} + \tilde{\theta}_{i,2}^{T}\varphi_{i,2} \\ + \theta_{i,2}^{T}\varphi_{i,2} - D^{\alpha}v_{i,2}\Bigg] + |s_{i,2}|(\tilde{\delta}_{i,2} + \delta_{i,2}) + \frac{3}{2}s_{i,2}^2 + \frac{1}{2}\left(s_{i,3}^2 + w_{i,3}^2\right) + \frac{k_{i,2}^2}{2}\|e_{i,1}\|^2 \\ - \frac{1}{\sigma_{i,2}}\tilde{\theta}_{i,2}^{T}(\sigma_{i,2}\varphi_{i,2}(\hat{X}_{i,2})s_{i,2} - \rho_{i,2}\theta_{i,2}) - \frac{1}{r_{i,2}}\tilde{\delta}_{i,2}(r_{i,2}|s_{i,2}| - \eta_{i,2}\delta_{i,2}) + w_{i,2}\left(-\frac{w_{i,2}}{\lambda_{i,2}} + B_{i,2}\right)\Bigg\}. \tag{49}$$

By Lemma 4, we have

$$w_{i,2}B_{i,2} \leq \frac{1}{2}w_{i,2}^2 + \frac{1}{2}M_{i,2}^2. \tag{50}$$

Then, we have

$$D^\alpha V_2 \le -q_2\|e\|^2 + \frac{1}{2}\|P\varepsilon\|^2 + \sum_{i=1}^{N}\sum_{l=1}^{n}\frac{1}{2}\tilde{\theta}_{i,l}^T\tilde{\theta}_{i,l} + \sum_{i=1}^{N}\Big\{ -c_{i1}s_{i,1}^2 - c_{i,2}s_{i,2}^2 + \frac{\rho_{i,1}}{\sigma_{i,1}}\tilde{\theta}_{i,1}^T\theta_{i,1} + \frac{\eta_{i,1}}{r_{i,1}}\tilde{\delta}_{i,1}\delta_{i,1} + \frac{\rho_{i,2}}{\sigma_{i,2}}\tilde{\theta}_{i,2}^T\theta_{i,2} + \frac{\eta_{i,2}}{r_{i,2}}\tilde{\delta}_{i,2}\delta_{i,2} + \sum_{j=1}^{N} a_{ij}\left(\frac{\rho_{j,1}}{\sigma_{j,1}}\tilde{\theta}_{j,1}^T\theta_{j,1} + \frac{\eta_{j,1}}{r_{j,1}}\tilde{\delta}_{j,1}\delta_{j,1}\right) - \left(\frac{1}{\lambda_{i,2}} - \frac{1}{2} - \frac{d_i{}^2}{2}\right)w_{i,2}^2 + \frac{1}{2}\left(s_{i,3}^2 + w_{i,3}^2\right) + \frac{1}{2}M_{i,2}^2\Big\} \tag{51}$$

where $q_2 = q_1 - \sum_{i=1}^{N} k_{i,2}^2$.

Similar to (36) ,we have

$$\lambda_{i,3}D^\alpha v_{i,3} + v_{i,3} = \alpha_{i,2}, \quad v_{i,3}(0) = \alpha_{i,2}(0). \tag{52}$$

By Equation (52), we can obtain

$$D^\alpha w_{i,3} = D^\alpha v_{i,3} - D^\alpha \alpha_{i,2} = -\frac{v_{i,3} - \alpha_{i,2}}{\lambda_{i,3}} - D^\alpha \alpha_{i,2} = -\frac{w_{i,3}}{\lambda_{i,3}} + B_{i,3} \tag{53}$$

where $B_{i,3} = -D^\alpha \alpha_{i,2}$. Furthermore, there exists an unknown constant M_{i3} such that $|B_{i3}| \le M_{i3}$ holds.

Step m. The Caputo fractional derivatives of $s_{i,m}$ are as follows:

$$D^\alpha s_{i,m} = D^\alpha \hat{x}_{i,m} - D^\alpha v_{i,m} = \hat{x}_{i,m+1} + k_{i,m}e_{i,1} + \tilde{\theta}_{i,m}^T\varphi_{i,m} + \theta_{i,m}^T\varphi_{i,m} + \varepsilon_{i,m}^q + \Delta f_{i,m}^q - D^\alpha v_{i,m}. \tag{54}$$

Substituting (16) into (54) produces

$$D^\alpha s_{i,m} = s_{i,m+1} + w_{i,m+1} + \alpha_{i,m} + k_{i,m}e_{i,1} + \tilde{\theta}_{i,m}^T\varphi_{i,m} + \theta_{i,m}^T\varphi_{i,m} + \varepsilon_{i,m}^q + \Delta_{i,m}^q - D^\alpha v_{i,m}. \tag{55}$$

We construct a Lyapunov function candidate as

$$V_m = V_{m-1} + \sum_{i=1}^{N} V_{i,m} = V_{m-1} + \frac{1}{2}\sum_{i=1}^{N}\left\{ s_{i,m}^2 + \frac{1}{\sigma_{i,m}}\tilde{\theta}_{i,m}^T\tilde{\theta}_{i,m} + \frac{1}{r_{i,m}}\tilde{\delta}_{i,m}^2 + w_{i,m}^2\right\}. \tag{56}$$

According to Lemma 3 and (55), we can obtain

$$\begin{aligned} D^\alpha V_m &\le D^\alpha V_{m-1} + \sum_{i=1}^{N}\left(s_{i,m}D^\alpha s_{i,m} + \frac{1}{\sigma_{i,m}}\tilde{\theta}_{i,m}^T D^\alpha\tilde{\theta}_{i,m} + \frac{1}{r_{i,m}}\tilde{\delta}_{i,m}D^\alpha\tilde{\delta}_{i,m} + w_{i,m}D^\alpha w_{i,m}\right) \\ &\le D^\alpha V_{m-1} + \sum_{i=1}^{N}\{s_{i,m}[s_{i,m+1} + w_{i,m+1} + \alpha_{i,m} + k_{i,m}e_{i,1} + \tilde{\theta}_{i,m}^T\varphi_{i,m} + \theta_{i,m}^T\varphi_{i,m} \\ &\quad + \varepsilon_{i,m}^q + \Delta f_{i,m}^q - D^\alpha v_{i,m}\Big] + \frac{1}{\sigma_{i,m}}\tilde{\theta}_{i,m}^T D^\alpha\tilde{\theta}_{i,m} + \frac{1}{r_{i,m}}\tilde{\delta}_{i,m}D^\alpha\tilde{\delta}_{i,m} + w_{i,m}D^\alpha w_{i,m}\Big\}. \end{aligned} \tag{57}$$

Similar to (22) and (23), the following inequalities hold

$$s_{i,m}k_{i,m}e_{i,1} \le \frac{1}{2}s_{i,m}^2 + \frac{1}{2}k_{i,m}^2\|e_{i,1}\|^2 \tag{58}$$

$$s_{i,m}(s_{i,m+1} + w_{i,m+1}) \le s_{i,m}^2 + \frac{1}{2}s_{i,m+1}^2 + \frac{1}{2}w_{i,m+1}^2 \tag{59}$$

$$s_{i,m}\Delta_{i,m} \le |s_{i,m}\Delta_{i,m}| \le |s_{i,m}||\Delta_{i,m}| \le |s_{i,m}|\delta_{i,m}^* = |s_{i,m}|\left(\tilde{\delta}_{i,m} + \delta_{i,m}\right). \tag{60}$$

Substituting (58)–(60) into (57) produces

$$\begin{aligned} D^{\alpha}V_m \leq & D^{\alpha}V_{m-1} + \sum_{i=1}^{N}\Big\{s_{i,m}\Big(\alpha_{i,m} + \tilde{\theta}_{i,m}^{T}\varphi_{i,m} + \theta_{i,m}^{T}\varphi_{i,m} - D^{\alpha}v_{i,m}\Big) \\ & + \frac{3}{2}s_{i,m}^2 + \frac{1}{2}k_{i,m}^2\|e_{i,1}\|^2 + |s_{i,m}|(\tilde{\delta}_{i,m} + \delta_{i,m}) + \frac{1}{2}s_{i,m+1}^2 + \frac{1}{2}w_{i,m+1}^2 \\ & - \frac{1}{\sigma_{i,m}}\tilde{\theta}_{i,m}^{T}D^{\alpha}\theta_{i,m} - \frac{1}{r_{i,m}}\tilde{\delta}_{i,m}D^{\alpha}\delta_{i,m} + w_{i,m}D^{\alpha}w_{i,m}\Big\}. \end{aligned} \tag{61}$$

We design the m-th virtual control function $\alpha_{i,m}$ and parameters adaptive laws

$$\alpha_{i,m} = -c_{i,m}s_{i,m} - 2s_{i,m} - \theta_{i,m}^{T}\varphi_{i,m} + \frac{\alpha_{i,m-1} - v_{i,m}}{\lambda_{i,m}} - sign(s_{i,m})\delta_{i,m} \tag{62}$$

$$D^{\alpha}\theta_{i,m} = \sigma_{i,m}\varphi_{i,m}(\hat{X}_{i,m})s_{i,m} - \rho_{i,m}\theta_{i,m} \tag{63}$$

$$D^{\alpha}\delta_{i,m} = r_{i,m}|s_{i,m}| - \eta_{i,m}\delta_{i,m}. \tag{64}$$

Substituting Equations (62)–(64) into (61), we can obtain

$$\begin{aligned} D^{\alpha}V_m \leq & D^{\alpha}V_{m-1} + \sum_{i=1}^{N}\Big\{s_{i,m}\Big[-c_{i,m}s_{i,m} - 2s_{i,m} - \theta_{i,m}^{T}\varphi_{i,m} + \frac{\alpha_{i,m-1} - v_{i,m}}{\lambda_{i,m}} \\ & - sign(s_{i,m})\delta_{i,m} + \tilde{\theta}_{i,m}^{T}\varphi_{i,m} + \theta_{i,m}^{T}\varphi_{i,m} - D^{\alpha}v_{i,m}\Big] + |s_{i,m}|(\tilde{\delta}_{i,m} + \delta_{i,m}) + \frac{3}{2}s_{i,m}^2 \\ & + \frac{1}{2}k_{i,m}^2\|e_{i,1}\|^2 + \frac{1}{2}s_{i,m+1}^2 + \frac{1}{2}w_{i,m+1}^2 - \frac{1}{\sigma_{i,m}}\tilde{\theta}_{i,m}^{T}(\sigma_{i,m}\varphi_{i,m}(\hat{X}_{i,m})s_{i,m} - \rho_{i,m}\theta_{i,m}) \\ & - \frac{1}{r_{i,m}}\tilde{\delta}_{i,m}(r_{i,m}|s_{i,m}| - \eta_{i,m}\delta_{i,m}) + w_{i,m}D^{\alpha}w_{i,m}\Big\}. \end{aligned} \tag{65}$$

Similar to (52), $v_{i,m}$ can be obtained as

$$\lambda_{i,m}D^{\alpha}v_{i,m} + v_{i,m} = \alpha_{i,m-1}, \quad v_{i,m}(0) = \alpha_{i,m-1}(0). \tag{66}$$

By Equation (66), we have

$$D^{\alpha}w_{i,m} = -\frac{w_{i,m}}{\lambda_{i,m}} + B_{i,m} \tag{67}$$

where $|B_{im}| \leq M_{im}$, and M_{im} is an unknown constant.

By employing Young's inequality, we have

$$w_{i,m}B_{i,m} \leq \frac{1}{2}w_{i,m}^2 + \frac{1}{2}M_{i,m}^2. \tag{68}$$

From (65)–(68), we have

$$\begin{aligned} D^{\alpha}V_m \leq & D^{\alpha}V_{m-1} + \sum_{i=1}^{N}\Big\{-c_{i,m}s_{i,m}^2 + \frac{\rho_{i,m}}{\sigma_{i,m}}\tilde{\theta}_{i,m}^{T}\theta_{i,m} + \frac{\eta_{i,m}}{r_{i,m}}\tilde{\delta}_{i,m}\delta_{i,m} + \frac{1}{2}s_{i,m+1}^2 \\ & + \frac{1}{2}w_{i,m+1}^2 - \Big(\frac{1}{\lambda_{i,m}} - \frac{1}{2}\Big)w_{i,m}^2 + \frac{1}{2}M_{i,m}^2 - \frac{1}{2}s_{i,m}^2 + \frac{1}{2}k_{i,m}^2\|e_{i,1}\|^2\Big\}. \end{aligned} \tag{69}$$

Combining (15), (35) and (51) together leads to

$$D^{\alpha}V_{m-1} \leq -q_{m-1}\|e\|^2 + \frac{1}{2}\|P\varepsilon\|^2 + \sum_{i=1}^{N}\sum_{l=1}^{n}\frac{1}{2}\tilde{\theta}_{i,l}^T\tilde{\theta}_{i,l}$$
$$+\sum_{i=1}^{N}\left\{\sum_{l=1}^{m-1}\left(-c_{i,l}s_{i,l}^2 + \frac{\rho_{i,l}}{\sigma_{i,l}}\tilde{\theta}_{i,l}^T\theta_{i,l} + \frac{\eta_{i,l}}{r_{i,l}}\tilde{\delta}_{i,l}\delta_{i,l}\right) + \sum_{j\in N_i}a_{ij}\left(\frac{\rho_{j,1}}{\sigma_{j,1}}\tilde{\theta}_{j,1}^T\theta_{j,1} + \frac{\eta_{j,1}}{r_{j,1}}\tilde{\delta}_{j,1}\delta_{j,1}\right)\right. \tag{70}$$
$$\left.-\left(\frac{1}{\lambda_{i,2}} - \frac{1}{2} - \frac{d_i^2}{2}\right)w_{i,2}^2 - \sum_{l=3}^{m-1}\left(\frac{1}{\lambda_{i,l}} - 1\right)w_{i,l}^2 + \frac{1}{2}\left(s_{i,m}^2 + w_{i,m}^2\right) + \sum_{l=2}^{m-1}\frac{1}{2}M_{i,l}^2\right\}.$$

Substituting (70) into (69), we can obtain

$$D^{\alpha}V_m \leq -q_m\|e\|^2 + \frac{1}{2}\|P\varepsilon\|^2 + \sum_{i=1}^{N}\sum_{l=1}^{n}\frac{1}{2}\tilde{\theta}_{i,l}^T\tilde{\theta}_{i,l}$$
$$+\sum_{i=1}^{N}\left\{\sum_{l=1}^{m}\left(-c_{i,l}s_{i,l}^2 + \frac{\rho_{i,l}}{\sigma_{i,l}}\tilde{\theta}_{i,l}^T\theta_{i,l} + \frac{\eta_{i,l}}{r_{i,l}}\tilde{\delta}_{i,l}\delta_{i,l}\right). + \sum_{j=1}^{N}a_{ij}\left(\frac{\rho_{j,1}}{\sigma_{j,1}}\tilde{\theta}_{j,1}^T\theta_{j,1} + \frac{\eta_{j,1}}{r_{j,1}}\tilde{\delta}_{j,1}\delta_{j,1}\right)\right. \tag{71}$$
$$\left.-\left(\frac{1}{\lambda_{i,2}} - \frac{1}{2} - \frac{d_i^2}{2}\right)w_{i,2}^2 - \sum_{l=3}^{m}\left(\frac{1}{\lambda_{i,l}} - 1\right)w_{i,l}^2 + \frac{1}{2}\left(s_{i,m+1}^2 + w_{i,m+1}^2\right) + \sum_{l=2}^{m}\frac{1}{2}M_{i,l}^2\right\}$$

where $q_m = q_{m-1} - \sum_{i=1}^{N}k_{i,m}^2$.

Step n. As in the previous design steps, we define the following equations:

$$s_{i,n} = \hat{x}_{i,n} - v_{i,n} \tag{72}$$

$$w_{i,n} = v_{i,n} - \alpha_{i,n-1}. \tag{73}$$

Similar to (66), we can obtain $v_{i,n}$ as

$$\lambda_{i,n}D^{\alpha}v_{i,n} + v_{i,n} = \alpha_{i,n-1}, \quad v_{i,n}(0) = \alpha_{i,n-1}(0). \tag{74}$$

By Equations (73) and (74), we have

$$D^{\alpha}w_{i,n} = -\frac{w_{i,n}}{\lambda_{i,n}} + B_{i,n}. \tag{75}$$

Further, the fractional derivative $D^{\alpha}s_{i,n}$ is given by

$$\begin{aligned} D^{\alpha}s_{i,n} = D^{\alpha}\hat{x}_{i,n} - D^{\alpha}v_{i,n} &= u_i(t) + k_{i,n}e_{i,1} + \tilde{\theta}_{i,n}^T\varphi_{i,n} + \theta_{i,n}^T\varphi_{i,n} + \varepsilon_{i,n}^q + \Delta f_{i,n}^q - D^{\alpha}v_{i,n} \\ &= q_i(\omega_i(t)) + k_{i,n}e_{i,1} + \tilde{\theta}_{i,n}^T\varphi_{i,n} + \theta_{i,n}^T\varphi_{i,n} + \varepsilon_{i,n}^q + \Delta f_{i,n}^q - D^{\alpha}v_{i,n}. \end{aligned} \tag{76}$$

We construct the Lyapunov function as follows:

$$V_n = V_{n-1} + \sum_{i=1}^{N}V_{i,n} = V_{n-1} + \frac{1}{2}\sum_{i=1}^{N}\left\{s_{i,n}^2 + \frac{1}{\sigma_{i,n}}\tilde{\theta}_{i,n}^T\tilde{\theta}_{i,n} + \frac{1}{r_{i,n}}\tilde{\delta}_{i,n}^2 + w_{i,n}^2\right\}. \tag{77}$$

Then, one has

$$\begin{aligned} D^{\alpha}V_n &= D^{\alpha}V_{n-1} + D^{\alpha}\left(\sum_{i=1}^{N}V_{i,n}\right) \\ &\leq D^{\alpha}V_{n-1} + \sum_{i=1}^{N}\left\{s_{i,n}D^{\alpha}s_{i,n} - \frac{1}{\sigma_{i,n}}\tilde{\theta}_{i,n}^T D^{\alpha}\theta_{i,n} - \frac{1}{r_{i,n}}\tilde{\delta}_{i,n}D^{\alpha}\delta_{i,n} + w_{i,n}D^{\alpha}w_{i,n}\right\}. \end{aligned} \tag{78}$$

Substituting Equation (76) into (78), we have

$$D^{\alpha}V_n \leq D^{\alpha}V_{n-1} + \sum_{i=1}^{N}\Big\{s_{i,n}[q_i(\omega_i(t)) + k_{i,n}e_{i,1} + \tilde{\theta}_{i,n}^{T}\varphi_{i,n} + \theta_{i,n}^{T}\varphi_{i,n} + \varepsilon_{i,n}^{q} + \Delta f_{i,n}^{q} - D^{\alpha}v_{i,n}] - \frac{1}{\sigma_{i,n}}\tilde{\theta}_{i,n}^{T}D^{\alpha}\theta_{i,n} - \frac{1}{r_{i,n}}\tilde{\delta}_{i,n}D^{\alpha}\delta_{i,n} + w_{i,n}D^{\alpha}w_{i,n}\Big\}. \tag{79}$$

According to (5), we have

$$D^{\alpha}V_n \leq D^{\alpha}V_{n-1} + \sum_{i=1}^{N}\Big\{s_{i,n}[H(\omega_i)\omega_i(t) + L_i(t) + k_{i,n}e_{i,1} + \tilde{\theta}_{i,n}^{T}\varphi_{i,n} - D^{\alpha}v_{i,n}] + \theta_{i,n}^{T}\varphi_{i,n} + \varepsilon_{i,n}^{q} + \Delta f_{i,n}^{q} - \frac{1}{\sigma_{i,n}}\tilde{\theta}_{i,n}^{T}D^{\alpha}\theta_{i,n} - \frac{1}{r_{i,n}}\tilde{\delta}_{i,n}D^{\alpha}\delta_{i,n} + w_{i,n}D^{\alpha}w_{i,n}\Big\}. \tag{80}$$

The actual controller $\omega_i(t)$ is designed as

$$D^{\alpha}\theta_{i,n} = \sigma_{i,n}\varphi_{i,n}(\hat{X}_{i,n})s_{i,n} - \rho_{i,n}\theta_{i,n} \tag{81}$$

$$D^{\alpha}\delta_{i,n} = r_{i,n}|s_{i,n}| - \eta_{i,n}\delta_{i,n} \tag{82}$$

$$\bar{\alpha}_{in} = c_{i,n}s_{i,n} + \frac{3}{2}s_{i,n} + \theta_{i,n}^{T}\varphi_{i,n} + sign(s_{i,n})\delta_{i,n} - \frac{\alpha_{i,n-1} - v_{i,n}}{\lambda_{i,n}} \tag{83}$$

$$\omega_i(t) = \frac{1}{1-d}\left(-\bar{\alpha}_{in} - \frac{s_{i,n}(\kappa_{i1}\bar{\alpha}_{in})^2}{\sqrt{(s_{i,n}\kappa_{i1}\bar{\alpha}_{in})^2 + \kappa_{i,2}^2}} - \frac{s_{i,n}M_{i,1}^2}{\sqrt{(s_{i,n}M_{i,1})^2 + \kappa_{i,2}^2}}\right). \tag{84}$$

Notice that, from (5) and (84), we can obtain

$$H(\omega_i)\omega_i(t) \leq -\bar{\alpha}_{in} - \frac{s_{i,n}(\kappa_{i1}\bar{\alpha}_{in})^2}{\sqrt{(s_{i,n}\kappa_{i1}\bar{\alpha}_{in})^2 + \kappa_{i,2}^2}} - \frac{s_{i,n}M_{i,1}^2}{\sqrt{(s_{i,n}M_{i,1})^2 + \kappa_{i,2}^2}}. \tag{85}$$

We define the event-triggered controller $u_i(t)$ as follows

$$u_i(t) = q_i(\omega_i(t_k))\forall \in [t_k, t_{k+1}). \tag{86}$$

The triggering condition for the sampling instants are as follows:

$$t_{k+1} = \inf\{t \in R||\Delta_i(t)| \geq \kappa_{i1}|u_i(t)| + H_{i1}\} \tag{87}$$

where $\Delta_i(t) = q_i(\omega_i(t)) - u_i(t)$ is the event sampling error, $0 < \kappa_{i1} < 1$, H_{i1} is a positive constant, and $t_k, k \in z^{+}$ is the controller update time.

3.3. Stability Analysis

From Equation (87), we have

$$\Delta_i(t) = q_i(\omega_i(t)) - u_i(t) = \beta_{i1}(t)\kappa_{i1}u_i(t) + \beta_{i2}(t)H_{i1} \tag{88}$$

where $\beta_{i1}(t)$, $\beta_{i2}(t)$ are time-varying parameters satisfying $|\beta_{i1}(t)| \leq 1$, $|\beta_{i2}(t)| \leq 1$. Accordingly, one can obtain

$$u_i(t) = \frac{q_i(\omega_i(t)) - \beta_{i2}(t)H_{i1}}{1 + \beta_{i1}(t)\kappa_{i1}}. \tag{89}$$

Thus, it follows that

$$D^\alpha V_n \le D^\alpha V_{n-1} + \sum_{i=1}^{N} \left\{ s_{i,n} \left[\frac{q_i(\omega_i(t)) - \beta_{i2}(t)H_{i1}}{1+\beta_{i1}(t)\kappa_{i1}} + k_{i,n}e_{i,1} + \tilde{\theta}_{i,n}^T \varphi_{i,n} + \theta_{i,n}^T \varphi_{i,n} \right.\right.$$
$$\left.\left. + \varepsilon_{i,n}^q + \Delta f_{i,n}^q - D^\alpha v_{i,n} \right] - \frac{1}{\sigma_{i,n}} \tilde{\theta}_{i,n}^T D^\alpha \theta_{i,n} - \frac{1}{r_{i,n}} \tilde{\delta}_{i,n} D^\alpha \delta_{i,n} + w_{i,n} D^\alpha w_{i,n} \right\}. \tag{90}$$

Substituting Equations (81) and (82) into (90), we can obtain

$$D^\alpha V_n \le D^\alpha V_{n-1} + \sum_{i=1}^{N} \left\{ s_{i,n} [\frac{q_i(\omega_i(t)) - \beta_{i2}(t)H_{i1}}{1+\beta_{i1}(t)\kappa_{i1}} + \theta_{i,n}^T \varphi_{i,n} - D^\alpha v_{i,n}] + s_{i,n}(k_{i,n}e_{i,1} + \tilde{\theta}_{i,n}^T \varphi_{i,n} \right.$$
$$\left. + \varepsilon_{i,n}^q + \Delta f_{i,n}^q) - \frac{1}{\sigma_{i,n}} \tilde{\theta}_{i,n}^T (\sigma_{i,n}\varphi_{i,n}s_{i,n} - \rho_{i,n}\theta_{i,n}) - \frac{1}{r_{i,n}} \tilde{\delta}_{i,n}(r_{i,n}|s_{i,n}| - \eta_{i,n}\delta_{i,n}) + w_{i,n} D^\alpha w_{i,n} \right\}. \tag{91}$$

Then, we can obtain

$$D^\alpha V_n \le D^\alpha V_{n-1} + \sum_{i=1}^{N} \left\{ s_{i,n} \left[\frac{q_i(\omega_i(t)) - \beta_{i2}(t)H_{i1}}{1+\beta_{i1}(t)\kappa_{i1}} + \bar{\alpha}_{in} \right] - c_{in}s_{i,n}^2 - \frac{3}{2}s_{i,n}^2 \right.$$
$$- |s_{i,n}|\delta_{i,n} + s_{i,n}\left(\varepsilon_{i,n}^q + \Delta f_{i,n}^q \right) + \frac{\rho_{i,n}}{\sigma_{i,n}} \tilde{\theta}_{i,n}^T \theta_{i,n} + s_{i,n}k_{i,n}e_{i,1}$$
$$\left. - \frac{1}{r_{i,n}} \tilde{\delta}_{i,n}(r_{i,n}|s_{i,n}| - \eta_{i,n}\delta_{i,n}) + w_{i,n} D^\alpha w_{i,n} \right\}. \tag{92}$$

Similar to the previous calculation, we have

$$s_{i,n}k_{i,n}e_{i,1} \le \frac{1}{2}s_{i,n}^2 + \frac{1}{2}k_{i,n}^2 \|e_{i,1}\|^2 \tag{93}$$

$$s_{i,n}\left(\varepsilon_{i,n}^q + \Delta f_{i,n}^q \right) \le |s_{i,n}|(\tilde{\delta}_{i,n} + \delta_{i,n}). \tag{94}$$

From Equations (92)–(94), we can obtain

$$D^\alpha V_n \le D^\alpha V_{n-1} + \sum_{i=1}^{N} \left\{ s_{i,n} \left[\frac{q_i(\omega_i(t)) - \beta_{i2}(t)H_{i1}}{1+\beta_{i1}(t)\kappa_{i1}} + \bar{\alpha}_{in} \right] - c_{in}s_{i,n}^2 - s_{i,n}^2 \right.$$
$$\left. + \frac{\rho_{i,n}}{\sigma_{i,n}} \tilde{\theta}_{i,n}^T \theta_{i,n} + \frac{\eta_{i,n}}{r_{i,n}} \tilde{\delta}_{i,n}\delta_{i,n} + \frac{1}{2}k_{i,n}^2 \|e_{i,1}\|^2 + w_{i,n}\left(-\frac{w_{i,n}}{\lambda_{i,n}} + B_{i,n} \right) \right\}. \tag{95}$$

By employing Young's inequality, we have

$$w_{i,n}B_{i,n} \le \frac{1}{2}w_{i,n}^2 + \frac{1}{2}M_{i,n}^2. \tag{96}$$

Then we have

$$D^\alpha V_n \le D^\alpha V_{n-1} + \sum_{i=1}^{N} \left\{ s_{i,n} \left[\frac{q_i(\omega_i(t)) - \beta_{i2}(t)H_{i1}}{1+\beta_{i1}(t)\kappa_{i1}} + \bar{\alpha}_{in} \right] - c_{in}s_{i,n}^2 - s_{i,n}^2 \right.$$
$$\left. + \frac{\rho_{i,n}}{\sigma_{i,n}} \tilde{\theta}_{i,n}^T \theta_{i,n} + \frac{\eta_{i,n}}{r_{i,n}} \tilde{\delta}_{i,n}\delta_{i,n} + \frac{1}{2}k_{i,n}^2 \|e_{i,1}\|^2 - \frac{w_{i,n}^2}{\lambda_{i,n}} + \frac{1}{2}w_{i,n}^2 + \frac{1}{2}M_{i,n}^2 \right\}. \tag{97}$$

Substituting Equations (5), (84) and (85) into (97), we have

$$D^\alpha V_n \le D^\alpha V_{n-1} + \sum_{i=1}^{N} \Big\{ -c_{in} s_{i,n}^2 - s_{i,n}^2 + \frac{\rho_{i,n}}{\sigma_{i,n}} \tilde{\theta}_{i,n}^T \theta_{i,n} + \frac{\eta_{i,n}}{r_{i,n}} \tilde{\delta}_{i,n} \delta_{i,n} + \frac{1}{2} k_{i,n}^2 \|e_{i,1}\|^2 - \frac{w_{i,n}^2}{\lambda_{i,n}} \\ + \frac{1}{2} w_{i,n}^2 + \frac{1}{2} s_{i,n}^2 + \frac{\omega_{\min}^2}{2(1-\kappa_{i1})^2} + \frac{1}{2} M_{i,n}^2 + \frac{2\kappa_{i2}}{1-\kappa_{i1}} \Big\}. \tag{98}$$

From Equation (71), we can obtain

$$D^\alpha V_{n-1} \le -q_{n-1}\|e\|^2 + \frac{1}{2}\|P\varepsilon\|^2 + \sum_{i=1}^{N}\sum_{l=1}^{n} \frac{1}{2} \tilde{\theta}_{i,l}^T \tilde{\theta}_{i,l} \\ + \sum_{i=1}^{N} \Big\{ \sum_{l=1}^{n-1} \Big(-c_{i,,l} s_{i,l}^2 + \frac{\rho_{i,l}}{\sigma_{i,l}} \tilde{\theta}_{i,l}^T \theta_{i,l} + \frac{\eta_{i,l}}{r_{i,l}} \tilde{\delta}_{i,l} \delta_{i,l} \Big) \\ + \sum_{j=1}^{N} a_{ij} \Big(\frac{\rho_{j,1}}{\sigma_{j,1}} \tilde{\theta}_{j,1}^T \theta_{j,1} + \frac{\eta_{j,1}}{r_{j,1}} \tilde{\delta}_{j,1} \delta_{j,1} \Big) - \Big(\frac{1}{\lambda_{i,2}} - \frac{1}{2} - \frac{d_i^2}{2} \Big) w_{i,2}^2 \\ - \sum_{l=3}^{n-1} \Big(\frac{1}{\lambda_{i,l}} - 1 \Big) w_{i,l}^2 + \frac{1}{2} \big(s_{i,n}^2 + w_{i,n}^2 \big) + \sum_{l=2}^{n-1} \frac{1}{2} M_{i,l}^2 \Big\}. \tag{99}$$

Substituting (99) into (98) yields

$$D^\alpha V_n \le -q_n\|e\|^2 + \frac{1}{2}\|P\varepsilon\|^2 + \sum_{i=1}^{N}\sum_{l=1}^{n} \frac{1}{2} \tilde{\theta}_{i,l}^T \tilde{\theta}_{i,l} + \sum_{i=1}^{N} \Big\{ \sum_{l=1}^{n} \Big(-c_{i,,l} s_{i,l}^2 + \frac{\rho_{i,l}}{\sigma_{i,l}} \tilde{\theta}_{i,l}^T \theta_{i,l} + \frac{\eta_{i,l}}{r_{i,l}} \tilde{\delta}_{i,l} \delta_{i,l} \Big) \\ + \sum_{j=1}^{N} a_{ij} \Big(\frac{\rho_{j,1}}{\sigma_{j,1}} \tilde{\theta}_{j,1}^T \theta_{j,1} + \frac{\eta_{j,1}}{r_{j,1}} \tilde{\delta}_{j,1} \delta_{j,1} \Big) - \Big(\frac{1}{\lambda_{i,2}} - \frac{1}{2} - \frac{d_i^2}{2} \Big) w_{i,2}^2 \\ - \sum_{l=3}^{n} \Big(\frac{1}{\lambda_{i,l}} - 1 \Big) w_{i,l}^2 + \frac{\omega_{\min}^2}{2(1-\kappa_{i1})^2} + \sum_{l=2}^{n} \frac{1}{2} M_{i,l}^2 + \frac{2\kappa_{i2}}{1-\kappa_{i1}} \Big\} \tag{100}$$

where $q_n = q_{n-1} - \sum_{i=1}^{N} k_{i,n}^2$. According to Lemma 4, we have

$$\tilde{\theta}_{*,l}^T \theta_{*,l} \le -\frac{1}{2} \tilde{\theta}_{*,l}^T \tilde{\theta}_{*,l} + \frac{1}{2} \theta_{*,l}^{*T} \theta_{*,l}^* \tag{101}$$

$$\tilde{\delta}_{*,l} \delta_{*,l} \le -\frac{1}{2} \tilde{\delta}_{*,l}^2 + \frac{1}{2} \delta_{*,l}{}^{*2}. \tag{102}$$

From Equations (100)–(102), we can obtain

$$D^\alpha V_n \le -q_n\|e\|^2 + \frac{1}{2}\|P\varepsilon\|^2 + \sum_{i=1}^{N}\sum_{l=1}^{n} \frac{1}{2} \tilde{\theta}_{i,l}^T \tilde{\theta}_{i,l} \\ + \sum_{i=1}^{N} \Big\{ \sum_{l=1}^{n} \Big(-c_{i,,l} s_{i,l}^2 - \frac{\rho_{i,l}}{2\sigma_{i,l}} \tilde{\theta}_{i,l}^T \tilde{\theta}_{i,l} - \frac{\eta_{i,l}}{2r_{i,l}} \tilde{\delta}_{i,l}^2 \Big) + \sum_{j=1}^{N} a_{ij} \Big(-\frac{\rho_{j,1}}{2\sigma_{j,1}} \tilde{\theta}_{j,1}^T \tilde{\theta}_{j,1} - \frac{\eta_{j,1}}{2r_{j,1}} \tilde{\delta}_{j,1}^2 \Big) \\ - \Big(\frac{1}{\lambda_{i,2}} - \frac{1}{2} - \frac{d_i^2}{2} \Big) w_{i,2}^2 - \sum_{l=3}^{n} \Big(\frac{1}{\lambda_{i,l}} - 1 \Big) w_{i,l}^2 \\ + \sum_{l=1}^{n} \Big(\frac{\rho_{i,l}}{2\sigma_{i,l}} \theta_{i,l}^{*T} \theta_{i,l}^* + \frac{\eta_{i,l}}{2r_{i,l}} \delta_{i,l}^{*2} \Big) + \sum_{j \in N_i} a_{ij} \Big(\frac{\rho_{j,1}}{2\sigma_{j,1}} \theta_{j,1}^{*T} \theta_{j,1}^* + \frac{\eta_{j,1}}{2r_{j,1}} \delta_{j,1}^{*2} \Big) \\ + \frac{\omega_{\min}^2}{2(1-\kappa_{i1})^2} + \sum_{l=2}^{n} \frac{1}{2} M_{i,l}^2 + \frac{2\kappa_{i2}}{1-\kappa_{i1}} \Big\}. \tag{103}$$

Denote

$$\xi = \frac{1}{2}\|P\varepsilon\|^2 + \sum_{i=1}^{N}\left\{\sum_{l=1}^{n}\left(\frac{\rho_{i,l}}{2\sigma_{i,l}}\theta_{i,l}^{*T}\theta_{i,l}^{*} + \frac{\eta_{i,l}}{2r_{i,l}}\delta_{i,l}^{*2}\right) + \sum_{j=1}^{N}a_{ij}\left(\frac{\rho_{j,1}}{2\sigma_{j,1}}\theta_{j,1}^{*T}\theta_{j,1}^{*} + \frac{\eta_{j,1}}{2r_{j,1}}\delta_{j,1}^{*2}\right)\right.$$
$$\left. + \frac{\omega_{\min}^2}{2(1-\kappa_{i1})^2} + \sum_{l=2}^{n}\frac{1}{2}M_{i,l}^2 + \frac{2\kappa_{i2}}{1-\kappa_{i1}}\right\}. \tag{104}$$

Then Equation (103) can be written as

$$D^{\alpha}V_n \le -q_n\|e\|^2 + \sum_{i=1}^{N}\left\{\sum_{l=1}^{n}\left(-c_{i,l}s_{i,l}^2 - \left(\frac{\rho_{i,l}}{2\sigma_{i,l}} - \frac{1}{2}\right)\tilde{\theta}_{i,l}^T\tilde{\theta}_{i,l}\right.\right.$$
$$\left. - \frac{\eta_{i,l}}{2r_{i,l}}\tilde{\delta}_{i,l}^2\right) + \sum_{j=1}^{N}a_{ij}\left(-\frac{\rho_{j,1}}{2\sigma_{j,1}}\tilde{\theta}_{j,1}^T\tilde{\theta}_{j,1} - \frac{\eta_{j,1}}{2r_{j,1}}\tilde{\delta}_{j,1}^2\right) \tag{105}$$
$$\left. - \left(\frac{1}{\lambda_{i,2}} - \frac{1}{2} - \frac{d_i^2}{2}\right)w_{i,2}^2 - \sum_{l=3}^{n}\left(\frac{1}{\lambda_{i,l}} - 1\right)w_{i,l}^2\right\} + \xi$$

where $c_{i,l} > 0, (l = 1, \ldots, n)$, $\left(\frac{1}{\lambda_{i,2}} - \frac{1}{2} - \frac{d_i^2}{2}\right) > 0$, $\left(\frac{1}{\lambda_{i,l}} - 1\right) > 0, l = 3, \ldots, n$, $\left(\frac{\rho_{i,l}}{2\sigma_{i,l}} - \frac{1}{\tau_i}\right) > 0$, $\frac{\eta_{i,l}}{2r_{i,l}} > 0$, $\frac{\rho_{i,l}}{2\sigma_{i,l}} > 0$.

Define

$$C = \min\left\{2q_n/\lambda_{\min}(P), 2c_{i,l}, 2\left(\frac{\rho_{i,l}}{2\sigma_{i,l}} - \frac{1}{2}\right), \frac{\eta_{i,l}}{r_{i,l}}, \frac{\rho_{i,l}}{\sigma_{i,l}}, 2\left(\frac{1}{\lambda_{i,2}} - \frac{1}{2} - \frac{{d_i}^2}{2}\right), 2\left(\frac{1}{\lambda_{i,l}} - 1\right)\right\}. \tag{106}$$

Then Equation (105) becomes

$$D^{\alpha}V_n \le -CV_n + \xi. \tag{107}$$

According to Equation (107), we can obtain

$$D^{\alpha}V_n + Q(t) = -CV_n + \xi \tag{108}$$

where $Q(t) \ge 0$.

According to Lemma 6, we can obtain

$$V_n \le V(0)E_{\alpha}(-Ct^{\alpha}) + \tfrac{\xi\mu}{C}. \tag{109}$$

Then, we have

$$\lim_{t\to\infty}|V_n(t)| \le \frac{\xi\mu}{C}. \tag{110}$$

Since $\frac{1}{2}|s_{i,1}|^2 \le V_n(t)$, and we can obtain $||s_{i,1}|| \le \sqrt{\frac{2\xi\mu}{C}}$, invoking $s_{i,1} = \sum_{j=1}^{N} a_{ij}(y_i - y_j) + \sum_{j=N+1}^{N+M} a_{ij}\left(y_i - y_{dj}(t)\right)$, note the fact that $s_1 = L_1 y + L_2 r(t)$, where $s_1 = [s_{1,1}, \ldots, s_{N,1}]^T$. Because the convex hull spanned by leaders is defined as $r_d(t) = -L_1^{-1}L_2 r(t)$, then, the containment errors satisfy $\|e\| = \|y - r_d(t)\| \le \frac{\sqrt{2\xi\mu/C}}{\|L_1\|_F}$.

The proof process that the proposed control method can avoid Zeno phenomenon is as follows:

By $\Delta_i(t) = q_i(\omega_i(t)) - u_i(t)$, we have $D^\alpha|\Delta_i| = D^\alpha(\sqrt{\Delta_i \cdot \Delta_i}) = sign(\Delta_i)D^\alpha(\Delta_i) \le |D^\alpha(q_i(\omega_i(t)))| = |D^\alpha(H(\omega_i)\omega_i(t))| \le (1+d)|D^\alpha(\omega_i(t))|$. According to Equation (84), $D^\alpha(\omega_i(t))$ is bounded in a closed interval $[0,t]$. Therefore, there exists a constant $\varsigma > 0$ such that $|D^\alpha(\omega_i(t))| \le \varsigma$. From $\Delta(t_k) = 0$ and $\lim_{t \to t_{k+1}} \Delta(t) = H_{i1}$, thus, there exists t^* such that $t^* \ge H_{i1}/\varsigma$. Therefore, there exists $t^* \ge 0$ such that $\forall k \in z^+$, $\{t_{k+1} - t_k\} \ge t^*$, the Zeno phenomenon will not occur.

Remark 1. *It should be noted that the classical local theories used in this paper do not have the ability to describe the material heterogeneities and the fluctuations of different scales. In future research, we will use a more appropriate definition of a fractional differential, such as the Atangana-Baleanu [50] or Caputo-Fabrizio [51] fractional derivative definition.*

4. Simulation

In this section, to verify the effectiveness of the proposed method, the following fractional Duffing-Holmes chaotic system [52] is considered.

$$\begin{cases} D^\alpha x_{i,1} = x_{i,2} + f_{i,1}^q(X_{i,1}) \\ D^\alpha x_{i,2} = u_i(t) + f_{i,2}^q(X_{i,2}) \\ \quad y_i = x_{i,1} \end{cases} \tag{111}$$

where the system order is $\alpha = 0.98$, $i = 1,2,3,4$. $y_{d1} = 0.2\sin t$ and $y_{d2} = \sin 0.3t$ are defined as the leaders. The unknown functions are $f_{1,1}^q = f_{2,1}^q = f_{3,1}^q = f_{4,1}^q = 0$, $f_{1,2}^1 = x_{1,1} - 0.25x_{1,2} - x_{1,1}^3 + 0.3\cos(t)$, $f_{1,2}^2 = 2x_{1,1} - 0.25x_{1,2} - x_{1,1}^3$, $f_{2,2}^1 = x_{2,1} - 0.25x_{2,2} - x_{2,1}^3 + 0.1\left(x_{2,1}^2 + x_{2,2}^2\right)^{1/2}$, $f_{2,2}^2 = x_{2,1}^2$, $f_{3,2}^1 = x_{3,1} - 0.25x_{3,2} - x_{3,1}^3 + 0.2\sin(t)\left(x_{3,1}^2 + 2x_{3,2}^2\right)^{1/2}$, $f_{3,2}^2 = x_{3,1}^2 - x_{3,1}^3$, $f_{4,2}^1 = x_{4,1}^2$, and $f_{4,2}^2 = x_{4,1} - 0.25x_{4,2} - x_{4,1}^3 + 0.2\sin(t)\left(2x_{4,1}^2 + 2x_{4,2}^2\right)^{1/2}$. We chose the design parameters as $c_{i,1} = 20$, $c_{i,2} = 30$, $\sigma_{i,2} = r_{i,2} = 1$, $\rho_{i,2} = 40$, $\eta_{i,2} = 20$, $\lambda_{i,2} = 0.05$, $\kappa_{i1} = 0.5$, $\kappa_{i2} = 2$, $M_{i,1} = 1$, $\omega_{min} = 1$, and $d = 0.4$. We chose the initial conditions of the system as $x_1(0) = [0.1, 0.1]^T$, $x_2(0) = [0.2, 0.2]^T$, $x_3(0) = [0.3, 0.3]^T$, and $x_4(0) = [0.4, 0.4]^T$. The observer initial conditions were chosen as $\hat{x}_1(0) = [0.2, 0.2]^T$, $\hat{x}_2(0) = [0.3, 0.3]^T$, $\hat{x}_3(0) = [0.4, 0.4]^T$, and $\hat{x}_4(0) = [0.5, 0.5]^T$.

The communication graph of the multiagent system is shown in Figure 1. Figures 2–13 show the simulation results. Figure 2 displays the trajectories of y_{d1}, y_{d2} and $x_{i,1} (i = 1, \cdots, 4)$. Figure 3 shows the trajectories of the containment tracking errors. Figure 3a shows the trajectories of the containment tracking errors based on the event-triggered quantized controller, and Figure 3b shows the trajectories of containment tracking errors based on the event-triggered controller without input quantization. Figure 4 shows the trajectories of the $x_{i,1} (i = 1, \cdots, 4)$ estimation values. Figure 5 gives the error surfaces $s_{i,1}$ of the two controllers. Figure 6 gives the trajectories of $x_{i,2}$ and $\hat{x}_{i,2}$. We use $x_{1,1}$ and $x_{1,2}$ as examples in Figure 7 to show the results of the neural network observer designed in this paper. Figures 8–11 show the trajectories of ω_i, $q(\omega_i)$, and u_i. Meanwhile, we compared the event-triggered control input without quantitative control technology with the control input mentioned in this article. From Figures 8–11, the triggered number of control input via the quanzited mechanism was reduced by 7% to 20%, among which u_1 was reduced by 20% (see Figure 8), and u_4 was reduced by 7% (see Figure 11). In order to better highlight the advantages of the method proposed in this paper, we have compared the triggered number under different sampling mechanisms. It can be seen from Figure 13 that the proposed method can significantly reduce the number of control input samples. This means that the combination of event-triggered control and quantized control mechanisms can effectively reduce the number of transmissions of control input signals, so it has more practical significance and potential engineering value. Figure 12 shows the trajectories of the switching signal $\sigma_i(t)$. From the simulation results, the proposed method can ensure all followers converge to the leaders' convex hull, and the control performance is satisfactory.

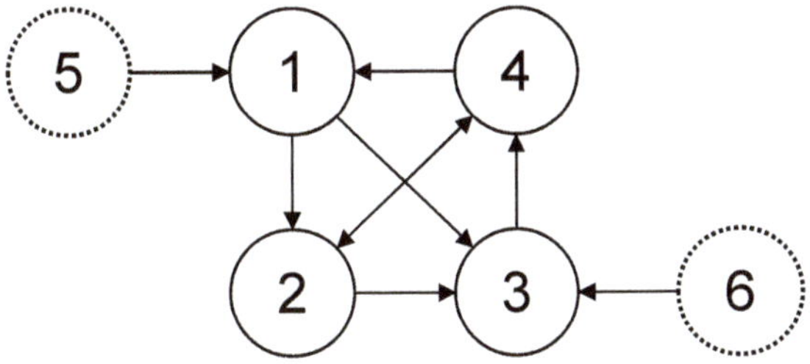

Figure 1. Communication graph.

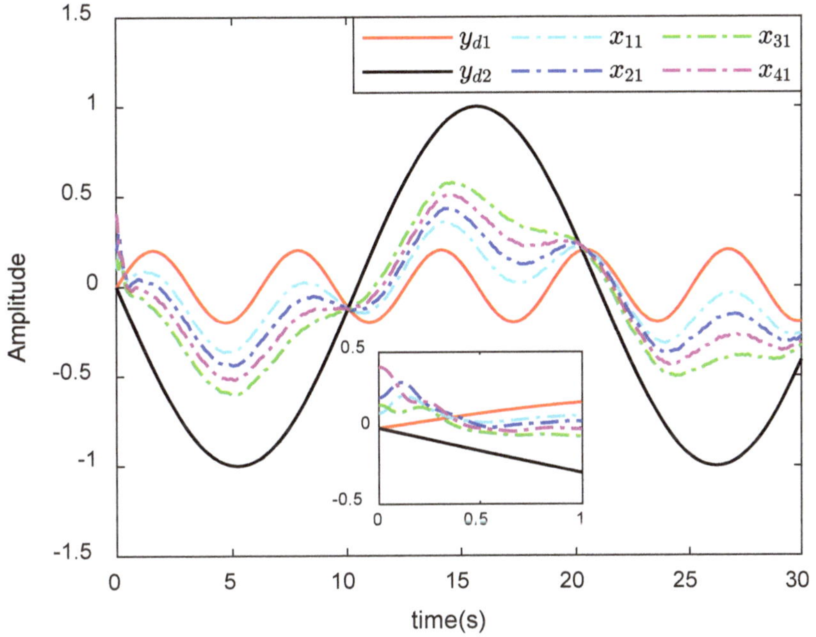

Figure 2. The trajectories of y_{d1},y_{d2} and $x_{i,1}(i = 1, \cdots, 4)$.

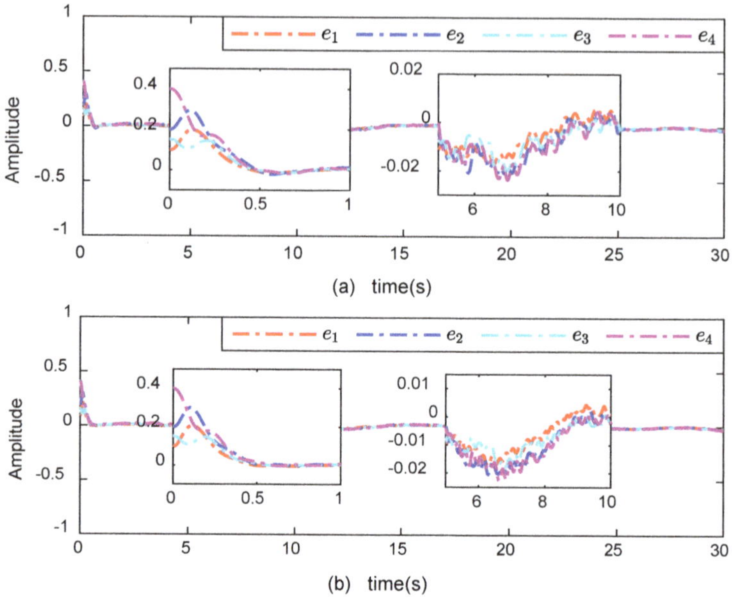

Figure 3. The trajectories of the containment tracking errors. (**a**) with quantized control. (**b**) without quantized control.

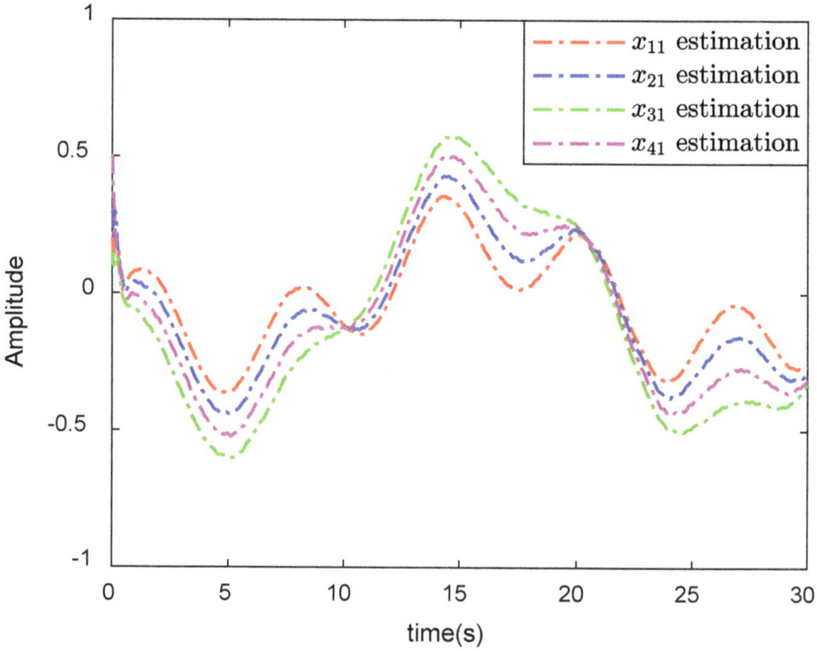

Figure 4. The trajectories of the $x_{i,1}(i = 1, \cdots, 4)$ estimation values.

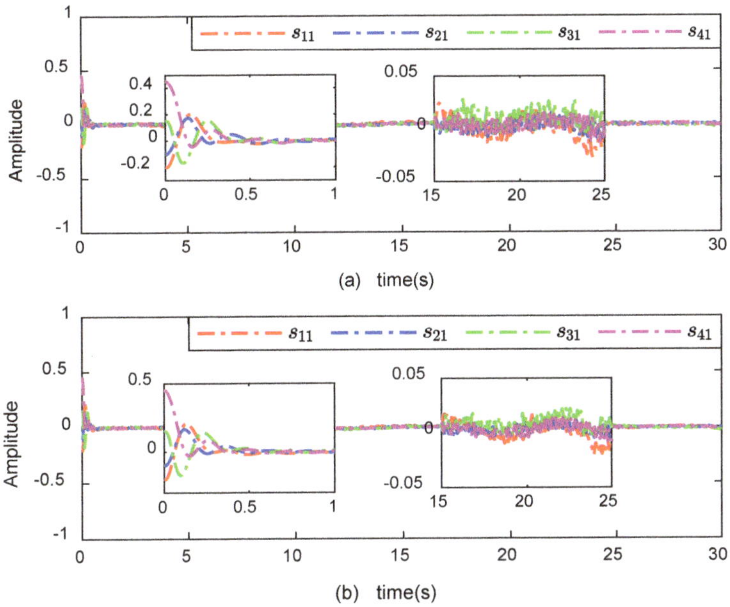

Figure 5. The trajectories of the error surfaces $s_{i,1}(i = 1, \cdots, 4)$. (**a**) with quantized control. (**b**) without quantized control.

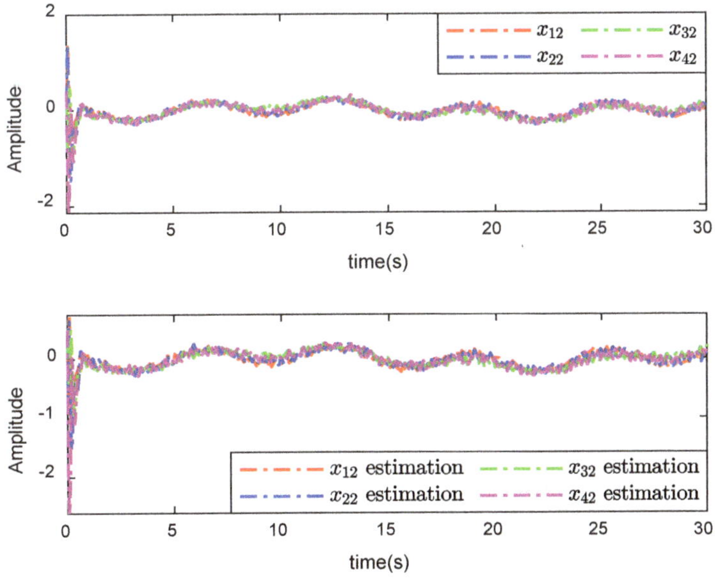

Figure 6. The trajectories of the $x_{i,2}(i = 1, \cdots, 4)$ and $x_{i,2}(i = 1, \cdots, 4)$ estimation values.

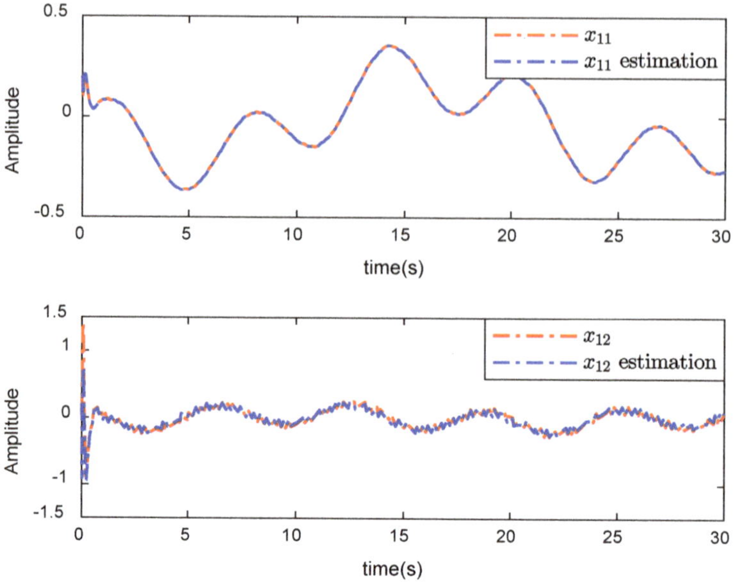

Figure 7. The trajectories of the $x_{1,1}$, $x_{1,1}$ estimation and $x_{1,2}$, $x_{1,2}$ estimation.

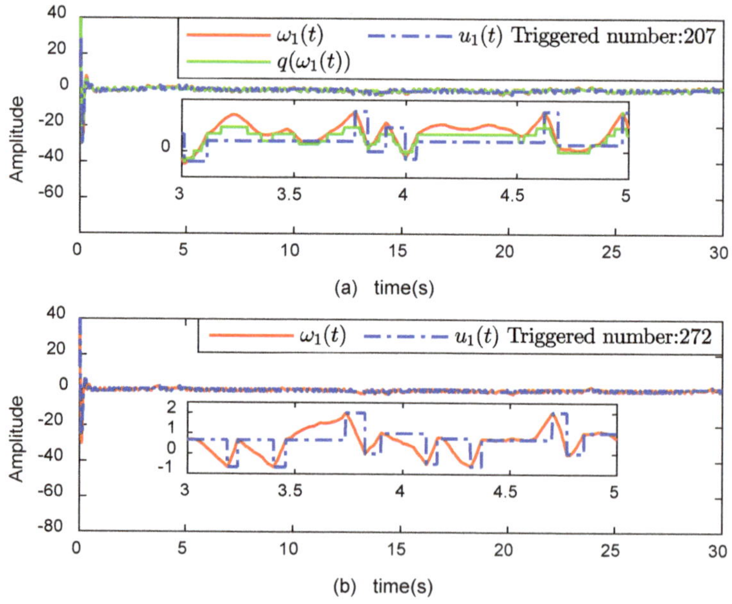

Figure 8. The trajectories of ω_1, $q(\omega_1)$, and u_1. (**a**) with quantized control. (**b**) without quantized control.

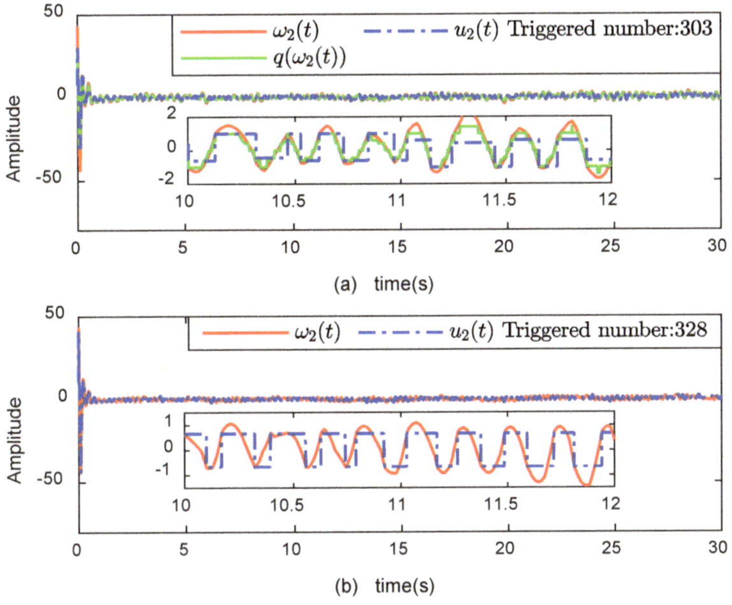

Figure 9. The trajectories of ω_2, $q(\omega_2)$, and u_2. (**a**) with quantized control. (**b**) without quantized control.

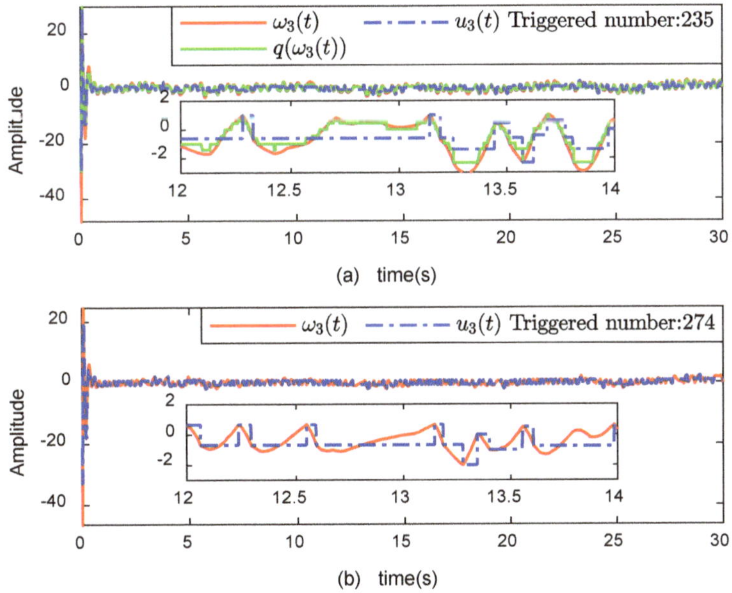

Figure 10. The trajectories of ω_3, $q(\omega_3)$, and u_3. (**a**) with quantized control. (**b**) without quantized control.

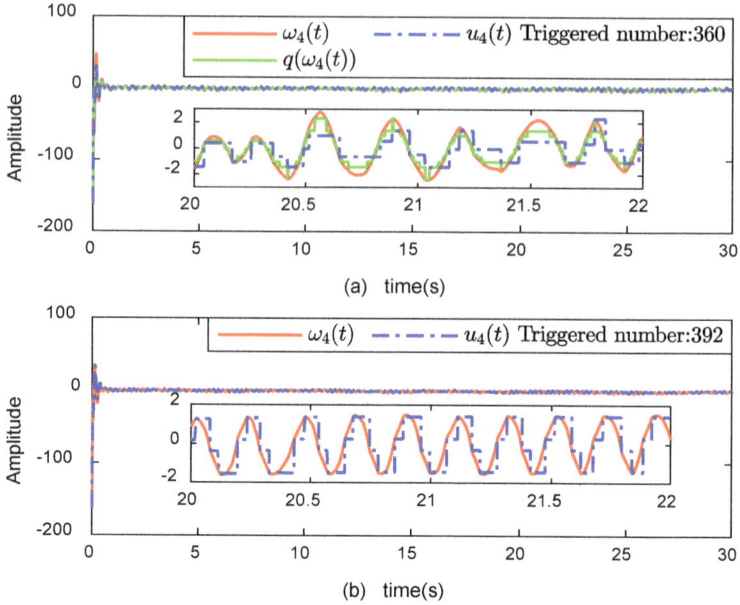

Figure 11. The trajectories of ω_4, $q(\omega_4)$, and u_4. (**a**) with quantized control. (**b**) without quantized control.

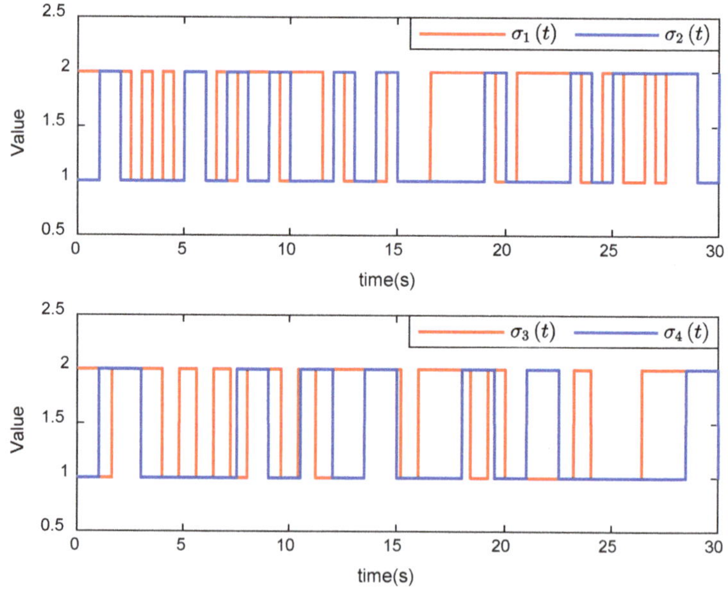

Figure 12. The switching signals $\sigma_i(t)$ of nonlinear functions.

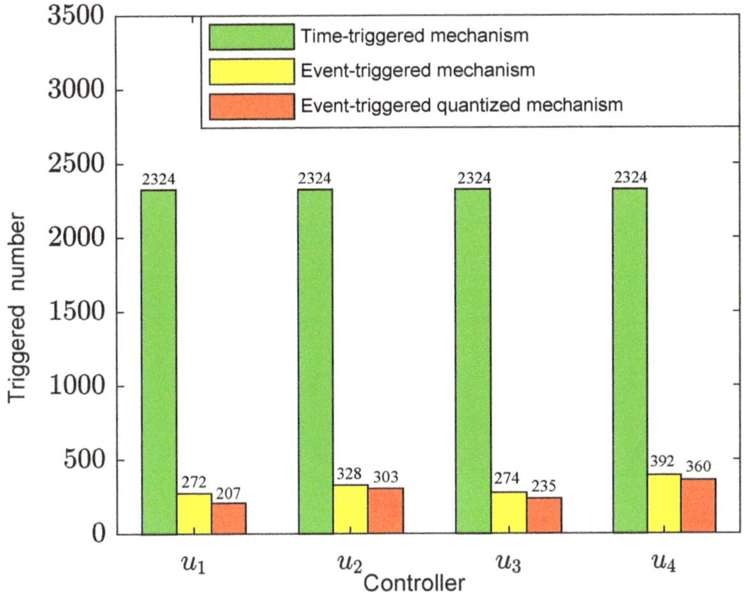

Figure 13. The triggered numbers of different mechanisms.

5. Conclusions

This paper proposed an event-triggered adaptive neural network dynamic surface quantized controller for the switched fractional order multiagent systems containment control problem. The followers considered were fractional order systems and contained arbitrarily switched nonlinear functions and unmeasured states. The hysteresis quantizer that we used can effectively avoid the chattering phenomena. An event-triggered scheme without Zeno behavior was considered, which reduced the utilization of communication resources. An RBF neural network was used to approximate unknown nonlinear functions and construct state observers to obtain unmeasurable states. Fractional derivatives of virtual control laws were obtained by fractional order DSC techniques, while avoiding "explosion of complexity". Example and simulation results showed that the proposed controller can not only ensure that all followers can converge to the leader's convex hull but also reduce the sampling frequency of the control input compared with the traditional event-triggered mechanism. With the consideration of dynamic uncertainties and the reduction in communication resources, the control algorithm in this study has a significant practical value, especially in the aspect of network control. Based on the previous work, this paper extended the adaptive dynamic surface control technology to the switched fractional order multiagent system and further studied the bipartite containment control problem under an event-triggered mechanism and control input quantization. Future research will apply this control scheme to real physical systems, such as wing vibration control of fixed-wing aircraft, robot formation control, etc.

Author Contributions: Conceptualization, J.Y.; Methodology, J.Y. and T.C.; Validation, T.C.; Writing—original draft, T.C.; Writing—review and editing, J.Y. All authors have read and agreed to the published version of the manuscript.

Funding: This research was funded by the opening project of Key Laboratory of Rotor Aerodynamics (China Aerodynamics Research and Development Center).

Institutional Review Board Statement: Not applicable.

Informed Consent Statement: Not applicable.

Data Availability Statement: Not applicable.

Acknowledgments: We would like to express our great appreciation to the editors and reviewers.

Conflicts of Interest: The authors declare no conflict of interest.

References

1. Sun, F.; Lei, C.; Kurths, J. Consensus of heterogeneous discrete-time multi-agent systems with noise over Markov switching topologies. *Int. J. Robust Nonlinear Control* **2021**, *31*, 1530–1541. [CrossRef]
2. Ma, L.; Wang, Z.; Lam, H.K. Event-triggered mean-square consensus control for time-varying stochastic multi-agent system with sensor saturations. *IEEE Trans. Autom. Control* **2016**, *62*, 3524–3531. [CrossRef]
3. Mao, J.; Yan, T.; Huang, S.; Li, S.; Jiao, J.g. Sampled-data output feedback leader-following consensus for a class of nonlinear multi-agent systems with input unmodeled dynamics. *Int. J. Robust Nonlinear Control* **2021**, *31*, 4203–4226. [CrossRef]
4. Deng, F.; Guo, S.; Zhou, R.; Chen, J. Sensor multifault diagnosis with improved support vector machines. *IEEE Trans. Autom. Sci. Eng.* **2015**, *14*, 1053–1063. [CrossRef]
5. Yao, D.; Dou, C.; Yue, D.; Zhao, N.; Zhang, T. Adaptive neural network consensus tracking control for uncertain multi-agent systems with predefined accuracy. *Nonlinear Dyn.* **2020**, *101*, 2249–2262. [CrossRef]
6. Guo, X.; Liang, H.; Pan, Y. Observer-Based Adaptive Fuzzy Tracking Control for Stochastic Nonlinear Multi-Agent Systems with Dead-Zone Input. *Appl. Math. Comput.* **2020**, *379*, 125269. [CrossRef]
7. Tian, Y.; Xia, Q.; Chai, Y.; Chen, L.; Lopes, A.M.; Chen, Y. Guaranteed Cost Leaderless Consensus Protocol Design for Fractional-Order Uncertain Multi-Agent Systems with State and Input Delays. *Fractal Fract.* **2021**, *5*, 141. [CrossRef]
8. Chen, T.; Yuan, J.; Yang, H. Event-triggered adaptive neural network backstepping sliding mode control of fractional-order multi-agent systems with input delay. *J. Vib. Control* **2021**. [CrossRef]
9. Yang, Y.; Liu, F.; Yang, H.; Li, Y.; Liu, Y. Distributed Finite-Time Integral Sliding-Mode Control for Multi-Agent Systems with Multiple Disturbances Based on Nonlinear Disturbance Observers. *J. Syst. Sci. Complex.* **2021**, *34*, 995–1013. [CrossRef]
10. Shahvali, M.; Azarbahram, A.; Naghibi-Sistani, M.B.; Askari, J. Bipartite consensus control for fractional-order nonlinear multi-agent systems: An output constraint approach. *Neurocomputing* **2020**, *397*, 212–223. [CrossRef]
11. González, A.; Aragüés, R.; López-Nicolás, G.; Sagüés, C. Weighted predictor-feedback formation control in local frames under time-varying delays and switching topology. *Int. J. Robust Nonlinear Control* **2020**, *30*, 3484–3500. [CrossRef]
12. Cui, G.; Xu, S.; Chen, X.; Lewis, F.L.; Zhang, B. Distributed containment control for nonlinear multiagent systems in pure-feedback form. *Int. J. Robust Nonlinear Control* **2018**, *28*, 2742–2758. [CrossRef]
13. Deng, X.; Cui, Y. Adaptive fuzzy containment control for nonlinear multi-agent systems with input delay. *Int. J. Syst. Sci.* **2021**, *52*, 1633–1645. [CrossRef]
14. Cui, Y.; Liu, X.; Deng, X.; Wang, L. Adaptive Containment Control for Nonlinear Strict-Feedback Multi-Agent Systems with Dynamic Leaders. *Int. J. Control* **2020**, 1–20. [CrossRef]
15. Li, Y.; Hua, C.; Wu, S.; Guan, X. Output feedback distributed containment control for high-order nonlinear multiagent systems. *IEEE Trans. Cybern.* **2017**, *47*, 2032–2043. [CrossRef]
16. Parsa, M.; Danesh, M. Containment control of high-order multi-agent systems with heterogeneous uncertainties, dynamic leaders, and time delay. *Asian J. Control* **2021**, *23*, 799–810. [CrossRef]
17. Pan, H.; Yu, X.; Yang, G.; Xue, L. Robust consensus of fractional-order singular uncertain multi-agent systems. *Asian J. Control* **2020**, *22*, 2377–2387. [CrossRef]
18. Lü, H.; He, W.; Han, Q.L.; Ge, X.; Peng, C. Finite-time containment control for nonlinear multi-agent systems with external disturbances. *Inf. Sci.* **2020**, *512*, 338–351. [CrossRef]
19. Xu, C.; Liao, M.; Li, P.; Yao, L.; Qin, Q.; Shang, Y. Chaos Control for a Fractional-Order Jerk System via Time Delay Feedback Controller and Mixed Controller. *Fractal Fract.* **2021**, *5*, 257. [CrossRef]
20. Jahanzaib, L.S.; Trikha, P.; Matoog, R.T.; Muhammad, S.; Al-Ghamdi, A.; Higazy, M. Dual Penta-Compound Combination Anti-Synchronization with Analysis and Application to a Novel Fractional Chaotic System. *Fractal Fract.* **2021**, *5*, 264. [CrossRef]
21. İlknur, K.; AKÇETİN, E.; Yaprakdal, P. Numerical approximation for the spread of SIQR model with Caputo fractional order derivative. *Turk. J. Sci.* **2020**, *5*, 124–139.
22. Dokuyucu, M.A. Caputo and atangana-baleanu-caputo fractional derivative applied to garden equation. *Turk. J. Sci.* **2020**, *5*, 1–7.
23. Butt, S.I.; Nadeem, M.; Farid, G. On Caputo fractional derivatives via exponential s-convex functions. *Turk. J. Sci.* **2020**, *5*, 140–146.
24. Zhao, S.; Butt, S.I.; Nazeer, W.; Nasir, J.; Umar, M.; Liu, Y. Some Hermite–Jensen–Mercer type inequalities for k-Caputo-fractional derivatives and related results. *Adv. Differ. Equ.* **2020**, *2020*, 262. [CrossRef]
25. Baleanu, D.; Fernandez, A.; Akgül, A. On a fractional operator combining proportional and classical differintegrals. *Mathematics* **2020**, *8*, 360. [CrossRef]
26. Sabir, Z.; Raja, M.A.Z.; Guirao, J.L.; Shoaib, M. A novel design of fractional Meyer wavelet neural networks with application to the nonlinear singular fractional Lane-Emden systems. *Alex. Eng. J.* **2021**, *60*, 2641–2659. [CrossRef]

27. Jiang, J.; Chen, H.; Cao, D.; Guirao, J.L. The global sliding mode tracking control for a class of variable order fractional differential systems. *Chaos Solitons Fractals* **2022**, *154*, 111674. [CrossRef]
28. Chen, J.; Guan, Z.H.; Yang, C.; Li, T.; He, D.X.; Zhang, X.H. Distributed containment control of fractional-order uncertain multi-agent systems. *J. Frankl. Inst.* **2016**, *353*, 1672–1688. [CrossRef]
29. Yuan, X.L.; Mo, L.P.; Yu, Y.G.; Ren, G.J. Distributed containment control of fractional-order multi-agent systems with double-integrator and nonconvex control input constraints. *Int. J. Control Autom. Syst.* **2020**, *18*, 1728–1742. [CrossRef]
30. Yang, W.; Yu, W.; Zheng, W.X. Fault-Tolerant Adaptive Fuzzy Tracking Control for Nonaffine Fractional-Order Full-State-Constrained MISO Systems With Actuator Failures. *IEEE Trans. Cybern.* **2021**, 1–14. [CrossRef]
31. Gong, P.; Lan, W. Adaptive robust tracking control for multiple unknown fractional-order nonlinear systems. *IEEE Trans. Cybern.* **2018**, *49*, 1365–1376. [CrossRef]
32. Wang, Y.; Yuan, Y.; Liu, J. Finite-time leader-following output consensus for multi-agent systems via extended state observer. *Automatica* **2021**, *124*, 109133. [CrossRef]
33. Yuan, X.; Mo, L.; Yu, Y. Observer-based quasi-containment of fractional-order multi-agent systems via event-triggered strategy. *Int. J. Syst. Sci.* **2019**, *50*, 517–533. [CrossRef]
34. Huo, X.; Ma, L.; Zhao, X.; Zong, G. Observer-based fuzzy adaptive stabilization of uncertain switched stochastic nonlinear systems with input quantization. *J. Frankl. Inst.* **2019**, *356*, 1789–1809. [CrossRef]
35. Zhang, X.; Wang, Z. Stability and robust stabilization of uncertain switched fractional order systems. *ISA Trans.* **2020**, *103*, 1–9. [CrossRef]
36. Tang, X.; Zhai, D.; Fu, Z.; Wang, H. Output Feedback Adaptive Fuzzy Control for Uncertain Fractional-Order Nonlinear Switched System with Output Quantization. *Int. J. Fuzzy Syst.* **2020**, *22*, 943–955. [CrossRef]
37. Li, Y.; Tong, S. Adaptive neural networks prescribed performance control design for switched interconnected uncertain nonlinear systems. *IEEE Trans. Neural Netw. Learn. Syst.* **2017**, *29*, 3059–3068. [CrossRef]
38. Sui, S.; Chen, C.L.P.; Tong, S. Neural-Network-Based Adaptive DSC Design for Switched Fractional-Order Nonlinear Systems. *IEEE Trans. Neural Netw. Learn. Syst.* **2021**, *32*, 4703–4712. [CrossRef]
39. Liu, W.; Ma, Q.; Xu, S.; Zhang, Z. Adaptive finite-time event-triggered control for nonlinear systems with quantized input signals. *Int. J. Robust Nonlinear Control* **2021**, *31*, 4764–4781. [CrossRef]
40. Liu, G.; Pan, Y.; Lam, H.K.; Liang, H. Event-triggered fuzzy adaptive quantized control for nonlinear multi-agent systems in nonaffine pure-feedback form. *Fuzzy Sets Syst.* **2021**, *416*, 27–46. [CrossRef]
41. Choi, Y.H.; Yoo, S.J. Quantized-Feedback-Based Adaptive Event-Triggered Control of a Class of Uncertain Nonlinear Systems. *Mathematics* **2020**, *8*, 1603. [CrossRef]
42. Xing, X.; Liu, J. Event-triggered neural network control for a class of uncertain nonlinear systems with input quantization. *Neurocomputing* **2021**, *440*, 240–250. [CrossRef]
43. Zhou, Q.; Wang, W.; Liang, H.; Basin, M.V.; Wang, B. Observer-Based Event-Triggered Fuzzy Adaptive Bipartite Containment Control of Multiagent Systems With Input Quantization. *IEEE Trans. Fuzzy Syst.* **2021**, *29*, 372–384. [CrossRef]
44. Li, Y.; Chen, Y.; Podlubny, I. Mittag–Leffler stability of fractional order nonlinear dynamic systems. *Automatica* **2009**, *45*, 1965–1969. [CrossRef]
45. Podlubny, I. *Fractional Differential Equations: An Introduction to Fractional Derivatives, Fractional Differential Equations, to Methods of Their Solution and Some of Their Applications*; Elsevier: Amsterdam, The Netherlands, 1998.
46. Duarte-Mermoud, M.A.; Aguila-Camacho, N.; Gallegos, J.A.; Castro-Linares, R. Using general quadratic Lyapunov functions to prove Lyapunov uniform stability for fractional order systems. *Commun. Nonlinear Sci. Numer. Simul.* **2015**, *22*, 650–659. [CrossRef]
47. Gao, H.; Zhang, T.; Xia, X. Adaptive neural control of stochastic nonlinear systems with unmodeled dynamics and time-varying state delays. *J. Frankl. Inst.* **2014**, *351*, 3182–3199. [CrossRef]
48. Wang, X.; Chen, Z.; Yang, G. Finite-time-convergent differentiator based on singular perturbation technique. *IEEE Trans. Autom. Control* **2007**, *52*, 1731–1737. [CrossRef]
49. Liu, W.; Lim, C.C.; Shi, P.; Xu, S. Backstepping fuzzy adaptive control for a class of quantized nonlinear systems. *IEEE Trans. Fuzzy Syst.* **2016**, *25*, 1090–1101. [CrossRef]
50. Algahtani, O.J.J. Comparing the Atangana–Baleanu and Caputo–Fabrizio derivative with fractional order: Allen Cahn model. *Chaos Solitons Fractals* **2016**, *89*, 552–559. [CrossRef]
51. Caputo, M.; Fabrizio, M. A new definition of fractional derivative without singular kernel. *Prog. Fract. Differ. Appl.* **2015**, *1*, 1–13.
52. Deepika, D.; Kaur, S.; Narayan, S. Uncertainty and disturbance estimator based robust synchronization for a class of uncertain fractional chaotic system via fractional order sliding mode control. *Chaos Solitons Fractals* **2018**, *115*, 196–203. [CrossRef]

Mathematical and Computational Applications

MDPI

Article

Equity Warrants Pricing Formula for Uncertain Financial Market

Foad Shokrollahi

Department of Mathematics and Statistics, University of Vaasa, P.O. Box 700, FIN-65101 Vaasa, Finland; foad.shokrollahi@uva.fi

Abstract: In this paper, inside the system of uncertainty theory, the valuation of equity warrants is explored. Different from the strategies of probability theory, the valuation problem of equity warrants is unraveled by utilizing the strategy of uncertain calculus. Based on the suspicion that the firm price follows an uncertain differential equation, a valuation formula of equity warrants is proposed for an uncertain stock model.

Keywords: equity warrants; uncertainty theory; uncertain stock model

1. Introduction

Warrants give the holder the right but not the obligation to purchase or sell the underlying assets by a specific date for a certain cost. Be that as it may, this right is not free. The warrant is one sort of exceptional option and it can be ordered in many types. Warrants can be partitioned into American warrants and European warrants as indicated by the distinction of the lapse date. Furthermore, they may be partitioned into call warrants and put warrants as indicated by the distinction of activity method. They may also be partitioned into equity warrants and covered warrants, agreeing with the distinction of the issuer. Covered warrants are as a rule given by sellers, which do not raise the organization's capital stock after their lapse dates. Valuing for this sort of warrant is like evaluating for normal options and, subsequently, numerous specialists use the Black–Scholes model [1] to value this sort of warrant. Yet, the value warrants are generally given by the recorded organization and the underlying capital is the given stock of its organization. The value warrants have a weakening impact and, consequently, valuing for this sort of warrant is in contrast to estimating for the standard European options in light of the fact that the organizations' equity warrants need to give new stock to meet the solicitation of the warrants' holder at the maturity date. All in all, the estimation cannot totally apply the works of art Black–Scholes model.

Uncertainty strategy was established by Liu [2] in 2007, and it has turned into a part of obvious mathematics for demonstrating belief degrees. As a part of obvious mathematics to manage belief degrees, the uncertainty hypothesis will assume a significant part in financial hypothesis and practice. Liu [3] started the pioneering work of uncertain finance in 2009. Thereafter, numerous analysts applied themselves to an investigation of financial issues by utilizing uncertainty strategy. For instance, Chen [4] explored the American alternative estimating issue and determined the evaluating formulae for Liu's uncertain stock model, and Chen and Gao [5] presented an uncertain term structure model of interest rate. Plus, in view of uncertainty strategy, Chen, Liu, and Ralescu [6] proposed an uncertain stock model with intermittent profits.

Previous studies of pricing equity warrants were mainly carried out with the method of stochastic finance based on the probability theory, and the firm price was usually assumed to follow some stochastic differential equation [7–9]. However, many empirical investigations showed that the firm value does not behave randomly, and it is often influenced by the belief degrees of investors since investors usually make their decisions

Citation: Shokrollahi, F. Equity Warrants Pricing Formula for Uncertain Financial Market. *Math. Comput. Appl.* **2022**, 27, 18. https://doi.org/10.3390/mca27020018

Academic Editors: António M. Lopes, Alireza Alfi, Liping Chen and Sergio A. David

Received: 17 January 2022
Accepted: 19 February 2022
Published: 22 February 2022

based on the degrees of belief rather than the probabilities. For example, one of the key elements in the Nobel Prize-winning theory of Kahneman and Tversky [10,11] is the finding of probability distortion which showed that decision makers usually make their decisions based on a nonlinear transformation of the probability scale rather than the probability itself, and people often overweight small probabilities and underweight large probabilities. Actually, we know that investors' belief degrees play an important role in decision making for financial practice [12–14]. Although a few models have been utilized in an equity warrant pricing, applying an uncertain stock strategy has not been considered. In this paper, inside the system of uncertain hypotheses, we examine the pricing issue of equity warrants. Based on the suspicion that the stock price satisfies an uncertain differential equation, we derive an uncertain model for estimating equity warrants.

The remainder of the paper is organized as follows: Some fundamental ideas of uncertain processes are reviewed in Section 2. In Section 3, a short presentation of an uncertain stock model is given. An uncertain value warrants model is proposed in Section 4. Finally, a concise rundown is given in Section 5.

2. Preliminary

A uncertain process is basically a sequence of uncertain variables indexed by time or space. In this segment, we review some essential realities about uncertain processes.

Definition 1 ([15]). *Let T be an index set and let $(\Gamma, \mathcal{M}, \mathcal{L})$ be an uncertainty space. An uncertain process is a measurable function from $T \times (\Gamma, \mathcal{M}, \mathcal{L})$ to the set of real numbers, i.e., for each $t \in T$ and any Borel set B of real numbers, the set*

$$\{X_t \in B\} = \{\gamma \in \Gamma | X_t(\gamma) \in B\}$$

is an event.

Definition 2 ([15]). *The uncertainty distribution Φ of an uncertain variable ξ is defined by*

$$\Phi(x) = \mathcal{M}\{\xi \leq x\}$$

for any real number x.

Definition 3 ([15]). *An uncertain variable ξ is called normal if it has a normal uncertainty distribution*

$$\Phi(x) = \left(1 + \exp\left(\frac{\pi(e - x)}{\sqrt{3}\sigma}\right)\right)^{-1}$$

denoted by $\mathcal{N}(e, \sigma)$ where e and σ are real numbers with $\sigma > 0$.

Definition 4 ([2]). *Let ξ be an uncertain variable. Then, the expected value of ξ is defined by*

$$E[\xi] = \int_0^{+\infty} \mathcal{M}\{\xi \geq r\}dr - \int_{-\infty}^0 \mathcal{M}\{\xi \leq r\}dr,$$

provided that at least one of the two integrals is finite.

Theorem 1 ([2]). *Let ξ be an uncertain variable with uncertainty distribution Φ. If the expected value exists, then*

$$E[\xi] = \int_0^{+\infty} (1 - \Phi(x))dx - \int_{-\infty}^0 \Phi(x)dx.$$

Theorem 2 ([16]). *Let ξ be an uncertain variable with regular uncertainty distribution Φ. Then,*

$$E[\xi] = \int_0^1 \Phi^{-1}(\alpha)d\alpha.$$

Definition 5 ([17]). *Let C_t be a canonical Liu process and let Z_t be an uncertain process. If there exist uncertain processes μ_t and σ_t such that*

$$Z_t = Z_0 + \int_0^t \mu_s ds + \int_0^t \sigma_s dC_s,$$

for any $t \geq 0$, then Z_t is called a Liu process with drift μ_t and diffusion σ_t. Furthermore, Z_t has an uncertain differential

$$dZ_t = \mu_t dt + \sigma_t dC_t.$$

Definition 6 ([15]). *Suppose C_t is a canonical Liu process, and f and g are two functions. Then,*

$$dX_t = f(t, X_t)dt + g(t, X_t)dC_t$$

is called an uncertain differential equation.

Definition 7 ([18]). *Let α be a number with $0 < \alpha < 1$. An uncertain differential equation*

$$dX_t = f(t, X_t)dt + g(t, X_t)dC_t$$

is said to have an α-path X_t^α if it solves the corresponding ordinary differential equation

$$dX_t^\alpha = f(t, X_t^\alpha)dt + |g(t, X_t^\alpha)|\Phi^{-1}(\alpha)dt,$$

where $\Phi^{-1}(\alpha)$ is the inverse standard normal uncertainty distribution, i.e.,

$$\Phi^{-1}(\alpha) = \frac{\sqrt{3}}{\pi}\ln\frac{\alpha}{1-\alpha}.$$

Theorem 3 ([18]). *Let X_t and X_t^α be the solution and α-path of the uncertain differential equation*

$$dX_t = f(t, X_t)dt + g(t, X_t)dC_t,$$

respectively. Then,

$$\begin{aligned} \mathcal{M}\{X_t \leq X_t^\alpha, \forall t\} &= \alpha \\ \mathcal{M}\{X_t > X_t^\alpha, \forall t\} &= 1 - \alpha. \end{aligned}$$

Theorem 4 ([18]). *Let X_t and X_t^α be the solution and α-path of the uncertain differential equation*

$$dX_t = f(t, X_t)dt + g(t, X_t)dC_t,$$

respectively. Then, the solution X_t has an inverse uncertainty distribution

$$\Psi_t^{-1}(\alpha) = X_t^\alpha.$$

Theorem 5 ([18]). *Let X_t and X_t^α be the solution and α-path of the uncertain differential equation*

$$dX_t = f(t, X_t)dt + g(t, X_t)dC_t,$$

respectively. Then, for any monotone (increasing or decreasing) function I, we have

$$E[I(X_t)] = \int_0^1 I(X_t^\alpha)d\alpha.$$

3. Uncertain Stock Model

Since the pioneer papers of Black, Scholes, and Merton on option evaluation were distributed in the mid-1970s, as a significant instrument, the Black–Scholes model was broadly utilized for estimating the financial derivatives by numerous specialists in which the stock value measure was portrayed by a stochastic differential equation as follows:

$$\begin{cases} dX_t = rX_t dt \\ dV_t = \mu V_t dt + \sigma V_t dB_t, \end{cases} \tag{1}$$

where X_t is the bond price, V_t is the stock price, r is the riskless interest rate, μ is the log-drift, σ is the log-diffusion, and B_t is a Wiener process.

Nonetheless, this assumption was tested among others by Liu [17] who proposed a contradiction showing that utilizing stochastic differential equations to depict stock value processes is not sensible. As an alternate tenet, Liu [3] generalized an uncertain differential equation to portray the fundamental stock value process and derived an uncertain stock model in which the bond value X_t and the stock cost V_t are described by

$$\begin{cases} dX_t = rX_t dt \\ dV_t = \mu V_t dt + \sigma V_t dC_t, \end{cases} \tag{2}$$

where C_t is a Liu process.

It follows from Equation (2) that the stock price is

$$V_t = V_0 e^{\mu t + \sigma C_t}, \quad 0 \le t \le T, \tag{3}$$

whose inverse uncertainty distribution is

$$\Phi^{-1}(\alpha) = V_0 \exp\left\{ \mu t + \frac{\sigma t\sqrt{3}}{\pi} \ln \frac{\alpha}{1-\alpha} \right\}.$$

4. The Pricing Model

Given an uncertainty space $(\Gamma, \mathcal{M}, \mathcal{L})$, we will suppose ideal conditions in the market for the firm's value and for the equity warrants:

(i) There are no transaction costs or taxes and all securities are perfectly divisible.
(ii) Dividends are not paid during the lifetime of the outstanding warrants, and the sequential exercise of the warrants is not optimal for warrant holders.
(iii) The warrant-issuing firm is an equity firm with no outstanding debt.
(iv) The total equity value of the firm, during the lifetime of the outstanding warrants, V_t, satisfies Equation (2).

In the case of equity warrants, the firm has N shares of common stock and M shares of equity warrants outstanding. Each warrant entitles the owner to receive k shares of stock at time T upon payment of J, the payoff of equity warrants is given by $\frac{1}{N+Mk}[kV_T - NJ]^+$, where V_T is the value of the firm's assets at time T. Considering the time value of money resulting from the bond, the present value of this payoff is

$$\frac{e^{-r(T-t)}}{N+Mk}[kV_T - NJ]^+.$$

Let f_w represent the price of the equity warrant. Then, the time-zero net return of the warrant holder is

$$-f_w + \frac{e^{-r(T-t)}}{N+Mk}[kV_T - NJ]^+.$$

On the other hand, the time-zero net return of the issuer is

$$f_w - \frac{e^{-r(T-t)}}{N+Mk}[kV_T - NJ]^+.$$

The fair price of this contract should make the holder of the equity warrant and the bank have an identical expected return, i.e.,

$$\begin{aligned} & f_w - E\left[\frac{e^{-r(T-t)}}{N+Mk}[kV_T - NJ]^+\right] \\ = & -f_w + E\left[\frac{e^{-r(T-t)}}{N+Mk}[kV_T - NJ]^+\right]. \end{aligned}$$

Thus, the price of an equity warrant can be defined as follows.

Definition 8. *Assume that there is a firm financed by N shares of stock and M shares of equity warrants. Each warrant gives the holder the right to buy k shares of stock at time $t = T$ in exchange for payment of an amount J. Let V_t be the asset value of the firm at time t. Then, the equity warrant price is*

$$f_w = \frac{e^{-r(T-t)}}{N+Mk} E\big[(kV_T - NJ)^+\big].$$

Theorem 6. *Based on all information from Definition (8), the price of an equity warrant at time t is given by*

$$\begin{aligned} f_w &= \frac{e^{-r(T-t)}}{N+Mk} \int_0^1 \bigg[kV_t \exp\{\mu(T-t) \\ &+ \frac{\sigma\sqrt{3}(T-t)}{\pi} \ln\frac{\alpha}{1-\alpha}\} - NJ \bigg]^+ d\alpha, \end{aligned}$$

where the optimal solutions σ^* and V_t^* satisfy the following system of nonlinear equations:

$$\begin{cases} NS_t = V_t - Mf_w \\ \sigma_S = \frac{\sigma V_t}{S_t}\left(\frac{1}{N} - \frac{M}{N}\frac{\partial f_w}{\partial V_t}\right). \end{cases} \tag{4}$$

Proof. Solving the ordinary differential equation

$$dV_t^\alpha = \mu V_t^\alpha dt + \sigma V_t^\alpha \Phi^{-1}(\alpha) dt,$$

where $0 < \alpha < 1$ and $\Phi^{-1}(\alpha)$ is the inverse standard normal uncertainty distribution, we have

$$V_t^\alpha = V_0 \exp\Big\{\mu t + \sigma \Phi^{-1}(\alpha) t\Big\}.$$

That means that the uncertain differential equation $dV_t = \mu V_t dt + \sigma V_t dC_t$ has an α-path

$$\begin{aligned} V_t^\alpha &= V_0 \exp\left\{\mu t + \sigma\Phi^{-1}(\alpha)t\right\} \\ &= V_0 \exp\left\{\mu t + \frac{\sigma\sqrt{3}}{\pi}\ln\frac{\alpha}{1-\alpha}\right\}. \end{aligned}$$

Since $I(x) = \frac{e^{-r(T-t)}}{N+Mk}[kV_T - NJ]^+$ is an increasing function, it follows from Theorem 5 and Definition (8) that the equity warrant price is

$$\begin{aligned} f_w &= E[I(V_T)] = \int_0^1 I(V_T^\alpha)d\alpha \\ &= \frac{e^{-r(T-t)}}{N+Mk}\int_0^1 [kV_T^\alpha - NJ]^+ d\alpha \\ &= \frac{e^{-r(T-t)}}{N+Mk}\int_0^1 \Bigg[kV_t \exp\{\mu(T-t) \\ &+ \frac{\sigma\sqrt{3}(T-t)}{\pi}\ln\frac{\alpha}{1-\alpha}\} - NJ\Bigg]^+ d\alpha. \end{aligned}$$

It is shown that the warrant pricing formula mentioned above depends on V_t and σ, which are unobservable. To obtain a pricing formula using observable values, we will make use of the following result.

Let β be the stock's elasticity, which gives the percentage change in the stock's value for a percentage change in the firm's value. Then, from a standard result in option pricing theory, we have

$$\beta = \frac{\sigma_s}{\sigma} = \frac{V_t \partial S_t}{S_t \partial V_t}. \tag{5}$$

From assumption (iii), we obtain $V_t = NS_t + Mf_w$. Consequently, we have

$$\frac{\partial S_t}{\partial V_t} = \frac{1}{N} - \frac{M}{N}\frac{\partial f_w}{\partial V_t}. \tag{6}$$

Now, from (5) and (6), it follows that

$$\sigma_s = \frac{\sigma V_t}{S_t}\left[\frac{1}{N} - \frac{M}{N}\frac{\partial f_w}{\partial V_t}\right]. \tag{7}$$

□

Theorem 7. *If $0 < \alpha < \frac{1}{2}$. Then, the nonlinear system (4) has a solution $(\sigma^*, V_t^*) \in (0, +\infty) \times (0, +\infty)$.*

Proof. First, it is clear that for any $\sigma \in (0, +\infty)$, there exists a unique $V_t \in (0, +\infty)$ which satisfies

$$NS_t = V_t - Mf_w.$$

Define a map $g : \sigma \to V_t$, which is given by an implicit function

$$G(\sigma, V_t) = V_t - Mf_w - NS_t.$$

The function $g : \sigma \mapsto V_t$ is increasing when $0 < \alpha < \frac{1}{2}$ since the following inequality holds:

$$\frac{dV_t}{d\sigma} = -\frac{\partial G/\partial\sigma}{\partial G/\partial V_t} = \frac{M\frac{\partial f_w}{\partial\sigma}}{1 - M\frac{\partial f_w}{\partial V_t}} > 0.$$

The inequality holds true because the function f_w is an increasing function of σ.

Second, it is obvious that for any $\sigma \in (0, +\infty)$, there exists a unique $V_t(\sigma) \in (0, +\infty)$, which satisfies

$$\sigma_s = \frac{\sigma V_t}{S_t}\left[\frac{1}{N} - \frac{M}{N}\frac{\partial f_w}{\partial V_t}\right].$$

Define a map $h : \sigma \mapsto V_t$, which is given by an implicit function

$$H(\sigma, V_t) = \frac{\sigma V_t}{S_t}\left[\frac{1}{N} - \frac{M}{N}\frac{\partial f_w}{\partial V_t}\right] - \sigma_s.$$

Function h is strictly continuous in V_t for all positive σ. Moreover, for all $\sigma > 0$, $\lim_{V_t \to 0} h(\sigma, V_t) = 0$ and $\lim_{V_t \to +\infty} h(\sigma, V_t) = +\infty$. Thus, we have

(1) g is one to one, continuous, and strictly increasing;
(2) h is continuous and attains any value in $(0, +\infty)$.

Hence, the intersection of g and h exists. This completes the proof. □

Different from a stochastic differential equation, an uncertain differential equation is driven by a Liu process. As a type of differential equation involving an uncertain process, it is very useful to deal with a dynamical process with uncertainty.

Figure 1 indicates that the equity warrant value is an increasing function with respect to the time T when other parameters remain unchanged. This is because the longer the time, the more likely it is to be executed and the higher the price of the equity warrant. This law is common sense in the financial markets.

Example 1. *Let* $N = 50, T - t = 3, M = 100, k = 1, S_t = 100, \sigma_s = 0.04, J = 50, r = 0.04$, $\mu = 0.02$. *Then, based on approximations* $V_t \approx NS_t$ *and* $\sigma \approx \sigma_s$, *the value of the equity warrant is*

$$f_w = 16.83.$$

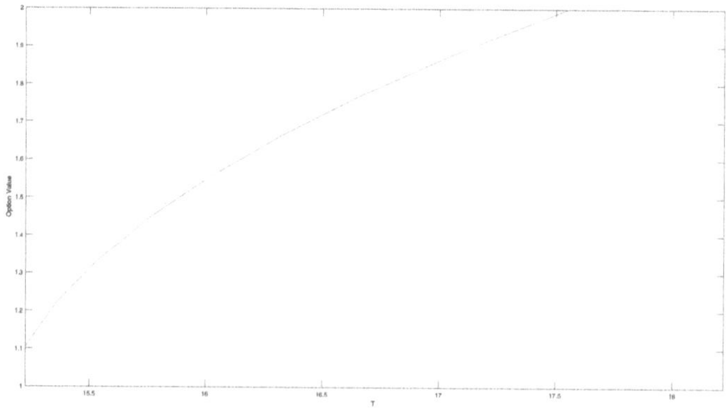

Figure 1. Equity warrant price f_w with respect to time.

5. Conclusions

The value of an equity warrant was examined within the structure of uncertainty probability in this paper. In light of the supposition that the firm's worth follows an uncertain differential equation, the model of equity warrants for an uncertain stock model was inferred with the strategy for uncertain analysis.

Funding: This research received no external funding.

Conflicts of Interest: The author declares that there are no conflicts of interest regarding the publication of this paper.

References

1. Black, F.; Scholes, M. The pricing of options and corporate liabilities. *J. Political Econ.* **1973**, *81*, 637–654. [CrossRef]
2. Liu, B. Uncertainty theory. In *Uncertainty Theory*; Springer: Berlin/Heidelberg, Germany, 2007; pp. 205–234.
3. Liu, B. Some research problems in uncertainty theory. *J. Uncertain Syst.* **2009**, *3*, 3–10.
4. Chen, X. American option pricing formula for uncertain financial market. *Int. J. Oper. Res.* **2011**, *8*, 32–37.
5. Chen, X.; Gao, J. Uncertain term structure model of interest rate. *Soft Comput.* **2013**, *17*, 597–604. [CrossRef]
6. Chen, X.; Liu, Y.; Ralescu, D.A. Uncertain stock model with periodic dividends. *Fuzzy Optim. Decis. Mak.* **2013**, *12*, 111–123. [CrossRef]
7. Xiao, W.; Zhang, W.; Xu, W.; Zhang, X. The valuation of equity warrants in a fractional Brownian environment. *Phys. A Stat. Mech. Appl.* **2012**, *391*, 1742–1752. [CrossRef]
8. Kremer, J.W.; Roenfeldt, R.L. Warrant pricing: Jump-diffusion vs. Black–Scholes. *J. Financ. Quant. Anal.* **1993**, *28*, 255–272. [CrossRef]
9. Zhang, W.G.; Xiao, W.L.; He, C.X. Equity warrants pricing model under Fractional Brownian motion and an empirical study. *Expert Syst. Appl.* **2009**, *36*, 3056–3065. [CrossRef]
10. Tversky, A.; Kahneman, D. Advances in prospect theory: Cumulative representation of uncertainty. *J. Risk Uncertain.* **1992**, *5*, 297–323. [CrossRef]
11. Tversky, A.; Kahneman, D. Advances in prospect theory: Cumulative representation of uncertainty. In *Readings in Formal Epistemology*; Springer: Cham, Switzerland, 2016; pp. 493–519.
12. Yao, K. No-arbitrage determinant theorems on mean-reverting stock model in uncertain market. *Knowl. Based Syst.* **2012**, *35*, 259–263. [CrossRef]
13. Zhang, Z.; Liu, W.; Sheng, Y. Valuation of power option for uncertain financial market. *Appl. Math. Comput.* **2016**, *286*, 257–264. [CrossRef]
14. Zhang, Z.; Liu, W.; Ding, J. Valuation of stock loan under uncertain environment. *Soft Comput.* **2017**, *22*, 5663–5669. [CrossRef]
15. Liu, B. Fuzzy process, hybrid process and uncertain process. *J. Uncertain Syst.* **2008**, *2*, 3–16.
16. Liu, B. *Uncertaint Theory: A Branch of Mathematics for Modeling Human Uncertainty*; Springer: Berlin/Heidelberg, Germany, 2010.
17. Chen, X.; Ralescu, D.A. Liu process and uncertain calculus. *J. Uncertain. Anal. Appl.* **2013**, *1*, 3. [CrossRef]
18. Yao, K.; Chen, X. A numerical method for solving uncertain differential equations. *J. Intell. Fuzzy Syst.* **2013**, *25*, 825–832. [CrossRef]

mathematics

Article

Parameter Identification and the Finite-Time Combination–Combination Synchronization of Fractional-Order Chaotic Systems with Different Structures under Multiple Stochastic Disturbances

Weiqiu Pan [1], Tianzeng Li [1,2,*], Muhammad Sajid [3], Safdar Ali [1] and Lingping Pu [4]

[1] College of Mathematics and Statistics, Sichuan University of Science and Engineering, Zigong 643000, China; 31907010403@suse.edu.cn (W.P.); Safdarkhan868@yanhoo.com (S.A.)
[2] South Sichuan Center for Applied Mathematics, Yibin 644000, China
[3] Faculty of Materials and Chemical Engineering, Yibin University, Yibin 644000, China; Engr.sajid80@gmail.com
[4] College of Liquor, Sichuan University of Science and Engineering, Zigong 643099, China; pulingping@163.com
* Correspondence: litianzeng@suse.edu.cn

Citation: Pan, W.; Li, T.; Sajid, M.; Ali, S.; Pu, L. Parameter Identification and the Finite-Time Combination–Combination Synchronization of Fractional-Order Chaotic Systems with Different Structures under Multiple Stochastic Disturbances. *Mathematics* **2022**, *10*, 712. https://doi.org/10.3390/math10050712

Academic Editors: António M. Lopes, Alireza Alfi, Liping Chen and Sergio A. David

Received: 21 January 2022
Accepted: 21 February 2022
Published: 24 February 2022

Abstract: This paper researches the issue of the finite-time combination-combination (C-C) synchronization (FTCCS) of fractional order (FO) chaotic systems under multiple stochastic disturbances (SD) utilizing the nonsingular terminal sliding mode control (NTSMC) technique. The systems we considered have different characteristics of the structures and the parameters are unknown. The stochastic disturbances are considered parameter uncertainties, nonlinear uncertainties and external disturbances. The bounds of the uncertainties and disturbances are unknown. Firstly, we are going to put forward a new FO sliding surface in terms of fractional calculus. Secondly, some suitable adaptive control laws (ACL) are found to assess the unknown parameters and examine the upper bound of stochastic disturbances. Finally, combining the finite-time Lyapunov stability theory and the sliding mode control (SMC) technique, we propose a fractional-order adaptive combination controller that can achieve the finite-time synchronization of drive-response (D-R) systems. In this paper, some of the synchronization methods, such as chaos control, complete synchronization, projection synchronization, anti-synchronization, and so forth, have become special cases of combination-combination synchronization. Examples are presented to verify the usefulness and validity of the proposed scheme via MATLAB.

Keywords: fractional-order chaotic system; finite-time synchronization; adaptive sliding mode control; stochastic disturbance

MSC: 34A08; 34D06

1. Introduction

Chaos is not an accidental or individual event, but a universal existence in various macro and micro systems in the universe. It promotes and relies on other sciences, which derive many interdisciplinary subjects, such as chaotic meteorology, chaotic economics, chaotic mathematics, and so forth. Because chaos is ubiquitous in many systems, the research on chaotic systems has drawn widespread attention of scholars. Thanks to the nonlinear nature of the chaotic system and the sensitivity to the initial value, the control and synchronization to the chaotic system has become a very difficult problem. Up to now, many valid synchronization methods were researched, such as drive-response synchronization [1], projective synchronization [2,3], adaptive fuzzy control [4–6], neural network synchronization [7,8], feedback synchronization [9] and pulse synchronization [10,11], sliding mode control [12,13] and so forth.

Some scholars have taken the above methods into consideration for the synchronization problem of FO chaotic systems [14–19]. However, the above research content does not consider the uncertainties of the system and external disturbances. Since the chaotic system is sensitive to the initial values; in practical applications, it is inevitable that the orbit of the system will change dramatically due to some small disturbances. One has adopted the active nonlinear control method to address the issue of modified projective synchronization for the FO chaotic systems with noise disturbance in Ref. [20]. Qin et al. established the system with the unknown nonlinear functions and uncertainties which are addressed by fuzzy logic method [4]. Meanwhile, replacing the FO chaotic systems in Ref. [4] with non-identical complex FO chaotic systems, the adaptive sliding mode synchronization has developed in Ref. [21]. Luo et al. derived some novel sufficient conditions for chaos synchronization of FO chaotic systems with nonlinear uncertainties and external disturbances [22]. In Ref. [23], the authors researched the multi-state uncertain synchronization of chaotic systems in which the structure is non-identical, parameters are unknown, and systems have a time-varying delay. This means the synchronization of the single master system with multiple slave systems which have more potential applications in real life. However, the master–slave system they considered was an integer order system and the synchronization of both systems is asymptotic and takes place in infinite time. This is also the case in Ref. [24]. It is generally found that fractional derivatives are better suited to describe memory and hereditary characteristics of different materials and processes than integer derivatives [25]. Mirrezapour et al. [26] used the sliding mode control to synchronize fractional-order chaotic systems with uncertainties and affected by disturbance. In Ref. [26], a new fractional sliding mode controller according to nonlinear FO controllers is proposed. However, there are some disadvantages here. Firstly, the author did not consider the effect of unknown parameters on the system. Then, from the numerical simulation results (synchronization errors converges to zero at $t = 10$ (approx)), it can be seen that the controller is not very effective in overcoming uncertainty and disturbance. On the contrary, the nonsingular terminal sliding mode control in our paper has a better transient performance, easy realization, rapid response, and insensitivity to external disturbances and so on. Of course, there are some studies on uncertain parameters of systems [27–29]. However, it can be seen from the above that for the uncertainties of the system, that is, parameter uncertainties and nonlinear uncertainties, and the influence of external disturbances on the system, most authors study some of the situations while a few authors have considered the three of them at the same time [30–32]. Furthermore, the above mentioned papers reveal that the convergence of the ideal dynamics is promised without time limit. We know that the finite time convergence with even existing disturbances has merits in strengthening the robustness, getting over the disturbance [33] and improving the security of information transmission in the field of chaotic communication [34]. Some more theoretical results about the synchronization of FO chaotic systems with uncertainties and external disturbances in finite-time can be seen in [35–42]. At present, with full consideration of system uncertainties and external disturbances in the given time as well as the unknown system parameters, no researchers have considered this situation.

There is another fact that we must note that the aforementioned papers focused on the single D-R system for the synchronization scheme. There are relatively few studies on multi-drive systems and multi-response systems, as well as the combination synchronization of each system. Actually, in engineering, communication theory, physics, electrical and many other fields, the combination–combination synchronization has more potential applications [43,44]. Just take the secure communication, for example, the transmitting signals can be understood as two basic ways. The first is to divide the transmission signals into multiple parts, each loaded with different drive systems. For example, assume the transmitted signal is $cost$, the signal $cost$ can be broken down into two parts: $\frac{1}{3}cost$ and $\frac{2}{3}cost$. The signal $\frac{1}{3}cost$ can be delivered to the first drive system, while $\frac{2}{3}cost$ can be delivered to the second drive system. The second way is to break down time into different intervals. Let the signals in different intervals load in different drive systems. It is clear to observe that the traditional master–slave synchronization schemes (one to one system) do not satisfy the above communication signals but can be transferred in our model. Thus, it is imperative to pay more attention to the synchronization research of multi-systems. Sun et al. [42] realized the parameter identification and C-C synchronization in a finite time. In [24], the authors handle a hybrid projective C-C synchronization scheme between four specific hyper-chaotic systems utilizing SMC. The idea of dual C-C multi switching synchronization adopted the eight chaotic systems was addressed in [45]. The global exponential multi switching combination synchronization was introduced in terms of three different chaotic systems, in [46]. There are also some papers here that also mention the issue of C-C synchronization [47–50]. However, the systems they consider are all integer order chaotic systems and some of them do not consider the SD.

In response to this situation, we are going to consider the finite-time combination–combination (C-C) synchronization (FTCCS) of FO chaotic systems with different structures and unknown parameters under multiple SD via the NTSMC technique. The multiple SD are explained as parameter uncertainties, nonlinear uncertainties and external disturbances. In the light of finite-time Lyapunov stability theory and the SMC technique, we propose an FO adaptive combination controller and some appropriate ACL.

Compared with other references, there are four advantages of the proposed method: (1) The finite-time control theory is different from the traditional stability theory and its control structure can be regarded as closed-loop feedback control. The complexity of the finite-time controller is relatively high, which is reflected in the anti-interference ability to the outside world and the robustness to the uncertainty of the system itself; (2) This paper extends the traditional drive-response synchronization schemes (single drive-response system) to combination–combination synchronization schemes. Thus, when the specific parameter values are gained to the D-R systems, the corresponding system or systems' combination are chose. The controller does not need to be redesigned for two systems or systems' combinations for every application. This not only has a wider range of applications but also saves too much time and effort. This advantage is reflected in Corollaries 1–3 in the paper; (3) In communication theory, comparing the traditional transmission model with the combination-combination synchronization model, our method has stronger anti-attack ability and anti-translated capability; (4) The nonsingular terminal sliding mode control avoids the singularity problem effectively that terminal sliding mode control (TSMC) would have and retains the characteristic of the finite-time convergence. Besides, the NTSMC has higher control accuracy than linear sliding mode control (SMC); (5) Based on the nonsingular terminal sliding mode control (NTSMC) and adaptive control, the combination–combination drive-response systems with unknown parameters and multiple stochastic disturbances is considered. The controller and parameter updating laws are designed to make the state of drive-response system gradually stable within a finite time. Our controller has good robustness and anti-interference performance.

This article is organized as follows. In Section 2, some definitions, lemmas and stability theories that need to be used are introduced. In Section 3, problem statements and assumptions are given. In Section 4, sliding mode synchronization controller and adaptive control laws are designed. In Section 5, the numerical simulations proved that our method is effective. In Section 6, there is a conclusion.

2. Preliminaries

2.1. Definitions and Lemmas of Fractional Derivative

Next, let us present the Riemann–Liouville (R-L) derivative and the Caputo derivative, which are equivalent if and only if the order α is a negative real number and a positive integer. The R–L definition is best suited for theoretical analysis and can simplify the computation of FO derivatives. The Caputo is more relevant to modern engineering and makes Laplace's transformation more concise. Thus, we only display the mathematical expression of the Caputo derivative with order α.

Definition 1 ([51]). *The mathematical expression of the fractional integral of the function $f(t)$ is following:*

$$I_t^{\alpha} f(t) = \frac{1}{\Gamma(\alpha)} \int_a^t \frac{f(v)}{(t-v)^{1-\alpha}} dv, \tag{1}$$

where $\Gamma(\alpha)$ indicates the Gamma function.

Definition 2 ([51]). *The mathematical expression of Caputo derivative with order α is given as:*

$${}_a^C D_t^{\alpha} f(t) = \frac{1}{\Gamma(p-\alpha)} \int_a^t (t-v)^{p-\alpha-1} f^{(p)}(v) dv, \tag{2}$$

where $p-1 < \alpha < p, p \in \mathbb{Z}^+$.

Lemma 1 ([18]). *When $\boldsymbol{x}(t) \in \mathbb{R}^n$ has a continuous first derivative, then*

$${}_a D_t^{\alpha} (\frac{1}{2} \boldsymbol{x}^T(t) Q \boldsymbol{x}(t)) \leq \boldsymbol{x}^T Q {}_a D_t^{\alpha} \boldsymbol{x}(t), \tag{3}$$

where $\alpha \in (0,1)$ and $Q \in R^n \times R^n$ indicate a positive definite matrix.

Lemma 2 ([52]). *For any real constants $a_i, i = 1, 2, \cdots, n$ and $\sigma \in (0,1)$, the following inequality exists:*

$$(|a_1| + |a_2| + \cdots + |a_n|)^{\sigma} \leq |a_1|^{\sigma} + |a_2|^{\sigma} + \cdots + |a_n|^{\sigma}. \tag{4}$$

2.2. Stability Theories of Fractional Order System

It follows that, if most things around us are nonlinear, we write the FO nonlinear system to be:

$${}_0 D_t^{\alpha} \boldsymbol{x}(t) = \boldsymbol{f}(t, \boldsymbol{x}(t)), \tag{5}$$

where $\alpha \in (0,1)$, $\boldsymbol{f} = (f_1, f_2, \cdots, f_n)^T$, $\boldsymbol{x}(t) \in \mathbb{R}^n$ and $f : [t_0, \infty] \times \Omega \to \mathbb{R}^n$ satisfies the requirements of Lipschitz conditions; the initial value is $x(t_0) = x_0, t_0 \geq 0$. The equilibrium point x^* of (5) can be calculated from $\boldsymbol{f}(\boldsymbol{x}^*) = 0$.

Theorem 1 ([53]). *Suppose that $\mathbb{D} \in \mathbb{R}^n$ is a domain that contains the origin. If there exists a locally bounded Lyapunov function $V(t, \boldsymbol{x}) : [t_0, \infty] \times \mathbb{D} \to \mathbb{R}$ which meets the local Lipschitz condition about x adapting to*

$$\eta_1(\|\boldsymbol{x}\|^a) \leq V(t, \boldsymbol{x}) \leq \eta_2(\|\boldsymbol{x}\|^{ab}), \tag{6}$$

$${}_0 D_t^{\alpha} V(t, \boldsymbol{x}) \leq -\eta_3(\|\boldsymbol{x}\|^{ab}), \tag{7}$$

where $\alpha \in (0,1)$, $a > 0$, $b > 0$, $\eta_i(i = 1,2,3) > 0$, then the system (5) is called Mittag-Leffler stable.

Theorem 2. *Suppose that $\mathbb{D} \subset \mathbb{R}^n$ is a domain that contains the origin. If there is a locally bounded Lyapunov function $V(t, \boldsymbol{x}) : [t_0, \infty] \times \mathbb{D} \to \mathbb{R}$ that meets the local Lipschitz condition about x adapting to*

$$\begin{aligned}(1)\eta_1(\|x\|^a) \le V(t,x) \le \eta_2(\|x\|^{ab}),\\ (2)_0D_t^\alpha V(t,x) \le -\eta_3(\|x\|^{ab}),\\ (3)_0D_t^\alpha V(t,x) \le -kV^{1/\beta}(t,x),\end{aligned} \tag{8}$$

where $\alpha \in (0,1)$, $a > 0$, $b > 0$, $k > 0$, $\beta > 1$, $\alpha > 1/\beta$, $\eta_i(i = 1,2,3) > 0$, then the system (5) is called finite-time stable. The system (5) will be stabilized in time T given by:

$$T \le \left[V^{\alpha-\frac{1}{\beta}}(0,x)\frac{\Gamma(1-\frac{1}{\beta})\Gamma(1+\alpha)}{\Gamma(\alpha-\frac{1}{\beta}+1)k}\right]^{\frac{1}{\alpha}}. \tag{9}$$

Proof. It is clear that the conditions (1) and (2) in Theorem 2 satisfy Theorem 1. Thus, the system (5) is Mittag–Leffler stable. Then, there is an equilibrium point $x(t_0)$ for system (5). According to condition (3), one obtained

$$V^{-1/\beta}(t,x)[_{t_0}D_t^\alpha V(t,x)] \le -k. \tag{10}$$

For convenience, let $v = 1/\beta$. Based on the property of Caputo fractional derivatives $D_t^\alpha x^\mu = \frac{\Gamma(\mu+1)}{\Gamma(\mu+1-\alpha)}x^{\mu-\alpha}D_t^\alpha x$ [54], we get

$$_aD_t^\alpha V^{\alpha-v}(t,x) = \frac{\Gamma(\alpha-v+1)}{\Gamma(1-v)}V^{-v}(t,x)_aD_t^\alpha V(t,x) \tag{11}$$

$$V^{-v}(t,x)_aD_t^\alpha V(t,x) = \frac{\Gamma(1-v)}{\Gamma(\alpha-v+1)}{_aD_t^\alpha} V^{\alpha-v}(t,x). \tag{12}$$

Then,

$$\frac{\Gamma(1-v)}{\Gamma(\alpha-v+1)}{_aD_t^\alpha} V^{\alpha-v}(t,x) \le -k, \tag{13}$$

$$_aD_t^\alpha V^{\alpha-v}(t,x) \le -k\frac{\Gamma(\alpha-v+1)}{\Gamma(1-v)}. \tag{14}$$

Integrating (14) from 0 to T gives:

$$V^{\alpha-v}(T,x) - V^{\alpha-v}(0,x) \le -k\frac{\Gamma(\alpha-v+1)}{\Gamma(1-v)\Gamma(1+\alpha)}T^\alpha. \tag{15}$$

Time T can be expressed as:

$$T \le \left[V^{\alpha-v}(0,x)\frac{\Gamma(1-v)\Gamma(1+\alpha)}{\Gamma(\alpha-v+1)k}\right]^{\frac{1}{\alpha}}. \tag{16}$$

Namely,

$$T \le \left[V^{\alpha-\frac{1}{\beta}}(0,x)\frac{\Gamma(1-\frac{1}{\beta})\Gamma(1+\alpha)}{\Gamma(\alpha-\frac{1}{\beta}+1)k}\right]^{\frac{1}{\alpha}}. \tag{17}$$

□

3. Problem Description and Assumptions

In this chapter, since the the initial values have a great influence on the initial values, in practical application, it is inevitable that the orbit of the system will change dramatically due to some small disturbances. Therefore, it is reasonable to treat them as bounded. This will also make our theory easier to understand.

The FO D-R systems with uncertainties and external disturbance are demonstrated as:

The two drive systems

$$ {}_0D_t^{\alpha} x_1(t) = F_1(x_1(t))(\theta_1 + \Delta\theta_1) + f_1(x_1(t)) + \Delta f_1(x_1(t)) + d_1(x_1, t), \tag{18} $$

$$ {}_0D_t^{\alpha} x_2(t) = F_2(x_2(t))(\theta_2 + \Delta\theta_2) + f_2(x_2(t)) + \Delta f_2(x_2(t)) + d_2(x_2, t). \tag{19} $$

and the two response systems

$$ {}_0D_t^{\alpha} y_1(t) = G_1(y_1(t))(\vartheta_1 + \Delta\vartheta_1) + g_1(y_1(t)) + \Delta g_1(y_1(t)) + \mu_1(y_1, t) + u_1(t), \tag{20} $$

$$ {}_0D_t^{\alpha} y_2(t) = G_2(y_2(t))(\vartheta_2 + \Delta\vartheta_2) + g_2(y_2(t)) + \Delta g_2(y_2(t)) + \mu_2(y_2, t) + u_2(t), \tag{21} $$

where $\theta_i = (\theta_{1i}, \theta_{2i}, \cdots, \theta_{ni})^T$ and $\vartheta_i = (\vartheta_{1i}, \vartheta_{2i}, \cdots, \vartheta_{ni})^T$ are the vectors of system parameters; $x_i(t) = (x_{1i}, x_{2i}, \cdots, x_{ni})^T$ and $y_i(t) = (y_{1i}, y_{2i}, \cdots, y_{ni})^T$; $F_i(x_i(t)) = (F_{1i}, F_{2i}, \cdots, F_{ni})^T$, $G_i(y_i(t)) = (G_{1i}, G_{2i}, \cdots, G_{ni})^T$, $F_{ji}, G_{ji} \in \mathbb{R}^{1\times n}, j = 1, 2, \cdots, n$, $f_i(x_i(t)) = (f_{1i}, f_{2i}, \cdots, f_{ni})^T, g_i(y_i(t)) = (g_{1i}, g_{2i}, \cdots, g_{ni})^T$ are the nonlinear continuous functions; $d_i(x_i) = (d_{1i}, d_{2i}, \cdots, d_{ni})^T$ and $\mu_i(y_i) = (u_{1i}, u_{2i}, \cdots, u_{ni})^T$ are the external disturbances; $\alpha_i \in (0, 1)$ represents the fractional order; $\Delta\theta_i$ and $\Delta\vartheta_i$, $\Delta f_i(x_i(t))$ and $\Delta g_i(y_i(t))$, are the parameter uncertainties and the nonlinear uncertainties. $u_i(t) = (u_{1i}, u_{2i}, \cdots, u_{ni})^T$ are the controllers. Then all of above satisfy $i = 1, 2$.

Definition 3. *Suppose that $A, B, C, D \in \mathbb{R}^n \times \mathbb{R}^n, C \neq 0$, or $D \neq 0$ are four constant matrices, then for $T > 0$, we have*

$$ \lim_{t\to T} \|e(t)\| = \lim_{t\to T} \|Cy_1(t) + Dy_2(t) - Ax_1(t) - Bx_2(t)\| = 0, \quad t < T, \tag{22} $$
$$ \|e(t)\| = 0, \quad t \geq T. $$

Then the FO error system, between a combination of drive systems (18), (19) and combination of response systems (20), (21) , can reach FTCCS.

Remark 1. *The matrices $A, B, C, D \in \mathbb{R}^n \times \mathbb{R}^n$ $C \neq 0$, or $D \neq 0$ indicating in (22) are named as the scaling matrices. They can also have different meanings, either as constant matrices or as functions of state variables x_1, x_2, y_1 and y_2.*

Remark 2. *If $C = D = I$, $A = B = \lambda I$, then it will be transformed into finite-time C-C complete synchronization with multiple SD for $\lambda = 1$; It will be transformed into finite-time C-C anti-synchronization with multiple SD for $\lambda = -1$; What's more, if $A = C = 0, D = I, B = \lambda I$, then it will be transformed into finite-time combination complete synchronization with multiple SD for $\lambda = 1$, the finite-time combination anti-synchronization with multiple SD for $\lambda = -1$.*

Remark 3. *If $C = 0, A = 0$ or $C = 0, B = 0$ or $D = 0, A = 0$ or $D = 0, B = 0$, then the issue of finite-time C-C synchronization with multiple SD will be transformed into the issue of finite-time synchronization with multiple SD.*

Remark 4. *If $A = 0, D = 0, C = I$ or $A = 0, C = 0, D = I$ or $B = 0, D = 0, C = I$ or $B = 0, C = 0, D = I$, then it will be transformed into finite-time combination projective synchronization.*

Remark 5. *It is supposed that $A = 0, B = 0, C = 0$ or $A = 0, B = 0, D = 0$, then finite-time C-C synchronization with multiple SD will be transformed into the issue of chaos control with multiple SD in the finite time .*

Remark 6. *Based on all the above synchronization methods, we can also consider $\Delta\boldsymbol{\theta}_i = 0, \Delta\boldsymbol{\vartheta}_i = 0$, or $\Delta f_i(x_i(t)) = 0, \Delta g_i(y_i(t)) = 0$, or $\boldsymbol{d}_i(x_i, t) = 0, \boldsymbol{\mu}_i(y_i, t) = 0$ or $\Delta\boldsymbol{\theta}_i = 0, \Delta\boldsymbol{\vartheta}_i = 0, \Delta f_i(x_i(t)) = 0, \Delta g_i(y_i(t)) = 0$ or $\Delta\boldsymbol{\theta}_i = 0, \Delta\boldsymbol{\vartheta}_i = 0, \boldsymbol{d}_i(x_i, t) = 0, \boldsymbol{\mu}_i(y_i, t) = 0$, or $\boldsymbol{d}_i(x_i, t) = 0, \boldsymbol{\mu}_i(y_i, t) = 0, \Delta f_i(x_i(t)) = 0, \Delta g_i(y_i(t)) = 0$, or all of the uncertainties and external disturbance equal to zero for $i = 1, 2$.*

Remark 7. *Starting from Definition 3, the number of D-R systems can be extended to three or more equations. Furthermore, D-R systems of the C-C synchronization scheme can be the same structure where $\boldsymbol{F}_i(x_i(t)) = \boldsymbol{G}_i(y_i(t))$ and $f_i(x_i(t)) = g_i(y_i(t))$ for $i = 1, 2$.*

It follows from the Equation (22) that the error system is rewritten as:

$$\begin{aligned} {}_0D_t^{\alpha} e(t) = {} & \boldsymbol{H}(x_1, x_2, y_1, y_2) + \boldsymbol{Q}(x_1, x_2, y_1, y_2) + \boldsymbol{R}(x_1, x_2, y_1, y_2) \\ & + \Delta\boldsymbol{R}(x_1, x_2, y_1, y_2) + \boldsymbol{V}(x_1, x_2, y_1, y_2) + Cu_1(t) + Du_2(t), \end{aligned} \tag{23}$$

where

$$\begin{aligned} \boldsymbol{H}(x_1, x_2, y_1, y_2) &= C\boldsymbol{G}_1(y_1(t))\boldsymbol{\vartheta}_1 + D\boldsymbol{G}_2(y_2(t))\boldsymbol{\vartheta}_2 - A\boldsymbol{F}_1(x_1(t))\boldsymbol{\theta}_1 - B\boldsymbol{F}_2(x_2(t))\boldsymbol{\theta}_2, \\ \boldsymbol{Q}(x_1, x_2, y_1, y_2) &= C\boldsymbol{G}_1(y_1(t))(\Delta\boldsymbol{\vartheta}_1) + D\boldsymbol{G}_2(y_2(t))(\Delta\boldsymbol{\vartheta}_2) - A\boldsymbol{F}_1(x_1(t))(\Delta\boldsymbol{\theta}_1) \\ &\quad - B\boldsymbol{F}_2(x_2(t))(\Delta\boldsymbol{\theta}_2), \\ \boldsymbol{R}(x_1, x_2, y_1, y_2) &= Cg_1(y_1(t)) + Dg_2(y_2(t)) - Af_1(x_1(t)) - Bf_2(x_2(t)), \\ \Delta\boldsymbol{R}(x_1, x_2, y_1, y_2) &= C\Delta g_1(y_1(t)) + D\Delta g_2(y_2(t)) - A\Delta f_1(x_1(t)) - B\Delta f_2(x_2(t)), \\ \boldsymbol{V}(x_1, x_2, y_1, y_2) &= C\boldsymbol{\mu}_1(y_1, t) + D\boldsymbol{\mu}_2(y_2, t) - A\boldsymbol{d}_1(x_1, t) - B\boldsymbol{d}_2(x_2, t). \end{aligned}$$

From the above discussion, we make the following assumptions to ensure that our conclusions are more realistic.

Assumption 1. *Assume that uncertain nonlinear vectors $\Delta f_i(x_i(t))$, $\Delta g_i(y_i(t))$, the external disturbances $\boldsymbol{d}_i(x_i, t)$, $\boldsymbol{\mu}_i(x_i, t)$ and the parameter uncertainties $\Delta\boldsymbol{\theta}_i$, $\Delta\boldsymbol{\vartheta}_i$ for $(i = 1, 2)$ all have a bounded norm. Namely, there are suitable positive constants h, l, q that satisfy:*

$$\begin{aligned} & \|C\Delta g_1(y_1(t)) + D\Delta g_2(y_2(t)) - A\Delta f_1(x_1(t)) - B\Delta f_2(x_2(t))\| \le h, \\ & \|C\boldsymbol{\mu}_1(y_1, t) + D\boldsymbol{\mu}_2(y_2, t) - A\boldsymbol{d}_1(x_1, t) - B\boldsymbol{d}_2(x_2, t)\| \le l, \\ & \|C\boldsymbol{G}_1(y_1(t))(\Delta\boldsymbol{\vartheta}_1) + D\boldsymbol{G}_2(y_2(t))(\Delta\boldsymbol{\vartheta}_2) - A\boldsymbol{F}_1(x_1(t))(\Delta\boldsymbol{\theta}_1) \\ & - B\boldsymbol{F}_2(x_2(t))(\Delta\boldsymbol{\theta}_2)\| \le q. \end{aligned} \tag{24}$$

Remark 8. *The parameter vectors of D-R systems $\boldsymbol{\theta}_i$, $\boldsymbol{\vartheta}_i$, $(i = 1, 2)$ and the three constants h, l, q are all unknown. Later, the parameters adaptive laws will be selected to identify them.*

Assumption 2. *Assume that the unknown vector parameters $\boldsymbol{\theta}_i$, $\boldsymbol{\vartheta}_i$, $(i = 1, 2)$ and the three unknown constants h, l, q satisfy:*

$$\|\boldsymbol{\theta}_1\| \le \delta_1, \quad \|\boldsymbol{\theta}_2\| \le \delta_2, \quad \|\boldsymbol{\vartheta}_1\| \le \delta_3, \quad \|\boldsymbol{\vartheta}_2\| \le \delta_4, \quad |h| \le h^*, \quad |l| \le l^*, \quad |q| \le q^*,$$

where $\delta_1, \delta_2, \delta_3, \delta_4, h^*, l^*, q^*$ is selected as a larger constant generally.

4. Sliding Mode Synchronization Controller Design within Finite Time

The main feature of the sliding mode control is that it directs the system states from their initial states towards the appropriate sliding surface which is specified and then it keeps the states in the corresponding sliding surface for all subsequent times. Designing a sliding mode controller consists of the following two steps : (1) To select a sliding mode surface; (2) To design a controller to make sure that the system's state converges to the sliding surface.

The nonsingular terminal FO sliding mode surfaces are designed as:

$$s(t) = \gamma e(t) + I_t^{\alpha} sgn(e(\tau))\|e(\tau)\|^{\xi} d\tau, \tag{25}$$

where $\gamma > 0, 0 < \alpha < 1$ and $0 < \xi < 1$ and its FO derivative with α satisfies:

$${}_0D_t^{\alpha} s(t) = \gamma[{}_0D_t^{\alpha} e(t)] + sgn(e(t))\|e(t)\|^{\xi}. \tag{26}$$

When the system is in the sliding mode surface, the following conditions should be satisfied:

$$s(t) = 0, \quad {}_0D_t^{\alpha} s(t) = 0. \tag{27}$$

Thus,

$${}_0D_t^{\alpha} e(t) = -\frac{1}{\gamma} sgn(e(t))\|e(t)\|^{\xi}. \tag{28}$$

Remark 9. *Now, the nonsingular terminal sliding mode control (NTSMC) technique is very popular in the study of stochastic disturbances of chaotic systems. This is a new technique. In addition, some the state-of-the-art methods have appeared in the study of the synchronization of chaotic systems, such as: based on the state decoupling strategy and the Lyapunov-based approach, the minimum-energy synchronization control for interconnected networks is addressed by Li et al. [55]. The synchronization of Henon maps using adaptive symmetry control has recently been proposed [56]. The finite-time and fixed-time synchronization analysis of shunting inhibitory memristive neural networks with time-varying delays is introduced via constructing Lyapunov functions and feedback control schemes [57]. Combining adaptive control theory with Lyapunov–Krasovskii theory, Yuan et al. [58] solved the problem of finite-time synchronization (FTS) for complex dynamical networks with time-varying delays and unknown internal coupling matrices. Furthermore, a novel decentralized non-integer order controller applied on nonlinear fractional-order composite system is addressed in [59]. Li et al. [60] explored the issue of network synchronization for an FO chaotic system based on an event-triggered mechanism for the first time.*

Theorem 3. *When Assumptions 1 and 2 are satisfied and assume that the error system (23) is controlled by following combination controller (30) and adaptive laws (31), then the state trajectory of the error systems (23) will arrive the sliding surface $s(t)$ in the finite time given by:*

$$T_1 \leq \left[V^{\alpha - \frac{1}{2}}(0, x) \frac{\Gamma(\frac{1}{2})\Gamma(1+\alpha)}{\sqrt{2}\varsigma\Gamma(\alpha + \frac{1}{2})} \right]^{\frac{1}{\alpha}}. \tag{29}$$

$$\begin{aligned} Cu_1(t) + Du_2(t) = & -R(x_1, x_2, y_1, y_2) + AF_1(x_1(t))\hat{\theta}_1 + BF_2(x_2(t))\hat{\theta}_2 \\ & - CG_1(y_1(t))\hat{\vartheta}_1 - DG_2(y_2(t))\hat{\vartheta}_2 - \frac{1}{\gamma} sgn(e(t))\|e(t)\|^{\xi} - \varsigma(\|\hat{\theta}_1\| \\ & + \|\hat{\theta}_2\| + \|\hat{\vartheta}_1\| + \|\hat{\vartheta}_2\| + \rho_1|\hat{h}| + \rho_2|\hat{l}| + \rho_3|\hat{q}| + \delta_1 + \delta_2 + \delta_3 + \delta_4 \\ & + \rho_1 h^* + \rho_2 l^* + \rho_3 q^*)(\frac{s}{\gamma\|s\|^2}) - (\hat{h} + \hat{l} + \hat{q}) sgn(s) - \frac{k}{\gamma}, \end{aligned} \tag{30}$$

where $k > \varsigma > 0$ and $\rho_1, \rho_2, \rho_3 \in (0,1)$. $\hat{\theta}_i, \hat{\vartheta}_i$ and $\hat{h}, \hat{l}, \hat{q}$ represent the estimations of θ_i, ϑ_i and h, l, q. Their errors defined as $\tilde{\theta}_i = \hat{\theta}_i - \theta_i$, $\tilde{\vartheta}_i = \hat{\vartheta}_i - \vartheta_i$, $\tilde{h} = \hat{h} - h$, $\tilde{l} = \hat{l} - l$, $\tilde{q} = \hat{q} - q$ where $i = 1, 2$.

$$
\begin{aligned}
{}_0D_t^{\alpha}\tilde{\boldsymbol{\theta}}_1 &= -\gamma \boldsymbol{F}_1^T(\boldsymbol{x}_1(t))A^T\boldsymbol{s}(t), \\
{}_0D_t^{\alpha}\tilde{\boldsymbol{\theta}}_2 &= -\gamma \boldsymbol{F}_2^T(\boldsymbol{x}_2(t))B^T\boldsymbol{s}(t), \\
{}_0D_t^{\alpha}\tilde{\boldsymbol{\vartheta}}_1 &= \gamma \boldsymbol{G}_1^T(\boldsymbol{y}_1(t))C^T\boldsymbol{s}(t), \\
{}_0D_t^{\alpha}\tilde{\boldsymbol{\vartheta}}_2 &= \gamma \boldsymbol{G}_2^T(\boldsymbol{y}_2(t))D^T\boldsymbol{s}(t) \\
{}_0D_t^{\alpha}\tilde{h} &= \gamma\rho_1\|\boldsymbol{s}(t)\|, \\
{}_0D_t^{\alpha}\tilde{l} &= \gamma\rho_2\|\boldsymbol{s}(t)\|, \\
{}_0D_t^{\alpha}\tilde{q} &= \gamma\rho_3\|\boldsymbol{s}(t)\|.
\end{aligned}
\tag{31}
$$

Proof. Adopting the Lyapunov function:

$$
\begin{aligned}
V(t) = {} & \frac{1}{2}\boldsymbol{s}^T(t)\boldsymbol{s}(t) + \frac{1}{2}\tilde{\boldsymbol{\theta}}_1^T\tilde{\boldsymbol{\theta}}_1 + \frac{1}{2}\tilde{\boldsymbol{\theta}}_2^T\tilde{\boldsymbol{\theta}}_2 + \frac{1}{2}\tilde{\boldsymbol{\vartheta}}_1^T\tilde{\boldsymbol{\vartheta}}_1 + \frac{1}{2}\tilde{\boldsymbol{\vartheta}}_2^T\tilde{\boldsymbol{\vartheta}}_2 + \frac{1}{2\rho_1}\tilde{h}^T\tilde{h} + \frac{1}{2\rho_2}\tilde{l}^T\tilde{l} \\
& + \frac{1}{2\rho_3}\tilde{q}^T\tilde{q}.
\end{aligned}
\tag{32}
$$

The FO derivative is expressed as:

$$
\begin{aligned}
{}_0D_t^{\alpha}V(t,\boldsymbol{x}(t)) \leq {} & \boldsymbol{s}^T{}_0D_t^{\alpha}\boldsymbol{s} + \tilde{\boldsymbol{\theta}}_1^T{}_0D_t^{\alpha}\tilde{\boldsymbol{\theta}}_1 + \tilde{\boldsymbol{\theta}}_2^T{}_0D_t^{\alpha}\tilde{\boldsymbol{\theta}}_2 + \tilde{\boldsymbol{\vartheta}}_1^T{}_0D_t^{\alpha}\tilde{\boldsymbol{\vartheta}}_1 + \tilde{\boldsymbol{\vartheta}}_2^T{}_0D_t^{\alpha}\tilde{\boldsymbol{\vartheta}}_2 \\
& + \frac{1}{\rho_1}\tilde{h}^T{}_0D_t^{\alpha}\tilde{h} + \frac{1}{\rho_2}\tilde{l}^T{}_0D_t^{\alpha}\tilde{l} + \frac{1}{\rho_3}\tilde{q}^T{}_0D_t^{\alpha}\tilde{q} \\
= {} & \boldsymbol{s}^T(\gamma{}_0D_t^{\alpha}\boldsymbol{e}(t) + sgn(\boldsymbol{e}(t))\|\boldsymbol{e}(t)\|^{\xi}) + \tilde{\boldsymbol{\theta}}_1^T(-\gamma\boldsymbol{F}_1^T(\boldsymbol{x}_1(t))A^T\boldsymbol{s}(t)) \\
& + \tilde{\boldsymbol{\theta}}_2^T(-\gamma\boldsymbol{F}_2^T(\boldsymbol{x}_2(t))B^T\boldsymbol{s}(t)) + \tilde{\boldsymbol{\vartheta}}_1^T(\gamma\boldsymbol{G}_1^T(\boldsymbol{y}_1(t))C^T\boldsymbol{s}(t)) \\
& + \tilde{\boldsymbol{\vartheta}}_2^T(\gamma\boldsymbol{G}_2^T(\boldsymbol{y}_2(t))D^T\boldsymbol{s}(t)) + \tilde{h}^T(\gamma\|\boldsymbol{s}(t)\|) + \tilde{l}^T(\gamma\|\boldsymbol{s}(t)\|) \\
& + \tilde{q}^T(\gamma\|\boldsymbol{s}(t)\|).
\end{aligned}
\tag{33}
$$

Substituting (30) into Equation (23), we obtain:

$$
\begin{aligned}
{}_0D_t^{\alpha}\boldsymbol{e}(t) = {} & -C\boldsymbol{G}_1(\boldsymbol{y}_1(t))\tilde{\boldsymbol{\vartheta}}_1 - D\boldsymbol{G}_2(\boldsymbol{y}_2(t))\tilde{\boldsymbol{\vartheta}}_2 + A\boldsymbol{F}_1(\boldsymbol{x}_1(t))\tilde{\boldsymbol{\theta}}_1 + B\boldsymbol{F}_2(\boldsymbol{x}_2(t))\tilde{\boldsymbol{\theta}}_2 \\
& + \boldsymbol{Q}(\boldsymbol{x}_1,\boldsymbol{x}_2,\boldsymbol{y}_1,\boldsymbol{y}_2) + \Delta\boldsymbol{R}(\boldsymbol{x}_1,\boldsymbol{x}_2,\boldsymbol{y}_1,\boldsymbol{y}_2) + \boldsymbol{V}(\boldsymbol{x}_1,\boldsymbol{x}_2,\boldsymbol{y}_1,\boldsymbol{y}_2) \\
& - \frac{1}{\gamma}sgn(\boldsymbol{e}(t))\|\boldsymbol{e}(t)\|^{\xi} - \varsigma(\|\hat{\boldsymbol{\theta}}_1\| + \|\hat{\boldsymbol{\theta}}_2\| + \|\hat{\boldsymbol{\vartheta}}_1\| + \|\hat{\boldsymbol{\vartheta}}_2\| + \rho_1|\hat{h}| + \rho_2|\hat{l}| + \rho_3|\hat{q}| \\
& + \delta_1 + \delta_2 + \delta_3 + \delta_4 + \rho_1 h^* + \rho_2 l^* + \rho_3 q^*)(\frac{\boldsymbol{s}}{\gamma\|\boldsymbol{s}\|^2}) \\
& - (\hat{h} + \hat{l} + \hat{q})sgn(\boldsymbol{s}) - \frac{k}{\gamma}.
\end{aligned}
\tag{34}
$$

Substituting (34) into Equation (33), we obtain:

$$
\begin{aligned}
{}_0D_t^{\alpha}V(t,\boldsymbol{x}(t)) \leq {} & \boldsymbol{s}^T[\gamma\boldsymbol{Q}(\boldsymbol{x}_1,\boldsymbol{x}_2,\boldsymbol{y}_1,\boldsymbol{y}_2) + \gamma\Delta\boldsymbol{R}(\boldsymbol{x}_1,\boldsymbol{x}_2,\boldsymbol{y}_1,\boldsymbol{y}_2) + \gamma\boldsymbol{V}(\boldsymbol{x}_1,\boldsymbol{x}_2,\boldsymbol{y}_1,\boldsymbol{y}_2) \\
& - \varsigma(\|\hat{\boldsymbol{\theta}}_1\| + \|\hat{\boldsymbol{\theta}}_2\| + \|\hat{\boldsymbol{\vartheta}}_1\| + \|\hat{\boldsymbol{\vartheta}}_2\| + \rho_1|\hat{h}| + \rho_2|\hat{l}| + \rho_3|\hat{q}| + \delta_1 + \delta_2 + \delta_3 \\
& + \delta_4 + \rho_1 h^* + \rho_2 l^* + \rho_3 q^*)(\frac{\boldsymbol{s}}{\|\boldsymbol{s}\|^2}) - \gamma(\hat{h} + \hat{l} + \hat{q})sgn(\boldsymbol{s}) - k] \\
& + \tilde{h}^T(\gamma\|\boldsymbol{s}(t)\|) + \tilde{l}^T(\gamma\|\boldsymbol{s}(t)\|) + \tilde{q}^T(\gamma\|\boldsymbol{s}(t)\|).
\end{aligned}
\tag{35}
$$

It follows from Assumption 1 that we get:

$$
\begin{aligned}
{}_0D_t^\alpha V(t,\boldsymbol{x}(t)) &\le \gamma\|\boldsymbol{s}\|(q+h+l-(\hat{h}+\hat{l}+\hat{q}))+\tilde{h}^T(\gamma\|\boldsymbol{s}(t)\|) \\
&+\tilde{l}^T(\gamma\|\boldsymbol{s}(t)\|)+\tilde{q}^T(\gamma\|\boldsymbol{s}(t)\|)-k\|\boldsymbol{s}\|-\boldsymbol{s}^T(\varsigma(\|\hat{\boldsymbol{\theta}}_1\| \\
&+\|\hat{\boldsymbol{\theta}}_2\|+\|\hat{\boldsymbol{\vartheta}}_1\|+\|\hat{\boldsymbol{\vartheta}}_2\|\rho_1|\hat{h}|+\rho_2|\hat{l}|+\rho_3|\hat{q}|+\delta_1+\delta_2+\delta_3 \\
&+\delta_4+\rho_1 h^*+\rho_2 l^*+\rho_3 q^*)(\frac{\boldsymbol{s}}{\|\boldsymbol{s}\|^2})) \\
&=-\varsigma(\|\hat{\boldsymbol{\theta}}_1\|+\|\hat{\boldsymbol{\theta}}_2\|+\|\hat{\boldsymbol{\vartheta}}_1\|+\|\hat{\boldsymbol{\vartheta}}_2\|+\rho_1|\hat{h}|+\rho_2|\hat{l}|+\rho_3|\hat{q}|+\delta_1 \\
&+\delta_2+\delta_3+\delta_4+\rho_1 h^*+\rho_2 l^*+\rho_3 q^*)-k\|\boldsymbol{s}\|.
\end{aligned}
\tag{36}
$$

It follows from Assumption 2 that we get:

$$
\begin{aligned}
&\|\hat{\boldsymbol{\theta}}_1-\boldsymbol{\theta}_1\|\le\|\hat{\boldsymbol{\theta}}_1\|+\|\boldsymbol{\theta}_1\|\le\|\hat{\boldsymbol{\theta}}_1\|+\delta_1, && \|\hat{\boldsymbol{\theta}}_2-\boldsymbol{\theta}_2\|\le\|\hat{\boldsymbol{\theta}}_2\|+\|\boldsymbol{\theta}_2\|\le\|\hat{\boldsymbol{\theta}}_2\|+\delta_2, \\
&\|\hat{\boldsymbol{\vartheta}}_1-\boldsymbol{\vartheta}_1\|\le\|\hat{\boldsymbol{\vartheta}}_1\|+\|\boldsymbol{\vartheta}_1\|\le\|\hat{\boldsymbol{\vartheta}}_1\|+\delta_4, && \|\hat{\boldsymbol{\vartheta}}_2-\boldsymbol{\vartheta}_2\|\le\|\hat{\boldsymbol{\vartheta}}_2\|+\|\boldsymbol{\vartheta}_2\|\le\|\hat{\boldsymbol{\vartheta}}_2\|+\delta_4, \\
&|\hat{h}-h|\le|\hat{h}|+|h|\le|\hat{h}|+h^*, && |\hat{l}-l|\le|\hat{l}|+|l|\le|\hat{l}|+l^*, \\
&|\hat{q}-q|\le|\hat{q}|+|q|\le|\hat{q}|+q^*.
\end{aligned}
$$

Finally,

$$
\begin{aligned}
{}_0D_t^\alpha V(t,\boldsymbol{x}(t)) &< -\varsigma(\|\hat{\boldsymbol{\theta}}_1\|+\|\hat{\boldsymbol{\theta}}_2\|+\|\hat{\boldsymbol{\vartheta}}_1\|+\|\hat{\boldsymbol{\vartheta}}_2\|+\hat{h}+\hat{l}+\hat{q}+\delta_1 \\
&+\delta_2+\delta_3+\delta_4+h^*+l^*+q^*)-k\|\boldsymbol{s}\| \\
&\le-\varsigma\|\boldsymbol{s}\|-\varsigma(\|\hat{\boldsymbol{\theta}}_1-\boldsymbol{\theta}_1\|+\|\hat{\boldsymbol{\theta}}_2-\boldsymbol{\theta}_2\|+\|\hat{\boldsymbol{\vartheta}}_1-\boldsymbol{\vartheta}_1\| \\
&+\|\hat{\boldsymbol{\vartheta}}_2-\boldsymbol{\vartheta}_2\|+\rho_1|\hat{h}-h|+\rho_2|\hat{l}-l|+\rho_3|\hat{q}-q|).
\end{aligned}
\tag{37}
$$

According to the Lemma 2:

$$
{}_0D_t^\alpha V(t,\boldsymbol{x}(t)) < -\sqrt{2}\varsigma V^{1/2}. \tag{38}
$$

Motivated by the Theorem 1, it is clear that the system (5) is Mittag–Leffler stable. Then, we can obtain that the combination drive-response systems (18)–(21) achieve finite-time synchronization. Additionally,

$$
T_1 \le \left[V^{\alpha-\frac{1}{2}}(0,x)\frac{\Gamma(\frac{1}{2})\Gamma(1+\alpha)}{\sqrt{2}\varsigma\Gamma(\alpha+\frac{1}{2})}\right]^{\frac{1}{\alpha}}, \tag{39}
$$

where $0<\alpha<1$. □

Theorem 4. *The dynamic of the sliding mode (28) is finite-time stable and the trajectories and state variables of the FO error system (23) converge to the equilibrium point in finite-time T_2.*

Proof. Adopting the Lyapunov function:

$$
V(t)=\frac{1}{2}\boldsymbol{e}^T(t)\boldsymbol{e}(t). \tag{40}
$$

The FO derivative is illustrated as:

$$
\begin{aligned}
{}_0D_t^\alpha V(t,\boldsymbol{x}(t)) &\le \boldsymbol{e}^T{}_0D_t^\alpha\boldsymbol{e} \\
&=\boldsymbol{e}^T(-\frac{1}{\gamma}sgn(\boldsymbol{e}(t))\|\boldsymbol{e}(t)\|^{\xi}) \\
&\le-\frac{1}{\gamma}\|\boldsymbol{e}(t)\|^{\xi+1} \\
&=-\frac{1}{\gamma}2^{(\xi+1)/2}V^{(\xi+1)/2}.
\end{aligned}
\tag{41}
$$

Thus, the error system (23) is Mittag–Leffler stable in finite-time T_1 under the sliding mode dynamics (28), described by:

$$T_2 \leq \left[V^{\alpha - \frac{\xi+1}{2}}(0,x) \frac{\Gamma(1-\frac{\xi+1}{2})\Gamma(1+\alpha)}{\frac{1}{\gamma} 2^{\frac{\xi+1}{2}} \Gamma(\alpha - \frac{\xi+1}{2}+1)} \right]^{\frac{1}{\alpha}}. \quad (42)$$

□

Remark 10. *According to Theorem 3, the FO error systems (23) can be driven to the sliding surface $s(t)$ via the controller (30) in finite time T_1, that is, the sliding mode surface has accessibility; when it is on the sliding mode surface, according to Theorem 4, the FO error system (23) converges to the equilibrium point in finite time T_2. So Theorem 3 and Theorem 4 achieve combination–combination synchronization within time $T \leq T_1 + T_2$.*

The following corollaries are successfully analyzed from Theorem 4 and their proofs are omitted here.

Corollary 1.

(i) *Assume the matrix $C = 0$, then the drive systems (18), (19) achieve the finite-time combination synchronization (FTCS) with the response system (21) provided the following controller:*

$$\begin{aligned} Du_2(t) = &-\boldsymbol{R}(\boldsymbol{x}_1,\boldsymbol{x}_2,\boldsymbol{y}_2) + AF_1(\boldsymbol{x}_1(t))\hat{\boldsymbol{\theta}}_1 + BF_2(\boldsymbol{x}_2(t))\hat{\boldsymbol{\theta}}_2 - DG_2(\boldsymbol{y}_2(t))\hat{\boldsymbol{\vartheta}}_2 \\ &- \frac{1}{\gamma} sgn(\boldsymbol{e}(t))\|\boldsymbol{e}(t)\|^{\xi} - \varsigma(\|\hat{\boldsymbol{\theta}}_1\| + \|\hat{\boldsymbol{\theta}}_2\| + \|\hat{\boldsymbol{\vartheta}}_2\| + \rho_1|\hat{h}| + \rho_2|\hat{l}| + \rho_3|\hat{q}| \\ &+ \delta_1 + \delta_2 + \delta_4 + \rho_1 h^* + \rho_2 l^* + \rho_3 q^*)(\frac{s}{\gamma\|s\|^2}) - (\hat{h} + \hat{l} + \hat{q})sgn(s) - \frac{k}{\gamma}, \end{aligned}$$

and the adaptive updating laws,

$$\begin{aligned} {}_0D_t^{\alpha}\tilde{\boldsymbol{\theta}}_1 &= -\gamma \boldsymbol{F}_1^T(\boldsymbol{x}_1(t))A^T\boldsymbol{s}(t), \\ {}_0D_t^{\alpha}\tilde{\boldsymbol{\theta}}_2 &= -\gamma \boldsymbol{F}_2^T(\boldsymbol{x}_2(t))B^T\boldsymbol{s}(t), \\ {}_0D_t^{\alpha}\tilde{\boldsymbol{\vartheta}}_2 &= \gamma \boldsymbol{G}_2^T(\boldsymbol{y}_2(t))D^T\boldsymbol{s}(t), \\ {}_0D_t^{\alpha}\tilde{h} &= \gamma\rho_1\|\boldsymbol{s}(t)\|, \\ {}_0D_t^{\alpha}\tilde{l} &= \gamma\rho_2\|\boldsymbol{s}(t)\|, \\ {}_0D_t^{\alpha}\tilde{q} &= \gamma\rho_3\|\boldsymbol{s}(t)\|. \end{aligned} \quad (43)$$

(ii) *Assume the matrix $D = 0$, then the drive systems (18), (19) achieve the FTCS with the response system (20) provided the following controller:*

$$\begin{aligned} Cu_1(t) = &-\boldsymbol{R}(\boldsymbol{x}_1,\boldsymbol{x}_2,\boldsymbol{y}_1) + AF_1(\boldsymbol{x}_1(t))\hat{\boldsymbol{\theta}}_1 + BF_2(\boldsymbol{x}_2(t))\hat{\boldsymbol{\theta}}_2 - CG_1(\boldsymbol{y}_1(t))\hat{\boldsymbol{\vartheta}}_1 \\ &- \frac{1}{\gamma} sgn(\boldsymbol{e}(t))\|\boldsymbol{e}(t)\|^{\xi} - \varsigma(\|\hat{\boldsymbol{\theta}}_1\| + \|\hat{\boldsymbol{\theta}}_2\| + \|\hat{\boldsymbol{\vartheta}}_1\| + \rho_1|\hat{h}| + \rho_2|\hat{l}| + \rho_3|\hat{q}| \\ &+ \delta_1 + \delta_2 + \delta_3 + \rho_1 h^* + \rho_2 l^* + \rho_3 q^*)(\frac{s}{\gamma\|s\|^2}) - (\hat{h} + \hat{l} + \hat{q})sgn(s) - \frac{k}{\gamma}, \end{aligned}$$

and the adaptive updating laws,

$$\begin{aligned}
{}_0D_t^{\alpha}\tilde{\boldsymbol{\theta}}_1 &= -\gamma \boldsymbol{F}_1^T(\boldsymbol{x}_1(t))A^T\boldsymbol{s}(t),\\
{}_0D_t^{\alpha}\tilde{\boldsymbol{\theta}}_2 &= -\gamma \boldsymbol{F}_2^T(\boldsymbol{x}_2(t))B^T\boldsymbol{s}(t),\\
{}_0D_t^{\alpha}\tilde{\boldsymbol{\vartheta}}_1 &= \gamma \boldsymbol{G}_1^T(\boldsymbol{y}_1(t))C^T\boldsymbol{s}(t),\\
{}_0D_t^{\alpha}\tilde{h} &= \gamma\rho_1\|\boldsymbol{s}(t)\|,\\
{}_0D_t^{\alpha}\tilde{l} &= \gamma\rho_2\|\boldsymbol{s}(t)\|,\\
{}_0D_t^{\alpha}\tilde{q} &= \gamma\rho_3\|\boldsymbol{s}(t)\|.
\end{aligned} \tag{44}$$

Corollary 2.

(i) *Assume the matrices $A = C = 0$, $D = I$ then the drive system (19) achieve the FTCS with the response system (21) provided the following controller:*

$$\begin{aligned}
\boldsymbol{u}_2(t) = &-\boldsymbol{R}(\boldsymbol{x}_2,\boldsymbol{y}_2) + B\boldsymbol{F}_2(\boldsymbol{x}_2(t))\hat{\boldsymbol{\theta}}_2 - \boldsymbol{G}_2(\boldsymbol{y}_2(t))\hat{\boldsymbol{\vartheta}}_2\\
&-\frac{1}{\gamma}sgn(\boldsymbol{e}(t))\|\boldsymbol{e}(t)\|^{\xi} - \varsigma(\|\hat{\boldsymbol{\theta}}_2\| + \|\hat{\boldsymbol{\vartheta}}_2\| + \rho_1|\hat{h}| + \rho_2|\hat{l}| + \rho_3|\hat{q}|\\
&+\delta_2 + \delta_4 + \rho_1 h^* + \rho_2 l^* + \rho_3 q^*)(\frac{\boldsymbol{s}}{\gamma\|\boldsymbol{s}\|^2}) - (\hat{h} + \hat{l} + \hat{q})sgn(\boldsymbol{s}) - \frac{k}{\gamma},
\end{aligned}$$

and the adaptive updating laws,

$$\begin{aligned}
{}_0D_t^{\alpha}\tilde{\boldsymbol{\theta}}_2 &= -\gamma \boldsymbol{F}_2^T(\boldsymbol{x}_2(t))B^T\boldsymbol{s}(t),\\
{}_0D_t^{\alpha}\tilde{\boldsymbol{\vartheta}}_2 &= \gamma \boldsymbol{G}_2^T(\boldsymbol{y}_2(t))\boldsymbol{s}(t),\\
{}_0D_t^{\alpha}\tilde{h} &= \gamma\rho_1\|\boldsymbol{s}(t)\|,\\
{}_0D_t^{\alpha}\tilde{l} &= \gamma\rho_2\|\boldsymbol{s}(t)\|,\\
{}_0D_t^{\alpha}\tilde{q} &= \gamma\rho_3\|\boldsymbol{s}(t)\|.
\end{aligned} \tag{45}$$

(ii) *Assume the matrices $A = D = 0$, $C = I$ then the drive system (19) achieve the FTCS with the response system (20) provided the following controller:*

$$\begin{aligned}
\boldsymbol{u}_1(t) = &-\boldsymbol{R}(\boldsymbol{x}_2,\boldsymbol{y}_1) + B\boldsymbol{F}_2(\boldsymbol{x}_2(t))\hat{\boldsymbol{\theta}}_2 - \boldsymbol{G}_1(\boldsymbol{y}_1(t))\hat{\boldsymbol{\vartheta}}_1\\
&-\frac{1}{\gamma}sgn(\boldsymbol{e}(t))\|\boldsymbol{e}(t)\|^{\xi} - \varsigma(\|\hat{\boldsymbol{\theta}}_2\| + \|\hat{\boldsymbol{\vartheta}}_1\| + \rho_1|\hat{h}| + \rho_2|\hat{l}| + \rho_3|\hat{q}|\\
&+\delta_2 + \delta_3 + \rho_1 h^* + \rho_2 l^* + \rho_3 q^*)(\frac{\boldsymbol{s}}{\gamma\|\boldsymbol{s}\|^2}) - (\hat{h} + \hat{l} + \hat{q})sgn(\boldsymbol{s}) - \frac{k}{\gamma},
\end{aligned}$$

and the adaptive updating laws,

$$\begin{aligned}
{}_0D_t^{\alpha}\tilde{\boldsymbol{\theta}}_2 &= -\gamma \boldsymbol{F}_2^T(\boldsymbol{x}_2(t))B^T\boldsymbol{s}(t),\\
{}_0D_t^{\alpha}\tilde{\boldsymbol{\vartheta}}_1 &= \gamma \boldsymbol{G}_1^T(\boldsymbol{y}_1(t))\boldsymbol{s}(t),\\
{}_0D_t^{\alpha}\tilde{h} &= \gamma\rho_1\|\boldsymbol{s}(t)\|,\\
{}_0D_t^{\alpha}\tilde{l} &= \gamma\rho_2\|\boldsymbol{s}(t)\|,\\
{}_0D_t^{\alpha}\tilde{q} &= \gamma\rho_3\|\boldsymbol{s}(t)\|.
\end{aligned} \tag{46}$$

(iii) *Assume the matrices* $B = D = 0$, $C = I$ *then the drive system (18) achieve the FTCS with the response system (20) provided the following controller:*

$$\begin{aligned} u_1(t) &= -R(x_1, y_1) + AF_1(x_1(t))\hat{\theta}_1 - G_1(y_1(t))\hat{\vartheta}_1 \\ &- \frac{1}{\gamma} sgn(e(t))\|e(t)\|^{\xi} - \varsigma(\|\hat{\theta}_1\| + \|\hat{\vartheta}_1\| + \rho_1|\hat{h}| + \rho_2|\hat{l}| + \rho_3|\hat{q}| \\ &+ \delta_1 + \delta_3 + \rho_1 h^* + \rho_2 l^* + \rho_3 q^*)(\frac{s}{\gamma\|s\|^2}) - (\hat{h} + \hat{l} + \hat{q})sgn(s) - \frac{k}{\gamma}, \end{aligned}$$

and the adaptive updating laws,

$$\begin{aligned} {}_0D_t^{\alpha}\tilde{\theta}_1 &= -\gamma F_1^T(x_1(t))A^T s(t), \\ {}_0D_t^{\alpha}\tilde{\vartheta}_1 &= \gamma G_1^T(y_1(t))s(t), \\ {}_0D_t^{\alpha}\tilde{h} &= \gamma\rho_1\|s(t)\|, \\ {}_0D_t^{\alpha}\tilde{l} &= \gamma\rho_2\|s(t)\|, \\ {}_0D_t^{\alpha}\tilde{q} &= \gamma\rho_3\|s(t)\|. \end{aligned} \tag{47}$$

(iv) *Assume the matrices* $B = C = 0$, $D = I$ *then the drive system (18) achieve the FTCS with the response system (21) provided the following controller:*

$$\begin{aligned} u_2(t) &= -R(x_1, y_2) + AF_1(x_1(t))\hat{\theta}_1 - G_2(y_2(t))\hat{\vartheta}_2 \\ &- \frac{1}{\gamma} sgn(e(t))\|e(t)\|^{\xi} - \varsigma(\|\hat{\theta}_1\| + \|\hat{\vartheta}_2\| + \rho_1|\hat{h}| + \rho_2|\hat{l}| + \rho_3|\hat{q}| \\ &+ \delta_1 + \delta_4 + \rho_1 h^* + \rho_2 l^* + \rho_3 q^*)(\frac{s}{\gamma\|s\|^2}) - (\hat{h} + \hat{l} + \hat{q})sgn(s) - \frac{k}{\gamma}, \end{aligned}$$

and the adaptive updating laws,

$$\begin{aligned} {}_0D_t^{\alpha}\tilde{\theta}_1 &= -\gamma F_1^T(x_1(t))A^T s(t), \\ {}_0D_t^{\alpha}\tilde{\vartheta}_2 &= \gamma G_2^T(y_2(t))s(t), \\ {}_0D_t^{\alpha}\tilde{h} &= \gamma\rho_1\|s(t)\|, \\ {}_0D_t^{\alpha}\tilde{l} &= \gamma\rho_2\|s(t)\|, \\ {}_0D_t^{\alpha}\tilde{q} &= \gamma\rho_3\|s(t)\|. \end{aligned} \tag{48}$$

Corollary 3.

(i) *Assume the matrices* $A = B = C = 0, D = I$, *then the equilibrium point* $(0,0,0,0)$ *of response system (21) is asymptotically stable provided the following controller:*

$$\begin{aligned} u_2(t) = -R(y_2) - G_2(y_2(t))\hat{\vartheta}_2 - \frac{1}{\gamma} sgn(e(t))\|e(t)\|^{\xi} - \varsigma(\|\hat{\vartheta}_2\| + \rho_1|\hat{h}| + \rho_2|\hat{l}| \\ + \rho_3|\hat{q}| + \delta_4 + \rho_1 h^* + \rho_2 l^* + \rho_3 q^*)(\frac{s}{\gamma\|s\|^2}) - (\hat{h} + \hat{l} + \hat{q})sgn(s) - \frac{k}{\gamma}, \end{aligned}$$

and the adaptive updating laws,

$$\begin{aligned} {}_0D_t^{\alpha}\tilde{\vartheta}_2 &= \gamma G_2^T(y_2(t))s(t) \\ {}_0D_t^{\alpha}\tilde{h} &= \gamma\rho_1\|s(t)\|, \\ {}_0D_t^{\alpha}\tilde{l} &= \gamma\rho_2\|s(t)\|, \\ {}_0D_t^{\alpha}\tilde{q} &= \gamma\rho_3\|s(t)\|. \end{aligned} \tag{49}$$

(ii) *Assume the matrices $A = B = D = 0, C = I$, then the equilibrium point $(0,0,0,0)$ of response system (20) is asymptotically stable provided the following controller:*

$$u_1(t) = -R(y_1) - G_1(y_1(t))\hat{\vartheta}_1 - \frac{1}{\gamma}sgn(e(t))\|e(t)\|^{\xi} - \varsigma(\|\hat{\vartheta}_1\| + \rho_1|\hat{h}| + \rho_2|\hat{l}|$$
$$+ \rho_3|\hat{q}| + \delta_3 + \rho_1 h^* + \rho_2 l^* + \rho_3 q^*)(\frac{s}{\gamma\|s\|^2}) - (\hat{h} + \hat{l} + \hat{q})sgn(s) - \frac{k}{\gamma},$$

and the adaptive updating laws,

$$\begin{aligned} {}_0D_t^{\alpha}\tilde{\vartheta}_1 &= \gamma G_1^T(y_1(t))s(t), \\ {}_0D_t^{\alpha}\tilde{h} &= \gamma\rho_1\|s(t)\|, \\ {}_0D_t^{\alpha}\tilde{l} &= \gamma\rho_2\|s(t)\|, \\ {}_0D_t^{\alpha}\tilde{q} &= \gamma\rho_3\|s(t)\|. \end{aligned} \tag{50}$$

Remark 11. *The scaling matrices $A, B, C, D \in \mathbb{R}^n \times \mathbb{R}^n$ could be the diagonal matrices or the identity matrices, or some of them are zero. As described in Remark 2, when $A = B = C = D = I \in \mathbb{R}^n \times \mathbb{R}^n$, then the topic will be transformed into finite-time C-C complete synchronization with multiple SD; the numerical simulation results are displayed in Section 5.*

5. Numerical Simulation

Let the FO hyperchaotic Lorenz and Chen system under multiple SD be the drive systems

$$\begin{pmatrix} {}_0D_t^{\alpha}x_{11} \\ {}_0D_t^{\alpha}x_{21} \\ {}_0D_t^{\alpha}x_{31} \\ {}_0D_t^{\alpha}x_{41} \end{pmatrix} = \begin{pmatrix} x_{21}-x_{11} & 0 & 0 & 0 \\ 0 & x_{11} & 0 & 0 \\ 0 & 0 & -x_{31} & 0 \\ 0 & 0 & 0 & x_{41} \end{pmatrix} \begin{pmatrix} a_1+\Delta a_1 \\ b_1+\Delta b_1 \\ c_1+\Delta c_1 \\ d_1+\Delta d_1 \end{pmatrix} + \begin{pmatrix} x_{41}+\Delta f_{11} \\ -x_{11}x_{31}-x_{21}+\Delta f_{21} \\ x_{11}x_{21}+\Delta f_{31} \\ -x_{21}x_{31}+\Delta f_{41} \end{pmatrix} + \begin{pmatrix} d_{11} \\ d_{21} \\ d_{31} \\ d_{41} \end{pmatrix}. \tag{51}$$

$$\begin{pmatrix} {}_0D_t^{\alpha}x_{12} \\ {}_0D_t^{\alpha}x_{22} \\ {}_0D_t^{\alpha}x_{32} \\ {}_0D_t^{\alpha}x_{42} \end{pmatrix} = \begin{pmatrix} x_{22}-x_{12} & 0 & 0 & 0 & 0 \\ 0 & 0 & x_{22} & x_{12} & 0 \\ 0 & -x_{32} & 0 & 0 & 0 \\ 0 & 0 & 0 & 0 & x_{42} \end{pmatrix} \begin{pmatrix} a_2+\Delta a_2 \\ b_2+\Delta b_2 \\ c_2+\Delta c_2 \\ d_2+\Delta d_2 \\ r+\Delta r \end{pmatrix} + \begin{pmatrix} x_{42}+\Delta f_{12} \\ -x_{11}x_{32}+\Delta f_{22} \\ x_{12}x_{22}+\Delta f_{32} \\ x_{22}x_{32}+\Delta f_{42} \end{pmatrix} + \begin{pmatrix} d_{12} \\ d_{22} \\ d_{32} \\ d_{42} \end{pmatrix}. \tag{52}$$

Let the FO hyper-chaotic Lü and Liu chaotic system under multiple SD and controller be the response systems

$$\begin{pmatrix} {}_0D_t^{\alpha}y_{11} \\ {}_0D_t^{\alpha}y_{21} \\ {}_0D_t^{\alpha}y_{31} \\ {}_0D_t^{\alpha}y_{41} \end{pmatrix} = \begin{pmatrix} y_{21}-y_{11} & 0 & 0 & 0 \\ 0 & y_{21} & 0 & 0 \\ 0 & 0 & -y_{31} & 0 \\ 0 & 0 & 0 & y_{41} \end{pmatrix} \begin{pmatrix} a_3+\Delta a_3 \\ b_3+\Delta b_3 \\ c_3+\Delta c_3 \\ d_3+\Delta d_3 \end{pmatrix} + \begin{pmatrix} y_{41}+\Delta g_{11} \\ -y_{11}y_{31}+\Delta g_{21} \\ y_{11}y_{21}+\Delta g_{31} \\ y_{11}y_{31}+\Delta g_{41} \end{pmatrix} + \begin{pmatrix} \mu_{11}+u_{11} \\ \mu_{21}+u_{21} \\ \mu_{31}+u_{31} \\ \mu_{41}+u_{41} \end{pmatrix}. \tag{53}$$

$$\begin{pmatrix} {}_0D_t^{\alpha}y_{12} \\ {}_0D_t^{\alpha}y_{22} \\ {}_0D_t^{\alpha}y_{32} \\ {}_0D_t^{\alpha}y_{42} \end{pmatrix} = \begin{pmatrix} y_{22}-y_{12} & 0 & 0 & 0 & 0 \\ 0 & y_{12} & 0 & 0 & 0 \\ 0 & 0 & -y_{32} & 0 & y_{12}^2 \\ 0 & 0 & 0 & -y_{12} & 0 \end{pmatrix} \begin{pmatrix} a_4+\Delta a_4 \\ b_4+\Delta b_4 \\ c_4+\Delta c_4 \\ d_4+\Delta d_4 \\ m+\Delta m \end{pmatrix} + \begin{pmatrix} \Delta g_{12} \\ -y_{12}y_{32}+y_{42}+\Delta g_{22} \\ \Delta g_{32} \\ \Delta g_{42} \end{pmatrix} + \begin{pmatrix} \mu_{12}+u_{12} \\ \mu_{22}+u_{22} \\ \mu_{32}+u_{32} \\ \mu_{42}+u_{42} \end{pmatrix}. \tag{54}$$

The chosen parameters are $a_1 = 10, b_1 = 28, c_1 = 8/3, d_1 = -1, a_2 = 35, b_2 = 3, c_2 = 12, d_2 = 7, r = 0.5, a_3 = 36, b_3 = 20, c_3 = 3, d_3 = 0.5, a_4 = 10, b_4 = 40, c_4 = 2.5, d_4 = 10, m = 4$. The initial values take as $\boldsymbol{x}_1(0) = (2, -2, 1, -1)$, $\boldsymbol{x}_2(0) = (1, 1, 2, 2)$, $\boldsymbol{y}_1(0) = (-1, 3, 1, 3)$, $\boldsymbol{y}_2(0) = (2, 1, 2, 1)$. The orders take as $\alpha = 0.99$. The combination D-R systems are in hyper-chaotic state which are presented in Figure 1.

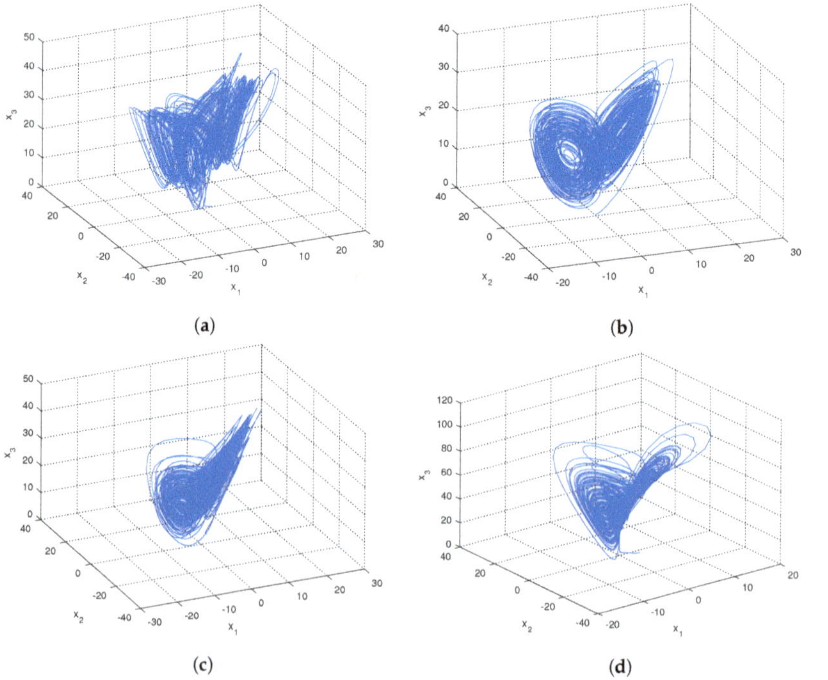

Figure 1. The attractors with respect to the FO hyper-chaotic Lorenz, Chen, Lü, Liu system indicating in sub-pictures (**a**–**d**) respectively for $\alpha = 0.99$.

Remark 12. *The ranges of fractional order that make the FO hyper-chaotic Chen, Lorenz, L and Liu chaotic system appear hyper-chaotic are chose as* $0.8 \leq \alpha < 1, 0.97 \leq \alpha < 1, 0.94 \leq \alpha \leq 1, 0.96 \leq \alpha \leq 1$ *respectively. If the drive-response systems are in hyper-chaotic, the influence of stochastic disturbances on the system can be better studied, and the effectiveness and robustness of the controller can be proved. It follows that the dynamic error has the same fractional-order as the drive and response systems that the fractional order* α *is chose as* $0.97 \leq \alpha < 1$ *which can ensure that the all drive-response systems are hyper-chaotic. Thus, in the numerical simulation section, we also consider the* $\alpha = 0.97$ *to validate the proposed method.*

According to the above equations, we consider:

$$\hat{\boldsymbol{\theta}}_1 = (\hat{a}_1, \hat{b}_1, \hat{c}_1, \hat{d}_1)^T, \quad \hat{\boldsymbol{\theta}}_2 = (\hat{a}_2, \hat{b}_2, \hat{c}_2, \hat{d}_2, \hat{r})^T,$$
$$\hat{\boldsymbol{\vartheta}}_1 = (\hat{a}_3, \hat{b}_3, \hat{c}_3, \hat{d}_3)^T, \quad \hat{\boldsymbol{\vartheta}}_2 = (\hat{a}_4, \hat{b}_4, \hat{c}_4, \hat{d}_4, \hat{m})^T,$$

The uncertain terms $\Delta\boldsymbol{\theta}_i$, $\Delta\boldsymbol{\vartheta}_i$, $\Delta \boldsymbol{f}_i(\boldsymbol{x}_i(t))$, $\Delta \boldsymbol{g}_i(\boldsymbol{y}_i(t))$ and external disturbance $\boldsymbol{d}_i(\boldsymbol{x}_i(t))$, $\boldsymbol{\mu}_i(\boldsymbol{y}_i(t))$ for $i = 1, 2$ are demonstrated as:

$$\begin{aligned}
&\Delta\boldsymbol{\theta}_1 = (0.2sin(t), 0.2sin(0.2t), 0.2sin(3t), 0.2sin(0.4t))^T,\\
&\Delta\boldsymbol{\theta}_2 = (0.2sin(5t), 0.2sin(0.6t), 0.2sin(0.8t), 0.2sin(2t), 0.2sin(10t))^T,\\
&\Delta\boldsymbol{\vartheta}_1 = (0.2sin(t), 0.2sin(2t), 0.2sin(3t), 0.2sin(4t))^T,\\
&\Delta\boldsymbol{\vartheta}_2 = (0.2sin(0.5t), 0.2sin(6t), 0.2sin(t), 0.2sin(0.2t), 0.2sin(3t))^T,\\
&\boldsymbol{d}_1(\boldsymbol{x}_1(t)) = (-0.1cos(t), -0.2cos(2t), 0.3sin(3t), 0.4sin(4t))^T,\\
&\boldsymbol{d}_2(\boldsymbol{x}_2(t)) = (-0.1sin(t), -0.2sin(2t), 0.3cos(3t), 0.4cos(4t))^T,\\
&\boldsymbol{\mu}_1(\boldsymbol{y}_1(t)) = (0.1cos(5t), 0.2cos(6t), 0.3sin(7t), 0.4sin(8t))^T,\\
&\boldsymbol{\mu}_2(\boldsymbol{y}_2(t)) = (0.1sin(5t), 0.2sin(6t), 0.3cos(7t), 0.4cos(8t))^T,\\
&\Delta\boldsymbol{f}_i(\boldsymbol{x}_i(t)) = (0.1cos(x_{1i}), 0.2cos(x_{2i}), 0.3cos(x_{3i}), 0.4cos(x_{4i}))^T,\\
&\Delta\boldsymbol{g}_i(\boldsymbol{y}_i(t)) = (0.1sin(y_{1i}), 0.2sin(y_{2i}), 0.3sin(y_{3i}), 0.4sin(y_{4i}))^T,
\end{aligned} \tag{55}$$

where $i = 1, 2$. It follows from (30), (31) and (34) that the error dynamics and the updating rules of unknown parameters are expressed as:

$$\begin{aligned}
{}_0D_t^{\alpha} e_1(t) =& [-(\hat{a}_3 - a_3) - 0.2sin(t)](y_{21} - y_{11}) - [(\hat{a}_4 - a_4) + 0.2sin(0.5t)](y_{22} - y_{12})\\
&+ [(\hat{a}_1 - a_1) - 0.2sin(t)](x_{21} - x_{11}) + [(\hat{a}_2 - a_2) - 0.2sin(5t)](x_{22} - x_{12})\\
&+ [0.1sin(y_{11}) + 0.1sin(y_{12}) - 0.1cos(x_{11}) - 0.1cos(x_{12})]\\
&+ [0.1cos(5t) + 0.1sin(5t) + 0.1cos(t) + 0.1sin(t)] - \frac{1}{\gamma} sgn(e_1(t))\|\boldsymbol{e}(t)\|^{\xi}\\
&- \varsigma(\|\hat{\boldsymbol{\theta}}_1\| + \|\hat{\boldsymbol{\theta}}_2\| + \|\hat{\boldsymbol{\vartheta}}_1\| + \|\hat{\boldsymbol{\vartheta}}_2\| + \rho_1|\hat{h}| + \rho_2|\hat{l}| + \rho_3|\hat{q}| + \delta_1 + \delta_2 + \delta_3\\
&+ \delta_4 + \rho_1 h^* + \rho_2 l^* + \rho_3 q^*)(\frac{s_1}{\gamma\|\boldsymbol{s}\|^2}) - (\hat{h} + \hat{l} + \hat{q}) sgn(s_1) - \frac{k}{\gamma}.
\end{aligned}$$

$$\begin{aligned}
{}_0D_t^{\alpha} e_2(t) =& \Big[-(\hat{b}_3 - b_3) + 0.2sin(2t)\Big] y_{21} - \Big[(\hat{b}_4 - b_4) - 0.2sin(6t)\Big] y_{12}\\
&+ \Big[(\hat{b}_1 - b_1) - 0.2sin(0.2t)\Big] x_{11} + [(\hat{c}_2 - c_2) - 0.2sin(0.6)] x_{22}\\
&+ \Big[(\hat{d}_2 - d_2) - 0.2sin(0.8)\Big] x_{12} + [0.2sin(y_{21}) + 0.2sin(y_{22})]\\
&[-0.2cos(x_{21}) - 0.2cos(x_{22})] + [0.2cos(6t) + 0.2sin(6t) + 0.2cos(2t) + 0.2sin(2t)]\\
&- \frac{1}{\gamma} sgn(e_2(t))\|\boldsymbol{e}(t)\|^{\xi} - \varsigma(\|\hat{\boldsymbol{\theta}}_1\| + \|\hat{\boldsymbol{\theta}}_2\| + \|\hat{\boldsymbol{\vartheta}}_1\| + \|\hat{\boldsymbol{\vartheta}}_2\| + \rho_1|\hat{h}| + \rho_2|\hat{l}| + \rho_3|\hat{q}| + \delta_1\\
&+ \delta_2 + \delta_3 + \delta_4 + \rho_1 h^* + \rho_2 l^* + \rho_3 q^*)(\frac{s_2}{\gamma\|\boldsymbol{s}\|^2}) - (\hat{h} + \hat{l} + \hat{q}) sgn(s_2) - \frac{k}{\gamma}.
\end{aligned}$$

$$
\begin{aligned}
{}_0D_t^{\alpha}e_3(t) &= [(\hat{c}_3 - c_3) - 0.2sin(3t)]y_{31} + [(\hat{c}_4 - c_4) - 0.2sin(t)]y_{32} \\
&- [(\hat{m} - m) - 0.2sin(3t)]y_{12}^2 - [(\hat{c}_1 - c_1) - 0.2sin(3t)]x_{31} \\
&- \Big[(\hat{b}_2 - b_2) - 0.2sin(0.6t)\Big]x_{32} + [0.3sin(y_{31}) + 0.3sin(y_{32}) - 0.3cos(x_{31}) - 0.3cos(x_{32})] \\
&+ [0.3cos(7t) + 0.3sin(7t) - 0.3cos(3t) - 0.3sin(3t)] - \frac{1}{\gamma}sgn(e_3(t))\|e(t)\|^{\xi} \\
&- \varsigma(\|\hat{\boldsymbol{\theta}}_1\| + \|\hat{\boldsymbol{\theta}}_2\| + \|\hat{\boldsymbol{\vartheta}}_1\| + \|\hat{\boldsymbol{\vartheta}}_2\| + \rho_1|\hat{h}| + \rho_2|\hat{l}| + \rho_3|\hat{q}| + \delta_1 + \delta_2 \\
&+ \delta_3 + \delta_4 + \rho_1 h^* + \rho_2 l^* + \rho_3 q^*)(\frac{s_3}{\gamma\|s\|^2}) - (\hat{h} + \hat{l} + \hat{q})sgn(s_3) - \frac{k}{\gamma}.
\end{aligned}
$$

$$
\begin{aligned}
{}_0D_t^{\alpha}e_4(t) &= \Big[-(\hat{d}_3 - d_3) + 0.2sin(4t)\Big]y_{41} + \Big[(\hat{d}_4 - d_4) + 0.2sin(0.2t)\Big]y_{12} \\
&+ \Big[(\hat{d}_1 - d_1) - 0.2sin(0.4t)\Big]x_{41} + [(\hat{r} - r) - 0.2sin(10t)]x_{42} \\
&+ [0.4sin(y_{41}) + 0.4sin(y_{42}) - 0.4cos(x_{41}) - 0.4cos(x_{42})] \\
&+ [0.4cos(8t) + 0.4sin(8t) - 0.4cos(4t) - 0.4sin(4t)] \\
&- \frac{1}{\gamma}sgn(e_4(t))\|e(t)\|^{\xi} - \varsigma(\|\hat{\boldsymbol{\theta}}_1\| + \|\hat{\boldsymbol{\theta}}_2\| + \|\hat{\boldsymbol{\vartheta}}_1\| + \|\hat{\boldsymbol{\vartheta}}_2\| \\
&+ \rho_1|\hat{h}| + \rho_2|\hat{l}| + \rho_3|\hat{q}| + \delta_1 + \delta_2 + \delta_3 + \delta_4 + \rho_1 h^* + \rho_2 l^* + \rho_3 q^*)(\frac{s_4}{\gamma\|s\|^2}) \\
&- (\hat{h} + \hat{l} + \hat{q})sgn(s_4) - \frac{k}{\gamma}.
\end{aligned}
$$

$$
\begin{aligned}
{}_0D_t^{\alpha}\tilde{\boldsymbol{\theta}}_1 &= \gamma\Big[((x_{11} - x_{21})s_1, -x_{11}s_2, x_{31}s_3, -x_{41}s_4)^T\Big], \\
{}_0D_t^{\alpha}\tilde{\boldsymbol{\theta}}_2 &= \gamma\Big[((x_{12} - x_{22})s_1, x_{32}s_3, -x_{22}s_2, -x_{12}s_2, -x_{42}s_4)^T\Big], \\
{}_0D_t^{\alpha}\tilde{\boldsymbol{\vartheta}}_1 &= \gamma\Big[((y_{21} - y_{11})s_1, y_{21}s_2, -y_{31}s_3, y_{41}s_4)^T\Big], \\
{}_0D_t^{\alpha}\tilde{\boldsymbol{\vartheta}}_2 &= \gamma\Big[((y_{22} - y_{12})s_1, y_{12}s_2, -y_{32}s_3, -y_{12}s_4, y_{12}^2 s_3)^T\Big], \\
{}_0D_t^{\alpha}\tilde{h} &= \gamma\rho_1\sqrt{(s_1^2 + s_2^2 + s_3^2 + s_4^2)}, \\
{}_0D_t^{\alpha}\tilde{l} &= \gamma\rho_2\sqrt{(s_1^2 + s_2^2 + s_3^2 + s_4^2)}, \\
{}_0D_t^{\alpha}\tilde{q} &= \gamma\rho_3\sqrt{(s_1^2 + s_2^2 + s_3^2 + s_4^2)},
\end{aligned}
$$

In the numerical simulation section, the method we adopted for the fractional order chaotic system is the Adams–Bashforth–Moulton type predictor-corrector scheme [25]. We use the Matlab software (R2016a) to solve them. For the simulation procedure, The initial values of D-R systems take as $\boldsymbol{x}_1(0) = (2, -2, 1, -1)$, $\boldsymbol{x}_2(0) = (1, 1, 2, 2)$, $\boldsymbol{y}_1(0) = (-1, 3, 1, 3)$, $\boldsymbol{y}_2(0) = (2, 1, 2, 1)$. The orders take as $\alpha = 0.99$. The time step is 0.003. The number of iterations is 3000. The initial conditions of parameters estimation are $(a_1(0), b_1(0), c_1(0), d_1(0)) = (1, 1, 1, 1)$, $(a_2(0), b_2(0), c_2(0), d_2(0), r(0)) = (1, 1, 1, 1, 1)$, $(a_3(0), b_3(0), c_3(0), d_3(0)) = (1, 1, 1, 1)$, $h(0)$, $l(0), q(0) = (1, 1, 1)$, $(a_4(0), b_4(0), c_4(0), d_4(0), m(0)) = (1, 1, 1, 1, 1)$. The constants are chosen as $\gamma = 1, \delta_1 = 100, \delta_2 = 100, \delta_3 = 100, \delta_4 = 100, h^* = 50, l^* = 50, q^* = 50, \rho_1 = 0.1, \rho_2 = 0.2, \rho_3 = 0.3, \xi = 0.5, \varsigma = 3, k = 4$. For $\alpha = 0.99$, the trajectories about the error variables $e_i(t), (i = 1, 2, 3, 4)$ are depicted in Figure 2 and the synchronization for the state trajectories of drive systems (18), (19) and response system (20), (21) are drawn in Figures 3. The trajectories of estimations $\hat{\boldsymbol{\theta}}_i$, $\hat{\boldsymbol{\vartheta}}_i$, $(i = 1, 2)$, $\hat{h}$, $\hat{l}$, $\hat{q}$ are depicted in Figure 4. Finally, in order to prove that the error variables converge completely to zero for $\alpha = 0.99$, the sum of squares of all errors $(e_1^2 + e_2^2 + e_3^2 + e_4^2)$ is conducted as shown in Figure 5. For $\alpha = 0.97$, the trajectories about the error variables $e_i(t), (i = 1, 2, 3, 4)$ are drawn in Figure 6 and the trajectories of estimations $\hat{\boldsymbol{\theta}}_i$, $\hat{\boldsymbol{\vartheta}}_i$, $(i = 1, 2)$, $\hat{h}$, $\hat{l}$, $\hat{q}$ are drawn in Figure 7. Finally, in order to prove that the error variables converge completely to zero for $\alpha = 0.97$, the sum of squares of all errors $(e_1^2 + e_2^2 + e_3^2 + e_4^2)$ is conducted as shown in Figure 8. It all demonstrates that the the error does converge completely to zero. Therefore, this controller and the updated rules of the parameters are effective.

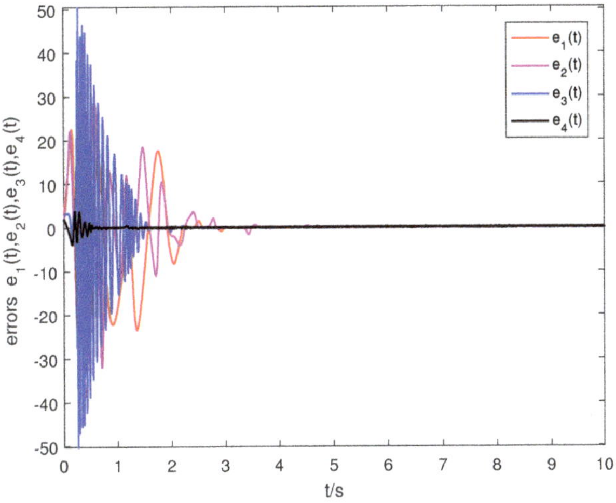

Figure 2. The C-C synchronization errors e_1, e_2, e_3, e_4 change with time t for $\alpha = 0.99$.

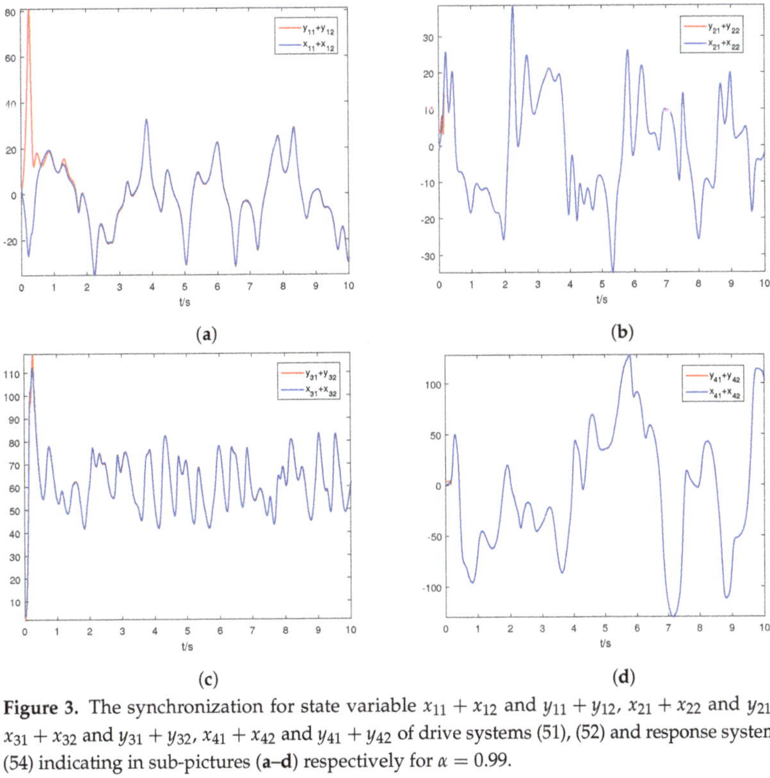

Figure 3. The synchronization for state variable $x_{11} + x_{12}$ and $y_{11} + y_{12}$, $x_{21} + x_{22}$ and $y_{21} + y_{22}$, $x_{31} + x_{32}$ and $y_{31} + y_{32}$, $x_{41} + x_{42}$ and $y_{41} + y_{42}$ of drive systems (51), (52) and response systems (53), (54) indicating in sub-pictures (**a–d**) respectively for $\alpha = 0.99$.

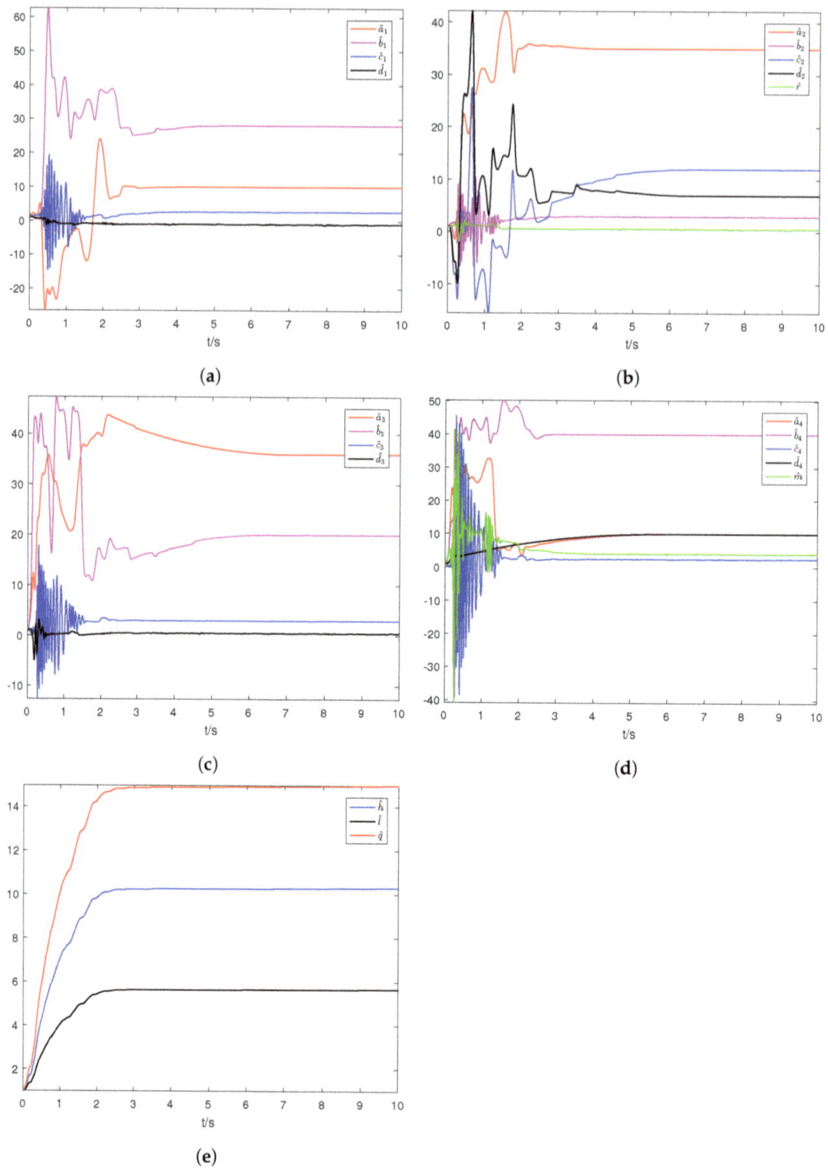

Figure 4. The estimation of parameters $\hat{a}_1, \hat{b}_1, \hat{c}_1, \hat{d}_1, \hat{a}_2, \hat{b}_2, \hat{c}_2, \hat{d}_2, \hat{r}$ of drive systems (51) (**a**) and (52) (**b**), $\hat{a}_3, \hat{b}_3, \hat{c}_3, \hat{d}_3, \hat{a}_4, \hat{b}_4, \hat{c}_4, \hat{d}_4, \hat{m}$ of response systems (53) (**c**) and (54) (**d**), $\hat{h}, \hat{l}, \hat{q}$ (**e**) for $\alpha = 0.99$.

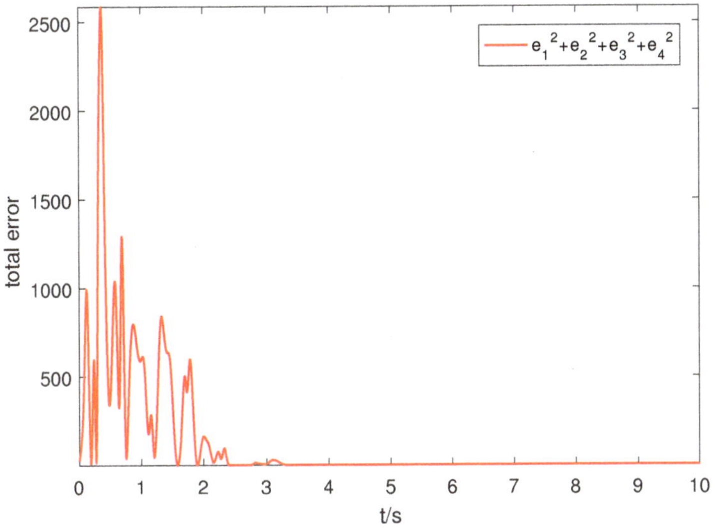

Figure 5. The C-C synchronization total error $e_1^2 + e_2^2 + e_3^2 + e_4^2$ changes with time t for $\alpha = 0.99$.

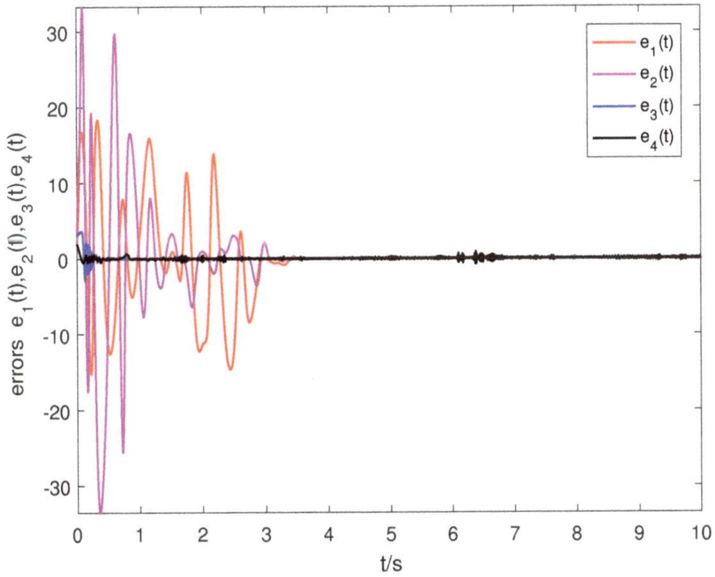

Figure 6. The C-C synchronization errors e_1, e_2, e_3, e_4 change with time t for $\alpha = 0.97$.

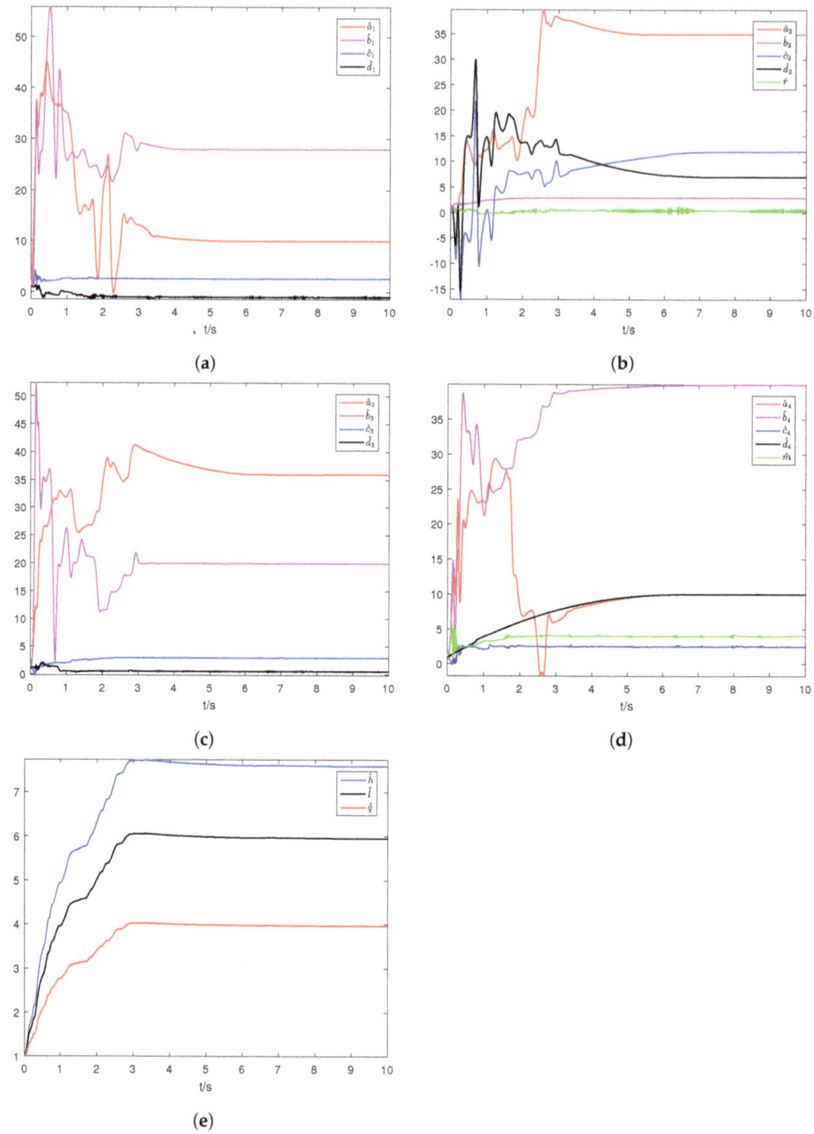

Figure 7. The estimation of parameters $\hat{a}_1, \hat{b}_1, \hat{c}_1, \hat{d}_1, \hat{a}_2, \hat{b}_2, \hat{c}_2, \hat{d}_2, \hat{r}$ of drive systems (51) (**a**) and (52) (**b**), $\hat{a}_3, \hat{b}_3, \hat{c}_3, \hat{d}_3, \hat{a}_4, \hat{b}_4, \hat{c}_4, \hat{d}_4, \hat{m}$ of response systems (53) (**c**) and (54) (**d**), $\hat{h}, \hat{l}, \hat{q}$ (**e**) for $\alpha = 0.97$.

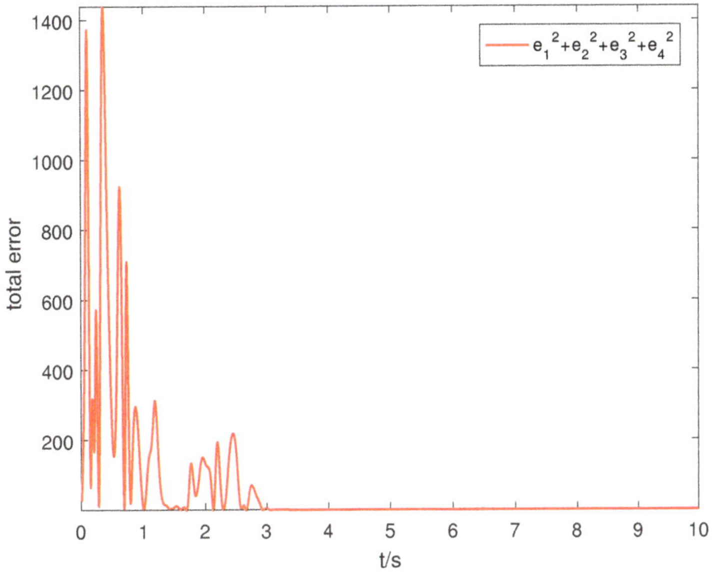

Figure 8. The C-C synchronization total error $e_1^2 + e_2^2 + e_3^2 + e_4^2$ changes with time t for $\alpha = 0.97$.

Remark 13. *In the numerical simulation section, the fractional order (FO) hyper-chaotic Lorenz and Chen system are the drive systems. The fractional order hyper-chaotic Lü and Liu chaotic system are the response systems. The equilibrium positions of drive-response systems are as follows. The FO hyper-chaotic Lorenz system* $E_1 = (0,0,0,0)$, $E_2 = (-1.17,-21.63,9.46,204.60)$, $E_3 = (1.17,21.63,9.46,-204.60)$. *The FO hyper-chaotic Chen system* $E_1 = (0,0,0,0)$. *The FO hyper-chaotic Lü system* $E_1 = (0,0,0,0)$, $E_2 = (7.75,9.30,3.60,55.77)$, $E_3 = (-7.75,-9.30,3.60,-55.77)$ *The FO hyper-chaotic Liu system* $E_1 = (0,0,0,0)$. *Now, there is a question worth thinking about, which is whether the proposed method is still valid for systems with a large number of equilibria. Thus, the numerical simulation for the systems with three equilibrium positions are conducted. They are the FO Lorenz system, the FO Lü system, the FO Genesio–Tesi system and the FO Arneodo system. The results are also valid. In fact, the adaptive combination controller has nothing to do with the number of equilibrium positions. In addition to the numerical simulation results we have obtained, there are also some references [45,46,49,61]. From the numerical simulation section of this literature, the choice of the drive-response system is arbitrary. Thus, the proposed method is still valid for systems with a large number of equilibria.*

A comparison analysis between the proposed finite-time combination–combination (C-C) synchronization (FTCCS) scheme and the earlier published work is as follows. In Ref. [62], the author applied the adaptive control method to achieve C-C synchronization among four identical hyper-chaotic systems where it noted that the synchronization states happened at $t = 5$ (approx). In Ref. [61], the author used the sliding mode control scheme to address multiple chaotic systems with unknown parameters and disturbances in which the synchronization happened at $t = 5$ (approx). Besides, in Ref. [63], the author solved a new type of C-C synchronization for four identical or different chaotic systems via adaptive control, where the desired synchronization happened at $t = 5.5$ (approx). The combination synchronization of FO non-autonomous chaotic systems with different dimensions adopting a scaling matrix is studied in Ref. [64], where the error synchronization happened at $t = 6$ (approx). Furthermore, the phase synchronization of FO complex chaotic systems with different structures is discussed in Ref. [65]; in the process of C-C synchronization, the desired synchronization happened at $t = 4.5$ (approx). The nonsingular terminal sliding mode control to achieve the finite-time synchronization between two complex-variable chaotic systems with unknown parameters is adopted in Ref. [66]; here it has been found that the synchronization error converges to zero at $t = 10$ (approx). In addition to the above studies, we have investigated the FTCCS scheme among fractional order (FO) chaotic systems under multiple stochastic disturbances (SD), utilizing the nonsingular terminal sliding mode control (NTSMC) technique in which it has been recorded that the synchronization occurs at $t = 3.1$ (approx) as depicted in Figure 5. Therefore, comparing the synchronization times discussed above with those obtained by our proposed scheme, our method is dominant. This also illustrates the vitality and effectivity of the considered methodology.

Remark 14. *After calculation, the finite synchronization time satisfies* $T_1 \leq 5.71$, $T_2 \leq 7.34$ *theoretically. Thus, we have* $T \leq T_1 + T_2 = 13.05$. *Comparing the numerical simulation results, we can see that our control scheme is effective.*

Remark 15. *The dynamic error has the same fractional-order as the D-R systems in our paper. It is worth considering that the non-integer order in the derivative of error is different from the D-R. If we only consider this situation, there are many papers that have discussed it. In Ref. [67], the author proposed a modified adaptive sliding-mode control technique to investigate the reduced-order and increased-order synchronization. Ouannas et al. [68] investigated the inverse full state hybrid function projective synchronization (IFSHFPS) of non-identical systems characterized by different dimensions and different orders. Furthermore, the hybrid projective synchronization of different dimensional fractional order chaotic systems with time delay and different orders is discussed by [69]. More research results can be found in Ref. [70–72]. All the above literature about the non-integer order in the derivative of error is different from the drive-response systems. Our next step will consider this situation.*

6. Conclusions

In this article, the FTCCS of FO chaotic systems among four systems with different structures and unknown parameters is solved. The most important point is that the conditions we consider are under multiple stochastic disturbances. Our thought for this topic is that under the action of the finite-time Lyapunov theory and the nonsingular terminal sliding mode control technique, we deduced a new FO sliding surface, adaptive combination controller and some parameter updating laws, which can achieve the combination–combination synchronization of systems under multiple stochastic disturbances in finite time. The unknown parameters are identified precisely. Moreover, the combination drive systems and combination response systems that we introduced are very general. The expression of the synchronization error system makes many synchronization methods, such as chaos control, complete synchronization, projection synchronization, anti-synchronization and so forth, become special cases of combination–combination synchronization. From the numerical simulation results, it is obvious that the error variables of the D-R systems quickly converge to the origin point in the given time. Therefore, this controller and the updated parameter laws are effective. Next, for the multiple stochastic disturbances, we will study the fractional order multi switching synchronization of eight chaotic systems with time-delay in which the systems' parameters are still unknown.

Author Contributions: W.P. proposed the main the idea and M.S. prepared the manuscript initially. T.L. gave the numerical simulation of this paper. S.A. and L.P. revised the English grammar of this paper. All authors have read and agreed to the published version of the manuscript.

Funding: This work is partly supported by the Project of the Science and Technology Department in Sichuan Province (Grant Nos. 2019YJ0456, 2021ZYD0004), Fund of Sichuan University of Science and Engineering (Grant Nos. 2020RC26, 2020RC42), College Student Innovation and Entrepreneurship Training Program of Sichuan University of Science and Engineering (Grant No. cx2020189).

Institutional Review Board Statement: Not applicable

Informed Consent Statement: Not applicable

Data Availability Statement: The data used to support the findings of this study are available from the corresponding author upon request

Acknowledgments: The authors would like to thank the editor and the anonymous reviewers for their constructive comments and suggestions to improve the quality of the paper.

Conflicts of Interest: The authors declare that they have no conflict of interest.

References

1. Ping, Z.; Peng, Z. Drive-response synchronization for chaotic systems. *J. Chong Qing Univ.* **2002**, *25*, 77–79.
2. Yu, J.; Hu, C.; Jiang, H. Projective synchronization for fractional neural networks. *Neural Netw.* **2014**, *49*, 87–95. [CrossRef] [PubMed]
3. Shao, K.; Guo, H.; Han, F. Finite-time projective synchronization of fractional-order chaotic systems via soft variable structure control. *J. Mech. Sci. Technol.* **2020**, *34*, 369–376. [CrossRef]
4. Qin, X.; Li, S.; Liu, H. Adaptive fuzzy synchronization of uncertain fractional-order chaotic systems with different structures and time-delays. *Adv. Diff. Equ.* **2019**, *2019*, 174. [CrossRef]
5. Bouzeriba, A.; Boulkroune, A.; Bouden, T. Fuzzy adaptive synchronization of a class of fractional-order chaotic systems. In Proceedings of the 2015 3rd International Conference on Control, Engineering & Information Technology (CEIT), Tlemcen, Algeria, 25–27 May 2015; Volume 7, pp. 1–16.
6. Liu, Y.J.; Gong, M.; Tong, S.; Chen, C.P.; Li, D.J. Adaptive fuzzy output feedback control for a class of nonlinear systems with full state constraints. *IEEE Trans. Fuzzy. Syst.* **2018**, *26*, 2607–2617. [CrossRef]
7. Ha, S.; Chen, L.; Liu, H. Command filtered adaptive neural network synchronization control of fractional-order chaotic systems subject to unknown dead zones. *J. Frankl. Inst.* **2021**, *358*, 3376–3402. [CrossRef]
8. Zeng, H.B.; Teo, K.L.; He, Y.; Xu, H.; Wang, W. Sampled-data synchronization control for chaotic neural networks subject to actuator saturation. *Neurocomputing* **2017**, *185*, 1656–1667. [CrossRef]
9. Wang, J.; Xu, C. Stochastic feedback coupling synchronization of networked harmonic oscillators. *Automatica* **2018**, *87*, 404–411. [CrossRef]
10. Li, H.L.; Jiang, Y.L.; Wang, Z.; Zhang, L.; Teng, Z. Parameter identification and adaptive-impulsive synchronization of uncertain complex networks with nonidentical topological structures. *Optik-Int. J. Light Electron. Opt.* **2015**, *126*, 5771–5776. [CrossRef]
11. Li, X.F.; Chu, Y.D.; Leung, A.Y.; Zhang, H. Synchronization of uncertain chaotic systems via complete-adaptive-impulsive controls. *Chaos Solitons Fractals* **2017**, *100*, 24–30. [CrossRef]
12. Kocamaz, U.E.; Cevher, B.; Uyaroğlu, Y. Control and synchronization of chaos with sliding mode control based on cubic reaching rule. *Chaos Solitons Fractals* **2017**, *105*, 92–98. [CrossRef]
13. Vaidyanathan, S. Anti-synchronization of 3-cells cellular neural network attractors via integral sliding mode control. *Int. J. PharmTech Res.* **2016**, *9*, 193–205.
14. Li, X.; Zhao, X.S. The chaotic synchronization of fractional-order and integer-order in a class of financial systems. *J. Sci. Teach. Coll. Univ.* **2020**, *40*, 1–4.
15. Jing, W.; Guang, P. Design of a sliding mode controller for synchronization of fractional-order chaotic systems with different structures. *J. Shanghai Jiaotong Univ.* **2016**, *50*, 849–860.
16. Jiang, N. The adaptive control synchronization of hyper-chaos lorenz system and hyper-chaos Rössler system. *J. Taiyuan Norm Univ.* **2014**, *13*, 47–50.
17. Wei, X. Adaptive control and synchronization of Lü hyper-chaotic system. *J. Honghe Univ.* **2015**, *13*, 23–27.
18. Li, T.; Wang, Y.; Zhao, C. Synchronization of fractional chaotic systems based on a simple Lyapunov function. *Adv. Diff. Equ.* **2017**, *2017*, 304. [CrossRef]
19. Wei, Y.H.; Chen, Y.Q. Lyapunov functions for nabla discrete fractional order systems. *ISA Trans.* **2019**, *88*, 82–90. [CrossRef]
20. Tirandaz, H.; Tavakoli, H.R.; Ahmadnia, M. modified projective synchronization of chaotic systems with noise disturbance, an active nonlinear control method. *Int. J. Electr. Comput. Eng.* **2017**, *7*, 3436–3445. [CrossRef]
21. Khan, A.; Jahanzaib, L.S. Synchronization on the adaptive sliding mode controller for fractional order complex chaotic systems with uncertainty and disturbances. *Int. J. Dyn. Control* **2019**, *7*, 1419–1433. [CrossRef]
22. Luo, R.; Su, H.; Zeng, Y. Synchronization of uncertain fractional-order chaotic systems via a novel adaptive controller. *Chin. J. Phys.* **2017**, *55*, 342–349. [CrossRef]
23. Kekha Javan, A.A.; Shoeibi, A.; Zare, A.; Hosseini Izadi, N.; Jafari, M.; Alizadehsani, R.; Moridian, P.; Mosavi, A.; Acharya, U.R.; Nahavandi, S. Design of Adaptive-Robust Controller for Multi-State Synchronization of Chaotic Systems with Unknown and Time-Varying Delays and Its Application in Secure Communication. *Sensors* **2021**, *21*, 254. [CrossRef] [PubMed]
24. Khan, A.; Chaudhary, H. Hybrid projective combination-combination synchronization in non-identical hyperchaotic systems using adaptive control. *Arab. J. Math.* **2020**, *9*, 597–611. [CrossRef]
25. Petras, I. *Fractional-Order Nonlinear Systems, Modeling, Analysis and Simulation*; Higher Education Press: Beijing, China, 2011.
26. Mirrezapour, S.Z.; Zare, A.; Hallaji, M. A new fractional sliding mode controller based on nonlinear fractional-order proportional integral derivative controller structure to synchronize fractional-order chaotic systems with uncertainty and disturbances. *J. Vib. Control* **2021**, 1–13. [CrossRef]

27. Zhang, R.; Yang, S. Robust chaos synchronization of fractional-order chaotic systems with unknown parameters and uncertain perturbations. *Nonlinear Dyn.* **2012**, *69*, 983–992. [CrossRef]
28. Ma, S.J.; Shen, Q.; Jing, H. Modified projective synchronization of stochastic fractional order chaotic systems with uncertain parameters. *Nonlinear Dyn.* **2013**, *73*, 93–100. [CrossRef]
29. Wang, Q.; Qi, D.L. Synchronization for fractional order chaotic systems with uncertain parameters. *Int. J. Control Autom. Syst.* **2016**, *14*, 211–216. [CrossRef]
30. Nian, F.; Liu, X.; Zhang, Y. Sliding mode synchronization of fractional-order complex chaotic system with parametric and external disturbances. *Chaos Solitons Fractals* **2018**, *116*, 22–28. [CrossRef]
31. Zhang, X.; Zhang, X.; Li, D.; Yang, D. Adaptive Synchronization for a Class of Fractional Order Time-delay Uncertain Chaotic Systems via Fuzzy Fractional Order Neural Network. *Int. J. Control Autom. Syst.* **2019**, *17*, 1209–1220. [CrossRef]
32. Deepika, D.; Sandeep, K.; Shiv, N. Uncertainty and disturbance estimator based robust synchronization for a class of uncertain fractional chaotic system via fractional order sliding mode control. *Chaos Solitons Fractals* **2018**, *115*, 196–203. [CrossRef]
33. Bhat, S.; Bernstein, D. Finite-time stability of homo-gencous systems. In Proceedings of the ACC, Albuquergue, NM, USA, 6 December 1997; pp. 2513–2514.
34. Velmurugan, G.; Rakkiyappan, R.; Cao, J. Finite-time synchronization of fractional-order memristor-based neural networks with time delays. *Neural Netw.* **2016**, *73*, 36–46. [CrossRef] [PubMed]
35. Lin, M.L.; Yuan, Z.Z.; Cai, J.P. Finite-time synchronization between two different chaotic systems with uncertainties. *J. Fujian Univ. Technol.* **2019**, *17*, 77–82.
36. Lan, T.L.; Wang, Y.J. Finite-time synchronization and parameters identification of a uncertain critical chaotic system. *Math. Pract. Theory* **2018**, *48*, 105–112.
37. Rashidnejad, Z.; Karimaghaee, P. Synchronization of a class of uncertain chaotic systems utilizing a new finite-time fractional adaptive sliding mode control. *Chaos Solitons Fractals* **2020**, *5*, 100042. [CrossRef]
38. Luo, Y.; Yao, Y. Finite-time synchronization of uncertain complex dynamic networks with time-varying delay. *Adv. Diff. Equ.* **2020**, *2020*, 32. [CrossRef]
39. Mishra, A.K.; Das, S.; Yadav, V.K. Finite-time synchronization of multi-scroll chaotic systems with sigmoid non-linearity and uncertain terms. *Chin. J. Phys.* **2020**, *75*, 235–245. [CrossRef]
40. Sweetha, S.; Sakthivel, R.; Harshavarthini, S. Finite-time synchronization of nonlinear fractional chaotic systems with stochastic actuator faults. *Chaos Solitons Fractals* **2020**, *142*, 110312. [CrossRef]
41. Li, H.L.; Cao, J.; Jiang, H.; Alsaedi, A. Finite-time synchronization and parameter identification of uncertain fractional-order complex networks. *Phys. A Stat. Mech. Appl.* **2019**, *533*, 122027. [CrossRef]
42. Sun, J.; Shen, Y.; Wang, X.; Chen, J. Finite-time combination-combination synchronization of four different chaotic systems with unknown parameters via sliding mode control. *Nonlinear Dyn.* **2014**, *76*, 383–397. [CrossRef]
43. Luo, R.Z.; Wang, Y.L.; Deng, S.C. Combination synchronization of three classic chaotic systems using active back-stepping design. *Chaos Interdiscip. J. Nonlinear Sci.* **2011**, *21*, 043114.
44. Luo, R.Z.; Wang, Y.L. Finite-time stochastic combination synchronization of three different chaotic systems and its application in secure communication. *Chaos Interdiscip. J. Nonlinear Sci.* **2012**, *22*, 821–824.
45. Khan, A.; Khattar, D.; Prajapati, N. Dual combination combination multi switching synchronization of eight chaotic systems. *Chin. J. Phys.* **2017**, *55*, 1209–1218. [CrossRef]
46. Ahmad, I.; Shafiq, M.; Al-Sawalha, M.M. Globally exponential multi switching-combination synchronization control of chaotic systems for secure communications. *Chin. J. Phys.* **2018**, *56*, 974–987. [CrossRef]
47. Khan, A.; Nigar, U. Adaptive hybrid complex projective combination-combination synchronization in non-identical hyper-chaotic complex systems. *Int. J. Dynam. Control* **2019**, *7*, 1404–1418. [CrossRef]
48. Vincent, U.E.; Saseyi, A.O.; Mcclintock, P. Multi-switching combination synchronization of chaotic systems. *Nonlinear Dyn.* **2015**, *80*, 845–854. [CrossRef]
49. Sun, J.; Cui, G.; Wang, Y.; Shen, Y. Combination complex synchronization of three chaotic complex systems. *Nonlinear Dyn.* **2015**, *79*, 953–965. [CrossRef]
50. Khan, A.; Budhraja, M.; Ibraheem, A. Combination-combination synchronisation of time-delay chaotic systems for unknown parameters with uncertainties and external disturbances. *Pramana* **2018**, *91*, 20. [CrossRef]
51. Podlubny, I. *Fractional Differential Equations*; Academic: New York, NY, USA, 1999.
52. Hardy, G.H.; Littlewood, J.E.; Polya, G. *Inequalities*; Cambridge University Press: Cambridge, UK, 1952.
53. Li, Y.; Chen, Y.Q.; Podlubny, I. Stability of fractional-order nonlinear dynamic systems: Lyapunov direct method and generalized Mittag-Leffler stability. *Comput. Math. Appl.* **2009**, *59*, 1810–1821. [CrossRef]
54. Li, C.P.; Deng, W.H. Remarks on fractional derivatives. *Appl. Math. Comput.* **2007**, *187*, 777–784. [CrossRef]
55. Li, J.L.; Xi, J.X.; Wang, L. Minimum-energy synchronization for interconnected networks with non-periodical information silence. *Neurocomputing* **2022**, *481*, 310–321. [CrossRef]
56. Aleksandra, V.; Lazaros, M.; Vyacheslav, G. Fast synchronization of symmetric Hnon maps using adaptive symmetry control. *Chaos Solitons Fractals* **2022**, *155*, 111732.
57. Kashkynbayev, A.; Issakhanov, A.; Otkel, M.; Kurths, J. Finite-time and fixed-time synchronization analysis of shunting inhibitory memristive neural networks with time-varying delays. *Chaos Solitons Fractals* **2022**, *156*, 111866. [CrossRef]

58. Yuan, W.Y.; Ma, Y.C. Finite-time $\mathcal{H}_\infty$ synchronization for complex dynamical networks with time-varying delays based on adaptive control. *ISA Trans.* **2021**. [CrossRef]
59. Zhang, Z.; Wang, Y.N.; Zhang, J. Novel fractional-order decentralized control for nonlinear fractional-order composite systems with time delays. *ISA Trans.* **2021**. [CrossRef]
60. Li, Q.; Liu, S.; Chen, Y. Combination event-triggered adaptive networked synchronization communication for nonlinear uncertain fractional-order chaotic systems. *Appl. Math. Comput.* **2018**, *333*, 521–535. [CrossRef]
61. Chen, X.; Park, J.H.; Cao, J.; Qiu, J. Adaptive synchronization of multiple uncertain coupled chaotic systems via sliding mode control. *Neurocomputing* **2017**, *273*, 9–21. [CrossRef]
62. Khan, A. Chaotic analysis and combination-combination synchronization of a novel hyperchaotic system without any equilibria. *Chin. J. Phys.* **2018**, *56*, 238–251. [CrossRef]
63. Sun, J.; Shen, Y.; Zhang, G.; Xu, C.; Cui, G. Combination-combination synchronization among four identical or different chaotic systems. *Nonlinear Dyn.* **2013**, *73*, 1211–1222. [CrossRef]
64. Zerimeche, H.; Houmor, T.; Berkane, A. Combination synchronization of different dimensions fractional-order non-autonomous chaotic systems using scaling matrix. *Int. J. Dyn. Control* **2021**, *9*, 788–796. [CrossRef]
65. Yadav, V.K.; Prasad, G.; Srivastava, M.; Das, S. Combination-combination phase synchronization among non-identical fractional order complex chaotic systems via nonlinear control. *Int. J. Dyn. Control* **2018**, *7*, 330–340. [CrossRef]
66. Sun, J.; Wang, Y.; Wang, Y.; Shen, Y. Finite-time synchronization between two complex-variable chaotic systems with unknown parameters via nonsingular terminal sliding mode control. *Nonlinear Dyn.* **2016**, *85*, 1105–1117. [CrossRef]
67. Mossa Al-sawalha, M. Synchronization of different order fractional-order chaotic systems using modify adaptive sliding mode control. *Adv. Differ. Equ.* **2020**, *2020*, 417. [CrossRef]
68. Ouannas, A.; Grassi, G.; Ziar, T. On a Function Projective Synchronization Scheme for non-identical Fractional-order chaotic (hyperchaotic) systems with different dimensions and orders. *Optik* **2017**, *136*, 513–523. [CrossRef]
69. Zhang, W.W.; Chen, D.Y. Hybrid Projective Synchronization of Different Dimensional Fractional Order Chaotic Systems with Time Delay and Different Orders. *Chin. J. Eng. Math.* **2017**, *34*, 321–330.
70. Song, S.; Song, X.N.; Pathak, N. Multi-switching adaptive synchronization of two fractional-order chaotic systems with different structure and different order. *Int. J. Control Autom. Syst.* **2017**, *15*, 1524–1535. [CrossRef]
71. Zhen, W.; Xia, H.; Zhao, Z. Synchronization of nonidentical chaotic fractional-order systems with different orders of fractional derivatives. *Nonlinear Dyn.* **2012**, *69*, 999–1007.
72. Si, G.; Sun, Z.; Zhang, Y.; Chen, W. Projective synchronization of different fractional-order chaotic systems with non-identical orders. *Nonlinear Anal. Real World Appl.* **2012**, *13*, 1761–1771. [CrossRef]

fractal and fractional

Article

A Numerical Study of the Fractional Order Dynamical Nonlinear Susceptible Infected and Quarantine Differential Model Using the Stochastic Numerical Approach

Thongchai Botmart [1], Zulqurnain Sabir [2], Muhammad Asif Zahoor Raja [3], Wajaree Weera [1], Rahma Sadat [4] and Mohamed R. Ali [5,6,*]

1 Department of Mathematics, Faculty of Science, Khon Kaen University, Khon Kaen 40002, Thailand; thongbo@kku.ac.th (T.B.); wajawe@kku.ac.th (W.W.)
2 Department of Mathematics and Statistics, Hazara University, Mansehra 21300, Pakistan; zulqurnain_maths@hu.edu.pk
3 Future Technology Research Center, National Yunlin University of Science and Technology, 123 University Road, Section 3, Douliou, Yunlin 64002, Taiwan; rajamaz@yuntect.edu.tw
4 Department of Mathematics, Zagazig Faculty of Engineering, Zagazig University, Ismailia 44519, Egypt; r.mosa@zu.edu.eg
5 Faculty of Engineering and Technology, Future University, Cairo 11835, Egypt
6 Department of Basic Science, Faculty of Engineering at Benha, Benha University, Benha 13512, Egypt
* Correspondence: mohamed.reda@fue.edu.eg or mohamed.reda@bhit.bu.edu.eg

Abstract: The theme of this study is to present the impacts and importance of the fractional order derivatives of the susceptible, infected and quarantine (SIQ) model based on the coronavirus with the lockdown effects. The purpose of these investigations is to achieve more accuracy with the use of fractional derivatives in the SIQ model. The integer, nonlinear mathematical SIQ system with the lockdown effects is also provided in this study. The lockdown effects are categorized into the dynamics of the susceptible, infective and quarantine, generally known as SIQ mathematical system. The fractional order SIQ mathematical system has never been presented before, nor solved by using the strength of the stochastic solvers. The stochastic solvers based on the Levenberg-Marquardt backpropagation scheme (LMBS) along with the neural networks (NNs), i.e., LMBS-NNs have been implemented to solve the fractional order SIQ mathematical system. Three cases using different values of the fractional order have been provided to solve the fractional order SIQ mathematical model. The data to present the numerical solutions of the fractional order SIQ mathematical model is selected as 80% for training and 10% for both testing and validation. For the correctness of the LMBS-NNs, the obtained numerical results have been compared with the reference solutions through the Adams–Bashforth–Moulton based numerical solver. In order to authenticate the competence, consistency, validity, capability and exactness of the LMB-NNs, the numerical performances using the state transitions (STs), regression, correlation, mean square error (MSE) and error histograms (EHs) are also provided.

Keywords: SIQ mathematical model; fractional order; coronavirus; Levenberg-Marquardt backpropagation scheme; neural networks; Adams–Bashforth–Moulton

Citation: Botmart, T.; Sabir, Z.; Raja, M.A.Z.; Weera, W.; Sadat, R.; Ali, M.R. A Numerical Study of the Fractional Order Dynamical Nonlinear Susceptible Infected and Quarantine Differential Model Using the Stochastic Numerical Approach. *Fractal Fract.* **2022**, *6*, 139. https://doi.org/10.3390/fractalfract6030139

Academic Editors: António M. Lopes, Alireza Alfi, Liping Chen and Sergio A. David

Received: 20 December 2021
Accepted: 24 February 2022
Published: 1 March 2022

1. Introduction

There are a number of dangerous and transmitted diseases like dengue, HIV and Ebola [1–3]. The coronavirus is a transmitted disease and has played a significant role in human lives for the last two years. It badly affected the economies, industries, sports, social activities, education sectors and each part of life [4,5]. The coronavirus disease spread quickly, and a number of casualties happened in a short time. The basic role of the coronavirus spreading is due to travel or transportations of individuals from defective countries to different areas [6,7]. The vaccination process was started as a hope to control this series viral disease. It is stated in the literature that the individual's migration has a vital role in the spreading of the infection. It has also been noted that immigration is not only an issue of the infections, but the other reasons may also affect the spread of the virus [8].

A number of the approaches have been used to solve the mathematical form of the coronavirus along with different features. Rhodes et al. [9] proposed the mathematical ODEs for the communal distresses due to coronavirus. Benvenuto et al. [10] implemented the ARIMA system for the coronavirus. Mustafa et al. [11] presented a mathematical system to forecast and analyze the coronavirus transmission. Sivakumar [12] analyzed the predictive control for the coronavirus in India. Nesteruk [13] assessed the dynamics of the coronavirus pandemic in Ukraine using the double data sets. Thompson [14] studied the epidemiologic system with the use of significant apparatus using the coronavirus interferences. Libotte [15] presented an administration plan for the coronavirus vaccine. Sadiq et al. [16] investigated the impacts of nanomaterial to handle the coronavirus disease. Gumel et al. [17] discovered a mathematical system for the coronavirus disease. Ortenzi et al. [18] presented a transdisciplinary discipline study of coronavirus in Italy. Sánchez et al. [19] designed a susceptible, infected, treatment and recovered (SITR) mathematical model using the sense of corona virus. In other studies, Sabir et al. [20] provided the stochastic performances of the SITR model-based coronavirus. Moore et al. [21] designed a mathematical coronavirus system to investigate a vaccination impact and a non-pharmaceutical intervention. Umar [22] studied theoretical performances to treat coronavirus. Anirudh [23] provided the transmission dynamics prediction based on the coronavirus. Chen et al. [24] provided the social distance effects using the mathematical form of the dynamics of coronavirus. Zhang et al. [25] expressed the coronavirus dynamics using the stochastic perturbation behavior. Soumia et al. [26] described the possible inhibitors of coronavirus.

In this study, the fractional order derivatives of susceptible, infected and quarantine (SIQ) model based on the coronavirus with the lockdown effects are presented using the stochastic numerical performances of the Levenberg–Marquardt backpropagation scheme (LMBS) along with the neural networks (NNs), i.e., LMBS-NNs.

The design of the fractional order SIQ model is presented in Section 2. The details of the stochastic applications are provided in Section 3. The LMBS-NNs structure is explained in Section 4. The simulations of the fractional order SIQ model are provided in Section 5. Finally, the conclusion is drawn in the Section 6.

2. Mathematical Design of the Fractional Order SIQ System

In this section, the lockdown impacts as protective measures have been provided in the SIQ model. The lockdown effects are categorized into the dynamics of the susceptible, infective and quarantine classes-based system of differential equations. The mathematical form of the SIQ model is provided as [27]:

$$\begin{cases} \frac{dS(x)}{dx} = a - \frac{\beta S(x)I(x)}{\alpha+\eta I(x)} - \mu S(x) + (1-\theta)m, & S_0 = c_1, \\ \frac{dI(x)}{dx} = m\theta - (\alpha_1 + \delta_1 + \mu + \sigma)I(x) + \frac{\beta(1-k)S(x)I(x)}{\eta I(x)+\alpha}, & I_0 = c_2, \\ \frac{dQ(x)}{dx} = \sigma I(x) + \frac{\beta k S(x)I(x)}{\eta I(x)+\alpha} - (\alpha_2 + \mu + \delta_2)Q(x), & Q_0 = c_3. \end{cases} \quad (1)$$

The necessary and exhaustive detail of the SIQ mathematical model together with the description of each parameter is given in Table 1. Moreover, the selection of the appropriate values given in the system (1) provided in [27] along with the theoretical details of optimal control, global and local stabilities.

Table 1. Description of each comprehensive detail of each specification of the SIQ mathematical model.

Parameters	Details
a	Recruitment rate
α	Half saturation constant
η	Positive value
m	Migrants number
β	Transmission infection rate
μ	Natural death rate
δ_1	Recovery of infective population
k	Contact tracing rate
θ	Infected migrants' rate
σ	0.59 per day
α_2	Disease associated quarantine's population death rate
α_1	Disease related infective population's death rate
δ_2	Quarantined population recovered rate
c_1, c_2 and c_3	Contents: Initial conditions (ICs)

In the current study, the numerical investigations of the fractional order derivatives of SIQ model based on the coronavirus with the lockdown effects (1) have been provided by using the artificial intelligence (AI) with the design of LMBS-NNs. The design of the fractional order derivatives of SIQ model is formulated for the in-depth analysis of the super slow evolution as well as superfast transitions by replacing the ordinary integer order derivation in set of Equation (1) by fractional orders. The modified system (1) is given as follows:

$$\begin{cases} \frac{d^{(v)}S(x)}{dx^{(v)}} = a - \frac{\beta S(x)I(x)}{\alpha+\eta I(x)} - \mu S(x) + (1-\theta)m, & S_0 = c_1, \\ \frac{d^{(v)}I(x)}{dx^{(v)}} = m\theta - (\alpha_1 + \delta_1 + \mu + \sigma)I(x) + \frac{\beta(1-k)S(x)I(x)}{\eta I(x)+\alpha}, & I_0 = c_2, \\ \frac{d^{(v)}Q(x)}{dx^{(v)}} = \sigma I(x) + \frac{\beta k S(x)I(x)}{\eta I(x)+\alpha} - (\alpha_2 + \mu + \delta_2)Q(x), & Q_0 = c_3. \end{cases} \tag{2}$$

where v shows the FO derivative in the above system.

3. Novel Topographies and Outline of the Stochastic Solvers

The numerical stochastic operators through the LMBS-NNs are provided to solve the fractional order derivatives of SIQ model based on the coronavirus with the lockdown effects. The local and global operator performances through the stochastic computing solvers have been exploited to solve the numerous nonlinear, complex, stiff and singular systems [28].

The aim of this study is to perform the numerical representations of the fractional order derivatives of SIQ model based on the coronavirus with the lockdown effects using the stochastic procedures of the LMBS-NNs. It is observed that the time-fractional order derivatives have a number of applications to define the system conditions. The derivative order form represents the remembrance, but the memory function represents the derivative of fractional order. These fractional derivatives indicate the real-world applications [29,30]. Some novel features of the LMBS-NNs for the mathematical fractional order system using the SIQ model are presented as:

- A novel design of the fractional order SIQ model based on the coronavirus with the lockdown effects is presented;
- The stochastic measures have not been applied before to solve the fractional order SIQ model based on the coronavirus with the lockdown effects;
- The numerical investigations through the stochastic paradigms are successfully presented using the fractional order SIQ mathematical model;
- AI with the design of LMBS-NNs is presented to solve the nonlinear fractional order SIQ mathematical model;

- Three different fractional order variations based on the SIQ model have been numerically solved to authenticate the reliability of the proposed scheme;
- The brilliance of the stochastic computing solver based LMBS-NNs is provided using the comparison of the obtained and reference (Adams–Bashforth–Moulton) solutions;
- The accuracy of the scheme is observed through the absolute error (AE) performances that is achieved in good order to solve the fractional order SIQ mathematical model;
- The regression, STs, MSE and EHs and correlation performances approve the dependability and constancy of the designed LMBS-NNs to solve the fractional order SIQ mathematical model.

4. Proposed Procedures: LMBS-NNs

The proposed LMBS-NNs structure for solving the fractional order SIQ mathematical model is explained in this section. The methodology is designed in two parts. First, the essential performances of the LMB-NNs operator are provided. Next, the execution method via LMBS-NNs is implemented to solve the fractional order SIQ mathematical model. The proposed LMBS-NN are executed with analysis on the similar pattern as given in reported studies [31,32].

Figure 1 presents the multi-layer optimization procedures using the numerical stochastic LMBS-NNs, while the single layer neuron structure is plotted in Figure 2. The LMBS-NNs procedures are provided using 'nftool' command in Matlab with the selection of data as 80% for training and 10% for both testing and authorization.

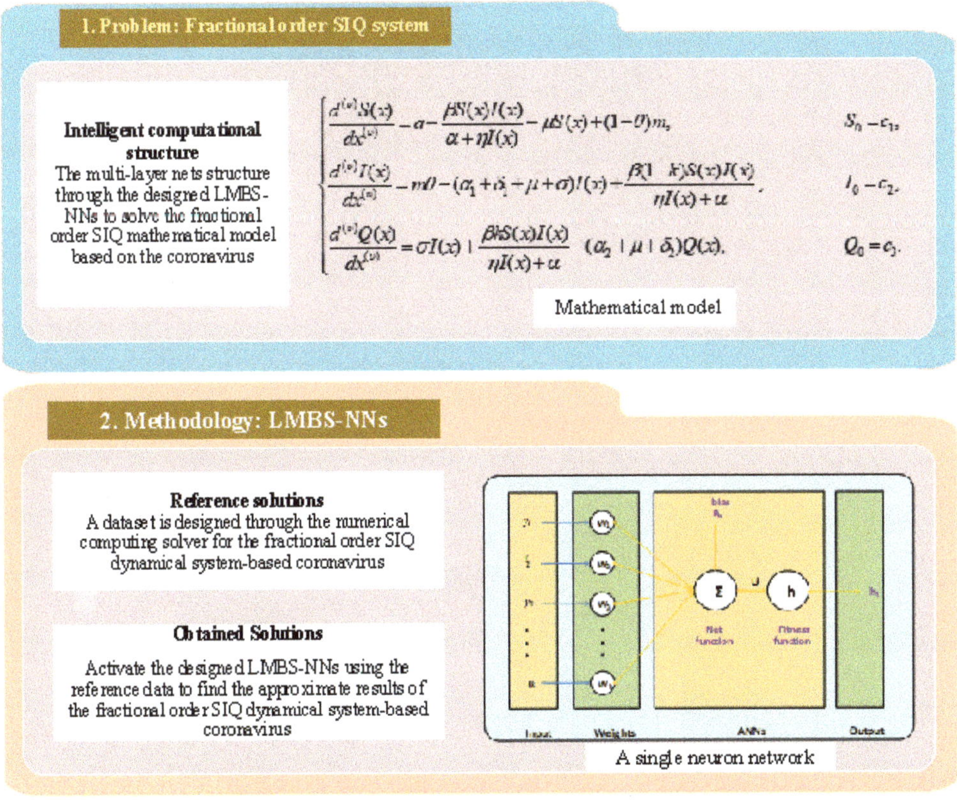

Figure 1. *Cont.*

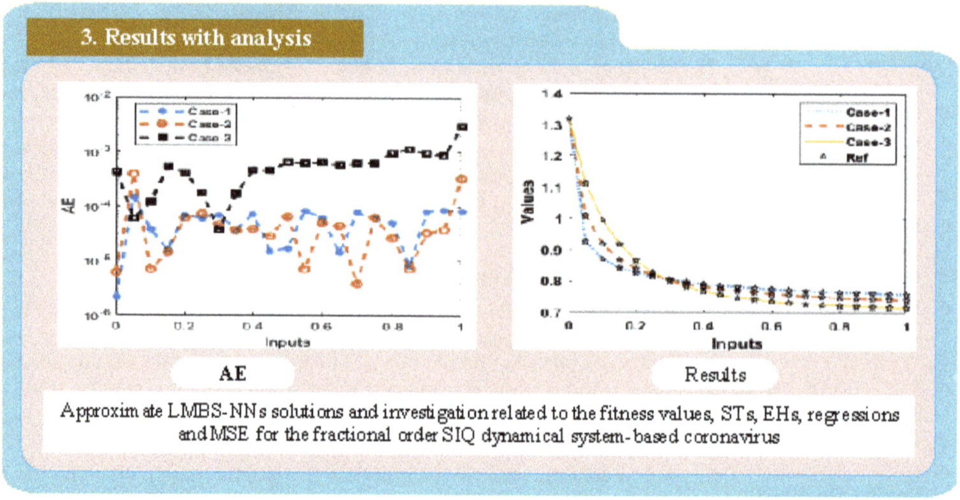

Figure 1. Workflow structure of LMBS-NNs to solve the fractional order SIQ model.

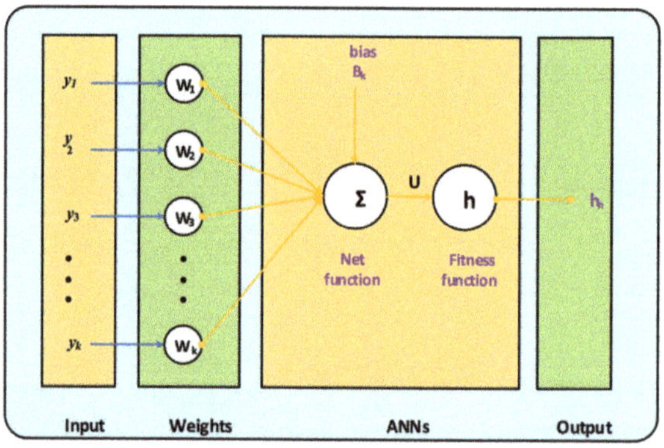

Figure 2. Construction of a single neuron.

5. Results through the Designed Method

This section shows the numerical performances of three different fractional order variations to solve the nonlinear SIQ mathematical system using the proposed LMBS-NNs. The mathematical representation of each variation is presented in the below cases as:

Case 1: Consider a fractional order coronavirus based SIQ mathematical model by taking the appropriate values $v = 0.5$, $a = 2.6$, $\beta = 2.1$, $\alpha = 5$, $\sigma = 0.59$, $\eta = 1$, $\alpha_1 = 1.78$, $\delta_1 = 0.4$, $\mu = 5.2$, $\alpha_2 = 1.78$, $\delta_2 = 0.4$, $\theta = 0.9$, $k = 0.1$, $m = 14$, $c_1 = 1.32$, $c_2 = 2.29$ and $c_3 = 3.5$ is provided as:

$$\begin{cases} \frac{d^{(0.5)}S(x)}{dx^{(0.5)}} = 4 - 5.2S(x) - \frac{2.1S(x)I(x)}{5+I(x)}, & S_0 = 1.32, \\ \frac{d^{(0.5)}I(x)}{dx^{(0.5)}} = 12.6 - 7.97I(x) + \frac{1.89I(x)S(x)}{I(x)+5}, & I_0 = 2.29, \\ \frac{d^{(0.5)}Q(x)}{dx^{(0.5)}} = 0.59I(x) + \frac{0.21S(x)I(x)}{5+I(x)} - 7.38Q(x), & Q_0 = 3.5. \end{cases} \tag{3}$$

Case 2: Consider a fractional order coronavirus based SIQ mathematical model by taking the appropriate values $v = 0.7$, $a = 2.6$, $\beta = 2.1$, $\alpha = 5$, $\sigma = 0.59$, $\eta = 1$, $\alpha_1 = 1.78$, $\delta_1 = 0.4$,

$\mu = 5.2$, $\alpha_2 = 1.78$, $\delta_2 = 0.4$, $\theta = 0.9$, $k = 0.1$, $m = 14$, $c_1 = 1.32$, $c_2 = 2.29$ and $c_3 = 3.5$ is provided as:

$$\begin{cases} \frac{d^{(0.7)}S(x)}{dx^{(0.7)}} = 4 - 5.2S(x) - \frac{2.1S(x)I(x)}{5+I(x)}, & S_0 = 1.32, \\ \frac{d^{(0.7)}I(x)}{dx^{(0.7)}} = 12.6 - 7.97I(x) + \frac{1.89I(x)S(x)}{I(x)+5}, & I_0 = 2.29, \\ \frac{d^{(0.7)}Q(x)}{dx^{(0.7)}} = 0.59I(x) + \frac{0.21S(x)I(x)}{5+I(x)} - 7.38Q(x), & Q_0 = 3.5. \end{cases} \tag{4}$$

Case 3: Consider a fractional order coronavirus based SIQ mathematical model by taking the appropriate values $v = 0.9$, $a = 2.6$, $\beta = 2.1$, $\alpha = 5$, $\sigma = 0.59$, $\eta = 1$, $\alpha_1 = 1.78$, $\delta_1 = 0.4$, $\mu = 5.2$, $\alpha_2 = 1.78$, $\delta_2 = 0.4$, $\theta = 0.9$, $k = 0.1$, $m = 14$, $c_1 = 1.32$, $c_2 = 2.29$ and $c_3 = 3.5$ is provided as:

$$\begin{cases} \frac{d^{(0.9)}S(x)}{dx^{(0.9)}} = 4 - 5.2S(x) - \frac{2.1S(x)I(x)}{5+I(x)}, & S_0 = 1.32, \\ \frac{d^{(0.9)}I(x)}{dx^{(0.9)}} = 12.6 - 7.97I(x) + \frac{1.89I(x)S(x)}{I(x)+5}, & I_0 = 2.29, \\ \frac{d^{(0.9)}Q(x)}{dx^{(0.9)}} = 0.59I(x) + \frac{0.21S(x)I(x)}{5+I(x)} - 7.38Q(x), & Q_0 = 3.5. \end{cases} \tag{5}$$

The numerical presentations through the simulations of coronavirus based SIQ mathematical model is presented by using the stochastic LMBS-NNs procedures with 8 numbers of neurons along with the selection of data as 80% for training and 10% for both testing and authorization. The hidden, output and input neuron's structure is given in Figure 3.

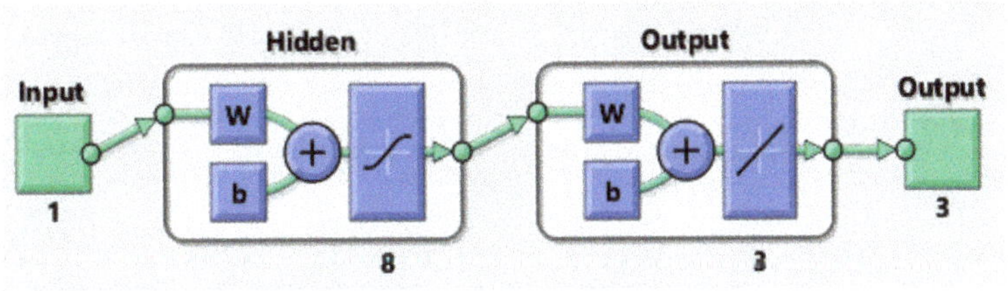

Figure 3. Proposed LMBS-NNs for the fractional order coronavirus based SIQ model.

The graphical representations are plotted in Figures 4–6 to solve the fractional order coronavirus based SIQ mathematical model by using the LMBS-NNs procedures. In order to check the best performances and STs, the graphical illustrations are provided in Figures 4 and 5. The MSE and STs values for training, best curves and authentication are derived in Figure 4 to solve the fractional order coronavirus based SIQ mathematical model. The obtained values of MSE based on the best performances of the fractional order coronavirus based SIQ mathematical model have been calculated at epochs 294, 1000 and 155 that are calculated as 1.2309×10^{-8}, 5.17679×10^{-9} and 1.9259×10^{-7}, respectively. The gradient measures are also plotted in Figure 4 to solve the fractional order coronavirus based SIQ mathematical model using the LMBS-NNs. These gradient performances have been calculated as 5.1656×10^{-6}, 1.9123×10^{-6} and 2.0104×10^{-5} for case 1, 2 and 3. These graphical representations indicate the convergence of proposed LMBS-NNs to solve the fractional order coronavirus based SIQ mathematical model using the LMBS-NNs. Figures 5–8 represents the values of the fitting curves to solve each case of fractional order coronavirus based SIQ mathematical model. These plots represent the comparative performances of the reference and obtained results. The error plots from the substantiation, testing and training to solve each case of fractional order coronavirus based SIQ mathematical model are provided in Figure 5 (a to c) while, the EHs are plotted in Figure 5d–f. The EHs are calculated as 2.38×10^{-4}, 7.10×10^{-5} and 4.29×10^{-4} for case 1, 2 and 3, respectively. The regression measures are provided in Figure 6a–c based on the fractional order coronavirus based SIQ mathematical model. The correlation is provided to validate the regression performance in Figure 6. It is clear in understanding that the correlation plots are calculated as 1 for the fractional order coronavirus based SIQ mathematical model. The training, testing and authentication representations denote the correctness of the stochastic LMBS-NNs procedure to solve the fractional order coronavirus based SIQ mathematical model. The convergence through MSE using the complexity, training, authentication, iterations, testing and backpropagation is provided in Table 2 Figure to solve the fractional order coronavirus based SIQ mathematical model. The brief description of the parameters tabulated is provided as follows; the validation performance means that the value of fitness, i.e., MSE, for the data samples used for the validation, i.e., 10% of total samples, validation checks being the controlling paper for the networks to stop further learning of the weights, Mu being the adaptive Levenberg–Marquardt parameter for convergence controlling coefficient of the algorithm, gradient being the first order optimality parameter, performance means fitness on MSE and time in seconds being the time complexity of adaption of the networks.

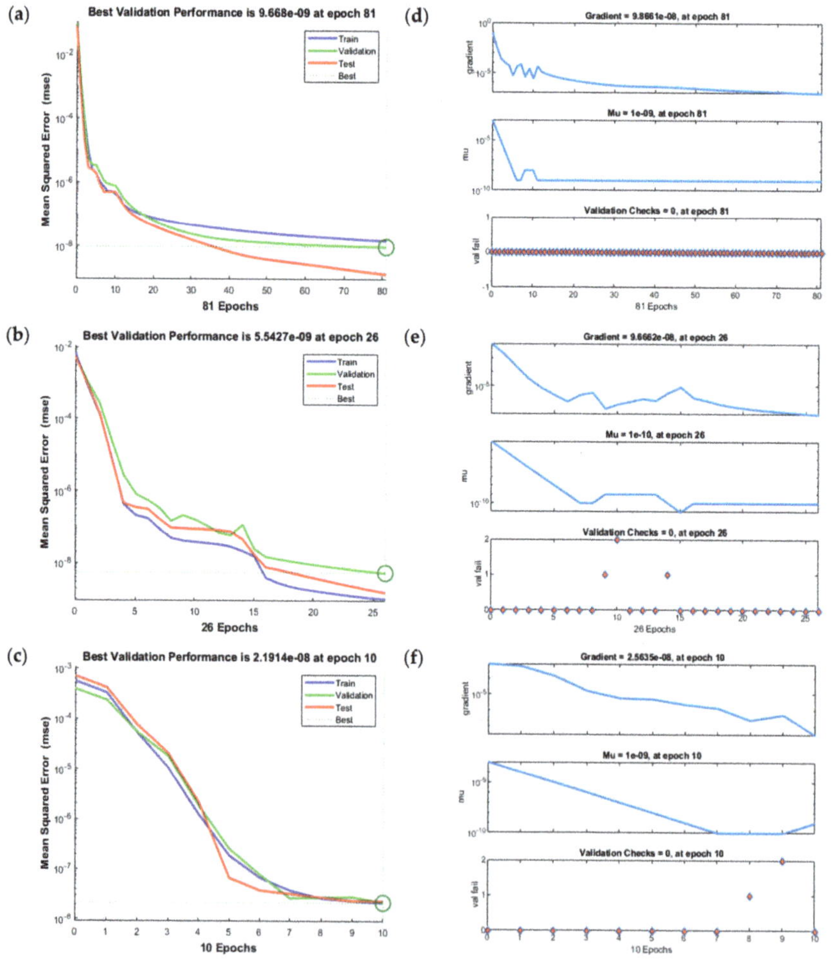

Figure 4. STs and MSE performances to solve the fractional order coronavirus based SIQ mathematical model. (**a**) Case 1 analysis on MSE. (**b**) Case 2: analysis on MSE. (**c**) Case 3: analysis on MSE. (**d**) Case I: algorithm parameter. (**e**) Case 2: algorithm parameter. (**f**) Case 3: algorithm parameter.

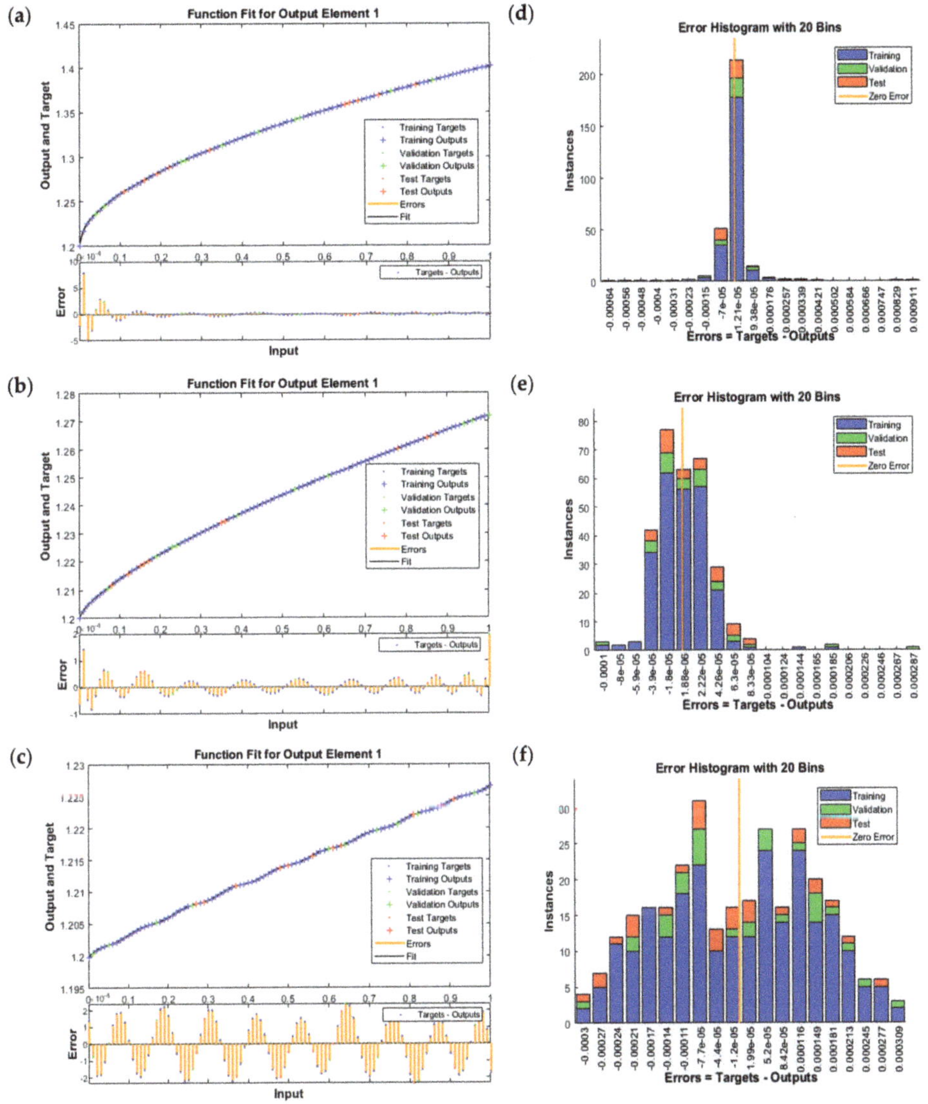

Figure 5. Valuations of the results and EHs for the STs to solve the fractional order coronavirus based SIQ mathematical model. (**a**) Case 1: Result assessments. (**b**) Case 2: Result assessments. (**c**) Case 3: Result assessments. (**d**) Case I: EH. (**e**) Case 2: EHs. (**f**) Case 3: EHs.

Table 2. LMBS-NNs procedure to solve the fractional order coronavirus based SIQ mathematical model.

Case	MSE			Gradient	Performance	Epoch	Mu	Time
	Training	Testing	Validation					
1	2.01×10^{-8}	4.14×10^{-6}	1.23×10^{-8}	5.17×10^{-6}	1.98×10^{-8}	300	1×10^{-8}	06
2	2.37×10^{-9}	1.64×10^{-7}	5.17×10^{-9}	1.91×10^{-6}	2.38×10^{-9}	1000	1×10^{-8}	06
3	1.45×10^{-7}	5.21×10^{-6}	1.92×10^{-7}	2.01×10^{-5}	1.37×10^{-7}	161	1×10^{-7}	03

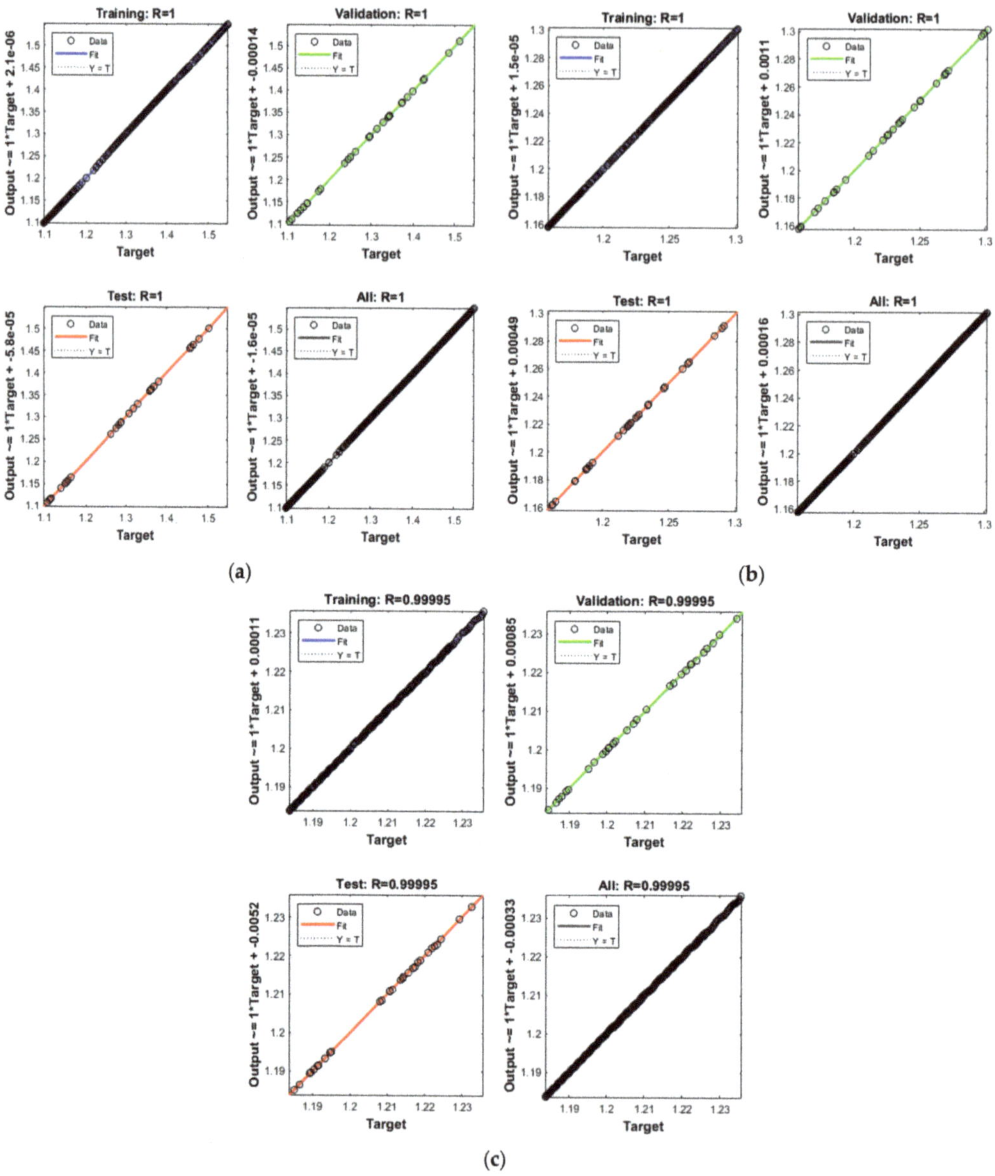

Figure 6. Regression plots STs to solve the fractional order coronavirus based SIQ mathematical model. (**a**) Regression plots: Case 1. (**b**) Regression plots: Case 2. (**c**) Regression plots: Case 3.

The plots of the result comparisons and AE values are provided in Figures 7 and 8. The numerical representations are provided to solve the fractional order coronavirus based SIQ mathematical model using the stochastic LMBS-NNs. The reference and obtained numerical performances are plotted in Figure 7 through the overlapping of the results. The result overlapping authenticates the exactness of the LMBS-NNs to solve the fractional order coronavirus based SIQ mathematical model. The AE values to solve the SIQ model are performed in Figure 8. The AE for the susceptible individuals $S(x)$ calculated as 10^{-4} to 10^{-7}, 10^{-4} to 10^{-6} and 10^{-4} to 10^{-5} for case 1 to 3. The AE for the infected individuals $I(x)$ calculated as 10^{-4} to 10^{-6}, 10^{-4} to 10^{-7} and 10^{-4} to 10^{-6} for case 1 to 3. Similarly, the AE for the quarantine individuals $Q(x)$ calculated as 10^{-4} to 10^{-6}, 10^{-4} to 10^{-5} and 10^{-3} to 10^{-5} for case 1 to 3. These AE values represent the exactness of the proposed LMBS-NNs to solve the fractional order coronavirus based SIQ mathematical model.

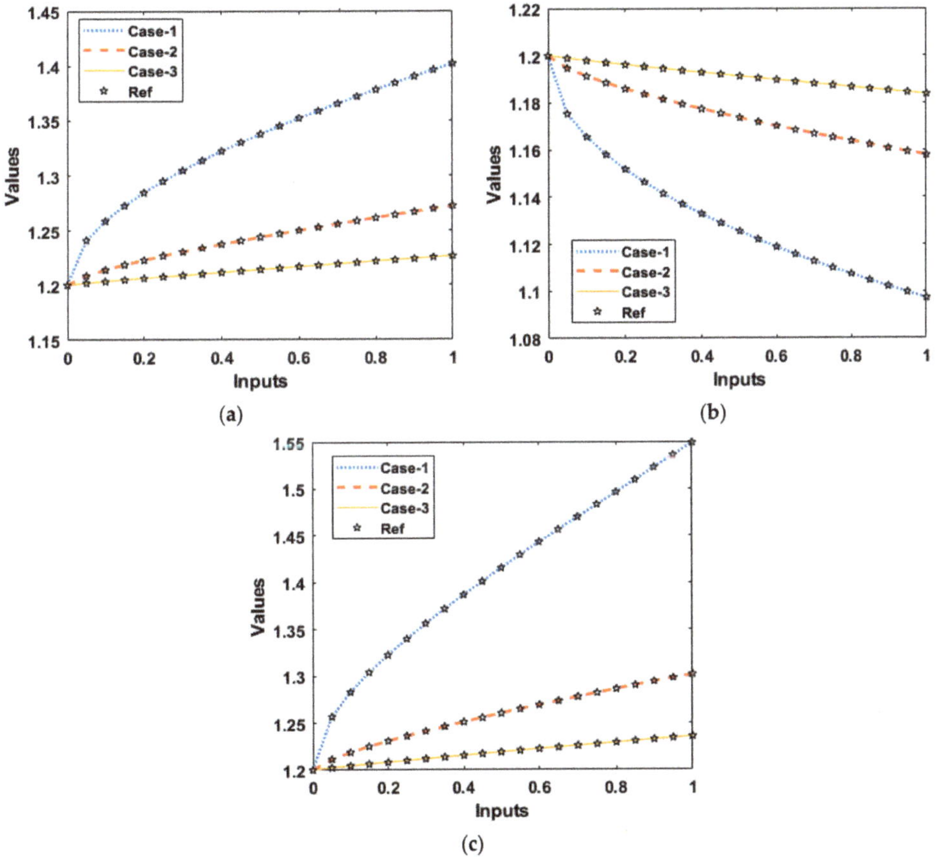

Figure 7. Results based on the fractional order coronavirus based SIQ mathematical model. (**a**) Results for $S(x)$. (**b**) Results for $I(x)$. (**c**) Results for $Q(x)$.

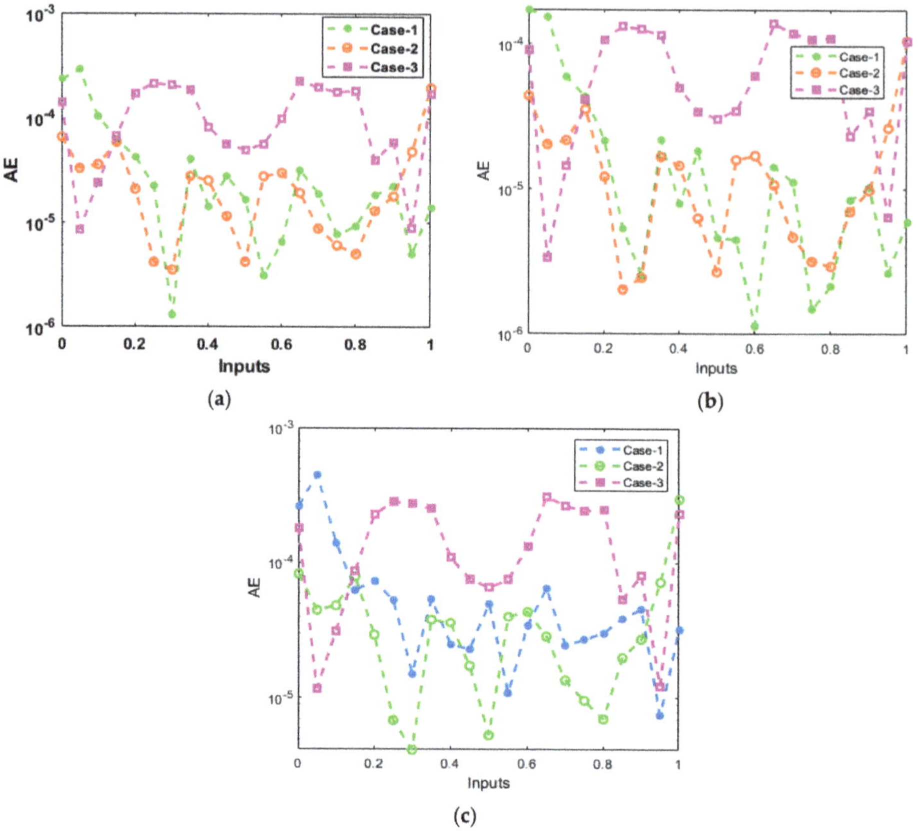

Figure 8. AE based on the fractional order coronavirus based SIQ mathematical model. (**a**) AE for $S(x)$. (**b**) AE for $I(x)$. (**c**) AE for $Q(x)$.

6. Concluding Remarks

In this work, the numerical presentations of the coronavirus based SIQ mathematical model are presented. The aim of this study is to provide the fractional order study using the dynamics of coronavirus based SIQ mathematical model to get more accurate performances of the system. The integer nonlinear mathematical SIQ system with the lockdown effects was also provided in this study. The fractional order coronavirus based SIQ mathematical model is classified into three dynamics, susceptible, infective and quarantine, generally known as the SIQ mathematical system. The numerical performances of the fractional order coronavirus based SIQ mathematical model have never been presented nor solved by using the stochastic Levenberg-Marquardt backpropagation neural networks. Three cases using different values of the fractional order have been provided to solve the fractional order SIQ mathematical model. The data to present the numerical solutions of the fractional order SIQ mathematical model were selected as 80% for training and 10% for both testing and authorization. Eight numbers of neurons were used to present the numerical performances of the fractional order SIQ mathematical system. The numerical results of the fractional order SIQ mathematical system have been compared with the Adams–Bashforth–Moulton solver. To reduce the MSE, the obtained numerical results have been performed by using the LMBS-NNs. The reliability and competence of LMBS-NNs and the numerical performances have been illustrated using the STs, regression, correlation, EHs and MSE. The correctness of the LMBS-NNs based on the fractional order SIQ mathematical model is observed via the matching of reference and obtained results. The performance of the scheme is verified based on the consistency and dependability of the proposed LMBS-NNs.

In future work, the LMBS-NNs can be implemented to present the numerical measures of the lonngren-wave, fluid mechanics systems, bioinformatics studies as well as information security models.

Author Contributions: T.B.: Simulate our proposed structures. Z.S.: Simulate our proposed structures. W.W.: Simulate our proposed structures. M.A.Z.R.: Do the calculations of CsPbBr3. R.S.: Do the calculations of CsPbBr3. M.R.A.: Provide the idea of this manuscript. Z.S.: Provide the idea of this manuscript. All authors have read and agreed to the published version of the manuscript.

Funding: This research received funding support from the NSRF via the Program Management Unit for Human Resources & Institutional Development, Research and Innovation (grant number B05F640088).

Institutional Review Board Statement: Not applicable.

Informed Consent Statement: Not applicable.

Data Availability Statement: No data were used to support this study.

Conflicts of Interest: The authors declare that they have no known competing financial interest or personal relationships that could have appeared to influence the work reported in this paper.

References

1. Guerrero–Sánchez, Y.; Umar, M.; Sabir, Z.; Guirao, J.L.G.; Raja, M.A.Z. Solving a class of biological HIV infection model of latently infected cells using heuristic approach. *Discret. Contin. Dyn. Syst.* **2021**, *14*, 3611. [CrossRef]
2. Umar, M.; Sabir, Z.; Amin, F.; Guirao, J.L.G.; Raja, M.A.Z. Stochastic numerical technique for solving HIV infection model of CD4+ T cells. *Eur. Phys. J. Plus* **2020**, *135*, 405. [CrossRef]
3. Berge, T.; Lubuma, J.-S.; Moremedi, G.; Morris, N.; Kondera-Shava, R. A simple mathematical model for Ebola in Africa. *J. Biol. Dyn.* **2017**, *11*, 42–74. [CrossRef] [PubMed]
4. Bhola, J.; Venkateswaran, V.R.; Koul, M. Corona epidemic in Indian context: Predictive mathematical modelling. *MedRxiv* **2020**. [CrossRef]
5. Li, Q.; Guan, X.; Wu, P.; Wang, X.; Zhou, L.; Tong, Y.; Ren, R.; Leung, K.S.; Lau, E.H.; Wong, J.Y.; et al. Early transmission dynamics in Wuhan, China, of novel coronavirus–infected pneumonia. *N. Engl. J. Med.* **2020**, *382*, 1199–1207. [CrossRef] [PubMed]
6. Bernasconi, A.; Grandi, S. A Conceptual Model for Geo-Online Exploratory Data Visualization: The Case of the COVID-19 Pandemic. *Information* **2021**, *12*, 69. [CrossRef]
7. Kucharski, A.J.; Russell, T.W.; Diamond, C.; Liu, Y.; Edmunds, J.; Funk, S.; Eggo, R.M.; Sun, F.; Jit, M.; Munday, J.D.; et al. Early dynamics of transmission and control of COVID-19: A mathematical modelling study. *Lancet Infect. Dis.* **2020**, *20*, 553–558. [CrossRef]
8. Spiteri, G.; Fielding, J.; Diercke, M.; Campese, C.; Enouf, V.; Gaymard, A.; Bella, A.; Sognamiglio, P.; Moros, M.J.S.; Riutort, A.N.; et al. First cases of coronavirus disease 2019 (COVID-19) in the WHO European Region, 24 January to 21 February 2020. *Eurosurveillance* **2020**, *25*, 2000178. [CrossRef] [PubMed]
9. Rhodes, T.; Lancaster, K. Mathematical models as public troubles in COVID-19 infection control: Following the numbers. *Health Sociol. Rev.* **2020**, *29*, 177–194. [CrossRef] [PubMed]
10. Benvenuto, D.; Giovanetti, M.; Vassallo, L.; Angeletti, S.; Ciccozzi, M. Application of the ARIMA model on the COVID-2019 epidemic dataset. *Data Brief.* **2020**, *29*, 105340. [CrossRef] [PubMed]
11. Mustafa, S.K.; Ahmad, M.A.; Sotnik, S.; Zeleniy, O.; Lyashenko, V.; Alzahrani, O. Brief review of the mathematical models for analyzing and forecasting transmission of COVID-19. *J. Crit. Rev.* **2020**, *7*, 4206–4210.
12. Sivakumar, A. Review of mathematical models to predict the rate of spread and control of COVID-19 in India. *Bullet. World Health Organ.* **2020**. [CrossRef]
13. Nesteruk, I. Estimates of the COVID-19 pandemic dynamics in Ukraine based on two data sets. *Medrxiv* **2021**. [CrossRef]
14. Thompson, R.N. Epidemiological models are important tools for guiding COVID-19 interventions. *BMC Med.* **2020**, *18*, 152. [CrossRef] [PubMed]
15. Libotte, G.B.; Lobato, F.S.; Platt, G.M.; Neto, A.J.S. Determination of an optimal control strategy for vaccine administration in COVID-19 pandemic treatment. *Comput. Methods Programs Biomed.* **2020**, *196*, 105664. [CrossRef] [PubMed]
16. Sadiq, I.Z.; Abubakar, F.S.; Dan-Iya, B.I. Role of nanoparticles in tackling COVID-19 pandemic: A bio-nanomedical approach. *J. Taibah Univ. Sci.* **2021**, *15*, 198–207. [CrossRef]
17. Gumel, A.B.; Iboi, E.A.; Ngonghala, C.N.; Elbasha, E.H. A primer on using mathematics to understand COVID-19 dynamics: Modeling, analysis and simulations. *Infect. Dis. Model.* **2021**, *6*, 148–168. [CrossRef] [PubMed]

18. Ortenzi, F.; Albanese, E.; Fadda, M. A Transdisciplinary Analysis of COVID-19 in Italy: The Most Affected Country in Europe. *Int. J. Environ. Res. Public Health* **2020**, *17*, 9488. [CrossRef]
19. Sánchez, Y.G.; Sabir, Z.; Guirao, J.L.G. Design of a nonlinear sitr fractal model based on the dynamics of a novel coronavirus (COVID-19). *Fractals* **2020**, *28*, 2040026. [CrossRef]
20. Sabir, Z.; Umar, M.; Raja, M.A.Z.; Baleanu, D. Applications of gudermannian neural network for solving the sitr fractal system. *Fractals* **2021**, *29*. [CrossRef]
21. Moore, S.; Hill, E.M.; Tildesley, M.J.; Dyson, L.; Keeling, M.J. Vaccination and non-pharmaceutical interventions for COVID-19: A mathematical modelling study. *Lancet Infect. Dis.* **2021**, *21*, 793–802. [CrossRef]
22. Umar, Y. Theoretical studies of the rotational and tautomeric states, electronic and spectroscopic properties of favipiravir and its structural analogues: A potential drug for the treatment of COVID-19. *J. Taibah Univ. Sci.* **2020**, *14*, 1613–1625. [CrossRef]
23. Anirudh, A. Mathematical modeling and the transmission dynamics in predicting the Covid-19—What next in combating the pandemic. *Infect. Dis. Model.* **2020**, *5*, 366–374. [CrossRef]
24. Chen, X.; Zhang, A.; Wang, H.; Gallaher, A.; Zhu, X. Compliance and containment in social distancing: Mathematical modeling of COVID-19 across townships. *Int. J. Geogr. Inf. Sci.* **2021**, *35*, 446–465. [CrossRef]
25. Zhang, Z.; Zeb, A.; Hussain, S.; Alzahrani, E. Dynamics of COVID-19 mathematical model with stochastic perturbation. *Adv. Differ. Equ.* **2020**, *2020*, 451. [CrossRef] [PubMed]
26. Soumia, M.; Hanane, Z.; Benaissa, M.; Younes, F.Z.; Chakib, A.; Mohammed, B.; Mohamed, B. Towards potential inhibitors of COVID-19 main protease Mpro by virtual screening and molecular docking study. *J. Taibah Univ. Sci.* **2020**, *14*, 1626–1636. [CrossRef]
27. Bhadauria, A.S.; Pathak, R.; Chaudhary, M. A SIQ mathematical model on COVID-19 investigating the lockdown effect. *Infect. Dis. Model.* **2021**, *6*, 244–257. [CrossRef] [PubMed]
28. Yuanlei, S.; Almohsen, B.; Sabershahraki, M.; Issakhov, A.; Raja, M.A.Z. Nanomaterial migration due to magnetic field through a porous region utilizing numerical modeling. *Chem. Phys. Lett.* **2021**, *785*, 139162. [CrossRef]
29. Ghanbari, B.; Djilali, S. Mathematical analysis of a fractional-order predator-prey model with prey social behavior and infection developed in predator population. *Chaos Solitons Fractals* **2020**, *138*, 109960. [CrossRef]
30. Ghanbari, B.; Djilali, S. Mathematical and numerical analysis of a three-species predator-prey model with herd behavior and time fractional-order derivative. *Math. Methods Appl. Sci.* **2020**, *43*, 1736–1752. [CrossRef]
31. Bolboacă, S.D.; Jäntschi, L. Sensitivity, specificity, and accuracy of predictive models on phenols toxicity. *J. Comput. Sci.* **2014**, *5*, 345–350. [CrossRef]
32. Jäntschi, L.; Bolboacă, S.D.; Sestraş, R.E. Meta-heuristics on quantitative structure-activity relationships: Study on polychlorinated biphenyls. *J. Mol. Model.* **2010**, *16*, 377–386. [CrossRef] [PubMed]

axioms

MDPI

Article

Multi-Point Boundary Value Problems for (k, ϕ)-Hilfer Fractional Differential Equations and Inclusions

Jessada Tariboon [1,*,†], Ayub Samadi [2,*,†] and Sotiris K. Ntouyas [3,†]

1 Intelligent and Nonlinear Dynamic Innovations, Department of Mathematics, Faculty of Applied Science, King Mongkut's University of Technology North Bangkok, Bangkok 10800, Thailand
2 Department of Mathematics, Miyaneh Branch, Islamic Azad University, Miyaneh, Iran
3 Department of Mathematics, University of Ioannina, 451 10 Ioannina, Greece; sntouyas@uoi.gr
* Correspondence: jessada.t@sci.kmutnb.ac.th (J.T.); ayubtoraj1366@gmail.com (A.S.)
† These authors contributed equally to this work.

Abstract: In this paper we initiate the study of boundary value problems for fractional differential equations and inclusions involving (k, ϕ)-Hilfer fractional derivative of order in $(1, 2]$. In the single-valued case the existence and uniqueness results are established by using classical fixed-point theorems, such as Banach, Krasnoselskiĭ and Leray-Schauder. In the multivalued case we consider both cases, when the right-hand side has convex or non-convex values. In the first case, we apply the Leray–Schauder nonlinear alternative for multivalued maps, and in the second, the Covit–Nadler fixed-point theorem for multivalued contractions. All results are well illustrated by numerical examples.

Keywords: (k, ϕ)-Hilfer fractional derivative; Riemann-Liouville fractional derivative; Caputo fractional derivative; existence; uniqueness; fixed point theorems

MSC: 26A33; 34A08; 34A60; 34B15

Citation: Tariboon, J.; Samadi, A.; Ntouyas, S.K. Multi-Point Boundary Value Problems for (k, ϕ)-Hilfer Fractional Differential Equations and Inclusions. *Axioms* **2022**, *11*, 110. https://doi.org/10.3390/axioms11030110

Academic Editors: António M. Lopes, Alireza Alfi, Liping Chen and Sergio A. David

Received: 8 February 2022
Accepted: 28 February 2022
Published: 2 March 2022

1. Introduction and Preliminaries

Fractional calculus and fractional differential equations have cashed substantial consideration owing to the broad applications of fractional derivative operators in the mathematical modelling, describing many real world processes more accurately than the classical-order differential equations. For a systematic development of the topic, see the monographs [1–9]. Fractional derivative operators are usually defined via fractional integral operators. In the literature, many fractional derivative operators have been proposed, such as Riemann–Liouville, Caputo, Hadamard, Erdélyi–Kober and Hilfer fractional operators, to name a few. The Riemann–Liouville fractional integral operator of order $\alpha > 0$ is one of the most used and studied operators, defined by

$$\mathfrak{I}^{\alpha}_{a+}\mathfrak{f}(w) = \frac{1}{\Gamma(\alpha)} \int_a^w (w-u)^{\alpha-1}\mathfrak{f}(u)du, \ \ w > a. \tag{1}$$

The Riemann–Liouvile and Caputo fractional derivative operators of order $\alpha > 0$ are defined in light of the above definition by

$$^{RL}\mathfrak{D}^{\alpha}_{a+}\mathfrak{f}(w) = \mathfrak{D}^n\mathfrak{I}^{n-\alpha}_{a+}\mathfrak{f}(w) = \frac{1}{\Gamma(n-\alpha)}\frac{d^n}{dw^n}\int_a^w (w-u)^{n-\alpha-1}\mathfrak{f}(u)du, \ \ w > a, \tag{2}$$

and

$$^{C}\mathfrak{D}^{\alpha}_{a+}\mathfrak{f}(w) = \mathfrak{I}^{n-\alpha}_{a+}\mathfrak{D}^n\mathfrak{f}(w) = \frac{1}{\Gamma(n-\alpha)}\int_a^w (w-u)^{n-\alpha-1}\mathfrak{f}^{(n)}(u)du, \ \ w > a, \tag{3}$$

respectively, where $n-1<\alpha\leq n$ and $n\in\mathbb{N}$. In [10], the Riemann–Liouville fractional integral operator was extended to k-Riemann–Liouville fractional integral of order $\alpha>0$ ($\alpha\in\mathbb{R}$) as

$$^{k}\mathfrak{I}^{\alpha}_{a+}\mathfrak{h}(w)=\frac{1}{k\Gamma_k(\alpha)}\int_a^w(w-u)^{\frac{\alpha}{k}-1}\mathfrak{h}(u)du, \tag{4}$$

where $\mathfrak{h}\in L^1([a,b],\mathbb{R})$, $k>0$ and Γ_k is the k-Gamma function for $w\in\mathbb{C}$ with $\Re(w)>0$ and $k\in\mathbb{R},k>0$ which is defined in [11] by

$$\Gamma_k(w)=\int_0^\infty s^{w-1}e^{-\frac{s^k}{k}}ds.$$

The following relations are well known.

$$\Gamma(\theta)=\lim_{k\to1}\Gamma_k(\theta),\ \Gamma_k(\theta)=k^{\frac{\theta}{k}-1}\Gamma\left(\frac{\theta}{k}\right)\text{ and }\Gamma_k(\theta+k)=\theta\Gamma_k(\theta).$$

In [12] the k-Riemann–Liouville fractional derivative was introduced as

$$^{k,RL}\mathfrak{D}^{\alpha}_{a+}\mathfrak{h}(w)=\left(k\frac{d}{dw}\right)^n\,{}^{k}\mathfrak{I}^{nk-\alpha}_{a+}\mathfrak{h}(w),\ \ n=\left\lceil\frac{\alpha}{k}\right\rceil, \tag{5}$$

where $\mathfrak{h}\in L^1([a,b],\mathbb{R})$, $k,\alpha\in\mathbb{R}^+$ and $\left\lceil\frac{\alpha}{k}\right\rceil$ is the ceiling function of $\frac{\alpha}{k}$.

On the other hand in [2] the ϕ-Riemann–Liouville fractional integral of the function $\mathfrak{h}\in L^1([a,b],\mathbb{R})$ and an increasing function $\phi:[a,b]\to\mathbb{R}$ with $\phi'(w)\neq0$ for all $w\in[a,b]$, was given by

$$\mathfrak{I}^{\overline{\alpha};\phi}\mathfrak{h}(w)=\frac{1}{\Gamma_k(\alpha)}\int_a^w\phi'(u)(\phi(w)-\phi(u))^{\overline{\alpha}-1}\mathfrak{h}(u)du. \tag{6}$$

Let $n-1<\overline{\alpha}\leq n$, $\phi\in C^n([a,b],\mathbb{R})$, $\phi'(w)\neq0,w\in[a,b]$, and $\mathfrak{h}\in C([a,b],\mathbb{R})$. Then the ϕ-Riemann–Liouville fractional derivative of the function $\mathfrak{h}$ of order $\overline{\alpha}$ was defined in [2] by

$$^{RL}\mathfrak{D}^{\overline{\alpha};\phi}\mathfrak{h}(w)=\left(\frac{1}{\phi'(w)}\frac{d}{dw}\right)^n\mathfrak{I}^{n-\overline{\alpha};\phi}_{a+}\mathfrak{h}(w), \tag{7}$$

and the ϕ-Caputo fractional derivative of the function $\mathfrak{h}$ of order α was defined in [13] by

$$^{C}\mathfrak{D}^{\overline{\alpha};\phi}\mathfrak{h}(w)=\mathfrak{I}^{n-\overline{\alpha};\phi}_{a+}\left(\frac{1}{\phi'(w)}\frac{d}{dw}\right)^n\mathfrak{h}(w), \tag{8}$$

respectively. In [14] the ϕ-Hilfer fractional derivative of the function $\mathfrak{h}\in C([a,b],\mathbb{R})$ of order $\overline{\alpha}\in(n-1,n]$ and type $\beta\in[0,1]$ and $\phi\in C^n([a,b],\mathbb{R})$, $\phi'(w)\neq0,w\in[a,b]$, was defined by

$$^{H}\mathfrak{D}^{\overline{\alpha},\beta;\phi}\mathfrak{h}(w)=\mathfrak{I}^{\beta(n-\overline{\alpha});\phi}_{a+}\left(\frac{1}{\phi'(w)}\frac{d}{dw}\right)^n\mathfrak{I}^{(1-\beta)(n-\overline{\alpha});\phi}_{a+}\mathfrak{h}(w). \tag{9}$$

In [15] was defined the (k,ϕ)-Riemann–Liouville fractional integral of order $\overline{\alpha}>0$ ($\alpha\in\mathbb{R}$) of the function $\mathfrak{h}\in L^1([a,b],\mathbb{R})$, $k>0$, as

$$^{k}\mathfrak{I}^{\overline{\alpha};\phi}_{a+}\mathfrak{h}(w)=\frac{1}{k\Gamma_k(\overline{\alpha})}\int_a^w\phi'(u)(\phi(w)-\phi(u))^{\frac{\overline{\alpha}}{k}-1}\mathfrak{h}(u)du. \tag{10}$$

Recently, in [16] introduced (k,ϕ)-Hilfer fractional derivative of the function $\mathfrak{h}\in C^n([a,b],\mathbb{R})$ of order $\overline{\alpha}>0,k>0$ and type $\beta\in[0,1]$, $\phi\in C^n([a,b],\mathbb{R})$, $\phi'(w)\neq0,w\in[a,b]$ as

$$^{k,H}\mathfrak{D}^{\overline{\alpha},\beta;\phi}\mathfrak{h}(w)={}^{k}\mathfrak{I}^{\beta(nk-\overline{\alpha});\phi}_{a+}\left(\frac{k}{\phi'(w)}\frac{d}{dw}\right)^n\,{}^{k}\mathfrak{I}^{(1-\beta)(nk-\overline{\alpha});\phi}_{a+}\mathfrak{h}(w),\ \ n=\left\lceil\frac{\overline{\alpha}}{k}\right\rceil. \tag{11}$$

Note that:

1. For $\beta = 0$, (11) reduces to (k,ϕ)-Riemann–Liouville fractional derivative operator

$$^{k,RL}\mathfrak{D}^{\overline{\alpha};\phi}\mathfrak{h}(w) = \left(\frac{k}{\phi'(w)}\frac{d}{dw}\right)^{n} {}^{k}\mathfrak{I}_{a+}^{(1-\beta)(nk-\overline{\alpha});\phi}\mathfrak{h}(w). \tag{12}$$

If we take in (12), $\phi(w) = w$, then we obtain k-Riemann–Liouville fractional derivative operator defined in [12];

2. For $\beta = 1$, (11) reduces to (k,ϕ)-Caputo fractional derivative operator [16]

$$^{k,C}\mathfrak{D}^{\overline{\alpha};\phi}\mathfrak{h}(w) = {}^{k}\mathfrak{I}_{a+}^{nk-\overline{\alpha};\phi}\left(\frac{k}{\phi'(w)}\frac{d}{dw}\right)^{n}\mathfrak{h}(w). \tag{13}$$

If we take $\phi(w) = w$ in (13), then we obtain k-Caputo fractional derivative operator [16]

$$^{k,C}\mathfrak{D}^{\overline{\alpha};\phi}\mathfrak{h}(w) = {}^{k}\mathfrak{I}_{a+}^{nk-\overline{\alpha};\phi}\left(k\frac{d}{dw}\right)^{n}\mathfrak{h}(w). \tag{14}$$

3. If $\phi(w) = w^{\rho}$, then (11) reduces to k-Hilfer–Katugampola fractional derivative operator:
   (a) If $\phi(w) = w^{\rho}$, $\beta = 0$, then (11) reduces to k-Katugampola fractional derivative operator [17];
   (b) If $\phi(w) = w^{\rho}$, $\beta = 1$, then (11) reduces to k-Caputo–Katugampola fractional derivative operator [17];
4. If $\phi(w) = \log w$, then (11) reduces to k-Hilfer–Hadamard fractional derivative operator:
   (a) If $\phi(w) = \log w$, $\beta = 0$, then (11) reduces to k-Hadamard fractional derivative operator [16];
   (b) If $\phi(w) = \log w$, $\beta = 1$, then (11) reduces to k-Caputo–Hadamard fractional derivative operator [16].

Remark 1. *If $\theta_k = \overline{\alpha} + \beta(nk - \overline{\alpha})$, then $\beta(nk - \overline{\alpha}) = \theta_k - \overline{\alpha}$ and $(1-\beta)(nk - \overline{\alpha}) = nk - \theta_k$ and hence the (k,ϕ)-Hilfer fractional derivative has been defined in the form of (k,ϕ)-Riemann-Liouville fractional derivative as follows*

$$\begin{aligned} ^{k,H}\mathfrak{D}^{\overline{\alpha},\beta;\phi}\mathfrak{h}(w) &= {}^{k}\mathfrak{I}_{a+}^{\theta_k-\overline{\alpha};\phi}\left(\frac{k}{\phi'(w)}\frac{d}{dw}\right)^{n} {}^{k}\mathfrak{I}_{a+}^{nk-\theta_k;\phi}\mathfrak{h}(w) \\ &= {}^{k}\mathfrak{I}_{a+}^{\theta_k-\overline{\alpha};\phi}\left({}^{k,RL}\mathfrak{D}^{\theta_k;\phi}\mathfrak{h}\right)(w). \end{aligned}$$

Note for $\beta \in [0,1]$ and $n-1 < \frac{\overline{\alpha}}{k} \le n$, we have $n-1 < \frac{\theta_k}{k} \le n$.

For some results on k-Riemann–Liouville fractional derivatives, we refer to [18–23] and the therein-cited references.

In [16] the authors proved several properties of (k,ϕ)-Hilfer fractional derivative operator. Moreover they studied the following nonlinear initial value problem involving (k,ϕ)-Hilfer fractional derivative of the form

$$\begin{cases} ^{k,H}\mathfrak{D}_{a+}^{\overline{\alpha},\beta;\phi}\vartheta(w) = \mathfrak{f}(w,\vartheta(w)), \ w \in (a,b], \ 0 < \overline{\alpha} < k, \ 0 \le \beta \le 1, \\ ^{k}\mathfrak{I}^{k-\theta_k;\phi}\vartheta(a) = x_a \in \mathbb{R}, \ \theta_k = \overline{\alpha} + \beta(k - \overline{\alpha}), \end{cases} \tag{15}$$

where $^{k,H}\mathfrak{D}^{\overline{\alpha},\beta;\phi}$ denotes the (k,ϕ)-Hilfer fractional derivative operator of order $\overline{\alpha}$, $0 < \overline{\alpha} \le 1$ and parameter β, $0 \le \beta \le 1$, and $\mathfrak{f} : [a,b] \times \mathbb{R} \to \mathbb{R}$ is a continuous function. By applying Banach's fixed point theorem they proved the existence of a unique solution for the problem (15).

In the present work, motivated by the paper [16], we study boundary value problems involving (k,ϕ)-Hilfer fractional derivative operator of order $\overline{\alpha}$ and parameter β, where $1 < \overline{\alpha} \le 2$ and $0 \le \beta \le 1$. To be more precisely, we consider in this paper the following (k,ϕ)-

Hilfer fractional boundary value problem with nonlocal multipoint boundary conditions of the form

$$\begin{cases} {}^{k,H}\mathfrak{D}^{\overline{\alpha},\beta;\phi}\vartheta(w) = \mathfrak{f}(w,\vartheta(w)), \quad w \in (a,b], \\ \vartheta(a) = 0, \quad \vartheta(b) = \sum_{i=1}^{m} \lambda_i \vartheta(\xi_i), \end{cases} \tag{16}$$

where ${}^{k,H}\mathfrak{D}^{\overline{\alpha},\beta;\phi}$ denotes the (k,ϕ)-Hilfer fractional derivative operator of order $\overline{\alpha}$, $1 < \overline{\alpha} < 2$ and parameter β, $0 \le \beta \le 1$, $k > 0$, $\mathfrak{f} : [a,b] \times \mathbb{R} \to \mathbb{R}$ is a continuous function, $\lambda_i \in \mathbb{R}$, and $a < \xi_i < b, i = 1,2,\ldots,m$. Our aim in this paper is to establish results concerning existence and uniqueness, by using Banach's and Krasnoselskiĭ's fixed point theorems, as well as a Leray–Schauder nonlinear alternative.

Next, we also study the multivalued problem

$$\begin{cases} {}^{k,H}\mathfrak{D}^{\overline{\alpha},\beta;\phi}\vartheta(w) \in \mathfrak{F}(w,\vartheta(w)), \quad w \in (a,b], \\ \vartheta(a) = 0, \quad \vartheta(b) = \sum_{i=1}^{m} \lambda_i \vartheta(\xi_i), \end{cases} \tag{17}$$

in which $\mathfrak{F} : [a,b] \times \mathbb{R} \to \mathcal{P}(\mathbb{R})$ is a multivalued map and the other parameters are as in problem (16). Here, $\mathcal{P}(\mathbb{R})$ denotes the family of all nonempty subsets of $\mathbb{R}$. We will study both cases, when the right-hand side is convex or nonconvex valued, and we will establish existence results by using Leray–Schauder nonlinear alternative for multivalued maps and the Covitz–Nadler fixed-point theorem for multivalued contractions, respectively.

Numerical examples are constructed illustrating the applicability of our obtained theoretical results.

The rest of our paper is organized as follows. In Section 2, we prove an ancillary result toward a linear variant of the (k,ϕ)-Hilfer fractional nonlocal boundary value problem (16). This lemma is important to transform the nonlinear boundary value problem (16) into an equivalent fixed-point problem. The main results for the single valued (k,ϕ)-Hilfer fractional nonlocal boundary value problem (16) are included in Section 3, while the results for the multivalued (k,ϕ)-Hilfer fractional nonlocal boundary value problem (17) are presented in Section 4. Finally, Section 5 is dedicated to illustrative examples.

2. An Auxiliary Result

In this section an auxiliary result is proved, which is the basic tool in transforming the nonlinear problem (16) into a fixed-point problem, and dealing with a linear variant of the problem (16). First we recall two useful lemmas.

Lemma 1 ([16]). *Let $\mu, k \in \mathbb{R}^+ = (0,\infty)$ and $n = \left\lceil \frac{\mu}{k} \right\rceil$. Assume that $\mathfrak{h} \in C^n([a,b],\mathbb{R})$ and ${}^{k}\mathfrak{J}^{nk-\mu;\phi}_{a+}\mathfrak{h} \in C^n([a,b],\mathbb{R})$. Then*

$$ {}^{k}\mathfrak{J}^{\mu;\phi}\left({}^{k,RL}\mathfrak{D}^{\mu;\phi}\mathfrak{h}(w)\right) = \mathfrak{h}(w) - \sum_{j=1}^{n} \frac{(\phi(w)-\phi(a))^{\frac{\mu}{k}-j}}{\Gamma_k(\mu - jk + k)} \left[\left(\frac{k}{\phi'(w)}\frac{d}{dw}\right)^{n-j} {}^{k}\mathfrak{J}^{nk-\mu;\phi}_{a+}\mathfrak{h}(w)\right]_{z=a}.$$

Lemma 2 ([16]). *Let $\alpha, k \in \mathbb{R}^+ = (0,\infty)$ with $\alpha < k$, $\beta \in [0,1]$ and $\theta_k = \alpha + \beta(k-\alpha)$. Then*

$${}^{k}\mathfrak{J}^{\theta_k;\phi}\left({}^{k,RL}\mathfrak{D}^{\theta_k;\phi}\mathfrak{h}\right)(w) = {}^{k}\mathfrak{J}^{\alpha;\phi}\left({}^{k,H}\mathfrak{D}^{\alpha,\beta;\phi}\mathfrak{h}\right)(w), \quad \mathfrak{h} \in C^n([a,b],\mathbb{R}).$$

Lemma 3. *Let $a < b$, $k > 0$, $1 < \overline{\alpha} \le 2$, $\beta \in [0,1]$, $\theta_k = \overline{\alpha} + \beta(2k - \overline{\alpha})$, $\mathfrak{g} \in C^2([a,b],\mathbb{R})$ and*

$$\mathcal{H} := \frac{1}{\Gamma_k(\theta_k)}\left[(\phi(b)-\phi(a))^{\frac{\theta_k}{k}-1} - \sum_{i=1}^{m} \lambda_i (\phi(\xi_i)-\phi(a))^{\frac{\theta_k}{k}-1}\right] \neq 0. \tag{18}$$

Then the function $\vartheta \in C([a,b],\mathbb{R})$ is a solution of the boundary value problem

$$\begin{cases} {}^{k,H}\mathfrak{D}^{\overline{\alpha},\beta;\phi}\vartheta(w) = \mathfrak{g}(w), \quad w \in (a,b], \\ \vartheta(a) = 0, \quad \vartheta(b) = \sum\limits_{i=1}^{m} \lambda_i \vartheta(\xi_i), \end{cases} \tag{19}$$

if and only if

$$\vartheta(w) = {}^{k}\mathfrak{J}^{\overline{\alpha};\phi}\mathfrak{g}(w) + \frac{(\phi(w)-\phi(a))^{\frac{\theta_k}{k}-1}}{\mathcal{H}\Gamma_k(\theta_k)}\left[\sum_{i=1}^{m}\lambda_i\, {}^{k}\mathfrak{J}^{\overline{\alpha};\phi}\mathfrak{g}(\xi_i) - {}^{k}\mathfrak{J}^{\overline{\alpha};\phi}\mathfrak{g}(b)\right]. \tag{20}$$

Proof. Assume that ϑ is a solution of the boundary value problem (19). Operating fractional integral ${}^{k}\mathfrak{J}^{\alpha;\phi}$ on both sides of equation in (19) and using Lemmas 1 and 2, we obtain

$$\begin{aligned} {}^{k}\mathfrak{J}^{\overline{\alpha};\phi}\left({}^{k,H}\mathfrak{D}^{\overline{\alpha},\beta;\phi}\vartheta\right)(w) &= {}^{k}\mathfrak{J}^{\theta_k;\phi}\left({}^{k,RL}\mathfrak{D}^{\theta_k;\phi}\vartheta\right)(w) \\ &= \vartheta(w) - \frac{(\phi(w)-\phi(a))^{\frac{\theta_k}{k}-1}}{\Gamma_k(\theta_k)}\left[\left(\frac{k}{\phi'(w)}\frac{d}{dw}\right){}^{k}\mathfrak{J}^{2k-\theta_k;\phi}\vartheta(w)\right]_{w=a} \\ &\quad - \frac{(\phi(w)-\phi(a))^{\frac{\theta_k}{k}-2}}{\Gamma_k(\theta_k-k)}\left[{}^{k}\mathfrak{J}^{2k-\theta_k;\phi}\vartheta(w)\right]_{w=a}. \end{aligned}$$

Consequently

$$\vartheta(w) = {}^{k}\mathfrak{J}^{\overline{\alpha};\phi}\mathfrak{g}(w) + c_0\frac{(\phi(w)-\phi(a))^{\frac{\theta_k}{k}-1}}{\Gamma_k(\theta_k)} + c_1\frac{(\phi(w)-\phi(a))^{\frac{\theta_k}{k}-2}}{\Gamma_k(\theta_k-k)}, \tag{21}$$

where

$$c_0 = \left[\left(\frac{k}{\phi'(w)}\frac{d}{dw}\right){}^{k}\mathfrak{J}^{2k-\theta_k;\phi}\vartheta(w)\right]_{w=a}, \quad c_1 = \left[{}^{k}\mathfrak{J}^{2k-\theta_k;\phi}\vartheta(w)\right]_{w=a}.$$

From the boundary condition $\vartheta(a) = 0$ we get $c_2 = 0$, since $\frac{\theta_k}{k} - 2 < 0$ by Remark 1. From the second boundary condition $\vartheta(b) = \sum_{i=1}^{m}\lambda_i\vartheta(\xi_i)$ we found

$$c_0 = \frac{1}{\mathcal{H}}\left[\sum_{i=1}^{m}\lambda_i {}^{k}\mathfrak{J}^{\overline{\alpha};\phi}\mathfrak{g}(\xi_i) - {}^{k}\mathfrak{J}^{\overline{\alpha};\phi}\mathfrak{g}(b)\right].$$

Replacing the values of c_0 and c_1 in (21), we get the solution (20). We can prove easily the converse by direct computation. The proof is finished. □

3. The Single Valued Problem

Let $C([a,b],\mathbb{R})$ be the Banach space of all continuous functions from $[a,b]$ to $\mathbb{R}$ endowed with the sup-norm $\|\vartheta\| = \sup_{w\in[a,b]}|\vartheta(w)|$. In view of Lemma 3, we define an operator $\mathcal{A} : C([a,b],\mathbb{R}) \to C([a,b],\mathbb{R})$ by

$$\begin{aligned} (\mathcal{A}\vartheta)(w) &= \frac{(\phi(w)-\phi(a))^{\frac{\theta_k}{k}-1}}{\mathcal{H}\Gamma_k(\theta_k)}\left[\sum_{i=1}^{m}\lambda_i\, {}^{k}\mathfrak{J}^{\overline{\alpha};\phi}\mathfrak{f}(\xi_i,\vartheta(\xi_i)) - {}^{k}\mathfrak{J}^{\overline{\alpha};\phi}\mathfrak{f}(b,\vartheta(b))\right] \\ &\quad + {}^{k}\mathfrak{J}^{\overline{\alpha};\phi}\mathfrak{f}(w,\vartheta(w)), \quad w \in [a,b]. \end{aligned} \tag{22}$$

It should be noticed that the solutions of the nonlocal (k,ϕ)-Hilfer fractional boundary value problem (16) will be fixed points of $\mathcal{A}$.

For convenience we put:

$$\begin{aligned}\mathfrak{G} &= \frac{(\phi(b)-\phi(a))^{\frac{\overline{\alpha}}{k}}}{\Gamma_k(\overline{\alpha}+k)} + \frac{(\phi(b)-\phi(a))^{\frac{\theta_k}{k}-1}}{|\mathcal{H}|\Gamma_k(\theta_k)}\Bigg[\sum_{i=1}^{m}|\lambda_i|\frac{(\phi(\xi_i)-\phi(a))^{\frac{\overline{\alpha}}{k}}}{\Gamma_k(\overline{\alpha}+k)} \\ &\quad + \frac{(\phi(b)-\phi(a))^{\frac{\overline{\alpha}}{k}}}{\Gamma_k(\overline{\alpha}+k)}\Bigg]. \end{aligned} \tag{23}$$

3.1. Existence of a Unique Solution

In our first result we will prove the existence of a unique solution of the problem (16). The basic tool is the Banach's contraction mapping principle [24].

Theorem 1. *Assume that:*
(H_1) $|\mathfrak{f}(w,\vartheta)-\mathfrak{f}(w,y)| \leq \mathfrak{L}|\vartheta - y|, \mathfrak{L} > 0$ *for each* $w \in [a,b]$ *and* $\vartheta, y \in \mathbb{R}$.

Then the (k,ϕ)*-Hilfer nonlocal multi-point fractional boundary value problem (16) has a unique solution on* $[a,b]$*, provided that*

$$\mathfrak{L}\mathfrak{G} < 1, \tag{24}$$

where $\mathfrak{G}$ *is defined by (23).*

Proof. We transform the (k,ϕ)-Hilfer nonlocal multipoint fractional boundary value problem (16) into a fixed-point problem, with the help of the operator $\mathcal{A}$ defined in (22). Then, we shall show that the operator $\mathcal{A}$ has a unique fixed point.

We let $\sup_{w\in[a,b]}|\mathfrak{f}(w,0)| = \mathfrak{M} < \infty$, and choose

$$r \geq \frac{\mathfrak{M}\mathfrak{G}}{1-\mathfrak{L}\mathfrak{G}}. \tag{25}$$

Let $B_r = \{\vartheta \in C([a,b],\mathbb{R}) : \|\vartheta\| \leq r\}$. In the first step we will show that $\mathcal{A}B_r \subset B_r$. We have, for $\vartheta \in B_r$, using (H_1), that

$$\begin{aligned} |\mathfrak{f}(w,\vartheta(w))| &\leq |\mathfrak{f}(w,\vartheta(w))-\mathfrak{f}(w,0)| + |\mathfrak{f}(w,0)| \\ &\leq \mathfrak{L}|\vartheta(w)| + \mathfrak{M} \leq \mathfrak{L}\|\vartheta\| + \mathfrak{M} \leq \mathfrak{L}r + \mathfrak{M}. \end{aligned}$$

For any $\vartheta \in B_r$, we have

$$\begin{aligned} |(\mathcal{A}\vartheta)(w)| &\leq \sup_{w\in[a,b]}\Bigg\{\frac{(\phi(w)-\phi(a))^{\frac{\theta_k}{k}-1}}{|\mathcal{H}|\Gamma_k(\theta_k)}\Bigg[\sum_{i=1}^{m}|\lambda_i|^k\mathfrak{J}^{\overline{\alpha};\phi}|\mathfrak{f}(\xi_i,\vartheta(\xi_i))| + {}^k\mathfrak{J}^{\overline{\alpha};\phi}|\mathfrak{f}(b,\vartheta(b))|\Bigg] \\ &\quad + {}^k\mathfrak{J}^{\overline{\alpha};\phi}|\mathfrak{f}(w,\vartheta(w))|\Bigg\} \\ &\leq {}^k\mathfrak{J}^{\overline{\alpha};\phi}(|\mathfrak{f}(w,\vartheta(w))-\mathfrak{f}(w,0)| + |\mathfrak{f}(w,0)|) \\ &\quad + \frac{(\phi(b)-\phi(a))^{\frac{\theta_k}{k}-1}}{|\mathcal{H}|\Gamma_k(\theta_k)}\Bigg(\sum_{i=1}^{m}|\lambda_i|^k\mathfrak{J}^{\overline{\alpha};\phi}|\mathfrak{f}(\xi_i,\vartheta(\xi_i))-\mathfrak{f}(\xi_i,0)| + |\mathfrak{f}(\xi_i,0)|) \\ &\quad + {}^k\mathfrak{J}^{\overline{\alpha};\phi}(|\mathfrak{f}(b,\vartheta(b))-\mathfrak{f}(b,0)| + |\mathfrak{f}(b,0)|)\Bigg) \\ &\leq \Bigg\{\frac{(\phi(b)-\phi(a))^{\frac{\overline{\alpha}}{k}}}{\Gamma_k(\alpha+k)} + \frac{(\phi(b)-\phi(a))^{\frac{\theta_k}{k}-1}}{|\mathcal{H}|\Gamma_k(\theta_k)}\Bigg[\sum_{i=1}^{m}|\lambda_i|\frac{(\phi(\xi_i)-\phi(a))^{\frac{\overline{\alpha}}{k}}}{\Gamma_k(\alpha+k)} \\ &\quad + \frac{(\phi(b)-\phi(a))^{\frac{\overline{\alpha}}{k}}}{\Gamma_k(\alpha+k)}\Bigg]\Bigg\}(\mathfrak{L}\|\vartheta\| + \mathfrak{M}) \\ &\leq (\mathfrak{L}r + \mathfrak{M})\mathfrak{G} \leq r. \end{aligned}$$

Consequently $\|\mathcal{A}\vartheta\| \leq r$ and thus $\mathcal{A}B_r \subset B_r$.

Now we will show that $\mathcal{A}$ is a contraction. For $w \in [a,b]$ and $\vartheta, y \in C([a,b],\mathbb{R})$, we have

$$\begin{aligned}
& |(\mathcal{A}\vartheta)(w) - (\mathcal{A}y)(w)| \\
\leq \; & {}^{k}\mathfrak{J}^{\overline{\alpha};\phi}|\mathfrak{f}(w,\vartheta(w)) - \mathfrak{f}(w,y(w))| \\
& + \frac{(\phi(b)-\phi(a))^{\frac{\theta_k}{k}-1}}{|\mathcal{H}|\Gamma_k(\theta_k)} \bigg(\sum_{i=1}^{m} |\lambda_i| {}^{k}\mathfrak{J}^{\overline{\alpha};\phi}|\mathfrak{f}(\xi_i,\vartheta(\xi_i)) - \mathfrak{f}(\xi_i,y(\xi_i))| \\
& + {}^{k}\mathfrak{J}^{\overline{\alpha};\phi}(|\mathfrak{f}(b,\vartheta(b)) - \mathfrak{f}(b,y(b))|\bigg) \\
\leq \; & \left\{ \frac{(\phi(b)-\phi(a))^{\frac{\overline{\alpha}}{k}}}{\Gamma_k(\overline{\alpha}+k)} + \frac{(\phi(b)-\phi(a))^{\frac{\theta_k}{k}-1}}{|\mathcal{H}|\Gamma_k(\theta_k)} \left[\sum_{i=1}^{m} |\lambda_i| \frac{(\phi(\xi_i)-\phi(a))^{\frac{\overline{\alpha}}{k}}}{\Gamma_k(\overline{\alpha}+k)} \right.\right. \\
& \left.\left. + \frac{(\phi(b)-\phi(a))^{\frac{\overline{\alpha}}{k}}}{\Gamma_k(\overline{\alpha}+k)} \right] \right\} \mathfrak{L}\|x-y\| \\
= \; & \mathfrak{L}\mathfrak{G}\|x-y\|.
\end{aligned}$$

Hence $\|\mathcal{A}x - \mathcal{A}y\| \leq \mathfrak{L}\mathfrak{G}\|x-y\|$ which implies that $\mathcal{A}$ is a contraction, since $\mathfrak{L}\mathfrak{G} < 1$. By the Banach's contraction-mapping principle, the operator $\mathcal{A}$ has a unique fixed point, which is the unique solution of (k,ϕ)-Hilfer nonlocal multipoint fractional boundary value problem (16). The proof is finished. □

3.2. Existence Results

In the forthcoming theorems we will prove existence results for the (k,ϕ)-Hilfer nonlocal multipoint fractional boundary value problem (16), utilizing Krasnoselskiĭ's fixed point theorem [25] and nonlinear alternative of Leray–Schauder type [26].

Theorem 2. *Let* $\mathfrak{f} : [a,b] \times \mathbb{R} \to \mathbb{R}$ *be a continuous function satisfying* (H_1). *In addition we assume that:*

(H_2) $|\mathfrak{f}(w,\vartheta)| \leq \varpi(w)$, $\forall (w,\vartheta) \in [a,b] \times \mathbb{R}$, *and* $\varpi \in C([a,b],\mathbb{R}^+)$.

Then the (k,ϕ)*-Hilfer nonlocal multi-point fractional boundary value problem (16) has at least one solution on* $[a,b]$, *if* $\mathfrak{G}_1\mathfrak{L} < 1$, *where*

$$\mathfrak{G}_1 := \frac{(\phi(b)-\phi(a))^{\frac{\theta_k}{k}-1}}{|\mathcal{H}|\Gamma_k(\theta_k)} \left[\sum_{i=1}^{m} |\lambda_i| \frac{(\phi(\xi_i)-\phi(a))^{\frac{\overline{\alpha}}{k}}}{\Gamma_k(\overline{\alpha}+k)} + \frac{(\phi(b)-\phi(a))^{\frac{\overline{\alpha}}{k}}}{\Gamma_k(\overline{\alpha}+k)} \right]. \tag{26}$$

Proof. Set $\sup_{w\in[a,b]} \varpi(w) = \|\varpi\|$ and $B_\rho = \{\vartheta \in C([a,b],\mathbb{R}) : \|\vartheta\| \leq \rho\}$, with $\rho \geq \|\varpi\|\mathfrak{G}$. We define on B_ρ two operators $\mathcal{A}_1$, $\mathcal{A}_2$ by

$$\mathcal{A}_1\vartheta(w) = {}^{k}\mathfrak{J}^{\overline{\alpha};\phi}\mathfrak{f}(w,\vartheta(w)), \quad w \in [a,b],$$

and

$$\mathcal{A}_2\vartheta(w) = \frac{(\phi(w)-\phi(a))^{\frac{\theta_k}{k}-1}}{\mathcal{H}\Gamma_k(\theta_k)} \left[\sum_{i=1}^{m} \lambda_i {}^{k}\mathfrak{J}^{\overline{\alpha};\phi}\mathfrak{f}(\xi_i,\vartheta(\xi_i)) - {}^{k}\mathfrak{J}^{\overline{\alpha};\phi}\mathfrak{f}(b,\vartheta(b)) \right], \quad w \in [a,b].$$

For any $\vartheta, y \in B_\rho$, we have

$$
\begin{aligned}
&|(\mathcal{A}_1\vartheta)(w)+(\mathcal{A}_2y)(w)| \\
\le\ & \sup_{w\in[a,b]}\left\{\frac{(\phi(w)-\phi(a))^{\frac{\theta_k}{k}-1}}{|\mathcal{H}|\Gamma_k(\theta_k)}\left[\sum_{i=1}^{m}|\lambda_i|^k\mathfrak{J}^{\overline{\alpha};\phi}|\mathfrak{f}(\xi_i,y(\xi_i))|+{}^k\mathfrak{J}^{\overline{\alpha};\phi}|\mathfrak{f}(b,y(b))|\right]\right. \\
& \left. +{}^k\mathfrak{J}^{\overline{\alpha};\phi}|\mathfrak{f}(w,\vartheta(w))|\right\} \\
\le\ & \left\{\frac{(\phi(b)-\phi(a))^{\frac{\overline{\alpha}}{k}}}{\Gamma_k(\overline{\alpha}+k)}+\frac{(\phi(b)-\phi(a))^{\frac{\theta_k}{k}-1}}{|\mathcal{H}|\Gamma_k(\theta_k)}\left[\sum_{i=1}^{m}|\lambda_i|\frac{(\phi(\xi_i)-\phi(a))^{\frac{\overline{\alpha}}{k}}}{\Gamma_k(\overline{\alpha}+k)}\right.\right. \\
& \left.\left.+\frac{(\phi(b)-\phi(a))^{\frac{\overline{\alpha}}{k}}}{\Gamma_k(\overline{\alpha}+k)}\right]\right\}\|\varpi\| \\
=\ & \mathfrak{G}\|\varpi\|\le\rho.
\end{aligned}
$$

Therefore $\|(\mathcal{A}_1\vartheta)+(\mathcal{A}_2y)\|\le\rho$, which shows that $\mathcal{A}_1\vartheta+\mathcal{A}_2y\in B_\rho$. Next we show that $\mathcal{A}_2$ is a contraction mapping. We omit the details since it is easy by using (26).

The operator $\mathcal{A}_1$ is continuous, since $\mathfrak{f}$ is continuous. Moreover, $\mathcal{A}_1$ is uniformly bounded on B_ρ as

$$
\|\mathcal{A}_1\vartheta\|\le\frac{(\phi(b)-\phi(a))^{\frac{\overline{\alpha}}{k}}}{\Gamma_k(\overline{\alpha}+k)}\|\varpi\|.
$$

To prove the compactness of the operator $\mathcal{A}_1$, we consider $w_1,w_2\in[a,b]$ with $w_1<w_2$. Then we have

$$
\begin{aligned}
&|(\mathcal{A}_1\vartheta)(w_2)-(\mathcal{A}_1\vartheta)(w_1)| \\
\le\ & \frac{1}{\Gamma_k(\overline{\alpha})}\left|\int_a^{w_1}\phi'(s)[(\phi(w_2)-\phi(s))^{\frac{\overline{\alpha}}{k}-1}-(\phi(w_1)-\phi(s))^{\frac{\overline{\alpha}}{k}-1}]\mathfrak{f}(s,\vartheta(s))ds\right. \\
& \left.+\int_{w_1}^{w_2}\phi'(s)(\phi(w_2)-\phi(s))^{\frac{\overline{\alpha}}{k}-1}\mathfrak{f}(s,\vartheta(s))ds\right| \\
\le\ & \frac{\|\varpi\|}{\Gamma_k(\overline{\alpha}+k)}[2(\phi(w_2)-\phi(w_1))^{\frac{\overline{\alpha}}{k}}+|(\phi(w_2)-\phi(a))^{\frac{\overline{\alpha}}{k}}-(\phi(w_1)-\phi(a))^{\frac{\overline{\alpha}}{k}}|],
\end{aligned}
$$

which tends to zero as $w_2-w_1\to0$, independently of ϑ. Thus, $\mathcal{A}_1$ is equicontinuous. By the Arzelá–Ascoli theorem, $\mathcal{A}_1$ is completely continuous. By Krasnoselskiĭ's fixed-point theorem the (k,ϕ)-Hilfer nonlocal multipoint fractional boundary value problem (16) has at least one solution on $[a,b]$. The proof is finished. □

Theorem 3. *Let $\mathfrak{f}:[a,b]\times\mathbb{R}\to\mathbb{R}$ be a continuous function. Assume that:*

(H_3) *there exist $\chi:[0,\infty)\to(0,\infty)$ which is continuous, nondecreasing function and a continuous positive function σ such that*

$$
|\mathfrak{f}(w,u)|\le\sigma(w)\chi(|u|)\quad \textit{for each}\quad (w,u)\in[a,b]\times\mathbb{R};
$$

(H_4) *there exists a constant $\mathfrak{K}>0$ such that*

$$
\frac{\mathfrak{K}}{\chi(\mathfrak{K})\|\sigma\|\mathfrak{G}}>1.
$$

Then the (k,ϕ)-Hilfer nonlocal multipoint fractional boundary value problem (16) has at least one solution on $[a,b]$.

Proof. In the first step we will show that the operator $\mathcal{A}$ maps bounded sets into bounded set in $C([a,b],\mathbb{R})$, where $\mathcal{A}$ is defined by (22). For $r>0$, let $B_r=\{\vartheta\in C([a,b],\mathbb{R}):\|\vartheta\|\leq r\}$. Then for $w\in[a,b]$ we have

$$\begin{aligned}
&|(\mathcal{A}\vartheta)(w)|\\
\leq\ & \sup_{w\in[a,b]}\left\{\frac{(\phi(w)-\phi(a))^{\frac{\theta_k}{k}-1}}{|\mathcal{H}|\Gamma_k(\theta_k)}\left[\sum_{i=1}^{m}|\lambda_i|^k\mathfrak{J}^{\bar{\alpha};\phi}|\mathfrak{f}(\xi_i,\vartheta(\xi_i))|+{}^k\mathfrak{J}^{\bar{\alpha};\phi}|\mathfrak{f}(b,\vartheta(b))|\right]\right.\\
&\left.+{}^k\mathfrak{J}^{\bar{\alpha};\phi}|\mathfrak{f}(w,\vartheta(w))|\right\}\\
\leq\ & \left\{\frac{(\phi(b)-\phi(a))^{\frac{\bar{\alpha}}{k}}}{\Gamma_k(\bar{\alpha}+k)}+\frac{(\phi(b)-\phi(a))^{\frac{\theta_k}{k}-1}}{|\mathcal{H}|\Gamma_k(\theta_k)}\left[\sum_{i=1}^{m}|\lambda_i|\frac{(\phi(\xi_i)-\phi(a))^{\frac{\bar{\alpha}}{k}}}{\Gamma_k(\bar{\alpha}+k)}\right.\right.\\
&\left.\left.+\frac{(\phi(b)-\phi(a))^{\frac{\bar{\alpha}}{k}}}{\Gamma_k(\bar{\alpha}+k)}\right]\right\}\|\sigma\|\chi(\|\vartheta\|),
\end{aligned}$$

and consequently,

$$\|\mathcal{A}x\|\leq\chi(r)\|\sigma\|\mathfrak{G}.$$

Now we will show that $\mathcal{A}$ maps bounded sets into equicontinuous sets of $C([a,b],\mathbb{R})$. Let $w_1,w_2\in[a,b]$ with $w_1<w_2$ and $\vartheta\in B_r$. Then we have

$$\begin{aligned}
&|(\mathcal{A}\vartheta)(w_2)-(\mathcal{A}\vartheta)(w_1)|\\
\leq\ & \frac{1}{\Gamma_k(\bar{\alpha})}\left|\int_a^{w_1}\phi'(s)[(\phi(w_2)-\phi(s))^{\frac{\bar{\alpha}}{k}-1}-(\phi(w_1)-\phi(s))^{\frac{\bar{\alpha}}{k}-1}]\mathfrak{f}(s,\vartheta(s))ds\right.\\
&\left.+\int_{w_1}^{w_2}\phi'(s)(\phi(w_2)-\phi(s))^{\frac{\bar{\alpha}}{k}-1}\mathfrak{f}(s,\vartheta(s))ds\right|\\
&+\frac{(\phi(w_2)-\phi(a))^{\frac{\theta_k}{k}-1}-(\phi(w_1)-\phi(a))^{\frac{\theta_k}{k}-1}}{|\mathcal{H}|\Gamma_k(\theta_k)}\left[\sum_{i=1}^{m}|\lambda_i|^k\mathfrak{J}^{\bar{\alpha};\phi}|\mathfrak{f}(\xi_i,\vartheta(\xi_i))|\right.\\
&\left.+{}^k\mathfrak{J}^{\bar{\alpha};\phi}|\mathfrak{f}(b,\vartheta(b))|\right]\\
\leq\ & \frac{\|\sigma\|\chi(r)}{\Gamma_k(\bar{\alpha}+k)}[2(\phi(w_2)-\phi(w_1))^{\frac{\bar{\alpha}}{k}}+|(\phi(w_2)-\phi(a))^{\frac{\bar{\alpha}}{k}}-(\phi(w_1)-\phi(a))^{\frac{\bar{\alpha}}{k}}|],\\
&+\frac{(\phi(w_2)-\phi(a))^{\frac{\theta_k}{k}-1}-(\phi(w_1)-\phi(a))^{\frac{\theta_k}{k}-1}}{|\mathcal{H}|\Gamma_k(\theta_k)}\left[\sum_{i=1}^{m}|\lambda_i|\frac{(\phi(\xi_i)-\phi(a))^{\frac{\bar{\alpha}}{k}}}{\Gamma_k(\bar{\alpha}+k)}\right.\\
&\left.+\frac{(\phi(b)-\phi(a))^{\frac{\bar{\alpha}}{k}}}{\Gamma_k(\bar{\alpha}+k)}\right]\|\sigma\|\chi(r).
\end{aligned}$$

As $w_2-w_1\to 0$ the right-hand side of the above inequality tends to zero independently of $\vartheta\in B_r$. Hence, the operator $\mathcal{A}:C([a,b],\mathbb{R})\to C([a,b],\mathbb{R})$ is completely continuous, by the Arzelá–Ascoli theorem.

Finally we will show the boundedness of the set of all solutions to equations $\vartheta=\lambda\mathcal{A}\vartheta$ for $\lambda\in(0,1)$.

Let ϑ be a solution. Then, for $w\in[a,b]$, and working as in the first step, we have

$$|\vartheta(w)|\leq\chi(\|\vartheta\|)\|\sigma\|\mathfrak{G},$$

or

$$\frac{\|\vartheta\|}{\chi(\|\vartheta\|)\|\sigma\|\mathfrak{G}}\leq 1.$$

In view of (H_4), there exists $\mathfrak{K}$ such that $\|\vartheta\| \neq \mathfrak{K}$. Let us set

$$U = \{\vartheta \in C([a,b],\mathbb{R}) : \|\vartheta\| < \mathfrak{K}\}.$$

We see that the operator $\mathcal{A} : \bar{U} \to C([a,b],\mathbb{R})$ is continuous and completely continuous. There is no $\vartheta \in \partial U$ such that $\vartheta = \lambda \mathcal{A}\vartheta$ for some $\lambda \in (0,1)$, from the choice of U. By the nonlinear alternative of Leray–Schauder type, we deduce that $\mathcal{A}$ has a fixed point $\vartheta \in \bar{U}$, which is a solution of the (k,ϕ)-Hilfer nonlocal multipoint fractional boundary value problem (16). This completes the proof. □

4. The Multivalued Problem

For a normed space $(\mathfrak{X}, \|\cdot\|)$, we define:

$\mathcal{P}_{cl}(\mathfrak{X}) = \{\mathfrak{R} \in \mathcal{P}(\mathfrak{X}) : \mathfrak{R} \text{ is closed}\}$, $\mathcal{P}_{cp}(\mathfrak{X}) = \{\mathfrak{R} \in \mathcal{P}(\mathfrak{X}) : \mathfrak{R} \text{ is compact}\}$, and $\mathcal{P}_{cp,c}(\mathfrak{X}) = \{\mathfrak{R} \in \mathcal{P}(\mathfrak{X}) : \mathfrak{R} \text{ is compact and convex}\}$.

For details of multivalued analysis we refer the reader to [27,28]. See also [7].

The set of selections of $\mathfrak{F}$, for each $\vartheta \in C([a,b],\mathbb{R})$, is defined by

$$S_{\mathfrak{F},\vartheta} := \{v \in L^1([a,b],\mathbb{R}) : v(w) \in \mathfrak{F}(w,\vartheta(w)) \text{ on } [a,b]\}.$$

Definition 1. *A function $\vartheta \in C([a,b],\mathbb{R})$ is said to be a solution of the (k,ϕ)-Hilfer nonlocal multipoint fractional boundary value problem (17) if there exists a function $v \in L^1([a,b],\mathbb{R})$ with $v(w) \in \mathfrak{F}(w,\vartheta)$ for a.e. $w \in [a,b]$ such that ϑ satisfies the differential equation ${}^{k,H}\mathfrak{D}^{\alpha,\beta;\phi}\vartheta(w) = v(w)$ on $[a,b]$ and the boundary conditions $\vartheta(a) = 0,\ \vartheta(b) = \sum_{i=1}^{m} \lambda_i \vartheta(\xi_i)$.*

In the first existence result, which concern the case when $\mathfrak{F}$ has convex values, we apply nonlinear alternative of Leray–Schauder type [26] with the assumption that $\mathfrak{F}$ is L^1-Carathéodory, that is, (i) $w \to \mathfrak{F}(w,u)$ is measurable for each $u \in \mathbb{R}$; (ii) $u \to \mathfrak{F}(w,u)$ is upper semicontinuous for almost all $w \in [a,b]$ and (iii) for each $r > 0$, there exists a function $m_r \in L^1([a,b],\mathbb{R}^+)$ such that

$$\|\mathfrak{F}(w,u)\| = \sup\{|v| : v \in \mathfrak{F}(w,u)\} < m_r(w),$$

for each $u \in \mathbb{R}$ with $|u| \le r$ and for almost every $w \in [a,b]$.

Theorem 4. *Assume that:*

(G_1) *$\mathfrak{F} : [a,b] \times \mathbb{R} \to \mathcal{P}_{cp,c}(\mathbb{R})$ is L^1-Carathéodory;*

(G_2) *there exists $z : [0,\infty) \to (0,\infty)$ a continuous nondecreasing function and a continuous positive function q such that*

$$\|\mathfrak{F}(w,\vartheta)\|_{\mathcal{P}} := \sup\{|v| : v \in \mathfrak{F}(w,\vartheta)\} \le q(w)z(\|\vartheta\|) \text{ for each } (w,\vartheta) \in [a,b] \times \mathbb{R};$$

(G_3) *there exists a constant $\mathfrak{K} > 0$ such that*

$$\frac{\mathfrak{K}}{\|q\|z(\mathfrak{K})\mathfrak{G}} > 1.$$

Then the (k,ϕ)-Hilfer nonlocal multi-point fractional boundary value problem (17) has at least one solution on $[a,b]$.

Proof. We define an operator $\mathcal{F} : C([a,b],\mathbb{R}) \longrightarrow \mathcal{P}(C([a,b],\mathbb{R}))$ by

$$\mathcal{F}(\vartheta) = \left\{ \begin{array}{l} h \in C([a,b],\mathbb{R}) : \\ h(w) = \left\{ \begin{array}{l} \dfrac{(\phi(w)-\phi(a))^{\frac{\theta_k}{k}-1}}{\mathcal{H}\Gamma_k(\theta_k)} \Big[\displaystyle\sum_{i=1}^{m} \lambda_i\, {}^{k}\mathfrak{J}^{\bar{\alpha};\phi} v(\xi_i) - {}^{k}\mathfrak{J}^{\bar{\alpha};\phi} v(b) \Big] \\ + {}^{k}\mathfrak{J}^{\bar{\alpha};\phi} v(w),\ w \in [a,b] \end{array} \right. \end{array} \right\}$$

and $v \in S_{\mathfrak{F},\vartheta}$. It is obvious that the solutions of the (k,ϕ)-Hilfer nonlocal multipoint fractional boundary value problem (17) are the fixed points of $\mathcal{F}$.

We will give the proof in several steps.

Step 1. For each $\vartheta \in C([a,b],\mathbb{R})$, the operator $\mathcal{F}(\vartheta)$ is convex.

We omit the proof, because it is obvious, since $\mathfrak{F}$ has convex values and thus $S_{F,\vartheta}$ is convex.

Step 2. $\mathcal{F}$ maps the bounded sets into bounded sets in $C([a,b],\mathbb{R})$.

Let $B_r = \{\vartheta \in C([a,b],\mathbb{R}) : \|\vartheta\| \leq r\}, r > 0$. Then, for each $h \in \mathcal{F}(\vartheta), \vartheta \in B_r$, there exists $v \in S_{\mathfrak{F},x}$ such that

$$h(w) = \frac{(\phi(w)-\phi(a))^{\frac{\theta_k}{k}-1}}{\mathcal{H}\Gamma_k(\theta_k)}\Big[\sum_{i=1}^{m}\lambda_i {}^k\mathfrak{J}^{\overline{\alpha};\phi}v(\xi_i,) - {}^k\mathfrak{J}^{\overline{\alpha};\phi}v(b)\Big] + {}^k\mathfrak{J}^{\overline{\alpha};\phi}v(w).$$

Then, for $w \in [a,b]$, we have

$$\begin{aligned}|h(w)| \leq & \sup_{w\in[a,b]}\left\{\frac{(\phi(w)-\phi(a))^{\frac{\theta_k}{k}-1}}{|\mathcal{H}|\Gamma_k(\theta_k)}\Big[\sum_{i=1}^{m}|\lambda_i|{}^k\mathfrak{J}^{\overline{\alpha};\phi}|v(\xi_i)| + {}^k\mathfrak{J}^{\overline{\alpha};\phi}|v(b)|\Big]\right.\\ & \left. + {}^k\mathfrak{J}^{\overline{\alpha};\phi}|v(w)|\right\}\\ \leq & \left\{\frac{(\phi(b)-\phi(a))^{\frac{\overline{\alpha}}{k}}}{\Gamma_k(\overline{\alpha}+k)} + \frac{(\phi(b)-\phi(a))^{\frac{\theta_k}{k}-1}}{|\mathcal{H}|\Gamma_k(\theta_k)}\left[\sum_{i=1}^{m}|\lambda_i|\frac{(\phi(\xi_i)-\phi(a))^{\frac{\overline{\alpha}}{k}}}{\Gamma_k(\overline{\alpha}+k)}\right.\right.\\ & \left.\left. + \frac{(\phi(b)-\phi(a))^{\frac{\overline{\alpha}}{k}}}{\Gamma_k(\overline{\alpha}+k)}\right]\right\}\|q\|z(\|\vartheta\|),\end{aligned}$$

and consequently,

$$\|h\| \leq z(r)\|q\|\mathfrak{G}.$$

Step 3. $\mathcal{F}$ maps bounded sets into equicontinuous sets of $C([a,b],\mathbb{R})$.

Let $w_1, w_2 \in [a,b]$ with $w_1 < w_2$ and $\vartheta \in B_r$. Then, for each $h \in \mathcal{F}(\vartheta)$, we obtain

$$\begin{aligned}& |h(w_2)-h(w_1)|\\ \leq & \frac{1}{\Gamma_k(\alpha)}\left|\int_a^{w_1}\phi'(s)[(\phi(w_2)-\phi(s))^{\frac{\overline{\alpha}}{k}-1} - (\phi(w_1)-\phi(s))^{\frac{\overline{\alpha}}{k}-1}]v(s)ds\right.\\ & \left. + \int_{w_1}^{w_2}\phi'(s)(\phi(w_2)-\phi(s))^{\frac{\overline{\alpha}}{k}-1}v(s)ds\right|\\ & + \frac{(\phi(w_2)-\phi(a))^{\frac{\theta_k}{k}-1} - (\phi(w_1)-\phi(a))^{\frac{\theta_k}{k}-1}}{|\mathcal{H}|\Gamma_k(\theta_k)}\Big[\sum_{i=1}^{m}|\lambda_i|{}^k\mathfrak{J}^{\overline{\alpha};\phi}|v(\xi_i)|\\ & + {}^k\mathfrak{J}^{\overline{\alpha};\phi}|v(b)|\Big]\\ \leq & \frac{\|q\|z(r)}{\Gamma_k(\overline{\alpha}+k)}[2(\phi(w_2)-\phi(w_1))^{\frac{\overline{\alpha}}{k}} + |(\phi(w_2)-\phi(a))^{\frac{\overline{\alpha}}{k}} - (\phi(w_1)-\phi(a))^{\frac{\overline{\alpha}}{k}}|],\\ & + \frac{(\phi(w_2)-\phi(a))^{\frac{\theta_k}{k}-1} - (\phi(w_1)-\phi(a))^{\frac{\theta_k}{k}-1}}{|\mathcal{H}|\Gamma_k(\theta_k)}\left[\sum_{i=1}^{m}|\lambda_i|\frac{(\phi(\xi_i)-\phi(a))^{\frac{\overline{\alpha}}{k}}}{\Gamma_k(\overline{\alpha}+k)}\right.\\ & \left. + \frac{(\phi(b)-\phi(a))^{\frac{\overline{\alpha}}{k}}}{\Gamma_k(\overline{\alpha}+k)}\right]\|q\|z(r).\end{aligned}$$

Hence, independently of $\vartheta \in B_r$ we have $|h(w_2) - h(w_1)| \to 0$ as $w_2 - w_1 \to 0$. By the Arzelá–Ascoli theorem that $\mathcal{F} : C([a,b],\mathbb{R}) \to \mathcal{P}(C([a,b],\mathbb{R}))$ is completely continuous.

By virtue of the Proposition 1.2 of [24], it is enough to prove that the $\mathcal{F}$ has a closed graph, which will imply that $\mathcal{F}$ is upper semicontinuous multivalued mapping.

Step 4. $\mathcal{F}$ has a closed graph.

Let $\vartheta_n \to \vartheta_*, h_n \in \mathcal{F}(\vartheta_n)$ and $h_n \to h_*$. Then we need to show that $h_* \in \mathcal{F}(\vartheta_*)$. Associated with $h_n \in \mathcal{F}(\vartheta_n)$, there exists $v_n \in S_{\mathfrak{F},\vartheta_n}$ such that for each $w \in [a,b]$,

$$h_n(w) = \frac{(\phi(w)-\phi(a))^{\frac{\theta_k}{k}-1}}{\mathcal{H}\Gamma_k(\theta_k)}\Big[\sum_{i=1}^{m}\lambda_i {}^k\mathfrak{J}^{\bar{\alpha};\phi}v_n(\xi_i,) - {}^k\mathfrak{J}^{\bar{\alpha};\phi}v_n(b)\Big] + {}^k\mathfrak{J}^{\bar{\alpha};\phi}v_n(w).$$

Thus it suffices to show that there exists $v_* \in S_{\mathfrak{F},\vartheta_*}$ such that for each $w \in [a,b]$,

$$h_*(w) = \frac{(\phi(w)-\phi(a))^{\frac{\theta_k}{k}-1}}{\mathcal{H}\Gamma_k(\theta_k)}\Big[\sum_{i=1}^{m}\lambda_i {}^k\mathfrak{J}^{\bar{\alpha};\phi}v_*(\xi_i) - {}^k\mathfrak{J}^{\bar{\alpha};\phi}v_*(b)\Big] + {}^k\mathfrak{J}^{\bar{\alpha};\phi}v_*(w).$$

Let us consider the linear operator $\Theta : L^1([a,b],\mathbb{R}) \to C([a,b],\mathbb{R})$ given by

$$v \mapsto \Theta(v)(w)\frac{(\phi(w)-\phi(a))^{\frac{\theta_k}{k}-1}}{\mathcal{H}\Gamma_k(\theta_k)}\Big[\sum_{i=1}^{m}\lambda_i {}^k\mathfrak{J}^{\bar{\alpha};\phi}v(\xi_i) - {}^k\mathfrak{J}^{\bar{\alpha};\phi}v(b)\Big] + {}^k\mathfrak{J}^{\bar{\alpha};\phi}v(w).$$

Observe that $\|h_n - h_*\| \to 0$, as $n \to \infty$. Therefore, it follows by a Lazota–Opial result [29], that $\Theta \circ S_{\mathfrak{F}}$ is a closed-graph operator. Further, we have $h_n(w) \in \Theta(S_{\mathfrak{F},\vartheta_n})$. Since $\vartheta_n \to \vartheta_*$, we have

$$h_*(w) = \frac{(\phi(w)-\phi(a))^{\frac{\theta_k}{k}-1}}{\mathcal{H}\Gamma_k(\theta_k)}\Big[\sum_{i=1}^{m}\lambda_i {}^k\mathfrak{J}^{\bar{\alpha};\phi}v_*(\xi_i) - {}^k\mathfrak{J}^{\bar{\alpha};\phi}v_*(b)\Big] + {}^k\mathfrak{J}^{\bar{\alpha};\phi}v_*(w),$$

for some $v_* \in S_{\mathfrak{F},\vartheta_*}$.

Step 5. There exists an open set $\mathcal{U} \subseteq C([a,b],\mathbb{R})$ with $\vartheta \notin \nu\mathcal{F}(\vartheta)$ for any $\nu \in (0,1)$ and all $\vartheta \in \partial\mathcal{U}$.

Let $\nu \in (0,1)$ and $\vartheta \in \nu\mathcal{F}(\vartheta)$. Then there exists $v \in L^1([a,b],\mathbb{R})$ with $v \in S_{\mathfrak{F},\vartheta}$ such that, for $w \in [a,b]$, we have

$$\vartheta(w) = \nu\frac{(\phi(w)-\phi(a))^{\frac{\theta_k}{k}-1}}{\mathcal{H}\Gamma_k(\theta_k)}\Big[\sum_{i=1}^{m}\lambda_i {}^k\mathfrak{J}^{\bar{\alpha};\phi}v(\xi_i) - {}^k\mathfrak{J}^{\bar{\alpha};\phi}v(b)\Big] + \nu\, {}^k\mathfrak{J}^{\bar{\alpha};\phi}v(w).$$

Working as in second step, we have

$$|\vartheta(w)| \leq \|p\|\omega(\|\vartheta\|)\mathfrak{G}.$$

Consequently

$$\|\vartheta\| \leq \|p\|\omega(\|\vartheta\|)\mathfrak{G},$$

or

$$\frac{\|\vartheta\|}{\|q\|z(\|\vartheta\|)\mathfrak{G}} \leq 1.$$

In view of (H_3), there exists $\mathfrak{K}$ such that $\|\vartheta\| \neq \mathfrak{K}$. Let us set

$$\mathcal{U} = \{\vartheta \in C([a,b],\mathbb{R}) : \|\vartheta\| < \mathfrak{K}\}.$$

The operator $\mathcal{F} : \overline{\mathcal{U}} \to \mathcal{P}(C([a,b],\mathbb{R}))$ is a compact multivalued map, upper semi-continuous with convex closed values. There is no $\vartheta \in \partial\mathcal{U}$ such that $\vartheta \in \nu\mathcal{F}(\vartheta)$ for some $\nu \in (0,1)$, from the choice of $\mathcal{U}$.

By the nonlinear alternative of Leray–Schauder type $\mathcal{F}$ has a fixed point $\vartheta \in \overline{\mathcal{U}}$ which is a solution of the (k,ϕ)-Hilfer nonlocal multi-point fractional boundary value problem (17). This ends the proof. □

In our second result, the existence of solutions for the (k,ϕ)-Hilfer nonlocal multipoint fractional boundary value problem (17) is showed when F is not necessarily nonconvex valued by using a fixed-point theorem for multivalued contractive maps due to Covitz and Nadler [30].

Theorem 5. *Assume that the following conditions hold:*

(A_1) $\mathfrak{F} : [a,b] \times \mathbb{R} \to \mathcal{P}_{cp}(\mathbb{R})$ *is such that* $\mathfrak{f}(\cdot,\vartheta) : [a,b] \to \mathcal{P}_{cp}(\mathbb{R})$ *is measurable for each* $\vartheta \in \mathbb{R}$.

(A_2) $H_d(\mathfrak{F}(w,\vartheta),\mathfrak{F}(w,\bar{\vartheta})) \leq m(w)|\vartheta - \bar{\vartheta}|$ *for almost all* $w \in [a,b]$ *and* $\vartheta, \bar{\vartheta} \in \mathbb{R}$ *with* $m \in C([a,b],\mathbb{R}^+)$ *and* $d(0,\mathfrak{f}(w,0)) \leq m(w)$ *for almost all* $w \in [a,b]$.

Then the (k,ϕ)-Hilfer nonlocal multipoint fractional boundary value problem (17) has at least one solution on $[a,b]$ if

$$\delta := \mathfrak{G}\|m\| < 1. \tag{27}$$

Proof. By the assumption (A_1), the set $S_{\mathfrak{F},\vartheta}$ is nonempty for each $\vartheta \in C([a,b],\mathbb{R})$. Hence $\mathfrak{F}$ has a measurable selection (see Theorem III.6 [31]). We show that $\mathcal{F}(\vartheta) \in \mathcal{P}_{cl}(C([a,b],\mathbb{R}))$ for each $\vartheta \in C([a,b],\mathbb{R})$. Let $\{u_n\}_{n\geq 0} \in \mathcal{F}(\vartheta)$ be such that $u_n \to u$ $(n \to \infty)$ in $C([a,b],\mathbb{R})$. Then $u \in C([a,b],\mathbb{R})$ and there exists $v_n \in S_{\mathfrak{F},\vartheta_n}$ such that, for each $w \in [a,b]$,

$$u_n(w) = \frac{(\phi(w)-\phi(a))^{\frac{\theta_k}{k}-1}}{\mathcal{H}\Gamma_k(\theta_k)}\Big[\sum_{i=1}^{m}\lambda_i {}^k\mathfrak{J}^{\bar{\alpha};\phi}v_n(\xi_i) - {}^k\mathfrak{J}^{\bar{\alpha};\phi}v_n(b)\Big] + {}^k\mathfrak{J}^{\bar{\alpha};\phi}v_n(w).$$

As $\mathfrak{F}$ has compact values, we pass onto a subsequence (if necessary) to obtain that v_n converges to v in $L^1([a,b],\mathbb{R})$. Thus, $v \in S_{\mathfrak{F},\vartheta}$ and for each $w \in [a,b]$, we have

$$u_n(w) \to u(w) = \frac{(\phi(w)-\phi(a))^{\frac{\theta_k}{k}-1}}{\mathcal{H}\Gamma_k(\theta_k)}\Big[\sum_{i=1}^{m}\lambda_i {}^k\mathfrak{J}^{\bar{\alpha};\phi}v_n(\xi_i) - {}^k\mathfrak{J}^{\bar{\alpha}\phi}v_n(b)\Big] + {}^k\mathfrak{J}^{\bar{\alpha};\phi}v_n(w).$$

Hence, $u \in \mathcal{F}(\vartheta)$.

Next we show that

$$H_d(\mathcal{F}(\vartheta),\mathcal{F}(\bar{\vartheta})) \leq \delta\|\vartheta - \bar{\vartheta}\|, \ \ \delta < 1, \ \ \textit{for each} \ \ \vartheta, \bar{\vartheta} \in C^2([a,b],\mathbb{R}).$$

Let $\vartheta, \bar{\vartheta} \in C^2([a,b],\mathbb{R})$ and $h_1 \in \mathcal{F}(x)$. Then there exists $v_1(w) \in \mathfrak{F}(w,\vartheta(w))$ such that, for each $w \in [a,b]$,

$$h_1(w) = \frac{(\phi(w)-\phi(a))^{\frac{\theta_k}{k}-1}}{\mathcal{H}\Gamma_k(\theta_k)}\Big[\sum_{i=1}^{m}\lambda_i {}^k\mathfrak{J}^{\bar{\alpha};\phi}v_1(\xi_i) - {}^k\mathfrak{J}^{\bar{\alpha};\phi}v_1(b)\Big] + {}^k\mathfrak{J}^{\bar{\alpha};\phi}v_1(w).$$

By (A_2), we have

$$H_d(\mathfrak{F}(w,\vartheta),\mathfrak{F}(w,\bar{\vartheta})) \leq m(w)|\vartheta(w) - \bar{\vartheta}(w)|.$$

So, there exists $\omega \in \mathfrak{f}(w,\bar{x}(w))$ such that

$$|v_1(w) - \omega| \leq m(w)|\vartheta(w) - \bar{\vartheta}(w)|, \ \ w \in [a,b].$$

Define $U : [a,b] \to \mathcal{P}(\mathbb{R})$ by

$$U(w) = \{w \in \mathbb{R} : |v_1(w) - \omega| \leq m(w)|\vartheta(w) - \bar{\vartheta}(w)|\}.$$

Since the multivalued operator $U(w) \cap \mathfrak{F}(w, \bar{\vartheta}(w))$ is measurable (Proposition III.4 [31]), there exists a function $v_2(w)$ which is a measurable selection for U. So $v_2(w) \in \mathfrak{F}(w, \bar{\vartheta}(w))$ and for each $w \in [a,b]$, we have $|v_1(w) - v_2(w)| \leq m(w)|\vartheta(w) - \bar{\vartheta}(w)|$.

For each $w \in [a,b]$, let us define

$$h_2(w) = \frac{(\phi(w) - \phi(a))^{\frac{\theta_k}{k}-1}}{\mathcal{H}\Gamma_k(\theta_k)}\Big[\sum_{i=1}^{m} \lambda_i {}^k\mathfrak{J}^{\bar{\alpha};\phi} v_2(\xi_i) - {}^k\mathfrak{J}^{\bar{\alpha};\phi} v_2(b)\Big] + {}^k\mathfrak{J}^{\bar{\alpha};\phi} v_2(w).$$

Thus,

$$\begin{aligned}
&|h_1(w) - h_2(w)| \\
\leq\ & \frac{(\phi(w) - \phi(a))^{\frac{\theta_k}{k}-1}}{\mathcal{H}\Gamma_k(\theta_k)}\Big[\sum_{i=1}^{m} \lambda_i {}^k\mathfrak{J}^{\bar{\alpha};\phi}(|v_1(s) - v_2(s)|)(\xi_i) + {}^k\mathfrak{J}^{\bar{\alpha};\phi}(|v_1(s) - v_2(s)|)(b)\Big] \\
& + {}^k\mathfrak{J}^{\bar{\alpha};\phi}(|v_1(s) - v_2(s)|)(w) \\
\leq\ & \Bigg\{\frac{(\phi(b) - \phi(a))^{\frac{\bar{\alpha}}{k}}}{\Gamma_k(\bar{\alpha} + k)} + \frac{(\phi(b) - \phi(a))^{\frac{\theta_k}{k}-1}}{|\mathcal{H}|\Gamma_k(\theta_k)}\Bigg[\sum_{i=1}^{m} |\lambda_i| \frac{(\phi(\xi_i) - \phi(a))^{\frac{\bar{\alpha}}{k}}}{\Gamma_k(\bar{\alpha} + k)} \\
& + \frac{(\phi(b) - \phi(a))^{\frac{\bar{\alpha}}{k}}}{\Gamma_k(\bar{\alpha} + k)}\Bigg]\Bigg\} \|m\| \|\vartheta - \bar{\vartheta}\| \\
=\ & \mathfrak{G}\|m\| \|\vartheta - \bar{\vartheta}\|.
\end{aligned}$$

Hence

$$\|h_1 - h_2\| \leq \mathfrak{G}\|m\| \|\vartheta - \bar{\vartheta}\|.$$

Analogously, interchanging the roles of x and $\bar{x}$, we obtain

$$H_d(\mathcal{F}(\vartheta), \mathcal{F}(\bar{\vartheta})) \leq \mathfrak{G}\|m\| \|\vartheta - \bar{v}\|.$$

So $\mathcal{F}$ is a contraction and by Covitz and Nadler theorem $\mathcal{F}$ has a fixed point ϑ which is a solution of the (k,ϕ)-Hilfer nonlocal multipoint fractional boundary value problem (17). This completes the proof. □

5. Examples

Now, we present some examples to show the applicability of our results.

Example 1. *Consider the following multipoint boundary value problems for (k,ϕ)-Hilfer fractional derivative of the form*

$$\begin{cases} {}^{\frac{1}{6},H}\mathfrak{D}^{\frac{3}{2},\frac{4}{5};w^7e^{-2w}}\vartheta(w) = \mathfrak{f}(w, \vartheta(w)), \quad \frac{1}{5} < w < \frac{8}{5}, \\ \vartheta\left(\frac{1}{5}\right) = 0, \quad \vartheta\left(\frac{8}{5}\right) = \frac{1}{11}\vartheta\left(\frac{2}{5}\right) + \frac{3}{22}\vartheta\left(\frac{3}{5}\right) \\ \qquad + \frac{5}{33}\vartheta\left(\frac{4}{5}\right) + \frac{7}{44}\vartheta\left(\frac{6}{5}\right) + \frac{9}{55}\vartheta\left(\frac{7}{5}\right). \end{cases} \tag{28}$$

Here $\bar{\alpha} = 3/2$, $\beta = 4/5$, $\phi(w) = w^7e^{-2w}$, $k = 1/6$, $a = 1/5$, $b = 8/5$, $m = 5$, $\lambda_1 = 1/11$, $\lambda_2 = 3/22$, $\lambda_3 = 5/33$, $\lambda_4 = 7/44$, $\lambda_5 = 9/55$, $\xi_1 = 2/5$, $\xi_2 = 3/5$, $\xi_3 = 4/5$, $\xi_4 = 6/5$, $\xi_5 = 7/5$. By direct computation, we get $\theta_{\frac{1}{6}} = 17/30$, $\Gamma_{\frac{1}{6}}(\theta_{\frac{1}{6}}) \approx 0.04044166691$, $\mathcal{H} \approx 29.03126784$, $\mathfrak{G} \approx 128.5303681$, $\mathfrak{G}_1 \approx 66.09288339$.

(i) Let a nonlinear unbounded $\mathfrak{f}(w,\vartheta)$ be given by

$$\mathfrak{f}(w,\vartheta) = \frac{e^{-(5w-1)^2}}{40(5w+6)}\left(\frac{\vartheta^2+|\vartheta|}{1+|\vartheta|}\right) + \frac{1}{3}w + \frac{1}{2}. \tag{29}$$

Then we can show that,

$$|\mathfrak{f}(w,\vartheta_1) - \mathfrak{f}(w,\vartheta_2)| \leq \frac{1}{140}|\vartheta_1 - \vartheta_2|,$$

for $w \in [1/5, 8/5]$ and $\vartheta_1, \vartheta_2 \in \mathbb{R}$. Therefore, for $\mathfrak{L} = 1/140$, we have $\mathfrak{L}\mathfrak{G} \approx 0.9180740579 < 1$. Thus by Theorem 1 the multipoint boundary value problem for (k,ϕ)-Hilfer fractional derivative (28) with (29) has a unique solution on the interval $[1/5, 8/5]$.

(ii) Let a nonlinear bounded $\mathfrak{f}(w,\vartheta)$ be defined as

$$\mathfrak{f}(w,\vartheta) = \frac{e^{-(5w-1)^2}}{10(5w+6)}\left(\frac{|\vartheta|}{1+|\vartheta|}\right) + \frac{1}{3}w + \frac{1}{2}. \tag{30}$$

Now, we observe that

$$|\mathfrak{f}(w,\vartheta)| \leq \frac{e^{-(5w-1)^2}}{10(5w+6)} + \frac{1}{3}w + \frac{1}{2} := \varpi(w),$$

which is bounded by the known function $\varpi(w)$, $w \in [1/5, 8/5]$. In addition, $\mathfrak{f}$ satisfies the Lipschitz condition (H_1) with Lipschitz constant $\mathfrak{L} = 1/70$. But we can not conclude the uniqueness result, because Theorem 1 can not be applied since $\mathfrak{L}\mathfrak{G} \approx 1.836148116 > 1$. However, since $\mathfrak{L}\mathfrak{G}_1 \approx 0.9441840484 < 1$, we deduce that the boundary value problem (28), with $\mathfrak{f}$ given by (30), has at least one solution on $[1/5, 8/5]$ by Theorem 2.

(iii) Let now a nonlinear $\mathfrak{f}(w,\vartheta)$ be presented by

$$\mathfrak{f}(w,\vartheta) = \frac{1}{2(5w+7)}\left(\frac{\vartheta^{182}}{15(1+\vartheta^{180})} + \frac{1}{18}\right). \tag{31}$$

Note that the nonlinear function can be bounded by quadratic term as

$$|\mathfrak{f}(w,\vartheta)| \leq \frac{1}{2(5w+7)}\left(\frac{1}{15}\vartheta^2 + \frac{1}{18}\right).$$

By setting $\sigma(w) = 1/(2(5w+7))$ and $\chi(u) = (1/15)u^2 + (1/18)$, we have $\|\sigma\| = 1/16$ and, then, there exists $\mathfrak{K} \in (0.7378396700, 1.129423324)$ satisfying condition (H_4) in Theorem 3. By application of Theorem 3, we conclude that the multipoint boundary value problem via (k,ϕ)-Hilfer fractional calculus (28), with $\mathfrak{f}$ given by (30), has at least one solution on $[1/5, 8/5]$.

(iv) Let the first equation of (28) be replaced by

$$_{\frac{1}{6}}{}^{H}\mathfrak{D}^{\frac{3}{2},\frac{4}{5};w^7e^{-2w}}\vartheta(w) \in \mathfrak{F}(w,\vartheta(w)), \quad \frac{1}{5} < w < \frac{8}{5}, \tag{32}$$

where

$$\mathfrak{F}(w,\vartheta) = \left[0, \frac{1}{20(5w+12)}\left(\frac{|\vartheta|}{1+|\vartheta|} + \sin\vartheta + 1\right)\right].$$

Now, we see that $\mathfrak{F}(w,\vartheta)$ is a measurable set. In addition, we have

$$H_d(\mathfrak{F}(w,\vartheta), \mathfrak{F}(w,\overline{\vartheta})) \leq \frac{1}{10(5w+12)}|\vartheta - \overline{\vartheta}|.$$

We set $m(w) = 1/(10(5w+12))$. Therefore, we can check that $d(0, \mathfrak{F}(w,0)) \leq 1/(20(5w+12)) \leq 1/(10(5w+12)) = m(w)$ for almost all $w \in [1/5, 8/5]$. As $\delta =$

$\mathfrak{G}\|m\| \approx 0.9886951392 < 1$, we get that (k,ϕ)-Hilfer fractional inclusion (32) with boundary conditions given in (28), has at least one solution on $[1/5, 8/5]$.

6. Conclusions

In the present research, we have investigated fractional boundary value problems consisting of (k,ϕ)-Hilfer fractional differential equations and inclusions, supplemented by nonlocal multipoint boundary conditions. First we considered the single valued case. After transforming the given problem into a fixed-point problem, we applied the Banach contraction-mapping principle, the Krasnoselskiĭ fixed-point theorem and the Leray–Schauder nonlinear alternative and established existence and uniqueness results. After that, we studied the multivalued case. We considered both cases, convex-valued and nonconvex-valued multivalued maps. In the first case, we established an existence result via a Leray–Schauder nonlinear alternative for multivalued maps, while in the second case the Covitz–Nadler fixed-point theorem for contractive multivalued maps was applied. Numerical examples illustrating the theoretical results are also presented. The used methods are standard, but their configuration in (k,ϕ)-Hilfer nonlocal multipoint fractional boundary value problems is new. To the best of our knowledge, our results in this paper are the only concerning boundary value problems involving (k,ϕ)-Hilfer fractional differential equations and inclusions of order in $(1,2]$. Hence our results will enrich the literature on this new research area.

Author Contributions: Conceptualization, J.T., A.S. and S.K.N.; methodology, J.T., A.S. and S.K.N.; validation, J.T., A.S. and S.K.N.; formal analysis, J.T., A.S. and S.K.N.; writing—original draft preparation, J.T., A.S. and S.K.N.; funding acquisition, J.T. All authors have read and agreed to the published version of the manuscript.

Funding: This research was funded by National Science, Research and Innovation Fund (NSRF), and King Mongkut's University of Technology North Bangkok with Contract no. KMUTNB-FF-65-36.

Institutional Review Board Statement: Not applicable.

Informed Consent Statement: Not applicable.

Data Availability Statement: Not applicable.

Conflicts of Interest: The authors declare no conflict of interest.

References

1. Diethelm, K. *The Analysis of Fractional Differential Equations*; Lecture Notes in Mathematics; Springer: New York, NY, USA, 2010.
2. Kilbas, A.A.; Srivastava, H.M.; Trujillo, J.J. *Theory and Applications of the Fractional Differential Equations*; North-Holland Mathematics Studies; Elsevier: Amsterdam, The Netherlands, 2006; Volume 204.
3. Lakshmikantham, V.; Leela, S.; Devi, J.V. *Theory of Fractional Dynamic Systems*; Cambridge Scientific Publishers: Cambridge, UK, 2009.
4. Miller, K.S.; Ross, B. *An Introduction to the Fractional Calculus and Differential Equations*; John Wiley: New York, NY, USA, 1993.
5. Podlubny, I. *Fractional Differential Equations*; Academic Press: New York, NY, USA, 1999.
6. Samko, S.G.; Kilbas, A.A.; Marichev, O.I. *Fractional Integrals and Derivatives*; Gordon and Breach Science: Yverdon, Switzerland, 1993.
7. Ahmad, B.; Alsaedi, A.; Ntouyas, S.K.; Tariboon, J. *Hadamard-Type Fractional Differential Equations, Inclusions and Inequalities*; Springer: Cham, Switzerland, 2017.
8. Ahmad, B.; Ntouyas, S.K. *Nonlocal Nonlinear Fractional-Order Boundary Value Problems*; World Scientific: Singapore, 2021.
9. Zhou, Y. *Basic Theory of Fractional Differential Equations*; World Scientific: Singapore, 2014.
10. Mubeen, S.; Habibullah, G.M. k–fractional integrals and applications. *Int. J. Contemp. Math. Sci.* **2012**, *7*, 89–94.
11. Diaz, R.; Pariguan, E. On hypergeometric functions and Pochhammer k-symbol. *Divulg. Mat.* **2007**, *2*, 179–192.
12. Dorrego, G.A. An alternative definition for the k-Riemann-Liouville fractional derivative. *Appl. Math. Sci.* **2015**, *9*, 481–491. [CrossRef]
13. Almeida, R. A Caputo fractional derivative of a function with respect to another function. *Commun. Nonlinear Sci. Numer. Simul.* **2017**, *44*, 460–481. [CrossRef]
14. Sousa, J.V.D.C.; De Oliveira, E.C. On the ψ-Hilfer fractional derivative. *Commun. Nonlinear Sci. Numer. Simul.* **2018**, *60*, 72–91. [CrossRef]

15. Kwun, Y.C.; Farid, G.; Nazeer, W.; Ullah, S.; Kang, S.M. Generalized Riemann-Liouville k-fractional integrals associated with Ostrowski type inequalities and error bounds of Hadamard inequalities. *IEEE Access* **2018**, *6*, 64946–64953. [CrossRef]
16. Kucche, K.D.; Mali, A.D. On the nonlinear (k, ψ)-Hilfer fractional differential equations. *Chaos Solitons Fractals* **2021**, *152*, 111335. [CrossRef]
17. Naz, S.; Naeem, M.N. On the generalization of k-fractional Hilfer-Katugampola derivative with Cauchy problem. *Turk. J. Math.* **2021**, *45*, 110–124. [CrossRef]
18. Mittal, E.; Joshi, S. Note on k-generalized fractional derivative. *Discret. Contin. Dyn. Syst.* **2020**, *13*, 797–804.
19. Magar, S.K.; Dole, P.V.; Ghadle, K.P. Pranhakar and Hilfer-Prabhakar fractional derivatives in the setting of ψ-fractional calculus and its applications. *Krak. J. Math.* **2024** , *48*, 515–533.
20. Agarwal, P.; Tariboon, J.; Ntouyas, S.K. Some generalized Riemann-Liouville k-fractional integral inequalities. *J. Ineq. Appl.* **2016**, *2016*, 122. [CrossRef]
21. Farid, G.; Javed, A.; ur Rehman, A. On Hadamard inequalities for n-times differentiable functions which are relative convex via Caputo k-fractional derivatives. *Nonlinear Anal. Forum* **2017**, *22*, 17–28.
22. Azam, M.K.; Farid, G.; Rehman, M.A. Study of generalized type k-fractional derivatives. *Adv. Differ. Equ.* **2017**, *2017*, 249. [CrossRef]
23. Romero, L.G.; Luque, L.L.; Dorrego, G.A.; Cerutti, R.A. On the k-Riemann-Liouville fractional derivative. *Int. J. Contemp. Math. Sci.* **2013**, *8*, 41–51. [CrossRef]
24. Deimling, K. *Nonlinear Functional Analysis*; Springer: New York, NY, USA, 1985.
25. Krasnosel'skiĭ, M.A. Two remarks on the method of successive approximations. *Uspekhi Mat. Nauk.* **1955**, *10*, 123–127.
26. Granas, A.; Dugundji, J. *Fixed Point Theory*; Springer: New York, NY, USA, 2005.
27. Deimling, K. *Multivalued Differential Equations*; Walter De Gruyter: Berlin, Germany; New York, NY, USA, 1992.
28. Hu, S.; Papageorgiou, N. *Handbook of Multivalued Analysis, Theory I*; Kluwer: Dordrecht, The Netherlands, 1997.
29. Lasota, A.; Opial, Z. An application of the Kakutani-Ky Fan theorem in the theory of ordinary differential equations. *Bull. Acad. Polon. Sci. Ser. Sci. Math. Astronom. Phys.* **1965**, *13*, 781–786.
30. Covitz, H.; Nadler, S.B., Jr. Multivalued contraction mappings in generalized metric spaces. *Isr. J. Math.* **1970**, *8*, 5–11. [CrossRef]
31. Castaing, C.; Valadier, M. *Convex Analysis and Measurable Multifunctions*; Lecture Notes in Mathematics 580; Springer: Berlin/Heidelberg, Germany; New York, NY, USA, 1977.

axioms

MDPI

Article

Existence of Mild Solutions for Hilfer Fractional Evolution Equations with Almost Sectorial Operators

Mian Zhou [1], Chengfu Li [1] and Yong Zhou [1,2,*]

1 Faculty of Mathematics and Computational Science, Xiangtan University, Xiangtan 411105, China; 201921001199@smail.xtu.edu.cn (M.Z.); cfli@xtu.edu.cn (C.L.)
2 Faculty of Information Technology, Macau University of Science and Technology, Macau 999078, China
* Correspondence: yzhou@xtu.edu.cn

Abstract: In this paper, we obtain new sufficient conditions of the existence of mild solutions for Hilfer fractional evolution equations in the cases that the semigroup associated with an almost sectorial operator is compact as well as noncompact. Our results improve and extend some recent results in references.

Keywords: fractional evolution equations; Hilfer derivative; almost sectorial operator; mild solutions

MSC: 26A33; 34A08; 34K37

Citation: Zhou, M.; Li, C.; Zhou, Y. Existence of Mild Solutions for Hilfer Fractional Evolution Equations with Almost Sectorial Operators. *Axioms* **2022**, *11*, 144. https://doi.org/10.3390/axioms11040144

Academic Editor: António M. Lopes

Received: 10 February 2022
Accepted: 15 March 2022
Published: 22 March 2022

1. Introduction

In the past two decades, fractional differential equations are widely used in the mathematical modeling of real-world phenomena. These applications have motivated many researchers in the field of differential equations to investigate fractional differential equations with different fractional derivatives, see the monographs [1–4] and the recent references.

The main motivation of studying fractional evolution equation comes from two aspects. Firstly, many mathematical models in physics and fluid mechanics are characterized by fractional partial differential equations. Secondly, many types of fractional partial differential equations, such as fractional diffusion equations, wave equations, Navier–Stokes equations, Rayleigh–Stokes equations, Fokker–Planck equations, Schrödinger equations, and so on, can be abstracted as fractional evolution equations, for example, see [5–7]. Therefore, the study of fractional evolution equations is very valuable in both theory and application. Indeed, the well-posedness of fractional evolution equations has become an important research topic of evolution equations (see [8–18]).

In this paper, we consider the Cauchy problem of fractional evolution equations with an almost sectorial operator

$$\begin{cases} {}^{H}D_{0+}^{\lambda,\nu}y(t) = Ay(t) + g(t, y(t)), \quad t \in (0, T], \\ I_{0+}^{(1-\lambda)(1-\nu)}y(0) = y_0, \end{cases} \tag{1}$$

where ${}^{H}D_{0+}^{\lambda,\nu}$ is the Hilfer fractional derivative of order $0 < \lambda < 1$ and type $0 \le \nu \le 1$, $I_{0+}^{(1-\lambda)(1-\nu)}$ is Riemann–Liouville fractional integral of order $(1-\lambda)(1-\nu)$, A is an almost sectorial operator in Banach space X, $g : [0, T] \times X \to X$ is a function to be defined later, $y_0 \in X, T \in (0, \infty)$.

The Hilfer fractional derivative is a natural generalization of Riemann–Liouville derivative and Caputo derivative, see [1]. It is obvious that fractional differential equations with Hilfer derivatives include fractional differential equations with Riemann–Liouville derivative or Caputo derivative as special cases. In the past few years, fractional differential equations with Hilfer fractional derivative received great attention from many researchers (see [8–18]).

In this paper, we will prove new existence theorems of mild solutions for (1) in the cases that the semigroup associated with the almost sectorial operator is compact as well as noncompact. In particular, our results obtained in this paper essentially improve and extend the known results in [4,9,10]. The rest of this paper is organized as follows: in Section 2, we will introduce almost sectorial operators, fractional calculus and the measure of noncompactness which will be used in this paper. In Section 3, we will give some useful lemmas before proving the main results. In Section 4, we will show some new existence results of mild solutions for Cauchy problem (1). In Section 5, we will point out that the definitions of the operators in [10,16–18] are inappropriate.

2. Preliminaries

We first introduce some notations and definitions about almost sectorial operators, fractional calculus and the Kuratowski's measure of noncompactness. For more details, we refer to [1,2,19,20].

Assume that X is a Banach space with the norm $|\cdot|$. Let $\mathbb{R} = (-\infty, \infty)$, $\mathbb{R}^+ = (0, \infty)$ and J be a finite interval of $\mathbb{R}$. By $C(J, X)$ we denote the Banach space of all continuous functions from J to X with the norm $\|u\| = \sup_{t\in J} |u(t)| < \infty$. We denote by $\mathcal{L}(X)$ the space of all bounded linear operators from X to X with the usual operator norm $\|\cdot\|_{\mathcal{L}(X)}$.

Let A be a linear operator from X to itself. Denote by $D(A)$ the domain of A, by $\sigma(A)$ its spectrum, while $\rho(A) := \mathbb{C} - \sigma(A)$ is the resolvent set of A. Let $S_\mu^0 = \{z \in \mathbb{C}\backslash\{0\} : |\arg z| < \mu\}$ be the open sector for $0 < \mu < \pi$, and S_μ be its closure, i.e., $S_\mu = \{z \in \mathbb{C}\backslash\{0\} : |\arg z| \leq \mu\} \cup \{0\}$.

Definition 1. *Let $0 < k < 1$ and $0 < \omega < \frac{\pi}{2}$. We denote $\Theta_\omega^{-k}(X)$ as a family of all closed linear operators $A : D(A) \subset X \to X$ such that*

(i) $\sigma(A) \subset S_\omega = \{z \in \mathbb{C} \setminus \{0\} : |\arg z| \leq \omega\} \cup \{0\}$ *and*

(ii) *for any $\mu \in (\omega, \pi)$, there exists C_μ such that*

$$\|R(z; A)\|_{\mathcal{L}(X)} \leq C_\mu |z|^{-k}, \text{ for all } z \subset \mathbb{C} \setminus S_\mu,$$

where $R(z; A) = (zI - A)^{-1}, z \in \rho(A)$ is the resolvent operator of A. The linear operator A will be called an almost sectorial operator on X if $A \in \Theta_\omega^{-k}(X)$.

Define the power of A as

$$A^\beta = \frac{1}{2\pi i} \int_{\Gamma_\rho} z^\beta R(z; A) dz, \quad \beta > 1 - k,$$

where $\Gamma_\rho = \{\mathbb{R}^+ e^{i\rho}\} \bigcup \{\mathbb{R}^+ e^{-i\rho}\}$ is an appropriate path oriented counterclockwise and $\omega < \rho < \mu$. Then, the linear power space $X_\beta := D(A^\beta)$ can be defined and X_β is a Banach space with the graph norm $\|y\|_\beta = |A^\beta y|, y \in D(A^\beta)$.

Next, let us introduce the semigroup associated with A. We denote the semigroup associated with A by $\{Q(t)\}_{t\geq 0}$. For $t \in S^0_{\frac{\pi}{2}-\omega}$

$$Q(t) = e^{-tz}(A) = \frac{1}{2\pi i} \int_{\Gamma_\rho} e^{-tz} R(z; A) dz,$$

where the integral contour $\Gamma_\rho = \{\mathbb{R}^+ e^{i\rho}\} \bigcup \{\mathbb{R}^+ e^{-i\rho}\}$ is oriented counter-clockwise and $\omega < \rho < \mu < \frac{\pi}{2} - |\arg t|$, forms an analytic semigroup of growth order $1 - k$.

Lemma 1 (see [19]). *Assume that $0 < k < 1$ and $0 < \omega < \frac{\pi}{2}$. Set $A \in \Theta_\omega^{-k}(X)$. Then*

(i) $Q(s + t) = Q(s)Q(t)$, *for any* $s, t \in S^0_{\frac{\pi}{2}-\omega}$;

(ii) *there exists a constant $C_0 > 0$ such that $\|Q(t)\|_{\mathcal{L}(X)} \leq C_0 t^{k-1}$, for any $t > 0$;*

(iii) *The range* $R(Q(t))$ *of* $Q(t)$, $t \in S^0_{\frac{\pi}{2}-\omega}$ *is contained in* $D(A^\infty)$. *Particularly,* $R(Q(t)) \subset D(A^\beta)$ *for all* $\beta \in \mathbb{C}$ *with* $Re(\beta) > 0$,

$$A^\beta Q(t)y = \frac{1}{2\pi i}\int_{\Gamma_\theta} z^\beta e^{-tz} R(z;A)y dz, \text{ for all } y \in X,$$

and hence there exists a constant $C' = C'(\gamma,\beta) > 0$ *such that*

$$\|A^\beta Q(t)\|_{B(X)} \le C' t^{-\gamma - Re(\beta) - 1}, \text{ for all } t > 0;$$

(iv) *If* $\beta > 1-k$, *then* $D(A^\beta) \subset \Sigma_Q = \{y \in X : \lim_{t\to 0+} Q(t)y = y\}$;
(v) $R(\lambda, A) = \int_0^\infty e^{-\lambda t} Q(t)dt$, *for every* $\lambda \in \mathbb{C}$ *with* $Re(\lambda) > 0$.

Definition 2 (Riemann-Liouville fractional integral, see [2]). *The fractional integral of order* λ *for a function* $y : [0,\infty) \to \mathbb{R}$ *is defined as*

$$I^\lambda_{0+} y(t) = \frac{1}{\Gamma(\lambda)}\int_0^t (t-s)^{\lambda-1} y(s)ds, \quad \lambda > 0,\ t > 0,$$

provided the right side is point-wise defined on $[0,\infty)$, *where* $\Gamma(\cdot)$ *is the gamma function.*

Definition 3 (Hilfer fractional derivative, see [1]). *Let* $0 < \lambda < 1$ *and* $0 \le \nu \le 1$. *The Hilfer fractional derivative of order* λ *and type* ν *for a function* $y : [0,\infty) \to \mathbb{R}$ *is defined as*

$$^H D^{\lambda,\nu}_{0+} y(t) = I^{\nu(1-\lambda)}_{0+} \frac{d}{dt} I^{(1-\lambda)(1-\nu)}_{0+} y(t).$$

In particular, when $\nu = 0$, $0 < \lambda < 1$, then

$$^H D^{\lambda,0}_{0+} y(t) = \frac{d}{dt} I^{1-\lambda}_{0+} y(t) =: {}^L D^\lambda_{0+} y(t),$$

where ${}^L D^\lambda_{0+}$ is Riemann–Liouville derivative.
If $\nu = 1$, $0 < \lambda < 1$, then

$$^H D^{\lambda,1}_{0+} y(t) = I^{1-\lambda}_{0+} \frac{d}{dt} y(t) =: {}^C D^\lambda_{0+} y(t),$$

where ${}^C D^\lambda_{0+}$ is Caputo derivative.

Let D be a nonempty subset of X. The Kuratowski's measure of noncompactness α is defined as follows:

$$\alpha(D) = \inf\left\{ d > 0 : D \subset \bigcup_{j=1}^n M_j \text{ and } \operatorname{diam}(M_j) \le d \right\},$$

where the diameter of M_j is given by $\operatorname{diam}(M_j) = \sup\{|x-y| : x,y \in M_j\}$, $j = 1,\dots,n$.

Lemma 2 ([21]). *Let* X *be a Banach space, and let* $\{u_n(t)\}_{n=1}^\infty : [0,T] \to X$ *be a continuous function family. If there exists* $\xi \in L[0,T]$ *such that*

$$|u_n(t)| \le \xi(t), \quad t \in [0,T],\ n = 1,2,\dots.$$

Then $\alpha(\{u_n(t)\}_{n=1}^\infty)$ *is integrable on* $[0,T]$, *and*

$$\alpha\left(\left\{ \int_0^t u_n(s)ds \right\}_{n=1}^\infty\right) \le 2\int_0^t \alpha(\{u_n(s)\}_{n=1}^\infty)ds.$$

Definition 4 ([22]). *Define the wright function* $M_\lambda(\theta)$ *by*

$$M_\lambda(\theta) = \sum_{n=1}^{\infty} \frac{(-\theta)^{n-1}}{(n-1)!\Gamma(1-\lambda n)}, \quad 0 < \lambda < 1, \, \theta \in \mathbb{C},$$

with the following property

$$\int_0^\infty \theta^\delta M_\lambda(\theta) d\theta = \frac{\Gamma(1+\delta)}{\Gamma(1+\lambda\delta)}, \quad \text{for } \delta \geq 0.$$

Lemma 3 ([9]). *The problem* (1) *is equivalent to the integral equation*

$$\begin{aligned} y(t) = & \frac{y_0}{\Gamma(\nu(1-\lambda)+\lambda)} t^{-(1-\lambda)(1-\nu)} \\ & + \frac{1}{\Gamma(\lambda)} \int_0^t (t-s)^{\lambda-1} [Ay(s) + g(s, y(s))] ds, \quad t \in (0, T]. \end{aligned} \tag{2}$$

Lemma 4. *Assume that* $y(t)$ *satisfies integral Equation* (2)*. Then*

$$y(t) = \mathcal{S}_{\lambda,\nu}(t) y_0 + \int_0^t \mathcal{K}_\lambda(t-s) g(s, y(s)) ds, \quad t \in (0, T],$$

where

$$\mathcal{S}_{\lambda,\nu}(t) = I_{0+}^{\nu(1-\lambda)} \mathcal{K}_\lambda(t), \; \mathcal{K}_\lambda(t) = t^{\lambda-1} \mathcal{Q}_\lambda(t), \text{ and } \mathcal{Q}_\lambda(t) = \int_0^\infty \lambda\theta M_\lambda(\theta) Q(t^\lambda \theta) d\theta.$$

Proof. This proof is similar to [9], so we omit it. □

In view of Lemma 4, we have the following definition.

Definition 5. *If* $y \in C((0, T], X)$ *satisfies*

$$y(t) = \mathcal{S}_{\lambda,\nu}(t) y_0 + \int_0^t \mathcal{K}_\lambda(t-s) g(s, y(s)) ds, \quad t \in (0, T],$$

then $y(t)$ *is called a mild solution of the Cauchy problem* (1).

Lemma 5 ([10]). *If* $\{Q(t)\}_{t>0}$ *is a compact operator, then* $\{\mathcal{S}_{\lambda,\nu}(t)\}_{t>0}$ *and* $\{\mathcal{Q}_\lambda(t)\}_{t>0}$ *are also compact operators.*

Lemma 6 ([4]). *Let* $\beta > 1 - k$*. For all* $y \in D(A^\beta)$*, we have* $\lim_{t \to 0+} \mathcal{Q}_\lambda(t) y = \frac{y}{\Gamma(\lambda)}$.

Lemma 7. *Assume that* $\{Q(t)\}_{t>0}$ *is a compact operator. Then* $\{Q(t)\}_{t>0}$ *is equicontinuous.*

Lemma 8 (See also [10]). *For any fixed* $t > 0$, $\mathcal{Q}_\lambda(t)$, $\mathcal{K}_\lambda(t)$ *and* $\mathcal{S}_{\lambda,\nu}(t)$ *are linear operators, and for any* $y \in X$,

$$|\mathcal{Q}_\lambda(t) y| \leq L_1 t^{\lambda(k-1)} |y|, \; |\mathcal{K}_\lambda(t) y| \leq L_1 t^{\lambda k - 1} |y|, \text{ and } |\mathcal{S}_{\lambda,\nu}(t) y| \leq L_2 t^{-1+\nu-\lambda\nu+\lambda k} |y|,$$

where

$$L_1 = \frac{C_0 \Gamma(k)}{\Gamma(\lambda k)}, \quad L_2 = \frac{C_0 \Gamma(k)}{\Gamma(\nu(1-\lambda)+\lambda k)}.$$

Proof. By

$$\int_0^\infty \theta^\delta M_\lambda(\theta) d\theta = \frac{\Gamma(1+\delta)}{\Gamma(1+\lambda\delta)}, \text{ for } \delta \geq 0,$$

we have

$$\begin{aligned}|\mathcal{Q}_\lambda(t)y| =& \left|\int_0^\infty \lambda\theta M_\lambda(\theta)Q(t^\lambda\theta)yd\theta\right| \\ \leq& \lambda C_0\int_0^\infty M_\lambda(\theta)\theta^k t^{\lambda(k-1)}|y|d\theta \\ \leq& L_1 t^{\lambda(k-1)}|y|, \text{ for } t\in(0,T] \text{ and } y\in X.\end{aligned}$$

Moreover, for $t \in (0,T]$ and $y \in X$,

$$|\mathcal{K}_\lambda(t)y| = |t^{\lambda-1}\mathcal{Q}_\lambda(t)y| \leq L_1 t^{\lambda k-1}|y|,$$

and

$$\begin{aligned}|\mathcal{S}_{\lambda,\nu}(t)y| = |I_{0+}^{\nu(1-\lambda)}\mathcal{K}_\lambda(t)y| =& \left|\frac{1}{\Gamma(\nu(1-\lambda))}\int_0^t (t-s)^{\nu(1-\lambda)-1}\mathcal{K}_\lambda(s)yds\right| \\ \leq& \frac{C_0\Gamma(k)}{\Gamma(\lambda k)\Gamma(\nu(1-\lambda))}\int_0^t (t-s)^{\nu(1-\lambda)-1}s^{\lambda k-1}|y|ds \\ \leq& L_2 t^{-1+\nu-\lambda\nu+\lambda k}|y|.\end{aligned}$$

This completes the proof. □

Lemma 9 ([10]). *Assume that $\{Q(t)\}_{t>0}$ is equicontinuous. Then $\{\mathcal{Q}_\lambda(t)\}_{t>0}$, $\{\mathcal{K}_\lambda(t)\}_{t>0}$ and $\{\mathcal{S}_{\lambda,\nu}(t)\}_{t>0}$ are strongly continuous, that is, for any $y \in X$ and $t'' > t' > 0$,*

$$\begin{aligned}&|\mathcal{Q}_\lambda(t')y - \mathcal{Q}_\lambda(t'')y| \to 0,\ |\mathcal{K}_\lambda(t')y - \mathcal{K}_\lambda(t'')y| \to 0, \\ &|\mathcal{S}_{\lambda,\nu}(t')y - \mathcal{S}_{\lambda,\nu}(t'')y| \to 0, \quad \text{as } t'' \to t'.\end{aligned}$$

3. Some Lemmas

Throughout this paper, we assume that $A \in \Theta_\omega^{-k}(X)$, $0 < k < 1$ and $0 < \omega < \frac{\pi}{2}$. Furthermore, we suppose that $y_0 \in D(A^\beta)$ with $\beta > 1-k$.

We introduce the following hypotheses:

(H1) $Q(t)$ is continuous in the uniform operator topology for $t > 0$, i.e., $\{Q(t)\}_{t>0}$ is equicontinuous.

(H2) the map $t \to g(t,y)$ is measurable for all $y \in X$ and the map $y \to g(t,y)$ is continuous for a.e. $t \in [0,T]$.

(H3) there exists a function $m \in L((0,T],\mathbb{R}^+)$ satisfying

$$I_{0+}^{\lambda k}m \in C((0,T],\mathbb{R}^+), \quad \lim_{t\to 0+} t^{1-\nu+\lambda\nu-\lambda k}I_{0+}^{\lambda k}m(t) = 0$$

and $|g(t,y)| \leq m(t)$, for a.e. $t \in (0,T]$ and any $y \in X$.

(H4) there exists a constant $r > 0$ such that

$$L_2|y_0| + L_1\sup_{t\in[0,T]}\left\{t^{1-\nu+\lambda\nu-\lambda k}\int_0^t (t-s)^{\lambda k-1}m(s)ds\right\} \leq r,$$

where

$$L_1 = \frac{C_0\Gamma(k)}{\Gamma(\lambda k)}, \quad L_2 = \frac{C_0\Gamma(k)}{\Gamma(\nu(1-\lambda)+\lambda k)}.$$

Let

$$C_\lambda((0,T],X) = \{y \in C((0,T],X) : \lim_{t\to 0+} t^{1-\nu+\lambda\nu-\lambda k}|y(t)| \text{ exists and is finite}\},$$

with the norm

$$\|y\|_\lambda = \sup_{t\in(0,T]} \{t^{1-\nu+\lambda\nu-\lambda k}|y(t)|\}.$$

Then $(C_\lambda((0,T],X), \|\cdot\|_\lambda)$ is a Banach space (see Lemma 3.2 of [23]).

For any $y \in C_\lambda((0,T],X)$, define an operator $\mathcal{T}$ as follows

$$(\mathcal{T}y)(t) = (\mathcal{T}_1 y)(t) + (\mathcal{T}_2 y)(t),$$

where

$$(\mathcal{T}_1 y)(t) = \mathcal{S}_{\lambda,\nu}(t)y_0, \quad (\mathcal{T}_2 y)(t) = \int_0^t \mathcal{K}_\lambda(t-s)g(s,y(s))ds, \quad \text{for } t \in (0,T].$$

Clearly, the problem (1) has a mild solution $y^* \in C_\lambda((0,T],X)$ if and only if $\mathcal{T}$ has a fixed point $y^* \in C_\lambda((0,T],X)$.

It is easy to show that

$$\lim_{t\to 0+} t^{1-\nu+\lambda\nu-\lambda k}\mathcal{S}_{\lambda,\nu}(t)y_0 = 0. \tag{3}$$

In fact,

$$\begin{aligned} t^{1-\nu+\lambda\nu-\lambda k}\mathcal{S}_{\lambda,\nu}(t)y_0 &= \frac{t^{1-\nu+\lambda\nu-\lambda k}}{\Gamma(\nu(1-\lambda))}\int_0^t (t-s)^{\nu(1-\lambda)-1}s^{\lambda-1}\mathcal{Q}_\lambda(s)y_0 ds \\ &= \frac{1}{\Gamma(\nu(1-\lambda))}\int_0^1 (1-z)^{\nu(1-\lambda)-1}z^{\lambda-1}t^{\lambda(1-k)}\mathcal{Q}_\lambda(tz)y_0 dz. \end{aligned}$$

By lemma 6, $\lim_{t\to 0+} t^{\lambda(1-k)}\mathcal{Q}_\lambda(tz)y_0 = 0$ and $\int_0^1 (1-z)^{\nu(1-\lambda)-1}z^{\lambda-1}dz$ exists, so (3) holds.

In addition, from Lemma 8 and (H3), we have

$$\begin{aligned} \left|t^{1-\nu+\lambda\nu-\lambda k}\int_0^t \mathcal{K}_\lambda(t-s)g(s,y(s))ds\right| &\le L_1 t^{1-\nu+\lambda\nu-\lambda k}\int_0^t (t-s)^{\lambda k-1}m(s)ds \\ &\to 0, \quad \text{as } t \to 0. \end{aligned} \tag{4}$$

For any $u \in C([0,T],X)$, set

$$y(t) = t^{-(1-\nu+\lambda\nu-\lambda k)}u(t), \quad t \in (0,T].$$

Clearly, $y \in C_\lambda((0,T],X)$. Define an operator $\mathcal{F}$ as follows

$$(\mathcal{F}u)(t) = (\mathcal{F}_1 u)(t) + (\mathcal{F}_2 u)(t),$$

where

$$(\mathcal{F}_1 u)(t) = \begin{cases} t^{1-\nu+\lambda\nu-\lambda k}(\mathcal{T}_1 y)(t), & \text{for } t \in (0,T], \\ 0, & \text{for } t = 0, \end{cases}$$

$$(\mathcal{F}_2 u)(t) = \begin{cases} t^{1-\nu+\lambda\nu-\lambda k}(\mathcal{T}_2 y)(t), & \text{for } t \in (0,T], \\ 0, & \text{for } t = 0. \end{cases}$$

Let

$$\Omega_r = \{u \in C([0,T],X) : \|u\| \le r\}.$$

and

$$\widetilde{\Omega}_r = \{y \in C_\lambda((0,T],X) : \|y\|_\lambda \le r\}.$$

Clearly, Ω_r and $\widetilde{\Omega}_r$ are nonempty, convex and closed subsets of $C([0,T],X)$ and $C_\lambda((0,T],X)$, respectively.

Before giving the main results, we first prove the following lemmas.

Lemma 10. *Assume that (H1)–(H4) hold. Then, the set* $\{\mathcal{F}u : u \in \Omega_r\}$ *is equicontinuous.*

Proof. Step I. We first prove that $\{\mathcal{F}_1 u : u \in \Omega_r\}$ is equicontinuous.

For $t_1 = 0$, $t_2 \in (0,T]$, by (3), we obtain

$$\left|(\mathcal{F}_1 u)(t_2) - (\mathcal{F}_1 u)(0)\right| \leq \left|{t_2}^{1-\nu+\lambda\nu-\lambda k}\mathcal{S}_{\lambda,\nu}(t_2)y_0 - 0\right| \to 0, \quad \text{as } t_2 \to 0.$$

For any $t_1, t_2 \in (0,T]$ and $t_1 < t_2$, we have

$$\begin{aligned}\left|(\mathcal{F}_1 u)(t_2) - (\mathcal{F}_1 u)(t_1)\right| \leq & \left|{t_2}^{1-\nu+\lambda\nu-\lambda k}\mathcal{S}_{\lambda,\nu}(t_2)y_0 - {t_1}^{1-\nu+\lambda\nu-\lambda k}\mathcal{S}_{\lambda,\nu}(t_1)y_0\right| \\ \leq & |{t_2}^{1-\nu+\lambda\nu-\lambda k}||\mathcal{S}_{\lambda,\nu}(t_2)y_0 - \mathcal{S}_{\lambda,\nu}(t_1)y_0| \\ & + |{t_2}^{1-\nu+\lambda\nu-\lambda k} - {t_1}^{1-\nu+\lambda\nu-\lambda k}||\mathcal{S}_{\lambda,\nu}(t_1)y_0| \\ \to & 0, \quad \text{as } t_2 \to t_1.\end{aligned}$$

Hence, $\{\mathcal{F}_1 u : u \in \Omega_r\}$ is equicontinuous.

Step II. We prove that $\{\mathcal{F}_2 u : u \in \Omega_r\}$ is equicontinuous.

Let $y(t) = t^{-(1-\nu+\lambda\nu-\lambda k)}u(t)$, for any $u \in \Omega_r$, $t \in (0,T]$. Then $y \in \widetilde{\Omega}_r$.

For $t_1 = 0$, $0 < t_2 < T$, by (4), we have

$$\begin{aligned}\left|(\mathcal{F}_2 u)(t_2) - (\mathcal{F}_2 u)(0)\right| = & \left|{t_2}^{1-\nu+\lambda\nu-\lambda k}\int_0^{t_2}\mathcal{K}_\lambda(t_2 - s)g(s,y(s))ds\right| \\ \to & 0, \quad \text{as } t_2 \to 0.\end{aligned}$$

For $0 < t_1 < t_2 \leq T$, we get

$$\begin{aligned}&|(\mathcal{F}_2 u)(t_2) - (\mathcal{F}_2 u)(t_1)| \\ \leq & \left|{t_1}^{1-\nu+\lambda\nu-\lambda k}\int_{t_1}^{t_2}(t_2 - s)^{\lambda-1}\mathcal{Q}_\lambda(t_2 - s)g(s,y(s))ds\right| \\ & + \left|{t_1}^{1-\nu+\lambda\nu-\lambda k}\int_0^{t_1}\left((t_2 - s)^{\lambda-1} - (t_1 - s)^{\lambda-1}\right)\mathcal{Q}_\lambda(t_2 - s)g(s,y(s))ds\right| \\ & + \left|{t_1}^{1-\nu+\lambda\nu-\lambda k}\int_0^{t_1}(t_1 - s)^{\lambda-1}(\mathcal{Q}_\lambda(t_2 - s) - \mathcal{Q}_\lambda(t_1 - s))g(s,y(s))ds\right| \\ & + \left|{t_2}^{1-\nu+\lambda\nu-\lambda k} - {t_1}^{1-\nu+\lambda\nu-\lambda k}\right|\left|\int_0^{t_2}(t_2 - s)^{\lambda-1}\mathcal{Q}_\lambda(t_2 - s)g(s,y(s))ds\right| \\ \leq & I_1 + I_2 + I_3 + I_4,\end{aligned}$$

where

$$\begin{aligned} I_1 = & L_1 {t_1}^{1-\nu+\lambda\nu-\lambda k}\left|\int_0^{t_2}(t_2 - s)^{\lambda k-1}m(s)ds - \int_0^{t_1}(t_1 - s)^{\lambda k-1}m(s)ds\right|, \\ I_2 = & 2L_1 {t_1}^{1-\nu+\lambda\nu-\lambda k}\int_0^{t_1}\left((t_1 - s)^{\lambda-1} - (t_2 - s)^{\lambda-1}\right)(t_2 - s)^{\lambda(k-1)}m(s)ds, \\ I_3 = & {t_1}^{1-\nu+\lambda\nu-\lambda k}\left|\int_0^{t_1}(t_1 - s)^{\lambda-1}(\mathcal{Q}_\lambda(t_2 - s) - \mathcal{Q}_\lambda(t_1 - s))g(s,y(s))ds\right|, \\ I_4 = & \left|{t_2}^{1-\nu+\lambda\nu-\lambda k} - {t_1}^{1-\nu+\lambda\nu-\lambda k}\right|\left|L_1\int_0^{t_2}(t_2 - s)^{\lambda k-1}m(s)ds\right|.\end{aligned}$$

One can deduce that $\lim_{t_2 \to t_1} I_1 = 0$, since $I_{0+}^{\lambda k} m \in C((0,T], \mathbb{R}^+)$. Noting that

$$((t_1-s)^{\lambda-1} - (t_2-s)^{\lambda-1})(t_2-s)^{\lambda(k-1)} m(s) \le (t_1-s)^{\lambda k-1} m(s), \quad \text{for } s \in [0,t_1),$$

then by Lebesgue dominated convergence theorem, we have

$$\int_0^{t_1} ((t_1-s)^{\lambda-1} - (t_2-s)^{\lambda-1})(t_2-s)^{\lambda(k-1)} m(s) ds \to 0, \quad \text{as } t_2 \to t_1,$$

which implies $I_2 \to 0$ as $t_2 \to t_1$.

By (H3), for $\varepsilon > 0$, we have

$$\begin{aligned}
I_3 \le& {t_1}^{1-\nu+\lambda\nu-\lambda k} \int_0^{t_1-\varepsilon} (t_1-s)^{\lambda-1} \|\mathcal{Q}_\lambda(t_2-s) - \mathcal{Q}_\lambda(t_1-s)\|_{\mathcal{L}(X)} |g(s,y(s))| ds \\
&+ {t_1}^{1-\nu+\lambda\nu-\lambda k} \left| \int_{t_1-\varepsilon}^{t_1} (t_1-s)^{\lambda-1} (\mathcal{Q}_\lambda(t_2-s) - \mathcal{Q}_\lambda(t_1-s)) g(s,y(s)) ds \right| \\
\le& {t_1}^{1-\nu+\lambda\nu-\lambda k} \int_0^{t_1} (t_1-s)^{\lambda-1} m(s) ds \sup_{s\in[0,t_1-\varepsilon]} \|\mathcal{Q}_\lambda(t_2-s) - \mathcal{Q}_\lambda(t_1-s)\|_{\mathcal{L}(X)} \\
&+ 2L_1 {t_1}^{1-\nu+\lambda\nu-\lambda k} \int_{t_1-\varepsilon}^{t_1} (t_1-s)^{\lambda k-1} m(s) ds \\
\le& I_{31} + I_{32} + I_{33},
\end{aligned}$$

where

$$\begin{aligned}
I_{31} =& {t_1}^{1-\nu+\lambda\nu-\lambda k} \int_0^{t_1} (t_1-s)^{\lambda-1} m(s) ds \sup_{s\in[0,t_1-\varepsilon]} \|\mathcal{Q}_\lambda(t_2-s) - \mathcal{Q}_\lambda(t_1-s)\|_{\mathcal{L}(X)}, \\
I_{32} =& 2L_1 {t_1}^{1-\nu+\lambda\nu-\lambda k} \left| \int_0^{t_1} (t_1-s)^{\lambda k-1} m(s) ds - \int_0^{t_1-\varepsilon} (t_1-\varepsilon-s)^{\lambda k-1} m(s) ds \right|, \\
I_{33} =& 2L_1 {t_1}^{1-\nu+\lambda\nu-\lambda k} \int_0^{t_1-\varepsilon} ((t_1-\varepsilon-s)^{\lambda k-1} - (t_1-s)^{\lambda k-1}) m(s) ds.
\end{aligned}$$

By (H1) and Lemma 9, it is easy to see that $I_{31} \to 0$ as $t_2 \to t_1$. Similar to the proof that I_1, I_2 tend to zero, we get $I_{32} \to 0$ and $I_{33} \to 0$ as $\varepsilon \to 0$. Thus, I_3 tends to zero as $t_2 \to t_1$. Clearly, $I_4 \to 0$ as $t_2 \to t_1$.

Therefore, $\{\mathcal{F}_2 u : u \in \Omega_r\}$ is equicontinuous. Furthermore, $\{\mathcal{F} u : u \in \Omega_r\}$ is equicontinuous. □

Lemma 11. *Assume that (H2)–(H4) hold. Then $\mathcal{F}\Omega_r \subset \Omega_r$.*

Proof. Let $y(t) = t^{-(1-\nu+\lambda\nu-\lambda k)} u(t)$, for $u \in \Omega_r$, $t \in (0,T]$. Then $y \in \widetilde{\Omega}_r$.

From Lemmas 10, we know that $\mathcal{F}\Omega_r \subset C([0,T],X)$. For $t > 0$ and any $u \in \Omega_r$, by (H4), we have

$$\begin{aligned}
|(\mathcal{F}u)(t)| \le& \left| t^{1-\nu+\lambda\nu-\lambda k} \mathcal{S}_{\lambda,\nu}(t) y_0 \right| + \left| t^{1-\nu+\lambda\nu-\lambda k} \int_0^t \mathcal{K}_\lambda(t-s) g(s,y(s)) ds \right| \\
\le& L_2 |y_0| + L_1 t^{1-\nu+\lambda\nu-\lambda k} \int_0^t (t-s)^{\lambda k-1} m(s) ds \le r.
\end{aligned}$$

For $t = 0$, we have $|(\mathcal{F}u)(0)| = 0 < r$. Therefore, $\mathcal{F}\Omega_r \subset \Omega_r$. □

Lemma 12. *Assume that (H2)–(H4) hold. Then $\mathcal{F}$ is continuous.*

Proof. Let $\{u_n\}_{n=1}^\infty$ be a sequence in Ω_r which is convergent to $u \in \Omega_r$. Consequently,

$$\lim_{n\to\infty} u_n(t) = u(t), \text{ and } \lim_{n\to\infty} t^{-(1-\nu+\lambda\nu-\lambda k)} u_n(t) = t^{-(1-\nu+\lambda\nu-\lambda k)} u(t), \text{ for } t \in (0,T].$$

Let $y(t) = t^{-(1-\nu+\lambda\nu-\lambda k)}u(t)$, $y_n(t) = t^{-(1-\nu+\lambda\nu-\lambda k)}u_n(t)$, $t \in (0,T]$. Then $y, y_n \in \widetilde{\Omega}_r$. In view of (H2), we have

$$\lim_{n\to\infty} g(t, y_n(t)) = \lim_{n\to\infty} g(t, t^{-(1-\nu+\lambda\nu-\lambda k)}u_n(t)) = g(t, t^{-(1-\nu+\lambda\nu-\lambda k)}u(t)) = g(t, y(t)).$$

For each $t \in (0,T]$, $(t-s)^{\lambda k-1}|g(s,y_n(s)) - g(s,y(s))| \le 2(t-s)^{\lambda k-1}m(s)$. By Lebesgue dominated convergence theorem, we obtain

$$\int_0^t (t-s)^{\lambda k-1}|g(s,y_n(s)) - g(s,y(s))|ds \to 0, \quad \text{as } n \to \infty.$$

Thus, for $t \in [0,T]$,

$$\begin{aligned}
&\Big|(\mathcal{F}u_n)(t) - (\mathcal{F}u)(t)\Big| \\
\le & t^{1-\nu+\lambda\nu-\lambda k} \int_0^t |\mathcal{K}_\lambda(t-s)(g(s,y_n(s)) - g(s,y(s)))|ds \\
\le & L_1 t^{1-\nu+\lambda\nu-\lambda k} \int_0^t (t-s)^{\lambda k-1}|g(s,y_n(s)) - g(s,y(s))|ds \to 0, \quad \text{as } n \to \infty.
\end{aligned}$$

Therefore, $\|\mathcal{F}u_n - \mathcal{F}u\| \to 0$ as $n \to \infty$. Hence, $\mathcal{F}$ is continuous. The proof is completed. □

4. Main Results

Theorem 1. *Assume that $Q(t)(t > 0)$ is compact. Furthermore suppose that (H2)–(H4) hold. Then the Cauchy problem (1) has at least one mild solution in $\widetilde{\Omega}_r$.*

Proof. Clearly, the problem (1) exists a mild solution $y \in \widetilde{\Omega}_r$ if and only if the operator $\mathcal{F}$ has a fixed point $u \in \Omega_r$, where $u(t) = t^{1-\nu+\lambda\nu-\lambda k}y(t)$. Hence, we only need to prove that the operator $\mathcal{F}$ has a fixed point in Ω_r. From Lemmas 11 and 12, we know that $\mathcal{F}\Omega_r \subset \Omega_r$ and $\mathcal{F}$ is continuous. In view of Lemma 10, the set $\{\mathcal{F}u : u \in \Omega_r\}$ is equicontinuous. It remains to prove that for $t \in [0,T]$, $\{(\mathcal{F}u)(t) : u \in \Omega_r\}$ is relatively compact in X. Clearly, $\{(\mathcal{F}u)(0) : u \in \Omega_r\}$ is relatively compact in X. We only consider the case $t > 0$. For any $\varepsilon \in (0,t)$ and $\delta > 0$, define $\mathcal{F}_{\varepsilon,\delta}$ on Ω_r as follows

$$\begin{aligned}
(\mathcal{F}_{\varepsilon,\delta}u)(t) :=& t^{1-\nu+\lambda\nu-\lambda k}(\mathcal{T}_{\varepsilon,\delta}y)(t) \\
:=& t^{1-\nu+\lambda\nu-\lambda k}\Bigg(\mathcal{S}_{\lambda,\nu}(t)y_0 + \int_0^{t-\varepsilon}\int_\delta^\infty \lambda\theta(t-s)^{\lambda-1}M_\lambda(\theta) \\
& \times Q((t-s)^\lambda\theta)g(s,y(s))d\theta ds\Bigg).
\end{aligned}$$

Thus,

$$\begin{aligned}
(\mathcal{F}_{\varepsilon,\delta}u)(t) =& t^{1-\nu+\lambda\nu-\lambda k}\Bigg(\mathcal{S}_{\lambda,\nu}(t)y_0 + Q(\varepsilon^\lambda\delta)\int_0^{t-\varepsilon}\int_\delta^\infty \lambda\theta(t-s)^{\lambda-1}M_\lambda(\theta) \\
& \times Q((t-s)^\lambda\theta - \varepsilon^\lambda\delta)g(s,y(s))d\theta ds\Bigg).
\end{aligned}$$

By Lemma 5, we know that $\mathcal{S}_{\lambda,\nu}(t)$ is compact because $Q(t)$ is compact for $t > 0$. Furthermore, $Q(\varepsilon^\lambda\delta)$ is compact, then the set $\{(\mathcal{F}_{\varepsilon,\delta}u)(t),\ u \in \Omega_r\}$ is relatively compact in X for any $\varepsilon \in (0,t)$ and for any $\delta > 0$. Moreover, for every $u \in \Omega_r$, we find

$$
\begin{aligned}
&|(\mathcal{F}u)(t)-(\mathcal{F}_{\varepsilon,\delta}u)(t)| \\
\leq & t^{1-\nu+\lambda\nu-\lambda k}\left|\int_0^t\int_0^\delta \lambda\theta(t-s)^{\lambda-1}M_\lambda(\theta)Q((t-s)^\lambda\theta)g(s,y(s))d\theta ds\right| \\
&+t^{1-\nu+\lambda\nu-\lambda k}\left|\int_{t-\varepsilon}^t\int_\delta^\infty \lambda\theta(t-s)^{\lambda-1}M_\lambda(\theta)Q((t-s)^\lambda\theta)g(s,y(s))d\theta ds\right| \\
\leq & \lambda C_0 t^{1-\nu+\lambda\nu-\lambda k}\int_0^t (t-s)^{\lambda k-1}|g(s,y(s))|ds\int_0^\delta \theta^k M_\lambda(\theta)d\theta \\
&+\lambda C_0 t^{1-\nu+\lambda\nu-\lambda k}\int_{t-\varepsilon}^t (t-s)^{\lambda k-1}|g(s,y(s))|ds\int_0^\infty \theta^k M_\lambda(\theta)d\theta \\
\leq & \lambda C_0 t^{1-\nu+\lambda\nu-\lambda k}\int_0^t (t-s)^{\lambda k-1}m(s)ds\int_0^\delta \theta^k M_\lambda(\theta)d\theta \\
&+\lambda C_0 t^{1-\nu+\lambda\nu-\lambda k}\int_{t-\varepsilon}^t (t-s)^{\lambda k-1}m(s)ds\int_0^\infty \theta^k M_\lambda(\theta)d\theta \\
\to & 0, \quad \text{as } \varepsilon\to 0,\ \delta\to 0.
\end{aligned}
$$

Therefore, $\{(\mathcal{F}u)(t):\ u\in\Omega_r\}$ is also a relatively compact set in X for $t\in[0,T]$. Thus, $\{\mathcal{F}u:\ u\in\Omega_r\}$ is relatively compact by Ascoli–Arzela Theorem. Hence, $\mathcal{F}$ is a completely continuous operator. Schauder's fixed point theorem shows that $\mathcal{F}$ has at least a fixed point $u^*\in\Omega_r$. Let $y^*(t)=t^{-(1-\nu+\lambda\nu-\lambda k)}u^*(t)$. Thus,

$$
y^*(t)=\mathcal{S}_{\lambda,\nu}(t)y_0+\int_0^t \mathcal{K}_\lambda(t-s)g(s,y^*(s))ds, \quad t\in(0,T],
$$

which implies that y^* is a mild solution of (1) in $\widetilde{\Omega}_r$. The proof is completed. □

In the case that $Q(t)$ is noncompact for $t>0$, we give an assumption as follows:

(H5) there exists a constant $K>0$ such that for any bounded $D\subseteq X$,

$$
\alpha(g(t,D))\leq Kt^{1-\nu+\lambda\nu-\lambda k}\alpha(D), \quad \text{for a.e. } t\in[0,T],
$$

where α is the Kuratowski's measure of noncompactness.

Theorem 2. *Assume that (H1)–(H5) hold. Then the Cauchy problem (1) has at least one mild solution in* $\widetilde{\Omega}_r$.

Proof. Let $u_0(t)=t^{1-\nu+\lambda\nu-\lambda k}\mathcal{S}_{\lambda,\nu}(t)y_0$ for all $t\in[0,T]$ and $u_{n+1}=\mathcal{F}u_n$, $n=0,1,2,\cdots$. By Lemma 11, $\mathcal{F}u_n\in\Omega_r$, for $u_n\in\Omega_r$. Consider set $\mathcal{V}=\{\mathcal{F}u_n\}:\ u_n\in\Omega_r\}_{n=0}^\infty$, and we will prove set $\mathcal{V}$ is relatively compact. In view of Lemmas 10, the set $\mathcal{V}$ is equicontinuous. We only need to prove $\mathcal{V}(t)=\{(\mathcal{F}u_n)(t),\ u_n\in\Omega_r\}_{n=0}^\infty$ is relatively compact in X for $t\in[0,T]$.

By the properties of measure of noncompactness, for any $t\in[0,T]$ we have

$$
\alpha\Big(\big\{u_n(t)\big\}_{n=0}^\infty\Big)=\alpha\Big(\big\{u_0(t)\big\}\cup\big\{u_n(t)\big\}_{n=1}^\infty\Big)=\alpha\Big(\big\{u_n(t)\big\}_{n=1}^\infty\Big)=\alpha(\mathcal{V}(t)). \tag{5}
$$

Let $y_n(t)=t^{-1+\nu-\lambda\nu+\lambda k}u_n(t)$, $t\in(0,T]$, $n=0,1,2,\cdots$. By the condition (H5) and Lemma 2, we have

$$\begin{aligned}\alpha(\mathcal{V}(t)) =&\alpha\Big(\Big\{(\mathcal{F}u_n)(t)\Big\}_{n=0}^{\infty}\Big)\\ =&\alpha\Big(\Big\{t^{1-\nu+\lambda\nu-\lambda k}\mathcal{S}_{\lambda,\nu}(t)y_0+t^{1-\nu+\lambda\nu-\lambda k}\int_0^t\mathcal{K}_\lambda(t-s)g(s,y_n(s))ds\Big\}_{n=0}^{\infty}\Big)\\ =&\alpha\Big(\Big\{t^{1-\nu+\lambda\nu-\lambda k}\int_0^t\mathcal{K}_\lambda(t-s)g(s,y_n(s))ds\Big\}_{n=0}^{\infty}\Big)\\ \le&2L_1t^{1-\nu+\lambda\nu-\lambda k}\int_0^t(t-s)^{\lambda k-1}\alpha\Big(g(s,\{s^{-1+\nu-\lambda\nu+\lambda k}u_n(s)\}_{n=0}^{\infty})\Big)ds\\ \le&2L_1KT^{1-\nu+\lambda\nu-\lambda k}\int_0^t(t-s)^{\lambda k-1}s^{1-\nu+\lambda\nu-\lambda k}\alpha\Big(\{s^{-1+\nu-\lambda\nu+\lambda k}u_n(s)\}_{n=0}^{\infty}\Big)ds\\ \le&2L_1KT^{1-\nu+\lambda\nu-\lambda k}\int_0^t(t-s)^{\lambda k-1}\alpha\Big(\Big\{u_n(s)\Big\}_{n=0}^{\infty}\Big)ds.\end{aligned}$$

In view of (5), we obtain

$$\alpha(\mathcal{V}(t))\le 2L_1KT^{1-\nu+\lambda\nu-\lambda k}\int_0^t(t-s)^{\lambda k-1}\alpha(\mathcal{V}(s))ds.$$

Therefore, by the inequality in ([24], p.188), we obtain that $\alpha(\mathcal{V}(t))=0$, then $\mathcal{V}(t)$ is relatively compact. Consequently, it follows from Ascoli–Arzela Theorem that set $\mathcal{V}$ is relatively compact, i.e., there exists a convergent subsequence of $\{u_n\}_{n=0}^{\infty}$. With no confusion, let $\lim_{n\to\infty}u_n=u^*\in\Omega_r$.

Thus, by continuity of the operator $\mathcal{F}$, we have

$$u^*=\lim_{n\to\infty}u_n=\lim_{n\to\infty}\mathcal{F}u_{n-1}=\mathcal{F}\Big(\lim_{n\to\infty}u_{n-1}\Big)=\mathcal{F}u^*.$$

Let $y^*(t)=t^{-1+\nu-\lambda\nu+\lambda k}u^*(t)$. Thus, y^* is a mild solution of (1) in $\widetilde{\Omega}_r$. The proof is completed. □

In the following, we prove the existence and uniqueness of a mild solution of the Cauchy problem (1).

(H6) There exists a function $L\in C([0,T],\mathbb{R}^+)$ such that $I_{0+}^{\lambda k}L\in C([0,T],\mathbb{R}^+)$,

$$|g(t,y_1(t))-g(t,y_2(t))|\le L(t)\|y_1-y_2\|_\lambda,\ \text{for any } y_1,y_2\in\widetilde{\Omega}_r,$$

and

$$\sup_{t\in[0,T]}\Big\{L_1T^{1-\nu+\lambda\nu-\lambda k}\int_0^t(t-s)^{\lambda k-1}L(s)ds\Big\}\le l_0<1.$$

Theorem 3. *Assume that the conditions (H2)–(H4) and (H6) hold. Then the Cauchy problem (1) has a unique mild solution in* $\widetilde{\Omega}_r$.

Proof. From Lemmas 11, we know that $\mathcal{F}\Omega_r\subset\Omega_r$. For any $u_1,u_2\in\Omega_r$, $t\in[0,T]$, we have

$$\begin{aligned}&\Big|(\mathcal{F}u_1)(t)-(\mathcal{F}u_2)(t)\Big|\\ \le&T^{1-\nu+\lambda\nu-\lambda k}\int_0^t|\mathcal{K}_\lambda(t-s)(g(s,y_1(s))-g(s,y_2(s)))|ds\\ \le&L_1T^{1-\nu+\lambda\nu-\lambda k}\int_0^t(t-s)^{\lambda k-1}|g(s,y_1(s))-g(s,y_2(s))|ds\\ \le&L_1T^{1-\nu+\lambda\nu-\lambda k}\int_0^t(t-s)^{\lambda k-1}L(s)\|y_1-y_2\|_\lambda ds\\ \le&l_0\|u_1-u_2\|.\end{aligned}$$

Thus
$$\|(\mathcal{F}u_1) - (\mathcal{F}u_2)\| \le l_0\|u_1 - u_2\|,$$
which implies that $\mathcal{F}$ is a contraction mapping. In view of the contraction mapping principle, $\mathcal{F}$ has the unique fixed point $u^* \in \Omega_r$. Let $y^*(t) = t^{-(1-\nu+\lambda\nu-\lambda k)}u^*(t)$. Thus, y^* is a unique mild solution of (1) in $\widetilde{\Omega}_r$. The proof is completed. □

5. Remarks

In recent paper [10], the authors studied the problem (1) and obtained the following result by Schauder's fixed point theorem.

Theorem 4 (see Theorem 3 in [10]). *Let $0 < k < 1$, $0 < \omega < \frac{\pi}{2}$ and $A \in \Theta_\omega^{-k}(X)$. If we assume, $Q(t)(t > 0)$ is compact and the following hypotheses hold:*

(h_1) *for each fixed $t \in (0, T]$, $g(t, \cdot) : X \to X$ is continuous function and for each $y \in C((0, T], X)$, $g(\cdot, y) : (0, T] \to X$ is strongly measurable.*

(h_2) *there exists a function $l \in L^1((0, T], \mathbb{R}^+)$ satisfying*
$$I_{0+}^{\lambda k} l \in C((0, T], \mathbb{R}^+), \quad \lim_{t\to 0+} t^{(1-\lambda k)(1-\nu)} I_{0+}^{\lambda k} l(t) = 0$$
and $|g(t, u)| \le l(t)$ for all $u \in \mathcal{B}_r^{\mathcal{Y}}((0, T])$ and almost all $t \in [0, T]$.

(h_3)
$$\sup_{t\in[0,T]} \left(t^{(1-\lambda k)(1-\nu)} |\mathcal{S}_{\lambda,\nu}(t) y_0| + t^{(1-\lambda k)(1-\nu)} \int_0^t (t-s)^{\lambda k - 1} l(s) ds \right) \le r,$$
for a constant $r > 0$ and $y_0 \in D(A^\theta)$, $\theta > 1 - k$, where $\mathcal{S}_{\lambda,\nu}(t) = I_{0+}^{\nu(1-\lambda)} t^{\lambda-1} \mathcal{Q}_\lambda(t)$.

Then there exist a mild solution of the Cauchy problem (1) in $\mathcal{B}_r^{\mathcal{Y}}((0, T])$ for every $y_0 \in D(A^\beta)$ with $\beta > 1 - k$.

Remark 1. *In [10], the authors claimed that $\lim_{t\to 0+} t^{(1-\lambda k)(1-\nu)} \mathcal{S}_{\lambda,\nu}(t) y_0 = 0$ (see, (12) in [10]). However, this claim is incorrect.*

In fact, when $\nu = 1$ and $y_0 \neq 0$, from Lemma 6, we know that $\lim_{t\to 0+} \mathcal{Q}_\lambda(t) y_0 = y_0/\Gamma(\lambda)$. Furthermore, we have
$$\begin{aligned}\lim_{t\to 0+} \mathcal{S}_{\lambda,1}(t) y_0 =& \frac{1}{\Gamma(1-\lambda)} \lim_{t\to 0+} \int_0^t (t-s)^{-\lambda} s^{\lambda-1} \mathcal{Q}_\lambda(s) y_0 ds \\ =& \frac{1}{\Gamma(1-\lambda)} \lim_{t\to 0+} \int_0^1 (1-z)^{-\lambda} z^{\lambda-1} \mathcal{Q}_\lambda(tz) y_0 dz \\ =& y_0 \neq 0.\end{aligned}$$

Therefore, the definition of the operator $\mathcal{E}$ in (14) of [10] is incorrect. Because there is the same shortcoming in the papers [16–18], the definitions of the operator $\mathcal{P}$ in [16], the operator Φ in the proof of Theorem 3.1 in [17] and the operator $\mathfrak{F}$ in the proof of Theorem 3 in [18] are inappropriate.

Remark 2. *The condition (h_3) contains the abstract operator $\mathcal{S}_{\lambda,\nu}(t)$. It is difficult to verify whether the condition (h_3) is satisfied for one fractional evolution equation.*

Remark 3. *The results obtained in this paper essentially improve and correct Theorem 3 in [10], and extend Theorem 2.1 in [4] and the known results in [9]. It is worth mentioning that all conditions of our theorems do not contain the abstract operator $\mathcal{S}_{\lambda,\nu}(t)$.*

Author Contributions: Conceptualization, M.Z. and Y.Z.; formal analysis, M.Z. and C.L.; investigation, M.Z. and Y.Z.; writing—review and editing, C.L. and Y.Z. All authors have read and agreed to the published version of the manuscript.

Funding: This research was funded by the National Natural Science Foundation of China (Nos. 12071396).

Institutional Review Board Statement: Not applicable.

Informed Consent Statement: Not applicable.

Data Availability Statement: No data was reported in this study.

Conflicts of Interest: The authors declare no conflict of interest.

References

1. Hilfer, R. *Applications of Fractional Calculus in Physics;* World Scientific: Singapore, 2000.
2. Kilbas, A.A.; Srivastava, H.M.; Trujillo, J.J. Theory and applications of fractional differential equations. In *North-Holland Mathematics Studies;* Elsevier Science B.V.: Amsterdam, The Netherlands, 2006; Volume 204.
3. Zhou, Y. *Basic Theory of Fractional Differential Equations;* World Scientific: Singapore, 2014.
4. Zhou, Y. *Fractional Evolution Equations and Inclusions: Analysis and Control;* Academic Press: London, UK, 2016.
5. Zhou, Y.; Wang, J.N. The nonlinear Rayleigh–Stokes problem with Riemann–Liouville fractional derivative. *Math. Meth. Appl. Sci.* **2021**, *44*, 2431–2438. [CrossRef]
6. Zhou, Y.; He, J.W.; Ahmad, B.; Tuan, N.H. Existence and regularity results of a backward problem for fractional diffusion equations. *Math. Meth. Appl. Sci.* **2019**, *42*, 6775–6790. [CrossRef]
7. Zhou, Y.; He, J.W. Well-posedness and regularity for fractional damped wave equations. *Mon. Math.* **2021**, *194*, 425–458. [CrossRef]
8. Zhou, Y. Infinite interval problems for fractional evolution equations. *Mathematics* **2022**, *10*, 900. [CrossRef]
9. Gu, H.B.; Trujillo, J.J. Existence of mild solution for evolution equation with Hilfer fractional derivative. *Appl. Math. Comput.* **2015**, *257*, 344–354. [CrossRef]
10. Jaiwal, A.; Bahuguna, D. Hilfer fractional differential equations with almost sectorial operators. *Differ. Equ. Dyn. Syst.* **2020**. [CrossRef]
11. Sousa, J.V.C.; Jarad, F.; Abdeljawad, T. Existence of mild solutions to Hilfer fractional evolution equations in Banach space. *Ann. Funct. Anal.* **2021**, *12*, 12. [CrossRef]
12. Yang, M.; Wang, Q. Existence of mild solutions for a class of Hilfer fractional evolution equations with nonlocal conditions. *Frac. Calc. Appl. Anal.* **2017**, *20*, 679–705. [CrossRef]
13. Kavitha, K.; Vijayakumar, V.; Udhayakumar, R.; Nisar, K.S. Results on the existence of Hilfer fractional neutral evolution equations with infinite delay via measures of noncompactness. *Math. Meth. Appl. Sci.* **2021**, *44*, 1438–1455. [CrossRef]
14. Furati, K.M.; Kassim, M.D.; Tatar, N.E. Existence and uniqueness for a problem involving Hilfer fractional derivative. *Comput. Math. Appl.* **2012**, *64*, 1616–1626. [CrossRef]
15. Saengthong, W.; Thailert, E.; Ntouyas, S.K. Existence and uniqueness of solutions for system of Hilfer-Hadamard sequential fractional differential equations with two point boundary conditions. *Adv. Diff. Equ.* **2019**, *2019*, 525. [CrossRef]
16. Bedi, P.; Kumar, A.; Abdeljawad, T.; Khan, Z.A.; Khan, A. Existence and approximate controllability of Hilfer fractional evolution equations with almost sectorial operators. *Adv. Diff. Equ.* **2020**, *2020*, 615. [CrossRef]
17. Varun Bose, C.S.; Udhayakumar, R. A note on the existence of Hilfer fractional differential inclusions with almost sectorial operators. *Math. Meth. Appl. Sci.* **2022**, *45*, 2530–2541. [CrossRef]
18. Karthikeyan, K.; Karthikeyan, P.; Patanarapeelert, N.; Sitthiwirattham, T. Mild solutions for impulsive integro-differential equations involving Hilfer fractional derivative with almost sectorial operators. *Axioms* **2021**, *10*, 313. [CrossRef]
19. Periago, F.; Straub, B. A functional calculus for almost sectorial operators and applications to abstract evolution equations. *J. Evol. Equ.* **2002**, *2*, 41–68. [CrossRef]
20. Markus, H. The Functional Valculus for Sectorial Operators. In *Operator Theory: Advances and Applications;* Birkhauser-Verlag: Basel, Switzerland, 2006; Volume 6.
21. Liu, Z.B.; Liu, L.S.; Zhao, J. The criterion of relative compactness for a class of abstract function groups in an infinite interval and its applications. *J. Syst. Sci. Math. Sci.* **2008**, *28*, 370–378.
22. Mainardi, F.; Paraddisi, P.; Gorenflo, R. Probability Distributions Generated by Fractional Diffusion Equations. In *Econophysics: An Emerging Science;* Kertesz, J., Kondor, I., Eds.; Kluwer: Dordrecht, The Netherlands, 2000.
23. Kou, C.H.; Zhou, H.C.; Yan, Y. Existence of solutions of initial problems for nonlinear fractional differential equations on the half-axis. *Nonlinear Anal.* **2011**, *74*, 5975–5986. [CrossRef]
24. Henry, D. *Geometric Theory of Semilinear Parabolic Equations, Lecture Notes in Math;* Springer: New York, NY, USA; Berlin/Heidelberg, Germany, 1981; Volume 840.

mathematics

MDPI

Article

Existence and Hyers–Ulam Stability for a Multi-Term Fractional Differential Equation with Infinite Delay

Chen Chen and Qixiang Dong *

School of Mathematical Sciences, Yangzhou University, Yangzhou 225002, China; ccyzu@outlook.com
* Correspondence: qxdong@yzu.edu.cn

Abstract: This paper is devoted to investigating one type of nonlinear two-term fractional order delayed differential equations involving Caputo fractional derivatives. The Leray–Schauder alternative fixed-point theorem and Banach contraction principle are applied to analyze the existence and uniqueness of solutions to the problem with infinite delay. Additionally, the Hyers–Ulam stability of fractional differential equations is considered for the delay conditions.

Keywords: fixed-point theorem; infinite delay; fractional differential equation; stability; existence and uniqueness; Caputo fractional derivative

MSC: 34A08; 26A33; 45M10

Citation: Chen, C.; Dong, Q. Existence and Hyers–Ulam Stability for a Multi-Term Fractional Differential Equation with Infinite Delay. *Mathematics* **2022**, *10*, 1013. https://doi.org/10.3390/math10071013

Academic Editors: António M. Lopes, Alireza Alfi, Liping Chen and Sergio A. David

Received: 1 March 2022
Accepted: 21 March 2022
Published: 22 March 2022

1. Introduction

In recent decades, relevant theories and applications of fractional differential equations [1–6] have developed rapidly. Generally, fractional differential equations are derived from the research of solid mechanics [7], chemistry [8], physics [9,10], electromechanics [11], finance [12], and so on. Abundant theoretical achievements have been made in the study of the existence and uniqueness of fractional differential equations by applying the fixed-pointed theorem, such as [12–16]. However, there are few articles in the research and application of fractional differential equations with time delay. The delay factor has an important influence on the solution to the fractional differential system. The change of the system solution not only depends on the present state but also is constrained by the past state. Therefore, it is of great significance to consider the delay effect on a fractional differential system. In [17], the authors discussed the stability of fractional differential equations with delay evolution inclusion. Li et al. [18] derived a comparison principle for functional differential equations with infinite delays. Additionally, note that the Hyers–Ulam stability property of delay differential equations can be mainly considered by the Gronwall inequality. It is worth mentioning that the mentioned method can be applied for the stability study of Caputo fractional delay differential equations (see, for example, in [19–21]).

In [22], Qixiang Dong et al. investigated a kind of weighted fractional differential equations with infinite delay, which can be expressed by

$$\begin{cases} D^{\alpha}y(t) = f(t, \widetilde{y}_t), & t \in (0, b], \\ \widetilde{y}_0 = \phi \in \mathscr{B}, \end{cases}$$

where $\alpha \in (0, 1]$, $\widetilde{y}(t) = t^{1-\alpha}y(t)$, D^{α} represents the Riemann–Liouville fractional derivative, $f : (0, b] \times \mathscr{B} \to \mathscr{B}$ is a given function satisfying some assumptions, and $\mathscr{B}$ is the phase space. A method named weighted delay is applied by the authors to study the properties of solutions to fractional differential equations whose initial value is not zero.

On the basis of these contents, we study the related properties of solutions to a class of nonlinear fractional differential equations with infinite delay, namely

$$\begin{cases} {}_cD^{\alpha}y(t) - a_cD^{\beta}y(t) = f(t, y_t), & t \in J = [0, b], \\ y(t) = \phi(t), & t \in (-\infty, 0], \end{cases} \quad (1)$$

where ${}_cD^{\alpha}$ and ${}_cD^{\beta}$ are Caputo fractional derivatives with $0 < \beta < \alpha \leqslant 1$, a is a certain constant, $f : J \times \mathscr{B} \to \mathbb{R}$ is a given function satisfying some assumptions that will be specified later, function $\phi \in \mathscr{B}$, and $\mathscr{B}$ is called a phase space, as defined later. Function y_t, which is an element $\mathscr{B}$, is defined as any function y on $(-\infty, b]$ as follows:

$$y_t(s) = y(t+s), \quad s \in (-\infty, 0], \quad t \in J. \quad (2)$$

Here, $y_t(\cdot)$ represents the preoperational state from time $-\infty$ up to time t. The notion of the phase space $\mathscr{B}$ plays an important role in the study of both qualitative and quantitative theories for functional differential equations. A common choice is the seminormed space satisfying suitable axioms, which was introduced by Hale and Kato [23].

Our approach is largely based on the alternative of Leray–Schauder and Banach fixed-point theorem. Due to the characteristic of delay equations, we need to give the proper form of the solutions when discussing the existence and uniqueness, which is one of the key and difficult points to solve the problem. Generally, delay differential equations can be transformed into integral equations. Under the definition of phase space, the solutions of the integral equations can be appropriately extended, and the constructed equations are still continuous at the point $x = 0$. Additionally, we study the Hyers–Ulam stability of fractional differential Equation (1) with infinite delay $y(t) = \phi(t)$. Due to the limitation of delay conditions, the research of the Hyers–Ulam stability becomes more complicated. In this paper, we verify the Hyers–Ulam stability of delay differential Equation (1) by using the related properties of phase space and obtain the stability conclusion by means of a class of Gronwall inequalities.

This paper is organized as follows. In Section 2, some basic mathematical tools are introduced that are used throughout the article. Section 3 is devoted to our main conclusions. The stability analysis is discussed in Section 4. Two examples are given at the end of the article to illustrate the conclusions.

2. Preliminaries and Lemmas

In order to facilitate readers in reading the following contents, we introduce some basic definitions and lemmas which are used throughout this paper in this section. First and foremost, we denote $C([a, b], \mathbb{R})$ the Banach space of all continuous functions $y : [a, b] \to \mathbb{R}$ with the norm $\|y\| = \sup\{|y(t)|, t \in [a, b]\}$. Additionally, we denote by $C^m([0, b]; \mathbb{R})$ the Banach space of all continuously differentiable functions, with the norm defined as usual.

Definition 1 ([24]). *The Riemann–Liouville integral with order $\alpha > 0$ of the given function $h : [a, b] \to \mathbb{R}$ is defined as*

$$J_a^{\alpha}h(t) = \frac{1}{\Gamma(\alpha)} \int_a^t (t-s)^{\alpha-1} h(s) ds, \quad t \in [a, b],$$

provided the other side is point-wisely defined, where $\Gamma(\cdot)$ is the Euler's gamma function; i.e, $\Gamma(z) = \int_0^{\infty} e^{-t} t^{z-1} dt$.

Definition 2 ([24]). *The Caputo derivative with order $\alpha > 0$ of the given function $h : [a, b] \to \mathbb{R}$ is defined as*

$${}_cD_a^{\alpha}h(t) = \frac{1}{\Gamma(m-\alpha)} \int_a^t (t-s)^{m-\alpha-1} h^{(m)}(s) ds, \quad t \in [a, b],$$

provided the other side is point-wisely defined, where m is a positive integer satisfying $m - 1 < \alpha \leqslant m$. Incidentally, ${}_cD_a^{\alpha}$ is called the Caputo fractional differential operator as well.

Lemma 1 ([24]). *Let $\alpha > 0$ and $m = [\alpha] + 1$. Then, the general solution to the fractional differential equation ${}_cD^\alpha u(t) = 0$ is given by*

$$u(t) = c_0 + c_1 t + c_2 t^2 + \cdots + c_{m-1} t^{m-1},$$

where $c_i \in \mathbb{R}, i = 0, 1, 2, \cdots, m-1$ are some constants. Further, assuming that $u \in C^m([0,b];\mathbb{R})$, we can get

$$J^\alpha {}_cD^\alpha u(t) = u(t) + c_0 + c_1 t + c_2 t^2 + \cdots + c_{m-1} t^{m-1},$$

for some $c_i \in \mathbb{R}, i = 0, 1, 2, \cdots, m-1$.

Definition 3 ([25]). *Let $\mathbb{X}$ be a Banach space; a linear topological space of functions from $(-\infty, 0]$ into $\mathbb{X}$, with the seminorm $\|\cdot\|_{\mathscr{B}}$, is called an admissible phase space if $\mathscr{B}$ has the following properties:*

(A1) There exists a positive constant H and functions $K(\cdot), M(\cdot) : [0, +\infty) \to [0, +\infty)$, with K continuous and M locally bounded, such that for any constant $a, b \in \mathbb{R}$ and $b > a$, if the function $x : (-\infty, b] \to \mathbb{X}, x_a \in \mathscr{B}$ and function $x(\cdot)$ is continuous on $[a, b]$, then for every $t \in [a, b]$, the following conditions (i)–(iii) hold:

(i) $x_t \in \mathscr{B}$;

(ii) $\|x(t)\| \leqslant H\|x_t\|_{\mathscr{B}}$ for some $H > 0$;

(iii) $\|x_t\|_{\mathscr{B}} \leqslant K(t-a)\sup_{a \leqslant s \leqslant t}\|x(s)\| + M(t-a)\|x_a\|_{\mathscr{B}}$.

(A2) For the function $x(\cdot)$ in $(A1)$, $t \mapsto x_t$ is a $\mathscr{B}$-valued continuous function for $t \in [a, b]$.

(B1) The space $\mathscr{B}$ is complete.

Lemma 2 ([26] Leray-Schauder alternative). *Let $\mathbb{X}$ be a Banach space, $\mathcal{C} \subset \mathbb{X}$ be a closed, convex subset of $\mathbb{X}$, $\mathcal{U}$ is an open subset of $\mathcal{C}$ and $0 \in \mathcal{U}$. Suppose $\mathcal{T} : \overline{\mathcal{U}} \to \mathcal{C}$ is a continuous, compact (in other words, $\mathcal{T}(\mathcal{U})$ is a relatively compact subset of $\mathcal{C}$) map. Then, either*

(i) $\mathcal{T}$ has a fixed point in $\mathcal{U}$, or

(ii) there is a $u \in \partial\mathcal{U}$ and $\lambda \in (0, 1)$ with $u = \lambda\mathcal{T}(u)$.

In general, Gronwall inequality plays a vital role in the study of Hyers–Ulam stability of differential equations. Next, we introduce an integral inequality which can be considered as a generalization of the Gronwall inequality.

Lemma 3 ([27]). *Suppose $\alpha > 0$, $a > 0$, $g(t,s)$ is a nonnegative continuous function defined on $[0, T] \times [0, T]$ with $g(t,s) \leqslant M$, and $g(t,s)$ is nondecreasing w.r.t. the first variable and nonincreasing w.r.t. the second variable. Assume that function $u(t)$ is nonnegative and integrable on $[0, T]$ with*

$$u(t) \leqslant a + \int_0^t g(t,s)(t-s)^{\alpha-1} u(s) ds, \quad t \in [0, T].$$

Then, we have

$$u(t) \leqslant a + a\int_0^t \sum_{n=1}^{\infty} \frac{(g(t,s)\Gamma(\alpha))^n}{\Gamma(n\alpha)} (t-s)^{n\alpha-1} ds,$$

where the notion "w.r.t." means "with respect to".

Lemma 4 ([22]). *Suppose $\alpha > 0$ and function $f \in C[0, b]$ is nonnegative and nondecreasing. Then, function $F(t) = J_0^\alpha f(t) = \frac{1}{\Gamma(\alpha)} \int_0^t (t-s)^{\alpha-1} f(s) ds$ is nondecreasing on $[0, b]$.*

Based on the Lemma 4 introduced above, the following inequality is proved to verify the Hyers–Ulam stability in Section 4.

Lemma 5. *For any nonnegative function $\omega \in C[a,b]$ and any $t \in [a,b]$, we have the following integral inequality*

$$\sup_{0\leqslant\tau\leqslant t}\int_0^{\tau}(\tau-s)^{\alpha-1}\omega(s)ds \leqslant \int_0^t (t-s)^{\alpha-1}\sup_{0\leqslant\sigma\leqslant s}\omega(\sigma)ds.$$

Proof of Lemma 5. Since function $\omega(\cdot)$ is nonnegative, $\sup_{0\leqslant\sigma\leqslant s}\omega(\sigma)$ is nondecreasing , which implies that the function $\int_0^t (t-s)^{\alpha-1}\sup_{0\leqslant\sigma\leqslant s}\omega(\sigma)ds$ is also nondecreasing , by Lemma 4. Now, fix $t \in [a,b]$. Then, for any $\tau \in [0,t]$, we have

$$\begin{aligned}\int_0^{\tau}(\tau-s)^{\alpha-1}\omega(s)ds &\leqslant \int_0^{\tau}(\tau-s)^{\alpha-1}\sup_{0\leqslant\sigma\leqslant s}\omega(s)ds\\ &\leqslant \int_0^{t}(t-s)^{\alpha-1}\sup_{0\leqslant\sigma\leqslant s}\omega(s)ds,\end{aligned}$$

which indicates that

$$\sup_{0\leqslant\tau\leqslant t}\int_0^{\tau}(\tau-s)^{\alpha-1}\omega(s)ds \leqslant \int_0^t (t-s)^{\alpha-1}\sup_{0\leqslant\sigma\leqslant s}\omega(\sigma)ds.$$

Thus, the Lemma is proved. □

3. Existence Results

In this section, we prove the existence results for problem (1) by using the alternative of Leray–Schauder theorem. Further, our results for the unique solution are based on the Banach contraction principle. Let us start by defining what we mean by a solution of problem (1). Define the space:

$$\Omega' = \{y : (-\infty,b] \to \mathbb{R} : y\mid_{(-\infty,0]} \in \mathscr{B} \textit{ and } y\mid_{[0,b]} \textit{ is contiunous}\}. \tag{3}$$

It can be easily verified that a function $y \in \Omega'$ is said to be a solution of (1) if y satisfies (1). For the existence results on (1), we need the following Lemma.

Lemma 6. *The solution y of the fractional differential Equation* (1) *has the following form:*

$$y(t) = aJ^{\alpha-\beta}y(t) + J^{\alpha}f(t,y_t) + \theta(t), \qquad t \in J = [0,b],$$

where $\theta(t) = c_0\left(\frac{at^{\alpha-\beta}}{\Gamma(\alpha-\beta+1)} - 1\right)$ is a polynomial type function, and c_0 is a certain constant.

Proof of Lemma 6. The proof is an immediate consequence of the Lemma 1. □

The following assumptions are essential to the results of existence.

Assumption 1. *$f : [0,b]\times\mathscr{B} \to \mathbb{R}$ is continuous, and there exists a bounded set $W_0 \subset \mathscr{B}$ such that $f : [0,b]\times W_0$ uniformly continuous.*

Assumption 2. *There exist function $g,l \in C(J,\mathbb{R}^+)$ such that $|f(t,u)| \leqslant g(t) + l(t)\|u\|_{\mathscr{B}}$ for $t \in J$ and every $u \in \mathscr{B}$.*

Assumption 3. *There exists a nonnegative function $\eta \in L^p[0,b]$ with $p > \frac{1}{\alpha}$ and a continuously non-decreasing function $\Omega : [0,+\infty) \to [0,+\infty)$ such that $|f(t,u)| \leqslant \eta(t)\Omega(\|u\|_{\mathscr{B}})$ for $t \in J$ and every $u \in \mathscr{B}$.*

Assumption 4. *There exists a constant L such that $|f(t,u)-f(t,v)| \leqslant L\|u-v\|_{\mathscr{B}}$ for $t \in J$ and every $u,v \in \mathscr{B}$.*

Theorem 1. *Suppose that Assumptions 1 and 2 hold. Additionally, assume that*

$$\frac{|a|b^{\alpha-\beta}}{\Gamma(\alpha-\beta+1)} + \frac{b^{\alpha}K_b}{\Gamma(\alpha+1)}\|l\| < 1 \tag{4}$$

holds. Then, the Equation (1) *has at least one solution on* $(-\infty, b]$.

Proof of Theorem 1. According to the content discussed above, we know that y is a solution to (1) if and only if y satisfies

$$y(t) = \begin{cases} aJ^{\alpha-\beta}y(t) + J^{\alpha}f(t, y_t) + \theta(t), & t \in [0, b], \\ \phi(t), & t \in (-\infty, 0]. \end{cases}$$

For any given function $\phi : (-\infty, 0]$ that belongs to $\mathscr{B}$, let $\widetilde{\phi}$ be a function defined by

$$\widetilde{\phi}(t) = \begin{cases} \phi(0), & t \in [0, b], \\ \phi(t), & t \in (-\infty, 0]. \end{cases}$$

For each $z \in C([0, b], \mathbb{R})$, we denote by $\widetilde{z}$ the function defined by

$$\widetilde{z}(t) = \begin{cases} z(t) - \phi(0), & t \in [0, b], \\ 0, & t \in (-\infty, 0]. \end{cases}$$

It can be easily seen that if $y(\cdot)$ satisfies the following integral equation

$$y(t) = aJ^{\alpha-\beta}y(t) + J^{\alpha}f(t, y_t) + \theta(t),$$

we can decompose $y(\cdot)$ as $y(t) = \widetilde{\phi}(t) + \widetilde{z}(t)$, $t \in [0, b]$, which implies that $y_t = \widetilde{\phi}_t + \widetilde{z}_t$, for every $t \in [0, b]$, and the function $z(\cdot)$ satisfies

$$z(t) = aJ^{\alpha-\beta}z(t) + J^{\alpha}f(t, \widetilde{z}_t + \widetilde{\phi}_t) + \theta(t).$$

Set $C_0 = \{z \in C([0, b], \mathbb{R}) : z(0) = \phi(0)\}$. Then C_0 is closed, and hence completed. Define an operator $P : C_0 \to C_0$ by

$$(Pz)(t) = aJ^{\alpha-\beta}z(t) + J^{\alpha}f(t, \widetilde{z}_t + \widetilde{\phi}_t) + \theta(t). \tag{5}$$

where $t \in [0, b]$. According to the Schauder's fixed point theorem, we show that the operator P is continuous and completely continuous in the following four steps.

Step 1. P is continuous.

Let $\{z_n\}$ be a sequence such that $z_n \to z$ in C_0. Then, we have for each $t \in [0, b]$

$$\begin{aligned} |Pz_n(t) - Pz(t)| \leqslant{}& \frac{|a|}{\Gamma(\alpha-\beta)}\int_0^t (t-s)^{\alpha-\beta-1}|z_n(s) - z(s)|ds \\ &+ \frac{1}{\Gamma(\alpha)}\int_0^t (t-s)^{\alpha-1}|f(s, \widetilde{(z_n)}_s + \widetilde{\phi}_s) - f(s, \widetilde{z}_s + \widetilde{\phi}_s)|ds. \end{aligned}$$

Set $W_0 = \{(z_n)_s : s \in [0, b],\ n \geqslant 1\} \subset \mathscr{B}$. It can be easily known from Assumption 1 that function f is uniformly continuous in $s \in [0, t]$, which implies that $\forall \varepsilon > 0$, $\exists \delta > 0$, $s.t$ $\forall z_1, z_2 \in W_0$, $|z_1 - z_2| < \delta$, we have $|f(s, z_1) - f(s, z_2)| < \varepsilon$. Since $z_n \to z$, then $\exists N > 0$, $s.t$ $\forall n > N$, we have $|z_n - z| < \delta$. Hence, for any $s \in [0, t]$, we can claim that $|f(s, z_n) - f(s, z)| < \varepsilon$. According to the definition $z(t) = \widetilde{z}(t) + \widetilde{\phi}(t)$ introduced above, it follows that $|f(s, \widetilde{(z_n)}_s + \widetilde{\phi}_s) - f(s, \widetilde{z}_s + \widetilde{\phi}_s)| < \varepsilon$, so we get

$$|Pz_n(t) - Pz(t)| \leqslant \frac{|a|b^{\alpha-\beta}}{\Gamma(\alpha-\beta+1)}\|z_n - z\| + \frac{b^{\alpha}}{\Gamma(\alpha+1)}\|f(s, \widetilde{(z_n)}_s + \widetilde{\phi}_s) - f(s, \widetilde{z}_s + \widetilde{\phi}_s)\|.$$

Hence, $|Pz_n(t) - Pz(t)| \to 0$ as $z_n \to z$, and P is continuous.

Step 2. P maps bounded sets into bounded sets in C_0.

Indeed, it is enough to show that for any $r > 0$ there exists a positive constant ξ such that for each $z \in B_r = \{z \in C_0 : \|z\| \leqslant r\}$ one has $\|Pz(t)\| \leqslant \xi$. Let $z \in B_r$. Since f is a continuous function, we have for each $t \in [0, b]$

$$
\begin{aligned}
|Pz(t)| &\leqslant \frac{|a|}{\Gamma(\alpha-\beta)}\int_0^t (t-s)^{\alpha-\beta-1}|z(s)|ds + \frac{1}{\Gamma(\alpha)}\int_0^t (t-s)^{\alpha-1}|f(s,\tilde{z}_s+\tilde{\phi}_s)|ds + |\theta(b)| \\
&\leqslant \frac{|a|b^{\alpha-\beta}}{\Gamma(\alpha-\beta+1)}\|z\| + \frac{1}{\Gamma(\alpha)}\int_0^t (t-s)^{\alpha-1}(g(s)+l(s)\|\tilde{z}_s+\tilde{\phi}_s\|_{\mathscr{B}})ds + |\theta(b)|.
\end{aligned}
$$

According to Definition 3, we can conclude that

$$
\begin{aligned}
\|\tilde{z}_s+\tilde{\phi}_s\|_{\mathscr{B}} &\leqslant \|\tilde{z}_s\|_{\mathscr{B}} + \|\tilde{\phi}_s\|_{\mathscr{B}} \\
&\leqslant K(s)\sup_{0\leqslant\tau\leqslant s}\|\tilde{z}(\tau)\| + M(s)\|\tilde{z}_0\|_{\mathscr{B}} + K(s)\sup_{0\leqslant\tau\leqslant s}\|\tilde{\phi}(\tau)\| + M(s)\|\tilde{\phi}_0\|_{\mathscr{B}} \\
&\leqslant K_b\sup_{0\leqslant\tau\leqslant s}\|z(\tau)-\phi(0)\| + K_b\|\phi(0)\| + M_b\|\phi\|_{\mathscr{B}} \\
&\leqslant K_b r + K_b\|\phi(0)\| + K_b\|\phi(0)\| + M_b\|\phi\|_{\mathscr{B}} \\
&\leqslant K_b r + 2K_bH\|\phi\|_{\mathscr{B}} + M_b\|\phi\|_{\mathscr{B}} \\
&= K_b r + (2K_bH + M_b)\|\phi\|_{\mathscr{B}} \\
&:= r_0,
\end{aligned}
$$

where $M_b = \sup\{|M(t)| : t \in [a,b]\}$, $K_b = \sup\{|K(t)| : t \in [a,b]\}$ and H is a positive constant. So we have

$$
|Pz(t)| \leqslant \frac{|a|b^{\alpha-\beta}}{\Gamma(\alpha-\beta+1)}r + \frac{b^{\alpha}\|g\|}{\Gamma(\alpha+1)} + \frac{b^{\alpha}\|l\|}{\Gamma(\alpha+1)}\Big(K_b r + (2K_bH+M_b)\|\phi\|_{\mathscr{B}}\Big) + |\theta(b)| := \xi.
$$

Hence, $|Pz(t)| \leqslant \xi$, which implies P maps bounded subsets into bounded subsets in C_0.

Step 3. P maps bounded sets into equicontinuous sets of C_0.

Let $t_1, t_2 \in [0,b]$, $t_1 < t_2$, and B_r be a bounded set of C_0 as in Step 2. Let $z \in B_r$. Then, for each $t \in [0,b]$, we have

$$
\begin{aligned}
&|(Pz)(t_2) - (Pz)(t_1)| \\
&\leqslant \frac{|a|\|z\|}{\Gamma(\alpha-\beta)}\left|\int_0^{t_1}\Big((t_2-s)^{\alpha-\beta-1} - (t_1-s)^{\alpha-\beta-1}\Big)ds + \int_{t_1}^{t_2}(t-s)^{\alpha-\beta-1}ds\right| \\
&\quad + \frac{1}{\Gamma(\alpha)}\left|\int_0^{t_1}\Big((t_2-s)^{\alpha-1} - (t_1-s)^{\alpha-1}\Big)f(s,\tilde{z}_s+\tilde{\phi}_s)ds\right. \\
&\quad \left.+ \int_{t_1}^{t_2}(t-s)^{\alpha-\beta-1}f(s,\tilde{z}_s+\tilde{\phi}_s)ds\right| + |\theta(t_2)-\theta(t_1)| \\
&\leqslant \frac{|a|\|z\|}{\Gamma(\alpha-\beta+1)}\Big({t_2}^{\alpha-\beta} - {t_1}^{\alpha-\beta} + 2(t_2-t_1)^{\alpha-\beta}\Big) \\
&\quad + \frac{\|g\|+\|l\|r_0}{\Gamma(\alpha+1)}({t_2}^{\alpha} - {t_1}^{\alpha} + 2(t_2-t_1)^{\alpha}) + |\theta(t_2)-\theta(t_1)|.
\end{aligned}
$$

As $t_1 \to t_2$, the right-hand side of the above inequality tends to zero, and the equicontinuity for the cases that $t_1 < t_2 \leqslant 0$ and $t_1 \leqslant 0 \leqslant t_2$ is obvious.

As a consequence of Steps 1–3, together with the Arzela–Ascoli theorem, we can conclude that $P : C_0 \to C_0$ is a completely continuous mapping.

Step 4. (A priori bounds). There exists an open set $U \subseteq C_0$ with $z \neq \lambda P(z)$ for $\lambda \in (0,1)$ and $z \in \partial U$.

According to the condition $\frac{|a|b^{\alpha-\beta}}{\Gamma(\alpha-\beta+1)} + \frac{b^{\alpha}K_b}{\Gamma(\alpha+1)}\|l\| < 1$, we can deduce that there exists a constant $N > 0$ such that

$$\frac{|a|b^{\alpha-\beta}}{\Gamma(\alpha-\beta+1)}N + \frac{b^{\alpha}K_b}{\Gamma(\alpha+1)}\|l\|N + \frac{b^{\alpha}}{\Gamma(\alpha+1)}\Big(\|g\| + \|l\|(2K_bH + M_b)\|\phi\|_{\mathscr{B}}\Big) + |\theta(b)| < N.$$

Define the set $\mathcal{E} = \{z \in C_0 : \|z\| < N\}$. Thus, the operator $P : \overline{\mathcal{E}} \to C_0$ satisfies the complete continuity. Assume the equation

$$z = \lambda P z$$

holds for some $z \in \overline{\mathcal{E}}$ and $\lambda \in (0,1)$. Then, we obtain

$$\begin{aligned}|z(t)| &= |\lambda P z(t)| \leqslant |Pz(t)| \\ &\leqslant \frac{|a|b^{\alpha-\beta}\|z\|}{\Gamma(\alpha-\beta+1)} + \frac{b^{\alpha}\|g\|}{\Gamma(\alpha+1)} + \frac{b^{\alpha}\|l\|}{\Gamma(\alpha+1)}\Big(K_b\|z\| + (2K_bH + M_b)\|\phi\|_{\mathscr{B}}\Big) + |\theta(b)|.\end{aligned}$$

Hence, the following inequality

$$\begin{aligned}\|z\| &\leqslant \frac{|a|b^{\alpha-\beta}\|z\|}{\Gamma(\alpha-\beta+1)} + \frac{b^{\alpha}K_b\|l\|\|z\|}{\Gamma(\alpha+1)} + \frac{b^{\alpha}}{\Gamma(\alpha+1)}\Big(\|g\| + \|l\|(2K_bH + M_b)\|\phi\|_{\mathscr{B}}\Big) + |\theta(b)| \\ &< N\end{aligned}$$

holds, which contradicts to $N = \|z\|$. Thus, we get

$$z \neq \lambda P z$$

for any $z \in \overline{\mathcal{E}}$ and λ. By the Leray–Schauder alternative, we infer that there exists at least one fixed point z of P, and $y = \tilde{z} + \tilde{\phi}$ is a solution to problem (1). The proof is thus complete. □

Remark 1. *In infinite dimensional space, continuous functions are not uniformly continuous in a bounded closed region. In order to verify the continuity of the operator P in the step 1, we give Assumption 1. The conclusion of continuity of the map P can be directly obtained by using the Lebesgue Dominated Convergence Theorem.*

Theorem 2. *Suppose that Assumptions 1 and 3 hold. Additionally, assume that*

$$\frac{|a|b^{\alpha-\beta}}{\Gamma(\alpha-\beta+1)} + \frac{b^{(\alpha-1)q+1}\|\eta\|_p}{\Gamma(\alpha)(1+(\alpha-1)q)^{\frac{1}{q}}}\limsup_{r\to\infty}\frac{\Omega(r)}{r} < 1 \tag{6}$$

holds. Then, the Equation (1) *has at least one solution on* $(-\infty, b]$.

Proof of Theorem 2. Let $P : C_0 \to C_0$ be defined as in (5). The conclusion can be verified analogously in the following four steps as well.

Step 1. P is continuous.

Similar to the proof of Theorem 1, it is not difficult to verify that P is continuous by Assumption 3 and the Lebesgue dominated convergence theorem.

Step 2. P maps bounded sets into bounded sets in C_0.

Let $B_r = \{z \in C_0 : \|z\| \leqslant r\}$. Then, for any $z \in B_r$ and $t \in [0,b]$, we have

$$|Pz(t)| \leqslant \frac{|a|}{\Gamma(\alpha-\beta)} \int_0^t (t-s)^{\alpha-\beta-1}|z(s)|ds + \frac{1}{\Gamma(\alpha)} \int_0^t (t-s)^{\alpha-1}|f(s,\tilde{z}_s+\tilde{\phi}_s)|ds + |\theta(b)|$$
$$\leqslant \frac{|a|b^{\alpha-\beta}}{\Gamma(\alpha-\beta+1)}\|z\| + \frac{1}{\Gamma(\alpha)} \int_0^t (t-s)^{\alpha-1}\eta(s)\Omega(\|\tilde{z}_s+\tilde{\phi}_s\|_{\mathscr{B}})ds + |\theta(b)|.$$

Since

$$\|\tilde{z}_s+\tilde{\phi}_s\|_{\mathscr{B}} \leqslant \|\tilde{z}_s\|_{\mathscr{B}} + \|\tilde{\phi}_s\|_{\mathscr{B}} \leqslant K_b r + (2K_bH + M_b)\|\phi\|_{\mathscr{B}} := r_0,$$

where $M_b = \sup\{|M(t)|: t \in [a,b]\}$, $K_b = \sup\{|K(t)|: t \in [a,b]\}$ and H is a positive constant. It follows from Holder's inequality and Assumption 3 that

$$\begin{aligned}
|Pz(t)| &\leqslant |\theta(b)| + \frac{|a|b^{\alpha-\beta}}{\Gamma(\alpha-\beta+1)}\|z\| \\
&\quad + \frac{1}{\Gamma(\alpha)} \int_0^t (t-s)^{\alpha-1}\eta(s)ds\Omega\Big(K_b r + (2K_bH+M_b)\|\phi\|_{\mathscr{B}}\Big) \\
&\leqslant |\theta(b)| + \frac{|a|b^{\alpha-\beta}}{\Gamma(\alpha-\beta+1)}\|z\| \\
&\quad + \frac{1}{\Gamma(\alpha)}\Omega\Big(K_b r + (2K_bH+M_b)\|\phi\|_{\mathscr{B}}\Big)\Big(\int_0^t (t-s)^{(\alpha-1)q}\Big)^{\frac{1}{q}}\|\eta\|_p \\
&\leqslant |\theta(b)| + \frac{|a|b^{\alpha-\beta}}{\Gamma(\alpha-\beta+1)}\|z\| \\
&\quad + \Omega\Big(K_b r + (2K_bH+M_b)\|\phi\|_{\mathscr{B}}\Big)\frac{b^{(\alpha-1)q+1}}{\Gamma(\alpha)(1+(\alpha-1)q)^{\frac{1}{q}}}\|\eta\|_p \\
&:= \xi,
\end{aligned}$$

where $\|\eta\|_p = (\int_0^b |\eta(s)|^p ds)^{\frac{1}{p}}$ and $\frac{1}{p}+\frac{1}{q}=1$, $(\alpha-1) > -1$. Therefore, $\|Pz\| \leqslant \xi$ for every $z \in B_r$, which implies that P maps bounded subsets into bounded subsets in C_0.

Step 3. P maps bounded sets into equicontinuous sets of C_0.

Let $t_1, t_2 \in [0,b]$, $t_1 < t_2$, and let B_r be a bounded set of C_0 as in the Step 2. Let $z \in B_r$. Then for each $t \in [0,b]$, we have

$$\begin{aligned}
&|(Pz)(t_2) - (Pz)(t_1)| \\
&\leqslant \frac{|a|\|z\|}{\Gamma(\alpha-\beta)}\Big|\int_0^{t_1}\Big((t_2-s)^{\alpha-\beta-1} - (t_1-s)^{\alpha-\beta-1}\Big)ds + \int_{t_1}^{t_2}(t-s)^{\alpha-\beta-1}ds\Big| \\
&\quad + \frac{1}{\Gamma(\alpha)}\Big|\int_0^{t_1}\Big((t_2-s)^{\alpha-1} - (t_1-s)^{\alpha-1}\Big)f(s,\tilde{z}_s+\tilde{\phi}_s)ds \\
&\quad + \int_{t_1}^{t_2}(t-s)^{\alpha-\beta-1}f(s,\tilde{z}_s+\tilde{\phi}_s)ds\Big| + |\theta(t_2)-\theta(t_1)| \\
&\leqslant \frac{|a|\|z\|}{\Gamma(\alpha-\beta+1)}\Big({t_2}^{\alpha-\beta} - {t_1}^{\alpha-\beta} + 2(t_2-t_1)^{\alpha-\beta}\Big) \\
&\quad + \frac{1}{\Gamma(\alpha)}\Big|\int_0^{t_1}\Big((t_2-s)^{\alpha-1} - (t_1-s)^{\alpha-1}\Big)\eta(s)\Omega(\|\tilde{z}_s+\tilde{\phi}_s\|_{\mathscr{B}})ds \\
&\quad + \int_{t_1}^{t_2}(t-s)^{\alpha-\beta-1}\eta(s)\Omega(\|\tilde{z}_s+\tilde{\phi}_s\|_{\mathscr{B}})ds\Big| + |\theta(t_2)-\theta(t_1)| \\
&\leqslant \frac{|a|\|z\|}{\Gamma(\alpha-\beta+1)}\Big({t_2}^{\alpha-\beta} - {t_1}^{\alpha-\beta} + 2(t_2-t_1)^{\alpha-\beta}\Big)
\end{aligned}$$

$$+\frac{\Omega(r_0)}{\Gamma(\alpha)}\left(\int_0^{t_1}((t_2-s)^{\alpha-1}-(t_1-s)^{\alpha-1})^q ds\right)^{\frac{1}{q}}\left(\int_0^{t_1}\eta^p(s)ds\right)^{\frac{1}{p}}$$
$$+\frac{\Omega(r_0)}{\Gamma(\alpha)}\left(\int_{t_1}^{t_2}(t_2-s)^{(\alpha-1)q}ds\right)^{\frac{1}{q}}\left(\int_{t_1}^{t_2}\eta^p(s)ds\right)^{\frac{1}{p}}+|\theta(t_2)-\theta(t_1)|$$
$$\leqslant\frac{|a|\|z\|}{\Gamma(\alpha-\beta+1)}\left({t_2}^{\alpha-\beta}-{t_1}^{\alpha-\beta}+2(t_2-t_1)^{\alpha-\beta}\right)$$
$$+\frac{\Omega(r_0)\|\eta\|_p}{\Gamma(\alpha)r_1}({t_2}^{r_2}-{t_1}^{r_2}+2(t_2-t_1)^{r_2})+|\theta(t_2)-\theta(t_1)|,$$

where $r_0=K_br+(2K_bH+M_b)\|\phi\|_{\mathscr{B}}$, $r_1=(1+(\alpha-1)q)^{\frac{1}{q}}$, $r_2=[(\alpha-1)q+1]/q>0$. As $t_1\to t_2$ the right-hand side of the above inequality tends to zero, and the equicontinuity for the cases that $t_1<t_2\leqslant 0$ and $t_1\leqslant 0\leqslant t_2$ is obvious.

As a consequence of Steps 1–3, together with the Arzela–Ascoli theorem, we can conclude that $P:C_0\to C_0$ is a completely continuous mapping.

Step 4. (A priori bounds). There exists an open set $U\subseteq C_0$ with $z\neq\lambda P(z)$ for $\lambda\in(0,1)$ and $z\in\partial U$.

According to the condition $\frac{|a|b^{\alpha-\beta}}{\Gamma(\alpha-\beta+1)}+\frac{b^{(\alpha-1)q+1}\|\eta\|_p}{\Gamma(\alpha)(1+(\alpha-1)q)^{\frac{1}{q}}}\lim_{r\to\infty}\sup\frac{\Omega(r)}{r}<1$, we can deduce that there exists a constant $N>0$ such that

$$\frac{|a|b^{\alpha-\beta}}{\Gamma(\alpha-\beta+1)}N+\frac{b^{(\alpha-1)q+1}\|\eta\|_p}{\Gamma(\alpha)(1+(\alpha-1)q)^{\frac{1}{q}}}\Omega(N)+|\theta(b)|<N.$$

Define the set $\mathcal{E}=\{z\in C_0:\|z\|<N\}$. So the operator $P:\overline{\mathcal{E}}\to C_0$ satisfies the complete continuity. Assume the equation

$$z=\lambda Pz$$

holds for some $z\in\overline{\mathcal{E}}$ and $\lambda\in(0,1)$. Then we obtain

$$|z(t)|=|\lambda Pz(t)|\leqslant|Pz(t)|$$
$$\leqslant\frac{|a|b^{\alpha-\beta}\|z\|}{\Gamma(\alpha-\beta+1)}+\frac{b^{(\alpha-1)q+1}\|\eta\|_p}{\Gamma(\alpha)(1+(\alpha-1)q)^{\frac{1}{q}}}\Omega\left(K_b\|z\|+(2K_bH+M_b)\|\phi\|_{\mathscr{B}}\right)+|\theta(b)|$$
$$<N.$$

Hence, the following inequality

$$\|z\|<N$$

holds, which contradicts $N=\|z\|$. Thus, we get

$$z\neq\lambda Pz$$

for any $z\in\overline{\mathcal{E}}$ and λ. By the Leray–Schauder alternative, we infer that there exists at least one fixed point z of P, and $y=\widetilde{z}+\widetilde{\phi}$ is a solution to problem (1). The proof is thus complete. □

Theorem 3. *Suppose that Assumptions 1 and 4 hold. Additionally, assume that*

$$0<\frac{|a|b^{\alpha-\beta}}{\Gamma(\alpha-\beta+1)}+\frac{Lb^{\alpha}K_b}{\Gamma(\alpha+1)}<1 \tag{7}$$

holds, Then, Equation (1) *has a unique solution on* $(-\infty,b]$.

Proof of Theorem 3. Let $P : C_0 \to C_0$ be defined as in (5). The operator P has a fixed point. which is equivalent to Equation (1) having a unique solution, and we turn to proving that P has a fixed point. We shall show that $P : C_0 \to C_0$ is a contraction map. Indeed, consider any $u, v \in C_0$. Then for each $t \in [0, b]$, we have

$$\begin{aligned} |(Pu)(t) - (Pv)(t)| &\leqslant \frac{|a|}{\Gamma(\alpha-\beta)} \int_0^t (t-s)^{\alpha-\beta-1} |u(s) - v(s)| ds \\ &+ \frac{1}{\Gamma(\alpha)} \int_0^t (t-s)^{\alpha-1} |f(s, \tilde{u}_s + \tilde{\phi}_s) - f(s, \tilde{v}_s + \tilde{\phi}_s)| ds \\ &\leqslant \frac{|a| b^{\alpha-\beta}}{\Gamma(\alpha-\beta+1)} \|u - v\| + \frac{L}{\Gamma(\alpha)} \int_0^t (t-s)^{\alpha-1} \|\tilde{u}(s) - \tilde{v}(s)\|_{\mathscr{B}} ds. \end{aligned}$$

Since

$$\begin{aligned} \|\tilde{u}(s) - \tilde{v}(s)\|_{\mathscr{B}} &\leqslant K(s) \sup_{0 \leqslant \tau \leqslant s} \|\tilde{u}(\tau) - \tilde{v}(\tau)\| + M(s) \|\tilde{u}_0 - \tilde{v}_0\|_{\mathscr{B}} \\ &\leqslant K_b \sup_{0 \leqslant \tau \leqslant s} \|u(\tau) - \phi(0) - v(\tau) + \phi(0)\| \\ &\leqslant K_b \|u - v\|, \end{aligned}$$

where $K_b = \sup\{|K(t)| : t \in [a, b]\}$, we get

$$\|Pu - Pv\| \leqslant \left(\frac{|a| b^{\alpha-\beta}}{\Gamma(\alpha-\beta+1)} + \frac{L b^{\alpha} K_b}{\Gamma(\alpha+1)} \right) \|u - v\|,$$

and P is a contraction. Therefore, P has a unique fixed point by applying the Banach contraction principle. □

4. Stability Analysis

In this section, the analysis of Hyers–Ulam stability of the fractional differential Equation (1) with infinite delay is presented. First and foremost, the definition given below is crucial to the proof of Hyers–Ulam stability.

Definition 4. *The problem* (1) *is said to be Hyers–Ulam stable if there exists a positive real number c such that for each $\varepsilon > 0$ and for each solution $u(\cdot)$ of the inequalities*

$$\begin{cases} \left| {}_cD^{\alpha} u(t) - a {}_cD^{\beta} u(t) = f(t, u_t) \right| \leqslant \varepsilon, & t \in J = [0, b], \\ u(t) = \phi(t), & t \in (-\infty, 0], \end{cases} \tag{8}$$

there exists a solution $v(\cdot)$ of the problem (1) *with*

$$|u(t) - v(t)| \leqslant c\varepsilon, \quad t \in J = [0, b].$$

Theorem 4. *Further, assume that the conditions of Theorem 3 are satisfied and the inequality* (8) *has at least one solution. Then, the problem* (1) *is Hyers–Ulam stable.*

Proof of Theorem 4. For each $\varepsilon > 0$, and each function u that satisfies the following inequalities

$$\left| {}_cD^{\alpha} u(t) - a {}_cD^{\beta} u(t) - f(t, u_t) \right| \leqslant \varepsilon, \quad t \in [0, b],$$

a function $g(t) = {}_cD^{\alpha} u(t) - a {}_cD^{\beta} u(t) - f(t, u_t)$ can be found; then, we have $|g(t)| \leqslant \varepsilon$, which implies that

$$u(t) = \theta(t) + a J^{\alpha-\beta} u(t) + J^{\alpha} f(t, u_t) + J^{\alpha} g(t),$$

where $\theta(t)$ is a polynomial function which is given in Lemma 6. According to Theorem 3, it has been verified that there is a unique solution $v(t)$ of problem (1), then function v can be expressed as

$$v(t) = \theta(t) + aJ^{\alpha-\beta}v(t) + J^{\alpha}f(t, v_t),$$

so we have

$$\begin{aligned}|u(t) - v(t)| \leqslant{}& \frac{|a|}{\Gamma(\alpha-\beta)}\int_0^t (t-s)^{\alpha-\beta-1}|u(s) - v(s)|ds \\ &+ \frac{1}{\Gamma(\alpha)}\int_0^t (t-s)^{\alpha-1}|f(s,u_s) - f(s,v_s)|ds + \frac{1}{\Gamma(\alpha)}\int_0^t (t-s)^{\alpha-1}|g(s)|ds.\end{aligned}$$

Since

$$|f(s,u_s) - f(s,v_s)| \leqslant L\|u_s - v_s\|_{\mathscr{B}},$$

together with Definition 3, we get

$$\begin{aligned}\|u_s - v_s\|_{\mathscr{B}} &= \|(\widetilde{u}_s + \widetilde{\phi}_s) - (\widetilde{v}_s + \widetilde{\phi}_s)\|_{\mathscr{B}} = \|\widetilde{u}_s - \widetilde{v}_s\|_{\mathscr{B}} \\ &\leqslant K(s)\sup_{0\leqslant\tau\leqslant s}\|\tilde{u}(\tau) - \tilde{v}(\tau)\| + M(s)\|\tilde{u}_0 - \tilde{v}_0\|_{\mathscr{B}} \\ &\leqslant K_b \sup_{0\leqslant\tau\leqslant s}\|u(\tau) - \phi(0) - v(\tau) + \phi(0)\| \\ &= K_b \sup_{0\leqslant\tau\leqslant s}|u(\tau) - v(\tau)|,\end{aligned}$$

where $K_b = \sup\{|K(t)|: t \in [a,b]\}$, it indicates that

$$\begin{aligned}|u(t) - v(t)| \leqslant{}& \frac{|a|}{\Gamma(\alpha-\beta)}\int_0^t (t-s)^{\alpha-\beta-1}|u(s) - v(s)|ds \\ &+ \frac{LK_b}{\Gamma(\alpha)}\int_0^t (t-s)^{\alpha-1}\sup_{0\leqslant\sigma\leqslant s}|u(\sigma) - v(\sigma)|ds + \frac{b^{\alpha}}{\Gamma(\alpha+1)}\varepsilon.\end{aligned}$$

According to Lemma 5, it immediately follows that

$$\begin{aligned}\sup_{0\leqslant\tau\leqslant t}|u(\tau) - v(\tau)| \leqslant{}& \frac{|a|}{\Gamma(\alpha-\beta)}\int_0^t (t-s)^{\alpha-\beta-1}\sup_{0\leqslant\sigma\leqslant s}|u(\sigma) - v(\sigma)|ds \\ &+ \frac{LK_b}{\Gamma(\alpha)}\int_0^t (t-s)^{\alpha-1}\sup_{0\leqslant\sigma\leqslant s}|u(\sigma) - v(\sigma)|ds + \frac{b^{\alpha}}{\Gamma(\alpha+1)}\varepsilon \\ ={}& \int_0^t \left[|a|\frac{(t-s)^{\alpha-\beta-1}}{\Gamma(\alpha-\beta)} + LK_b\frac{(t-s)^{\alpha-1}}{\Gamma(\alpha)}\right]\sup_{0\leqslant\sigma\leqslant s}|u(\sigma) - v(\sigma)|ds \\ &+ \frac{b^{\alpha}}{\Gamma(\alpha+1)}\varepsilon,\end{aligned}$$

let $\varphi(t) := \sup_{0\leqslant\tau\leqslant t}|u(\tau) - v(\tau)|$, $M := \frac{b^{\alpha}}{\Gamma(\alpha+1)}$, and $g(t,s) := |a|\frac{1}{\Gamma(\alpha-\beta)} + LK_b\frac{(t-s)^{\beta}}{\Gamma(\alpha)}$, we can get

$$\varphi(t) \leqslant M\varepsilon + \int_0^t g(t,s)(t-s)^{\alpha-\beta-1}\varphi(s)ds.$$

It is not difficult to note that $g(t,s) \leqslant |a|\frac{1}{\Gamma(\alpha-\beta)} + LK_b\frac{b^{\beta}}{\Gamma(\alpha)}(:= M_0)$. Hence, in view of Lemma 3,

$$\begin{aligned}\varphi(t) &\leqslant M\varepsilon + M\varepsilon\int_0^t \sum_{n=1}^{\infty}\frac{(g(t,s)\Gamma(\alpha-\beta))^n}{\Gamma(n(\alpha-\beta))}(t-s)^{n(\alpha-\beta)-1}ds \\ &\leqslant M\varepsilon + M\varepsilon\int_0^t \sum_{n=1}^{\infty}\frac{(M_0\Gamma(\alpha-\beta))^n}{\Gamma(n(\alpha-\beta))}(t-s)^{n(\alpha-\beta)-1}ds\end{aligned}$$

$$\leqslant M\varepsilon + M\varepsilon \sum_{n=1}^{\infty} \frac{(M_0\Gamma(\alpha-\beta))^n}{\Gamma(n(\alpha-\beta)+1)} b^{n(\alpha-\beta)}$$
$$\leqslant M\varepsilon E_{\alpha-\beta}\big(M_0 b^{(\alpha-\beta)}\Gamma(\alpha-\beta)\big),$$

let $c := ME_{\alpha-\beta}\big(M_0 b^{(\alpha-\beta)}\Gamma(\alpha-\beta)\big)$, then the inequality

$$\varphi(t) \leqslant c\varepsilon$$

holds, which implies that Hyers-Ulam stability of problem (1) is proved. □

5. Examples

Two examples are presented in this section to illustrate the conclusions. To begin with, let $\gamma > 0$ be a real constant and

$$E_\gamma = \{y \in C((-\infty,0],\mathbb{R}) : \lim_{\theta\to-\infty} e^{\gamma\theta} y(\theta) \text{ exists in } \mathbb{R}\}.$$

Accordingly, the norm of E_γ is given by

$$|y|_\gamma = \sup_{-\infty<\theta\leqslant 0} e^{\gamma\theta}|y(\theta)|.$$

By [28], E_γ satisfies the conditions in Definition 3 with $K = M = H = 1$. It can be easily claimed that E_γ is a phase space.

Example 1. *Consider the following nonlinear Caputo-type fractional differential equation with infinite delay of the form*

$$_cD^{0.8}y(t) - \frac{1}{2}{}_cD^{0.4}y(t) = \frac{e^{-\gamma t}}{10}(|y_t| + \frac{1}{2}cost), \quad t \in J = [0,1], \tag{9}$$

$$y(t) = \phi(t) \in E_\gamma, \quad t \in (-\infty, 0]. \tag{10}$$

According to the given data, it can be easily found that Assumptions 1 and 2 are satisfied with function $l(t) = \frac{e^{-\gamma t}}{10}$. Furthermore, we have $\frac{|a|b^{\alpha-\beta}}{\Gamma(\alpha-\beta+1)} + \frac{b^\alpha K_b}{\Gamma(\alpha+1)}\|l\| < \frac{1}{2\Gamma(1.4)} + \frac{1}{10\Gamma(1.8)} \approx 0.6707 < 1$. Therefore, all the conditions of Theorem 1 hold true, and consequently the problems (9) and (10) with $f(t,y_t)$ given by the equation $f(t,y_t) = \frac{e^{-\gamma t}}{10}(|y_t| + \frac{1}{2}cost)$ have at least one solution on $(-\infty,1]$.

Example 2. *We can investigate the following nonlinear delayed fractional differential equation*

$$_cD^{0.7}y(t) - \frac{1}{3}{}_cD^{0.5}y(t) = \frac{\tilde{c}e^{-\gamma t+t}|y|_\gamma}{(e^t+e^{-t})(1+|y|_\gamma)}, \quad t \in J = [0,1], \tag{11}$$

$$y(t) = \phi(t) \in E_\gamma, \quad t \in (-\infty, 0], \tag{12}$$

where $\tilde{c}$ is a given positive constant. Set

$$f(t,x) = \frac{e^{-\gamma t+t}x}{\tilde{c}(e^t+e^{-t})(1+x)}, \ (t,x) \in [0,1] \times \mathbb{R}^+.$$

Then, for any $x, y \in E_\gamma$, we have

$$|f(t,x) - f(t,y)| = \frac{e^{-\gamma t+t}}{\tilde{c}(e^t+e^{-t})}\left|\frac{x}{1+x} - \frac{y}{1+y}\right|$$
$$\leqslant \frac{e^{-\gamma t+t}|x-y|}{\tilde{c}(e^t+e^{-t})(1+x)(1+y)}$$

$$\leqslant \frac{e^t|x-y|}{\widetilde{c}(e^t+e^{-t})}$$
$$\leqslant \frac{1}{\widetilde{c}}|x-y|.$$

Hence, the condition Assumption 4 holds. Since $K=1$, *assume that* $\widetilde{c} > \frac{3\Gamma(1.2)}{\Gamma(1.7)(3\Gamma(1.2)-1)} \approx 1.7269$, *and Equation* (7) *holds. Thus, it can be verified that problems* (11) *and* (12) *have a unique solution on* $(-\infty, 1]$ *by applying Theorem 3.*

On the basis of the conclusions, we further discuss the Hyers–Ulam stability of problem (11) *and* (12). *For any* $\varepsilon > 0$ *and each function* y *that satisfies the following inequalities*

$$\left|{}_cD^{0.7}y(t) - \frac{1}{3}{}_cD^{0.5}y(t) - \frac{\widetilde{c}e^{-\gamma t+t}|y|_\gamma}{(e^t+e^{-t})(1+|y|_\gamma)}\right| \leqslant \varepsilon, \quad t \in J = [0,1],$$

let $g(t)$ *represent the right side of the inequality above. Additionally, let* $x(t)$ *be the unique solution of problem* (11) *and* (12); *then, we have*

$$\sup_{0\leqslant\tau\leqslant t}|y(\tau)-x(\tau)| \leqslant \int_0^t \left(\frac{(t-s)^{-0.8}}{3\Gamma(0.2)} + \frac{(t-s)^{-0.3}}{\widetilde{c}\Gamma(0.7)}\right)\sup_{0\leqslant\sigma\leqslant s}|y(\sigma)-x(\sigma)|ds + \frac{1}{\Gamma(1.7)}\varepsilon,$$

let $\varphi(t) := \sup_{0\leqslant\tau\leqslant t}|y(\tau)-x(\tau)|$, $g(t,s) := \frac{1}{3\Gamma(0.2)} + \frac{(t-s)^{0.5}}{\widetilde{c}\Gamma(0.7)}$ *and* $M := \frac{1}{\Gamma(1.7)}$, *then it is easy to get that* $g(t,s) \leqslant \frac{1}{3\Gamma(0.2)} + \frac{1}{\widetilde{c}\Gamma(0.7)} (:= M_0)$, *and in view of Lemma 3,*

$$\begin{aligned}
\varphi(t) &\leqslant M\varepsilon + \int_0^t g(t,s)(t-s)^{-0.8}\varphi(s)ds \\
&\leqslant M\varepsilon + M\varepsilon\int_0^t \sum_{n=1}^{\infty}\frac{(g(t,s)\Gamma(0.2))^n}{\Gamma(0.2n)}(t-s)^{0.2n-1}ds \\
&\leqslant M\varepsilon + M\varepsilon\int_0^t \sum_{n=1}^{\infty}\frac{(M_0\Gamma(\alpha-\beta))^n}{\Gamma(0.2n)}(t-s)^{0.2n-1}ds \\
&\leqslant M\varepsilon + M\varepsilon\sum_{n=1}^{\infty}\frac{(M_0\Gamma(0.2))^n}{\Gamma(0.2n+1)} \\
&\leqslant M\varepsilon E_{0.2}(M_0\Gamma(0.2)),
\end{aligned}$$

let $c := ME_{0.2}(M_0\Gamma(0.2)) = \frac{1}{\Gamma(1.7)}E_{0.2}\left(\frac{1}{3} + \frac{\Gamma(0.2)}{\widetilde{c}\Gamma(0.7)}\right)$, *it follows that* $\varphi(t) \leqslant c\varepsilon$, *which implies that the problem* (11) *and* (12) *is Hyers-Ulam stable.*

6. Conclusions

This paper mainly discusses and investigates a class of nonlinear fractional differential equations with infinite time delay. Based on the properties of Green's function, we give the form of a solution to the differential equations. In addition to applying the fixed point theorem and Gronwall inequality, the related properties of the phase space are explored to investigate the nature and Hyers–Ulam stability of the solutions of fractional order differential equations under time delay conditions. Generally, various types of Gronwall inequalities can be utilized to explore the stability of fractional differential equations. However, we have found that only applying Gronwall inequalities is not enough to get stability conclusions in this paper. Therefore, we prove a comparative property of fractional calculus as an auxiliary tool to verify the stability of solutions. Furthermore, two examples are listed to confirm the conclusions.

Author Contributions: Conceptualization, Q.D.; validation, C.C.; formal analysis, Q.D.; methodology, Q.D.; writing—original draft preparation, C.C.; writing—review and editing, Q.D. and C.C. All authors have read and agreed to the published version of the manuscript.

Funding: This work was supported by the National Natural Science Foundation of China [Grant No. 11871064] and the Graduate Research and Innovation Projects of Jiangsu Province [Grant No. XKYCX20_010].

Institutional Review Board Statement: Not applicable.

Informed Consent Statement: Not applicable.

Data Availability Statement: Not applicable.

Acknowledgments: The authors thank the reviewers for their useful comments, which led to the improvement of the content of the paper.

Conflicts of Interest: The authors declare no conflict of interest.

References

1. Sun, H.; Chang, A.;Zhang, Y.; Chen, W.; Mahmudov, N.I. A review on variable-order fractional differential equations: Mathematical foundations, physical models, numerical methods and applications. *Fract. Calc. Appl. Anal.* **2019**, *22*, 27–59. [CrossRef]
2. Diethelm, K.; Ford, N.J. Analysis of fractional differential equations. *J. Math. Anal. Appl.* **2002**, *265*, 229–248. [CrossRef]
3. Plekhanova, M.V. Nonlinear equations with degenerate operator at fractional Caputo derivative. *Math. Methods Appl. Sci.* **2016**, *40*, 41–44. [CrossRef]
4. Fedorov, V.E.; Nagumanova, A.V.; Avilovich, A.S. A class of inverse problems for evolution equations with the Riemann–Liouville derivative in the sectorial case. *Math. Methods Appl. Sci.* **2021**, *44*, 11961–11969. [CrossRef]
5. Dzielinski, A.; Sierociuk, D.; Sarwas, G. Some applications of fractional order calculus. *Bull. Pol. Acad. Sci. Tech. Sci.* **2010**, *58*, 583–592. [CrossRef]
6. Li, C.P.; Sarwar, S. Existence and continuation of solutions for Caputo type fractional differential equations. *Electron. J. Differ. Equ.* **2016**, *207*, 1–14.
7. Moghaddam, B.P.; Machado, J.A.T. Computational scheme for solving nonlinear fractional stochastic differential equations with delay. *Stoch. Anal. Appl.* **2019**, *37*, 893–908. [CrossRef]
8. Maleknejad, K.; Hashemizadeh, E. Numerical solution of the dynamic model of a chemical reactor by hybrid functions. *Procedia Comput. Sci.* **2011**, *3*, 908–912. [CrossRef]
9. Moghaddam, B.P.; Machado, J.A.T. Time analysis of forced variable-order fractional Vander Pol oscillator. *Eur. Physucal J. Spec. Top.* **2017**, *226*, 3803–3810. [CrossRef]
10. Moghaddam, B.P.; Dabiri, A.; Lopes, A.M.; Machado, J.A.T. Numerical solution of mixed-type fractional functional differential equations using modified Lucas polynomials. *Comput. Appl. Math.* **2019**, *38*, 1–12. [CrossRef]
11. Moghaddam, B.P.; Mostaghim, Z.S. Modified finite difference method for solving fractional delay differential equations. *Bol. Soc. Parana. Matemática* **2017**, *35*, 49–58. [CrossRef]
12. Tuan, N.H.; Ngoc, T.B.; Huynh, L.N.; Kirane, M. Existence and uniqueness of mild solution of time-fractional semilinear differential equations with a nonlocal final condition. *Comput. Math. Appl.* **2019**, *78*, 1651–1668. [CrossRef]
13. Gou, H.; Li, B. Existence of Mild Solutions for Sobolev-Type Hilfer Fractional Nonautonomous Evolution Equations with Delay. *Int. J. Nonlinear. Sci. Numer. Simul.* **2018**, *19*, 481–492. [CrossRef]
14. Zhu, B.; Han, B.; Yu, W. Existence of Mild Solutions for a Class of Fractional Non-autonomous Evolution Equations with Delay. *Acta Math. Appl. Sin. Engl. Ser.* **2020**, *36*, 870–878. [CrossRef]
15. Wang, X.; Zhu, B. Existence Results for Fractional Semilinear Integrodifferential Equations of Mixed Type with Delay. *J. Funct. Spaces* **2021**, *2021*, 5519992. [CrossRef]
16. Hristova, S.; Dobreva, A. Existence, continuous dependence and finite time stability for Riemann-Liouville fractional differential equations with a constant delay. *AIMS Math.* **2020**, *5*, 3809–3824. [CrossRef]
17. Harrat, A.; Nieto, J.J.; Debbouche, A. Solvability and optimal controls of impulsive Hilfer fractional delay evolution inclusions with Clarke sub-differential. *J. Comput. Appl. Math.* **2018**, *344*, 725–737. [CrossRef]
18. Li, X.; Shen, J.; Akca, H.; Rakkiyappan, R. Comparison principle for impulsive functional differential equations with infinite delays and applications. *Commun. Nonlinear Sci. Numer. Simul.* **2018**, *57*, 309–321. [CrossRef]
19. Baleanu, D.; Ranjbar, A.; Sadati, S.J.; Delavari, H.; Maraaba, T.A.; Gejji, V. Lyapunov-Krasovskii stability theorem for fractional systems with delay. *Rom. J. Phys.* **2011**, *56*, 636–643.
20. Baleanu, D.; Sadati, S.J.; Ghaderi, R.; Ranjbar, A.; Maraaba, T.A.; Jarad, F. Razumikhin stability theorem for fractional systems with delay. *Abstr. Appl. Anal.* **2010**, *2010*, 124812. [CrossRef]
21. Chen, B.; Chen, J. Razumikhin-type stability theorems for functional fractional-order differential systems and applications. *Appl. Math. Comput.* **2015**, *254*, 63–69. [CrossRef]
22. Dong, Q.; Liu, C.; Fan, Z. Weighted fractional differential equations with infinite delay in Banach spaces. *Open Math.* **2016**, *14*, 370–383. [CrossRef]
23. Hale, J.K.; Kato, J. Phase Space for Retarded Equations with Infinite Delay. *Funkcial. Ekvac.* **1978**, *21*, 11–41.

24. Diethelm, K. *The Analysis of Fractional Differential Equations: An Application-Oriented Exposition Using Differential Operators of Caputo Type*; Springer Science & Business Media: New York, NY, USA, 2010.
25. Hino, Y.; Murakami, S.; Naito, T. *Functional Differential Equations with Infinite Delay*; Springer: Berlin/Heidelberg, Germany, 1991.
26. Smart, D.R. *fixed-Point Theorems, Cambridge Tracts in Mathematics*; Cambridge University Press: London, UK; New York, MY, USA, 1974.
27. Xu, L.; Dong, Q.; Li, G. Existence and Hyers-Ulam stability for three-point boundary value problems with Riemann-Liouville fractional derivatives and integrals. *Adv. Differ. Equ.* **2018**, *2018*, 458. [CrossRef]
28. Benchohra, M.; Henderson, H.; Ntouyas, S.T.; Ouahab, A. Existence results for fractional order functional differential equations with infinite delay. *J. Math. Anal. Appl.* **2008**, *338*, 1340–1350. [CrossRef]

fractal and fractional

MDPI

Article

Impact of Al_2O_3 in Electrically Conducting Mineral Oil-Based Maxwell Nanofluid: Application to the Petroleum Industry

Hanifa Hanif [1,2,*] and Sharidan Shafie [2,*]

[1] Department of Mathematics, Sardar Bahadur Khan Women's University, Quetta 87300, Pakistan
[2] Department of Mathematical Sciences, Faculty of Science, Universiti Teknologi Malaysia, Johor Bahru 81310, Johor, Malaysia
* Correspondence: hanifahanif@outlook.com (H.H.); sharidan@utm.my (S.S.)

Abstract: Alumina nanoparticles (Al_2O_3) are one of the essential metal oxides and have a wide range of applications and unique physio-chemical features. Most notably, alumina has been shown to have thermal properties such as high thermal conductivity and a convective heat transfer coefficient. Therefore, this study is conducted to integrate the adsorption of Al_2O_3 in mineral oil-based Maxwell fluid. The ambitious goal of this study is to intensify the mechanical and thermal properties of a Maxwell fluid under heat flux boundary conditions. The novelty of the research is increased by introducing fractional derivatives to the Maxwell model. There are various distinct types of fractional derivative definitions, with the Caputo fractional derivative being one of the most predominantly applied. Therefore, the fractoinal-order derivatives are evaluated using the fractional Caputo derivative, and the integer-order derivatives are evaluated using the Crank–Nicolson method. The obtained results are graphically displayed to demonstrate how all governing parameters, such as nanoparticle volume fraction, relaxation time, fractional derivative, magnetic field, thermal radiation, and viscous dissipation, have a significant impact on fluid flow and temperature distribution.

Keywords: Maxwell fluid; fractional derivative; nanofluid; Crank–Nicolson method

Citation: Hanif, H.; Shafie, S. Impact of Al_2O_3 in Electrically Conducting Mineral Oil-Based Maxwell Nanofluid: Application to the Petroleum Industry. *Fractal Fract.* **2022**, *6*, 180. https://doi.org/10.3390/fractalfract6040180

Academic Editors: António M. Lopes, Alireza Alfi, Liping Chen and Sergio A. David

Received: 10 February 2022
Accepted: 7 March 2022
Published: 24 March 2022

1. Introduction

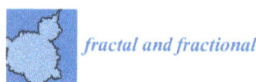

Nanotechnology has been a well-known subject of study since the last century. There have been numerous groundbreaking developments in the field of nanotechnology since Nobel laureate Richard P. Feynman introduced the term in their well-known 1959 lecture "There's Plenty of Room at the Bottom" [1]. Nanotechnology can generate a wide variety of new materials and devices with applications in nanomedicine, nanoelectronics, biomaterials, energy production, and consumer products. A decade ago, nanoparticles were studied because of their size-dependent physical and chemical properties. Now they have entered a period of commercial exploration [2]. In 1993, when industries and science needed better thermal capacities in fluids used daily for multiple jobs, Masuda et al. [3] proposed using ultra-fine particles in ordinary fluids. Later, Choi and Eastman [4] introduced the groundbreaking concept of nanofluid, which involves incorporating metallic nanoparticles with an average size of 100 nm into traditional fluids to improve thermal conductivity; this concept has modernized the worlds of engineering and industry. A nanofluid is an effective and practical approach to enhance heat transfer in a thermal system. However, research has shown that heat transfer efficiency varies between nanoparticles. Islam et al. [5] discussed the natural convection flow and heat transfer of Cu–water nanofluid into a square enclosure with the dominance of periodic magnetic effects. They observed that the heat transfer rate rises by 18.71% for Cu–water nanofluid with 1% nanoparticle volume. Wakif et al. [6] numerically investigated Couette flow with heat transfer for a Cu–water nanofluid in the presence of a magnetic field and thermal radiation with variable thermo-physical properties. Their results showed that heat transfer rates could enhance by increasing the nanoparticle volume fraction and the value of the radiation parameter. Xia et al. [7] discussed the dynamics of an unsteady reactive flow of a viscous nanomaterial subjected to Ohmic heating, heat source, and viscous dissipation. Their findings indicate that the temperature increases for the Eckert number, whereas the magnetic parameter shows the opposite pattern. Precisely, nanoparticle type, shape, and size have proven to play an important role [8–10].

Alumina (Al_2O_3), often known as aluminum oxide, is an amphoteric oxide found in nature in the minerals corundum and gibbsite. Alumina nanoparticles offer several desirable qualities, including high thermal conductivity, thermal stability, oxidation, high strength and stiffness, mechanical strength, high adsorption capacity, and electrical insulation. Most importantly, it is a low-cost, non-toxic, and pretty abrasive nanoparticle [11]. Haridas et al. [12] have experimentally evaluated the performance of Al_2O_3 and SiO_2 in deionized water-based nanofluids for their ability to influence heat transfer phenomena in small channels. They found an increase of $\approx$41% in the average heat transfer coefficient for the 0.02 Vol.% of Al_2O_3 at Re = 342, In contrast, the corresponding enhancement for SiO_2 nanoparticles was limited to 6% in the lower Reynolds number range. Animasaun [13] used a modified version of the buoyancy-induced model to study the flow of 47 nm alumina–water nanofluid along a horizontal paraboloid of revolution under the effects of Lorentz force, non-linear radiation, and chemical reaction. He concluded that the heat capacity and other features of 47 nm alumina–water nanofluid considerably create more heat energy at large values of volume fraction, which accounts for the overshoot in temperature and velocity curves. Kabeel and Abdelgaied [14] have numerically explored the impact of Al_2O_3–water concentration on sharp-edge orifice flow characteristics in cavitation and non-cavitation turbulent flow regimes. According to their findings, when the nanofluid concentration increases from 0.0% to 2%, the turbulent kinetic energy and turbulent intensity increase by 160% and 74%, respectively, in the separation zone downstream of the orifice. Hawwash et al. [15] looked into the effectiveness of employing alumina nanofluids as a working fluid for solar water heaters. Sheikholeslami and Ebrahimpour [16] used Al_2O_3/water together with multi-way twisted tape for thermal improvement of a linear Fresnel solar system. Bahari et al. [17] presented research on the synthesis of Al_2O_3 to SiO_2/water hybrid nanofluid and effects of anionic (SDS), cationic (CTAB), and nonionic (PVP) surfactants toward dispersion and stability. They concluded that SDS could positively affect the dispersion and stability of the nanofluids, and the best ratio of Al_2O_3:SiO_2 was at 30:70. Moreover, the electrical conductivity increased with temperature, and nanofluid containing CTAB and SDS had a higher increment in conductivity. Recently, Ho et al. [18] investigated the cooling efficiency and entropy generation of Al_2O_3–water flow and heat transfer in a circular tube with wall conduction effects. They stated that the irreversibility of a system could reduce using nanofluid.

In the late nineteenth and early twentieth centuries, it had recognized that the stress in a fluid could have a nonlinear or temporal dependency on the rate of deformation or both; we now refer to such materials as non-Newtonian fluids [19]. Non–Newtonian fluids are usually considered more suitable and sufficient in industrial processes due to their diverse range of uses, including exotic lubricants, polymer fluid extrusion, colloidal and suspension solutions, slurry fuels, and more. Unlike Newtonian fluids, it is not easy to imagine a single mathematical model that encompasses all of the properties of non-Newtonian fluids. Therefore, several mathematical models for non-Newtonian fluids have been proposed. The Maxwell fluid model, which can predict stress relaxation, has received much attention among these models. In 1867, James Clerk Maxwell proposed the concept of Maxwell fluid, and a few years later, James G. Oldroyd popularized the idea [20,21]. Researchers have drawn to the Maxwell fluid model because of its simplicity. Megahed [22] has theoretically analyzed the steady flow of Maxwell fluid along a permeable stretching sheet subject to convective boundary conditions. The consequences of the inclined magnetohydrodynamic flow of a Maxwell fluid through a penetrable stretched plate had discussed by Shafiq and

Khalique [23]. Specifically, the heat generation and absorption effects are investigated in the heat transfer phenomenon using Lie group methods.

Fractional calculus is not a new concept; its history is nearly identical to classical calculus. However, it has become more popular in the constitutive modeling of non-Newtonian fluids over the last two decades. The fundamental reason for this development is that a fractional model could express the complex properties of viscoelastic material simply and elegantly. For example, many materials have an algebraic decay during the relaxation process, which cannot be adequately characterized by the exponential relaxation moduli of conventional ordinary models [24]. However, experiments indicate that fractional models can accurately capture and link these behaviors [25,26]. According to Heymans [27], complex module expressions can result in fractional derivative constitutive models that can numerically integrate the overall loading history. Liu et al. [28] introduced a unique constitution equation comprising relaxation time parameters and distributed-order fractional operators to analyze flow and heat transfer of an incompressible Maxwell fluid over a moving plate. Yang et al. [29] explored heat transfer characteristics of a double-fraction Maxwell fluid flow subject to slip boundary conditions. Their findings showed that the fractional Maxwell fluid has a higher viscosity against fractional parameters and that the oscillation phenomenon would gradually decrease as slip parameters grow. Razzaq et al. [30] addressed the heat transfer of fractional Maxwell fluid in a circular cylinder using Laplace and Hankel transformations. Hanif [31] studied two-dimensional boundary layer flow and heat transfer of fractional Maxwell fluid with constant heating. Asjad et al. [32] investigated the effects of clay nanoparticles on an unsteady natural convection flow of Maxwell nanofluids over an infinite vertical surface. They found that oil-based nanofluid had minimal velocity compared to water-based nanofluid. Saqib et al. [33] discussed the heat-transfer properties of a Maxwell fluid in the presence of a magnetic field using the fractional Cattaneo–Friedrich Model. Bayones et al. [34] studied the peristaltic flow of fractional Maxwell fluid in a circular cylinder tube in the presence of a magnetic filed.

In this research, the physical model is based on fractional Maxwell fluid flow with accompanying heat transport over a horizontal plate with significant physical assumptions. This research is motivated by improved cooling processes caused by the interaction of Al_2O_3 nanoparticles in mineral oil. The applied magnetic field and viscous dissipation contribute to the novelty of the fractional fluid model. Moreover, there are a few instances where exact analytic solutions to the Navier–Stokes equations can be found. Therefore, the inspiring goal of this research is to introduce the Crank–Nicolson-based L1 algorithm to solve the fractional Maxwell fluid flow model. There are various distinct types of fractional derivative definitions, with the Riemann–Liouville fractional derivative and the Caputo fractional derivative being two of the most prominent in applications. Therefore, the Caputo fractional derivative has been used to integrate the fractional-order derivatives, whereas integer-order derivatives are evaluated using the Crank–Nicolson finite difference method.

2. Mathematical Formulation

This section is devoted to the detailed mathematical modeling of the fractional Maxwell nanofluid. In this regard, the following definitions will be helpful.

Definition 1. *Let $\Gamma(\cdot)$ denote the Gamma function defined by the integral (see for instance Podlubny [35])*

$$\Gamma(\eta) = \int_{\mathbb{R}} e^{-\psi}\psi^{\eta-1}d\psi, \quad \forall\eta \in \mathbb{C} \quad \text{such that} \quad \Re(\eta) > 0. \tag{1}$$

Definition 2. *Let $n \in \mathbb{N}$ and $\alpha \in \mathbb{C}$ with $\Re(\alpha) > 0$ such that $n-1 < \alpha < n$. Then for a function f in $C^n(\mathbb{R})$, the Caputo fractional derivative of order α is given by:*

$$\frac{\partial^\alpha f(t)}{\partial t^\alpha} = \partial_t^\alpha f(t) := \frac{1}{\Gamma(n-\alpha)}\int_0^t (t-\tau)^{n-\alpha-1}\frac{\partial^n}{\partial t^n}f(\tau)d\tau, \tag{2}$$

where $\Gamma(\cdot)$ is the gamma function; refer to the book [35] for detailed analysis of fractional derivatives.

2.1. Flow Configuration and Governing Equations

Assume that the Maxwell nanofluid is in the space above an infinite plate parallel to the xz-plane and is confined by two parallel sidewalls perpendicular to the plate. A pressure gradient is applied to the fluid along the x-axis at time $t > 0$, which initiates the mainstream flow. As a result, flow velocity takes the following form

$$V = \big(u(y,z,t), 0, 0\big), \tag{3}$$

along with the extra stress tensor

$$\mathcal{T} = \mathcal{T}(y,z,t), \tag{4}$$

in the absence of a cross flow. The graphical representation of the flow model is presented in Figure 1.

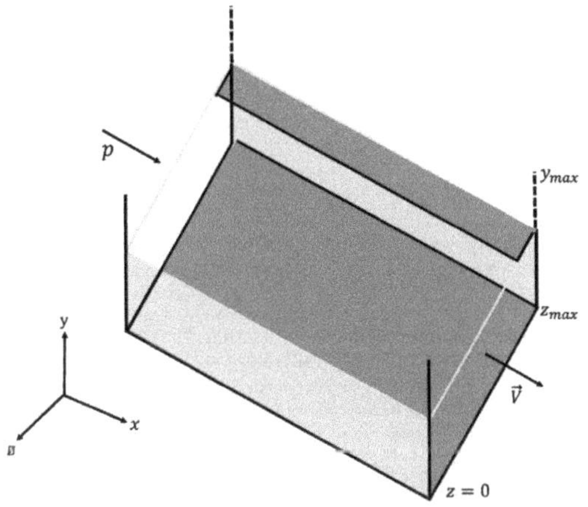

Figure 1. Graphical representation of the flow model.

If a fluid with the density ρ is moving with the velocity V, then the continuity equation is defined as [31]

$$\frac{\partial \rho}{\partial t} + \nabla \cdot (\rho V) = 0. \tag{5}$$

For an incompressible fluid, Equation (5) reduces to the following form

$$\nabla \cdot V = 0. \tag{6}$$

It is simple to verify that the velocity field of the form (3) automatically meets the incompressibility condition. The non-relativistic momentum transport in any continuum is predicted by Cauchy momentum equation, defined by [36]:

$$\rho\left(\frac{\partial V}{\partial t} + V \cdot \nabla V\right) = -\nabla \mathcal{P} + \nabla \cdot \mathcal{T}, \tag{7}$$

where $\mathcal{P}$ is the pressure. The extra stress tensor $\mathcal{T}$ is represented by the following relationship [34]:

$$\mathcal{T} + \lambda^{\alpha}\left(\partial_t^{\alpha}\mathcal{T} + V \cdot \nabla \mathcal{T} - (\nabla V)\mathcal{T} - \mathcal{T}(\nabla V)^{\dagger}\right) = \mu \mathcal{A}. \tag{8}$$

Here $\mathcal{A} = \nabla V + (\nabla V)^{\dagger}$ is the first Rivlin–Erickson tensor, μ is the dynamic viscosity of Maxwell fluid, λ is the relaxation time parameter, and the subscript $\dagger$ is the transpose of a matrix. In the presence of magnetic field $B = B_0 + B_1$, Equation (7) can be modified as

$$\rho\left(\frac{\partial V}{\partial t} + V \cdot \nabla V\right) = -\nabla \mathcal{P} + \nabla \cdot \mathcal{T} + J \times B. \tag{9}$$

Ohm's law describes the current density J as [37]

$$J = \sigma E_r, \tag{10}$$

where σ is the electrical conductivity of the fluid and E_r is the electric field experienced by the fluid. Applying the Lorentz transformation to the fluid traveling at velocity V concerning the external magnetic field gives us

$$E_r = E + V \times B. \tag{11}$$

The electric field vector $E = 0$ because no applied or polarization voltage is imposed on the flow field. Further, the magnetic Reynolds number is considered to be too small for the induced magnetic field B_1 to be negligible, and therefore the current density J is reduced to

$$J = \sigma(V \times B), \tag{12}$$

and the cross product $(V \times B)$ can be obtained as

$$(V \times B) = \begin{vmatrix} i & j & k \\ u & 0 & 0 \\ 0 & B_0 & 0 \end{vmatrix} = (0, 0, B_0 u). \tag{13}$$

With Equations (12) and (13), $(J \times B)$ is given as

$$(J \times B) = \begin{vmatrix} i & j & k \\ 0 & 0 & B_0 u \\ 0 & B_0 & 0 \end{vmatrix} = (-B_0^2 u, 0, 0). \tag{14}$$

In reference with the velocity field (3), extra stress tensor (4) and Lorentz force (14), the momentum Equation (9) reduces to the following form

$$\rho_{nf}\frac{\partial u}{\partial t} = -\frac{\partial \mathcal{P}}{\partial x} + \frac{\partial \tau_{xy}}{\partial y} + \frac{\partial \tau_{xz}}{\partial z} - B_0^2 u, \tag{15}$$

where τ_{xy} and τ_{xz} are nonzero components of $\mathcal{T}$. Introducing Equation (3) into the extra stress tensor relation (8) gives us

$$\left(1 + \lambda_1^{\alpha}\partial_t^{\alpha}\right)\tau_{xy} = \mu\frac{\partial u}{\partial y}, \quad \left(1 + \lambda_1^{\alpha}\partial_t^{\alpha}\right)\tau_{xz} = \mu\frac{\partial u}{\partial z}. \tag{16}$$

Now, operating the differential operator $\left(1 + \lambda_1^{\alpha}\partial_t^{\alpha}\right)$ to Equation (15) and utilizing Equation (16) results in

$$\rho\left(1 + \lambda_1^{\alpha}\partial_t^{\alpha}\right)\frac{\partial u}{\partial t} = -\left(1 + \lambda_1^{\alpha}\partial_t^{\alpha}\right)\frac{\partial \mathcal{P}}{\partial x} + \mu\left(\frac{\partial^2 u}{\partial y^2} + \frac{\partial^2 u}{\partial z^2}\right) - B_0^2\sigma\left(1 + \lambda_1^{\alpha}\partial_t^{\alpha}\right)u. \tag{17}$$

The applied pressure in the x-direction is

$$\frac{\partial \mathcal{P}}{\partial x} = p_0 \mathcal{H}(t), \tag{18}$$

with the Heaviside function

$$\mathcal{H}(t) = \begin{cases} 1, \; t > 0, \\ 0, \; t < 0. \end{cases} \tag{19}$$

Next, the internal (heat) energy balance law can be stated in terms of T as [31]

$$\rho C_p \left(\frac{\partial T}{\partial t} + V \cdot \nabla T \right) = k \nabla T + \mathcal{T} : \nabla V. \tag{20}$$

Here k is the thermal conductivity and C_p is the specific heat at constant pressure. In the presence of thermal radiation and Ohmic heating, the energy Equation (20) can be modified as

$$\rho C_p \left(\frac{\partial T}{\partial t} + V \cdot \nabla T \right) = k \nabla T - \frac{\partial q_r}{\partial y} + \frac{1}{\sigma} J \cdot J + \mathcal{T} : \nabla V. \tag{21}$$

Using the Roseland approximation, the radiative heat flux q_r in Equation (21) is expressed as

$$q_r = -\frac{4\sigma_b}{3k_b} \frac{\partial T^4}{\partial y}. \tag{22}$$

Let us consider that the temperature difference $T - T_\infty$ within the flow domain to be small enough that T^4 can be reasonably expanded about T_∞ using the Taylor series as follows:

$$T^4 \approxeq T_\infty^4 + 4T_\infty^3 (T - T_\infty) + 6T_\infty^2 (T - T_\infty)^2 + \ldots \tag{23}$$

The higher-order terms are ignored because the temperature gradient is believed to be small enough, resulting in

$$T^4 \approxeq T_\infty^4 + 4T_\infty^3 (T - T_\infty). \tag{24}$$

In Equation (22), the simplified version of T^4 is employed and differentiated w.r.t y, yielding

$$\frac{\partial q_r}{\partial y} = -\frac{16\sigma_b T_\infty^3}{3k_b} \frac{\partial T^2}{\partial y^2}. \tag{25}$$

Invoking Equations (3), (12) and (25) for the energy Equation (21) leads us to

$$\rho C_p \frac{\partial T}{\partial t} = k \left(\frac{\partial^2 T}{\partial y^2} + \frac{\partial^2 T}{\partial z^2} \right) + \frac{\partial^2 T}{\partial y^2} + B_0^2 \sigma u^2 + \tau_{xy} \frac{\partial u}{\partial y} + \tau_{xz} \frac{\partial u}{\partial z}. \tag{26}$$

Furthermore, the governing equation for a nanofluid flow can be obtained by replacing the properties of a regular fluid with the corresponding properties of a nanofluid. Hence Equations (17) and (26) can be revised as

$$\rho_{nf} \left(1 + \lambda_1^\alpha \partial_t^\alpha \right) \frac{\partial u}{\partial t} = -\left(1 + \lambda_1^\alpha \partial_t^\alpha \right) \frac{\partial \mathcal{P}}{\partial x} + \mu_{nf} \left(\frac{\partial^2 u}{\partial y^2} + + \frac{\partial^2 u}{\partial z^2} \right) - B_0^2 \sigma_{nf} \left(1 + \lambda_1^\alpha \partial_t^\alpha \right) u. \tag{27}$$

$$(\rho C_p)_{nf} \frac{\partial T}{\partial t} = k_{nf} \left(\frac{\partial^2 T}{\partial y^2} + \frac{\partial^2 T}{\partial z^2} \right) + \frac{\partial^2 T}{\partial y^2} + B_0^2 \sigma_{nf} u^2 + \tau_{xy} \frac{\partial u}{\partial y} + \tau_{xz} \frac{\partial u}{\partial z}. \tag{28}$$

The mathematical expressions for nanofluid properties, $\mu_{nf}, \rho_{nf}, \sigma_{nf}, (\rho C_p)_{nf}$, and k_{nf} are presented in Table 1, and thermo-physical properties of mineral oil and Al_2O_3 are provided in Table 2.

Initially, the fluid is at rest. Therefore, the zero initial conditions are considered:

$$u(y,z,t) = 0 = \frac{\partial u(y,z,t)}{\partial t},\ T(y,z,t),\ t \leq 0,\ (y,z) \in [0,\infty) \times [0, z_{max}]. \tag{29}$$

We impose a no-slip velocity condition along the plate and the walls so that:

$$\begin{cases} u(0,z,t) = 0,\ k_{nf}\dfrac{\partial T(0,z,t)}{\partial y} = -q_w,\ t > 0,\ z \in [0, z_{max}], \\ u(y,0,t) = 0 = u(y, z_{max}, t),\ t > 0,\ y \in [0,\infty), \\ T(y,0,t) = T_\infty = T(y, z_{max}, t),\ t > 0,\ y \in [0,\infty). \end{cases} \tag{30}$$

The natural far field conditions are:

$$u(y,z,t) \to 0,\ T(y,z,t) \to T_\infty \text{ as } y \to \infty. \tag{31}$$

Table 1. Mathematical expression of nanofluid properties [5].

Properties	Mathematical Expressions
Viscosity	$\mu_{nf} = \mu_f(1-\varphi)^{-2.5}$
Density	$\rho_{nf} = (1-\varphi)\rho_f + \varphi\rho_s$
Heat capacitance	$(\rho C_p)_{nf} = (1-\varphi)(\rho C_p)_f + \varphi(\rho C_p)_s$
Thermal conductivity	$\dfrac{k_{nf}}{k_f} = \dfrac{(k_s + 2k_f) + 2\varphi(k_s - k_f)}{(k_s + 2k_f) - \varphi(k_s - k_f)}$
Electrical conductivity	$\dfrac{\sigma_{nf}}{\sigma_f} = \dfrac{(\sigma_s + 2\sigma_f) + 2\varphi(\sigma_s - \sigma_f)}{(\sigma_s + 2\sigma_f) - \varphi(\sigma_s - \sigma_f)}$

Table 2. Thermo-physical properties of mineral oil and nanoparticles [38,39].

Materials	Mineral Oil	Al_2O_3
ρ (kg/m^3)	861	3970
k (W/mK)	0.157	40
C_p (J/kgK)	1860	765
σ (S/m)	$\approx 0.3310^{-9}$	35×10^6
μ (Pa.s)	0.01335	–

2.2. Non-Dimensional Modeling

Non-dimensional representation is imperative to highlight the physics of the stated problem. Therefore, the following non-dimensional parameters are introduced:

$$\begin{gathered} y^* = \frac{y}{z_{max}},\quad z^* = \frac{z}{z_{max}},\quad t^* = \frac{\nu_f t}{z_{max}^2},\quad u^* = \frac{u z_{max}}{\nu_f}, \\ T^* = \frac{T - T_\infty}{q_w z_{max}/k_f},\quad \lambda^* = \frac{\lambda \nu_f}{z_{max}^2},\quad \tau_{xy}^* = \frac{z_{max}^2 \tau_{xy}}{\mu_f \nu_f},\quad \tau_{xz}^* = \frac{z_{max}^2 \tau_{xz}}{\mu_f \nu_f}. \end{gathered} \tag{32}$$

Using the set of non-dimensional parameters (32) in Equations (27)–(31), we arrived at

$$\phi_1\left(1 + \lambda^\alpha \frac{\partial^\alpha}{\partial t^\alpha}\right)\frac{\partial u}{\partial t} = p\left(\mathcal{H}(t) + \lambda^\alpha \frac{t^{-\alpha}}{\Gamma(1-\alpha)}\right) + \phi_2\left(\frac{\partial^2 u}{\partial y^2} + \frac{\partial^2 u}{\partial z^2}\right) - \phi_3 M\left(1 + \lambda^\alpha \frac{\partial^\alpha}{\partial t^\alpha}\right)u, \tag{33}$$

$$Pr\phi_4 \frac{\partial T}{\partial t} = \left(\phi_5 + Rd\right)\frac{\partial^2 T}{\partial y^2} + \phi_5 \frac{\partial^2 T}{\partial z^2} + \phi_3 M u^2 + \mathcal{E}\left\{\tau_{xy}\frac{\partial u}{\partial y} + \tau_{xz}\frac{\partial u}{\partial z}\right\}, \tag{34}$$

subject to the initial and boundary conditions

$$\begin{cases} u(y,z,t) = 0 = \dfrac{\partial u(y,z,t)}{\partial t}, \; T(y,z,t) = 0, t < 0, \; (y,z) \in [0,\infty) \times [0, z_{max}], \\ u(0,z,t) = 0, \; \phi_4 \dfrac{\partial T(0,z,t)}{\partial y} = -1, \; t > 0, \; z \in [0, z_{max}], \\ u(y,0,t) = 0 = u(y, z_{max}, t), \; T(y,0,t) = 0 = T(y, z_{max}, t), \; t > 0, \; y \in [0,\infty), \\ u(y,z,t) \to 0, \; T(y,z,t) \to 0 \text{ as } y \to \infty. \end{cases} \tag{35}$$

Provided that

$$\begin{aligned} &\phi_1 = (1-\varphi) + \varphi\rho_s/\rho_f, \; \phi_2 = (1-\varphi)^{-2.5}, \phi_3 = \frac{\sigma_{nf}}{\sigma_f}, \; \phi_4 = (1-\varphi) + \varphi(\rho C_p)_s/(\rho C_p)_f, \\ &\phi_5 = \frac{k_{nf}}{k_f}, \; p = \frac{p_0 z_{max}^3}{v_f^2}, \; M = \frac{\sigma_f B_0^2 z_{max}}{\mu_f}, Rd = \frac{16\sigma_b}{3k_b k_f}, \; \mathcal{E} = \frac{\mu_f v_f^2}{q_w z_{maz}^3}, \; Pr = \frac{\mu_f C_{p_f}}{k_f}. \end{aligned} \tag{36}$$

3. Numerical Scheme

The aim of this section is to devise a scheme for approximating Equations (33)–(35) over a finite time interval.

Define $t_k = k\hbar, k = 0,1,\cdots,\mathfrak{n}$, $y_i = i\mathfrak{p}, i = 1,2,\cdots,\mathfrak{r}$, $z_j = j\mathfrak{q}, j = 1,2,\cdots,\mathfrak{s}$, where $\hbar = t_{\mathfrak{f}}/n$, is the time step, $\mathfrak{p} = y_{max}/\mathfrak{r}$, and $\mathfrak{q} = z_{max}/\mathfrak{s}$ are the mesh size in (y,z) direction. The integer-order derivatives are approximated using the Crank–Nicolson finite difference method as follows:

$$\frac{\partial u}{\partial t}\Big|_{t_k} = \frac{u_{i,j}^k - u_{i,j}^{k-1}}{\hbar}, \quad \frac{\partial T}{\partial t}\Big|_{t_k} = \frac{T_{i,j}^k - T_{i,j}^{k-1}}{\hbar}. \tag{37}$$

$$\frac{\partial^2 u}{\partial y^2}\Big|_{t_k} = \frac{u_{i-1,j}^k - 2u_{i,j}^k + u_{i+1,j}^k + u_{i-1,j}^{k-1} - 2u_{i,j}^{k-1} + u_{i+1,j}^{k-1}}{2\mathfrak{p}^2}. \tag{38}$$

$$\frac{\partial^2 u}{\partial z^2}\Big|_{t_k} = \frac{u_{i,j-1}^k - 2u_{i,j}^k + u_{i,j+1}^k + u_{i,j-1}^{k-1} - 2u_{i,j}^{k-1} + u_{i,j+1}^{k-1}}{2\mathfrak{q}^2}. \tag{39}$$

$$\frac{\partial^2 T}{\partial y^2}\Big|_{t_k} = \frac{T_{i-1,j}^k - 2T_{i,j}^k + T_{i+1,j}^k + T_{i-1,j}^{k-1} - 2T_{i,j}^{k-1} + T_{i+1,j}^{k-1}}{2\mathfrak{p}^2}. \tag{40}$$

$$\frac{\partial^2 T}{\partial z^2}\Big|_{t_k} = \frac{T_{i,j-1}^k - 2T_{i,j}^k + T_{i,j+1}^k + T_{i,j-1}^{k-1} - 2T_{i,j}^{k-1} + T_{i,j+1}^{k-1}}{2\mathfrak{q}^2}. \tag{41}$$

The L1 algorithm of Caputo fractional derivative (2) is given as

$$\begin{aligned} \frac{\partial^\alpha f(t_k)}{\partial t^\alpha} &= \frac{\hbar^{-\alpha}}{\Gamma(2-\alpha)} \textstyle\sum_{\mathrm{m}=0}^{k-1} b_{\mathrm{m}} \left[f(t_{k-\mathrm{m}} - f(t_{k-\mathrm{m}-1}) \right], \\ &= \frac{\hbar^{-\alpha}}{\Gamma(2-\alpha)} \left[b_0 f(t_k) - b_{k-1} f(t_0) - \textstyle\sum_{\mathrm{m}=1}^{k-1} (b_{\mathrm{m}-1} - b_{\mathrm{m}}) f(t_{k-\mathrm{m}}) \right], \end{aligned} \tag{42}$$

where $b_{\mathrm{m}} = (\mathrm{m}+1)^{1-\alpha} - \mathrm{m}^{1-\alpha}, \mathrm{m} = 0,1,2,\cdots,\mathfrak{n}$. Now, the fractional derivatives in Equation (33) can be approximated using the L1 algorithm (42) as follows:

$$\frac{\partial^\alpha u}{\partial t^\alpha}\Big|_{t_k} = \frac{\hbar^{-\alpha}}{\Gamma(2-\alpha)} \left[\mathcal{U}(t_k) - \sum_{\mathrm{m}=1}^{k-1} a_{\mathrm{m}} \mathcal{U}(t_{k-\mathrm{m}}) \right], \tag{43}$$

$$\frac{\partial^{\alpha+1} u}{\partial t^{\alpha+1}}\Big|_{t_k} = \frac{\hbar^{-\alpha-1}}{\Gamma(2-\alpha)} \left[\mathcal{U}(t_k) - \mathcal{U}(t_{k-1}) - \sum_{\mathrm{m}=1}^{k-1} a_{\mathrm{m}} \big(\mathcal{U}(t_{k-\mathrm{m}}) - \mathcal{U}(t_{k-\mathrm{m}-1}) \big) \right], \tag{44}$$

where $a_{\mathrm{m}} = (b_{\mathrm{m}-1} - b_{\mathrm{m}})$.

$$\begin{aligned}
\frac{\phi_1}{\hbar}\left(1+\frac{\lambda^{\alpha}\hbar^{-\alpha}}{\Gamma(2-\alpha)}\right)\left[u_{i,j}^{k}-u_{i,j}^{k-1}\right] &= \frac{\phi_1 p_0}{2}\left[\mathcal{H}(t_k)+\mathcal{H}(t_{k+1})+\lambda^{\alpha}\frac{t_k^{-\alpha}+t_{k+1}^{-\alpha}}{\Gamma(1-\alpha)}\right] \\
&+\frac{\phi_2}{2\mathrm{p}^2}\left[u_{i-1,j}^{k}-2u_{i,j}^{k}+u_{i+1,j}^{k}+u_{i-1,j}^{k-1}\right. \\
&\left.-2u_{i,j}^{k-1}+u_{i+1,j}^{k-1}\right]+\frac{\phi_2}{2\mathrm{q}^2}\left[u_{i,j-1}^{k}-2u_{i,j}^{k}\right. \\
&\left.+u_{i,j+1}^{k}+u_{i,j-1}^{k-1}-2u_{i,j}^{k-1}+u_{i,j+1}^{k-1}\right] \\
&-\left(\phi_3 M+\phi_3 M\lambda^{\alpha}\frac{\hbar^{-\alpha}}{\Gamma(2-\alpha)}\right)\left[u_{i,j}^{k}+u_{i,j}^{k-1}\right] \\
&+\phi_3 M\lambda^{\alpha}\frac{\hbar^{-\alpha}}{\Gamma(2-\alpha)}\sum_{\mathrm{m}=1}^{k-1}\mathfrak{b}_{\mathrm{m}}\left[u_{i,j}^{k-\mathrm{m}}+u_{i,j}^{k-\mathrm{m}-1}\right] \\
&+\phi_1\lambda^{\alpha}\frac{\hbar^{-(\alpha+1)}}{\Gamma(2-\alpha)}\sum_{\mathrm{m}=1}^{k-1}\mathfrak{b}_{\mathrm{m}}\left[u_{i,j}^{k-\mathrm{m}}-u_{i,j}^{k-\mathrm{m}-1}\right].
\end{aligned} \tag{45}$$

$$\begin{aligned}
\frac{\phi_3 Pr}{\hbar}\left[T_{i,j}^{k}-T_{i,j}^{k-1}\right] &= \frac{(\phi_4+Rd)}{2\mathrm{p}^2}\left[T_{i-1,j}^{k}-2T_{i,j}^{k}+T_{i+1,j}^{k}+T_{i,j+1}^{k-1}-2T_{i,j}^{k-1}+T_{i,j}^{k-1}\right] \\
&+\frac{\phi_4}{2\mathrm{q}^2}\left[T_{i,j-1}^{k}-2T_{i,j}^{k}+T_{i,j+1}^{k}+T_{i,j-1}^{k-1}-2T_{i,j}^{k-1}+T_{i,j+1}^{k-1}\right] \\
&+\frac{\phi_3 M}{4}\left(u_{i,j}^{k}+u_{i,j}^{k-1}\right)^2+\frac{\mathcal{E}}{4\mathrm{p}}\left(\tau_{xy}^{k}+\tau_{xy}^{k-1}\right)\left[u_{i+1,j}^{k}-u_{i,j}^{k}+u_{i+1,j}^{k-1}\right. \\
&\left.-u_{i,j}^{k-1}\right]+\frac{\mathcal{E}}{8\mathrm{q}}\left(\tau_{xz}^{k}+\tau_{xz}^{k-1}\right)\left[u_{i,j+1}^{k}-u_{i,j-1}^{k}+u_{i,j+1}^{k-1}-u_{i,j-1}^{k-1}\right].
\end{aligned} \tag{46}$$

$$\begin{aligned}
u_{i,j}^{0} &= 0 = T_{i,j}^{0},\ u_{0,j}^{k} = u_{i,0}^{k} = u_{i,\mathfrak{s}}^{k} = u_{\mathfrak{r},j}^{k} = 0, \\
T_{-1,j}^{k}+T_{-1,j}^{k-1} &= 4\mathrm{p}+T_{1,j}^{k}+T_{1,j}^{k-1},\ T_{i,0}^{k} = T_{i,\mathfrak{s}}^{k} = T_{\mathfrak{r},j}^{k} = 0.
\end{aligned} \tag{47}$$

4. Results and Discussion

Using the framework of an unsteady two-dimensional fluid flow, the purpose of this section is to help the reader understand the explanation of the graphical illustrations of Maxwell nanofluid flow over a horizontal plate. The theoretical aspects of nanoparticles, magnetic fields, thermal radiation, viscous dissipation, and Joule heating concerning fluid flow and heat transfer are also discussed in this section. Figures 2–13 are presented to investigate the impact of regulating parameters on the velocity and the temperature profiles of Maxwell nanofluid. The following numerical values for the parameters are assumed to be fixed unless stated otherwise: $\alpha = 0.5$ [32], $\lambda = 0.1$ [32], $\varphi = 0.01$ [32], $M = 2$ [6], $Rd = 0.1$ [7], and $\mathcal{E} = 0.1$ [7].

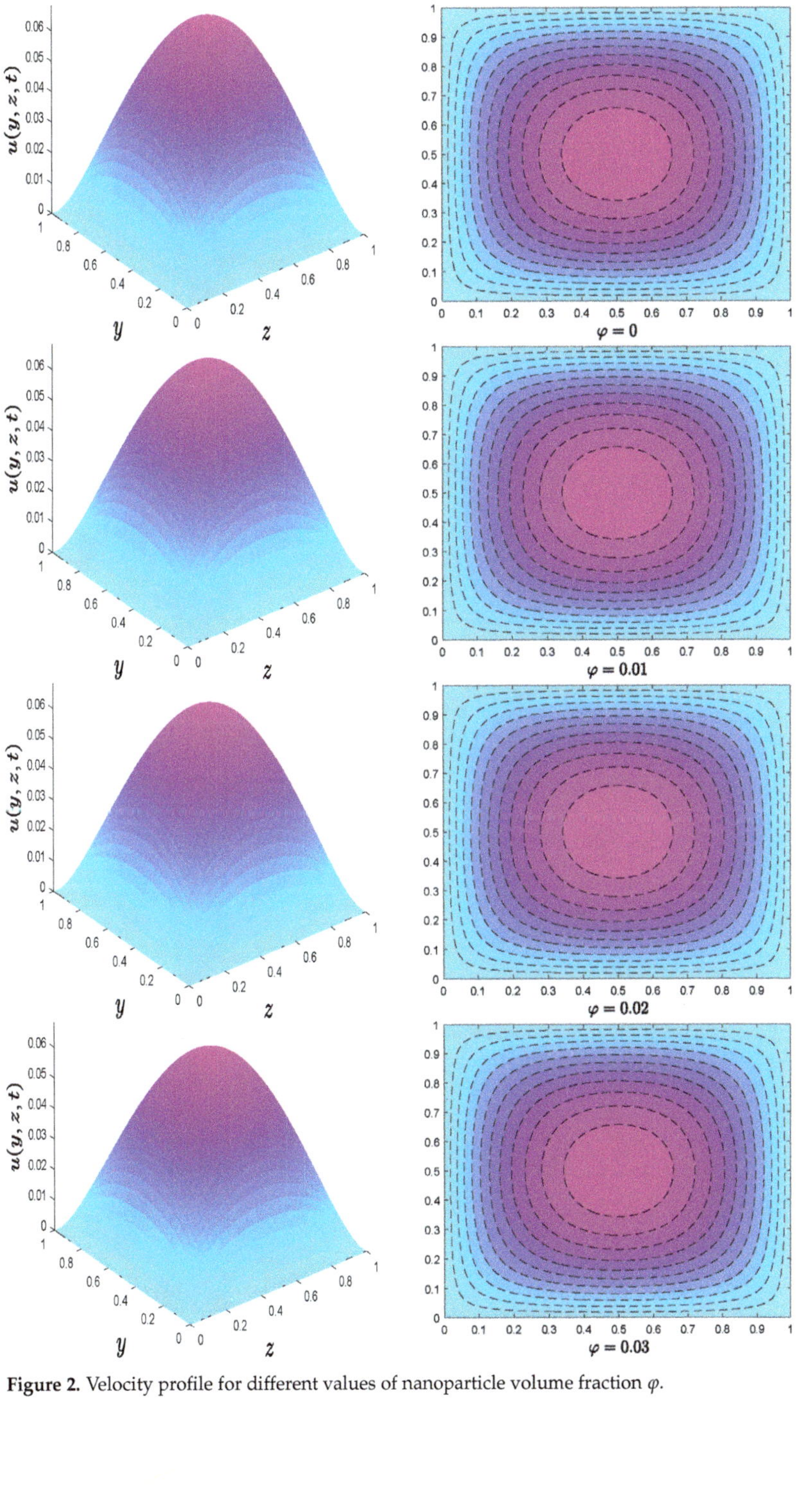

Figure 2. Velocity profile for different values of nanoparticle volume fraction φ.

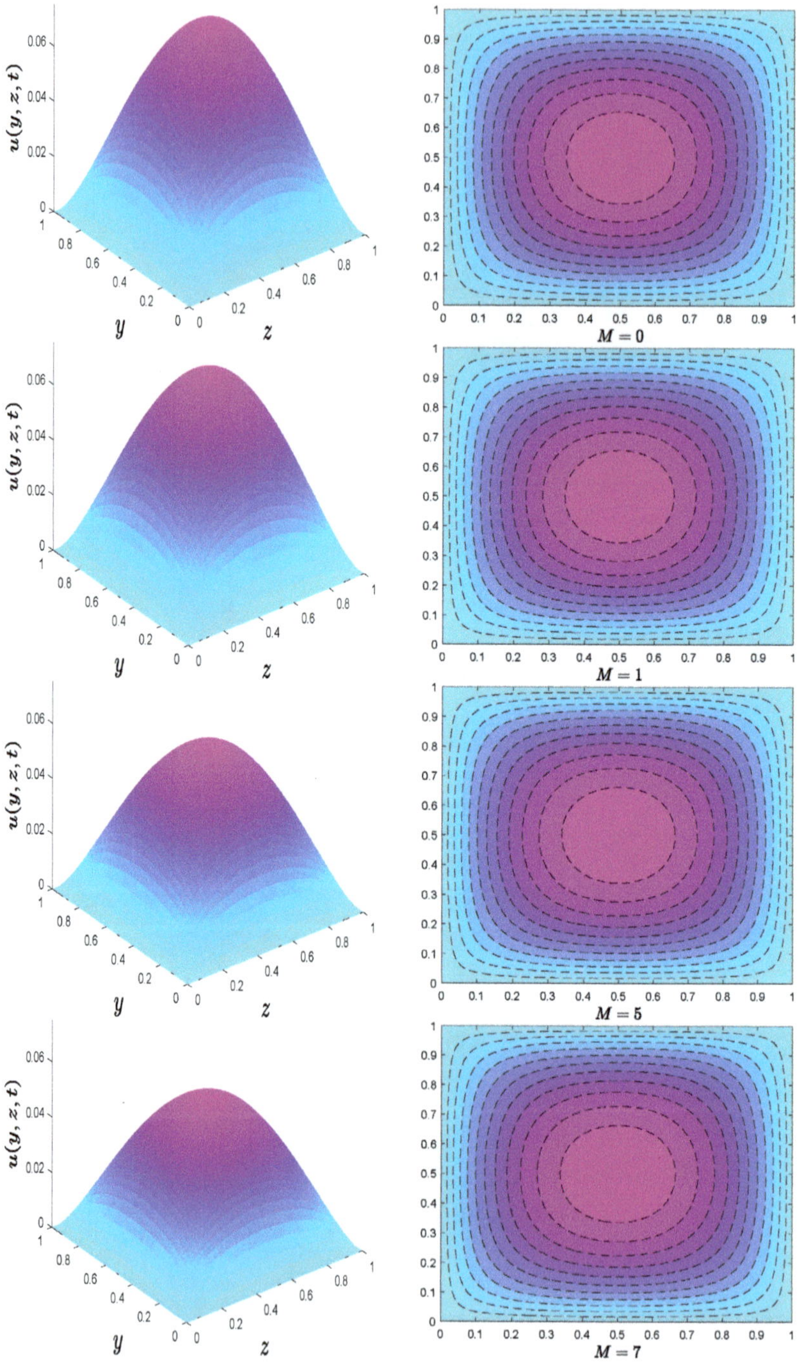

Figure 3. Velocity profile for different values of magnetic parameter M.

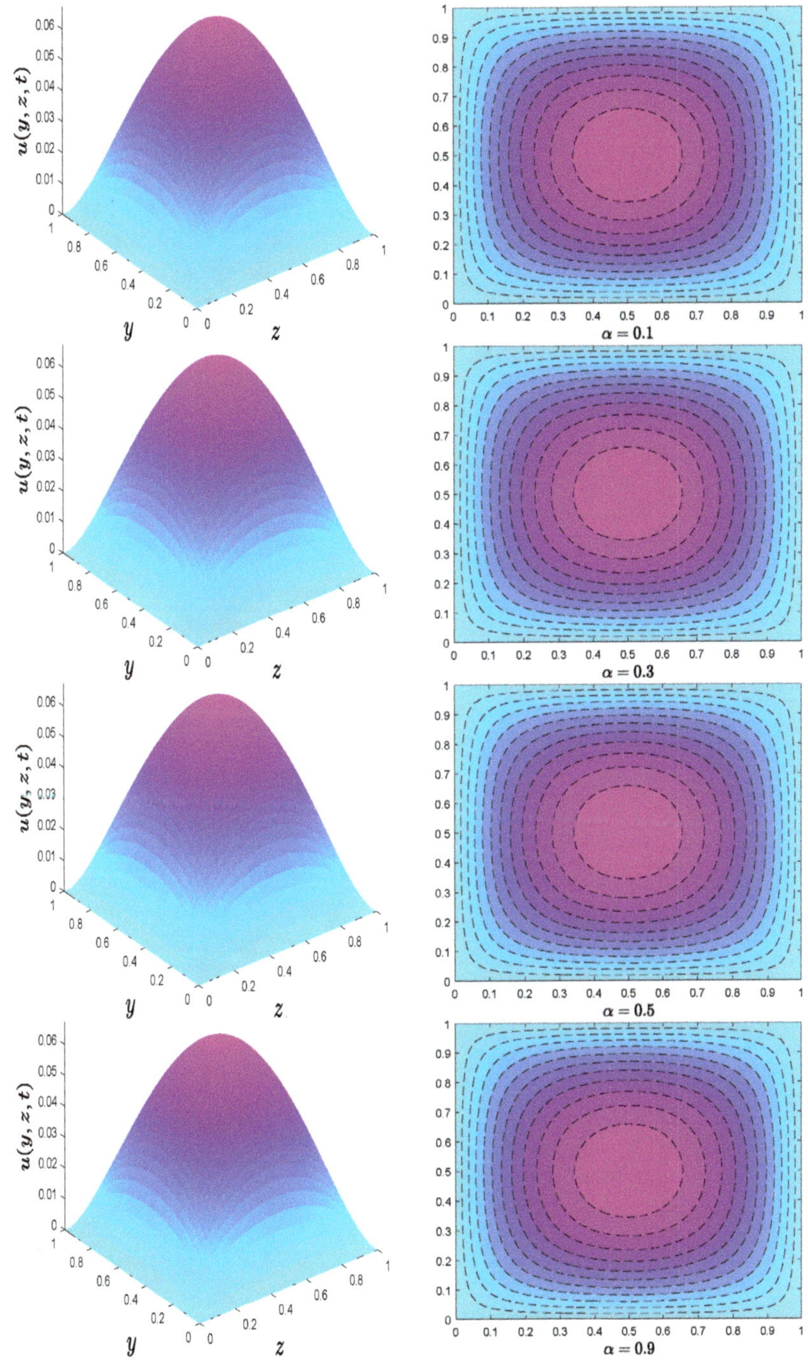

Figure 4. Velocity profile for different values of fractional derivative parameter α.

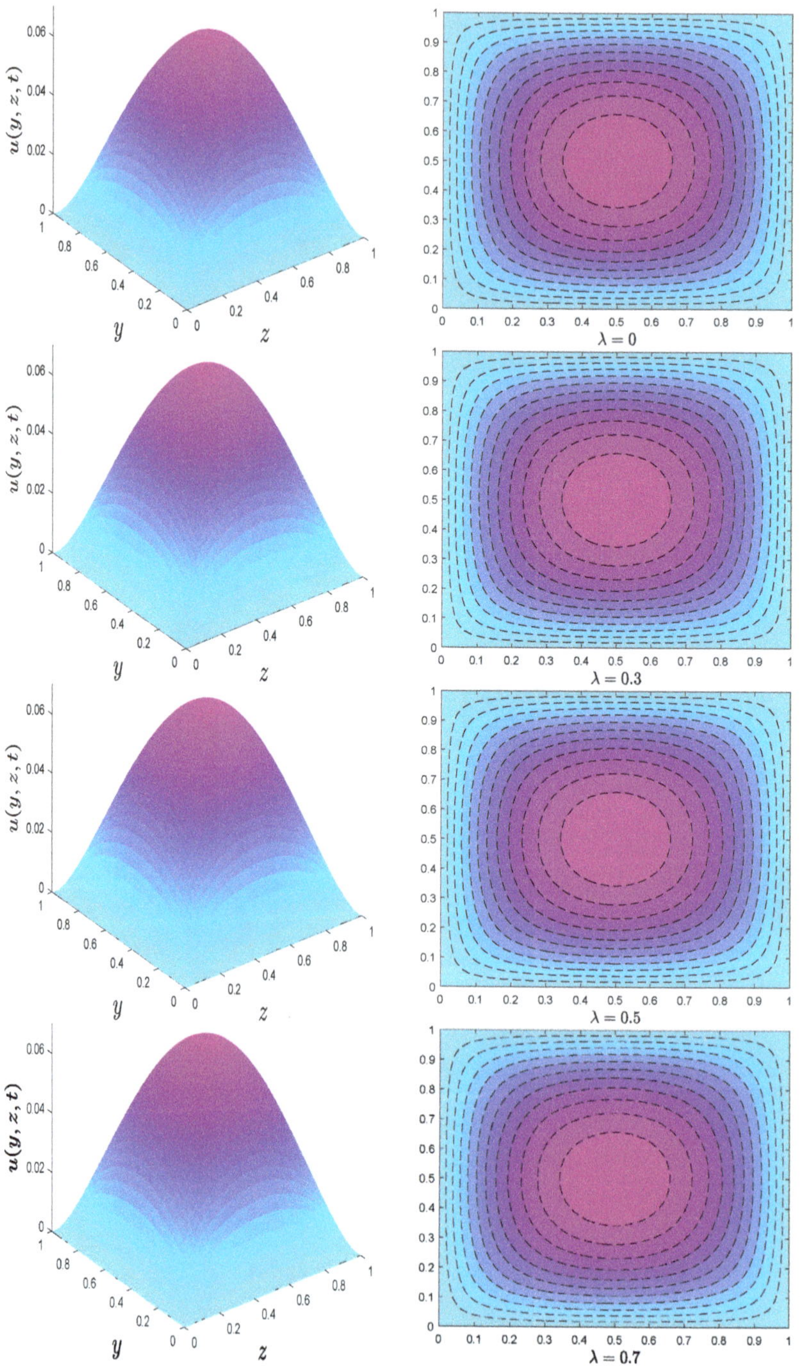

Figure 5. Velocity profile for different values of relaxation time parameter λ.

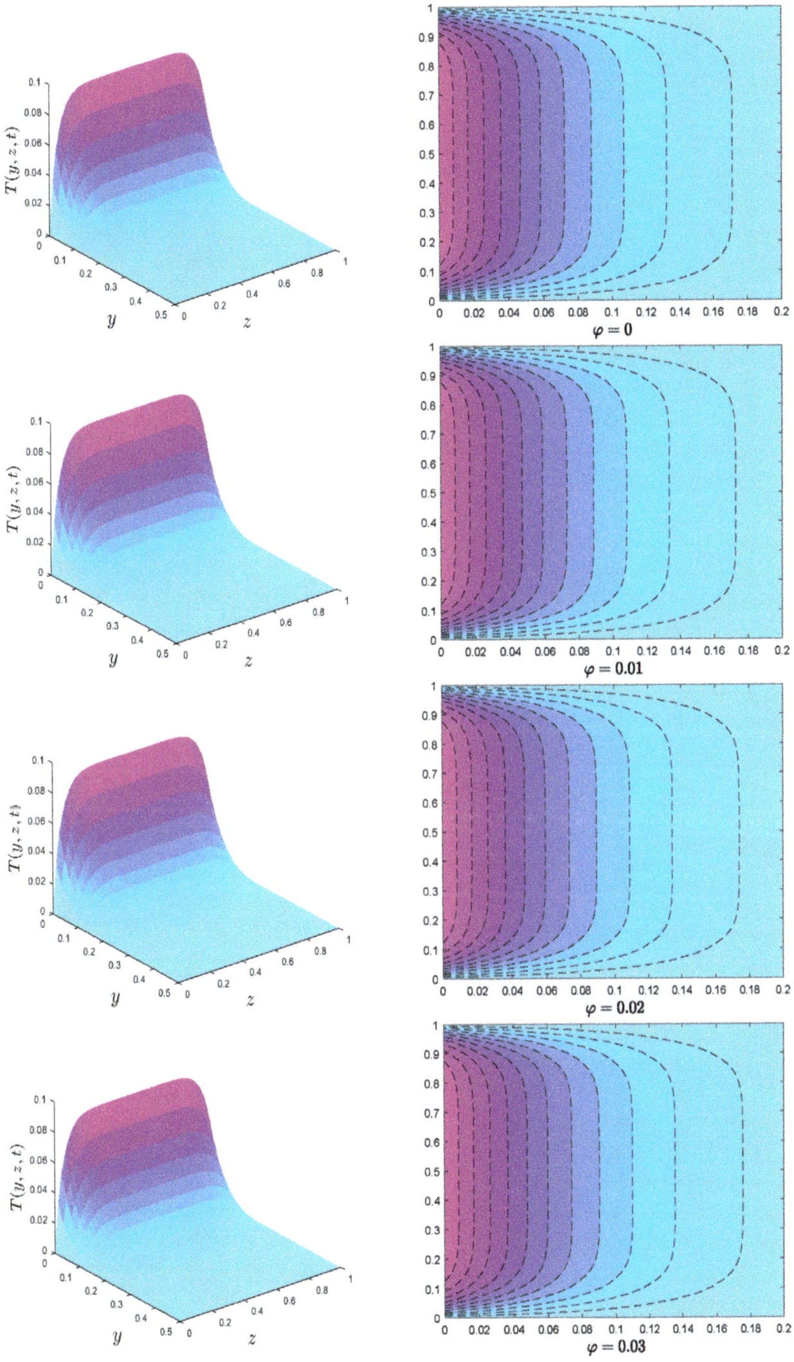

Figure 6. Temperature profile for different values of nanoparticle volume fraction φ.

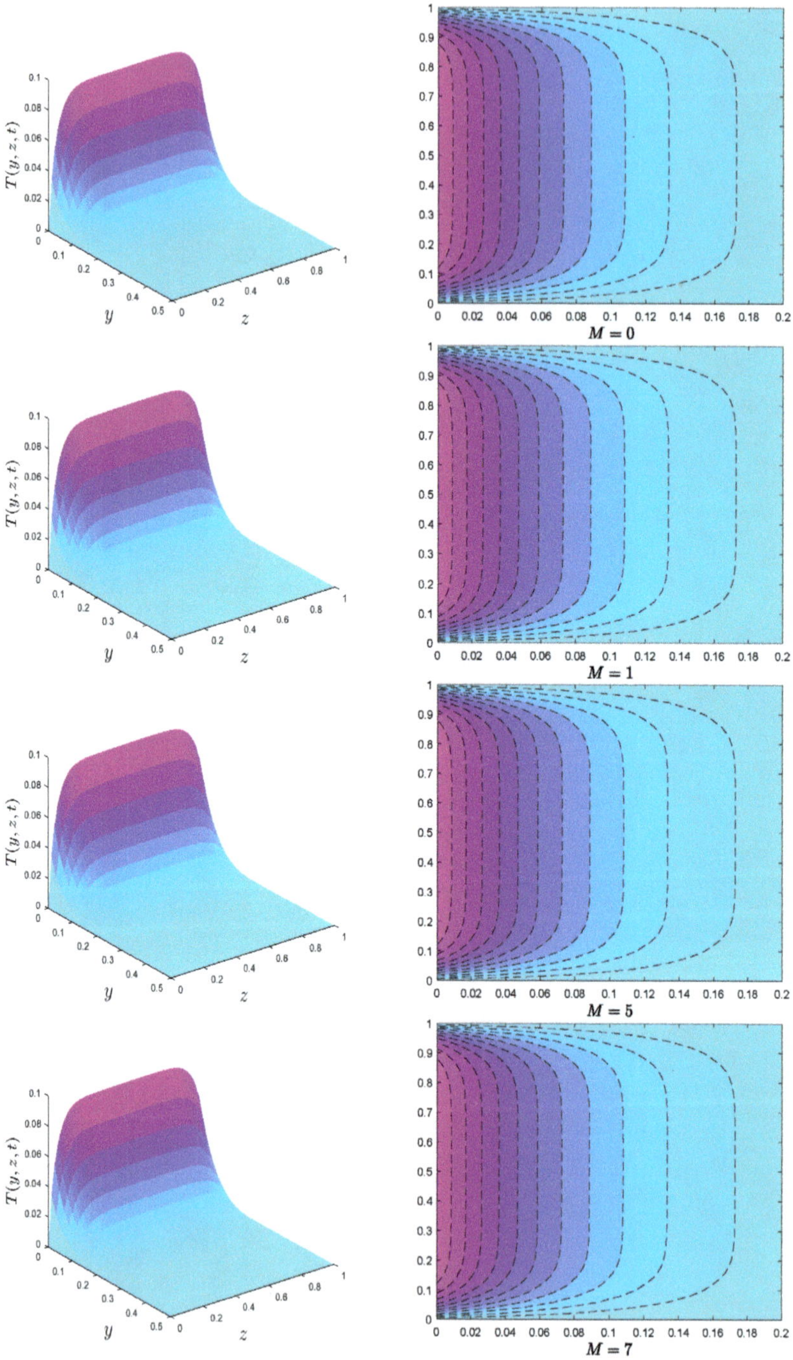

Figure 7. Temperature profile for different values of magnetic parameter M.

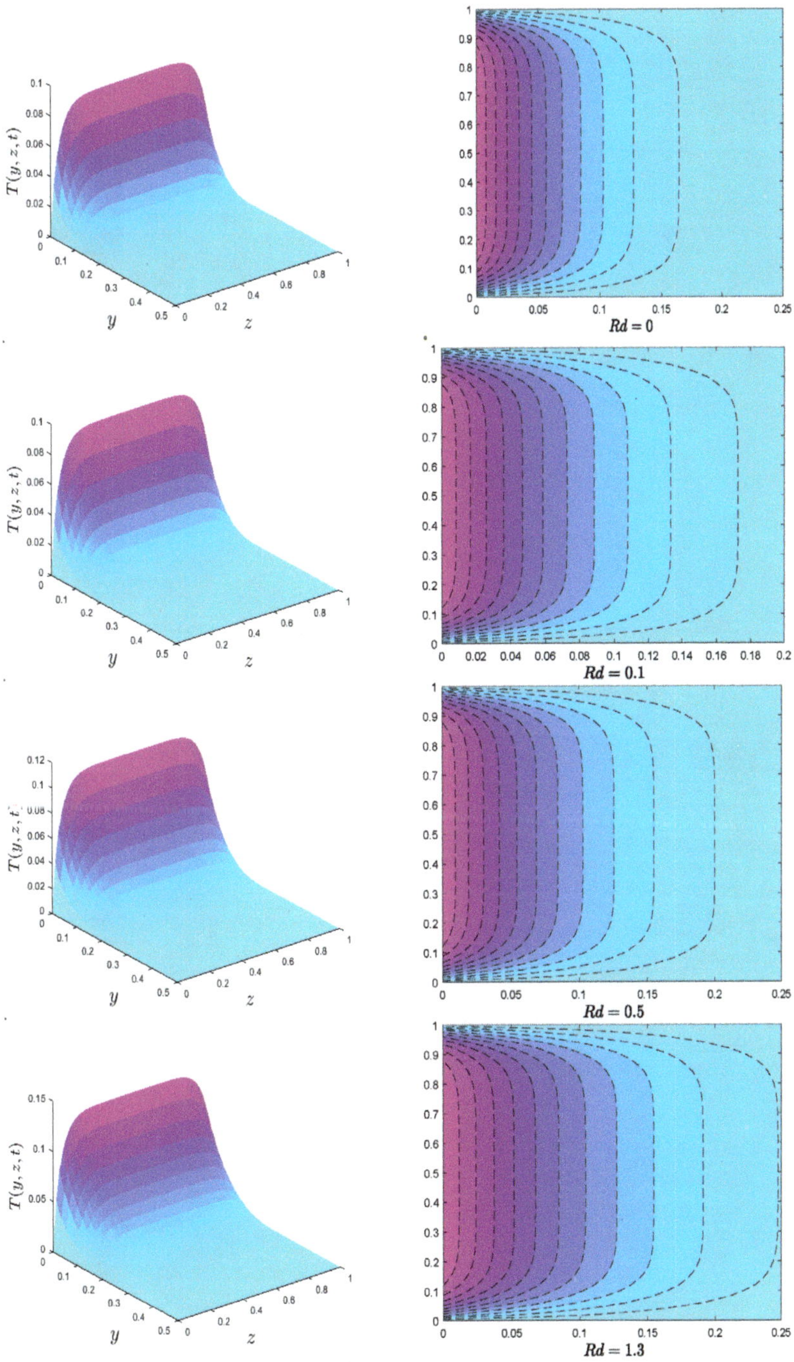

Figure 8. Temperature profile for different values of thermal radiation parameter Rd.

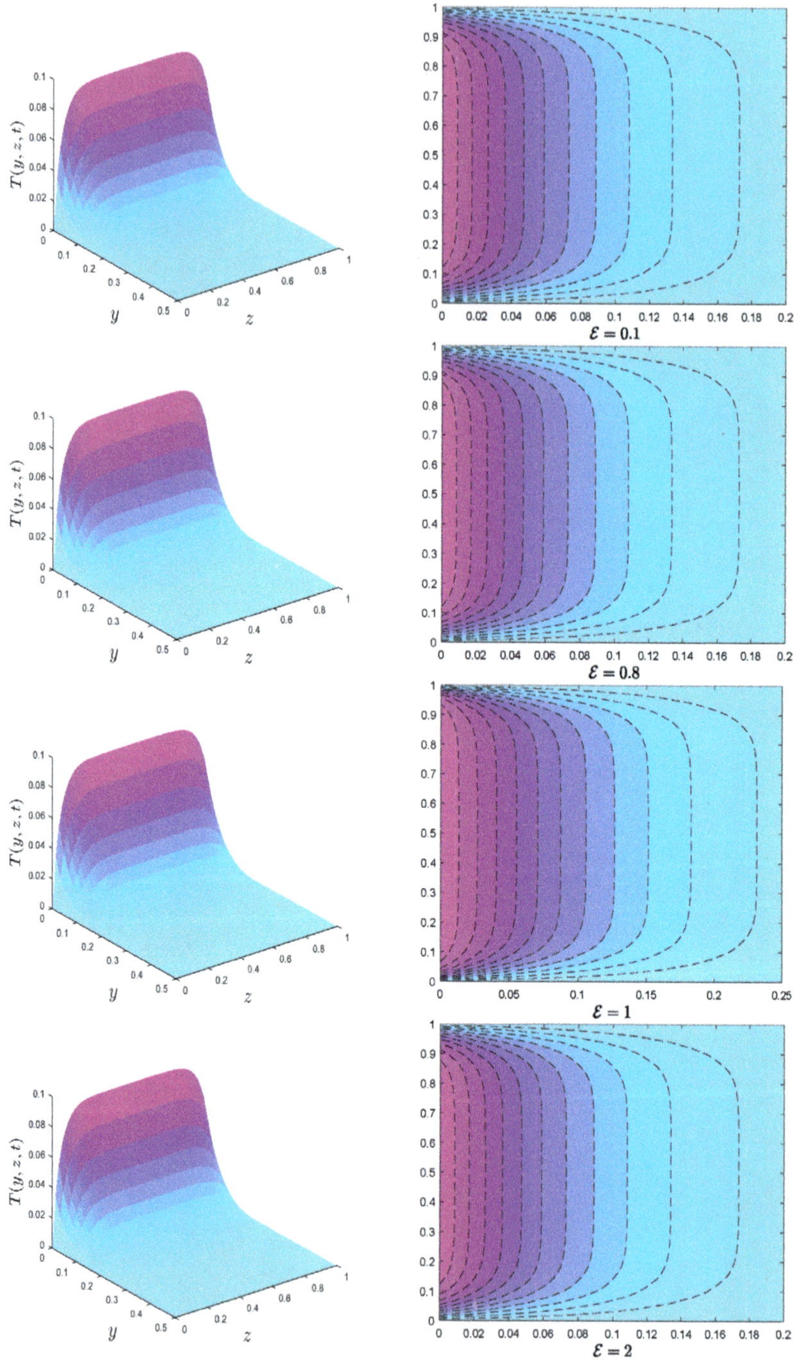

Figure 9. Temperature profile for different values of dissipation parameter $\mathcal{E}$.

The effects are $\varphi, M, \alpha, \lambda$ are elucidated in Figures 2–5. The suspension of Al_2O_3 nanoparticles in the fluid decreased the velocity flow; see Figure 2. Physically, this was expected because increasing the volume concentration of nanomaterials inside the fluid makes the fluid more viscous; as a result, velocity flow decreases. By drawing Figure 3, an attempt has been made to evoke the influence of a magnetic field on the Maxwell fluid velocity. The result shows that the velocity field reaches a maximum without a magnetic field ($M = 0$) but slows down as M increases. Physically, when the magnetic number increases, the Lorentz force increases and gives rise to magnetic resistance; as a result, the velocity is slowed. The impact of fractional derivative α on velocity is depicted in Figure 4, and it is worth noticing that as α grows higher, the amplitude of velocity decreases. On the other hand, an increase in fluid velocity is visible for more significant estimations of the relaxation time parameter λ; see Figure 5. Moreover, it deserves to mention that $\lambda = 0$ refers to Newtonian fluid flow.

Next, Figures 6–9 are provided to show the variations in the temperature distribution for several governing parameters, including nanoparticle volume fraction φ, magnetic field parameter M, thermal radiation Rd, and viscous dissipation factor $\mathcal{E}$. Figure 6 is shown to analyze the variations in the temperature of the fluid when Al_2O_3 nanoparticles are added. In Figure 7, the fluctuations in the temperature distribution due to the magnetic field are sketched. Unlike the velocity profile, the fluid temperature significantly increases when M increases. This might be because high resistance produces more heat due to increased friction force. Figure 8 depicts the aspects of the radiation parameter Rd on the temperature profile. As one might expect, increasing the value of Rd causes the material particles to have more kinetic energy, which increases the temperature distribution. The effects of viscous dissipation on temperature distribution are shown with the help of surface and contour plots, provided in Figure 9. Physically, if there is a lot of friction between the fluid layers, viscous dissipation solely influences the fluid temperature. As seen from the results, viscous dissipation causes both the surface temperature and the temperature of the fluid layers to rise.

By fixing the y-coordinate, the one-dimensional velocity profile of Al_2O_3/mineral oil is drawn; see Figures 10 and 11. The same conclusions as the surface plots are drawn; however, the Maxwell fluid had a high-velocity profile than the Newtonian fluid. On the other hand, the Newtonian fluid temperature is higher than that of the Maxwell fluid, as shown in Figures 12 and 13.

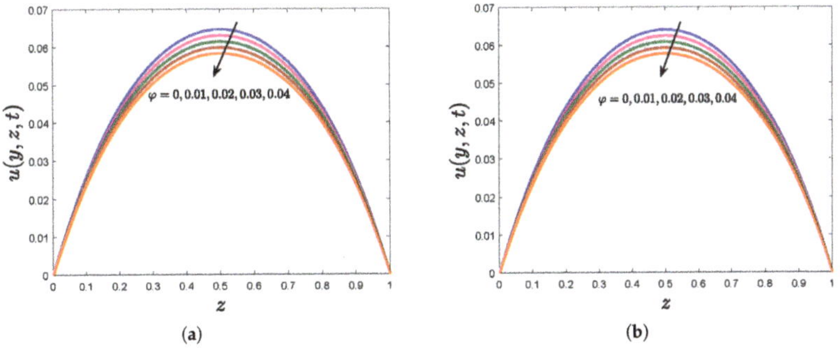

Figure 10. One-dimensional velocity profile for various values of φ. (**a**) Maxwell fluid, (**b**) Newtonian fluid.

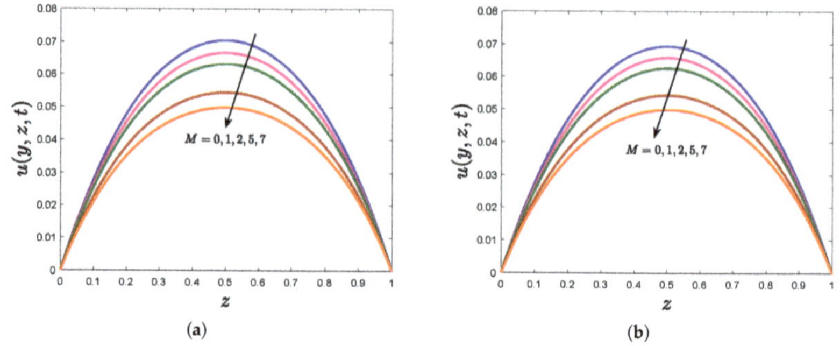

Figure 11. One-dimensional velocity profile for various values of M. (**a**) Maxwell fluid, (**b**) Newtonian fluid.

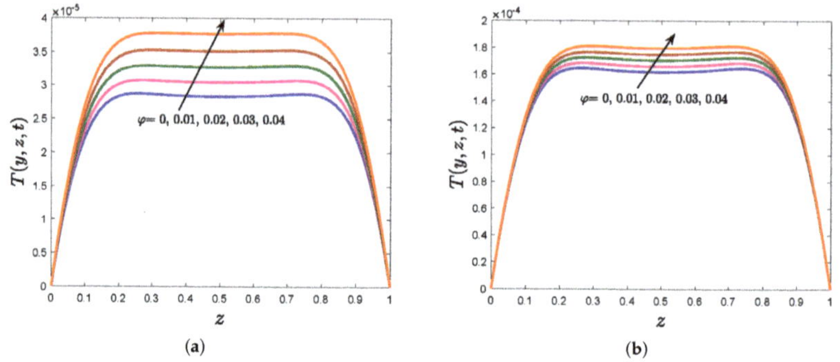

Figure 12. One-dimensional temperature profile for various values of φ. (**a**) Maxwell fluid, (**b**) Newtonian fluid.

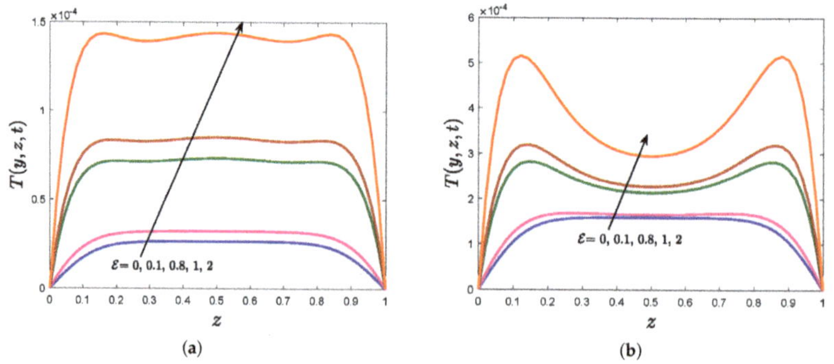

Figure 13. One-dimensional temperature profile for various values of $\mathcal{E}$. (**a**) Maxwell fluid, (**b**) Newtonian fluid.

5. Conclusions

The numerical simulation of mineral oil-based nanofluid flow with Al_2O_3 nanoparticles across a horizontal plate, accompanied by an external magnetic field, thermal radiation, viscous dissipation, and heat flux boundary conditions, is addressed. The following are the most affirmative outcomes:

- Small values of the nanoparticle volume fraction and the magnetic parameter may often predict Maxwell fluid flow augmentation.

- The relaxation time parameter increases the amplitude of the velocity.
- To manifest a surface heat enhancement, the nanoparticle volume fraction, magnetic number, thermal radiation, and viscous dissipation parameters must all be substantial.

Author Contributions: H.H. formulated the problem, solved the problem, and plotted the graphs. S.S. discussed the results. H.H. wrote the manuscript. S.S. proofread the manuscript. All authors have read and agreed to the published version of the manuscript.

Funding: This research was funded by the Ministry of Higher Education Malaysia and Research Management Center, Universiti Teknologi Malaysia (UTM) for financial support through vote numbers FRGS/1/2019/STG06/UTM/02/22 and 08G33.

Institutional Review Board Statement: Not applicable.

Informed Consent Statement: Not applicable.

Data Availability Statement: Not applicable.

Acknowledgments: The authors would like to acknowledge the Ministry of Higher Education Malaysia and Research Management Center, Universiti Teknologi Malaysia (UTM) for financial support through vote numbers FRGS/1/2019/STG06/UTM/02/22 and 08G33.

Conflicts of Interest: The authors declare no conflict of interest.

References

1. Feynman, R. There is plenty of room at the bottom: An invitation to enter a new field of physics. Presented at the Lecture at American Physical Society Meeting, Pasadena, CA, USA, 29 December 1959.
2. Salata, O.V. Applications of nanoparticles in biology and medicine. *J. Nanobiotechnol.* **2004**, *2*, 3. [CrossRef] [PubMed]
3. Masuda, H.; Ebata, A.; Teramae, K. Alteration of thermal conductivity and viscosity of liquid by dispersing ultra-fine particles. Dispersion of Al_2O_3, SiO_2 and TiO_2 ultra-fine particles. *J-STAGE* **1993**, *7*, 227–233. [CrossRef]
4. Choi, U.S.U.; Eastman, J.A. Enhancing thermal conductivity of fluids with nanoparticles. In Proceedings of the International Mechanical Engineering Congress and Exhibition, San Francisco, CA, USA, 12–17 November 1995.
5. Islam, T.; Yavuz, M.; Parveen, N.; Fayz-Al-Asad, M. Impact of Non-Uniform Periodic Magnetic Field on Unsteady Natural Convection Flow of Nanofluids in Square Enclosure. *Fractal Fract.* **2022**, *6*, 101. [CrossRef]
6. Wakif, A.; Boulahia, Z.; Ali, F.; Eid, M.R.; Sehaqui, R. Numerical analysis of the unsteady natural convection MHD Couette nanofluid flow in the presence of thermal radiation using single and two-phase nanofluid models for Cu–water nanofluids. *Int. J. Appl. Comput. Math.* **2018**, *4*, 81. [CrossRef]
7. Xia, W.-F.; Khan, M.I.; Khan, S.U.; Shah, F.; Khan, M.I. Dynamics of unsteady reactive flow of viscous nanomaterial subject to Ohmic heating, heat source and viscous dissipation. *Ain Shams Eng. J.* **2021**, *12*, 3997–4005. [CrossRef]
8. Hanif, H.; Khan, I.; Shafie, S.; Khan, W.A. Heat Transfer in Cadmium Telluride-Water Nanofluid over a Vertical Cone under the Effects of Magnetic Field inside Porous Medium. *Processes* **2020**, *8*, 7. [CrossRef]
9. Shi, Y.; Abidi, A.; Khetib, Y.; Zhang, L.; Sharifpur, M.; Cheraghian, G. The computational study of nanoparticles shape effects on thermal behavior of H_2O-Fe nanofluid: A molecular dynamics approach. *J. Mol. Liq.* **2022**, *346*, 117093. [CrossRef]
10. Hanif, H. A finite difference method to analyze heat and mass transfer in kerosene based γ-oxide nanofluid for cooling applications. *Phys. Scr.* **2021**, *96*, 095215. [CrossRef]
11. Mallakpour, S.; Khadem, E. Recent development in the synthesis of polymer nanocomposites based on nano-alumina. *Prog. Polym. Sci.* **2015**, *51*, 74–93. [CrossRef]
12. Haridas, D.; Rajput, N.S.; Srivastava, A. Interferometric study of heat transfer characteristics of Al_2O_3 and SiO_2-based dilute nanofluids under simultaneously developing flow regime in compact channels. *Int. J. Heat Mass Transf.* **2015**, *88*, 713–727. [CrossRef]
13. Animasaun, I.L. 47 nm alumina–water nanofluid flow within boundary layer formed on upper horizontal surface of paraboloid of revolution in the presence of quartic autocatalysis chemical reaction. *Alex. Eng. J.* **2016**, *55*, 2375–2389. [CrossRef]
14. Kabeel, A.; Abdelgaied, M. Study on the effect of alumina nano-fluid on sharp-edge orifice flow characteristics in both cavitations and non-cavitations turbulent flow regimes. *Alex. Eng. J.* **2016**, *55*, 1099–1106. [CrossRef]
15. Hawwash, A.; Abdel-Rahman, A.K.; Ookawara, S.; Nada, S. Experimental study of alumina nanofluids effects on thermal performance efficiency of flat plate solar collectors. *J. Eng. Technol. (JET)* **2016**, *4*, 123–131.
16. Sheikholeslami, M.; Ebrahimpour, Z. Thermal improvement of linear Fresnel solar system utilizing Al_2O_3-water nanofluid and multi-way twisted tape. *Int. J. Therm. Sci.* **2022**, *176*, 107505. [CrossRef]
17. Bahari, N.M.; Che Mohamed Hussein, S.N.; Othman, N.H. Synthesis of Al_2O_3–SiO_2/water hybrid nanofluids and effects of surfactant toward dispersion and stability. *Part. Sci. Technol.* **2021**, *39*, 844–858. [CrossRef]

18. Ho, C.; Cheng, C.Y.; Yang, T.F.; Rashidi, S.; Yan, W.M. Cooling characteristics and entropy production of nanofluid flowing through tube. *Alex. Eng. J.* **2022**, *61*, 427–441. [CrossRef]
19. Denn, M.M. Fifty years of non-Newtonian fluid dynamics. *AIChE J.* **2004**, *50*, 2335–2345. [CrossRef]
20. Mackosko, C.W. *Rheology: Principles, Measurements and Applications*; VCH Publishers, Inc.: New York, NY, USA, 1994.
21. Adegbie, K.S.; Omowaye, A.J.; Disu, A.B.; Animasaun, I.L. Heat and mass transfer of upper convected Maxwell fluid flow with variable thermo-physical properties over a horizontal melting surface. *Appl. Math.* **2015**, *6*, 1362. [CrossRef]
22. Megahed, A.M. Improvement of heat transfer mechanism through a Maxwell fluid flow over a stretching sheet embedded in a porous medium and convectively heated. *Math. Comput. Simul.* **2021**, *187*, 97–109. [CrossRef]
23. Shafiq, A.; Khalique, C.M. Lie group analysis of upper convected Maxwell fluid flow along stretching surface. *Alex. Eng. J.* **2020**, *59*, 2533–2541. [CrossRef]
24. Hilfer, R. *Applications of Fractional Calculus in Physics*; World Scientific Publishing: Singapore, 2000. [CrossRef]
25. Meral, F.; Royston, T.; Magin, R. Fractional calculus in viscoelasticity: An experimental study. *Commun. Nonlinear Sci. Numer. Simul.* **2010**, *15*, 939–945. [CrossRef]
26. Yang, P.; Lam, Y.C.; Zhu, K.Q. Constitutive equation with fractional derivatives for the generalized UCM model. *J. Non-Newton. Fluid Mech.* **2010**, *165*, 88–97. [CrossRef]
27. Heymans, N. Hierarchical models for viscoelasticity: Dynamic behaviour in the linear range. *Rheol. Acta* **1996**, *35*, 508–519. [CrossRef]
28. Liu, L.; Feng, L.; Xu, Q.; Zheng, L.; Liu, F. Flow and heat transfer of generalized Maxwell fluid over a moving plate with distributed order time fractional constitutive models. *Int. Commun. Heat Mass Transf.* **2020**, *116*, 104679. [CrossRef]
29. Yang, W.; Chen, X.; Jiang, Z.; Zhang, X.; Zheng, L. Effect of slip boundary condition on flow and heat transfer of a double fractional Maxwell fluid. *Chin. J. Phys.* **2020**, *68*, 214–223. [CrossRef]
30. Razzaq, A.; Seadawy, A.R.; Raza, N. Heat transfer analysis of viscoelastic fluid flow with fractional Maxwell model in the cylindrical geometry. *Phys. Scr.* **2020**, *95*, 115220. [CrossRef]
31. Hanif, H. A computational approach for boundary layer flow and heat transfer of fractional Maxwell fluid. *Math. Comput. Simul.* **2022**, *191*, 1–13. [CrossRef]
32. Asjad, M.I.; Ali, R.; Iqbal, A.; Muhammad, T.; Chu, Y.M. Application of water based drilling clay-nanoparticles in heat transfer of fractional Maxwell fluid over an infinite flat surface. *Sci. Rep.* **2021**, *11*, 18833. [CrossRef]
33. Saqib, M.; Hanif, H.; Abdeljawad, T.; Khan, I.; Shafie, S.; Nisar, K.S. Heat transfer in mhd flow of maxwell fluid via fractional cattaneo-friedrich model: A finite difference approach. *Comput. Mater. Contin* **2020**, *65*, 1959–1973. [CrossRef]
34. Bayones, F.; Abd-Alla, A.; Thabet, E.N. Effect of heat and mass transfer and magnetic field on peristaltic flow of a fractional Maxwell fluid in a tube. *Complexity* **2021**, *2021*, 9911820. [CrossRef]
35. Podlubny, I. *Fractional Differential Equations: An Introduction to Fractional Derivatives, Fractional Differential Equations, to Methods of Their Solution and Some of Their Applications*; Academic Press: Cambridge, MA, USA, 1999.
36. Hanif, H. Cattaneo–Friedrich and Crank–Nicolson analysis of upper-convected Maxwell fluid along a vertical plate. *Chaos Solitons Fractals* **2021**, *153*, 111463. [CrossRef]
37. Davidson, P.A. An introduction to magnetohydrodynamics. *Am. J. Phys.* **2002**, *70*, 781. [CrossRef]
38. Fontes, D.H.; Ribatski, G.; Bandarra Filho, E.P. Experimental evaluation of thermal conductivity, viscosity and breakdown voltage AC of nanofluids of carbon nanotubes and diamond in transformer oil. *Diam. Relat. Mater.* **2015**, *58*, 115–121. [CrossRef]
39. Devi, S.A.; Devi, S.S.U. Numerical investigation of hydromagnetic hybrid Cu–Al_2O_3/water nanofluid flow over a permeable stretching sheet with suction. *Int. J. Nonlinear Sci. Numer. Simul.* **2016**, *17*, 249–257. [CrossRef]

fractal and fractional

MDPI

Article

Continuum Damage Dynamic Model Combined with Transient Elastic Equation and Heat Conduction Equation to Solve RPV Stress

Wenxing Chen [1], Shuyang Dai [1,2,*] and Baojuan Zheng [3]

1 School of Mathematics and Statistics, Wuhan University, Wuhan 430072, China; wenxingchen@whu.edu.cn
2 Hubei Key Laboratory of Computational Science, Wuhan University, Wuhan 430072, China
3 Commerical Vehicle Technology Center, SAIC Motor Group Co., Ltd., Shanghai 200041, China; zhengbaojuan2020@163.com
* Correspondence: shuyang_dai@whu.edu.cn

Abstract: The development of the world cannot be separated from energy: the energy crisis has become a major challenge in this era, and nuclear energy has been applied to many fields. This paper mainly studies the stress change of reaction pressure vessels (RPV). We established several different physical models to solve the same mechanical problem. Numerical methods range from 1D to 3D; the 1D model is mainly based on the mechanical equilibrium equations established by the internal pressure of RPV, the hoop stress, and the axial stress. We found that the hoop stress is twice the axial stress; this model is a rough estimate. For 2D RPV mechanical simulation, we proposed a new method, which combined the continuum damage dynamic model with the transient cross-section finite element method (CDDM-TCFEM). The advantage is that the temperature and shear strain can be linked by the damage factor effect on the elastic model and Poission ratio. The results show that with the increase of temperature (damage factor $\hat{\mu}, \hat{d}$), the Young's modulus decreases point by point, and the Poisson's ratio increases with the increase of temperature (damage factor $\hat{\mu}, \mathcal{E}_t$). The advantage of the CDDM-TCFEM is that the calculation efficiency is high. However, it is unable to obtain the overall mechanical cloud map. In order to solve this problem, we established the axisymmetric finite element model, and the results show that the stress value at both ends of RPV is significantly greater than that in the middle of the container. Meanwhile, the shape changes of 2D and 3D RPV are calculated and visualized. Finally, a 3D thermal–mechanical coupling model is established, and the cloud map of strain and displacement are also visualized. We found that the stress of the vessel wall near the nozzle decreases gradually from the inside surface to the outside, and the hoop stress is slightly larger than the axial stress. The main contribution of this paper is to establish a CDDM-TCFEM model considering the influence of temperature on elastic modulus and Poission ratio. It can dynamically describe the stress change of RPV; we have given the fitting formula of the internal temperature and pressure of RPV changing with time. We also establish a 3D coupling model and use the adaptive mesh to discretize the pipe. The numerical discrete theory of FDM-FEM is given, and the numerical results are visualized well. In addition, we have given error estimation for h-type and p-type adaptive meshes. So, our research can provide mechanical theoretical support for nuclear energy safety applications and RPV design.

Keywords: RPV; FDM-FEM; damage model; adaptive mesh; axisymmetric method; stress cloud map; multi-physics model

Citation: Chen, W.; Dai, S.; Zheng, B. Continuum Damage Dynamic Model Combined with Transient Elastic Equation and Heat Conduction Equation to Solve RPV Stress. *Fractal Fract.* **2022**, *6*, 215. https://doi.org/10.3390/fractalfract6040215

Academic Editors: Norbert Herencsar, António M. Lopes, Alireza Alfi, Liping Chen and Sergio A. David

Received: 23 February 2022
Accepted: 2 April 2022
Published: 11 April 2022

1. Introduction

1.1. Research Motivation and Significance

Nuclear energy plays an important role in today's energy system, especially nuclear power generation. Nuclear energy is a safe, clean, and economical energy source [1]. Meanwhile, it has many advantages, such as the small size of reaction equipment, slowing down the greenhouse effect, and releasing huge energy in a short time. The main negative impact is that nuclear accidents are prone to nuclear radiation and nuclear pollution. Therefore, the quality of nuclear pressure vessels must be up to standard before they can be used, including operating specifications, regular security inspections, etc. The design of pressure vessels and safety performance evaluation is also an important research topic [2,3]. The force analysis of RPV will also use some knowledge of extreme mechanics, especially for the welding joints of nuclear reactor nozzles. Due to the limited load, stress concentration and various cracks are prone to occur here. The ultimate load is mainly determined by the overall plastic yield of the shell material [4,5]. When the yield strength is low, it has almost no effect on the crack size. As yields increase, cracks will also increase. Since the pressure vessel is operated in a high-temperature environment, many physical parameters will change, such as the density, Young modulus, Poisson ratio, and so on. In fact, during normal operation, nuclear pressure vessels are in a multi-physics environment, such as operating under the combined effects of high temperature, thermal shock, coolant, nuclear radiation, etc. In addition, temperature and thermal shock may cause corrosion and damage to the RPV cladding. These factors are essential in the design of RPV and in the later stage of quality inspection. However, there are few theories and models in this field that need to be improved urgently, which is the purpose and significance of our research.

1.2. Related Work

In addition, pressure vessel is the core component of the design and operation of next-generation reactors. Fatigue damage analysis, crack propagation simulation, and pipe opening stress calculation are usually required for RPV. However, many models belong to static mechanical analysis, and the Young's modulus and Poisson's ratio of the model are calculated according to fixed values. A damage model was established to describe the dynamic changes of Young's modulus and Poisson's ratio. The reliability of RPV also includes some uncertain factors, including the existence of the coupling of internal pressure and inertial force, combined with probabilistic fracture mechanics, estimation of stress intensity factors, and in turn, these works can help to analyze the pressure vessel's fracture and reliability analysis [6,7]. The mechanical properties and electromagnetic properties are the external performance under irradiation [8]. These advantages are beneficial to establish the nondestructive evaluation technology of embrittlement. Numerical calculation combined with the local nonlinear dynamics method and this criterion based on the critical splitting stress have greatly improved the global static method to describe the crack propagation.

The structural damage dynamic model is usually used in combination with the fatigue analysis model. In continuum mechanics, the damage is calculated as a post-processing of elastic or elastoplastic macroscopic analysis. However, this important work has not been cited in the mechanical research of RPV, which also reflects the uniqueness of our work. The damage is considered to be isotropic, and there is a micro-defect closure effect on both macro and micro scales [9]. Secondly, the damage evolution equation can explain different damage mechanisms when forging alloy materials. The numerical results show that the damage evolution equation can reflect the anisotropic accelerated creep and creep fracture time under different stress levels and loading directions [10]. Through the numerical simulation of the representative volume element (RVE) of quasi-brittle materials, an anisotropic damage model with the least internal variables can be constructed [11]. The orientation distribution function of the two elastic modulus is numerically determined, and the influence of the nucleation and propagation of microcracks is considered by the phase field method. In reference [12], an energy-based damage model is proposed to simulate the crack propagation of very low cycle fatigue (VLCF). This model can be used to predict the failure period, and the comparison of fracture surfaces also shows good consistency. The above model is only applicable to the damage model of a mechanical single field independent of temperature change, which also reflects that the research work in this paper is different from the current model. We consider the influence of physical information such as temperature and shear strain on the material. The fatigue damage analysis of RPV requires a variety of theories to solve, including prediction of the crack growth of steel RPV based on the maximum main stress propagation standard and combination with the probability direction standard to predict the unstable crack path [13–15].

The cross-section FEM has the characteristics of fast calculation, stratification, and local mechanics, and it has been widely used to solve various engineering problems [16–18]. However, they are all numerical theories of the static cross-section FEM, and there are few transient cross-section FEM methods. Transient energy studies the mechanical changes in each time period, which is wider than the static practical range. This is also the reason why this paper uses the transient cross-section FEM to study the nuclear pressure vessel. Changsik provides a simple method to estimate the cross-section stress distribution of the nozzle designed according to Section 3 of the ASME code. This method requires the geometric information of pressure vessels and nozzles. The limitation of this method is that the stress distribution in the cross-section needs to use accurate stress concentration factors, and the method discussed is only effective under internal pressure [19]. The error of the RPV stress theoretical analysis method for 2D cross-section FEM analysis is relatively large at the edge. Reference [20] derived the accurate theoretical formulas of radial and axial displacement of cylindrical vessels and pipelines under thermal stress through the fourth-order differential equation. The edge effect has an important influence on the geometric deformation of pressure vessels and pipelines under thermal mechanical load. The maximum relative error of radial displacement at the edge reaches 42.2%, and the maximum relative error of axial displacement reaches 28.5%. Sectional FEM is also used to study the influence of buckling and post-buckling behavior of composite laminates [21]. The results are compared with those of two finite element models. Residual stresses have a significant influence on the buckling and post-buckling behavior of closed-section thin-walled laminated structures.

Recently, there have been some simulation models of RPV. The study of stress intensity of the RPV pipe mouth is generally controlled by parameters such as size, shape, inner radius and thickness of the nozzle, etc. It is concluded that the optimal design of the nozzle can minimize the stress intensity (Tresca yield criterion) and conflict between the quality of RPV [22]. However, the working environment of RPV belongs to multi-physics and needs to consider the interaction of temperature and stress, which is also the difference of the nozzle model established in our paper. In addition, we also compare the axial stress and hoop stress. What is more, through simulation, three-dimensional thermal hydraulic parameter distributions can be obtained; with the increase of the injection rate, the disturbance of the temperature field and the velocity field becomes more intense, and it is more likely to cause thermal fatigue [23,24].

Pressurized thermal shock (PTS) also affects the structural integrity of the pressurized water RPV. The literature [25,26] studies the pressurization–thermal shock phenomenon in pressure vessels (RPV). The results show that the assessment of crack initiation, stopping, and tearing instability in thermal shock (PTS) events (of RPV) is studied. According to the new results, the tearing process of RPV is still stable even for large initial cracks larger than the maximum assumed crack size in the code [27,28]. The most important performance factor is mainly the application of fluid and probabilistic fracture mechanics to comprehensively evaluate the structural integrity of RPV under hypothetical PTS accidents. When the emergency nuclear cooling (ECC) water is injected, a large temperature gradient will be generated, which will lead to a large thermal stress in the RPV wall. Predicting the thermo-mechanical behavior of the pressure vessel can also improve the safe coefficient, optimizing the ECCS performance [29,30]. Other literature work thermal shock force is generally in the form of a graph. In this paper, the fitting formula of thermal shock force and temperature is given, which is convenient for outputting the function value corresponding to any moment during the simulation process.

In addition, regarding the issue of stress prediction, synchronization accelerator X-ray diffraction measures the stress generated by the clad pressure vessel steel during thermal shock. Experimental measurements show that the peak stress intensity factor occurs during thermal shock, rather than in a steady state [31]. The internal structure of the pressure vessel is more complicated and accompanied by robust radiation, so the experimental measurement is relatively difficult. At present, ultrasonic technology can be used to measure the stress of the pressure vessel, and ultrasonic transducers with different frequency ranges are used to evaluate the hoop and axial residual stress [32]. The experiment indicates that it is limited, the calculated stress and ultrasonic measurement results have a high degree of consistency. In addition, the elements added in RPV steel will affect the toughness and crack resistance of the material. Figure 1 below shows the evolution of the main chemical elements of RPV in China in the last 40 years. The key properties of nuclear RPV are high strength, good toughness, corrosion resistance, good compatibility with coolant, stable microstructure, good welding, hot and cold processing performance, and developing to an ultra-high strength direction.

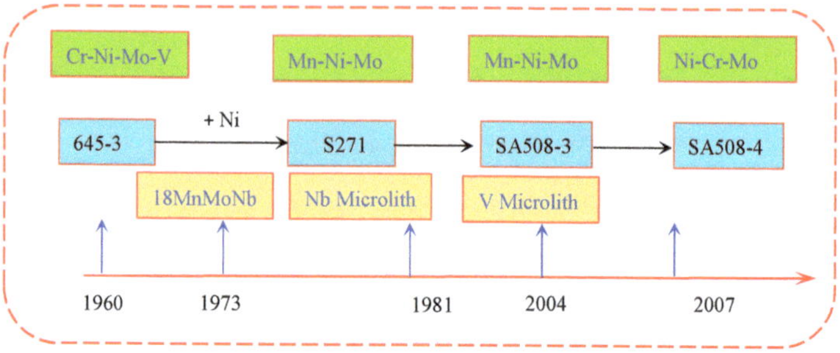

Figure 1. Development history of main metal elements of RPV in China.

Furthermore, there are also many numerical methods for pressure vessel stress evaluation, such as the extended 3D finite element method (XFEM) to calculate the stress field of the reactor pressure vessel (RPV). The sub-model contains three types of cracks: axial, circumferential, and inclined directions [33]. However, there are a few coupling field simulation models with time term for RPV. In this paper, the transient thermal–mechanical coupling model is studied, which is different from other research work. We use FDM-FEM to discrete the 3D pipeline port area. In addition, there are also multi-scale coupled numerical methods for force analysis of pressure vessels [34], and simulation of thermo-hydraulic phenomena (such as heat, mass, and dissolution transmission in nuclear pressure vessels (RPV)). Four subsystems have been solved; the parameter correlation of RPV can more realistically react the heat transfer simulation of the pressure vessel. Reference [35] FVM is reliable for solving the neutron diffusion equation, and it can obtain an accurate three-dimensional distribution of neutron flux and power of the core. For a metal pressure vessel, generally, corrosion-resistant materials are used to prevent the material from becoming fragile due to rust and chemical attack, and the tensile strength will be reduced. Eventually, it will cause bursting under high internal pressure. Actual nuclear pressure vessels are composite materials. There are many finite element methods for pressure vessel structures/components and pipelines [36]. They even include linear and nonlinear, static and dynamic, stress and deflection analysis, thermal problems, fracture mechanics problems, and solid coupling [37,38]. COMSOL, ANSYS, ABAQUES, etc. are commonly used in the finite element analysis software of pressure vessels and pipelines.

1.3. Contributions

The main contributions of this article are four points. Firstly, this paper proposed a simplified one-dimensional RPV estimation formulas for axial and hoop stress and introduces the working principle of RPV. The second contribution is that we proposed the continuous damage dynamics model combined with the transient cross-section FEM Method (CDDM-

TCFEM), which can adapt to the variable parameter mechanical calculation model in the high-temperature environment. The change trend of Young's modulus and Poisson ratio is calculated and visualized. The third contribution is that we use axisymmetric FEM to analyze the nuclear pressure vessel, which not only improves the calculation speed but also obtains the overall mechanical change cloud map. A variable parameter model is more accurate than traditional fixed parameter calculation. In addition, we found that the stress at both ends of the RPV was significantly greater than that in the middle. The fourth contribution is that we build the physical model of the mechanical and thermal coupling, analyze the mechanical change of the RPV pipe mouth, and calculate the difference between the pipe mouth axial stress and loop stress, and finally the specific temperature and mechanical change cloud diagrams are given. In a word, our work is beneficial to the structural design and the RPV's security assessment.

1.4. Structure and Framework of This Paper

The structural arrangement and design of this paper consists of five sections. Section 2 mainly consists of two parts. Part one is a one-dimensional simplified mechanical equilibrium problem, which describes the internal pressure and axial stress, and the equilibrium problem of hoop stress. Part two mainly introduces the continuous damage dynamic model and the numerical theory of cross-section finite element (DDM-TSFEM). We convert it into a two-dimensional section to solve. Section 3 mainly introduces the axisymmetric finite element method. We obtained the three-dimensional stress–strain cloud map of the pressure vessel through thermal shock force, which is more intuitive than the section finite element method. Another feature of this model is the addition of deformation. Section 4 is mainly about the thermal field–force field coupling of the RPV pipe mouth physical model. By establishing three-dimensional transient solid heat transfer and elastic mechanics equations, the axial and radial stress variation trends are finally obtained at different times. The biggest feature of this example is that the stress change at the RPV nozzle is considered. Section 5 is mainly a summary and outlook and provides the relevant research conclusions of this paper and the problems that need to be studied subsequently.

2. RPV Working Principle and Internal Structure of Nuclear Power

2.1. RPV Working Principle of Nuclear Power

Nuclear power plants can convert nuclear energy into electrical energy for life and industrial use. The core component of nuclear power plants is nuclear pressure vessels. Common nuclear power plants can be divided into pressurized water reactor nuclear power plants, heavy water reactor nuclear power plants, boiling water reactor nuclear power plants, and fast reactor nuclear power plants according to different reactor principles. At present, China's main nuclear power plants are composed of pressurized water reactor nuclear power plants and heavy water reactor nuclear power plants. More than 60% of the world 's nuclear power plants are PWR nuclear power plants, which are mainly composed of reactors, steam generators, steam turbines, generators, and related system equipment.

At present, in nuclear power plants, the role of reactors is to conduct nuclear fission and convert nuclear energy into heat energy from water. Water as a coolant absorbs the heat generated by nuclear fission in the reactor, and water at high temperature and high pressure becomes saturated steam. The steam pressure promotes the rotation of the steam turbine, and the heat energy is converted into mechanical energy. Then, the steam turbine drives the generator to rotate and converts mechanical energy into electrical energy. The cooled water is pumped back to the reactor by the main pump and heated again. Thus, the cycle is repeated to form a closed cycle of heat absorption and heat release. The pressure of the loop is controlled by the regulator. Usually, the primary circuit and its auxiliary systems and plants are collectively referred to as nuclear islands (NIs). In summary, the PWR nuclear power plant converts nuclear energy into electrical energy in four steps, which are implemented by four main devices:

(a) Reactor—converting nuclear energy into water heat.

(b) Steam generator—transferring the heat from the high-temperature and high-pressure water in the first loop to the water in the second loop, so that it becomes saturated steam.
(c) Steam turbine—converting the heat energy of saturated steam into the mechanical energy of high-speed rotation of a steam turbine rotor.
(d) Generator—converting mechanical energy from the steam turbine into electrical energy. To use power generation, they need to go through multiple complex processes. The working principle diagram of the pressurized water reactor nuclear power plant is shown in Figure 2.

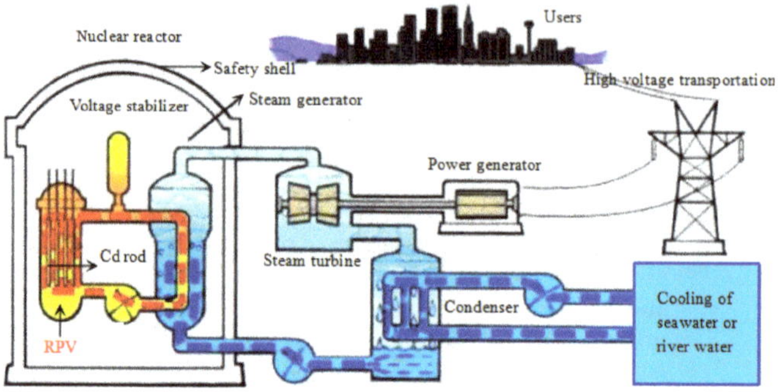

Figure 2. Working principle diagram of the pressurized water reactor nuclear power plant.

2.2. RPV Classification and Internal Structure

The nuclear pressure vessel is an important device of nuclear power plants. High-strength alloy steel (Fe, Mn, C, Zn, and other elements) is generally used in the vessel. The internal material of the nuclear pressure vessel will encounter thermal impact force, high temperature, strong radiation, crack propagation, chemical corrosion, and other factors when working. It is difficult to measure the internal force by a direct experiment method. Therefore, the finite element method can be used to solve the numerical solution according to the elastic equation and boundary information. Example 1 mainly introduces the geometric two-dimensional transient elastic equation of the continuum damage dynamic model to solve the internal force of the nuclear pressure vessel. Common pressure vessels can be divided into four grades according to temperature and internal pressure. The classification results and scope standards are shown in Table 1.

Table 1. Classification of nuclear pressure vessels by temperature and pressure.

Pressure Classification	Pressure Range	Temperature Classification	Temperature Range
Low-pressure vessel (L)	0.1 Mpa $\leq P <$ 1.6 Mpa	Cryogenic container	$t < -20$ °C
Medium-pressure vessel (M)	1.6 Mpa $\leq P <$ 10 Mpa	Normal-temperature vessel	-20 °C $\leq t <$ 150 °C
High-pressure vessel (H)	10 Mpa $\leq P <$ 100 Mpa	Medium-temperature vessel	150 °C $\leq t <$ 450 °C
Super-high-pressure vessels (U)	$P \geq$ 100 Mpa	High-temperature vessels	$t \geq$ 450 °C

The geometric dimensions of common nuclear reactor pressure vessels are generally ellipsoidal spherical vessels. The inner shell of the pressure vessel is made of harder steel materials such as austenitic stainless steel. Pressure vessels are commonly used key equipment in the nuclear power plant, petrochemical, metallurgical, power generation and aerospace sectors. They generally work in high temperature, high pressure, corrosion and radiation environments. Especially nuclear pressure vessels, strong neutron radiation will also cause continuous damage to the material and cause brittle fracture. In severe cases, there is a risk of explosion. Therefore, pressure vessel design and internal load control must be strictly implemented in accordance with the regulations. Currently, nuclear power plants mainly use nuclear fission to release energy. The internal structure of the nuclear pressure vessel is shown in Figure 3.

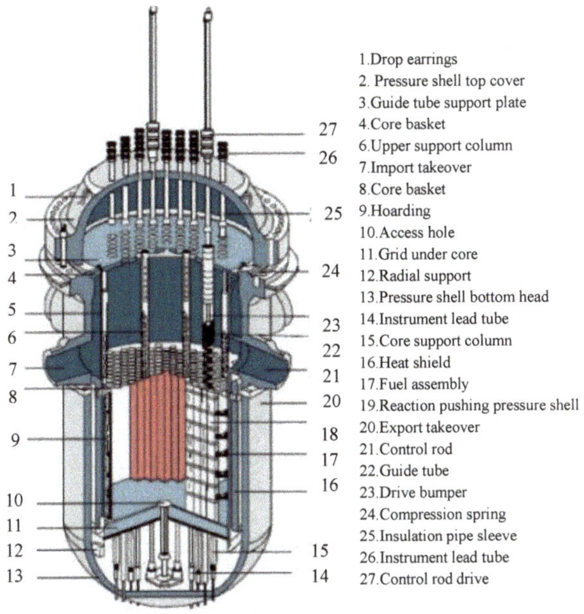

Figure 3. Ilustration of the internal structure and important parts of the pressure vessel.

2.3. Four Model Assumptions of RPV

Before establishing the RPV model in this article, we need to give the assumptions of each model, which will help the model to describe the scope of use more accurately.

Model 1: This model assumes that the material is isotropic, the internal pressure is uniform, and the thickness of the container wall is greater than $d_m \geq 0.05$ m.

Model 2: The CDDM-TCFEM method assumes that the obtained cross-sections are all continuous and uniform, isotropic materials. It satisfies the six assumptions of linear elasticity theory, including continuity, complete elasticity, uniformity, isotropy, slight deformation, and no initial stress. It is assumed that the continuous damage is a small defect, no obvious crack is formed, and the temperature will not cause the creep of the RPV vessel wall.

Model 3: The axisymmetric model assumes that the RPV shell is a symmetrical geometry, and the interior is subjected to a uniform outward pressure P.

Model 4: The thermal–mechanical coupling model of the pipe mouth assumes that the RPV material is isotropic; the process we study only emits hot steam and does not release the cooling liquid, because the release of the cooling liquid requires the addition of the hydrodynamic Navier–Stokes equation. We assume that at each moment, the temperature and pressure values remain relatively stable, and there is no sudden increase or decrease.

3. RPV Stress by the Simple Mechnical Balance

Model 1: Considering a simplified pressure vessel force analysis model, this vessel with radius r and wall thickness d is subjected to an internal gage pressure or thermal shock p along the longitudinal direction and hoop direction of the vessel to analyze the longitudinal stress σ_l and hoop stress σ_θ. This model has axisymmetric coordinates; there is no shear stress. When the working condition of the nuclear pressure vessel is stable, we make a cut across the section of the RPV to analyze the longitudinal stress σ_l of the spherical pressure vessel.

Although the derivation process of the problem borrows the area to represent the axial stress σ_l and the surface pressure F generated by the internal pressure P, the final formula shows that the radius R and the thickness d_m of the vessel are constant, and the final change of the axial stress depends only on the internal pressure of the RPV. Therefore, the axial stress obtained by the model belongs to a simplified one-dimensional approximation.

$$\sigma_l \cdot d_m \cdot 2\pi r = p \cdot \pi r^2, \quad \sigma_l = \frac{pr}{2d_m}. \tag{1}$$

Similarly, the circumferential stress is also symmetrical. We cut the vessel along any axis. The tangential direction of the cylinder is the circumferential stress σ_θ, and the equilibrium equation is established along the z direction. D is the diameter of the RPV, the pressure P acts on the projection of the half section, and $S = \frac{D}{2} l \sin\alpha$ is balanced with the circumferential stress σ_θ acting on the two sections. We can finally get:

$$\int_0^\pi pl\frac{D}{2}\sin\alpha d\alpha = p \cdot 2r \cdot d_m = 2d_m l\sigma_\theta, \quad \sigma_\theta = \frac{pr}{d_m}. \tag{2}$$

The above model is only a one-dimensional static analysis on the cross section, and the calculated stress results are rough estimates. In fact, the three-dimensional force analysis of the nuclear RPV cannot be obtained by this method. We also want to get the local stress defects of the pressure vessel and the overall stress changes. When the nuclear vessel reacts, the inside is affected by thermal shock. The following sections will introduce the other two nuclear pressure vessel force analysis methods in detail. They are the cross-section method and the axisymmetric method. The hoop stress and axial stress in static equilibrium are illustrated in Figure 4.

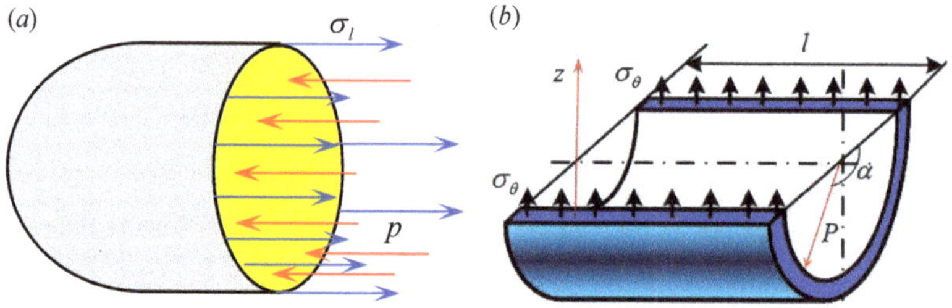

Figure 4. Stress estimation of capsule shaped nuclear pressure vessel. (**a**) Hoop stress of RPV. (**b**) Axial stress of RPV.

4. Continuum Damage Dynamics Model with Transient Cross-Section FEM

4.1. Continuum Damage Dynamics Model

This section will introduce our proposed method continuum damage dynamics model with transient cross-section FEM in detail, which is referred to as the CDDM-TCFEM method. This model mainly assumes that the nuclear pressure vessel is an isotropic material. A large amount of heat will be released instantaneously during the nuclear fission reaction. The surrounding gas will form thermal shock, long-term erosion, high-temperature effects, and microscopic cracks formed on the inner surface of the pressure vessel. Residual stress cannot be ignored and will have a certain impact on the container itself. In order to accurately describe the magnitude of the impact, we established a continuum dynamic damage model [39,40]. First, the degree of damage of the material needs to be defined, that is, the volume fraction of the part containing microscopic defects on the surface of the material, which can be marked as $w(t)$; then, the effective area of the material is $\widetilde{A} = A(1 - w(t))$. Through the stress definition, it is not difficult to obtain the effective stress expression:

$$\tilde{\sigma} = \frac{F}{A(1 - w(t))} = \frac{\sigma}{1 - w(t)}. \tag{3}$$

This model introduces a symmetric fourth-order damage effect tensor $\boldsymbol{M}$, that can connect Cauchy stress σ with real stress $\tilde{\sigma}$. Their relationship is shown in Equation (4).

$$\begin{cases} \tilde{\sigma} = \boldsymbol{M}\sigma & \tilde{\sigma} = M_{ijkl}\sigma_{kl}. \\ M_{ijkl} = \frac{1}{1-\hat{d}}\left((1 - \hat{u})\delta_{ik}\delta_{jl} + u\delta_{ij}\delta_{kl}\right) \end{cases} \tag{4}$$

Considering the symmetry of the stress tensor, the Cauchy stress vector and real stress vector are expressed as:

$$\sigma^T = \begin{bmatrix} \sigma_{11} & \sigma_{22} & \sigma_{33} & \sigma_{12} & \sigma_{23} & \sigma_{31} \end{bmatrix}. \tag{5}$$

$$\tilde{\sigma}^T = \begin{bmatrix} \tilde{\sigma}_{11} & \tilde{\sigma}_{22} & \tilde{\sigma}_{33} & \tilde{\sigma}_{12} & \tilde{\sigma}_{23} & \tilde{\sigma}_{31} \end{bmatrix}. \tag{6}$$

In the matrix form of the damage effect tensor $\boldsymbol{M}$, the variables $\hat{u}$ and $\hat{d}$ represent the two damage parameters. The variable $\hat{u}$ represents the damage effect of the Poisson-dependent transverse shear deformation. The variable $\hat{d}$ is a loss parameter related to the internal temperature of the RPV [41–43]. Of course, we can refer to some of the work of Lemaitre and Chaboche for related damage models. The damage effect tensor $\boldsymbol{M}$ is shown in Equation (7).

$$\boldsymbol{M} = \frac{1}{1-\hat{d}}\begin{bmatrix} 1 & \hat{u} & \hat{u} & & & \\ \hat{u} & 1 & \hat{u} & & & \\ \hat{u} & \hat{u} & 1 & 1-\hat{u} & & \\ & & & & 1-\hat{u} & \\ & & & & & 1-\hat{u} \end{bmatrix} \tag{7}$$

In Equation (8), $\hat{u}$ and $\hat{d}$ are two damage parameters; $\hat{u}$ represents the Poisson ratio and transverse shear strain-related damage effect in the initial state. E_0 and v_0 are the undamaged elastic modulus and Poisson's ratio, and the corresponding initial values are $E_0 = 206$ Gpa and $v_0 = 0.3$. After the material is damaged, the real elastic modulus and the Poisson ratio are nonlinear functions as follows:

$$\begin{cases} E(\hat{u}, \hat{d}) = \frac{E_0(1-\hat{d})^2}{1-4v_0\hat{u}+2(1-v_0)\hat{u}^2} \\ v(\hat{u}, \varepsilon_t) = -\frac{v_0-2(1-v_0)\hat{u}-(1-3v_0)\hat{u}^2}{1-4v_0\hat{u}+2(1-v_0)\hat{u}^2} + \Delta\varepsilon_t \end{cases} \tag{8}$$

The internal temperature T of the nuclear pressure vessel is generally controlled at 20–300 °C. This numerical experiment simulates the temperature change of [20, 600]. The change of temperature will affect some physical parameters in the material, including the Young's modulus, yield strength, thermal conductivity, and thermal expansion coefficient. In this model, the influence factor d of the damage dynamics model is modified to a function that is positively correlated with temperature. This model only studies the part of the internal temperature of the pressure vessel that is linearly increased, and it is in a periodic high-temperature state for a long time in the later period. It belongs to a nonlinear change, and the deformation will creep. This change can be described by the nonlinear relationship between strain and time:

$$\hat{u} = \alpha \ln(\gamma T(t) + 1). \tag{9}$$

The damage caused by temperature to the container material is a nonlinear change process. The functional relationship between the nonlinear part damage factor $\hat{d}$ and temperature is:

$$\hat{d} = \kappa e^{1-\frac{T_i - T_{\min}}{T_{\max} - T_{\min}}}. \tag{10}$$

In Equation (8), where ε_t is a weak white noise, then ε_t obeys the standard normal distribution, which can be denoted as $\varepsilon_t \sim N(\xi, \sigma^2)$, and it satisfies the relationship $E(\varepsilon_t) = \xi, \quad E(\varepsilon_t^2) = \sigma^2$; the probability density function is shown in Equation (11):

$$f(\varepsilon_t) = \frac{1}{\sqrt{2\pi\sigma}} \exp\left(-\frac{\varepsilon_t}{2\sigma^2}\right). \tag{11}$$

In addition, the random disturbance sequence is added, which is equivalent to a correction of Poisson' s v value, making it closer to the actual real value. The model assumes that the range of random disturbance is $\Delta\varepsilon_t = \varepsilon_t - \varepsilon_{t-1} = 10^{-4}$. The sources of uncertainty include the increase of martensite integral as well as the influence of uncertain factors such as thermal shock force and crack propagation on the material. The value of this model is to dynamically characterize the changes of Young's modulus E and Poisson's ratio v with temperature T and shear strain γ. The nuclear pressure vessel works in a high-temperature and high-pressure environment for a long time, and it is easy for the material inside the vessel to encounter thermal shock and chemical corrosion as well as the radiation of nuclear fuel and many other effects. Hence, it is essential to establish a dynamic damage model to describe this physical damage.

The traditional method considers that the elastic modulus E and Poisson's ratio v change very little or as a constant value to calculate the stress of RPV. However, in practice, these parameters change with temperature. Based on the continuous damage model, some more appropriate parameter values can be obtained from our proposed model. The influence of temperature on the material structure parameters is primarily considered. The parameters $\left(\hat{u}, \hat{d}, \varepsilon_t\right)$ represent a temperature-dependent variable. The temperature and pressure inside the nuclear pressure vessel indicate a dynamic nonlinear change trend. In the initial stage, the pressure vessel will instantly release a large amount of heat, but with the addition of the coolant system, the temperature will gradually decrease.

4.2. *Transient Cross-Section FEM Method*

In this section, we will introduce a two-dimensional transient cross-section FEM method. In other words, we use the CTFEM method to solve a two-dimensional linear elastic equation with finite difference approximation for the time term and finite element approximation for the space term. The pressure vessel can be divided into different sections according to the radial and axial direction. So, this problem has been simplified to many thin rings and rectangular slices: that is, turning a three-dimensional problem into a two-dimensional problem [44,45]. The advantage of this method is that local details can be observed and the solution time is relatively fast. If FEM combined with ARIMA method can also be applied to the variable force prediction of RPV [46]. The time term $T > 0$ of linear elasticity equation is discretized by the finite difference method, and the spatial term $\Omega \subset R^2$ is discretized by the finite element method. The boundary area is denoted as $\partial\Omega$. Partial parameters of the elasticity equation need to be combined with the model of continuum damage dynamics. For the displacement of two-dimensional transient elastic mechanics, there are two degrees of freedom on each mesh node, and the displacement components along the x and y directions can be written in the form of vectors as follows Equation (12).

$$u(x, y, t) = (u_1(x, y, t), u_2(x, y, t)). \tag{12}$$

Here, we use displacement $\boldsymbol{u}$ to represent the two-dimensional strain tensor matrix $\varepsilon(\boldsymbol{u})$.

$$\varepsilon(\boldsymbol{u}) = \begin{pmatrix} \varepsilon_{xx}(\boldsymbol{u}) & \varepsilon_{xy}(\boldsymbol{u}) \\ \varepsilon_{yx}(\boldsymbol{u}) & \varepsilon_{yy}(\boldsymbol{u}) \end{pmatrix} = \begin{pmatrix} \frac{\partial u_1}{\partial x} & \frac{1}{2}\left(\frac{\partial u_1}{\partial y} + \frac{\partial u_2}{\partial x}\right) \\ \frac{1}{2}\left(\frac{\partial u_2}{\partial x} + \frac{\partial u_1}{\partial y}\right) & \frac{\partial u_2}{\partial y} \end{pmatrix} \tag{13}$$

In the same way, we can use variable displacement $\boldsymbol{u}$ to represent the stress tensor matrix $\sigma(\boldsymbol{u})$.

$$\begin{aligned} \sigma(\boldsymbol{u}) &= \begin{pmatrix} \sigma_{xx}(\boldsymbol{u}) & \sigma_{xy}(\boldsymbol{u}) \\ \sigma_{yx}(\boldsymbol{u}) & \sigma_{yy}(\boldsymbol{u}) \end{pmatrix} = \lambda\,\mathrm{tr}(\varepsilon(\boldsymbol{u}))\boldsymbol{I} + 2\mu\varepsilon(\boldsymbol{u}) \\ &= \begin{pmatrix} \lambda(\varepsilon_{xx}(\boldsymbol{u}) + \varepsilon_{yy}(\boldsymbol{u})) + 2\mu\varepsilon_{xx}(\boldsymbol{u}) & 2\mu\varepsilon_{xy}(\boldsymbol{u}) \\ 2\mu\varepsilon_{yx}(\boldsymbol{u}) & \lambda(\varepsilon_{xx}(\boldsymbol{u}) + \varepsilon_{yy}(\boldsymbol{u})) + 2\mu\varepsilon_{yy}(\boldsymbol{u}) \end{pmatrix} \end{aligned} \tag{14}$$

The λ and μ are the Lame coefficients, and the elastic modulus $\hat{E}$ and the possion rate $\hat{\vartheta}$ represent the parameters solved in the structural damage model.

$$\lambda = \frac{\hat{\vartheta}\hat{E}}{(1-2\hat{\vartheta})(1+\hat{\vartheta})}, \quad \mu = \frac{\hat{E}}{2(1+\hat{\vartheta})}. \tag{15}$$

The two-dimensional transient elastic equation can be simplified as:

$$\rho\boldsymbol{u}_{tt} - \nabla\sigma = \boldsymbol{f}. \tag{16}$$

Then, the solution space of the transient elasticity equation exists in $\boldsymbol{u} \in [0,T] \times \Omega$; differential Equation (16) can also be written in the form of a component equation.

$$\begin{cases} \hat{\rho}(t)\frac{\partial^2 \boldsymbol{u}}{\partial t^2} - \left(\frac{\partial \sigma_{xx}(\boldsymbol{u})}{\partial x} + \frac{\partial \sigma_{yx}(\boldsymbol{u})}{\partial y}\right) = f_x \\ \hat{\rho}(t)\frac{\partial^2 \boldsymbol{u}}{\partial t^2} - \left(\frac{\partial \sigma_{xy}(\boldsymbol{u})}{\partial x} + \frac{\partial \sigma_{yy}(\boldsymbol{u})}{\partial y}\right) = f_y \end{cases} \tag{17}$$

Boundary conditions include displacement boundary and force boundary conditions; they are shown in Equations (18) and (19). The effect of the two boundary conditions can indicate the initial state of the pressure vessel, and it clearly describes the boundary force position and constraint conditions:

$$\boldsymbol{u}_i(x,y,t) = \boldsymbol{b}_i(x,y,t), \quad (x,y,t) \in \Gamma_D \times [0,T], \quad i = 1,2. \tag{18}$$

$$\begin{pmatrix} \sigma_{xx}(\boldsymbol{u}) & \sigma_{xy}(\boldsymbol{u}) \\ \sigma_{yx}(\boldsymbol{u}) & \sigma_{yy}(\boldsymbol{u}) \end{pmatrix}\begin{pmatrix} n_x \\ n_y \end{pmatrix} = \begin{pmatrix} p_x \\ p_y \end{pmatrix} \quad \Gamma_N \times [0,T]. \tag{19}$$

The initial conditions corresponding to the displacement and velocity are as follows:

$$u_1(x,y,0) = g_1(x,y), \quad u_2(x,y,0) = g_2(x,y) \quad (x,y) \in \Gamma_D = \partial\Omega. \tag{20}$$

$$\frac{\partial u_1}{\partial t}(x,y,0) = v_{b1}(x,y), \quad (x,y) \text{ in } \Gamma_1. \tag{21}$$

$$\frac{\partial u_2}{\partial t}(x,y,0) = v_{b2}(x,y), \quad (x,y) \text{ in } \Gamma_2. \tag{22}$$

In Equation (17), $\hat{\rho}(t) > 0$ is the density of the pressure vessel, and the density decreases slightly with the increase of temperature [47,48]. The right end function can be denoted as $\boldsymbol{f} = (f_x, f_y)^T, \Omega \times [0,T] \to R^2$, and the displacement function in the initial boundary condition can be expressed as $\boldsymbol{b} = (b_1, b_2) : \Gamma_D \times [0,T] \to R^2$; the force boundary condition is $\boldsymbol{p} = (p_x, p_y)^T, \Gamma_N \times [0,T] \to R^2$. Under the initial condition, when $t = 0$, the corresponding displacement term function is $\boldsymbol{g} = (g_1, g_2)^T$. The corresponding boundary initial velocity is $\boldsymbol{v}_b = (\boldsymbol{v}_{b1}, \boldsymbol{v}_{b2})^T$.

Then, when combined with the variational principle, the transient elastic equation is discretized. For any $\boldsymbol{u} = (u_1, u_2), \boldsymbol{v} = (v_1, v_2)$, and it satisfies the spatial relationship $u_i \in V \quad i = 1,2$, V is a Hilbert space; for any $v_i \in V \quad i = 1,2, (\boldsymbol{u}, \boldsymbol{v}) \in V \times V \to B(\boldsymbol{u}, \boldsymbol{v}) \in R$ is a bilinear functional. $F(v) =< f, v >$ is a continuous functional, and the following relationship satisfies Equation (23).

$$B(\boldsymbol{u}, \boldsymbol{v}) = \langle \boldsymbol{f}, \boldsymbol{v} \rangle \quad \forall \boldsymbol{v} \in V. \tag{23}$$

$$\begin{aligned} B(\boldsymbol{u}, \boldsymbol{v}) &= \int_{\Omega} \hat{\rho}(t) \left(\frac{\partial^2 u_1}{\partial t^2} v_1 + \frac{\partial^2 u_2}{\partial t^2} v_2 \right) dxdy + a(\boldsymbol{u}, \boldsymbol{v}) \\ &= \int_{\Omega} f_1 v_1 dxdy + \int_2 f_2 v_2 dxdy + \int_{\Gamma_N} h_1 v_1 ds + h_2 v_2 ds. \end{aligned} \tag{24}$$

Among them, $B(\boldsymbol{u}, \boldsymbol{v})$ and $a(\boldsymbol{u}, \boldsymbol{v})$ are bilinear functions, and the specific expressions of $\boldsymbol{u} = (u_1, u_2) : \bar{\Omega} \times [0, T]$. $\forall v_1 : \bar{\Omega} \to R^2, v_1|_{\Gamma_D} = 0$ and $\forall v_2 : \bar{\Omega} \to R^2, v_2|_{\Gamma_D} = 0, a(\boldsymbol{u}, \boldsymbol{v})$ are as follows in Equation (25).

$$\begin{aligned} a(\boldsymbol{u}, \boldsymbol{v}) &= \int_{\Omega} \sigma(\mathbf{symbol}u) : \nabla \boldsymbol{v} dxdy = \int_{\Omega} \sigma(\boldsymbol{u}) : \varepsilon(\boldsymbol{v}) dxdy \\ &= \int_{\Omega} \lambda (\nabla \cdot \boldsymbol{u})(\nabla \cdot \boldsymbol{v}) dxdy + \int_{\Omega} 2\mu\varepsilon(\boldsymbol{u}) : \varepsilon(\boldsymbol{v}) dxdy \\ &= \int_{\Omega} \lambda \left(\frac{\partial u_1}{\partial x} + \frac{\partial u_2}{\partial y} \right) \left(\frac{\partial v_1}{\partial x} + \frac{\partial v_2}{\partial y} \right) dxdy \\ &+ 2\mu \int_{\Omega} \left(\frac{\partial u_1}{\partial x} \frac{\partial v_1}{\partial x} + \frac{1}{2} \left(\frac{\partial u_1}{\partial y} + \frac{\partial u_2}{\partial x} \right) \left(\frac{\partial v_1}{\partial y} + \frac{\partial v_2}{\partial x} \right) + \frac{\partial u_2}{\partial y} \frac{\partial v_2}{\partial y} \right) dxdy. \end{aligned} \tag{25}$$

Of course, it can also be calculated directly, and the results obtained in the two forms of Equations (25) and (26) are equivalent.

$$\sigma(\boldsymbol{u}) : \nabla \mathbf{v} = \begin{pmatrix} \sigma_{11}(\boldsymbol{u}) & \sigma_{12}(\boldsymbol{u}) \\ \sigma_{21}(\boldsymbol{u}) & \sigma_{22}(\boldsymbol{u}) \end{pmatrix} : \begin{pmatrix} \frac{\partial v_1}{\partial x} & \frac{\partial v_1}{\partial y} \\ \frac{\partial v_2}{\partial x} & \frac{\partial v_2}{\partial y} \end{pmatrix} \tag{26}$$

After finishing, we can get Equation (27)

$$\begin{aligned} &\int_{\Omega} \sigma(\boldsymbol{u}) : \nabla v dxdy \\ &= \int_{\Omega} \left(\lambda \frac{\partial u_1}{\partial x} \frac{\partial v_1}{\partial x} + 2\mu \frac{\partial u_1}{\partial x} \frac{\partial v_1}{\partial x} + \lambda \frac{\partial u_2}{\partial y} \frac{\partial v_1}{\partial x} + \mu \frac{\partial u_1}{\partial y} \frac{\partial v_1}{\partial y} \right) \\ &+ \mu \frac{\partial u_2}{\partial x} \frac{\partial v_1}{\partial y} + \mu \frac{\partial u_1}{\partial y} \frac{\partial v_2}{\partial x} + \mu \frac{\partial u_2}{\partial x} \frac{\partial v_2}{\partial x} + \lambda \frac{\partial u_1}{\partial x} \frac{\partial v_2}{\partial y} + \\ &\lambda \frac{\partial u_2}{\partial y} \frac{\partial v_2}{\partial y} + 2\mu \frac{\partial u_2}{\partial y} \frac{\partial v_2}{\partial y} \Bigg) dxdy \end{aligned} \tag{27}$$

The right-hand function of variational Equation (23) can be written as Equation (28).

$$< f, v >= \int_{\Omega} f_1 v_1 + f_2 v_2 dxdy. \tag{28}$$

The backward Euler scheme is used to discrete the time term. As for the time step $\Delta\tau = \frac{T}{N}, N \in N^+$, the time used in step n is $t_n = n\Delta t$, and the corresponding function value is $f^{n+1}, u \in C^0([0, T], V) \bigcap C^2([0, T], H)$.

$$\left(\frac{d^2 \boldsymbol{u}(t)}{dt^2}, \boldsymbol{v} \right) + \alpha(\boldsymbol{u}(t), \boldsymbol{v}) = (\boldsymbol{f}(t), \boldsymbol{v}) \quad \forall \boldsymbol{v} \in V, t \in [0, T]. \tag{29}$$

The initial conditions of the transient linear elastic equation are divided into displacement and velocity.

$$u(0) = \boldsymbol{u}_0, \quad \boldsymbol{u}_0 \in V. \quad v_{b1} = \frac{du(0)}{dt} = \boldsymbol{u}_1, \quad \boldsymbol{u}_1 \in H. \tag{30}$$

The time term is discreted by the central difference scheme, and the terms $\boldsymbol{u}^{n+1} \in V, \quad 1 \leq n \leq N-1$ are to be solved such that we can get a semi-discrete variational equation as follows in Equation (31).

$$\left(\hat{\rho}(t)\frac{\boldsymbol{u}_h^{n+1} - 2\boldsymbol{u}_h^n + \boldsymbol{u}_h^{n-1}}{\Delta t^2}, \boldsymbol{v}\right) + a(\boldsymbol{u}_h^n, \boldsymbol{v}) = (\boldsymbol{f}^n, \boldsymbol{v}) \quad \forall v \in V_h. \tag{31}$$

$$u(0) = u_0, \quad u_0 \in V. \quad v_{b1} = u_0 + \Delta t u_1, \quad u_1 \in H. \tag{32}$$

The basis function of elastic plate displacement constitutes the finite element solution space $\boldsymbol{u}_h^n = \left(u_{1h}^n, u_{2h}^n\right)^{\mathrm{T}}$, which satisfies the relationship $u_{1h}, u_{2h} \in U_h = \mathrm{span}\{\varphi_j\}_{j=1}^{NF}$. NF is expressed as the number of displacement components; then, the finite element solution of the displacement component can be written as shown in Equation (33).

$$u_{1h}^n = \sum_{j=1}^{NF} u_{1j}^n \varphi_j, \quad u_{2h}^n = \sum_{j=1}^{NF} u_{2j}^n \varphi_j. \tag{33}$$

We choose the text function $\boldsymbol{v}_h = (\varphi_i, 0)^{\mathrm{T}}, \quad (i = 1, 2, \ldots, NF)$; this is equivalent to $v_{1h} = \varphi_i, \quad v_{2h} = 0$. By moving terms and sorting equations, $\forall v_{1h} \in V_h, i = 1, 2$, we can obtain the form of the discrete function as follows in Equation (34).

$$\left(\hat{\rho}(t)\left(u_{1h}^{n+1} - 2u_{1h}^n + u_{1h}^{n-1}\right), v_{1h}\right) + \Delta t^2 a(u_{ih}^n, v_{1h}) = \Delta t^2 (f^n, v_{1h}). \tag{34}$$

Then, we bring Equation (33) into Equation (34), and we can get a displacement component Equation (35).

$$\begin{aligned}
&\int_\Omega \hat{\rho}(t)\left(\sum_{j=1}^{NF} u_{1h}^{n+1}\varphi_j\varphi_i - 2\sum_{j=1}^{NF} u_{1h}^n \varphi_j\varphi_i + \sum_{j=1}^{NF} u_{1h}^{n-1}\varphi_j\varphi_i\right)dxdy + \\
&\Delta t^2\left[\left(\lambda\left(\sum_{j=1}^{NF} u_{1j}^n \frac{\partial \varphi_j}{\partial x}\right)\frac{\partial \varphi_i}{\partial x} dxdy + 2\int_\Omega \mu\left(\sum_{j=1}^{NF} u_{1j}^n \frac{\partial \varphi_j}{\partial x}\right)\frac{\partial \varphi_i}{\partial x} dxdy + \right.\right. \\
&\int_\Omega \lambda\left(\sum_{j=1}^{NF} u_{2j}^n \frac{\partial \varphi_j}{\partial y}\right)\frac{\partial \varphi_i}{\partial x} dxdy + \int_\Omega \mu\left(\sum_{j=1}^{NF} u_{1j}^n \frac{\partial \varphi_j}{\partial y}\right)\frac{\partial \varphi_i}{\partial y} dxdy + \\
&\left.\int_\Omega \mu\left(\sum_{j=1}^{NF} u_{2j}^n \frac{\partial \varphi_j}{\partial x}\right)\frac{\partial \varphi_i}{\partial y} dxdy\right] = \Delta t^2 \int_\Omega f_1^n \varphi_i dxdy.
\end{aligned} \tag{35}$$

Similarly, we choose the test function $\boldsymbol{v}_h = (0, \varphi_i)^{\mathrm{T}}, \quad (i = 1, 2, \ldots, NF)$; this is equivalent to $v_{1h} = 0, v_{2h} = \varphi_i$. $\forall v_{2h} \in V_h, i = 1, 2$. The numerical discretization results of the FDM-FEM method are as follows in Equation (36).

$$\left(\hat{\rho}(t)\left(u_{2h}^{n+1} - 2u_{2h}^n + u_{2h}^{n-1}\right), v_{2h}\right) + \Delta t^2 a(u_{ih}^n, v_{2h}) = \Delta t^2 (f^n, v_{2h}). \tag{36}$$

Bring Equation (33) into Equation (36), and we can get another displacement component, as shown in Equation (37).

$$\begin{aligned}
&\int_{\Omega}\hat{\rho}(t)\left(\sum_{j=1}^{NF}u_{2h}^{n+1}\varphi_j\varphi_i-2\sum_{j=1}^{NF}u_{2h}^{n}\varphi_j\varphi_i+\sum_{j=1}^{NF}u_{2h}^{n-1}\varphi_j\varphi_i\right)dxdy+\\
&\Delta t^2\left[\left(\mu\left(\sum_{j=1}^{NF}u_{1j}^{n}\frac{\partial\varphi_j}{\partial y}\right)\frac{\partial\varphi_i}{\partial x}dxdy+\int_{\Omega}\mu\left(\sum_{j=1}^{NF}u_{2j}^{n}\frac{\partial\varphi_j}{\partial x}\right)\frac{\partial\varphi_i}{\partial x}dxdy+\right.\right.\\
&\int_{\Omega}\lambda\left(\sum_{j=1}^{NF}u_{1j}^{n}\frac{\partial\varphi_j}{\partial x}\right)\frac{\partial\varphi_i}{\partial y}dxdy+\int_{\Omega}\lambda\left(\sum_{j=1}^{NF}u_{2j}^{n}\frac{\partial\varphi_j}{\partial y}\right)\frac{\partial\varphi_i}{\partial y}dxdy+\\
&\left.2\int_{\Omega}\mu\left(\sum_{j=1}^{NF}u_{2j}^{n}\frac{\partial\varphi_j}{\partial y}\right)\frac{\partial\varphi_i}{\partial y}dxdy\right]=\Delta t^2\int_{\Omega}f_2^n\varphi_i dxdy.
\end{aligned} \tag{37}$$

Then, we can integrate Equations (35) and (36), so it is easily to obtain the vector iteration formulas.

$$\boldsymbol{X}^{n+1}=\left(\left[u_{1j}^{n+1}\right]_{j=1}^{NF},\left[u_{2j}^{n+1}\right]_{j=1}^{NF}\right)^{\mathrm{T}},\boldsymbol{X}^{n}=\left(\left[u_{1j}^{n}\right]_{j=1}^{NF},\left[u_{2j}^{n}\right]_{j=1}^{NF}\right)^{\mathrm{T}}. \tag{38}$$

$$\boldsymbol{X}^{n-1}=\left(\left[u_{1j}^{n-1}\right]_{j=1}^{NF},\left[u_{2j}^{n-1}\right]_{j=1}^{NF}\right)^{\mathrm{T}},\quad \boldsymbol{b}=\left(\int_{\Omega}f_1^n\varphi_i dxdy,\int_{\Omega}f_2^n\varphi_i dxdy\right)^{\mathrm{T}}. \tag{39}$$

Using the same method, we can get the sparse matrices $\boldsymbol{A},\boldsymbol{B}$, and $\boldsymbol{C}$. Finally, we transform the elastic differential equation into an algebraic iterative equation.

$$\boldsymbol{A}\boldsymbol{X}^{n+1}+\boldsymbol{B}\boldsymbol{X}^{n}+\boldsymbol{C}\boldsymbol{X}^{n-1}=\boldsymbol{b}. \tag{40}$$

Further sorting out Equation (40), we can get vector $\boldsymbol{X}^{n-1}$.

$$\boldsymbol{X}^{n+1}=-\boldsymbol{A}^{-1}\boldsymbol{B}\boldsymbol{X}^{n}-\boldsymbol{A}^{-1}\boldsymbol{C}\boldsymbol{X}^{n-1}+\boldsymbol{A}^{-1}\boldsymbol{b}. \tag{41}$$

The initial iteration value can be obtained according to the boundary conditions, such as $\boldsymbol{X}^0=\left(u_{11}^0,u_{12}^0,\ldots,u_{1NF}^0,u_{21}^0,u_{22}^0,\ldots,u_{2NF}^0\right)^{\mathrm{T}}$. Similarly, $\boldsymbol{X}^1=(u_{11}^1,u_{12}^1,\ldots,u_{1NF}^1,u_{21}^1,u_{22}^1,\ldots,u_{2NF}^1)^{\mathrm{T}}$. Finally, we can obtain the N-1 group transient displacement solutions by iteration, which can be denoted as $\boldsymbol{X}^k,\quad (k=1,2,\ldots N-1)$.

4.3. Numerical Simulation with CDDM-TCFEM Method

4.3.1. RPV Axial Section Solved by CDDM-TCFEM Method

The middle part and both ends of the vessel are the key positions of mechanical analysis. The nuclear pressure vessel cuts n equal parts along the longitudinal direction, and each section is actually a rectangular slice. The inner side is subjected to thermal shock, and the outer side is a free end. The upper and lower sides of the rectangle are fixed. Then, the transient linear elastic equation is discretized according to the FEM-FDM theory [49,50]. According to the material parameters, size, and boundary information of the nuclear pressure vessel, the structural mechanics problem is solved according to the principle of minimum potential energy or the variational method. In this example, the ring area and the axial direction are considered. The rectangular regions are all discretized by triangular elements of the upgraded spectrum. The two-dimensional transient elastic equations can be written as shown in Equation (42).

$$\begin{cases}\hat{\rho}(t)\frac{\partial^2\boldsymbol{u}}{\partial t^2}-\left(\frac{\partial\sigma_{xx}(\boldsymbol{u})}{\partial x}+\frac{\partial\sigma_{yx}(\boldsymbol{u})}{\partial y}\right)=f_x\\ \hat{\rho}(t)\frac{\partial^2\boldsymbol{u}}{\partial t^2}-\left(\frac{\partial\sigma_{xy}(\boldsymbol{u})}{\partial x}+\frac{\partial\sigma_{yy}(\boldsymbol{u})}{\partial y}\right)=f_y\end{cases} \tag{42}$$

The displacement boundary conditions and the force boundary conditions corresponding to the numerical examples are as follows:

(1) The displacement boundary conditions.

$$u(x,y,t)|_{x=x_0,y=y_0,t} = u_t(x,y,t)|_{x=x_0,y=y_0,t} = \bar{u} = 0 \quad (x,y,t) \in \Gamma_{up}. \tag{43}$$

$$v(x,y,t)|_{x=x_0,y=y_0,t} = v_t(x,y,t)|_{x=x_0,y=y_0,t} = \bar{v} = 0, \quad (x,y,t) \in \Gamma_{\text{down}}. \tag{44}$$

$$v|_{x=x_0,y=y_0,t} = u|_{x=x_0,y=y_0,t} = 0, \quad (x,y,t) \in \Gamma_{\text{outer}}. \tag{45}$$

$$\Gamma_{up} = \left\{(x,y,t) \mid x_i = \frac{d}{n}i, y_i = \frac{H}{n}i, i = 0,1,2,\ldots n, t > 0\right\}. \tag{46}$$

$$\Gamma_{\text{down}} = \left\{(x,y,t) \mid x_i = 0, y_i = \frac{H}{n}i, i = 0,1,2,\ldots n, t > 0\right\}. \tag{47}$$

$$\Gamma_{\text{outer}} = \left\{(x,y,t) \mid x_i = a, y_i = \frac{H}{n}i, i = 0,1,2,..n, t > 0\right\}. \tag{48}$$

Among them, Γ_{up} and Γ_{down} represent the upper and lower boundaries of the rectangle. d is the thickness, and H is the height of the longitudinal section of the pressure vessel.

(2) The force boundary conditions.

The thermal shock force (the exterior force per unit volume) on the inside of the rectangular section is $f = (f_x, f_y)^T$; since the problem is a transient equation, f is a function of t, and the corresponding force boundary conditions are:

$$n_x\sigma_{xx}(x_b,y_b,t) + n_y\tau_{xy}(x_b,y_b,t) = \bar{p}_x, \quad (x_b,y_b,t) \in \Gamma_{\text{inner}}. \tag{49}$$

$$n_x\tau_{xy}(x_b,y_b,t) + n_y\sigma_{xx}(x_b,y_b,t) = \bar{p}_y, \quad (x_b,y_b,t) \in \Gamma_{\text{inner}}. \tag{50}$$

$$\Gamma_{\text{inner}} = \left\{(x_b,y_b,t) \mid x_{bi} = d, y_{bi} = \frac{H}{n}i, i = 1,2,\ldots n, t > 0\right\}. \tag{51}$$

$$n_x = -1, n_y = 0, \quad \bar{p}_x = f_x(t), \bar{p}_y = 0N. \tag{52}$$

4.3.2. Radial Section Solved by CDDM-TCFEM Method

The radial section of the nuclear pressure vessel is a circle, the outer boundary belongs to the free end, and the inner side is subjected to the thermal shock force f, which also satisfies the two-dimensional transient elastic equation.

(1) The displacement boundary conditions.

The outer side of the circular section is a fixed end, the two components of the displacement are zero, and the corresponding displacement boundary conditions are:

$$u(x,y,t)|_{x=x_0,y=y_0,t} = \bar{u} = 0 \quad (x,y,t) \in \Gamma_1. \tag{53}$$

$$v(x,y,t)|_{x=x_0,y=y_0} = \bar{v} = 0, \quad (x,y,t) \in \Gamma_1. \tag{54}$$

$$\Gamma_1 = \left\{(x,y) \mid x_i = R\cos\theta_i, y_i = R\sin\theta_i, \theta_i = \frac{2\pi i}{n}, i = 0,1,2,\ldots n\right\}. \tag{55}$$

(2) The force boundary condition.

We denoted R as the outer radius and r as the inner radius; then, the thickness of the pressure vessel can be written as $d = R - r$. The thermal shock force on the inside of the pressure vessel is uniformly variable force of outward extrusion. For the thermal shock force $f = (f_x, f_y)^{\text{T}}$ acting on the inner side of the radial cross-section of pressure vessel, the force boundary condition is as follows:

$$n_x\sigma_{xx}(x_b,y_b,t) + n_y\tau_{xy}(x_b,y_b,t) = \bar{p}_x, \quad (x_b,y_b,t) \in \Gamma_2. \tag{56}$$

$$n_x\tau_{xy}(x_b,y_b,t) + n_y\sigma_{xx}(x_b,y_b,t) = \bar{p}_y, \quad (x_b,y_b,t) \in \Gamma_2. \tag{57}$$

$$\bar{p}_x = f_x(t_j)\cos\theta_i, \quad \bar{p}_y = f_y(t_j)\sin\theta_i. \tag{58}$$

$$\Gamma_2 = \left\{ (x,y) \mid x_i = r\cos\theta_i, y_i = r\sin\theta_i, \theta_i = \frac{2\pi i}{n}, i = 0,1,2,\dots n \right\}. \tag{59}$$

For the two-dimensional transient elastic mechanics problem, the numerical solution can be solved according to the FDM-FEM theory; the time term is approximated by the second-order central difference, and the space term is discretized by a finite element. Items are discretized by triangular elements. For rectangular areas, they are finally divided into 380 domain elements, 58 edge elements, and 220 mesh vertices. As for the circular sections, they are divided into 344 elements and 256 mesh vertices. For rectangular areas and circles, all ring sections use LST elements, and the displacement field function can be expressed in the following Equation (60).

$$u = \sum_{i=1}^{6} u_i N_i(\xi,\eta) \quad , v = \sum_{i=1}^{6} v_i N_i(\xi,\eta). \tag{60}$$

The six-node isoparametric LST element is composed of three vertices of a triangle and the midpoints of three sides, and its shape function is as follows:

$$N_1 = (2L_1 - 1)L_1 \quad N_2 = 4(1 - L_1 - L_2)L_1. \tag{61}$$

$$N_3 = [2(1 - L_1 - L_2) - 1](1 - L_1 - L_2) \quad N_4 = 4L_2(1 - L_1 - L_2). \tag{62}$$

$$N_5 = (2L_1 - 1)L_2. \tag{63}$$

Among them, L_1, L_2 are area coordinates, which can be solved according to the relationship between area coordinates and rectangular coordinates.

$$\begin{pmatrix} L_i \\ L_j \\ L_k \end{pmatrix} = \frac{1}{2A} \begin{pmatrix} a_i & b_i & c_i \\ a_j & b_j & c_j \\ a_k & b_k & c_k \end{pmatrix}. \tag{64}$$

a_i, b_i, c_i are replaced by the vertex coordinates of the triangular element.

$$a_i = x_j y_k - x_k y_j, \quad b_i = y_j - y_k, \quad c_i = x_k - x_j. \tag{65}$$

Then, according to Section 4.2, the transient linear elasticity theory of this paper can be solved. This numerical experiment is mainly a dimensionality reduction processing method, which simplifies the three-dimensional problem into a two-dimensional plane problem, which makes the original problem easier to solve and improves the calculation speed. At the same time, the rectangular section and circular section use the LST quadratic element ratio. The accuracy of the approximation of the CST linear element is higher, and some preprocessing of the parameters is required before the numerical solution. The outer radius $R = 3$ of this numerical experiment, the inner radius $r = 2.75$ m, and the thickness of the pressure vessel is $d = R - r = 0.25$ m. The material selected for the pressure vessel is A508 metal, and its density will decrease with the increase of temperature. We fit the density $\hat{\rho}(t)$ of the material with respect to the temperature T and find that it satisfies the following functional relationship shown in Equation (66).

$$\hat{\rho}(T) = \sum_{i=1}^{3} \alpha_i T^i = \alpha_0 + \alpha_1 T + \alpha_2 T^2 + \dots + \alpha_3 T^3. \tag{66}$$

The fitting coefficient is $\alpha_0 = 7865$, $\alpha_1 = -0.522$, $\alpha_2 = 4.69 \times 10^{-4}$, $\alpha_3 = -2.78 \times 10^{-7}$. The Root Mean Square Error (RMSE) is $E_{rmse} = 13.64$, and the goodness-of-fit $R^2 = 0.991$. The fitting error is very small, which also shows that the variable density function relationship established by us is reliable. In fact, the density $\hat{\rho}(t)$ of our model is a function of change with time t, the varying density values can be obtained from Table 2. Equation (67) obtains the functional relationship expression of temperature.

According to the test data of the change of temperature inside the pressure vessel with time, we found the fitting function of temperature with time t, which is in the form of a piecewise function.

$$\mathrm{T}(t) = \begin{cases} \frac{-29.3t^2+45.14t+162.9}{t+1.185} & 0 < t \leq 6000 \\ 31.32t + 83.33 & 6000 < t \leq 15000 \end{cases} \tag{67}$$

The variation trend of the internal parameters of the pressure vessel under the structural damage model is shown in Figure 5 below. Figure 5a shows the relationship between the internal temperature and thermal shock force of the pressure vessel with time. The function relationship of temperature change with time can be used. Equation (67) describes that the internal pressure of the pressure vessel is mainly generated by thermal shock, and we use a nonlinear function to approximate the change of the thermal shock $f(t)$ inside the pressure vessel within 7250–7350s.

$$f(t) = \frac{15}{1 + e^{-\frac{1}{5}(x-7300)}} + 3, \quad 7250 \leq \mathrm{t} \leq 7350. \tag{68}$$

Figure 5b contains the graph of the Young's modulus of the cladding and the parent material as a function of temperature obtained through experimental tests. According to the data trend, the Young's modulus E will decrease with the increase of temperature. Figure 5c shows (under the continuous damage model) the three-dimensional variation of the elastic modulus with the influencing variables u and d; while u and d are both temperature-related functions, the change of u has a significant effect. The numerical results show that the elastic modulus of the model with damage will decrease with the increase of u. For Figure 5d, it is the change trend of Poisson rate under the model with damage.

In traditional linear elasticity theory, Young's modulus and the Poisson rate are constant. However, in the high-temperature and high-pressure environment, these physical parameters usually change. This paper not only considers the influence of temperature but also combines the damage factor. Therefore, the improved continuous structural damage model satisfies this change rule. Figure 5d can observe that with the increase of u, the Poisson rate increases, and u has a proportional relationship with the temperature function. In other words, when the temperature range is 20–600, the Poisson rate will increase with the increase of temperature. It exists in the range of $v \in [0.305, 0.357]$; from the definition of Poisson rate, it can also show that the change value of transverse strain with the increase of temperature is greater than that of longitudinal strain.

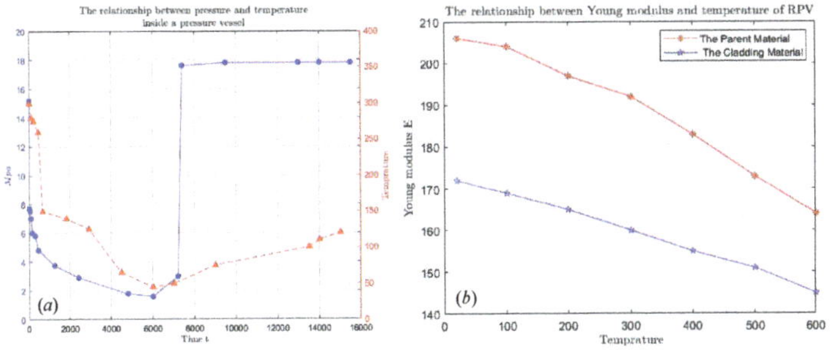

Figure 5. *Cont.*

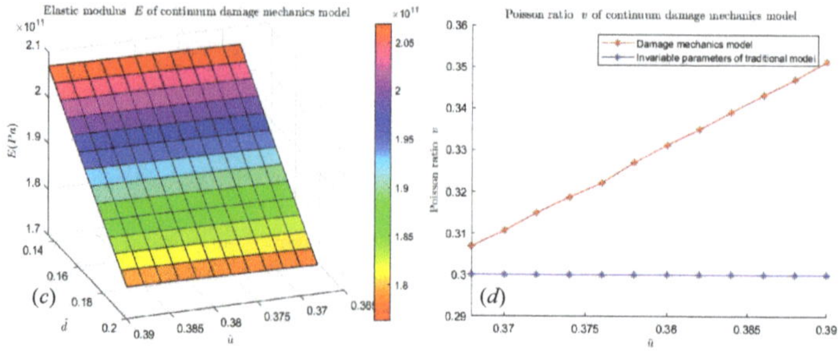

Figure 5. Variation of internal parameters of pressure vessel with temperature in structural damage dynamic model. (**a**) Variation trend of internal temperature and pressure of RPV with time t. (**b**) Variation diagram of Young's modulus and temperature. (**c**) Young's modulus for solving damage dynamic model of continuous structure. (**d**) Comparing the Possion rate v of the traditional model with the damage model.

4.4. Numerical Example 1 Result Display

When the temperature is from 20 to 600 °C, the specific heat coefficient, heat transfer coefficient, thermal expansion coefficient, and density inside the nuclear pressure vessel will change dynamically [49–51]. The experimental data are shown in Table 2. From the table, we can see that the coefficient of thermal expansion α increases with the increase of temperature, and the density, thermal conductivity, and specific heat capacity all increase with temperature. The experimental data are shown in Table 2.

Table 2. Statistical table of changes in relevant material parameters of nuclear pressure vessels with temperature.

Temperature T (°C)	Specific Heat Capacity C (J/kg/°C)	Heat Conduction K (J/kg/°C)	Thermal Expansion α $(10^{-6}$ 1/k)	Density (g/cm^3)
20	63.5	454	13.1	7846
100	68.6	485	13.4	7817
200	52.7	528	13.8	7788
300	46.7	592	14.0	7753
400	40.8	680	14.5	7717
500	37.4	703	14.8	7681
600	34.0	880	11.9	7643

For the two-dimensional transient linear elastic equation, through the continuous damage variable parameter model established above combined with the FDM-FEM numerical theory, we can obtain the stress analysis of the two-dimensional section of the pressure vessel along the radial and axial direction [52,53]. The second-order central difference is used in the time term, and the finite element is used in the space term. The mesh generation and the application of boundary load can be referred to Figure 6a,b. The force $F_1(t)$ and $F_2(t)$ loaded by the boundary are uniform transient forces, and the force increases gradually with the increase of time. The time step $\tau = \frac{T}{N}$, where T = 100s, N = 50 s.

Figure 6c shows that when $t_3 = 7254$ s, the rectangular section is subjected to the horizontal right transient thermal shock force $F_1(t_3) = 3 \times 10^6$ N/m^2, and the stress variation diagram is generated under this force. Figure 6d shows that when $t_{36} = 7320$ s, the rectangular section is subjected to the horizontal right transient thermal shock force $F_1(t_{36}) = 1.77 \times 10^7$ N/m^2, and the stress diagram is generated by the right boundary of the rectangular section. In addition, the loading strain of the ring section is different from that of the rectangular section, which is subjected to uniform radiation transient force F_2. In the actual solution process, it needs to be decomposed F_2 into two horizontal and vertical components: that is, $(f_{2x}, f_{2y}) = (F_2(t)\cos\theta_2, F_2(t)\sin\theta_2)$. Figure 6e is the strain of the circular section under the boundary force of $F_2(t_3) = 3 \times 10^6$ N/m^2, respectively. Similarly, when $t_{36} = 7320$ s, the variable force $F_2(t_{36}) = 1.77 \times 10^7$ N/m^2 is the boundary force loaded on the inner side of the circular section and Figure 6f shows the strain ε_{xx} of the circumferential section of RPV.

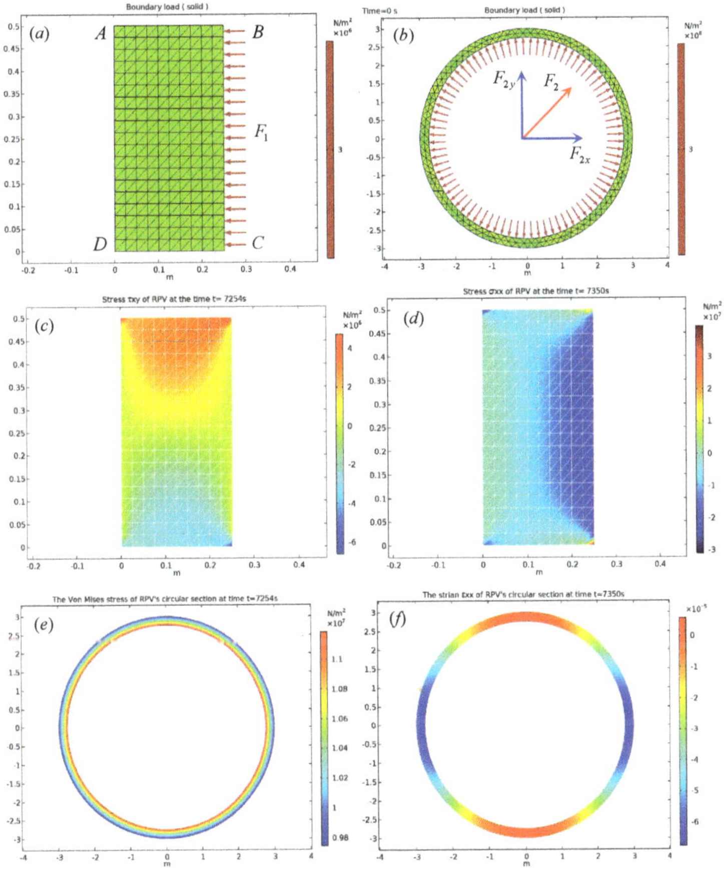

Figure 6. The axial stress and radial stress of RPV are solved by FEM combined with the damage dynamic model. (**a**) The diagram of inner load on a axial section. (**b**) The diagram of inner load on a radial section. (**c**) The axial section stress τ_{xy} diagram of RPV. (**d**) The axial section stress σ_{xx} diagram of RPV. (**e**) The Von Mises stress of radial section of RPV. (**f**) The strain ε_{xx} of radial section of RPV.

In this example, we mainly use the CMMD-TCFEM method to solve the axial and radial stress of RPV. The solution idea belongs to the dimensionality reduction method, and the three-dimensional RPV is divided into a section in the radial and axial directions for mechanical modeling. Then, through the continuous structural dynamic model with damage, we can obtain a more accurate Young modulus and Poisson rate. This numerical solution conclusion is that the elastic modulus E will decrease with the increase of temperature T, while the Poisson ratio will increase with the increase of temperature. At the same time, the fitting function of density with temperature is given in this numerical experiment. The real density corresponding to each time step can be accurately solved. Finally, through numerical comparison, it is found that the stress and strain of the pressure vessel wall material will increase with the increase of the internal thermal shock force, and the position of the boundary fixed connection has the phenomenon of stress concentration. The advantage of this numerical experiment is that it can quickly analyze how the stress of the pressure vessel changes under the transient force. This example transforms the three-dimensional problem into a two-dimensional problem. The calculation speed is improved. The defect is that only the change of local force can obtain the overall stress. In order to make up for the analysis defect, the axisymmetric finite element method is considered in Example 2, and the detailed theoretical and simulation results are in Section 5.

5. Axisymmetric FEM Method to Solve RPV Stress

5.1. The Theories Axisymmetric FEM Method of RPV

Pressure vessels are similar to capsule vessels, which have the characteristics of geometric symmetry. Therefore, in addition to the section method mentioned above, the axisymmetric finite element method can also be used to solve this problem [54,55]. The stress of three-dimensional pressure vessels can be quickly obtained, since the calculation amount of the axisymmetric method is relatively small, which is more intuitive than the section method to reflect the change of internal mechanical properties of pressure vessels. The displacement function of the axisymmetric problem can be expressed as:

$$\left\{ \begin{array}{l} u = \alpha_1 + \alpha_2 r + \alpha_3 z \\ w = \alpha_4 + \alpha_5 r + \alpha_6 z \end{array} \right. \tag{69}$$

Similar to the plane problem, for axisymmetric problems, we take one arbitrary element, and the numbers of three nodes are i, j, m, and the coordinates of nodes are respectively (r_i, z_i), (r_j, z_j), (r_m, z_m). Let the corresponding node displacements be (u_i, w_i), (u_j, w_j), (u_m, w_m). Bring the node coordinates and displacements into Equation (69), respectively.

$$\left\{ \begin{array}{l} u = N_i u_i + N_j u_j + N_m u_m \\ w = N_i w_i + N_j w_j + N_m w_m \end{array} \right. \tag{70}$$

The shape function matrix $\mathbf{N}$ and the node displacement vector $\{q\}^e$ can be written as Equations (71) and (72).

$$\mathbf{N} = \begin{pmatrix} N_i & 0 & N_j & 0 & N_m & 0 \\ 0 & N_i & 0 & N_j & 0 & N_m \end{pmatrix} \tag{71}$$

$$\{q\}^e = \{ u_i \quad w_i \quad u_j \quad w_j \quad u_m \quad w_m \}^T \tag{72}$$

Then, the matrix form of the nodal displacements on the final axisymmetric element is $\{u\}^e = [N]\{q\}^e$. In Equation (71), N_i, N_j, N_m is the shape function. As for the axisymmetric problem, there are four stress components $\{\sigma\} = \{\sigma_r, \sigma_\theta, \sigma_z, \tau_{rz}\}^T$. Similarly, the corresponding strain is still a function of u and w, so the strain vector can be written as $\{\varepsilon\} = \{\varepsilon_{rr}, \varepsilon_{zz}, \varepsilon_\theta, \gamma_{rz}\}$, and radial deformation causes circumferential strain, which is $\varepsilon_\theta = \frac{2\pi(r+u)-2\pi r}{2\pi r} = \frac{u}{r}$. Therefore, the element strain can be expressed by displacement.

$$\{\varepsilon\} = \{\varepsilon_r, \varepsilon_\theta, \varepsilon_z, \gamma_{rz}\}^T = \left\{ \frac{\partial u}{\partial r} \quad \frac{u}{r} \quad \frac{\partial w}{\partial z} \quad \frac{\partial u}{\partial r} + \frac{\partial u}{\partial r} \right\}^T = \boldsymbol{B}q^e. \tag{73}$$

Among them, $\boldsymbol{B} = \begin{bmatrix} B_i & B_j & B_m \end{bmatrix}$, and each node satisfies the relationships shown in Equations (74) and (75).

$$\boldsymbol{B}_l = \frac{1}{2A} \begin{bmatrix} b_l & 0 \\ f_l & 0 \\ 0 & c_l \\ c_l & b_l \end{bmatrix} \quad (l = i, j, m). \tag{74}$$

$$f_l(r,z) = \frac{a_l + b_l r + c_l z}{r} \quad (l = i,j,m). \tag{75}$$

We need to emphasize that the constitutive equation is written as $\boldsymbol{\sigma} = \boldsymbol{D}(\boldsymbol{\varepsilon} - \boldsymbol{\varepsilon}_0) + \boldsymbol{\sigma}_0$; This formula takes into account the initial stress $\boldsymbol{\sigma}_0$ and initial strain $\boldsymbol{\varepsilon}_0$, but our model considers the values of initial stress and initial strain is zero. At the same time, it is assumed that the RPV material in the axisymmetric model is isotropic. According to the relationship between stresses and strains, we can bring Equation (73) into $\{\boldsymbol{\sigma}\} = \boldsymbol{D\varepsilon}$; then, the element stress matrix can be written as:

$$\{\boldsymbol{\sigma}\} = \boldsymbol{D\varepsilon} = \boldsymbol{DBq}^e = \boldsymbol{Sq}^e = \begin{bmatrix} \boldsymbol{S}_i & \boldsymbol{S}_j & \boldsymbol{S}_m \end{bmatrix} \boldsymbol{q}^e. \tag{76}$$

In Equation (76), $\boldsymbol{S}$ is a stress matrix, and $\hat{E}$ and $\hat{u}$ are the Young's modulus and Poisson's ratio, which can be calculated from the damage model, respectively.

$$\boldsymbol{S}_k = \frac{\hat{E}(1-\hat{u})}{2A(1+\hat{u})(1-2\hat{u})} \begin{bmatrix} b_l + A_1 f_l & A_1 c_l \\ A_1 b_l + f_l & A_1 c_l \\ A_1(c_l + f) & c_l \\ A_2 c_l & A_2 b_l \end{bmatrix} \quad (k = i,j,m). \tag{77}$$

$$A_1 = \frac{\hat{u}}{1-\hat{u}} \quad A_2 = \frac{1-2\hat{u}}{2(1-\hat{u})}. \tag{78}$$

The axisymmetric single element stiffness matrix can be obtained by the principle of virtual work.

$$\{\boldsymbol{F}\}^e\{\delta \boldsymbol{q}^e\} = \iiint_{Ve} \{\delta\boldsymbol{\varepsilon}\}^T\{\boldsymbol{\sigma}\} r dr d\theta dz. \tag{79}$$

The virtual work expression for 3D elasticity includes the volume integrals terms, which can be written as $dV = rd\theta(drdz) = rd\theta dA$.

Then, the virtual strain of the element becomes Equation (80).

$$\{\delta\boldsymbol{\varepsilon}\}^e = [\boldsymbol{B}]\{\delta\boldsymbol{q}\}^e. \tag{80}$$

The mechanical equilibrium equation is established based on virtual work principle, and then, we can obtain Equation (81).

$$\iint_A \int_0^{2\pi} \delta\varepsilon^T \boldsymbol{\sigma} r d\theta dA = \iint_A \int_0^{2\pi} \delta\boldsymbol{u}^T \boldsymbol{b} r d\theta dA + \oint_l \int_0^{2\pi} \delta\boldsymbol{u}^T \boldsymbol{T} d\theta ds + \sum_i \int_0^{2\pi} \delta\boldsymbol{u}^T \boldsymbol{p}_i r_i d\theta. \tag{81}$$

In Equation (81), A is the bounary and area of the region of integration.

$$\boldsymbol{b} = \begin{pmatrix} b_r \\ b_z \end{pmatrix} \quad \boldsymbol{T} = \begin{pmatrix} t_r \\ t_z \end{pmatrix} \quad \boldsymbol{P} = \begin{pmatrix} P_{ri} \\ P_{zi} \end{pmatrix} \tag{82}$$

The sum of the above three vectors represents the external forces $\{\boldsymbol{F}\}$, which consists of body forces, surface tractions, and point loads, respectively [56,57]. The equivalent nodal force of the triangular element is denoted as $\{\boldsymbol{F}\}$ and the virtual displacement is $\{\delta\boldsymbol{q}^e\}$; then, the virtual strain of the element can be written as $\{\delta\varepsilon^e\} = \boldsymbol{B}\{\delta\boldsymbol{q}\}^e$. At the same time, the virtual displacement $\{\delta\boldsymbol{u}^e\} = \boldsymbol{N}\{\delta\boldsymbol{q}^e\}$ is eliminated on both sides, and we can obtain Equation (83).

$$\iiint_{Ve} [\boldsymbol{B}]^T\{\boldsymbol{\sigma}\} r dr d\theta dz \{\boldsymbol{q}^e\} = 2\pi \iint_{Ae} [\boldsymbol{B}]^T[\boldsymbol{D}][\boldsymbol{B}] r dr dz \{\boldsymbol{q}^e\} = [\boldsymbol{K}^e]\{\boldsymbol{q}^e\}. \tag{83}$$

Among them, the stiffness matrix of the triangular element is:

$$\{\boldsymbol{K}^e\} = 2\pi \iint_{Ae} [\boldsymbol{B}]^T[\boldsymbol{D}][\boldsymbol{B}] r dr dz = \begin{pmatrix} k_{11} & k_{12} & k_{13} \\ k_{21} & k_{22} & k_{23} \\ k_{31} & k_{32} & k_{33} \end{pmatrix}. \tag{84}$$

The elements stiffness matrix satisfies the relationship shown in Equation (85).

$$k_{rs} = 2\pi \int_A \mathbf{B}_r^T \mathbf{D} \mathbf{B}_s r dA = 2\pi \mathbf{B}_r^T \mathbf{D} \mathbf{B}_s \bar{r} A, \quad (r, s = 1, 2, 3), \bar{r} = \frac{1}{3}(r_1 + r_2 + r_3). \tag{85}$$

Then, the shape function $\mathbf{N}$ includes the external force terms of the element. After finishing, we can get Equation (86).

$$\{\mathbf{F}^e\} = 2\pi \iint_{Ae} \mathbf{B}^T \sigma r dA - 2\pi \iint_{Ae} \mathbf{N}^T \mathbf{b} r dA - 2\pi \oint_{le} \mathbf{N}^T \mathbf{T} r ds. \tag{86}$$

Finally, each element matrix is assembled into a total stiffness matrix. Thus, we can get the final algebraic equation $\mathbf{K}\mathbf{q} = \mathbf{F}$.

5.2. *Axisymmetric Numerical Simulation Example*

This section will give examples of three-dimensional pressure vessels. The advantages of the axisymmetric method can make up for the defect of the poor overall evaluation effect of the section method, and it is more intuitive to show the stress state of three-dimensional vessels. The advantages of the axisymmetric method can make up for the defects of the poor overall evaluation effect of the section method, and it is more intuitive to show the stress state of three-dimensional vessels. The axisymmetric problem has distinct characteristics: the geometric structure and the boundary constraint condition are symmetrical about the central axis. The axisymmetric problem has different characteristics: the geometric structure and the boundary constraint condition are symmetrical about the central axis.

The thickness $d = 25$ mm of the wall of the nuclear pressure vessel in this numerical experiment, and Young's modulus of continuous structural damage model is $\hat{E}$. Similarly, Poisson's ratio of the continuous structural damage model is $\hat{v}$. The material density of the pressure vessel changes with the increase in temperature. The specific function expression is shown in Equations (67) and (68), and the variable density function is denoted as $\hat{\rho}(t)$. As for the geometric parameter of the nuclear pressure vessel, the simplified nuclear pressure vessel can be considered a combination of a hollow cylinder and a semi-ellipsoid. The geometric parameters and dimensions are as follows: the thickness $t = 0.25$ m of the vessel wall, the radius of the bottom of the vessel is $R_1^A = \frac{D_1}{2} = 5m$, the radius of the inner wall is $R_2^A = \frac{D_2}{2} = 4.75m$, and the dome height formula with a curved radian that satisfies the following relation is:

$$h_i = R_c - \sqrt{(R_c - R_2^A)(R_c + R_2^A - 2R_k)} = 1.997m \tag{87}$$

Among them, $R_k = 0.1D_1 = 1m, R_c = 0.9D_2 = 8.55m$, the maximum angle between the tangent of the dome and the vertical direction of the container wall is α.

$$\alpha = \arctan\left(\frac{R_2^A - R_k}{R_c - h_i}\right) \tag{88}$$

After calculation $\alpha = 0.519$ rad, the height of the container wall is $H_A = 10$ m. For a pressure vessel, the axisymmetric method is mainly used to solve the problem. The displacement boundary conditions can also be called boundary constraints.

$$u(r,\theta,z)|_{r=r_0,\theta=\theta_0,z=z_0} = \bar{u} = 0 \tag{89}$$

$$v(r,\theta,z)|_{r=r_0,\theta=\theta_0,z=z_0} = \bar{v} = 0 \tag{90}$$

$$w(r,\theta,z)|_{r=r_0,\theta=\theta_0,z=z_0} = \bar{w} = 0 \tag{91}$$

$$\Gamma_1 = \{(r,\theta,z) \mid 0 \le \theta \le 2\pi, r = R_1, 0 \le z \le H_A\} \tag{92}$$

$$\Gamma_2 = \{(r,\theta,z) \mid 0 \le \theta \le 2\pi, r = r_a, 0 \le z \le h_i\} \tag{93}$$

The impact force generated during the reaction of the pressure vessel is assumed to be uniformly acting on the inner wall of the vessel, and this mode of action is generated along the normal direction of the vessel wall surface. The forces received by the three-dimensional nuclear pressure vessel are all face forces, which are different in actual applications. The impact force on the inner wall of the nuclear pressure vessel is different. At a certain moment, the impact force on the inner wall of the nuclear pressure vessel by gas is a constant force P. The surface force is the force on the surface of the object. Motion is an internal force, and only boundary elements may have surface forces. The two components of surface force $\bar{P} = \{P_r, P_z\}$; if the surface force on the edge of the element is $\boldsymbol{q}$, the equivalent nodal load of the element is:

$$\bar{P}_e = 2\pi \int_L \mathbf{N}^T q r d s \tag{94}$$

In this example, the face force is linearly distributed perpendicular to the surface of the object. This face force is very common, such as dams hitting a flood, the air flow of the aircraft engine hitting the outer wall, and the wheel pressing the ground. The effect placed on the edge of the unit ij is perpendicular to the linearly distributed surface force on the surface of the object, the force at node i is q_i, the force at node j is q_j, and the surface force at any point on the ij side of the element is decomposed into hoop and axial components.

$$\boldsymbol{q}^e = \left\{ \begin{array}{c} q_r \\ q_z \end{array} \right\} = \left\{ \begin{array}{c} (N_i q_i + N_j q_j)\frac{b_m}{l_{ij}} \\ (N_i q_i + N_j q_j)\frac{c_m}{l_{ij}} \end{array} \right\} \tag{95}$$

Then, we determine the linearly distributed surface force perpendicular to the surface of the object, and the equivalent nodal load of node i is:

$$\bar{\boldsymbol{P}}_{ei} = \left\{ \begin{array}{c} \bar{P}_{ri} \\ \bar{P}_{zi} \end{array} \right\} = \frac{1}{6}\pi[(3r_i + r_j)q_i + (r_i + r_j)q_j]\left\{ \begin{array}{c} z_i - z_j \\ r_j - r_i \end{array} \right\} \tag{96}$$

The equivalent nodal load of the linearly distributed surface force node j perpendicular to the surface of the object is:

$$\bar{\boldsymbol{P}}_{ej} = \left\{ \begin{array}{c} \bar{P}_{rj} \\ \bar{P}_{zj} \end{array} \right\} = \frac{1}{6}\pi[(r_i + r_j)q_i + (r_i + 3r_j)q_j]\left\{ \begin{array}{c} z_i - z_j \\ r_j - r_i \end{array} \right\} \tag{97}$$

Finally, the axisymmetric stress tensor can be calculated according to the following equation:

$$\{\sigma\} = \boldsymbol{D}\varepsilon = \boldsymbol{D}\boldsymbol{B}\boldsymbol{q}^e = \boldsymbol{S}\boldsymbol{q}^e = \left[\begin{array}{ccc} S_i & S_j & S_m \end{array} \right]\boldsymbol{q}^e \tag{98}$$

The axisymmetric finite element method is used to solve the pressure vessel. The solution steps are carried out according to the following points: material parameter definition, geometric region construction, mesh division, and physical field selection. Then, load conditions and fixed constraints are added. Finally, it is transformed into algebraic equations and output stress cloud diagrams. The geometric cross-section is divided into elements on the rz plane, and quadrilateral elements are used for distillation. The discretized area contains 575 domain elements and 250 boundary elements, the number of degrees of freedom is 2541, the total time is $t = 10$ s, and the symmetric axis is $r = 0$. As for the fixed constraint condition of the vessel, the outer boundary displacement is 0, and the load boundary load conditions are that the inner side is subjected to uniform outward pressure; the range is from $\bar{P} = 3 \times 10^6$pa to $\bar{P} = 1.68 \times 10^7$pa.

Figure 7a shows the stress and deformation of the 2D symmetry plane of the pressure vessel. The output result contains two physical quantities: stress and deformation. The deformation is mainly the displacement change, and its amplification factor is $\alpha = 128.6$. The purpose is to observe the largest displacement change position more clearly. Similarly, the greater value of stress is also concentrated in the middle part. Figure 7b shows the radial strain ε_{rr} cloud diagram of the pressure vessel at F = 13 Mpa, which can also reflect that the 2D section stress results are consistent with the 3D results. The center of the cylinder is larger, and the surrounding forces are relatively large, stable, and uniform. Figure 7c shows the von Mises stress figure of the pressure vessel at F = 3 Mpa. Figure 7d shows the von Mises stress of the pressure vessel at F = 16.8 Mpa. The solution process is also to first calculate the single stiffness matrix, including the application of boundary conditions, and then assemble the total stiffness matrix to form a large sparse matrix and finally solve the linear system.

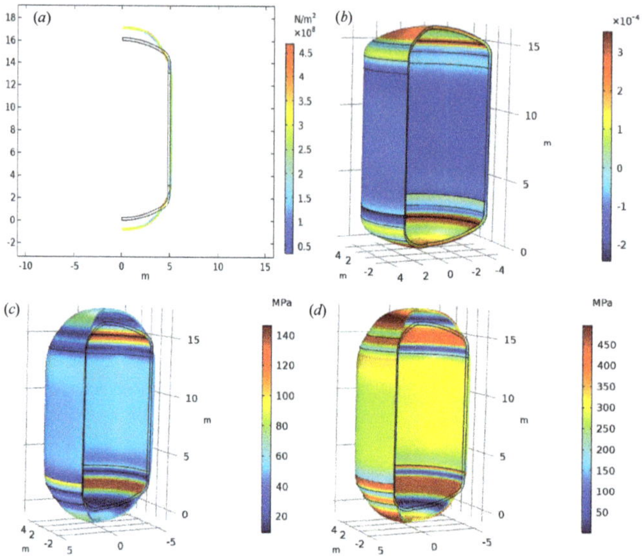

Figure 7. Numerical results of mechanical change of RPV solved by axisymmetric FEM. (**a**) Deformation diagram of the symmetrical half-section of the pressure vessel at F = 15.2 Mpa. (**b**) The radial strain ε_{rr} cloud diagram of the pressure vessel at F = 13 Mpa. (**c**) von Mises stress nephogram of the pressure vessel at F = 3 Mpa. (**d**) von Mises stress nephogram of the pressure vessel at F = 16.8 Mpa.

6. Three-Dimensional (3D) Multi-Physics Field Model of RPV

The working environment of the real pressure vessel is relatively complex. After nuclear fission, a large amount of heat is released in a short time. Generally speaking, there are four exhaust pipes on the wall of the pressure vessel, two pipes are the inlet and outlet of the coolant, and the other two pipes are the hot steam inlet and outlet. In the initial state, the temperature inside the pressure vessel is very high. With the addition of a cooling system (ECC), the temperature gradually drops from 350 to about 100 °C. The first two examples only consider pressure related to the force condition of the container, the established geometric model does not consider the temperature change around the exhaust pipe and the state of stress distribution, and the stress change of the pipe port is more important for the sealing of the entire container and the pressure distribution. Therefore, it is very important that it is necessary to study the state of stress and temperature changes at the pipe mouth of RPV. Example 3 established an coupled model of three-dimensional temperature field and stress field [58–60]. The FDM-FEM numerical method is used to solve the problem, and the output is the corresponding temperature and stress.

6.1. Three-Dimensional Transient Elastic Equation

In fact, the three-dimensional nuclear pressure vessel internal force analysis is a rather complicated analysis process. Due to some uncertainty of the impact force inside the vessel, the geometric structure is not completely symmetrical, and there are multiple pipes near the top of the nuclear pressure vessel. These interfaces are mainly responsible for the discharge of exhaust steam, the input of coolant, etc. The stress change analysis near the interface has always been the focus of scholars. Due to the relatively high surface temperature of the interface, the final force analysis is not simply a mechanical problem. It is more scientific to use the knowledge of multi-physics coupling to solve the problem. This example is mainly responsible for the coupled modeling of the thermal field and the force field, and it analyzes the force situation near the pipe mouth of the pressure vessel.

The solution of nuclear pressure vessels in the thermal–mechanical coupling field contains two important equations: namely, the convective–diffusion equation and the equilibrium equation of solid mechanics. When the reaction of the pressure vessel is stable, the overall internal temperature tends to be balanced, but the local temperature changes are quite different due to the action of the coolant and the position very close to the core. Since the nuclear reactor reaction is a continuous process and is closely related to time, the analysis of temperature change should consider the transient 3D heat conduction equation and the 3D transient mechanical equilibrium equation. The following will give the 3D transient heat conduction equation.

First, we establish the force field balance equation of the nuclear pressure vessel under the action of thermal shock. Among them, $\boldsymbol{u} = (u, v, w)^T$ is the displacement field function. Since this model belongs to the multi-physics coupling model, the RPV material $\rho(t)$ is a nonlinear function of time t, which will decrease with the increase of temperature, σ is the three-dimensional stress tensor matrix, $\boldsymbol{F} = (f_x(t), f_y(t), f_z(t))^T$ is the corresponding thermal shock force. The three-dimensional gradient operator can be expressed as $\nabla = \left(\frac{\partial}{\partial x}, \frac{\partial}{\partial y}, \frac{\partial}{\partial z}\right)$; then, the three-dimensional transient mechanical equation is expressed as shown in Equaiton (99):

$$\rho(t)\frac{\partial^2 \boldsymbol{u}}{\partial t^2} = \nabla \cdot \sigma + \boldsymbol{F}, \quad \boldsymbol{u} \in \Omega \times [0, T_m] \tag{99}$$

The Cauchy stress tensor introduced by a three-dimensional deformable solid is expressed as:

$$\sigma = \begin{pmatrix} \sigma_{xx} & \sigma_{xy} & \sigma_{xz} \\ \sigma_{yx} & \sigma_{yy} & \sigma_{yz} \\ \sigma_{zx} & \sigma_{zy} & \sigma_{zz} \end{pmatrix} \tag{100}$$

For the 3D stress tensor and strain, the relationship satisfies Equation (101).

$$\sigma_{ij} = \delta_{ij}\lambda\nabla \cdot \boldsymbol{u} + 2\mu\varepsilon_{ij} = \frac{\partial u_k}{\partial x_k}\lambda\delta_{ij} + \mu\left(\frac{\partial u_i}{\partial x_j} + \frac{\partial u_j}{\partial x_i}\right) \tag{101}$$

where E is the Young's modulus of the elastomer, u is the Poisson ratio, and the Lamé constant formula is:

$$\lambda = \frac{Ev}{(1+v)(1-2v)} \tag{102}$$

The relationship between the three-dimensional stress tensor and strain is $\sigma = \boldsymbol{D}\varepsilon$, where $\boldsymbol{D}$ is the elastic matrix, and the final stress can be expressed in the form of displacement:

$$\begin{pmatrix} \sigma_{xx} \\ \sigma_{yy} \\ \sigma_{zz} \\ \sigma_{xy} \\ \sigma_{xz} \\ \sigma_{yz} \end{pmatrix} = \frac{E}{1+v}\begin{pmatrix} \frac{1-v}{2v-1} & \frac{-v}{2v-1} & \frac{-v}{2v-1} & 0 & 0 & 0 \\ \frac{-v}{2v-1} & \frac{1-v}{2v-1} & \frac{-v}{2v-1} & 0 & 0 & 0 \\ \frac{-v}{2v-1} & \frac{-v}{2v-1} & \frac{1-v}{2v-1} & 0 & 0 & 0 \\ 0 & 0 & 0 & 1 & 0 & 0 \\ 0 & 0 & 0 & 0 & 1 & 0 \\ 0 & 0 & 0 & 0 & 0 & 1 \end{pmatrix}\begin{pmatrix} \varepsilon_{xx} \\ \varepsilon_{yy} \\ \varepsilon_{zz} \\ \varepsilon_{xy} \\ \varepsilon_{xz} \\ \varepsilon_{yx} \end{pmatrix} = \frac{\boldsymbol{D}}{2}\begin{pmatrix} 2\frac{\partial u}{\partial x} \\ 2\frac{\partial v}{\partial y} \\ 2\frac{\partial w}{\partial z} \\ \frac{\partial u}{\partial x} + \frac{\partial v}{\partial y} \\ \frac{\partial u}{\partial x} + \frac{\partial w}{\partial z} \\ \frac{\partial v}{\partial y} + \frac{\partial w}{\partial z} \end{pmatrix} \tag{103}$$

Then, by substituting Equation (103) into Equation (104), we can convert the three-dimensional linear elastic stress equation into three displacement classification equations. Then, using the linear weighted form of the displacement basis function in place of the displacement in the equation, the weak form of the Galerkin finite element is obtained. The scalar equations along the x, y, and z directions are:

$$\begin{cases} \rho(t)\frac{\partial^2 u}{\partial t^2} - \left(\frac{\partial \sigma_{xx}}{\partial x} + \frac{\partial \sigma_{yx}}{\partial y} + \frac{\partial \sigma_{zx}}{\partial z}\right) - f_x(t) = 0 \\ \rho(t)\frac{\partial^2 v}{\partial t^2} - \left(\frac{\partial \sigma_{xy}}{\partial x} + \frac{\partial \sigma_{yy}}{\partial y} + \frac{\partial \sigma_{zy}}{\partial z}\right) - f_y(t) = 0 \\ \rho(t)\frac{\partial^2 w}{\partial t^2} - \left(\frac{\partial \sigma_{xz}}{\partial x} + \frac{\partial \sigma_{yz}}{\partial y} + \frac{\partial \sigma_{zz}}{\partial z}\right) - f_z(t) = 0 \end{cases} \tag{104}$$

For the boundary conditions of the exhaust pipe of the RPV, there are two cases of displacement boundary conditions and force boundary conditions. The displacement boundary of the outer side of the pipe and the outer wall of the RPV can be assumed to have an initial value of 0, which can be expressed as:

$$\boldsymbol{u}|_{(x,y,z,t)} = 0 \quad (x, y, z, t) \in \Gamma_{\text{out}} \times [0, T_m] \tag{105}$$

The wall of the RPV container is mainly subjected to radial impact force, and there is also a small shear force in the z direction. The inner side of the pipe wall will also be subjected to thermal shock force. If there is cooling liquid inside the pipe, gravity must also be considered, which belongs to fluid–solid coupled heating conduction model. This example only considers the force and temperature changes at the nozzle of the RPV exhaust steam, which satisfies the following mechanical boundary conditions:

$$\begin{cases} \sigma_{xx}n_x + \sigma_{xy}n_y + \sigma_{xy}n_z = f_x(t) \\ \sigma_{yx}n_x + \sigma_{yy}n_y + \sigma_{yz}n_z = f_y(t) \\ \sigma_{zx}n_x + \sigma_{zy}n_y + \sigma_{zz}n_z = f_z(t) \end{cases} (x, y, z, t) \in \Gamma_{\text{RPV}} \times [0, T_m] \tag{106}$$

As for Equation (106), the time term is discreted by the central difference scheme, the terms $\boldsymbol{u}^{n+1} \in V, \quad 1 \le n \le N-1$ are to be solved such that we can get a semi-discrete variational equation as follows in Equation (107).

$$\left(\hat{\rho}(t)\frac{\boldsymbol{u}_h^{n+1} - 2\boldsymbol{u}_h^n + \boldsymbol{u}_h^{n-1}}{\Delta t^2}, \boldsymbol{v}\right) + a(\boldsymbol{u}_h^n, \boldsymbol{v}) = (\boldsymbol{f}^n, \boldsymbol{v}) \quad \forall \boldsymbol{v} \in V_h. \tag{107}$$

The basis function of elastic plate displacement constitutes the finite element solution space $\boldsymbol{u}_h^n = \left(u_{1h}^n, u_{2h}^n, u_{3h}^n\right)^{\mathrm{T}}$, which satisfies the relationship $u_{1h}, u_{2h}, u_{3h} \in U_h = \text{span}\{\varphi_j\}_{j=1}^{NF}$. NF is expressed as the number of displacement components.

The discrete form of the space term of the 3D linear elastic equation is similar to the two-dimensional term, and there are two differences. The first point, The 3D linear elastic equation has one more equation about the displacement w component than the 2D linear elastic equation when the equation is discretized. The second point, When the space term of the 3D linear elastic equation is discretized by FEM, the basis function selected is different from that of the 2D. The 3D lowest-order basis function is a tetrahedral element, while the 2D discretization is a linear CST element. Then, according to the variational principle, the variational form is obtained, and then the basis function is brought in to obtain the Galerkin weak form. This continuous differential equation is transformed into a discrete algebraic equation. Finally, we can obtain a matrix iterative equation, and each iteration needs to solve a linear equation.

6.2. Three-Dimensional Stress Analysis Model of RPV

The 3D elastic force analysis model is similar to the 2D model. For spatial dispersion of the 3D pressure vessel, we can use the tetrahedral element to discretize it. When the asymmetric 3D structure is discrete, the axisymmetric method is not feasible, and a Cartesian coordinate system needs to be established, using the general finite element discrete model, the displacement linear function of the tetrahedral element can be expressed as the following form:

$$\begin{cases} u = \alpha_1 + \alpha_2 x + \alpha_3 y + \alpha_4 z \\ v = \alpha_5 + \alpha_6 x + \alpha_7 y + \alpha_8 z \\ w = \alpha_9 + \alpha_{10} x + \alpha_{11} y + \alpha_{12} z \end{cases} \tag{108}$$

Then, we combined with the four nodal coordinates of the tetrahedral element, and we use the shape function to represent the element displacement

$$u = \sum_{i=1}^{4} N_i u_i, \quad v = \sum_{i=1}^{4} N_i v_i, \quad w = \sum_{i=1}^{4} N_i w_i \tag{109}$$

The matrix form of the element displacement can be expressed as $\{d^e\} = \{\begin{array}{ccc} u & v & w \end{array}\}^T = \boldsymbol{N}\boldsymbol{q}^e$, and the element stress matrix is

$$\{\sigma\} = \boldsymbol{D}\{\varepsilon\} = \boldsymbol{D}\boldsymbol{B}\{\boldsymbol{q}^e\} = \boldsymbol{S}\{q^e\} = \left[\begin{array}{cccc} S_i & S_j & S_m & S_p \end{array}\right]\{q^e\} \tag{110}$$

The value of the matrix $\boldsymbol{S}$ is mainly related to the tetrahedral node coordinates

$$\boldsymbol{S}_l = \boldsymbol{D}\boldsymbol{B}_l = \frac{6A_3}{V}\begin{bmatrix} b_l & A_1 b_l & A_1 b_l & A_2 c_l & 0 & A_2 d_l \\ A_1 c_l & c_l & A_2 c_l & A_2 b_l & A_2 d_l & 0 \\ A_1 d_l & A_1 d_l & d_l & 0 & A_2 c_l & A_2 b_l \end{bmatrix}^T \quad (l = i, j, m, p) \tag{111}$$

In Equation (111), the following relational expression is satisfied

$$A_1 = \frac{\mu}{1-\mu} \quad A_2 = \frac{1-2\mu}{2(1-\mu)} \quad A_3 = \frac{E(1-\mu)}{36(1+\mu)(1-2\mu)} \tag{112}$$

Similarly, the expression form of the stiffness matrix can be obtained according to the principle of virtual work:

$$\boldsymbol{K}^e = \iiint_V \boldsymbol{B}^T \boldsymbol{D}\boldsymbol{B} dxdydz = \boldsymbol{B}^T \boldsymbol{D}\boldsymbol{B} V \tag{113}$$

The total equivalent nodal load array of the element due to body force, surface force, and concentrated force is:

$$\{\boldsymbol{F}^e\} = \{\boldsymbol{F}_v^e\} + \{\boldsymbol{F}_s^e\} + \{\boldsymbol{F}_c^e\} = \iiint_V \boldsymbol{N}_l \boldsymbol{P}_v dv + \iint_S \boldsymbol{N}_l \boldsymbol{P}_s dA + \sum_l^4 \boldsymbol{N}_l \boldsymbol{P}_c \quad (l = i, j, m, p) \tag{114}$$

After obtaining the stiffness matrix of the element, it is necessary to synthesize the total stiffness matrix, the stiffness matrix of the N_e tetrahedral elements on the three-dimensional solution area, and the node load according to the element node coding rules from the total stiffness matrix. Then, finally, we get a large sparse system of linear equations $\boldsymbol{K}\boldsymbol{q} = \boldsymbol{F}$.

$$\boldsymbol{K} = \sum_{i=1}^{N_e} \boldsymbol{K}_i^e, \quad \boldsymbol{F} = \sum_{i=1}^{N_e} \boldsymbol{F}_i^e, \quad i = 1, 2, \ldots, N_e \tag{115}$$

The above is the stress solution of 3D RPV from the perspective of a virtual work principle. It is convenient to solve the steady-state problem, for the transient problem, we need to change the force $F(t)$ of the integral term in each calculation. In Section 4.3.2, we will introduce another method to solve the stress at different times according to the transient elastic equation.

6.3. Three-Dimensional Transient Heat Conduction Equation

The temperature variable $T(x,y,z,t)$ is a multivariate function of coordinates and time. When $T(x,y,z,t)$, it indicates that Q does not change with time, and it indicates that the temperature of the thermally conductive object does not change with time after heat exchange. This process is called the steady-state temperature field. When $\frac{\partial T}{\partial t} \neq 0$ is the transient temperature field, the difference between the transient temperature field and the steady-state temperature field is time variable t. According to the Fourier heat transfer law and the energy conservation law, the energy balance differential equation in the rectangular coordinate system satisfies the following relationship:

The heat transfer equation [61–63] satisfied by the heat transfer inside the RVP material, its equation, and related parameters are as follows:

$$\rho c\frac{\partial T}{\partial t} + \rho c u \cdot \nabla T + \nabla \cdot (-\boldsymbol{k}\nabla T) - Q = 0 \tag{116}$$

For Equation (116), ρ is the material density, the unit is $\mathrm{kg/m^3}$, and c is the specific heat capacity at constant pressure of the RPV material $\mathrm{J/(kg \cdot k)}$. The internal nuclear reaction of RPV produces enormous heat; Q is the heat generated by the internal heat source. $\boldsymbol{k} = (k_x, k_y, k_z)$ is the thermal conductivity vector along different directions x, y, z. Furthermore, $\frac{\partial T}{\partial x}, \frac{\partial T}{\partial y}, \frac{\partial T}{\partial z}$ respectively represent the heat that flows in the x, y, z direction, $\boldsymbol{u}_c = (u_x, u_y, u_z)$ is the convection velocity terms. Furthermore, we can get that the equivalent form of Equation (116) is the differential Equation (117).

$$\rho c\left[\frac{\partial T}{\partial t} + \left(u_x\frac{\partial T}{\partial x} + u_y\frac{\partial T}{\partial y} + u_z\frac{\partial T}{\partial z}\right)\right] = \left(\frac{\partial}{\partial x}\left(k_x\frac{\partial T}{\partial x}\right) + \frac{\partial}{\partial y}\left(k_y\frac{\partial T}{\partial y}\right) + \frac{\partial}{\partial z}\left(k_z\frac{\partial T}{\partial z}\right)\right) + Q \tag{117}$$

In addition, the temperature field distribution in the solution domain Ω needs to meet certain boundary conditions.

(1) Class I boundary conditions: The solid surface temperature is a known function of the time t.

$$T_1(x,y,z,t) = \bar{T}(x,y,z,t), \quad T_1(x,y,z,t) \in \Gamma \tag{118}$$

(2) Class II boundary conditions: The thermal flow density of the solid surface is equal to the change value of the temperature T in the direction of each component.

$$k_x\frac{\partial T_2}{\partial x}n_x + k_y\frac{\partial T_2}{\partial y}n_y + k_z\frac{\partial T_2}{\partial z}n_z = k\boldsymbol{n} \cdot \nabla T = q(x) \quad T_2 \in \Gamma_2 \tag{119}$$

(3) Class III boundary conditions: The difference between the heat flow density of the solid surface is proportional to the surface temperature T and the fluid surface temperature T_c.

$$k_x\frac{\partial T_3}{\partial x}n_x + k_y\frac{\partial T_3}{\partial y}n_y + k_z\frac{\partial T_3}{\partial z}n_z = h(T_a - T_3) \quad T_3 \in \Gamma_3 \tag{120}$$

n_x, n_y, n_z is the direction cosine of the normal line outside the boundary, $\bar{T}(x,y,z,t)$ is a given temperature, ∇T_3 is the heat flow density vector on the boundary Γ_3, h is the thermal conductivity coefficient $W/(m^2 \cdot K)$ on the boundary, T_a is the insulating temperature of the boundary layer under natural convection conditions, and the combination of all boundaries can be expressed as $\Gamma = \Gamma_1 + \Gamma_2 + \Gamma_3$.

Then, it is assumed that the three-dimensional RPV is a homogeneous material; that is, the thermal conductivity along different directions is the same [64], and there is $k_x = k_y = k_z$. So, the convection–diffusion equation can also be written as (117), which is equivalent to Equation (121).

$$\frac{\partial T}{\partial t} + \boldsymbol{u} \cdot \nabla T = \nabla \cdot (\boldsymbol{k} \nabla T) + \frac{Q}{\rho c} \tag{121}$$

Perform Galerkin integration, multiply both sides of Equation (120) by the test function $\varphi(x, y, z)$, obtain the corresponding discrete equation according to the variational principle, and consider the right-hand term of Equation (120).

$$D_f = \iiint_\Omega \varphi_i \left[\nabla \cdot (k \nabla T) + \frac{Q}{\rho c} \right] dV = \iiint_\Omega k(\varphi_i \nabla \cdot (k \nabla T)) + \varphi_i \frac{Q}{\rho c} dxdydz \tag{122}$$

Using the Gauss divergence theorem to further simplify the equation, we can get

$$D_f = k \oint_S \varphi_i \boldsymbol{n} \cdot (\nabla T) dS + \iiint_\Omega -k(\nabla \varphi_i \cdot \nabla T) + \varphi_i \frac{Q}{\rho c} dxdydz \tag{123}$$

After considering the left-hand term of Equation (124), the discrete form of Galerkin can be finally obtained:

$$\hat{T}(x, y, z, t) = \sum_{j=1}^{N} T_j(t) \varphi_j(x, y, z) \tag{124}$$

The tetrahedral element (4-NQ) is used to discrete the RPV, and the discrete equation in the whole region is obtained.

$$\sum_{j=1}^{N} \boldsymbol{A}_{ij} \frac{d\boldsymbol{T}_j}{dt} + \sum_{j=1}^{N} \boldsymbol{C}_{ij} \boldsymbol{T}_j = -k \sum_{j=1}^{N} \boldsymbol{B}_{ij} \boldsymbol{T}_j + \frac{1}{\rho c} \oint_S \varphi_i q dS + \frac{1}{\rho c} \sum_{j=1}^{N} \boldsymbol{M}_{ij} \varphi_i Q_j \tag{125}$$

Then, we abbreviate the diffusion matrix of Equation (126) as:

$$\boldsymbol{B}_{ij} = \iiint_\Omega \nabla \varphi_i \cdot \nabla \varphi_j dv = \iiint_\Omega \nabla \varphi_i \cdot \nabla \varphi_j dxdydz \tag{126}$$

Meanwhile, M_{ij} of Equation (127) is called the mass matrix

$$\boldsymbol{M}_{ij} = \iiint_\Omega \varphi_i \cdot \varphi_j dv = \iiint_\Omega \varphi_i \cdot \varphi_j dxdydz \tag{127}$$

The matrix C_{ij} is the convection matrix:

$$\boldsymbol{C}_{ij} = \iiint_\Omega \varphi_i u \cdot \nabla \varphi_j dv = \iiint_\Omega \varphi_i u \cdot \nabla \varphi_j dxdydz \tag{128}$$

Finally, the partial differential Equation (129) is transformed into a system of ordinary differential equations, and the specific form is as follows:

$$\boldsymbol{M} \cdot \frac{d\boldsymbol{T}}{dt} + \boldsymbol{CT} = k(-\boldsymbol{B} \cdot \boldsymbol{T} + \boldsymbol{b}) \tag{129}$$

Neumann boundary conditions are imposed on the right-hand term components of Equation (130); its components are of the form:

$$b_i = \frac{1}{k} \left(\oint_S \varphi_i q dS + \sum_{j=1}^{N} M_{ij} Q_j \right) \tag{130}$$

The boundary temperature of the outer surface of the RPV belongs to the Drichlet boundary condition, and the substitution method can be used. If there is a known function

$T = T_i(x_b, y_b, z_b, t_b)$, the $i-th$ equation of the overall discrete Equation (129) can be replaced by the Drichlet boundary function T_i and the corresponding mass matrix $\boldsymbol{M}$. The $i-th$ row diagonal element of the convection matrix $\boldsymbol{C}$ and matrix $\boldsymbol{B}$ is i.

6.4. *h-p Method Error Estimate*

(1) *p*-type adaptive error analysis

The finite element cluster is denoted as $\{e, p_e, \Sigma_e\}$, the continuous function space can be written as Ω, and the adaptive mesh discretization of the region is denoted as $\widetilde{T}_h$; for any element in the region $\widetilde{T}_h$, it satisfies $\forall e \in \widetilde{T}_h, h_e \to 0, \quad h_e > 0, \frac{h_e}{p_e} \leq const$ [65,66]. If π_e is a higher-order approximation operator on the element, π_h is a higher-order approximation operator on the overall region, then there is a constant C such that the following interpolation error estimation holds:

$$|v - \pi_e v|_{m,q,e} \leq C(\widetilde{T}_h) h_e^{k+1-m+n\left(\frac{1}{q}+\frac{1}{p}\right)} |v|_{k+1,p,e} \quad v \in H^{k+1,p}(e) \tag{131}$$

When $p = q, \quad H^{k+1,p}(\Omega)$ and $H^{m,p}(\Omega)$ are two Sobolev spaces, and we have the following relation established:

$$|v - \pi_h v|_{m,p,\Omega} \leq C(\widetilde{T}_h) h^{k+1-m} |v|_{k+1,p,\Omega} \quad v \in H^{k+1,p}(\Omega) \tag{132}$$

Among them, the constant C is related to m, n and the reference element $\hat{e}, \sigma_n$ is the unit sphere volume in the space R^n; then, the $C(\widetilde{T}_h)$ range satisfies the following expression:

$$\sigma_n C_1 p^n \leq C(\widetilde{T}_h) \leq \sigma_n C_2 h^n \tag{133}$$

(2) *h*-type adaptive error.

h - type finite element, where h represents the maximum size of the element. In the calculation process, the method does not change the type of element but improves the calculation results by continuously reducing the geometric size of the element, that is, refinement mesh. Because the order of elements in this method is generally low, it is also called low-order finite element method.

If $v \in H^{k+1}(\Omega) \bigcap V, \forall e \in \widetilde{T}_h, \quad h_e \to 0, \quad h_e > 0, \quad \frac{h_e}{p_e} \leq const$. Then, the following estimation formula is established.

$$\|u - u_h\|_{1,\Omega} \leq C\bar{h}^k |u|_{k+1,\Omega} \tag{134}$$

Among them, $\bar{h}$ is the average side length of the cells of the adaptive mesh, and N_A represents the total number of cells in the adaptive mesh region $\widetilde{\Omega}$.

$$\bar{h} = \frac{1}{N_A} \sum_{i=1}^{N_A} \max(l_1^e, l_2^e, l_3^e) \tag{135}$$

When the order of the basis function is p-order, the numerical error of adaptive FEM generally has a relationship with the quality of the adaptive mesh [67]. If the size of the element side length of the adaptive mesh varies from the edge to the center point O where the mesh size is the smallest, and decreases exponentially, the mathematical formula is written as:

$$h_i = e^{-\xi} h_{i-1}, \quad \xi > 0, \quad i = 2, ..N_A. \tag{136}$$

Then, the newly formed adaptive grid error also has the characteristics of exponential change. The specific error estimation expression is:

$$\|e\|_{1,\Omega} = \|u - u_h\|_{1,\Omega} \leq C_0 N^{-\beta} |u|_{k+1,\Omega}, \quad \beta > 0, \quad \beta \in \boldsymbol{R} \tag{137}$$

6.5. Numerical Result Display

The RPV parameters are divided into geometric parameters and basic material property parameters. For the RPV radius $R = 5$ m we simulated, the wall thickness $d = 15$ cm, the radius of the pipe mouth $r_{pip} = 10$ cm, the thickness of the pipe wall $d_{pip} = 4$ cm, and the height of the RPV calculation area $H = 0.6$ m. This example uses tetrahedral elements, and we perform discretization. Figure 8 below shows the mesh quality evaluation diagram. This example simulates an RPV with four nozzles. The structure contains 58,910 domain elements, 30,345 boundary elements, and 3985 edge elements. The green mesh in Figure 8a indicates that the mesh quality is relatively good, and the yellow part belongs to the part with poor mesh quality. The overall quality of the mesh divided in this example is relatively good. Due to the symmetry of RPV, we only need to study the stress and temperature changes of a nozzle. Figure 8b is the result of meshing the tetrahedral element of one nozzle. The vicinity of the nozzle is the focus of our research, so the adaptive meshing method is adopted. It has a total of 9735 domain elements, 3297 boundary elements, and 471 edge elements, and the mesh has the characteristics of self-adaptation, which can not only ensure the advantages of fast calculation speed but also ensure the accurate description of the details of stress changes at the interface of the pipe wall. It can smoothly transition the numerical results of positions with large stress gradient changes, which makes the visualization effect better. The mesh quality evaluation chart shows that the mesh effect near the exhaust pipe is relatively poor, and the geometric change of the RPV container wall is gentle, so the mesh quality of the element is better.

Regarding other numerical results, Figure 8c shows the inner temperature variation diagram of the RPV nozzle at the calculation time t = 420 s, which reflects that the temperature of the nozzle is relatively lower than that of other positions. The reason is that the coolant added at the nozzle can reduce the temperature near the nozzle. Figure 8d is the isothermal line diagram of the three-dimensional nozzle. The outer side of the RPV is shown in the figure, and different colors represent different temperatures. Similarly, it can be seen from the figure that the temperature near the nozzle is relatively low, and there is a cooling effect caused by the combined action of air cooling and coolant. Figure 8e is the displacement cloud map of an RPV nozzle at t − 7200 s, which reflects the initial starting time; the force generated by the internal pressure is large, and the temporary change of the cooling system is not very obvious. Figure 8f is the strain ε_{xx} of RPV, and the change range near the nozzle is significantly larger than the change of the internal value of the nozzle. The change of strain and displacement is mainly affected by the thickness of the material, the external load, the elastic modulus of the material, the Poisson ratio, and other basic properties. The results show a comprehensive response; not only the embodiment of the load change but also the change of the displacement is significantly larger than the strain. This can also be reflected from the geometric constitutive equation.

The symmetrical geometric appearance is helpful for element calculation, and the numerical results show that the stress change is relatively large at the intersection of the pipe of the RPV. In the actual application process, the RPV is accompanied by multiple exhaust pipes, which can exhaust gas, add coolant, etc. Therefore, the third numerical model of this paper is mainly to analyze the stress change near the pipe mouth, and we have established a three-dimensional finite element model of thermal–mechanical coupling. The adaptive mesh is used to discretize the pipe mouth area. Finally, the numerical solution cloud map of the stress, strain, and displacement of the RPV pipe mouth is obtained. Then, we compared the radial and hoop stress changes of RPV at different times. The physical model established in this paper and the new numerical method proposed in this paper have important reference values for the stress analysis of RPV, and the method can also be transferred to other coupled physical models. The safe control of nuclear energy production is a meaningful research topic.

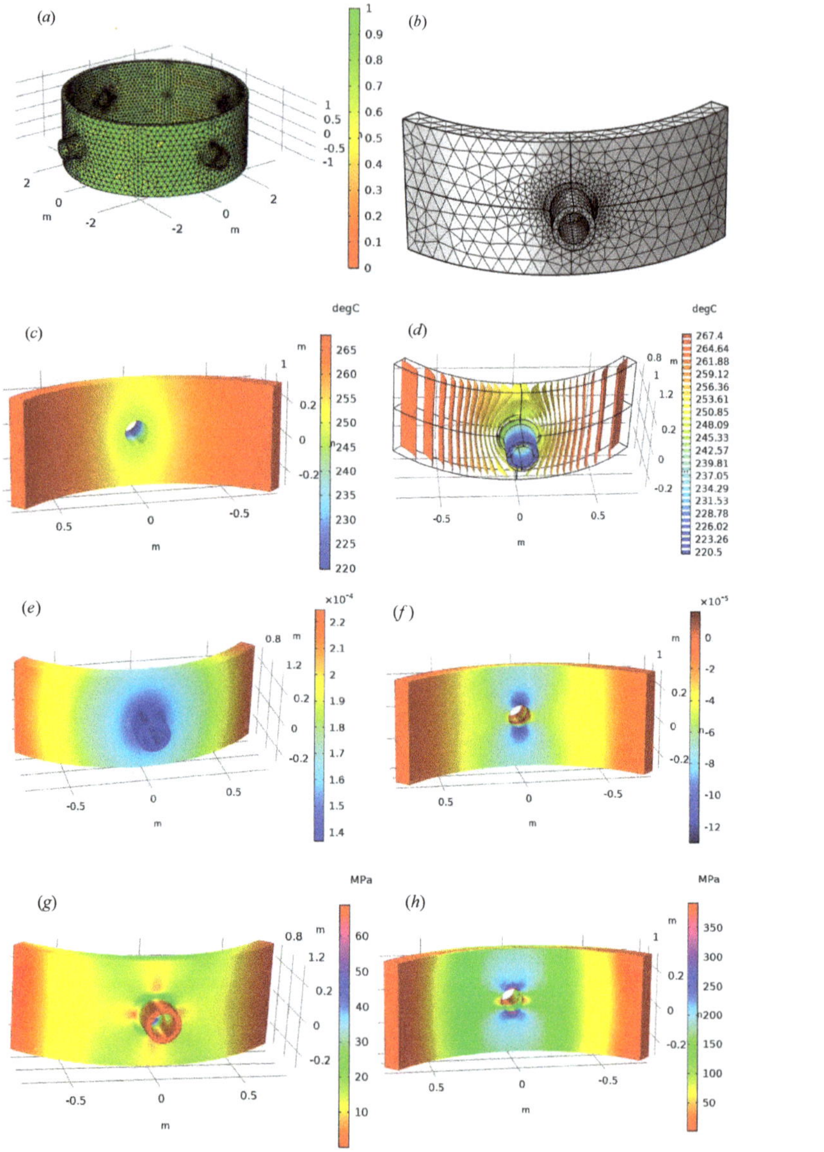

Figure 8. Numerical simulation of RPV by 3D thermal-mechanics coupled model. (**a**) Mesh quality assessment of all pipe outlets. (**b**) 4-NQ element grid division of RPV single pipe outlet and adjacent area. (**c**) Temperature T nephogram of RPV pipe mouth. (**d**) Isothermal line diagram of RPV pipe mouth. (**e**) Displacement of RPV nozzle U. (**f**) Strain ε_{xx} nephogram near RPV nozzle. (**g**) Von Mises stress of RPV pipe. (**h**) Stress nephogram of σ_{yy}.

Figure 9a is the circumferential stress of the RPV vessel wall. We choose four time points: $t = 1200$ s, $t = 2400$ s, $t = 3600$ s, and $t = 7200$ s. From the curve trend, it can be seen in the initial $t = 1200$ s and subsequent $t = 7200$ s, the hoop stress is larger, mainly because the internal pressure is larger. Of course, the thermal stress formed by temperature will also have a partial influence. It should be noted that the distance from the outer surface of the RPV (d = 150 mm) will produce reverse stress on the vessel wall, which is formed by the interaction between internal stresses. Similarly, Figure 9a,b form a set of stress comparison diagrams. Figure 9b is the axial stress above the pipe mouth. The trend is basically similar to that in Figure 9a, and the stress gradually decreases. The difference is that the stress near the pipe mouth changes obviously, the gradient value is relatively large, and the other positions decrease slowly, which is mainly due to the stress concentration at the pipe mouth. This also shows that the numerical results are in good agreement with the actual situation.

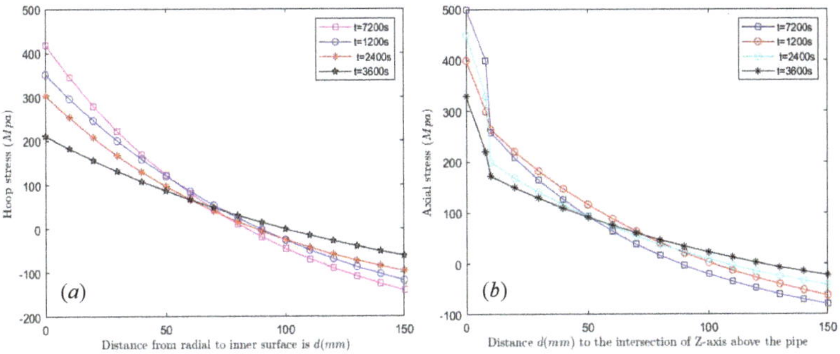

Figure 9. Variation trend of radial stress and circumferential stress of RPV with calculation distance. (**a**) Hoop stress on the RPV wall. (**b**) Axial stress above the nozzle.

7. Conclusions

The purpose of this paper is to study the stress variation of nuclear pressure vessels. The mechanical models of pressure vessels established in this paper are from one-dimensional to three-dimensional. The theory of each model and three numerical examples are given. For a one-dimensional model, the equilibrium equation is mainly established according to the internal pressure, axial stress, and circumferential stress of RPV. The model belongs to the rough estimation of stress, and the error is too large. The conclusion of the theoretical model is that the circumferential stress is twice the axial stress. In this paper, the continuous damage dynamic model with cross-section finite element method (CMMD-TCFEM) is proposed. The advantage of this model is that it can dynamically describe the change of physical parameters of RPV under the action of the loss factor. The model has the characteristics of fast calculation, layered, and localized display. The model can obtain the stress distribution cloud map of axial and radial 2D sections. The numerical conclusion is that the Poisson's ratio increases with the increase of temperature ($\hat{u}$,$\mathcal{E}_t$), and the Young's modulus decreases with the increase of temperature ($\hat{u}$, $\hat{d}$).

In the second numerical example, axisymmetric theory is mainly given. After giving the geometric parameters and material parameters, the model can output the stress and strain nephogram of RPV under different internal pressures. The other contribution is to compare the initial state of RPV and the deformation of RPV after internal pressure. Compared with the CMMD-TCFEM method, the 3D axisymmetric method can obtain the overall stress and strain cloud map, which is more complete and intuitive. The numerical results show that the stress change at both ends of RPV is significantly greater than that of the middle vessel wall, and the reinforcement method should be adopted at both ends of the RPV. In practical application, RPV is accompanied by multiple exhaust pipes to release steam and add coolant, and stress modeling and solution near the exhaust pipe are also very important. Therefore, in example 3, a three-dimensional finite element model of thermal–mechanical coupling is established, and the adaptive mesh is used to discrete the solution area. Finally, the stress, strain, displacement, and other information of the RPV pipe mouth are obtained. We also compare the changes of radial stress and circumferential stress near the RPV pipe mouth. The numerical results show that the distance d from the inner surface is from inside to outside, and the radial stress and circumferential stress near the RPV pipe mouth gradually decrease.

In short, the new numerical method proposed in this paper corresponds to a number of different models, from one-dimensional to three-dimensional, from a single physical field to a multi-physical field. The continuous damage dynamic model is successfully combined with the finite element method, which can better characterize the elastic modulus and Poisson ratio with the change of the damage factor. The axisymmetric model and the coupling model of the nozzle can provide theoretical and simulation experience for RPV design and stress simulation. Our method reflects the multidisciplinary intersection and can solve the same problem from different angles. Our future work will focus on the intelligent application of nuclear energy. It includes optimizing fuel metering and periodically automatically detecting the performance of RPV materials. Machine learning is used to predict the internal temperature of RPV in real time, and multi-scale theory is used to analyze the defects and crack propagation of RPV materials. The application of these problems will contribute to the effective improvement of nuclear technology and provide a good theoretical basis for the application and design of a new generation of nuclear energy, so that nuclear energy can better benefit mankind and create more energy value for society.

Author Contributions: Conceptualization, W.C., S.D. and B.Z.; methodology and experiments, W.C.; writing—original draft preparation, W.C.; writing—review and editing, W.C. and S.D.; visualization, W.C.; supervision, B.Z. and S.D.; funding acquisition, S.D. All authors have read and agreed to the published version of the manuscript.

Funding: This research was funded by the Science and Technology Major Project of Hubei Province under Grant 2021AAA010 and by the National Natural Science Foundation of China (Grant No. 12071363).

Institutional Review Board Statement: Not applicable.

Informed Consent Statement: Informed consent was obtained from all subjects involved in the study.

Data Availability Statement: Data for this article can be accessed publicly.

Acknowledgments: This research was funded by the Science and Technology Major Project of Hubei Province under Grant 2021AAA010, and by the National Natural Science Foundation of China (Grant No. 12071363). At last, we extend our thanks to the anonymous reviewers for their professional advice.

Conflicts of Interest: The authors declare that they have no known competing financial interest or personal relationships that could have appeared to influence the work reported in this paper.

References

1. Wang, Z. Hybridized Heuristic Heterogeneous Mathematical modeling for sustainable International comparison of the economic efficiency in nuclear energy. *Sustain. Energy Technol. Assess.* **2022**, *50*, 101578. [CrossRef]
2. Niu, X.; Zhu, S.; He, J.; Ai, Y.; Shi, K.; Zhang, L. Fatigue reliability design and assessment of reactor pressure vessel structures: Concepts and validation. *Int. J. Fatigue* **2021**, *153*, 106524. [CrossRef]
3. Solazzi, L.; Vaccari, M. Reliability design of a pressure vessel made of composite materials. *Compos. Struct.* **2022**, *279*, 114726. [CrossRef]
4. Onizawa, K.; Nishikawa, H.; Itoh, H. Development of probabilistic fracture mechanics analysis codes for reactor pressure vessels and piping considering welding residual stress. *Int. J. Press. Vessel. Pip.* **2010**, *87*, 2–10. [CrossRef]
5. Kanto, Y.; Onizawa, K.; Machida, H.; Isobe, Y.; Yoshimura, S. Recent Japanese research activities on probabilistic fracture mechanics for pressure vessel and piping of nuclear power plant. *Int. J. Press. Vessel. Pip.* **2010**, *87*, 11–16. [CrossRef]
6. Chou, H.; Chang, C. Probabilistic fracture analysis for boiling water reactor vessels considering seismic loads during decommissioning transition period. *Ann. Nucl. Energy* **2022**, *167*, 108827. [CrossRef]
7. Huang, C.; Chou, H.; Chen, B.; Liu, R.; Lin, H. Probabilistic fracture analysis for boiling water reactor pressure vessels subjected to low temperature over-pressure event. *Ann. Nucl. Energy* **2012**, *43*, 61–67. [CrossRef]
8. Li, C.; Shu, G.; Liu, W.; Duan, Y. The unified model for irradiation embrittlement prediction of reactor pressure vessel. *Ann. Nucl. Energy* **2020**, *139*, 107246. [CrossRef]
9. Bhattacharyya, M.; Fau, A.; Desmorat, R.; Alameddin, S.; Néron, D.; Ladevèze, P.; Nackenhorst, U. A kinetic two-scale damage model for high-cycle fatigue simulation using multi-temporal Latin framework. *Eur. J. Mech. Solids* **2019**, *77*, 103808. [CrossRef]

10. Naumenko, K.; Gariboldi, E. Experimental analysis and constitutive modeling of anisotropic creep damage in a wrought age-hardenable Alalloy. *Eng. Fract. Mech.* **2022**, *259*, 108119. [CrossRef]
11. Yvonnet, J.; He, Q.; Li, P. A data-driven harmonic approach to constructing anisotropic damage models with a minimum number of internal variables. *J. Mech. Phys. Solids* **2022**, *162*, 104828. [CrossRef]
12. Murtaza, U.T.; Hyder, M.J. Optimization of the size and shape of the set-in nozzle for a PWR reactor pressure vessel. *Nucl. Eng. Des.* **2015**, *284*, 219–227. [CrossRef]
13. Lu, B.T.; Song, F.; Gao, M.; Elboujdaini, M. Crack growth prediction for underground high pressure gas lines exposed to concentrated carbonate–bicarbonate solution with high pH. *Eng. Fract. Mech.* **2011**, *78*, 1452–1465. [CrossRef]
14. Singh, R.; Singh, V.; Arora, A.; Mahajan, D.K. In-situ investigations of hydrogen influenced crack initiation and propagation under tensile and low cycle fatigue loadings in RPV steel. *J. Nucl. Mater.* **2020**, *529*, 151912. [CrossRef]
15. Vukojević, N.; Gubeljak, N.; Terzic, M.; Hadžikadunić, F. Analysis of the impact of position in fatigue cracks on the fracture toughness of thick-walled pressure vessel material. *Procedia Struct. Integr.* **2016**, *2*, 2982–2988. [CrossRef]
16. Czapski, P. Influence of laminate code and curing process on the stability of square cross-section, composite columns—Experimental and FEM studies. *Compos. Struct.* **2020**, *250*, 112564. [CrossRef]
17. Kundrák, J.; Karpuschewski, B.; Pálmai, Z.; Felhő, C.; Makkai, T.; Borysenko, D. The energetic characteristics of milling with changing cross-section in the definition of specific cutting force by FEM method. *CIRP J. Manuf. Sci. Technol.* **2021**, *32*, 61–69. [CrossRef]
18. Dodig, H. A boundary integral method for numerical computation of radar cross section of 3D targets using hybrid BEM/FEM with edge elements. *J. Comput. Phys.* **2017**, *348*, 790–802. [CrossRef]
19. Oh, C.; Lee, S.; Jhung, M.J. Analytical method to estimate cross-section stress profiles for reactor vessel nozzle corners under internal pressure. *Nucl. Eng. Technol.* **2022**, *54*, 1, 401–413. [CrossRef]
20. Wu, X.; Wang, Z.; Fan, H.; Liu, P. Investigation on theoretical solution of geometric deformation of pressure vessel and pipe subjected to thermo-mechanical loadings. *Int. J. Press. Vessel. Pip.* **2021**, *194*, 104564. [CrossRef]
21. Moskovka, A.; Valdman, J. Fast MATLAB evaluation of nonlinear energies using FEM in 2D and 3D: Nodal elements. *Appl. Math. Comput.* **2022**, *424*, 127048. [CrossRef]
22. Hwang, Ji.; Kim, Yu.; Kim, Ji. Energy-based damage model incorporating failure cycle and load ratio effects for very low cycle fatigue crack growth simulation. *Int. J. Mech. Sci.* **2022**, *221*, 107223. [CrossRef]
23. González-Albuixech, V.F.; Qian, G.; Sharabi, M.; Niffenegger, M.; Niceno, B.; Lafferty, N. Coupled RELAP5, 3D CFD and FEM analysis of postulated cracks in RPVs subjected to PTS loading. *Nucl. Eng. Des.* **2016**, *297*, 111–122. [CrossRef]
24. González-Albuixech, V.F.; Qian, G.; Sharabi, M.; Niffenegger, M.; Niceno, B.; Lafferty, N. Comparison of PTS analyses of RPVs based on 3D-CFD and RELAP5. *Nucl. Eng. Des.* **2015** *291*, 168–178. [CrossRef]
25. Chouhan, R.; Kansal, A.K.; Maheshwari, N.K.; Sharma, A. Computational studies on pressurized thermal shock in reactor pressure vessel. *Ann. Nucl. Energy* **2021**, *152*, 107987. [CrossRef]
26. Chen, M.; Yu, W.; Qian, G.; Shi, J.; Cao, Y.; Yu, Y. Crack initiation, arrest and tearing assessments of a RPV subjected to PTS events. *Ann. Nucl. Energy* **2018**,*116*, 143–151. [CrossRef]
27. Huang, P.; Chou, H.; Ferng, Y.; Kang, C. Large thermal gradients on structural integrity of a reactor pressure vessel subjected to pressurized thermal shocks. *Int. J. Press. Vessel. Pip.* **2020**, *179*, 103942. [CrossRef]
28. Sun, X.; Lu, W.; Chai, G.; Bao, Y. Effect of cladding thickness on brittle fracture prevention of the base wall of reactor pressure vessel. *Thin-Walled Struct.* **2021**, *158*, 107163. [CrossRef]
29. Christian, R.; Lee, Y.; Kang, H.G. Emergency core cooling system performance criteria for Multi-Layered Silicon Carbide nuclear fuel cladding. *Nucl. Eng. Des.* **2019**, *353*, 110280. [CrossRef]
30. Wang, J.; Zhang, L.; Qu, J.; Tong, J.; Wu, G. Rapid accident source term estimation (RASTE) for nuclear emergency response in high temperature gas cooled reactor. *Ann. Nucl. Energy* **2020**, *147*, 107654. [CrossRef]
31. Oliver, S.; Simpson, C.; Collins, D.M.; Reinhard, C.; Pavier, M.; Mostafavi, M. In-situ measurements of stress during thermal shock in clad pressure vessel steel using synchrotron X-ray diffraction. *Int. J. Mech. Sci.* **2021**, *192*, 106136. [CrossRef]
32. Zhao, P.; Ji, K.; Zhang, J.; Chen, Y.; Dong, Z.; Zheng, J.; Fu, J. In-situ ultrasonic measurement of molten polymers during injection molding. *J. Mater. Process. Technol.* **2021**, *293*, 117081. [CrossRef]
33. Tasavori, M.; Maleki, A.T.; Ahmadi, I. Composite coating effect on stress intensity factors of aluminum pressure vessels with inner circumferential crack by X-FEM. *Int. J. Press. Vessel. Pip.* **2021**, *194*, 104445. [CrossRef]
34. Zhang, K.; Sanchez-Espinoza, V.H. The Dynamic-Implicit-Additional-Source (DIAS) method for multi-scale coupling of thermal-hydraulic codes to enhance the prediction of mass and heat transfer in the nuclear reactor pressure VESSEL. *Int. J. Heat Mass Transf.* **2020**, *147*, 118987. [CrossRef]
35. Huo, Y.; Yu, H.; Wang, M.; Tian, W.; Qiu, S.; Su, G.H. Development and application of TaSNAM 2.0 for advanced pressurized water reactor. *Ann. Nucl. Energy* **2022**, *166*, 108801. [CrossRef]
36. Mackerle, J. Finite elements in the analysis of pressure vessels and piping—A bibliography (1976–1996). *Int. J. Press. Vessel. Pip.* **1996**, *69*, 279–339. [CrossRef]
37. Mohanavel, V.; Prasath, S.; Arunkumar, M.; Pradeep, G.M.; Babu, S.S. Modeling and stress analysis of aluminium alloy based composite pressure vessel through ANSYS software. *Mater. Today Proc.* **2021**, *37*, 1911–1916. [CrossRef]

38. You, Q.; Mo, N.; Liu, X.; Luo, H.; Shi, Z. Experiments on helium breakdown at high pressure and temperature in uniform field and its simulation using COMSOL Multiphysics and FD-FCT. *Ann. Nucl. Energy* **2020**, *141*, 107351. [CrossRef]
39. Yang, Z.; Liu, H. A continuum fatigue damage model for the cyclic thermal shocked ceramic-matrix composites. *Int. J. Fatigue* **2020**, *134*, 105507. [CrossRef]
40. Damhof, F.; Brekelmans, W.A.M.; Geers, M.G.D. Non-local modeling of thermal shock damage in refractory materials. *Eng. Fract. Mech.* **2008**, *75*, 4706–4720. [CrossRef]
41. Zhu, C.; Li, Y.; Tan, H.; Shi, J.; Nie, Y.; Qiu, Q. Multi-field coupled effect of thermal disturbance on quench and recovery characteristic along the hybrid energy pipe. *Energy* **2022**, *246*, 123362. [CrossRef]
42. Lemaitre, J.; Chaboche, J.L.; Maji, A.K. Mechanics of Solid Materials. *J. Eng. Mech.* **1992**, *119*, 642–643. [CrossRef]
43. Almasi, A.; Baghani, M.; Moallemi, A. Thermomechanical analysis of hyperelastic thick-walled cylindrical pressure vessels, analytical solutions and FEM. *Int. J. Mech. Sci.* **2017**, *130*, 426–436. [CrossRef]
44. Yang, Z.; Lui, H. A continuum damage mechanics model for 2-D woven oxide/oxide ceramic matrix composites under cyclic thermal shocks. *Ceram. Int.* **2020**, *46*, 6029–6037 [CrossRef]
45. Yang, Y.; Schiavone, P.; Li, Xi. Effect of surface elasticity on transient elastic field around a mode-III crack-tip under impact loads. *Eng. Fract. Mech.* **2021**, *258*, 108062. [CrossRef]
46. Chen, W.; Dai, S.; Zheng, B. ARIMA-FEM Method with Prediction Function to Solve the Stress-Strain of Perforated Elastic Metal Plates. *Metals* **2022**, *12*, 179. [CrossRef]
47. Demirbas, M.D. Thermal stress analysis of functionally graded plates with temperature-dependent material properties using theory of elasticity. *Engineering* **2017**, *131*, 100–124. [CrossRef]
48. Li, C.; Guo, H.; Tian, X.; He, T. Time-domain finite element method to generalized diffusion-elasticity problems with the concentration-dependent elastic constants and the diffusivity. *Appl. Math. Model.* **2020**, *87*, 55–76. [CrossRef]
49. Si, H.M.; Cho, C.; Kwahk, S.Y. A hybrid method for casting process simulation by combining FDM and FEM with an efficient data conversion algorithm. *J. Mater. Process. Technol.* **2003**, *133*, 311–321. [CrossRef]
50. Zhang, H.; Tong, L.; Addo, M.A.; Liang, J.; Wang, L. Research on contact algorithm of unbonded flexible riser under axisymmetric load. *Int. J. Press. Vessel. Pip.* **2020**, *188*, 104248. [CrossRef]
51. Que, Z.; Seifert, H.P.; Spätig, P.; Zhang, A.; Holzer, J.; Rao, G.S.; Ritter, S. Effect of dynamic strain ageing on environmental degradation of fracture resistance of low-alloy RPV steels in high-temperature water environments. *Corros. Sci.* **2019**, *152*, 172–189. [CrossRef]
52. Li, Y.; Jin, T.; Wang, Z.; Wang, D. Engineering critical assessment of RPV with nozzle corner cracks under pressurized thermal shocks. *Nucl. Eng. Technol.* **2020**, *52*, *11*, 2638–2651. [CrossRef]
53. Sun, X.; Chai, G.; Bao, Y. Ultimate bearing capacity analysis of a reactor pressure vessel subjected to pressurized thermal shock with XFEM. *Eng. Fail. Anal.* **2017**, *80*, 102–111. [CrossRef]
54. Bao, W.; Garcke, H.; Nürnberg, R.; Zhao, Q. Volume-preserving parametric finite element methods for axisymmetric geometric evolution equations. *J. Comput. Phys.* **2022**, *460*, 111180. [CrossRef]
55. Li, Q.; Hou, P.; Shang, S. Accurate 3D thermal stress analysis of thermal barrier coatings. *Int. J. Mech. Sci.* **2022**, *217*, 107024. [CrossRef]
56. Upadhyay, K.; Subhash, G.; Spearot, D. Hyperelastic constitutive modeling of hydrogels based on primary deformation modes and validation under 3D stress states. *Int. J. Eng. Sci.* **2020**, *154*, 103314. [CrossRef]
57. Zhou, F.; You, Y.; Li, G.; Xie, G.; Li, G. The precise integration method for semi-discretized equation in the dual reciprocity method to solve three-dimensional transient heat conduction problems. *Eng. Anal. Bound. Elem.* **2018**, *95*, 160–166. [CrossRef]
58. Wu, Q.; Peng, M.J.; Fu, Y.D.; Cheng, Y.M. The dimension splitting interpolating element-free Galerkin method for solving three-dimensional transient heat conduction problems. *Eng. Anal. Bound. Elem.* **2021**, *128*, 326–341. [CrossRef]
59. Zhang, H.; Yang, Y.; Huang, W. Influence of the thermal insulation layer on radial stress and collapse resistance of subsea wet insulation pipe. *Ocean Eng.* **2021**, *235*, 109374. [CrossRef]
60. Chen, W.; Dai, S.; Zheng, B.; Lin, H. An Efficient Evaluation Method for Automobile Shells Design Based on Semi-supervised Machine Learning Strategy. *J. Phys. Conf. Ser. ICCBD2021* **2022**, *2171*, 012026. [CrossRef]
61. Duru, K.L; Rannabauer, L.; Gabriel, A.; Ling, O.K.A.; Igel, H.; Bader, M. A stable discontinuous Galerkin method for linear elastodynamics in 3D geometrically complex elastic solids using physics based numerical fluxes. *Comput. Methods Appl. Mech. Eng.* **2022**, *389*, 114386. [CrossRef]
62. Yalameha, S.; Nourbakhsh, Z.; Vashaee, D. ElATools: A tool for analyzing anisotropic elastic properties of the 2D and 3D materials. *Comput. Phys. Commun.* **2022**, *271*, 108195. [CrossRef]
63. Xu, F.; Liu, Q.; Shibahara, M. Transient and steady-state heat transfer for forced convection of helium gas in minichannels with various inner diameters. *Int. J. Heat Mass Transf.* **2022**, *191*, 122813. [CrossRef]
64. Solin, P.; Dubcova,L.; Kruis, J. Adaptive hp-FEM with dynamical meshes for transient heat and moisture transfer problems. *J. Comput. Appl. Math.* **2010**, *12*, 3103–3112. [CrossRef]
65. Erath, C.; Gantner, G.; Praetorius, D. Optimal convergence behavior of adaptive FEM driven by simple-type error estimators. *Comput. Math. Appl.* **2020**, *79*, 623–642. [CrossRef]

66. Bériot, H.; Gabard, G. Anisotropic adaptivity of the p-FEM for time-harmonic acoustic wave propagation. *J. Comput. Phys.* **2019**, *378*, 234–256. [CrossRef]
67. Giani, S.; Solin, P. Solving elliptic eigenproblems with adaptive multimesh hp-FEM. *J. Comput. Appl. Math.* **2021**, *394*, 113528. [CrossRef]

fractal and fractional

MDPI

Article

Epidemic Dynamics of a Fractional-Order SIR Weighted Network Model and Its Targeted Immunity Control

Na Liu *, Jie Fang, Junwei Sun and Sanyi Li

School of Electric and Information Engineering, Zhengzhou University of Light Industry, Zhengzhou 450002, China; fangjie@zzuli.edu.cn (J.F.); sunjunwei@zzuli.edu.cn (J.S.); lisanyi@zzuli.edu.cn (S.L.)
* Correspondence: 2014034@zzuli.edu.cn

Abstract: With outbreaks of epidemics, an enormous loss of life and property has been caused. Based on the influence of disease transmission and information propagation on the transmission characteristics of infectious diseases, in this paper, a fractional-order SIR epidemic model is put forward on a two-layer weighted network. The local stability of the disease-free equilibrium is investigated. Moreover, a conclusion is obtained that there is no endemic equilibrium. Since the elderly and the children have fewer social tiers, a targeted immunity control that is based on age structure is proposed. Finally, an example is presented to demonstrate the effectiveness of the theoretical results. These studies contribute to a more comprehensive understanding of the epidemic transmission mechanism and play a positive guiding role in the prevention and control of some epidemics.

Keywords: fractional-order; weighted networks; SIR network models; targeted immunity; epidemic dynamics

Citation: Liu, N.; Fang, J.; Sun, J.; Li, S. Epidemic Dynamics of a Fractional-Order SIR Weighted Network Model and Its Targeted Immunity Control. *Fractal Fract.* **2022**, *6*, 232. https://doi.org/10.3390/fractalfract6050232

Academic Editors: António M. Lopes, Alireza Alfi, Liping Chen and Sergio Adriani David

Received: 27 March 2022
Accepted: 19 April 2022
Published: 22 April 2022

1. Introduction

Infectious diseases, especially the outbreak and pandemic of emerging infectious diseases, have become a major public health problem around the world. Neither modern science nor technology can predict when and where a new infection will occur. However, once this occurs, it is often not possible to respond in a timely and effective manner due to a lack of understanding of the epidemic. For example, COVID-19, at the end of 2019, with its high infection rate and rapid onset of the cycle, has posed a huge threat to human lives and caused immeasurable losses to the economy of China and even the entire world. Therefore, the study of pathogenesis, the law of transmission, as well as strategies for the prevention and treatment of infectious diseases are of great practical importance and perspective.

The network model is one of the most widely studied models in recent years. Individuals in a crowd are treated as nodes in the network, and the relationship between individuals is described by edges between the nodes. The most influential research was carried out by Pastor-Satorras and Vespignani in [1], where SIS (susceptible-infected-susceptible) and SIR (susceptible-infected-recovered) models were studied using mean field theory. Moreover, in order to better analyze the characteristics of disease transmission in the population, not only the evolution of the population network was taken into account but also the transmission of information about the disease. Recently, some researchers [2–5] have extended the dynamics of transmission of infectious disease to a multi-layer network, which led to a deeper study of mathematical epidemiology. Kan et al. [6] introduced a self-consciousness variable and found that the infection threshold and the infected density are influenced by the consciousness network, the topology of the disease network, and the effective transmission rate. In addition, some scientists proposed a transmission model of infectious diseases in a multi-layer coupling network from a new perspective in [7–9]. The transmission probability among the set of possible node states and the influence of network topology on the transmission threshold were analyzed in a multi-layer network.

In [10], the awareness of infection risk was incorporated into the Volz–Miller SIR epidemic model, to study the effect of awareness on disease dynamics.

As the above research progressed, it became clear that the strength of the relationship between people can seriously affect the transmission of the epidemic. Edge weights indicate the familiarity or intimacy of interactive individuals. The larger the weight of the edge between two nodes is, the easier the susceptible can be infected and the quicker the unknown individual can acquire the disease message. In [11–14], some methods for estimating disease transmission along the edges in weighted networks were presented. A modified epidemic SIS model with a birth–death process and nonlinear infectivity in an adaptive and weighted contact network was proposed in [15]. The model indicated that the intimacy or familiarity between two related individuals would decrease as the disease progresses. To estimate the epidemic threshold and epidemic size on networks with general degree and weight distributions, a new edge-weight-based compartmental approach was developed in [16]. It was found in [17] that the weight exponent can contribute to the transmission of the epidemic by increasing the basic reproduction number, and the effect of the internal rate of infectiousness on the prevalence of the epidemic was greater than the effect of the rate of cross-infection for various network structures.

It can be found that the weight of the network has a great influence on the spread of disease. However, these studies did not put forward a control strategy to control the disease from the perspective of network weights. Therefore, in order for the transmission process to represent a realistic system, in this paper, we build a model of the epidemic on a weighted two-layer network and evaluate the impact of network weights on disease transmission, and try to propose an effective control method based on the network weights.

Since the fractional-order epidemic model is an extension of the integer-order epidemic model and it is more advantageous to describe processes that have memory and heritability, many scientists [18–20] have used fractional order differential equations to analyze the dynamics of transmission of infectious diseases. Based on the basic reproduction number and Lyapunov's theory of stability, Zafar et al. [21] analyzed the stability of the equilibrium point of a fractional-order HIV/AIDS model and the control of its spread. Rostamy et al. [22] discussed the existence of multiple equilibrium points in the SIR model and showed that choosing appropriate fractional order parameters can extend the stable region of the equilibrium points. In [23], a mathematical model consisting of a system of nonlinear fractional order differential equations was presented, in which bats were considered as the origin of the virus that spread the disease into the human population. A fractional-order SIR model, which employs the Caputo fractional derivative and incorporates infectious and noninfectious abandonment dynamics, was discussed in [24]. Furthermore, fractional-order SIR systems in the context of COVID-19 were built [25,26], especially, a novel modified predictor-corrector method was proposed to capture the nature of the obtained solution for a suitable nonlinear fractional dynamical system with different arbitrary orders [27]. However, few studies [28,29] have analyzed the specific influence of fractional order on transmission dynamics. Therefore, quantifying the effect of fractional order on the transmission threshold for a specific model is a significant supplement to the dynamics of infectious diseases.

In addition, for fractional-order infectious disease models, some researchers have proposed vaccination control strategies to prevent the spread of the disease. If the immunity control objects are different, the control effect will be different. Age-targeted immunity [30,31], internet-information-driven immunity [32–34], and dynamic immunity of human behavior [35] are common control methods. A few studies [36–38] have shown that people with low immunity are more likely to be infected and are less treatable. From the perspective of a complex network, people with low immunity are the nodes with low weights in the network. Therefore, the implementation of vaccination control for the nodes whose weight is less than a certain threshold can play a great role in controlling the spread of infectious diseases. Based on the fractional-order epidemic model on a two-layer weighted network, a targeted immunity control strategy is proposed for nodes whose weight is less than a certain value, which can not only suppress the spread of the epidemics but also save the cost of control.

The paper is organized as follows. In Section 2, we propose a fractional-order SIR model for two-layer weighted networks. In Section 3, the stability of the disease-free equilibrium and endemic equilibrium on weighted networks are analyzed separately. In Section 4, a linear vaccine control based on age structure is presented to inoculate the nodes whose weights are less than a certain value. Numerical confirmation of the theoretical predictions is provided in Section 5. Some conclusions are made in Section 6.

2. Model Description

The nodes of the disease network can be divided into three categories: susceptible nodes S, infected nodes I, and recovery nodes R. The law of transmission is shown in Figure 1. Social network nodes can also be divided into three categories: A represents the nodes that know the disease message and spread it out, C represents the nodes that know the disease message but do not spread it; U represents the nodes that do not know the disease message. The law of transmission between them is shown in Figure 2.

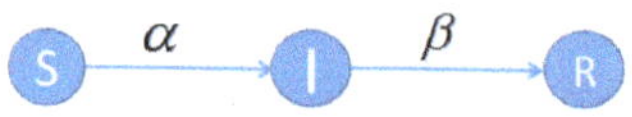

Figure 1. State transmission diagram between nodes of a disease network.

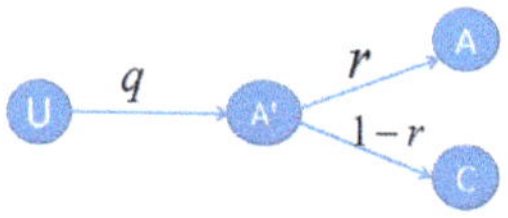

Figure 2. State transmission diagram between nodes of a social network.

In a social network for a node i with the degree k, its connection weight with node j is ω_{ij}. If node i is connected with node j, then $\omega_{ij} \neq 0$; on the contrary, then $\omega_{ij} = 0$. Here, we will only focus on undirected networks, namely $\omega_{ij} = \omega_{ji}$. According to previous research, the weight of nodes has a strong influence on disease transmission.

By combining the states of nodes in a social-disease network, all nodes can be divided into the following states: US, UR, AS, AI, AR, CS, CI, and CR. The law of transmission between states is shown in Figure 3.

From Figure 3, we can find that for a susceptible node i, the probability of its infection by the neighboring infected nodes is equal to $\lambda_I(\omega_{ij}) = 1 - (1-\alpha)^{\omega_{ij}}$, based on the weight (the weight is determined by the social network). If there are p infected nodes with degree k, then the overall probability of infection is $1 - \prod_{j=1}^{p}(1-\lambda_I(\omega_{ij}))$. Likewise, for a node i, which does not know the disease message, the probability that it will receive a disease message from a neighboring node is $\lambda_A(\omega_{ij}) = 1 - (1-q\gamma)^{\omega_{ij}}$. If the degree of the node is k, where there are l nodes that know and transmit a message about the disease to other people, then the total probability of receiving information is $1 - \prod_{j=1}^{l}(1-\lambda_A(\omega_{ij}))$. Thus, the law of transmission between the eight states is shown in Figure 4.

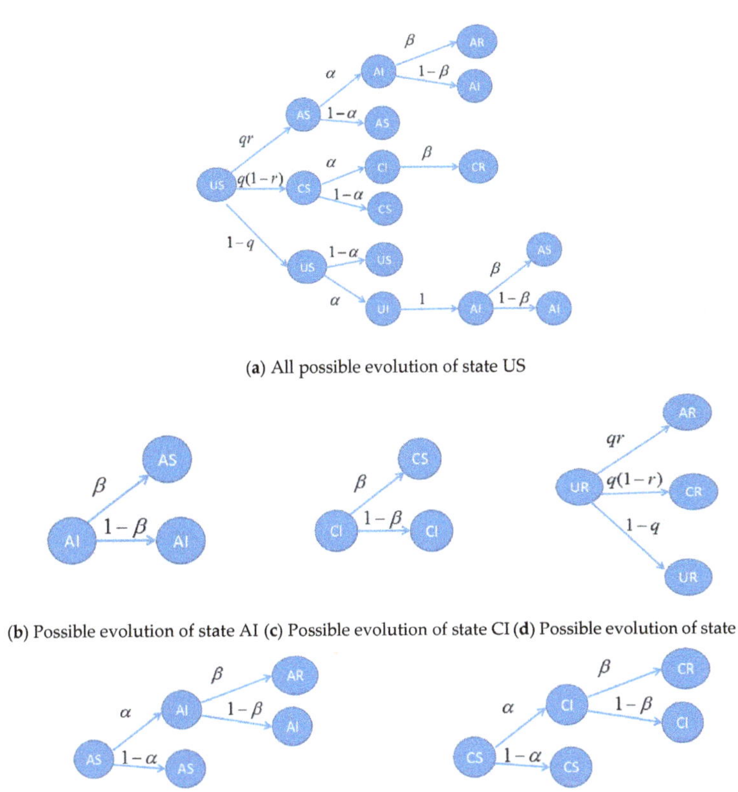

(**a**) All possible evolution of state US

(**b**) Possible evolution of state AI (**c**) Possible evolution of state CI (**d**) Possible evolution of state UR

(**e**) Possible evolution of state AS (**f**) Possible evolution of state CS

Figure 3. Propagation possibilities between states in a two-layer network.

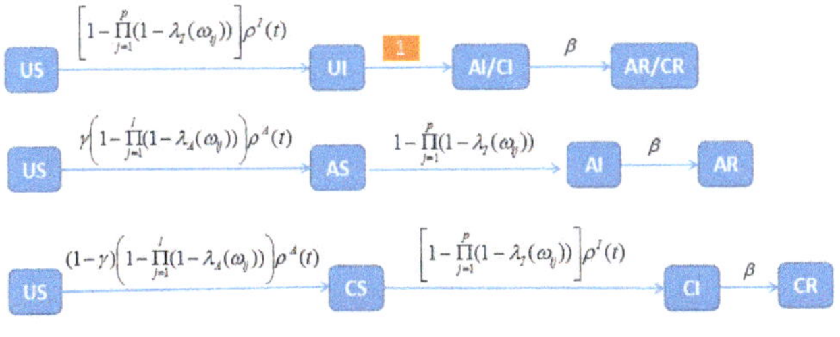

Figure 4. The law of transmission between eight states under a weighted network.

According to the relationship between disease transmission and information propagation, a fractional-order SIR network model in a two-layer network is established as follows:

$$D^m \rho^{US} = -\rho^I \left[1 - \prod_{j=1}^{p} (1 - \lambda_I)\right] \rho^{US} - \rho^A \left[1 - \prod_{j=1}^{l} (1 - \lambda_A)\right] \rho^{US}, \quad (1a)$$

$$D^m \rho^{UR} = -\rho^A \left[1 - \prod_{j=1}^{l} (1 - \lambda_A)\right] \rho^{UR}, \quad (1b)$$

$$D^m \rho^{AS} = \rho^A \left[1 - \prod_{j=1}^{l} (1 - \lambda_A)\right] \rho^{US} \gamma - \rho^I \left[1 - \prod_{j=1}^{p} (1 - \lambda_I)\right] \rho^{AS}, \quad (1c)$$

$$D^m\rho^{AI} = \rho^I\left[1 - \prod_{j=1}^{p}(1-\lambda_I)\right]\rho^{AS} - \rho^{AI}\beta, \tag{1d}$$

$$D^m\rho^{AR} = \rho^A\left[1 - \prod_{j=1}^{l}(1-\lambda_A)\right]\rho^{UR}\gamma + \rho^{AI}\beta, \tag{1e}$$

$$D^m\rho^{CS} = \rho^A\left[1 - \prod_{j=1}^{l}(1-\lambda_A)\right]\rho^{US}(1-\gamma) - \rho^I\left[1 - \prod_{j=1}^{p}(1-\lambda_I)\right]\rho^{CS}, \tag{1f}$$

$$D^m\rho^{CI} = \rho^I\left[1 - \prod_{j=1}^{p}(1-\lambda_I)\right]\rho^{CS} - \rho^{CI}\beta, \tag{1g}$$

$$D^m\rho^{CR} = \rho^A\left[1 - \prod_{j=1}^{l}(1-\lambda_A)\right]\rho^{UR}(1-\gamma) + \rho^{CI}\beta. \tag{1h}$$

where $D^m(\bullet)$ is the Caputo differential with $0 < m < 1$, $\rho(t)$ is the density of the corresponding state at the time t. For example, $\rho^I(t)$ represents an infectious density at time t. The factor $\lambda_I = 1-(1-\alpha)^{w_{ij}}$, $j = 1, \cdots, p$ represents the probability of infection of a node i in the disease network, p is the number of infected nodes in the neighboring nodes of a node i in the disease network. The factor $\lambda_A = 1-(1-q\gamma)^{w_{ij}}$, $j = 1, \cdots, l$ represents the probability of node i in the social network receiving a message, l is the number of nodes that know and distribute messages to the neighboring nodes of a node i in a social network.

Remark 1. *If $m = 1$, then system (1) changes to an integer order system, which is the further generalization of the models proposed in [2,7] since it contains more possibilities for node states. Compared with the fractional-order models in [21–24], it not only considers the transmission of information between people but also considers the impact of the closeness of the connection between people on the transmission of information, e.g., the network weight. Therefore, the proposed model in this paper is more realistic and has practical significance.*

3. Stability Analysis

Let $\overline{\lambda}_A = 1 - \prod_{j=1}^{l}(1-\lambda_A)$ and $\overline{\lambda}_I = 1 - \prod_{j=1}^{p}(1-\lambda_I)$, then system (1) can be rewritten as follows:

$$\begin{aligned}
D^m\rho^{US} &= -\rho^I\overline{\lambda}_I\rho^{US} - \rho^A\overline{\lambda}_A\rho^{US},\\
D^m\rho^{UR} &= -\rho^A\overline{\lambda}_A\rho^{UR},\\
D^m\rho^{AS} &= \rho^A\overline{\lambda}_A\rho^{US}\gamma - \rho^I\overline{\lambda}_I\rho^{AS},\\
D^m\rho^{AI} &= \rho^I\overline{\lambda}_I\rho^{AS} - \rho^{AI}\beta,\\
D^m\rho^{AR} &= \rho^A\overline{\lambda}_A\rho^{UR}\gamma + \rho^{AI}\beta,\\
D^m\rho^{CS} &= \rho^A\overline{\lambda}_A\rho^{US}(1-\gamma) - \rho^I\overline{\lambda}_I\rho^{CS},\\
D^m\rho^{CI} &= \rho^I\overline{\lambda}_I\rho^{CS} - \rho^{CI}\beta,\\
D^m\rho^{CR} &= \rho^A\overline{\lambda}_A\rho^{UR}(1-\gamma) + \rho^{CI}\beta.
\end{aligned} \tag{2}$$

For system (2), the Jacobian matrix J at equilibrium has the form

$$J = \begin{bmatrix}
-\overline{\lambda}_I\rho^I - \overline{\lambda}_A\rho^A & 0 & -\overline{\lambda}_A\rho^{US} & -\overline{\lambda}_I\rho^{US} - \overline{\lambda}_A\rho^{US} & -\overline{\lambda}_A\rho^{US} & 0 & -\overline{\lambda}_I\rho^{US} & 0\\
0 & -\overline{\lambda}_A\rho^A & -\overline{\lambda}_A\rho^{UR} & -\overline{\lambda}_A\rho^{UR} & -\overline{\lambda}_A\rho^{UR} & 0 & 0 & 0\\
\overline{\lambda}_A\rho^A\gamma & 0 & -\overline{\lambda}_I\rho^I + \overline{\lambda}_A\rho^{US}\gamma & -\overline{\lambda}_I\rho^{AS} + \overline{\lambda}_A\rho^{US}\gamma & \overline{\lambda}_A\rho^{US}\gamma & 0 & -\overline{\lambda}_I\rho^{AS} & 0\\
0 & 0 & \overline{\lambda}_I\rho^I & \overline{\lambda}_I\rho^{AS} - \beta & 0 & 0 & \overline{\lambda}_I\rho^{AS} & 0\\
0 & \overline{\lambda}_A\rho^A\gamma & \overline{\lambda}_A\rho^{UR}\gamma & \overline{\lambda}_A\rho^{UR}\gamma + \beta & \overline{\lambda}_A\rho^{UR}\gamma & 0 & 0 & 0\\
0 & \overline{\lambda}_A\rho^A(1-\gamma) & \overline{\lambda}_A\rho^{US}(1-\gamma) & \overline{\lambda}_A\rho^{US}(1-\gamma) - \overline{\lambda}_I\rho^{CS} & \overline{\lambda}_A\rho^{US}(1-\gamma) & -\overline{\lambda}_I\rho^I & -\overline{\lambda}_I\rho^{CS} & 0\\
0 & 0 & 0 & \overline{\lambda}_I\rho^{CS} & 0 & \overline{\lambda}_I\rho^I & -\beta & 0\\
0 & \overline{\lambda}_A\rho^A(1-\gamma) & \overline{\lambda}_A\rho^{UR}(1-\gamma) & \overline{\lambda}_A\rho^{UR}(1-\gamma) & \overline{\lambda}_A\rho^{UR}(1-\gamma) & 0 & \beta & 0
\end{bmatrix}$$

with $\rho^I = \rho^{AI} + \rho^{CI}$, $\rho^A = \rho^{AS} + \rho^{AI} + \rho^{AR}$.

3.1. The Disease-Free Equilibrium

Let the right side of Equation (1) be equal to zero, then from (1a) and (1b) we can obtain that

$$\begin{aligned}(\rho^{AR}+\rho^{AS})\rho^{US}=0,\\(\rho^{AR}+\rho^{AS})\rho^{UR}=0.\end{aligned} \tag{3}$$

From Equation (3), if $\rho^{AR}+\rho^{AS}\neq 0$, then $\rho^{US}=0$ and $\rho^{UR}=0$, and the disease-free equilibrium is $E^{01}=(0,\,0,\,\rho^{AS},\,0,\,\rho^{AR},\,\rho^{CS},\,0,\,\rho^{CR})$.

If $\rho^{AR}+\rho^{AS}=0$, then $\rho^{AS}=0$ and $\rho^{AR}=0$, and the disease-free equilibrium is

$$E^{02}=(\rho^{US},\,\rho^{UR},\,0,\,0,\,0,\,\rho^{CS},\,0,\,\rho^{CR}).$$

Firstly, we will analyze the stability of disease-free equilibrium E^{01}.

When the disease-free equilibrium is $E^{01}=(0,\,0,\,\rho^{AS},\,0,\,\rho^{AR},\,\rho^{CS},\,0,\,\rho^{CR})$, the Jacobian matrix J is simplified to

$$J=\begin{bmatrix}-\overline{\lambda}_A\rho^A & 0 & 0 & 0 & 0 & 0 & 0 & 0\\ 0 & -\overline{\lambda}_A\rho^A & 0 & 0 & 0 & 0 & 0 & 0\\ \overline{\lambda}_A\rho^A\gamma & 0 & 0 & -\overline{\lambda}_I\rho^{AS} & 0 & 0 & -\overline{\lambda}_I\rho^{AS} & 0\\ 0 & 0 & 0 & \overline{\lambda}_I\rho^{AS}-\beta & 0 & 0 & \overline{\lambda}_I\rho^{AS} & 0\\ 0 & \overline{\lambda}_A\rho^A\gamma & 0 & \beta & 0 & 0 & 0 & 0\\ 0 & \overline{\lambda}_A\rho^A(1-\gamma) & 0 & -\overline{\lambda}_I\rho^{CS} & 0 & 0 & -\overline{\lambda}_I\rho^{CS} & 0\\ 0 & 0 & 0 & \overline{\lambda}_I\rho^{CS} & 0 & 0 & -\beta & 0\\ 0 & \overline{\lambda}_A\rho^A(1-\gamma) & 0 & 0 & 0 & 0 & \beta & 0\end{bmatrix}.$$

The eigenvalues $\lambda_j (j=1,\,2,\,\cdots,\,8)$ of the matrix J can be calculated as follows:

$$\lambda_1=\lambda_2=\lambda_3=0,$$

$$\lambda_4=\lambda_5=-\rho^A\overline{\lambda}_A,$$

$$\lambda_6-0,$$

$$\lambda_7=\frac{\overline{\lambda}_I\rho^{AS}}{2}-\beta-\frac{\overline{\lambda}_I\sqrt{\rho^{AS}(\rho^{AS}+4\rho^{CS})}}{2},$$

$$\lambda_8=\frac{\overline{\lambda}_I\rho^{AS}}{2}-\beta+\frac{\overline{\lambda}_I\sqrt{\rho^{AS}(\rho^{AS}+4\rho^{CS})}}{2}.$$

It is easy to judge that λ_4, λ_5 and λ_7 are all negative. If

$$\lambda_8=\frac{\overline{\lambda}_I\rho^{AS}}{2}-\beta+\frac{\overline{\lambda}_I\sqrt{\rho^{AS}(\rho^{AS}+4\rho^{CS})}}{2}>0,$$

then the system is unstable at equilibrium E^{01}.

Suppose $\lambda_8=\frac{\overline{\lambda}_I\rho^{AS}}{2}-\beta+\frac{\overline{\lambda}_I\sqrt{\rho^{AS}(\rho^{AS}+4\rho^{CS})}}{2}=0$, for matrix J, the minimal polynomial of $f(\lambda)=-\lambda(\lambda+\overline{\lambda}_A\rho^A)(-\lambda^2+\overline{\lambda}_I\rho^{AS}\lambda-2\beta\lambda-\beta^2+\overline{\lambda}_I{}^2\rho^{AS}\rho^{CS}+\beta\overline{\lambda}_I\rho^{AS})$ could be simplified to

$f(\lambda)=-\lambda(\lambda+\overline{\lambda}_A\rho^A)(-\lambda^2+\overline{\lambda}_I\rho^{AS}\lambda-2\beta\lambda+3\beta^2-3\beta\overline{\lambda}_I\rho^{AS})$. Since $\rho^A=\rho^{AR}+\rho^{AS}\neq 0$, then $f(\lambda)=-\lambda(\lambda+\overline{\lambda}_A\rho^A)(-\lambda^2+\overline{\lambda}_I\rho^{AS}\lambda-2\beta\lambda+3\beta^2-3\beta\overline{\lambda}_I\rho^{AS})=0$, only has one zero root, that is to say, the system is locally stable at E^{01}.

Suppose $\lambda_8=\frac{\overline{\lambda}_I\rho^{AS}}{2}-\beta+\frac{\overline{\lambda}_I\sqrt{\rho^{AS}(\rho^{AS}+4\rho^{CS})}}{2}<0$, similarly, we can deduce that the minimal polynomial $f(\lambda)=-\lambda(\lambda+\overline{\lambda}_A\rho^A)(-\lambda^2+\overline{\lambda}_I\rho^{AS}\lambda-2\beta\lambda-\beta^2+\overline{\lambda}_I{}^2\rho^{AS}\rho^{CS}+\beta\overline{\lambda}_I\rho^{AS})$ only has one zero root, and the system is locally stable at E^{01}.

Thus, when:

$$\lambda_8 = \frac{\overline{\lambda}_I \rho^{AS}}{2} - \beta + \frac{\sqrt{\overline{\lambda}_I \rho^{AS}(\overline{\lambda}_I \rho^{AS} + \overline{\lambda}_I \rho^{CS})}}{2} \leq 0,$$

then

$$\overline{\lambda}_I{}^2 \rho^{AS} \rho^{CS} + 4\beta \overline{\lambda}_I{}^2 \rho^{AS} \leq 4\beta^2.$$

Since $\rho^{AS} < 1$ and $\rho^{CS} < 1$, if

$$\overline{\lambda}_I{}^2 + 4\beta \overline{\lambda}_I{}^2 < 4\beta^2, \tag{4}$$

then inequality $\overline{\lambda}_I{}^2 \rho^{AS} \rho^{CS} + 4\beta \overline{\lambda}_I{}^2 \rho^{AS} < 4\beta^2$ holds.

From inequality (4), we can obtain:

$$\overline{\lambda}_I < \frac{2\beta}{\sqrt{1+4\beta}}$$

Since $\overline{\lambda}_I = 1 - \prod_{j=1}^{p} (1 - \lambda_I)$, $\lambda_I = 1 - (1-\alpha)^{w_{ij}}$, $j = 1, \cdots, p$, therefore, if

$$1 - \prod_{j=1}^{p} (1-\alpha)^{w_{ij}} < \frac{2\beta}{\sqrt{1+4\beta}}.$$

holds, all eigenvalues in the disease-free equilibrium E^{01} are no more than zero and we can conclude that the system is locally stable at E^{01}.

Based on the above analysis, we can obtain the following theorem.

Theorem 1. *For node i, if* $1 - \prod_{j=1}^{p} (1-\alpha)^{w_{ij}} < \frac{2\beta}{\sqrt{1+4\beta}}$ *is satisfied, while* w_{ij} *is the weight between node i and node* $j (j = 1, 2, \cdots, p)$*, and p is the number of infectious neighboring nodes of node i, then system (1) is locally stable on disease-free equilibrium* $E^{01} = (0, 0, \rho^{AS}, 0, \rho^{AR}, \rho^{CS}, 0, \rho^{CR})$.

Secondly, we will analyze the stability of disease-free equilibrium E^{02}.

When the disease-free equilibrium is $E^{02} = (\rho^{US}, \rho^{UR}, 0, 0, 0, \rho^{CS}, 0, \rho^{CR})$, the Jacobian matrix J' is

$$J' = \begin{bmatrix} 0 & 0 & -\overline{\lambda}_A \rho^{US} & -\overline{\lambda}_I \rho^{US} - \overline{\lambda}_A \rho^{US} & -\overline{\lambda}_A \rho^{US} & 0 & -\overline{\lambda}_I \rho^{US} & 0 \\ 0 & 0 & -\overline{\lambda}_A \rho^{UR} & -\overline{\lambda}_A \rho^{UR} & -\overline{\lambda}_A \rho^{UR} & 0 & 0 & 0 \\ 0 & 0 & \overline{\lambda}_A \rho^{US} \gamma & \overline{\lambda}_A \rho^{US} \gamma & \overline{\lambda}_A \rho^{US} \gamma & 0 & 0 & 0 \\ 0 & 0 & 0 & -\beta & 0 & 0 & 0 & 0 \\ 0 & 0 & \overline{\lambda}_A \rho^{UR} \gamma & \overline{\lambda}_A \rho^{UR} \gamma + \beta & \overline{\lambda}_A \rho^{UR} \gamma & 0 & 0 & 0 \\ 0 & 0 & \overline{\lambda}_A \rho^{US}(1-\gamma) & \overline{\lambda}_A \rho^{US}(1-\gamma) - \overline{\lambda}_I \rho^{CS} & \overline{\lambda}_A \rho^{US}(1-\gamma) & 0 & -\overline{\lambda}_I \rho^{CS} & 0 \\ 0 & 0 & 0 & \overline{\lambda}_I \rho^{CS} & 0 & 0 & -\beta & 0 \\ 0 & 0 & \overline{\lambda}_A \rho^{UR}(1-\gamma) & \overline{\lambda}_A \rho^{UR}(1-\gamma) & \overline{\lambda}_A \rho^{UR}(1-\gamma) & 0 & \beta & 0 \end{bmatrix}.$$

At this point, the eigenvalues $\lambda'_j (j = 1, 2, \cdots, 8)$ of the matrix J' can be calculated as follows:

$$\lambda'_1 = \lambda'_2 = \lambda'_3 = \lambda'_4 = \lambda'_5 = 0,$$
$$\lambda'_6 = (\overline{\lambda}_I + \overline{\lambda}_A) \rho^{US} \gamma,$$
$$\lambda'_7 = \lambda'_8 = -\beta.$$

Obviously, if $\rho^{US} = 0$, by the same method, all the eigenvalues at disease-free equilibrium E^{02} are not more than zero, and the system (1) is locally stable.

However, if $\rho^{US} > 0$, then $\lambda'_6 > 0$, then the system (1) at disease-free equilibrium E^{02} is unstable.

3.2. The Endemic Equilibrium

Suppose there is an endemic equilibrium, then $\rho^{CI} \neq 0$ should be satisfied. From (1a), (1c), (1d) and (1g), we can obtain that $\rho^{US} = 0$, $\rho^{AS} = 0$, $\rho^{AI} = 0$ and

$$\rho^{CS} = \frac{1 - \prod_{j=1}^{p} (1 - \lambda_I)}{\beta}.$$

In addition, from (1b) and (1e), we have $\rho^{UR} = 0$ or $\rho^{AR} = 0$. If $\rho^{UR} = 0$, then substituting it into equation (1h) we have $\rho^{CI} = 0$, which contradicts the hypothesis. If $\rho^{AR} = 0$, then substituting it into (1c) and (1d), we also have $\rho^{CI} = 0$, which contradicts the hypothesis.

Thus, for system (1) there is no endemic equilibrium, and there is only a disease-free equilibrium.

4. Targeted Immunity Based on Age Structure

For the infants and the elderly, their immunity is relatively poor and their influence on their surroundings is relatively small, which is reflected in complex networks that these special nodes have a relatively small weight. Taking targeted immunization against these special nodes with a small weight is a very effective control method to suppress the spread of infectious diseases in a wide range. Based on this, we propose a step function $\delta(\omega)$ related to the node weight, which is described as follows:

$$\delta(\omega_i) = \begin{cases} 0, & \sum_{j=1}^{k} \omega_{ij} > \Omega; \\ 1, & \sum_{j=1}^{k} \omega_{ij} \leq \Omega. \end{cases}$$

where $\omega_i = \sum_{j=1}^{k} \omega_{ij}$ is the sum of weights of node i, k is the degree of node i, Ω is the given threshold value of weight. When the weight of a node in the network is less than or equal to Ω, the node is vaccinated with probability σ. At this time, the transformation relationship among states of the network node is shown in Figure 5.

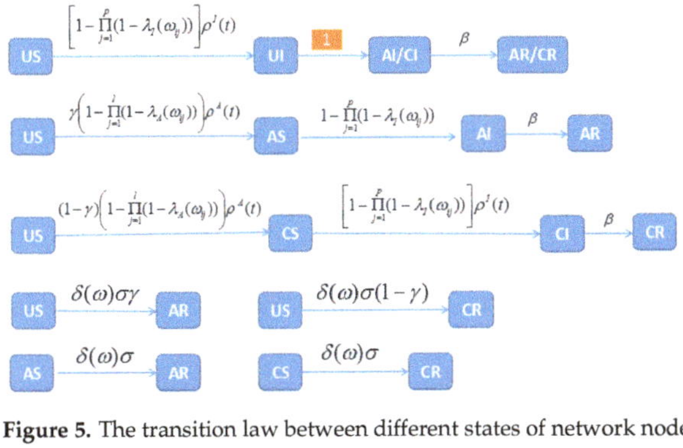

Figure 5. The transition law between different states of network nodes under control.

Thus, the fractional-order SIR network model (1) can be rewritten as follows:

$$
\begin{aligned}
D^m\rho^{US} &= -\rho^I\left[1-\prod_{j=1}^{p}(1-\lambda_I)\right]\rho^{US} - \rho^A\left[1-\prod_{j=1}^{l}(1-\lambda_A)\right]\rho^{US} - \delta(\omega)\sigma\rho^{US},\\
D^m\rho^{UR} &= -\rho^A\left[1-\prod_{j=1}^{l}(1-\lambda_A)\right]\rho^{UR},\\
D^m\rho^{AS} &= \rho^A\left[1-\prod_{j=1}^{l}(1-\lambda_A)\right]\rho^{US}\gamma - \rho^I\left[1-\prod_{j=1}^{p}(1-\lambda_I)\right]\rho^{AS} - \delta(\omega)\sigma\rho^{AS},\\
D^m\rho^{AI} &= \rho^I\left[1-\prod_{j=1}^{p}(1-\lambda_I)\right]\rho^{AS} - \rho^{AI}\beta,\\
D^m\rho^{AR} &= \rho^A\left[1-\prod_{j=1}^{l}(1-\lambda_A)\right]\rho^{UR}\gamma + \rho^{AI}\beta + \delta(\omega)\sigma\rho^{AS} + \delta(\omega)\sigma\gamma\rho^{US},\\
D^m\rho^{CS} &= \rho^A\left[1-\prod_{j=1}^{l}(1-\lambda_A)\right]\rho^{US}(1-\gamma) - \rho^I\left[1-\prod_{j=1}^{p}(1-\lambda_I)\right]\rho^{CS} - \delta(\omega)\sigma\rho^{CS},\\
D^m\rho^{CI} &= \rho^I\left[1-\prod_{j=1}^{p}(1-\lambda_I)\right]\rho^{CS} - \rho^{CI}\beta,\\
D^m\rho^{CR} &= \rho^A\left[1-\prod_{j=1}^{l}(1-\lambda_A)\right]\rho^{UR}(1-\gamma) + \rho^{CI}\beta + \delta(\omega)\sigma\rho^{CS} + \delta(\omega)\sigma(1-\gamma)\rho^{US}.
\end{aligned}
\tag{5}
$$

Similarly, for model (5), the disease-free equilibrium is $E^{01} = (0, 0, 0, 0, \rho^{AR}, 0, 0, \rho^{CR})$ and $E^{02} = (0, \rho^{UR}, 0, 0, 0, 0, 0, \rho^{CR})$.

For $E^{01} = (0, 0, 0, 0, \rho^{AR}, 0, 0, \rho^{CR})$, the Jacobian matrix J is

$$
J = \begin{bmatrix}
-\overline{\lambda}_A\rho^{AR} - \delta(\omega)\sigma & 0 & 0 & 0 & 0 & 0 & 0 & 0\\
0 & -\overline{\lambda}_A\rho^{AR} & 0 & 0 & 0 & 0 & 0 & 0\\
\overline{\lambda}_A\rho^{AR}\gamma & 0 & -\delta(\omega)\sigma & 0 & 0 & 0 & 0 & 0\\
0 & 0 & 0 & -\beta & 0 & 0 & 0 & 0\\
\delta(\omega)\sigma\gamma & \overline{\lambda}_A\rho^{AR}\gamma & \delta(\omega)\sigma & \beta & 0 & 0 & 0 & 0\\
\overline{\lambda}_A\rho^{AR}(1-\gamma) & 0 & 0 & 0 & 0 & -\delta(\omega)\sigma & 0 & 0\\
0 & 0 & 0 & 0 & 0 & 0 & -\beta & 0\\
\delta(\omega)\sigma(1-\gamma) & \overline{\lambda}_A\rho^{AR}(1-\gamma) & 0 & 0 & 0 & \delta(\omega)\sigma & \beta & 0
\end{bmatrix}.
$$

For node i, when $\sum_{j=1}^{k}\omega_{ij} > \Omega$ and $\delta(\omega_i) = 0$, the Jacobian matrix J at $E^{01} = (0, 0, 0, 0, \rho^{AR}, 0, 0, \rho^{CR})$ can be written as

$$
J = \begin{bmatrix}
-\overline{\lambda}_A\rho^{AR} & 0 & 0 & 0 & 0 & 0 & 0 & 0\\
0 & -\overline{\lambda}_A\rho^{AR} & 0 & 0 & 0 & 0 & 0 & 0\\
\overline{\lambda}_A\rho^{AR}\gamma & 0 & 0 & 0 & 0 & 0 & 0 & 0\\
0 & 0 & 0 & -\beta & 0 & 0 & 0 & 0\\
0 & \overline{\lambda}_A\rho^{AR}\gamma & 0 & \beta & 0 & 0 & 0 & 0\\
\overline{\lambda}_A\rho^{AR}(1-\gamma) & 0 & 0 & 0 & 0 & 0 & 0 & 0\\
0 & 0 & 0 & 0 & 0 & 0 & -\beta & 0\\
0 & \overline{\lambda}_A\rho^{AR}(1-\gamma) & 0 & 0 & 0 & 0 & \beta & 0
\end{bmatrix},
$$

and the eigenvalues $\lambda_j (j = 1, 2, \cdots, 8)$ of the matrix J can be calculated as follows:

$$
\begin{aligned}
\lambda_1 = \lambda_2 = \lambda_3 = \lambda_4 &= 0,\\
\lambda_5 = \lambda_6 &= -\overline{\lambda}_A\rho^{AR},\\
\lambda_7 = \lambda_8 &= -\beta.
\end{aligned}
$$

When $\sum_{j=1}^{k} \omega_{ij} \leq \Omega$ and $\delta(\omega_i) = 1$, the Jacobian matrix J can be rewritten as

$$J = \begin{bmatrix} -\overline{\lambda}_A\rho^{AR} - \sigma & 0 & 0 & 0 & 0 & 0 & 0 & 0 \\ 0 & -\overline{\lambda}_A\rho^{AR} & 0 & 0 & 0 & 0 & 0 & 0 \\ \overline{\lambda}_A\rho^{AR}\gamma & 0 & -\sigma & 0 & 0 & 0 & 0 & 0 \\ 0 & 0 & 0 & -\beta & 0 & 0 & 0 & 0 \\ \sigma\gamma & \overline{\lambda}_A\rho^{AR}\gamma & \sigma & \beta & 0 & 0 & 0 & 0 \\ \overline{\lambda}_A\rho^{AR}(1-\gamma) & 0 & 0 & 0 & 0 & -\sigma & 0 & 0 \\ 0 & 0 & 0 & 0 & 0 & 0 & -\beta & 0 \\ \sigma(1-\gamma) & \overline{\lambda}_A\rho^{AR}(1-\gamma) & 0 & 0 & 0 & \sigma & \beta & 0 \end{bmatrix},$$

and the eigenvalues $\lambda_j (j = 1, 2, \cdots, 8)$ of the matrix J can be calculated as follows:

$$\lambda_1 = \lambda_2 = \lambda_3 = 0,$$
$$\lambda_4 = -\overline{\lambda}_A\rho^{AR},\ \lambda_5 = -\sigma,$$
$$\lambda_7 = \lambda_8 = -\beta,\ \lambda_6 = -\overline{\lambda}_A\rho^{AR} - \sigma.$$

Therefore, applying the same method, system (2) is always locally stable at $E^{01} = (0, 0, 0, 0, \rho^{AR}, 0, 0, \rho^{CR})$.

Moreover, for $E^{02} = (0, \rho^{UR}, 0, 0, 0, 0, 0, \rho^{CR})$, the Jacobian matrix J is

$$J = \begin{bmatrix} -\delta(\omega)\sigma & 0 & 0 & 0 & 0 & 0 & 0 & 0 \\ 0 & 0 & -\overline{\lambda}_A\rho^{UR} & -\overline{\lambda}_A\rho^{UR} & -\overline{\lambda}_A\rho^{UR} & 0 & 0 & 0 \\ 0 & 0 & -\delta(\omega)\sigma & 0 & 0 & 0 & 0 & 0 \\ 0 & 0 & 0 & -\beta & 0 & 0 & 0 & 0 \\ \delta(\omega)\sigma\gamma & 0 & \overline{\lambda}_A\rho^{UR}\gamma & \overline{\lambda}_A\rho^{UR}\gamma + \beta & \overline{\lambda}_A\rho^{UR}\gamma & 0 & 0 & 0 \\ 0 & 0 & 0 & 0 & 0 & -\delta(\omega)\sigma & 0 & 0 \\ 0 & 0 & 0 & 0 & 0 & 0 & -\beta & 0 \\ \delta(\omega)\sigma(1-\gamma) & 0 & \overline{\lambda}_A\rho^{UR}(1-\gamma) & \overline{\lambda}_A\rho^{UR}(1-\gamma) & \overline{\lambda}_A\rho^{UR}(1-\gamma) & \delta(\omega)\sigma & \beta & 0 \end{bmatrix}.$$

Thus, system (2) is also locally stable at $E^{02} = (0, \rho^{UR}, 0, 0, 0, 0, 0, \rho^{CR})$.

In the same way, we can deduce that there is also no endemic equilibrium under targeted immunity based on age structure, either.

$$\lambda_6 = -\overline{\lambda}_A\rho^{UR}\gamma,\ \lambda_7 = \lambda_8 = -\beta.$$

When $\sum_{j=1}^{k} \omega_{ij} \leq \Omega$, we can obtain the eigenvalues of the Jacobian matrix

$$\lambda_1 = \lambda_2 = 0,\ \lambda_3 = -\overline{\lambda}_A\rho^{UR}\gamma,$$

$$\lambda_4 = \lambda_5 = \lambda_6 = -\sigma,$$

$$\lambda_7 = \lambda_8 = -\beta.$$

Thus, system (2) is also locally stable at $E^{02} = (0, \rho^{UR}, 0, 0, 0, 0, 0, \rho^{CR})$.

Corollary 1. *If the network weight $\omega_{ij} = \omega$ is a constant, then system (2) is always local stable at the disease-free equilibrium point.*

Remark 2. *Compared with the theoretical results in [16,17], the results present that the infected density is affected by the network weights and the node degree. In this paper, if the basic reproduction number is less than 1, we can conclude that the degree of decay is also influenced by the network weights, and even more, the infectious density is gradually truncated to zero, eventually. This result further simplifies the propagation law of infectious disease under-weighted networks.*

5. Examples and Simulations

In this section, numerical simulations are presented to illustrate the theoretical results mentioned above.

Example 1. *Without loss of generality, for a node i, suppose that* $\alpha = 0.04$, $\beta = 0.35$, $q = 0.4$, $\gamma = 0.88$. *The number of infectious neighboring nodes is equal* $l = 10$, *and the number of nodes that know and distribute messages is* $p = 13$. *The weights* ω_{ij} *are valued as a random number between 0 and 1. The initial condition is [0.122, 0.1, 0.038, 0.019, 0.432, 0.231, 0.010, 0.038].*

We can calculate that $\lambda_1 = 0.2010$ and $\frac{2\beta}{\sqrt{1+4\beta}} = 0.4516$, which satisfies Theorem 1, thus there is only a disease-free equilibrium, and system (1) is locally stable. From Figure 6, we can find that the disease-free equilibrium point is globally asymptotically stable. To be clear, Figure 7 shows that the infectious states AI and CI converge to zero when $m = 0.98$, which means that the disease will eventually disappear. From the above, we can conclude that the theoretical results are correct and the simulation results are effective.

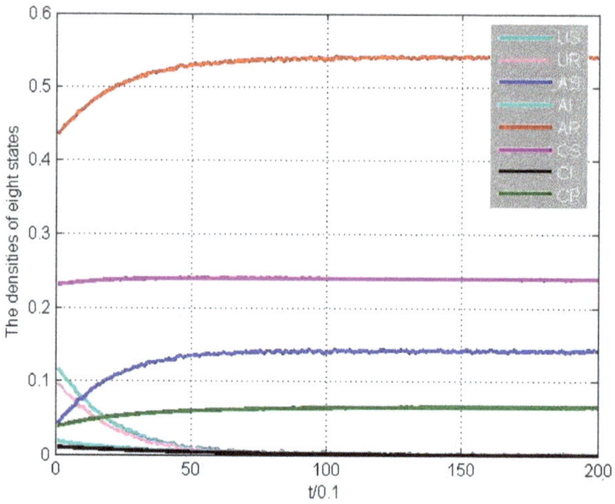

Figure 6. The simulation results for all the states of model (1) at $m = 0.98$.

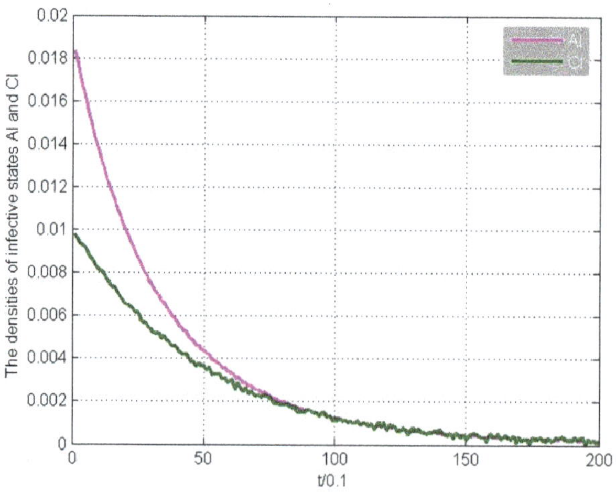

Figure 7. The graphical results for the infectious states at $m = 0.98$.

Remark 3. *Compared with the results in [16,17], the simulation in Figure 6 not only presents that the infectious will disappear in the future but also shows how all the states evolve over time. We also find that all people know the information about the disease, which signifies that they will voluntarily take measures to prevent the epidemic.*

In addition, we also simulate the effect of the fractional order parameter on disease transmission. When we choose $m = 0.6$, from Figure 8, we can also find that the disease-free equilibrium point is globally asymptotically stable. However, Figure 9 shows that the infectious states AI and CI converge much slower compared with Figure 7. Moreover, we can conclude that the smaller the fractional order parameter, the slower the infective rate converges, as can be seen from Figure 10.

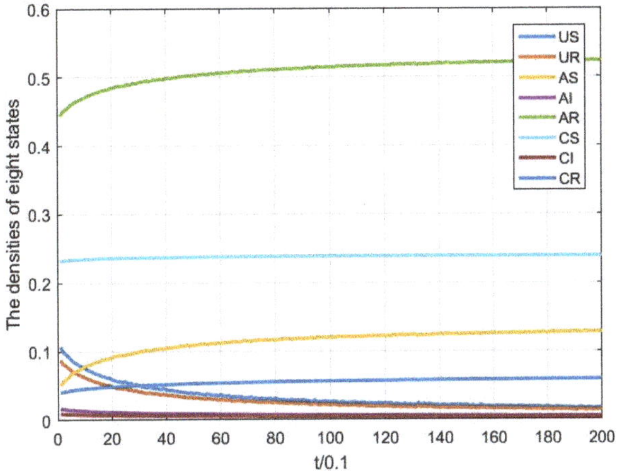

Figure 8. The simulation results for all the states of the model (1) at $m = 0.6$.

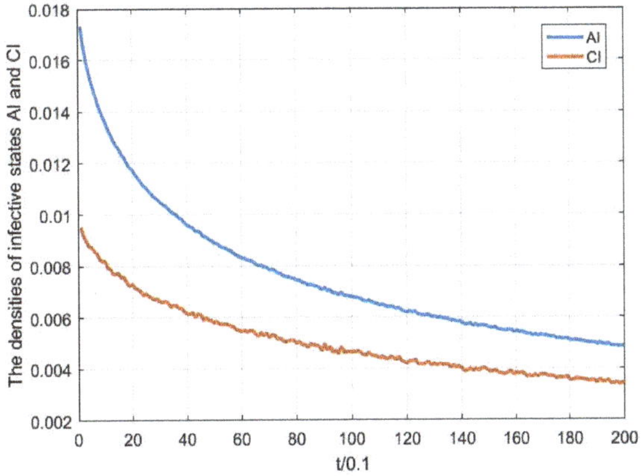

Figure 9. The graphical results for the infectious states at $m = 0.6$.

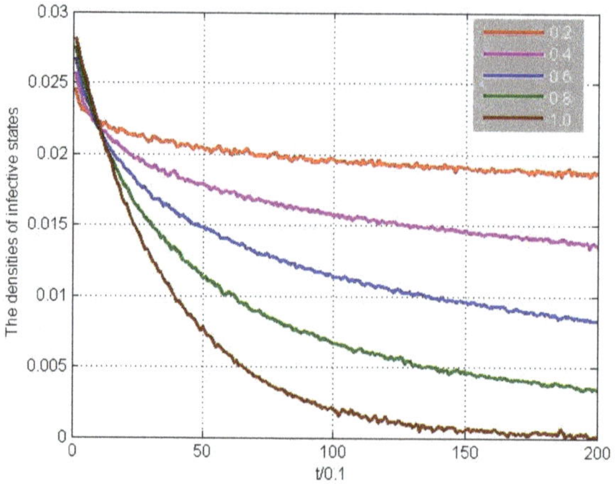

Figure 10. Effect of the fractional order parameter on infectious density.

Figure 11 indicates that under targeted immunity control, not only will the disease disappear, but everyone will know about the outbreak of the disease.

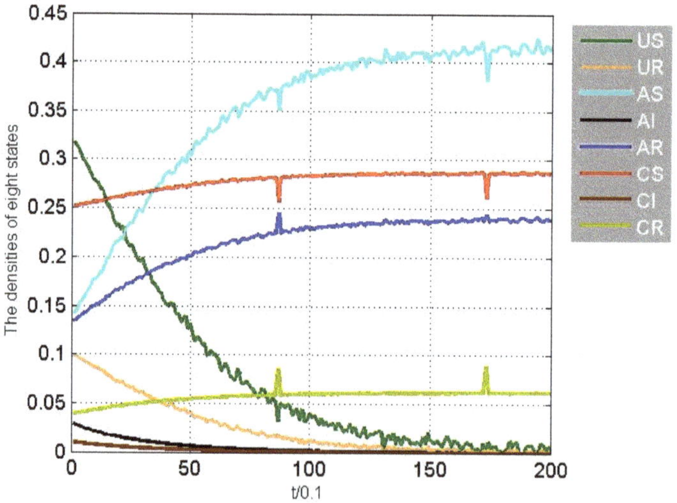

Figure 11. The simulation results for all the states under targeted immunity control.

Remark 4. *Comparing Figures 6 and 11, it is obvious that the disease dies out much more quickly under control than no control, although it is roughly specified about the control node weight and control proportion. In the next step, we will build a real network to seek the optimal control nodes and control proportion, according to the actual situation of node weight.*

Example 2. *For node i, suppose that* $\alpha = 0.25$, $\beta = 0.2$, $q = 0.4$, $\gamma = 0.88$. *Other parameters are the same as Example 1, that is to say,* $m = 0.98$, $l = 10$, $p = 13$ *weights* ω_{ij} *are valued as a random number from 0 to 1, and the initial condition is also [0.122, 0.1, 0.038, 0.019, 0.432, 0.231, 0.010, 0.038]. In this case, we can calculate that* $\lambda_1 = 0.8451$ *and* $\frac{2\beta}{\sqrt{1+4\beta}} = 0.2985$, *which did not satisfy Theorem 1. From Figures 12 and 13, we observe that without control, the infectious states do not decline to zero, and even have a trend of rising for a period of time.*

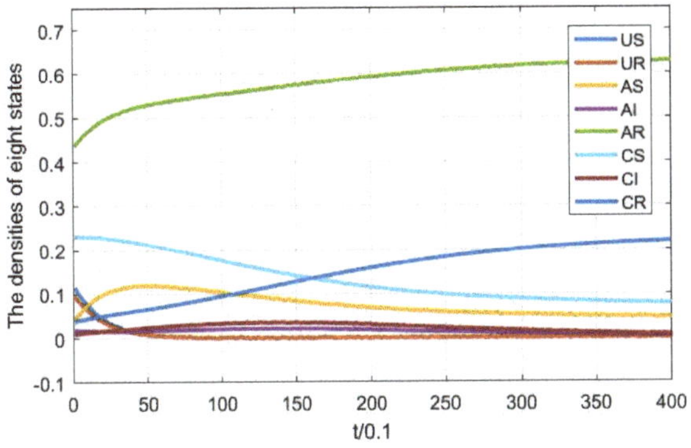

Figure 12. The simulation results for all the states without targeted immunity control.

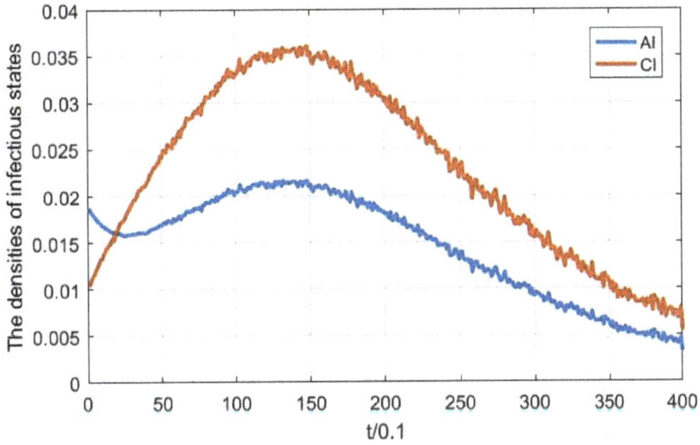

Figure 13. The infectious simulation results without targeted immunity control.

Remark 5. *Comparing Figures 7 and 13, it is easy to see that as the disease propagation rates* α *and* β *are different, then for the infectious density, one is obviously stable, the other may be unstable in a period. In a word, the disease network topology has a great influence on the epidemic transmission dynamics.*

Similarly, for the purpose of suppressing the spread of the disease among the elderly and young, targeted immunity control with $\Omega = 1, \sigma = 0.8$ is still taken. At this moment, the simulation result is shown in Figure 14, which indicates that the disease will disappear ultimately and the control method is effective. Moreover, with different control rates, from Figure 15, we can observe that the larger the control rate, the more quickly the infectious state decreases. The best control effect happens when $\sigma = 1$, but the control cost is the highest.

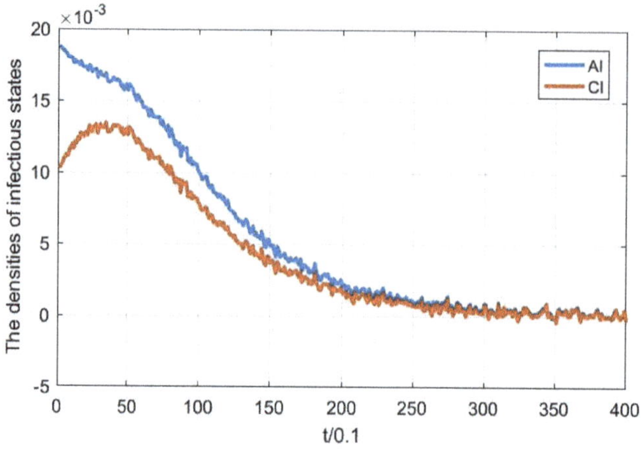

Figure 14. The simulation results for infectious states under targeted immunity control.

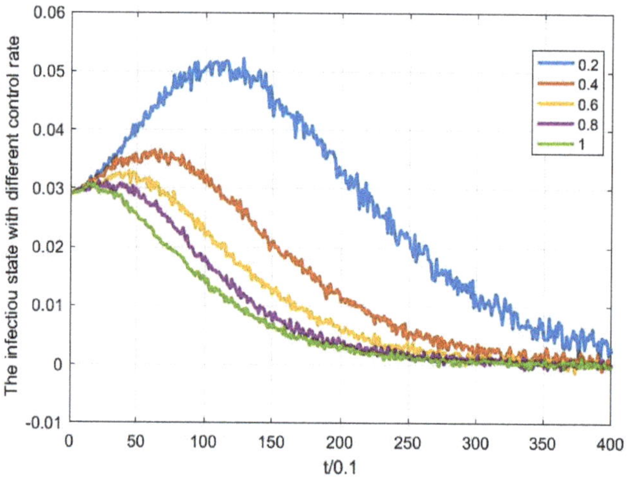

Figure 15. The infectious simulation results under different targeted immunity control rates.

6. Conclusions

The connection between individuals has a significant impact on the spread of disease. In order to quantitatively investigate the effect of edge weight on the spread of an epidemic, this article presents a fractional SIR model with a two-layer weighted network. On the basis of the Jacobian matrix, the stability of disease-free equilibrium is analyzed in detail. Under certain conditions, the disease-free equilibrium is locally stable, which means that the disease will eventually die out, regardless of the initial density of the infected individuals. Furthermore, we conclude that there exists no endemic equilibrium. Since the elderly and the children have lower immunity, a targeted immunity controller based on age structure is proposed. In addition, its transmission dynamics are analyzed in detail. Finally, numerical simulations are presented to illustrate the theoretical results, and the effect of the fractional order parameter on the infection rate is simulated.

Note, that since the weight has a large influence on the propagation dynamics, it may be necessary to further build a specific model and develop control strategies for certain specific infectious diseases. Many scientific disciplines are currently investigating and forecasting the spread of COVID-19. They found that older people and young children are more susceptible to COVID-19. Susceptible people have a relatively small weight in the population network. In this case, the idea is to prioritize vaccination to the nodes with less weight to prevent widespread COVID-19 infection. This strategy has worked in Zhejiang Province, China, and after a period of observation, it will be extended to the entire country. Therefore, the next research work is to analyze the critical weight parameter and calculate the optimal inoculation ratio in a real environment, although a little work has been done in this paper.

Author Contributions: Methodology, N.L. and J.F.; software, simulation, N.L. and S.L.; validation, N.L. and J.S.; formal analysis, N.L., S.L. and J.F.; writing—original draft preparation, N.L., J.F. and J.S.; writing—review and editing, N.L. and J.F. All authors have read and agreed to the published version of the manuscript.

Funding: This work was funded by the National Natural Science Foundation of China under Grants 61775198. This work was also sponsored by the Science and Technology Project in Henan province under Grant 202102310203.

Institutional Review Board Statement: Not applicable.

Informed Consent Statement: Not applicable.

Data Availability Statement: Not applicable.

Acknowledgments: The authors would like to thank the reviewers for their valuable comments and suggestions that greatly improved the presentation of this work.

Conflicts of Interest: The authors declare no conflict of interest.

References

1. Pastor-Satorras, R.; Vespignani, A. Epidemic spreading in scale-free networks. *Phys. Rev. Lett.* **2000**, *86*, 3200–3203. [CrossRef] [PubMed]
2. Granell, C.; Gómez, S.; Arenas, A. Competing spreading processes on multiplex networks: Awareness and epidemics. *Phys. Rev. E* **2014**, *90*, 012808. [CrossRef] [PubMed]
3. Wang, Z.; Andrews, M.A.; Wu, Z.-X.; Wang, L.; Bauch, C.T. Coupled disease-behavior dynamics on complex networks: A review. *Phys. Life Rev.* **2015**, *15*, 1–29. [CrossRef]
4. Ma, W.C.; Zhang, P.; Zhao, X.; Xue, L. The coupled dynamics of information dissemination and SEIR-based epidemic spreading in multiplex networks. *Phys. A* **2022**, *588*, 126558. [CrossRef] [PubMed]
5. Wang, W.; Liu, Q.H.; Liang, J.; Hu, Y.; Zhou, T. Coevolution spreading in complex networks. *Phys. Rep.* **2019**, *820*, 1–51. [CrossRef]
6. Kan, J.; Zhang, H. Effects of awareness diffusion and self-initiated awareness behavior on epidemic spreading-An approach based on multiplex networks. *Commun. Nonlinear Sci. Numer. Simul.* **2017**, *44*, 193–203. [CrossRef]
7. Liu, Y.; Ding, L.; An, X.; Hu, P.; Du, F. Epidemic spreading on midscopic multi-layer network with optimal control mechanism. *Phys. A* **2019**, *537*, 122775. [CrossRef]
8. Scatà, M.; Di Stefano, A.; Liò, P.; La Corte, A. The Impact of Heterogeneity and Awareness in Modeling Epidemic Spreading on Multiplex Networks. *Sci. Rep.* **2016**, *6*, 37105. [CrossRef]
9. Gao, C.; Tang, S.; Li, W.; Yang, Y.; Zheng, Z. Dynamical Processes and Epidemic Threshold on Nonlinear Coupled Multiplex Networks. *Phys. A* **2018**, *496*, 330–338. [CrossRef]
10. Li, M.; Wang, M.; Xue, S.; Ma, J. The influence of awareness on epidemic spreading on random networks. *J. Theor. Biol.* **2020**, *486*, 110090. [CrossRef]
11. Jing, W.; Li, Y.; Zhang, X.; Zhang, J.; Jin, Z. A rumor spreading pairwise model on weighted networks. *Phys. A* **2022**, *585*, 126451. [CrossRef]
12. Barrat, A.; Barthelemy, M.; Vespignani, A. Modeling the evolution of weighted networks. *Phys. Rev. E* **2004**, *70*, 066149. [CrossRef] [PubMed]
13. Chu, X.; Zhang, Z.; Guan, J.; Zhou, S. Epidemic spreading with nonlinear infectivity in weighted scale-free networks. *Phys. A* **2009**, *390*, 471–481. [CrossRef]
14. Yang, Z.; Zhou, T. Epidemic spreading in weighted networks: An edge-based mean-field solution. *Phys. Rev. E* **2011**, *85*, 056106. [CrossRef]
15. Zhu, G.H.; Chen, G.R.; Xu, X.J.; Fu, X.C. Epidemic spreading on contact networks with adaptive weights. *J. Theor. Biol.* **2013**, *317*, 133–139. [CrossRef]
16. Wang, W.; Tang, M.; Zhang, H.F.; Gao, H.; Liu, Z.H. Epidemic spreading on complex networks with general degree and weight distributions. *Phys. Rev. E* **2014**, *90*, 042803. [CrossRef]

17. Xu, Z.; Wang, Y.; Wu, N.; Fu, X. Propagation dynamics of a periodic epidemic model on weighted interconnected networks. *IEEE Trans. Netw. Sci. Eng.* **2019**, *7*, 1545–1556. [CrossRef]
18. Huo, J.J.; Zhao, H.Y. Dynamical analysis of a fractional SIR model with birth and death on heterogeneous complex networks. *Phys. A* **2016**, *448*, 41–56. [CrossRef]
19. Balzotti, C.; D'Ovidio, M.; Loreti, P. Fractional SIS Epidemic Models. *Fractal Fract.* **2020**, *4*, 44. [CrossRef]
20. Farhadi, A.; Hanert, E. Front Propagation of Exponentially Truncated Fractional-Order Epidemics. *Fractal Fract.* **2022**, *6*, 53. [CrossRef]
21. Zafar, Z.U.A.; Rehan, K.; Mushtaq, M. HIV/AIDS epidemic fractional-order model. *J. Differ. Equ. Appl.* **2017**, *23*, 1298–1315. [CrossRef]
22. Rostamy, D.; Mottaghi, E. Stability analysis of a fractional-order epidemics model with multiple equilibrium. *Adv. Differ. Equ.* **2016**, *2016*, 170. [CrossRef]
23. Torres, D. Fractional-Order Modelling and Optimal Control of Cholera Transmission. *Fractal Fract.* **2021**, *5*, 261.
24. Jrg, A.; Lk, A.; Al, A.; Min, W.B. Stability analysis of a fractional online social network model. *Math. Comput. Simul.* **2020**, *178*, 625–645.
25. Majee, S.; Adak, S.; Jana, S.; Mandal, M.; Kar, T.K. Complex dynamics of a fractional-order SIR system in the context of COVID-19. *J. Appl. Math. Comput.* **2022**, 1–24. [CrossRef]
26. Alqahtani, R.T. Mathematical model of SIR epidemic system (COVID-19) with fractional derivative: Stability and numerical analysis. *Adv. Differ. Equ.* **2021**, *2021*, 2. [CrossRef]
27. Gao, W.; Veeresha, P.; Cattani, C.; Baishya, C.; Baskonus, H.M. Modified Predictor-Corrector Method for the Numerical Solution of a Fractional-Order SIR Model with 2019-nCoV. *Fractal Fract.* **2022**, *6*, 92. [CrossRef]
28. Liu, N.; Li, Y.L.; Sun, J.W.; Fang, J.; Liu, P. Epidemic Dynamics of a Fractional-Order SIS Infectious Network Model. *Discret. Dyn. Nat. Soc.* **2021**, *2021*, 5518436. [CrossRef]
29. Liu, N.; Liu, P. Epidemic dynamics of a fractional multistage SIR network model. *Univ. Politeh. Buchar. Sci. Bull.-Ser. A-Appl. Math. Phys.* **2021**, *83*, 215–226.
30. Tsuzuki, S.; Baguelin, M.; Pebody, R.; van Leeuwen, E. Modelling the optimal target age group for seasonal influenza vaccination in Japan. *Vaccine* **2020**, *38*, 752–762. [CrossRef]
31. Zhou, L.H.; Wang, Y.; Xiao, Y.Y.; Li, M.Y. Global dynamics of a discrete age-structured SIR epidemic model with applications to measles vaccination strategies. *Math. Biosci.* **2019**, *308*, 27–37. [CrossRef] [PubMed]
32. Yang, Y.; McKhann, A.; Chen, S.; Harling, G.; Onnela, J.-P. Efficient vaccination strategies for epidemic control using network information. *Epidemics* **2019**, *27*, 115–122. [CrossRef] [PubMed]
33. Kabir, K.; Kuga, K.; Tanimoto, J. The impact of information spreading on epidemic vaccination game dynamics in a heterogeneous complex network-A theoretical approach. *Chaos Solitons Fractals* **2020**, *132*, 109548. [CrossRef]
34. Kumar, A.; Srivastava, P.K.; Gupta, R.P. Nonlinear dynamics of infectious diseases via information-induced vaccination and saturated treatment. *Math. Comput. Simul.* **2019**, *157*, 77–99. [CrossRef]
35. Peng, X.-L.; Zhang, Z.-Q.; Yang, J.; Jin, Z. An SIS epidemic model with vaccination in a dynamical contact network of mobile individuals with heterogeneous spatial constraints. *Commun. Nonlinear Sci. Numer. Simul.* **2019**, *73*, 52–73. [CrossRef]
36. Kwon, H.D.; Lee, J.; Yang, S.D. Optimal control of an age-structured model of HIV infection. *Appl. Math. Comput.* **2012**, *219*, 2766–2779. [CrossRef]
37. Kwon, H.D.; Lee, J.; Yoon, M. An Age-Structured Model with Immune Response of HIV Infection: Modeling and Optimal Control Approach. *Discret. Contin. Dyn. Syst. B* **2017**, *19*, 153–172. [CrossRef]
38. Hisashi, I.; Ryohei, S.; Nicolas, B. An age-structured epidemic model for the demographic transition. *J. Math. Boil.* **2018**, *77*, 1299–1339.

fractal and fractional

MDPI

Article

Investigating a Generalized Fractional Quadratic Integral Equation

Basim N. Abood [1], Saleh S. Redhwan [2,*], Omar Bazighifan [3,4] and Kamsing Nonlaopon [5]

1 Department of Mathematics, College of Education of Pure Science, University of Wasit, Kut 52001, Iraq; basim.nasih@yahoo.com
2 Department of Mathematics, Dr. Babasaheb Ambedkar Marathwada University, Aurangabad 431001, India
3 Department of Mathematics, Faculty of Science, Hadhramout University, Hadhramout 50512, Yemen; o.bazighifan@gmail.com
4 Department of Mathematics, Faculty of Education, Seiyun University, Hadhramout 50512, Yemen
5 Department of Mathematics, Faculty of Science, Khon Kaen University, Khon Kaen 40002, Thailand; nkamsi@kku.ac.th
* Correspondence: saleh.redhwan909@gmail.com

Abstract: In this article, we investigate the analytical and approximate solutions for a fractional quadratic integral equation in the frame of the generalized Riemann–Liouville fractional integral operator with respect to another function. The existence and uniqueness results obtained. Moreover, some new special results corresponding to suitable values of the parameters ζ and q are given. The main results are proved by applying Banach's fixed point theorem, the Adomian decomposition method, and Picard's method. In the end, we present a numerical example to justify our results.

Keywords: fractional differential equations; fixed point theorems; ζ-fractional derivative; monotone operator

Citation: Abood, B.N.; Redhwan, S.S.; Bazighifan, O.; Nonlaopon, K. Investigating a Generalized Fractional Quadratic Integral Equation. *Fractal Fract.* **2022**, *6*, 251. https://doi.org/10.3390/fractalfract6050251

Academic Editors: António M. Lopes, Alireza Alfi, Liping Chen and Sergio Adriani David

Received: 17 March 2022
Accepted: 27 April 2022
Published: 1 May 2022

Publisher's Note: MDPI stays neutral with regard to jurisdictional claims in published maps and institutional affiliations.

1. Introduction

Fractional differential equations (FDEs) with initial/boundary conditions arise from a set of applications included in different fields of science and engineering, e.g., practical problems, conservative systems, concerning mechanics, physics, harmonic oscillator, biology, economy, control systems, chemistry, atomic energy, medicine, information theory, nonlinear oscillations, the engineering technique fields; this is because FDEs characterize many real-world processes linked to memory and hereditary properties of different materials more carefully as compared to classical order differential equations. For further details [1–5].

In [6], Hilfer was given a generalization of fractional derivatives (FDs) of Riemann–Liouville (RL) and Caputo, with the so-called Hilfer FD of order q and a type p, $0 < p < 1$. More specifics on this FD mentioned above can be found in [7,8]. In Ref. [9], the researchers introduced the FD with another function in the frame of Hilfer FD, with the so-called $\zeta-$Hilfer FD. For some new results of ζ-Hilfer type initial value problems (IVPs), see [10–13] and, for boundary value problems (BVPs), see [14–16].

In recent decades, there has been a lot of enthusiasm for the Adomian decomposition method (ADM), which is an analytical technique for solving broad types of functional equations. The method was successfully applied to a lot of employments in applied sciences. Here, we also refer to some recent works [17–20] dealing with the technique and its application.

In [21], Picard's Method (PM) creates a sequence of increasingly specific algebraic approximations of the curtained precise solution of the first-order differential equation with an initial value.

First, they compare the PM method with the ADM by [20,22] on a group of examples. In [23], the researchers contrasted the two techniques for a quadratic integral equation (QIE).

The QIEs can be widely applicable in more applications like the dynamic theory of gases, the theory of radiative exchange, the traffic theory, etc. The QIEs have been the focus of several papers and monographs, see [23–28].

For example, the researchers in [23] proved the existence and uniqueness of the solution for

$$\varkappa(\vartheta) = h(\vartheta) + \mathfrak{g}(\vartheta, \varkappa(\vartheta)) \int_0^{\vartheta} \mathcal{F}(v, \varkappa(v))dv,$$

by using the Adomian method and Picard method. In [29], the investigators discussed the analytical and approximate solutions for the fractional quadratic integral equation (FQIE)

$$x(\vartheta) = h(\vartheta) + \mathfrak{g}(\vartheta, x(\vartheta))\, \mathbb{I}_{0^+}^{q;\rho} \mathcal{F}(\vartheta, x(\vartheta)),\ \vartheta \in \mathcal{J} = [0,1],\ q > 0,$$

where $\mathbb{I}_{0^+}^{q;\rho}$ is the Katugampola fractional integral.

In this article, we give the analytical and approximate solutions for the following fractional quadratic integral equation (FQIE)

$$\varkappa(\vartheta) = h(\vartheta) + g(\vartheta, \varkappa(\vartheta))\mathbb{I}_{0^+}^{q;\zeta} \mathcal{F}(\vartheta, \varkappa(\vartheta)),\ \vartheta \in \mathcal{J} = [0,1],\ q > 0, \tag{1}$$

where $\mathbb{I}_{0^+}^{q;\zeta}$ is the left sided ζ-RL fractional integral of order q defined by

$$\mathbb{I}_{0^+}^{q;\zeta} \mathcal{F}(\vartheta, \varkappa(\vartheta)) = \frac{1}{\Gamma(q)} \int_0^{\vartheta} \zeta'(v)(\zeta(\vartheta) - \zeta(v))^{q-1} \mathcal{F}(v, \varkappa(v))dv.$$

Observe that the considered equation is investigated under the Riemann–Liouville integral of fractional order and with respect to another function. In fact, for problem (1), the existence and uniqueness of solutions can be proved readily by using fixed point theorems. However, in general, it is difficult to obtain the exact solutions of (1) directly, due to the Riemann–Liouville operator not having good regularities. Relying on this motivation, recently Kilbas et al. [1] and Almeida [30] provided generalized definitions of fractional calculus involving another function. In this regard, we first give recent results on existence and uniqueness of (1) based on Banach's fixed point theorem and then apply the Adomian decomposition method and Picard method to obtain an approximate solution for (1). Particularly, if $\zeta(\vartheta) = \vartheta$, $\zeta(\vartheta) = log(\vartheta)$, and $\zeta(\vartheta) = \vartheta^{\rho}$, then our results will reduce to the classical Riemann–Liouville, Hadamard, and Katugampola fractional quadratic integral equation, respectively.

The article is formed as follows. In Section 2, we present some notations and definitions used all through the article. Our main results for the generalized FQIE (1) are addressed in Section 3. An example to explain the acquired results is constructed in Section 4.

2. Preliminaries

In this section, we set some notations and introductory facts that will be applied in the proofs of the subsequent results.

Let $C(\mathcal{J}, \mathbb{R})$ be the Banach space of continuous functions and $L(\mathcal{J}, \mathbb{R})$ are Lebesgue integrable functions from $\mathcal{J}$ into $\mathbb{R}$ with the norms

$$\|z\|_{\infty} = \sup\{|z(\vartheta)| : \vartheta \in \mathcal{J}\},$$

and

$$\|z\|_{L} = \int_a^b |z(\vartheta)|d\vartheta,$$

respectively.

For $\varsigma = q + 2p - qp$, where $1 < q < 2$, and $0 \leq p \leq 1$, then $1 < \varsigma \leq 2$. Let $\zeta \in C^1(\mathcal{J}, \mathbb{R})$ be an increasing function with $\zeta'(\vartheta) \neq 0$, for all $\vartheta \in \mathcal{J}$.

Definition 1 ([1]). *Let $q > 0$ and $\mathcal{F} \in L^1(\mathcal{J}, \mathbb{R})$. The ζ-RL fractional integral of order q of a function $\mathcal{F}$ is given by*

$$\mathbb{I}^{q;\zeta}\mathcal{F}(\vartheta, \varkappa(\vartheta)) = \frac{1}{\Gamma(q)} \int_a^\vartheta \zeta'(v)(\zeta(\vartheta) - \zeta(v))^{q-1}\mathcal{F}(\vartheta, \varkappa(\vartheta))dv,$$

where $\Gamma(\cdot)$ denotes the Gamma function.

Lemma 1 ([1,9]). *Let $q, \eta, \delta > 0$. Then,*

1. $\mathbb{I}^{q;\zeta}\mathbb{I}^{\eta;\zeta}\mathcal{F}(\vartheta, \varkappa(\vartheta)) = \mathbb{I}^{q+\eta;\zeta}\mathcal{F}(\vartheta, \varkappa(\vartheta))$.
2. $\mathbb{I}^{q;\zeta}(\zeta(\vartheta) - \zeta(a))^{\delta-1} = \frac{\Gamma(\delta)}{\Gamma(q+\delta)}(\zeta(\vartheta) - \zeta(a))^{q+\delta-1}$.

Here, we can suffice to refer to Banach's fixed point theorem [31] and Krasnoselskii's fixed point theorem [31].

3. Main Results

Let us introduce the following hypotheses which are used to investigate the FQDE (1).

1. $h : \mathcal{J} \to \mathbb{R}$ is a continuous function on $\mathcal{J}$.
2. $\mathcal{F}, g : \mathbb{J} \times \mathbb{R} \to \mathbb{R}$ are a bounded and continuous function with $\mu_1 = \sup_{(\vartheta,\varkappa)\in\mathcal{J}\times\mathbb{R}}|g(\vartheta, \varkappa)|$, and $\mu_2 = \sup_{(\vartheta,\varkappa)\in\mathcal{J}\times\mathbb{R}}|\mathcal{F}(\vartheta, \varkappa)|$.
3. There exist two constants $\hbar_1, \hbar_2 > 0$ such that

$$\begin{aligned} |g(\vartheta, \varkappa) - g(\vartheta, \mathrm{y})| &\leq \hbar_1|\varkappa - \mathrm{y}|, \\ |\mathcal{F}(\vartheta, \varkappa) - \mathcal{F}(\vartheta, \mathrm{y})| &\leq \hbar_2|\varkappa - \mathrm{y}|, \end{aligned}$$

for all $\vartheta \in \mathcal{J}$ and $\varkappa, \mathrm{y} \in \mathbb{R}$.

Our first result is based on Banach's fixed point theorem to obtain the uniqueness solution of the nonlinear FQIE (1).

3.1. Existence and Uniqueness of Solutions

Theorem 1. *Suppose* (1), (2) *and* (3) *hold. If*

$$\Upsilon := \left(\frac{\hbar_1\mu_2 + \hbar_2\mu_1}{\Gamma(q+1)}\right) < 1,$$

then the nonlinear FQIE (1) has a unique solution $\varkappa \in C(\mathcal{J})$.

Proof. It is easy to see that $\Pi : C(\mathcal{J}) \to C(\mathcal{J})$, where

$$(\Pi\varkappa)(\vartheta) = h(\vartheta) + g(\vartheta, \varkappa(\vartheta)) \int_0^\vartheta \frac{\zeta'(v)}{\Gamma(q)}(\zeta(\vartheta) - \zeta(v))^{q-1}\mathcal{F}(v, \varkappa(v))dv, \ \vartheta \in \mathcal{J}, \ q > 0.$$

Now, let $\mathcal{B}_r \subset C(\mathcal{J})$ where $\mathcal{B}_r$ is defined as

$$\mathcal{B}_r = \{\varkappa(\vartheta) \in C(\mathcal{J}) : |\varkappa(\vartheta) - h(\vartheta)| \leq r, \text{ for } \vartheta \in \mathcal{J}\}.$$

If we choose $r = \frac{\mu_1\mu_2}{\Gamma(q+1)}$, then the operator $\Pi : \mathcal{B}_r \to \mathcal{B}_r$. Indeed, for $\varkappa \in \mathcal{B}_r$, we have

$$\begin{aligned}
|\varkappa(\vartheta) - h(\vartheta)| &\leq |g(\vartheta, \varkappa(\vartheta))| \int_0^\vartheta \frac{\zeta'(v)}{\Gamma(q)}(\zeta(\vartheta) - \zeta(v))^{q-1}|\mathcal{F}(v, \varkappa(v))|dv \\
&\leq \mu_1\mu_2 \int_0^\vartheta \frac{\zeta'(v)}{\Gamma(q)}(\zeta(\vartheta) - \zeta(v))^{q-1}dv \\
&\leq \frac{\mu_1\mu_2}{\Gamma(q+1)}(\zeta(\vartheta))^q \\
&\leq \frac{\mu_1\mu_2}{\Gamma(q+1)} = r.
\end{aligned}$$

In addition, $\mathcal{B}_r$ is a closed subset of $C(\mathcal{J})$. In order to prove that Π is a contraction, we have

$$\begin{aligned}
(\Pi\varkappa)(\vartheta) - (\Pi y)(\vartheta) &= g(\vartheta, \varkappa(\vartheta)) \int_0^\vartheta \frac{\zeta'(v)}{\Gamma(q)}(\zeta(\vartheta) - \zeta(v))^{q-1}\mathcal{F}(v, \varkappa(v))dv \\
&\quad -g(\vartheta, y(\vartheta)) \int_0^\vartheta \frac{\zeta'(v)}{\Gamma(q)}(\zeta(\vartheta) - \zeta(v))^{q-1}\mathcal{F}(v, y(v))dv \\
&\quad +g(\vartheta, \varkappa(\vartheta)) \int_0^\vartheta \frac{\zeta'(v)}{\Gamma(q)}(\zeta(\vartheta) - \zeta(v))^{q-1}\mathcal{F}(v, y(v))dv \\
&\quad -g(\vartheta, \varkappa(\vartheta)) \int_0^\vartheta \frac{\zeta'(v)}{\Gamma(q)}(\zeta(\vartheta) - \zeta(v))^{q-1}\mathcal{F}(v, y(v))dv \\
&= [g(\vartheta, \varkappa(\vartheta) - g(\vartheta, y(\vartheta)] \int_0^\vartheta \frac{\zeta'(v)}{\Gamma(q)}(\zeta(\vartheta) - \zeta(v))^{q-1}\mathcal{F}(v, y(v))dv \\
&\quad +g(\vartheta, \varkappa(\vartheta)) \int_0^\vartheta \frac{\zeta'(v)}{\Gamma(q)}(\zeta(\vartheta) - \zeta(v))^{q-1}[\mathcal{F}(v, \varkappa(v)) - \mathcal{F}(v, \varkappa(v)]dv.
\end{aligned}$$

Then,

$$\begin{aligned}
&|(\Pi\varkappa)(\vartheta) - (\Pi y)(\vartheta)| \\
\leq\ & |g(\vartheta, \varkappa(\vartheta) - g(\vartheta, y(\vartheta)| \int_0^\vartheta \frac{\zeta'(v)}{\Gamma(q)}(\zeta(\vartheta) - \zeta(v))^{q-1}|\mathcal{F}(v, y(v))|dv \\
&+|g(\vartheta, \varkappa(\vartheta))| \int_0^\vartheta \frac{\zeta'(v)}{\Gamma(q)}(\zeta(\vartheta) - \zeta(v))^{q-1}|\mathcal{F}(v, \varkappa(v)) - \mathcal{F}(v, \varkappa(v)|dv \\
\leq\ & \frac{\hbar_1\mu_2}{\Gamma(q+1)}(\zeta(\vartheta))^q|\varkappa(\vartheta) - y(\vartheta)| + \hbar_2\mu_1 \int_0^\vartheta \frac{\zeta'(v)}{\Gamma(q)}(\zeta(\vartheta) - \zeta(v))^{q-1}|\varkappa(v) - y(v)|dv \\
\leq\ & \frac{\hbar_1\mu_2}{\Gamma(q+1)}|\varkappa(\vartheta) - y(\vartheta)| + \hbar_2\mu_1 \int_0^\vartheta \frac{\zeta'(v)}{\Gamma(q)}(\zeta(\vartheta) - \zeta(v))^{q-1}|\varkappa(v) - y(v)|dv,
\end{aligned}$$

which implies □

$$\begin{aligned}
\|(\Pi\varkappa)(\vartheta) - (\Pi y)(\vartheta)\| &= \sup_{\vartheta\in\mathcal{J}}|(\Pi\varkappa)(\vartheta) - (\Pi y)(\vartheta)| \\
&\leq \frac{\hbar_1\mu_2}{\Gamma(q+1)}\|\varkappa - y\| + \hbar_2\mu_1\|\varkappa - y\| \int_0^\vartheta \frac{\zeta'(v)}{\Gamma(q)}(\zeta(\vartheta) - \zeta(v))^{q-1}dv \\
&\leq \frac{\hbar_1\mu_2}{\Gamma(q+1)}\|\varkappa - y\| + \frac{\hbar_2\mu_1}{\Gamma(q+1)}\|\varkappa - y\| \\
&= \Upsilon\|\varkappa - y\|.
\end{aligned}$$

Since $\Upsilon < 1$, the operator Π is a contraction mapping. Hence, as a consequence of Banach's fixed point theorem, the FQIE (1) has a unique solution $\varkappa \in C(\mathcal{J})$. This complete the proof.

3.2. Picard Method (PM)

By applying the PM to the FQEI (1), the solution is framed by the sequence

$$\begin{cases} \varkappa_n(\vartheta) = h(\vartheta) + g(\vartheta, \varkappa_{n-1}(\vartheta)) \int_0^\vartheta \frac{\zeta'(v)}{\Gamma(q)}(\zeta(\vartheta) - \zeta(v))^{q-1}\mathcal{F}(v, \varkappa_{n-1}(v))dv, \ n = 1, 2, \ldots \\ \varkappa_0(\vartheta) = h(\vartheta) \end{cases}. \tag{2}$$

The functions $\varkappa_n$ can be written as

$$\varkappa_n = \varkappa_0 + \sum_{j=1}^{n} [\varkappa_j - \varkappa_{j-1}],$$

where the functions $\{\varkappa_n(\vartheta)\}_{n\geq 1}$ are continuous.

If the infinite series $\sum[\varkappa_j - \varkappa_{j-1}]$ converges, then the sequence functions $\varkappa_n(\vartheta)$ will converge to $\varkappa(\vartheta)$. Consequently, the solution will be

$$\varkappa(\vartheta) = \lim_{n\to\infty} \varkappa_n(\vartheta).$$

Now, we show that $\{\varkappa_n(\vartheta)\}_{n\geq 1}$ has uniform convergence. Consider the infinite series

$$\sum_{n=1}^{\infty} [\varkappa_n(\vartheta) - \varkappa_{n-1}(\vartheta)].$$

From (2) for $n = 1$, we achieve

$$\varkappa_1(\vartheta) - \varkappa_0(\vartheta) = g(\vartheta, \varkappa_0(\vartheta)) \int_0^\vartheta \frac{\zeta'(v)}{\Gamma(q)}(\zeta(\vartheta) - \zeta(v))^{q-1}\mathcal{F}(v, \varkappa_0(v))dv.$$

Consequently,

$$|\varkappa_1(\vartheta) - \varkappa_0(\vartheta)| \leq \mu_1\mu_2 \int_0^\vartheta \frac{\zeta'(v)}{\Gamma(q)}(\zeta(\vartheta) - \zeta(v))^{q-1}dv < \frac{\mu_1\mu_2}{\Gamma(q+1)}(\zeta(\vartheta))^q. \tag{3}$$

Here, we find the expression $\varkappa_n(\vartheta) - \varkappa_{n-1}(\vartheta)$, for $n \geq 2$ as

$$\begin{aligned}
&\varkappa_n(\vartheta) - \varkappa_{n-1}(\vartheta) \\
= \ & g(\vartheta, \varkappa_{n-1}(\vartheta)) \int_0^\vartheta \frac{\zeta'(v)}{\Gamma(q)}(\zeta(\vartheta) - \zeta(v))^{q-1}\mathcal{F}(v, \varkappa_{n-1}(v))dv \\
& - g(\vartheta, \varkappa_{n-2}(\vartheta)) \int_0^\vartheta \frac{\zeta'(v)}{\Gamma(q)}(\zeta(\vartheta) - \zeta(v))^{q-1}\mathcal{F}(v, \varkappa_{n-2}(v))dv \\
& + g(\vartheta, \varkappa_{n-1}(\vartheta)) \int_0^\vartheta \frac{\zeta'(v)}{\Gamma(q)}(\zeta(\vartheta) - \zeta(v))^{q-1}\mathcal{F}(v, \varkappa_{n-2}(v))dv \\
& - g(\vartheta, \varkappa_{n-1}(\vartheta)) \int_0^\vartheta \frac{\zeta'(v)}{\Gamma(q)}(\zeta(\vartheta) - \zeta(v))^{q-1}\mathcal{F}(v, \varkappa_{n-2}(v))dv \\
= \ & g(\vartheta, \varkappa_{n-1}(\vartheta)) \int_0^\vartheta \frac{\zeta'(v)}{\Gamma(q)}(\zeta(\vartheta) - \zeta(v))^{q-1}[\mathcal{F}(v, \varkappa_{n-1}(v)) - \mathcal{F}(v, \varkappa_{n-2}(v)]dv \\
& + [g(\vartheta, \varkappa_{n-1}(\vartheta) - g(\vartheta, \varkappa_{n-2}(\vartheta)] \int_0^\vartheta \frac{\zeta'(v)}{\Gamma(q)}(\zeta(\vartheta) - \zeta(v))^{q-1}\mathcal{F}(v, \varkappa_{n-2}(v))dv.
\end{aligned}$$

Using Hypotheses (2) and (3), we attain

$$
\begin{aligned}
&|\varkappa_n(\vartheta) - \varkappa_{n-1}(\vartheta)| \\
\leq\ & |g(\vartheta, \varkappa_{n-1}(\vartheta))| \int_0^\vartheta \frac{\zeta'(v)}{\Gamma(q)}(\zeta(\vartheta) - \zeta(v))^{q-1} |\mathcal{F}(v, \varkappa_{n-1}(v)) - \mathcal{F}(v, \varkappa_{n-2}(v)| dv \\
& + |g(\vartheta, \varkappa_{n-1}(\vartheta)) - g(\vartheta, \varkappa_{n-2}(\vartheta))| \int_0^\vartheta \frac{\zeta'(v)}{\Gamma(q)}(\zeta(\vartheta) - \zeta(v))^{q-1} |\mathcal{F}(v, \varkappa_{n-2}(v))| dv \\
\leq\ & \hbar_2 \mu_1 \int_0^\vartheta \frac{\zeta'(v)}{\Gamma(q)}(\zeta(\vartheta) - \zeta(v))^{q-1} |\varkappa_{n-1}(v) - \varkappa_{n-2}(v)| dv \\
& + \hbar_1 \mu_2 |\varkappa_{n-1}(\vartheta) - \varkappa_{n-2}(\vartheta)| \int_0^\vartheta \frac{\zeta'(v)}{\Gamma(q)}(\zeta(\vartheta) - \zeta(v))^{q-1} dv.
\end{aligned}
$$

By taking $n = 2$, and using (3), we obtain

$$
\begin{aligned}
|\varkappa_2(\vartheta) - \varkappa_1(\vartheta)| \leq\ & \hbar_2 \mu_1 \int_0^\vartheta \frac{\zeta'(v)}{\Gamma(q)}(\zeta(\vartheta) - \zeta(v))^{q-1} |\varkappa_1(v) - \varkappa_0(v)| dv \\
& + \hbar_1 \mu_2 |\varkappa_1(\vartheta) - \varkappa_0(\vartheta)| \int_0^\vartheta \frac{\zeta'(v)}{\Gamma(q)}(\zeta(\vartheta) - \zeta(v))^{q-1} dv \\
\leq\ & \frac{\hbar_2 \mu_1^2 \mu_2}{\Gamma(q+1)} \int_0^\vartheta \frac{\zeta'(v)}{\Gamma(q)}(\zeta(\vartheta) - \zeta(v))^{q-1} (\zeta(v))^q dv \\
& + \frac{\hbar_1 \mu_2^2 \mu_1}{\Gamma(q+1)} (\zeta(\vartheta))^q \frac{(\zeta(\vartheta))^q}{\Gamma(q+1)} \\
\leq\ & \frac{\hbar_2 \mu_1^2 \mu_2}{\Gamma(q+1)} \frac{\Gamma(q+1)}{\Gamma(2q+1)} (\zeta(\vartheta))^{2q} \\
& + \frac{\hbar_1 \mu_2^2 \mu_1}{\Gamma(q+1)\Gamma(q+1)} (\zeta(\vartheta))^{2q} \\
\leq\ & \frac{\mu_1 \mu_2}{\Gamma(q+1)} \left[\hbar_2 \mu_1 \frac{\Gamma(q+1)}{\Gamma(2q+1)} + \frac{\hbar_1 \mu_2}{\Gamma(q+1)} \right] (\zeta(\vartheta))^{2q}.
\end{aligned}
$$

Similarly, for $n = 3$,

$$
\begin{aligned}
|\varkappa_3(\vartheta) - \varkappa_2(\vartheta)| \leq\ & \hbar_2 \mu_1 \int_0^\vartheta \frac{\zeta'(v)}{\Gamma(q)}(\zeta(\vartheta) - \zeta(v))^{q-1} |\varkappa_2(\vartheta) - \varkappa_1(\vartheta)| dv \\
& + \hbar_1 \mu_2 |\varkappa_2(\vartheta) - \varkappa_1(\vartheta)| \int_0^\vartheta \frac{\zeta'(v)}{\Gamma(q)}(\zeta(\vartheta) - \zeta(v))^{q-1} dv \\
\leq\ & \frac{\mu_1 \mu_2}{\Gamma(q+1)} \left(\hbar_2 \mu_1 \frac{\Gamma(q+1)}{\Gamma(2q+1)} + \frac{\hbar_1 \mu_2}{\Gamma(q+1)} \right) \\
& \times \left(\hbar_2 \mu_1 \frac{\Gamma(2q+1)}{\Gamma(3q+1)} + \frac{\hbar_1 \mu_2}{\Gamma(q+1)} \right) (\zeta(\vartheta))^{3q}.
\end{aligned}
$$

Repeating this process, we obtain

$$\begin{aligned}
|\varkappa_n(\vartheta) - \varkappa_{n-1}(\vartheta)| &\leq \frac{\mu_1\mu_2}{\Gamma(q+1)}\left(\hbar_2\mu_1\frac{\Gamma(q+1)}{\Gamma(2q+1)} + \frac{\hbar_1\mu_2}{\Gamma(q+1)}\right) \\
&\times\left(\hbar_2\mu_1\frac{\Gamma(2q+1)}{\Gamma(3q+1)} + \frac{\hbar_1\mu_2}{\Gamma(q+1)}\right)\times\dots \\
&\times\left(\hbar_2\mu_1\frac{\Gamma((n-1)q+1)}{\Gamma(nq+1)} + \frac{\hbar_1\mu_2}{\Gamma(q+1)}\right)(\zeta(\vartheta))^{nq} \\
&\leq \frac{\mu_1\mu_2}{\Gamma(q+1)}\left(\hbar_2\mu_1\frac{\Gamma(q+1)}{\Gamma(q+1)} + \frac{\hbar_1\mu_2}{\Gamma(q+1)}\right) \\
&\times\left(\hbar_2\mu_1\frac{\Gamma(2q+1)}{\Gamma(q+1)} + \frac{\hbar_1\mu_2}{\Gamma(q+1)}\right)\times\dots \\
&\times\left(\hbar_2\mu_1\frac{\Gamma((n-1)q+1)}{\Gamma((n-1)q+1)} + \frac{\hbar_1\mu_2}{\Gamma(q+1)}\right) \\
&\leq \frac{\mu_1\mu_2}{\Gamma(q+1)}((\hbar_2\mu_1+\hbar_1\mu_2))\times((\hbar_2\mu_1+\hbar_1\mu_2))\times\dots \\
&\times((\hbar_2\mu_1+\hbar_1\mu_2)) \\
&\leq \frac{\mu_1\mu_2}{\Gamma(q+1)}((\hbar_2\mu_1+\hbar_1\mu_2))^n.
\end{aligned}$$

Since $\left(\frac{\hbar_1\mu_2+\hbar_2\mu_1}{\Gamma(q+1)}\right) < 1$, then the series $\sum_{n=1}^{\infty}[\varkappa_n(\vartheta) - \varkappa_{n-1}(\vartheta)]$ and the sequence $\{\varkappa_n(\vartheta)\}$ are uniformly convergent.

Because $\mathcal{F}(\vartheta,\varkappa)$ and $g(\vartheta,\varkappa)$ are continuous in $\varkappa$, it follows that

$$\begin{aligned}
\varkappa(\vartheta) &= \lim_{n\to\infty} g(\vartheta,\varkappa_n(\vartheta))\int_0^{\vartheta}\frac{\zeta'(v)}{\Gamma(q)}(\zeta(\vartheta)-\zeta(v))^{q-1}\mathcal{F}(v,\varkappa_n(v))dv \\
&= g(\vartheta,\varkappa(\vartheta))\int_0^{\vartheta}\frac{\zeta'(v)}{\Gamma(q)}(\zeta(\vartheta)-\zeta(v))^{q-1}\mathcal{F}(v,\varkappa(v))dv.
\end{aligned}$$

This shows the existence of a solution. Here, we need to show that this solution is unique; let $y(\vartheta)$ be a continuous solution of the FQEI (1) that is

$$y(\vartheta) = h(\vartheta) + g(\vartheta,y(\vartheta))\int_0^{\vartheta}\frac{\zeta'(v)}{\Gamma(q)}(\zeta(\vartheta)-\zeta(v))^{q-1}\mathcal{F}(v,y(v))dv,\ \ \vartheta\in[0,1],\ q>0.$$

Hence,

$$\begin{aligned}
y(\vartheta)-\varkappa_n(\vartheta) &= g(\vartheta,y(\vartheta))\int_0^{\vartheta}\frac{\zeta'(v)}{\Gamma(q)}(\zeta(\vartheta)-\zeta(v))^{q-1}\mathcal{F}(v,y(v))dv \\
&-g(\vartheta,\varkappa_{n-1}(\vartheta))\int_0^{\vartheta}\frac{\zeta'(v)}{\Gamma(q)}(\zeta(\vartheta)-\zeta(v))^{q-1}\mathcal{F}(v,\varkappa_{n-1}(v))dv \\
&+g(\vartheta,y(\vartheta))\int_0^{\vartheta}\frac{\zeta'(v)}{\Gamma(q)}(\zeta(\vartheta)-\zeta(v))^{q-1}\mathcal{F}(v,\varkappa_{n-1}(v))dv \\
&-g(\vartheta,y(\vartheta))\int_0^{\vartheta}\frac{\zeta'(v)}{\Gamma(q)}(\zeta(\vartheta)-\zeta(v))^{q-1}\mathcal{F}(v,\varkappa_{n-1}(v))dv \\
&= g(\vartheta,y(\vartheta))\int_0^{\vartheta}\frac{\zeta'(v)}{\Gamma(q)}(\zeta(\vartheta)-\zeta(v))^{q-1}[\mathcal{F}(v,y(v))-\mathcal{F}(v,\varkappa_{n-1}(v)]dv \\
&+[g(\vartheta,y(\vartheta)-g(\vartheta,\varkappa_{n-1}(\vartheta)]\int_0^{\vartheta}\frac{\zeta'(v)}{\Gamma(q)}(\zeta(\vartheta)-\zeta(v))^{q-1}\mathcal{F}(v,\varkappa_{n-1}(v))dv.
\end{aligned}$$

By using assumptions (2) and (3), we obtain

$$
\begin{aligned}
|\mathrm{y}(\vartheta)-\varkappa_n(\vartheta)| &\leq |g(\vartheta,\mathrm{y}(\vartheta))|\int_0^\vartheta \frac{\zeta'(v)}{\Gamma(q)}(\zeta(\vartheta)-\zeta(v))^{q-1}|\mathcal{F}(v,\mathrm{y}(v))-\mathcal{F}(v,\varkappa_{n-1}(v)|dv \\
&\quad +|g(\vartheta,\mathrm{y}(\vartheta)-g(\vartheta,\varkappa_{n-1}(\vartheta)|\int_0^\vartheta \frac{\zeta'(v)}{\Gamma(q)}(\zeta(\vartheta)-\zeta(v))^{q-1}|\mathcal{F}(v,\varkappa_{n-1}(v))|dv \\
&\leq \hbar_2\mu_1\int_0^\vartheta \frac{\zeta'(v)}{\Gamma(q)}(\zeta(\vartheta)-\zeta(v))^{q-1}|\mathrm{y}(v)-\varkappa_{n-1}(v)|dv \\
&\quad +\hbar_1\mu_2|\mathrm{y}(\vartheta)-\varkappa_{n-1}(\vartheta)|\int_0^\vartheta \frac{\zeta'(v)}{\Gamma(q)}(\zeta(\vartheta)-\zeta(v))^{q-1}dv. \qquad (4)
\end{aligned}
$$

However, we have

$$|\mathrm{y}(\vartheta)-h(\vartheta)|\leq \frac{\mu_1\mu_2}{\Gamma(q+1)}\zeta(\vartheta)^q.$$

Hence, using (4), we obtain

$$|\mathrm{y}(\vartheta)-\varkappa_n(\vartheta)|\leq \frac{\mu_1\mu_2}{\Gamma(q+1)}[(\hbar_2\mu_1+\hbar_1\mu_2)]^n.$$

Consequently,

$$\lim_{n\to\infty}\varkappa_n(\vartheta)=\mathrm{y}(\vartheta)=\varkappa(\vartheta).$$

This ends the proof.

Corollary 1. *Under the assumptions of Theorem 1, if $\zeta(\vartheta)=\vartheta^\rho$, then the FQEI (1) reduces to*

$$\varkappa(\vartheta)=h(\vartheta)+g(\vartheta,\varkappa(\vartheta))\int_0^\vartheta \frac{v^{\rho-1}}{\Gamma(q)}\left(\frac{\vartheta^\rho-v^\rho}{\rho}\right)^{q-1}\mathcal{F}(v,\varkappa(v))dv,$$

which has a unique solution; see [29].

3.3. AD Method (ADM)

In this section, we will analyze ADM for the FQEI (1). The solution algorithm of the FQEI (1) by applying ADM is

$$\varkappa_0(\vartheta)=h(\vartheta), \qquad (5)$$

$$\varkappa_\ell(\vartheta)=\varpi_{(\ell-1)}(\vartheta)\,\mathbb{I}_{0^+}^{q;\zeta}\omega_{(\ell-1)}(\vartheta), \qquad (6)$$

where ϖ_ℓ and ω_ℓ are Adomian polynomials of the nonlinear terms $g(\vartheta,\varkappa)$ and $\mathcal{F}(v,\varkappa)$, respectively, which forms as follows:

$$\varpi_n=\frac{1}{n!}\left[\frac{d^n}{d\lambda^n}\left(g\left(\vartheta,\sum_{\ell=0}^{\infty}\lambda^\ell\varkappa_\ell\right)\right)\right]_{\lambda=0}, \qquad (7)$$

$$\omega_n=\frac{1}{n!}\left[\frac{d^n}{d\lambda^n}\left(\mathcal{F}\left(\vartheta,\sum_{\ell=0}^{\infty}\lambda^\ell\varkappa_\ell\right)\right)\right]_{\lambda=0}. \qquad (8)$$

Now, we will show the solution as

$$\varkappa(\vartheta)=\sum_{\ell=0}^{\infty}\varkappa_\ell. \qquad (9)$$

3.4. Convergence Analysis

Theorem 2. *Let $\varkappa(\vartheta)$ be a solution of the FQIE (1) and there exists a positive constant $\mathbb{M}$ satisfying $|\varkappa_1(\vartheta)|<\mathbb{M}$. Then, solution (9) of the FQIE (1) applying ADM converges.*

Proof. Let $\{\mathbb{S}_{\varrho_1}\}$ be a sequence such that $\{\mathbb{S}_{\varrho_1}\} = \sum_{\ell=0}^{\varrho_1} \varkappa_\ell$ is a sequence of partial sums from the series (9) and we have

$$\begin{aligned} g(\vartheta,\varkappa) &= \sum_{\ell=0}^{\infty} \varpi_\ell, \\ \mathcal{F}(\vartheta,\varkappa) &= \sum_{\ell=0}^{\infty} \omega_\ell. \end{aligned}$$

Set $\mathbb{S}_{\varrho_1}$ and let $\mathbb{S}_{\varrho_2}$ be two partial sums with $\varrho_1 > \varrho_2$. Now, we show that $\mathbb{S}_{\varrho_1}$ is a Cauchy sequence in $C(\mathcal{J})$.

$$\begin{aligned} \mathbb{S}_{\varrho_1} - \mathbb{S}_{\varrho_2} &= \sum_{\ell=0}^{\varrho_1} \varkappa_\ell - \sum_{\ell=0}^{\varrho_2} \varkappa_\ell \\ &= \sum_{\ell=0}^{\varrho_1} \varpi_{(\ell-1)}(\vartheta)\left(\mathbb{I}_{0^+}^{q;\zeta} \sum_{\ell=0}^{\varrho_1} \omega_{(\ell-1)}(\vartheta)\right) - \sum_{\ell=0}^{\varrho_2} \varpi_{(\ell-1)}(\vartheta)\left(\mathbb{I}_{0^+}^{q;\zeta} \sum_{\ell=0}^{\varrho_2} \omega_{(\ell-1)}(\vartheta)\right) \\ &= \sum_{\ell=0}^{\varrho_1} \varpi_{(\ell-1)}(\vartheta)\left(\mathbb{I}_{0^+}^{q;\zeta} \sum_{\ell=0}^{\varrho_1} \omega_{(\ell-1)}(\vartheta)\right) - \sum_{\ell=0}^{\varrho_2} \varpi_{(\ell-1)}(\vartheta)\left(\mathbb{I}_{0^+}^{q;\zeta} \sum_{\ell=0}^{\varrho_1} \omega_{(\ell-1)}(\vartheta)\right) \\ &\quad + \sum_{\ell=0}^{\varrho_2} \varpi_{(\ell-1)}(\vartheta)\left(\mathbb{I}_{0^+}^{q;\zeta} \sum_{\ell=0}^{\varrho_1} \omega_{(\ell-1)}(\vartheta)\right) - \sum_{\ell=0}^{\varrho_2} \varpi_{(\ell-1)}(\vartheta)\left(\mathbb{I}_{0^+}^{q;\zeta} \sum_{\ell=0}^{\varrho_2} \omega_{(\ell-1)}(\vartheta)\right) \\ &= \left[\sum_{\ell=0}^{\varrho_1} \varpi_{(\ell-1)}(\vartheta) - \sum_{\ell=0}^{\varrho_2} \varpi_{(\ell-1)}(\vartheta)\right]\left(\mathbb{I}_{0^+}^{q;\zeta} \sum_{\ell=0}^{\varrho_1} \omega_{(\ell-1)}(\vartheta)\right) \\ &\quad + \sum_{\ell=0}^{\varrho_2} \varpi_{(\ell-1)}(\vartheta)\left(\mathbb{I}_{0^+}^{q;\zeta}\left[\sum_{\ell=0}^{\varrho_1} \omega_{(\ell-1)}(\vartheta) - \sum_{\ell=0}^{\varrho_2} \omega_{(\ell-1)}(\vartheta)\right]\right) \end{aligned}$$

However,

$$\begin{aligned} \|\mathbb{S}_{\varrho_1} - \mathbb{S}_{\varrho_2}\| &\le \max_{\vartheta\in\mathcal{J}}\left|\sum_{\ell=\varrho_2+1}^{\varrho_1} \varpi_{(\ell-1)}(\vartheta)\left(\mathbb{I}_{0^+}^{q;\zeta} \sum_{\ell=0}^{\varrho_1} \omega_{(\ell-1)}(\vartheta)\right)\right| \\ &\quad + \max_{\vartheta\in\mathcal{J}}\left|\sum_{\ell=0}^{\varrho_2} \varpi_{(\ell-1)}(\vartheta)\left(\mathbb{I}_{0^+}^{q;\zeta} \sum_{\ell=\varrho_2+1}^{\varrho_1} \omega_{(\ell-1)}(\vartheta)\right)\right| \\ &\le \max_{\vartheta\in\mathcal{J}}\left|\sum_{\ell=\varrho_2}^{\varrho_1-1} \varpi_\ell(\vartheta)\right|\left|\mathbb{I}_{0^+}^{q;\zeta} \sum_{\ell=0}^{\varrho_1} \omega_{(\ell-1)}(\vartheta)\right| + \max_{\vartheta\in\mathcal{J}}\left|\sum_{\ell=0}^{\varrho_2} \varpi_{(\ell-1)}(\vartheta)\right|\left|\sum_{\ell=\varrho_2}^{\varrho_1-1} \omega_\ell(\vartheta)\right| \\ &\le \max_{\vartheta\in\mathcal{J}}|g(\vartheta,\mathbb{S}_{\varrho_1-1}) - g(\vartheta,\mathbb{S}_{\varrho_2-1})| \int_0^\vartheta \frac{\zeta'(v)}{\Gamma(q)}(\zeta(\vartheta)-\zeta(v))^{q-1}|\mathcal{F}(v,\mathbb{S}_{\varrho_1})|dv \\ &\quad + \max_{\vartheta\in\mathcal{J}}|g(\vartheta,\mathbb{S}_{\varrho_2})| \int_0^\vartheta \frac{\zeta'(v)}{\Gamma(q)}(\zeta(\vartheta)-\zeta(v))^{q-1}|\mathcal{F}(v,\mathbb{S}_{\varrho_1-1}) - \mathcal{F}(v,\mathbb{S}_{\varrho_2-1})|dv \\ &\le \hbar_1\mu_2 \max_{\vartheta\in\mathcal{J}}|\mathbb{S}_{\varrho_1-1} - \mathbb{S}_{\varrho_2-1}| \int_0^\vartheta \frac{\zeta'(v)}{\Gamma(q)}(\zeta(\vartheta)-\zeta(v))^{q-1}dv \\ &\quad + \hbar_2\mu_1 \max_{\vartheta\in\mathcal{J}}|\mathbb{S}_{\varrho_1-1} - \mathbb{S}_{\varrho_2-1}| \int_0^\vartheta \frac{\zeta'(v)}{\Gamma(q)}(\zeta(\vartheta)-\zeta(v))^{q-1}dv \\ &\le \frac{1}{\Gamma(q+1)}[(\hbar_2\mu_1 + \hbar_1\mu_2)] \max_{\vartheta\in\mathcal{J}}|\mathbb{S}_{\varrho_1-1} - \mathbb{S}_{\varrho_2-1}| \\ &\le \Upsilon\|\mathbb{S}_{\varrho_1-1} - \mathbb{S}_{\varrho_2-1}\|. \end{aligned}$$

Let $\varrho_1 = \varrho_2 + 1$; then,

$$\|\mathbb{S}_{\varrho_2+1} - \mathbb{S}_{\varrho_2}\| \le \Upsilon\|\mathbb{S}_{\varrho_2} - \mathbb{S}_{\varrho_2-1}\| \le \Upsilon^2\|\mathbb{S}_{\varrho_2-1} - \mathbb{S}_{\varrho_2-2}\| \le \cdots \le \Upsilon^{\varrho_2}\|\mathbb{S}_1 - \mathbb{S}_0\|.$$

In addition, we have

$$\begin{aligned}\|\mathbb{S}_{\varrho_1}-\mathbb{S}_{\varrho_2}\| &\leq \|\mathbb{S}_{\varrho_2+1}-\mathbb{S}_{\varrho_2}\|+\|\mathbb{S}_{\varrho_2+2}-\mathbb{S}_{\varrho_2+1}\|+\cdots+\|\mathbb{S}_{\varrho_1}-\mathbb{S}_{\varrho_1-1}\| \\ &\leq \left[\Upsilon^{\varrho_2}+\Upsilon^{\varrho_2+1}+\cdots+\Upsilon^{\varrho_1-1}\right]\|\mathbb{S}_1-\mathbb{S}_0\| \\ &\leq \Upsilon^{\varrho_2}\left[1+\Upsilon+\cdots+\Upsilon^{\varrho_1-\varrho_2-1}\right]\|\mathbb{S}_1-\mathbb{S}_0\| \\ &\leq \Upsilon^{\varrho_2}\left[\frac{1-\Upsilon^{\varrho_1-\varrho_2}}{1-\Upsilon}\right]\|\varkappa_1\|.\end{aligned}$$

The assumptions $0<\Upsilon<1$, and $\varrho_1>\varrho_2$ lead to $(1-\Upsilon^{\varrho_1-\varrho_2})\leq 1$. Hence,

$$\begin{aligned}\|\mathbb{S}_{\varrho_1}-\mathbb{S}_{\varrho_2}\| &\leq \frac{\Upsilon^{\varrho_2}}{1-\Upsilon}\|\varkappa_1\| \\ &\leq \frac{\Upsilon^{\varrho_2}}{1-\Upsilon}\max_{\vartheta\in\mathcal{J}}|\varkappa_1(\vartheta)|.\end{aligned}$$

However, $|\varkappa_1(\vartheta)|<\mathbb{M}$ and as $\varrho_2\to\infty$, then $\|\mathbb{S}_{\varrho_1}-\mathbb{S}_{\varrho_2}\|\to 0$ and hence $\{\mathbb{S}_{\varrho_1}\}$ is a Cauchy sequence in $C(\mathcal{J})$, and the series $\sum_{\ell=0}^{\infty}\varkappa_\ell(\vartheta)$ converges. □

4. Numerical Example

In this part, we will study numerical example via Picard and ADM methods.

Example 1. *Consider the following nonlinear FQIE:*

$$\varkappa(\vartheta)=\left(\vartheta^3-\frac{104\vartheta^{\frac{17}{2}}}{750}\right)+\frac{1}{4}\varkappa(\vartheta)\mathbb{I}_{0^+}^{\frac{1}{2};\zeta}\varkappa^4(\vartheta). \tag{10}$$

Here, the $\varkappa(\vartheta)=\vartheta^3$ is the exact solution for (10).

Taking $\zeta=\frac{1}{2}$, and applying PM to (10), we obtain

$$\varkappa_n(\vartheta)=\left(\vartheta^3-\frac{104\vartheta^{\frac{17}{2}}}{750}\right)+\frac{1}{4}\varkappa_{n-1}(\vartheta)\mathbb{I}_{0^+}^{\frac{1}{2};\frac{1}{2}}\varkappa_{n-1}^4(\vartheta),\quad n=1,2,\cdots,$$

$$\varkappa_0(\vartheta)=\left(\vartheta^3-\frac{104\vartheta^{\frac{17}{2}}}{750}\right).$$

and the solution will be in the form

$$\varkappa(\vartheta)=\varkappa_n(\vartheta).$$

Again, applying ADM to (10), we obtain

$$\varkappa_0(\vartheta)=\left(\vartheta^3-\frac{104\vartheta^{\frac{17}{2}}}{750}\right),$$

$$\varkappa_i(\vartheta)=\frac{1}{4}\varkappa_{i-1}(\vartheta)\mathbb{I}_{0^+}^{\frac{1}{2};\frac{1}{2}}\varpi_{i-1}(\vartheta),\quad i=1,2,\ldots\ldots\ldots$$

where ϖ_i are Adomian polynomials of the nonlinear term $\varkappa^4$, and the solution will be

$$\varkappa(\vartheta)=\sum_{i=0}^{p}\varkappa_i(\vartheta).$$

5. Conclusions

In this article, we have considered the FQIE (1) in the frame of the generalized Riemann–Liouville fractional integral operator. First, the existence and uniqueness of solutions for the proposed equations were obtained. Next, we have given some special results corresponding to suitable values of the parameters ζ and q. Moreover, the main results have been proven based on Banach's fixed point theorem, the Adomian decomposition method, and Picard's method. Finally, we have presented an example. The present results are new for some special cases. The proposed techniques can be extended to other ζ-Hilfer fractional quadratic integral equations [32].

Author Contributions: B.N.A.: Formal Analysis, Methodology, Visualization, Writing—original draft; S.S.R.: Supervision, Investigation, Review & Editing; O.B.: Formal Analysis of revised manuscript, Improve English writing for the revised manuscript, Supervision for revised manuscript; K.N.: Supervision for the revised manuscript, Investigation of the revised manuscript, Visualization, Editing. All authors have read and agreed to the published version of the manuscript.

Funding: This research received no external funding.

Institutional Review Board Statement: Not applicable.

Informed Consent Statement: Not applicable.

Data Availability Statement: Not applicable.

Conflicts of Interest: The authors declare no conflict of interest.

References

1. Kilbas, A.A.; Srivastava, H.M.; Trujillo, J.J. *Theory and Applications of Fractional Differential Equations*; Elsevier: Amsterdam, The Netherlands, 2006; Volume 204.
2. Podlubny, I. *Fractional Differential Equations: An Introduction to Fractional Derivatives, Fractional Differential Equations, to Methods of Their Solution and Some of Their Applications*; Elsevier: Amsterdam, The Netherlands, 1998.
3. Redhwan, S.S.; Shaikh, S.L.; Abdo, M.S. Implicit fractional differential equation with anti-periodic boundary condition involving Caputo-Katugampola type. *Aims Math.* **2020**, *5*, 3714–3730. [CrossRef]
4. Redhwan, S.S.; Shaikh, S.L.; Abdo, M.S. Some properties of Sadik transform and its applications of fractional-order dynamical systems in control theory. *Adv. Theory Nonlinear Anal. Appl.* **2019**, *4*, 51–66. [CrossRef]
5. Redhwan, S.S.; Shaikh, S.L.; Abdo, M.S. coupled non-separated system of Hadamard-type fractional differential equations. *Adv. Theory Nonlinear Anal. Its Appl.* **2021**, *6*, 33–44.
6. Hilfer, R. *Applications of Fractional Calculus in Physics*; World Scientific: Singapore, 2000.
7. Hilfer, R. Experimental evidence for fractional time evolution in glass forming materials. *J. Chem. Phys.* **2002**, *284*, 399–408. [CrossRef]
8. Sousa, J.V.D.C.; de Oliveira, E.C. A Gronwall inequality and the Cauchy-type problem by means of ζ-Hilfer operator. *arXiv* **2017**, arXiv:1709.03634.
9. Sousa, J.V.D.C.; De Oliveira, E.C. On the $\zeta-$Hilfer fractional derivative, Commun. *Nonlinear Sci. Numer. Simul.* **2018**, *60*, 72–91. [CrossRef]
10. da Vanterler, C.; Sousa J.; Kucche K.D.; Capelas de Oliveira, E. On the Ulam-Hyers stabilities of the solutions of $\zeta-$Hilfer fractional differential equation with abstract Volterra operator. *Math. Methods Appl. Sci.* **2019**, *42*, 3021–3032.
11. Luo, D.; Shah, K.; Luo, Z. On the Novel Ulam–Hyers Stability for a Class of Nonlinear $\zeta-$Hilfer Fractional Differential Equation with Time-Varying Delays. *Mediterr. J. Math.* **2019**, *16*, 1–15. [CrossRef]
12. Almalahi, M.A.; Abdo, M.S.; Panchal, S.K. ζ-Hilfer fractional functional differential equation by Picard operator method. *J. Appl. Nonlinear Dyn* **2020**, *9*, 685–702. [CrossRef]
13. Redhwan, S.S.; Shaikh, S.L.; Abdo, M.S.; Shatanawi, W.; Abodayeh, K.; Almalahi, M.A.; Aljaaidi, T. Investigating a generalized Hilfer-type fractional differential equation with two-point and integral boundary conditions. *AIMS Math.* **2022**, *7*, 1856–1872. [CrossRef]
14. Asawasamrit, S.; Kijjathanakorn, A.; Ntouyas, S.K.; Tariboon, J. Nonlocal boundary value problems for Hilfer fractional differential equations. *Bull. Korean Math. Soc.* **2018**, *55*, 1639–1657.
15. Mali, A.D.; Kucche, K.D. Nonlocal boundary value problem for generalized Hilfer implicit fractional differential equations. *Math. Methods Appl. Sci.* **2020**, *43*, 8608–8631. [CrossRef]
16. Ntouyas, S.K.; Vivek, D. Existence and uniqueness results for sequential ζ-Hilfer fractional differential equations with multi-point boundary conditions. *Acta Math. Univ.* **2021**, *90*, 171–185.
17. Adomian, G. *Stochastic System*; Academic Press: New York, NY, USA, 1983.
18. Adomian, G. *Nonlinear Stochastis System Theory and Applications to Physics*; Springer Dordrecht: New York, NY, USA, 1989.
19. Cherruault, Y. Convergence of Adomian's Method. *Kybernetes* **1989**, *18*, 31–38. [CrossRef]
20. Rach, R. On the Adomian (decomposition) method and comparisons with Picard's method. *J. Math. Anal. Appl.* **1987**, *128*, 480–483. [CrossRef]

21. Curtain, R.F.; Pritchard, A.J. *Functional Analysis in Modern Applied Mathematics*; Academic Press: Cambridge, MA, USA, 1977.
22. Bellomo, N.; Sarafyan, D. On Adomian's decomposition method and some comparisons with Picard's iterative scheme. *J. Math. Anal. Appl.* **1987**, *123*, 389–400. [CrossRef]
23. El-Sayed, A.M.A.; Hashem, H.H.G.; Ziada, E.A.A. Picard and Adomian methods for quadratic integral equation. *Comput. Appl. Math.* **2010**, *29*, 447–463. [CrossRef]
24. Banaś, J.; Lecko, M.; El-Sayed, W. G. Existence theorems for some quadratic integral equations. *J. Math. Anal. Appl.* **1998**, *222*, 276–285. [CrossRef]
25. El-Sayed, A.M.A.; Saleh, M.M.; Ziada, E.A.A. Numerical and analytic solution for nonlinear quadratic integral equations. *Math. Sci. Res. J.* **2008**, *12*, 183–191.
26. El-Sayed, A.; Hashem, H.H.G. Integrable and continuous solutions of a nonlinear quadratic integral equation. *Electron. Qual. Theory Differ. Equ.* **2008**, *25*, 1–10. [CrossRef]
27. Mohamed Abdalla, D. On quadratic integral equation of fractional orders. *J. Math. Anal. Appl.* **2005**, *311*, 112–119.
28. Mohamed, D.; Henderson, J. Existence and asymptotic stability of solutions of a perturbed quadratic fractional integral equation. *Fract. Calc. Appl. Anal.* **2009**, *12*, 71–86.
29. Abood, B.N.; Redhwan, S.S.; Abdo, M.S. Analytical and Approximate solutions for a generalized fractional quadratic integral equation. *Nonlinear Funct. Anal. Appl.* **2021** , *26*, 497–512.
30. Almeida R. A Caputo fractional derivative of a function with respect to another function. *Commun. Nonlinear Sci. Numer. Simul.* 2017, **44**, 460–481. [CrossRef]
31. Burton, T. A.; KirkÙ, C. A fixed point theorem of Krasnoselskii Schaefer type. *Math. Nachrichten* **1998**, *189*, 23–31. [CrossRef]
32. Miller, K.S.; Ross, B. *An Introduction to the Fractional Calculus and Fractional Differential Equations*; Wiley: Hoboken, NJ, USA, 1993.

fractal and fractional

Article

Abundant Exact Travelling Wave Solutions for a Fractional Massive Thirring Model Using Extended Jacobi Elliptic Function Method

Mohammed Shqair [1,*], Mohammed Alabedalhadi [2], Shrideh Al-Omari [3] and Mohammed Al-Smadi [4,5]

1 Department of Physics, College of Science and Humanities in Al-Kharj, Prince Sattam Bin Abdulaziz University, Al-Kharj 11942, Saudi Arabia
2 Department of Applied Science, Ajloun College, Al-Balqa Applied University, Ajloun 26816, Jordan; mohmdnh@gmail.com
3 Department of Physics and Basic Sciences, Faculty of Engineering Technology, Al-Balqa Applied University, Amman 11183, Jordan; s.k.q.alomari@fet.edu.jo
4 College of Commerce and Business, Lusail University, Doha 122104, Qatar; malsmadi@lu.edu.qa or mhm.smadi@yahoo.com
5 Nonlinear Dynamics Research Center (NDRC), Ajman University, Ajman 20550, United Arab Emirates
* Correspondence: shqeeeer@gmail.com

Abstract: The fractional massive Thirring model is a coupled system of nonlinear PDEs emerging in the study of the complex ultrashort pulse propagation analysis of nonlinear wave functions. This article considers the NFMT model in terms of a modified Riemann–Liouville fractional derivative. The novel travelling wave solutions of the considered model are investigated by employing an effective analytic approach based on a complex fractional transformation and Jacobi elliptic functions. The extended Jacobi elliptic function method is a systematic tool for restoring many of the well-known results of complex fractional systems by identifying suitable options for arbitrary elliptic functions. To understand the physical characteristics of NFMT, the 3D graphical representations of the obtained propagation wave solutions for some free physical parameters are randomly drawn for a different order of the fractional derivatives. The results indicate that the proposed method is reliable, simple, and powerful enough to handle more complicated nonlinear fractional partial differential equations in quantum mechanics.

Keywords: fractional massive Thirring model; Jacobi expansion method; nonlinear partial differential equation; travelling wave solution; quantum field theory

Citation: Shqair, M.; Alabedalhadi, M.; Al-Omari, S.; Al-Smadi, M. Abundant Exact Travelling Wave Solutions for a Fractional Massive Thirring Model Using Extended Jacobi Elliptic Function Method. *Fractal Fract.* **2022**, *6*, 252. https://doi.org/10.3390/fractalfract6050252

Academic Editors: António M. Lopes, Alireza Alfi, Liping Chen and Sergio Adriani David

Received: 22 March 2022
Accepted: 28 April 2022
Published: 5 May 2022

1. Introduction

Physics can be typically classified into two branches: classical and modern physics. Modern physics can be distinguished by considering spatiotemporal requirements for joint interaction, whereas, in classical physics, we can consider time and space separately because they are independent and absolute. Furthermore, classical physics usually deals with the macroscopic scale, while modern physics deals with microscopic or sub-microscopic scales. Although classical physics has different applications in science and engineering, modern physics can be considered a revolution in applied physics, as it can elucidate many essential phenomena, such as black body radiation, photoelectric effect, Compton's effect and stability of atoms that cannot be explained from a classical physics point of view. However, modern physics focuses on quantum mechanics and the theory of relativity; quantum mechanics considers the physical quantities restricted to be discrete values, where the thinking of the probability is dominant instead of certain measurements, which is represented mathematically by the Schrödinger wave equation. The theory of relativity studies the physical quantities moving at a speed near the speed of light, the time dilation, and the dimensions contraction started to be important concepts, and Einstein's mass-energy equation makes a revolution in the science [1–4].

The contemporary revolution in theoretical and applied physics combines quantum mechanics with the theory of relativity in a multi-body system, which establishes quantum field theory. Quantum field equations represent a general form of the Schrödinger wave equation, where the wavefunction is generalized to an infinite-dimensional space of field configurations [2]. Motivated by this, in this work, we consider the massive Thirring model (MTM) as an important application of the quantum field theory, which was derived by W. Thirring in 1958 [3]. Thereafter, many theoretical and applied studies of such a complex system were conducted. For example, but not limited to, Kondo 1995 studied the bosonization and duality of the MTM with a four-fermion interaction of the current type [4], and the Thirring model was also considered in a separate work as a gauge theory [5]. In 2018, Joshi et al. introduced an integrable semi-discretization of the MTM for the first time in laboratory coordinates [6].

Nevertheless, to find out an alternative methodology for the Schrodinger equation, Dirac discovered the integral path approach, similar to Lagrangian's least-action principle technique in classical mechanics; this approach was developed by Feynman to create Feynman diagrams. Feynman diagrams were modified to Wiener's path integral, which is equivalent to the Brownian path integral in classical mechanics. Recently, the Levy flight random process has been introduced to understand difficult classical and quantum physics phenomena, where the Levy index α is introduced. Now, the consequences of the path integral for the Levy flight paths' studies are an essential issue in fractional quantum mechanics and consequently in fractional quantum field theory [7]. Examining research to obtain novel and additional exact traveling-wave solutions for fractional models is prospering. Indeed, this is not an easy task and is one of the pivotal challenging problems in mathematics and physics. Hence, resorting to sophisticated analytical and digital methods is inevitable. In this direction, many effective and accurate analytical methods for solving these equations have been considered thus far, for example, the Bäcklund transformation method, the Riccati sub-equation method, the extended tanh-function method, the G′/G-expansion method, the Kudryashov method [8–11] and so forth.

The analysis in this paper highlights the complex behavior of nonlinear wavefunction, which is notably dependent on the genetic properties and temporal memory that can be explored with great skill using fractional calculus.

In this direction, consider the following semi-discrete nonlinear massive Thirring model (MTM) that can be typically provided by a complex triple system of difference equations:

$$\begin{gathered}
4i\tfrac{d\chi_n}{dt}+\phi_{n+1}+\phi_n+\tfrac{2i}{\nu}(\psi_{n+1}-\psi_n)+\chi_n^2(\check{\psi}_n+\check{\psi}_{n+1})-\chi_n\left(|\phi_{n+1}|^2+|\phi_n|^2+|\psi_{n+1}|^2+|\psi_n|^2\right)\\
-\tfrac{i\nu}{2}\chi_n^2(\check{\phi}_n+\check{\phi}_{n+1})=0,\\
\tfrac{2i}{\nu}(\phi_{n+1}-\phi_n)-2\chi_n+|\chi_n|^2(\phi_{n+1}+\phi_n)=0,\\
\psi_{n+1}+\psi_n-2\chi_n+\tfrac{i\nu}{2}(\psi_{n+1}-\psi_n)=0,
\end{gathered} \tag{1}$$

where n denotes the discrete lattice to index iterates, ν denotes the lattice-spacing parameter of aspace discretization, and the symbol i is an imaginary unit. The complex-conjugates of ψ_n and ϕ_n are denoted respectively by $\check{\psi}_n$ and $\check{\phi}_n$. The first equation refers to the case of temporal evolution, while the last two difference equations refer to the semi-discrete massive Thirring equations constrained with the components of $\{\psi_n\}_{n\in\mathbb{Z}}$ and $\{\phi_n\}_{n\in\mathbb{Z}}$, which can be defined in terms of $\{\chi_n\}_{n\in\mathbb{Z}}$ in the temporal and spatial coordinates [6]. With the continuity of $\nu\to 0$, the slowly changing solutions between the lattice nodes can be written as:

$$\chi_n(t)=\chi(x=\nu n,t),\psi_n(t)=\psi(x=\nu n,\ t),\ \phi_n(t)=\phi(x=\nu n,\ t), \tag{2}$$

where continuous variables fulfill the following system of partial equations:

$$\begin{aligned} 2i\tfrac{\partial\chi}{\partial t} + i\tfrac{\partial\psi}{\partial x} + \phi + \chi^2\check{\psi} - \chi\left(|\phi|^2 + |\psi|^2\right) &= 0, \\ i\tfrac{\partial\phi}{\partial x} - \chi + |\chi|^2\phi &= 0, \\ \psi - \chi &= 0, \end{aligned} \tag{3}$$

which leads to an MTM system of two semi-linear equations for $(F, G) \in \mathbb{C}^2$ in terms of the variables $\psi(x,t) = \mathrm{F}(x, t-x)$ and $\phi(x,t) = G(x, t-x)$ in the normalized form:

$$\begin{aligned} i\left(\tfrac{\partial F}{\partial t} + \tfrac{\partial F}{\partial x}\right) + G &= |G|^2 F, \\ i\left(\tfrac{\partial G}{\partial t} - \tfrac{\partial G}{\partial x}\right) + F &= |F|^2 G. \end{aligned} \tag{4}$$

This paper deals with the fractional version of such a system. Therefore, we consider the following nonlinear space–time fractional MTM system:

$$\begin{aligned} i\left(D_t^{\alpha} F + \tfrac{\partial F}{\partial x}\right) + G &= |G|^2 F, \\ i\left(D_t^{\alpha} G - \tfrac{\partial G}{\partial x}\right) + F &= |F|^2 G. \end{aligned} \tag{5}$$

Considerable analytical and numerical investigations of the MTM have been made in the literature using various techniques. The construction of the MTM using the functional integral scheme within quantum field theory was discussed in [12]. The physical states, as well as a solution of the MTM, by means of many-body wave functions, are presented in [13]. In [14], Bethe ansatz solutions of the MTM were tested numerically by solving periodic boundary value problems. Delepine et al. [15] demonstrated that the MTM is equivalent to the quantum sine-Gordon model in quantum field theories at a finite temperature. The white noise of the oscillator MTM was examined in [16] in terms of the phase–space displays. In [17], the non-thermal phase structure of the MTM was studied using ansatz matrix-product states. Using the N-fold Darboux transform, the rogue wave solutions of the MTM equations were derived in [18]. On the other side as well, the fractional versions of the nonlinear complex MTM were numerically solved using advanced semi-analytical and approximate methods; for example, the q-HAM was applied in [19] to solve the fractional massive Thirring model in Caputo sense. In [20], the fractional residual power series method was implemented to solve a class of the fractional MTM with conformable derivatives. For more details regarding the numerical and analytical solutions of different fractional models, we refer to [21–31].

Almost all scientific problems can be solved using different fractional calculus techniques, where one or many suitable methods can be chosen for each problem; some problems that are solved using modified Riemann–Liouville fractional calculus techniques were noted as incorrect conditions [32–35]. Although these cases are not related to this work, this note must be mentioned here. These cases do not affect the Riemann–Liouville fractional calculus technique, which solves a huge number of problems successfully, as do other methods, such as the Mittag–Leffler function, the fractional Riccati method, the fractional double function method, and the fractional Y-function expansion method [36,37].

The novelty of this paper is to explore new travelling wave solutions for fractional MTM equations (5) by employing an effective analytic approach based on a complex fractional transformation and Jacobi elliptic functions. It is worth noting that the previous study of soliton for the fractional MTM equations was performed to provide an approximate solution for or study a special case of the MTM equations [4–6]. This paper introduces a general case exact solution for MTM equations for the first time; this study can be considered as a strong motivation to provide the obtained results.

The outline of this analysis has the following sections: In Section 2, some basic definitions and characteristics of the considered fractional operator are presented. In Section 3, the key idea of the proposed method is described. Then, in Section 4, we apply this method to create new sets of exact traveling wave solutions to the fractional massive Thirring model. Finally, a brief conclusion is also provided.

2. Preliminaries

Recently, many researchers have used various fractional operators to study several models associated with the functions of complex variables, and they proved that these fractional operators are more influential than the classical ones while analyzing the natural behavior of those models. Herein, we introduce the basic definition and some properties of Jumarie's modification of Riemann–Liouville derivative [38–41] that are very useful for displaying this work in a standardized way.

Definition 1. *Let* $\omega : \mathbb{R} \to \mathbb{R}$ *be a continuous function. Then, the modified Riemann–Liouville derivative of the order* α *is as follows*

$$D_t^{\alpha}\omega(t) = \begin{cases} \frac{1}{\Gamma(-\alpha)}\frac{d}{dt}\int_0^t (t-\xi)^{-\alpha-1}(\omega(\xi)-\omega(0))d\xi, \ \alpha < 0, \\ \frac{1}{\Gamma(1-\alpha)}\frac{d}{dt}\int_0^t (t-\xi)^{-\alpha}(\omega(\xi)-\omega(0))d\xi, \ 0 < \alpha < 1, \\ \left[\omega^{(\alpha-n)}(t)\right]^{(n)}, \ n \le \alpha < n+1, \ n \ge 1. \end{cases}$$

In this work, if $\omega(t)$ has a modified Riemann–Liouville derivative of the order α, it will be defined as D_t^{α}-differentiable. Further, it is obvious that the operator D_t^{α} of Jumarie's modification satisfies the following interesting properties:

Theorem 1. *Let* $\omega_1 : \mathbb{R} \to \mathbb{R}$ *be* D_t^{α} *-differentiable function at a point* $t > 0$ *and* $\omega_2 : \mathbb{R} \to \mathbb{R}$ *be* D_t^{α} *-differentiable and defined in the range of* ω_1*. Then, we have:*

(I) *If* $\omega_1(t) = t^{\gamma}$, *then* $D_t^{\alpha}t^{\gamma} = \frac{\Gamma(\gamma+1)}{\Gamma(\gamma+1-\alpha)}t^{\gamma-\alpha}$ *for* $\gamma > 0$.

(II) $D_t^{\alpha}(\omega_1(t)\omega_2(t)) = \omega_2(t)D_t^{\alpha}\omega_1(t) + \omega_1(t)D_t^{\alpha}\omega_2(t)$.

(III) $D_t^{\alpha}\omega_1(\omega_2(t)) = \frac{d}{d\omega_2}\omega_1(\omega_2(t))D_t^{\alpha}\omega_2(t) = D_{\omega_2}^{\alpha}\omega_1(\omega_2(t))\left(\frac{d}{dt}\omega_2(t)\right)^{\alpha}$.

3. The Extended Jacobi Elliptic Equation Method

This section presents the definition of Jacobi elliptic functions and reviews some important properties that we will use within the framework of this paper. Then, we introduce the algorithm of the proposed method.

3.1. The Jacobi Elliptic Functions

The Jacobi elliptic functions are the standard forms of elliptic functions. There are three double periodic functions, namely the Jacobian elliptic sine function, Jacobian elliptic cosine function, and Jacobian elliptic function of a third kind denoted by $sn(u,\delta) = sn(u)$, $cn(u,\delta) = cn(u)$ and $dn(u,\delta) = dn(u)$, respectively, where δ is the elliptic modulus. In the next segment, we provide the details of the derivation of these functions. To this end, we consider the following nonlinear partial differential equation (PDE):

$$\frac{\partial^2\varphi}{\partial x\partial t} = \lambda\sin(\varphi). \tag{6}$$

By substituting the linear transformation $\eta = \theta(x-\mu t)$ into PDE (6), we get the following nonlinear ordinary differential equation (NODE):

$$\frac{d^2\varphi}{d\eta^2} = \frac{-\lambda}{\theta^2\mu}\sin(\varphi). \tag{7}$$

Then, some simplifications lead to the following equivalent NODE:

$$\left(\frac{1}{2}\frac{d\varphi}{d\eta}\right)^2 = \frac{-\lambda}{\theta^2\mu}\sin^2\frac{1}{2}(\varphi) + c. \tag{8}$$

Letting $c = 1, -\lambda/\theta^2\mu = -\delta^2$ and $\omega = \varphi/2$, then Equation (8) takes the form

$$\frac{d\omega}{d\eta} = \sqrt{1 - \delta^2\sin^2\omega}, \tag{9}$$

which is equivalent to

$$\int \frac{1}{\sqrt{1 - \delta^2\sin^2\omega}}d\omega = \int d\eta, \tag{10}$$

where the integral in Equation (10) is called the Legendre elliptic integral of the first kind. Now, we define

$$u = \int_0^{\varphi} \frac{1}{\sqrt{1 - \delta^2\sin^2 y}}dy = \int_0^{t\,\equiv \sin\xi} \frac{1}{\sqrt{(1 - x^2)(1 - \delta^2x^2)}}dx. \tag{11}$$

Provided that $u = f(t)$ so that $t = f^{-1}(u) = sn(u)$, which is the Jacobi elliptic sine function. Nevertheless, the Jacobi elliptic cosine function can be defined by letting

$$u = \int_0^{\varphi} \frac{1}{\sqrt{1 - \delta^2\cos^2 y}}dy = \int_0^{\sqrt{1-t^2}\,\equiv \cos y} \frac{1}{\sqrt{(1 - x^2)(1 - \delta^2x^2)}}dx. \tag{12}$$

Provided that $u = f\left(\sqrt{1-t^2}\right)$ so that $\sqrt{1-t^2} = f^{-1}(u) = cn(u)$. Consequently, one can write the following argument

$$t = sn(u),\ \sqrt{1-t^2} = cn(u),\ \sqrt{1-\delta^2t^2} = dn(u). \tag{13}$$

On the other side as well, Jacobi elliptic functions $sn(u)$, $cn(u)$ and $dn(u)$ can be defined respectively as solutions to

$$\begin{aligned} y'' &= (2-\delta^2)y - 2y^3, \\ y'' &= -(1-2\delta^2)y - 2\delta^2y^3, \\ y'' &= -(1+\delta^2)y + 2\delta^2y^3, \end{aligned} \tag{14}$$

and possess the following properties in terms of their singular points:

$$\begin{aligned} sc(u) &= \tfrac{sn(u)}{cn(u)},\ sd(u) = \tfrac{sn(u)}{dn(u)},\ cd(u) = \tfrac{cn(u)}{dn(u)}, \\ cs(u) &= \tfrac{1}{sc(u)}, ds(u) = \tfrac{1}{sd(u)}, dc(u) = \tfrac{1}{cd(u)}, \\ ns(u) &= \tfrac{1}{sn(u)},\ nc(u) = \tfrac{1}{cn(u)}, nd(u) = \tfrac{1}{dn(u)}. \end{aligned} \tag{15}$$

when $\delta \to 1$, the Jacobi elliptic functions turn into hyperbolic functions as follows

$sn(u) \to \tanh u$,	$cn(u) \to \operatorname{sech} u$,	$dn(u) \to \operatorname{sech} u$,
$ns(u) \to \coth u$,	$nc(u) \to \cosh u$,	$nd(u) \to \cosh u$,
$sc(u) \to \sinh u$,	$sd(u) \to \sinh u$,	$cd(u) \to 1$,
$cs(u) \to \operatorname{csch} u$,	$ds(u) \to \operatorname{csch} u$,	$dc(u) \to 1$.

when $\delta \to 0$, they turn into trigonometric functions as follows

$sn(u) \to \sin u$,	$cn(u) \to \cos u$,	$dn(u) \to 1$,
$ns(u) \to \csc u$,	$nc(u) \to \sec u$,	$nd(u) \to 1$,
$sc(u) \to \tan u$,	$sd(u) \to \sin u$,	$cd(u) \to \cos u$,
$cs(u) \to \cot u$,	$ds(u) \to \csc u$,	$dc(u) \to \sec u$.

Furthermore, one can obtain the following identities:

$cn^2(u) + sn^2(u) = 1,$ $\quad dn^2(u) = 1 - \delta^2 sn^2(u),$
$ns^2(u) - cs^2(u) = 1,$ $\quad nd^2(u) = 1 + \delta^2 sd^2(u),$
$nc^2(u) - sc^2(u) = 1,$ $\quad cd^2(u) + (1-\delta^2)sd^2(u) = 1,$
$ns^2(u) - ds^2(u) = \delta^2,$ $\quad dc^2(u) - (1-\delta^2)sc^2(u) = 1,$
$ds^2(u) - cs^2(u) = 1 - \delta^2,$ $\quad dc^2(u) - (1-\delta^2)nc^2(u) = \delta^2,$
$\delta^2(cn^2(u) - 1) - dn^2(u) = 1,$ $\quad \delta^2 cd^2(u) + (1-\delta^2)nd^2(u) = 1.$

The derivatives of the Jacobi elliptic functions are as follows

$(sn\ u)' = cn(u)dn(u),$ $\quad (cn\ u)' = -sn(u)dn(u),$ $\quad (dn\ u)' = -\delta^2 sn(u)cn(u),$
$(ns\ u)' = -cs(u)ds(u),$ $\quad (nc\ u)' = sc(u)dc(u),$ $\quad (nd\ u)' = \delta^2 cd(u)sd(u),$
$(sc\ u)' = nc(u)dc(u),$ $\quad (sd\ u)' = nd(u)cd(u),$ $\quad (cd\ u)' = (\delta^2 - 1)sd(u)nd(u),$
$(cs\ u)' = -ns(u)ds(u),$ $\quad (ds\ u)' = -ns(u)cs(u),$ $\quad (dc\ u)' = (1-\delta^2)nc(u)sc(u).$

3.2. Extended Jacobi Elliptic Function Expansion Method

Herein, the algorithm of the extended Jacobi elliptic function expansion method will be illustrated to obtain the exact travelling wave solutions of NFPDEs. To this end, let us consider FPDE in the the following form

$$P\left(u, D_t^{\alpha}u, D_x^{\beta}u,\ D_y^{\gamma}u, D_t^{2\alpha}u, D_x^{2\beta}u, \ldots\right) = 0,\ t \geq 0,\ 0 < \alpha, \beta, \gamma < 1, \tag{16}$$

where $u = u(t, x, y)$, P is a polynomial in u, and its partial derivatives, including fractional derivatives, D_t^{α}, D_x^{β} and D_y^{γ}, are a modified Riemann–Liouville derivative of u with respect to the independent variables t, x and y. In the following, the main steps of the proposed algorithm are presented to find out the exact travelling wave solutions of FPDE (16):

Step 1. Use the fractional wave transformation

$$u(t, x, y) = U(\xi), \xi = \frac{x^{\beta}}{\Gamma(\beta+1)} + \frac{y^{\gamma}}{\Gamma(\gamma+1)} + \frac{vt^{\alpha}}{\Gamma(\alpha+1)}, \tag{17}$$

where v is the wave velocity that will later be determined. This permits us to reduce FPDE (16) into the following ODE of integer order in terms of ξ:

$$\tilde{P}\left(U, dU/d\xi, d^2U/d\xi^2, d^3U/d\xi^3, \ldots\right) = 0, \tag{18}$$

Step 2. Propose that Equation (18) has a solution in the following form

$$U(\xi) = b_0 + b_1 Q_{\jmath}(\xi) + b_2 R_{\jmath}(\xi) + b_3 S_{\jmath}(\xi) + \sum_{\hbar=2}^{L} Q_{\jmath}^{\hbar-2}(\xi)\left[p_{\hbar} Q_{\jmath}^2(\xi) + r_{\hbar} R_{\jmath}(\xi) S_{\jmath}(\xi)\right], \tag{19}$$

where $\jmath = 1, 2, \ldots, 12$, in which L is a positive integer,b_0, b_1, b_2, b_3, and $p_{\hbar}$, $r_{\hbar}$, $\hbar = 2, 3, \ldots, L$ and are constants to be determined afterwards. The functions $Q_{\jmath}(\xi)$, $R_{\jmath}(\xi)$ and $S_{\jmath}(\xi)$, $\jmath = 1, 2, \ldots, 12$ can be expressed in terms of Jacobi elliptic functions (15) as follows

$$\begin{aligned}
Q_1(\xi) &= \tfrac{1}{\rho+dn(\xi)}, R_1(\xi) = \tfrac{sn(\xi)}{\rho+dn(\xi)}, S_1(\xi) = \tfrac{cn(\xi)}{\rho+dn(\xi)},\\
Q_2(\xi) &= \tfrac{1}{\rho+sd(\xi)}, R_2(\xi) = \tfrac{cd(\xi)}{\rho+sd(\xi)}, S_2(\xi) = \tfrac{nd(\xi)}{\rho+sd(\xi)},\\
Q_3(\xi) &= \tfrac{1}{\rho+cd(\xi)}, R_3(\xi) = \tfrac{sd(\xi)}{\rho+cd(\xi)}, S_3(\xi) = \tfrac{nd(\xi)}{\rho+cd(\xi)},\\
Q_4(\xi) &= \tfrac{1}{\rho+ns(\xi)}, R_4(\xi) = \tfrac{cs(\xi)}{\rho+ns(\xi)}, S_4(\xi) = \tfrac{ds(\xi)}{\rho+ns(\xi)},\\
Q_5(\xi) &= \tfrac{1}{\rho+nd(\xi)}, R_5(\xi) = \tfrac{sd(\xi)}{\rho+nd(\xi)}, S_5(\xi) = \tfrac{cd(\xi)}{\rho+nd(\xi)},\\
Q_6(\xi) &= \tfrac{1}{\rho+sc(\xi)}, R_6(\xi) = \tfrac{nc(\xi)}{\rho+sc(\xi)}, S_6(\xi) = \tfrac{dc(\xi)}{\rho+sc(\xi)},\\
Q_7(\xi) &= \tfrac{1}{\rho+cn(\xi)}, R_7(\xi) = \tfrac{sn(\xi)}{\rho+cn(\xi)}, S_7(\xi) = \tfrac{dn(\xi)}{\rho+cn(\xi)},\\
Q_8(\xi) &= \tfrac{1}{\rho+dc(\xi)}, R_8(\xi) = \tfrac{sc(\xi)}{\rho+dc(\xi)}, S_8(\xi) = \tfrac{nc(\xi)}{\rho+dc(\xi)},\\
Q_9(\xi) &= \tfrac{1}{\rho+nc(\xi)}, R_9(\xi) = \tfrac{sc(\xi)}{\rho+nc(\xi)}, S_9(\xi) = \tfrac{dc(\xi)}{\rho+nc(\xi)},\\
Q_{10}(\xi) &= \tfrac{1}{\rho+sn(\xi)}, R_{10}(\xi) = \tfrac{cn(\xi)}{\rho+sn(\xi)}, S_{10}(\xi) = \tfrac{dn(\xi)}{\rho+sn(\xi)},\\
Q_{11}(\xi) &= \tfrac{1}{\rho+cs(\xi)}, R_{11}(\xi) = \tfrac{ds(\xi)}{\rho+cs(\xi)}, S_{11}(\xi) = \tfrac{ns(\xi)}{\rho+cs(\xi)},\\
Q_{12}(\xi) &= \tfrac{1}{\rho+ds(\xi)}, R_{12}(\xi) = \tfrac{cs(\xi)}{\rho+ds(\xi)}, S_{12}(\xi) = \tfrac{ns(\xi)}{\rho+ds(\xi)},
\end{aligned} \tag{20}$$

where ρ is an arbitrary constant.

Step 3. Determine the integer L in the predicted solution (19) by balancing the highest order nonlinear terms

$$O\left(U^{l_1}\frac{d^{l_2}}{d\xi^r}U\right) = (l_1+1)L + l_2 \text{ for } l_1,\ l_2 = 0,1,2,\ldots, \tag{21}$$

and the highest-order derivatives

$$O\left(\frac{d^{l_2}}{d\xi^{l_2}}U\right) = L + l_2 \text{for } l_2 = 0,1,2,\ldots. \tag{22}$$

Step 4. Substitute the predicted solution (19) back into ODE (18) to obtain an expression in terms of $sn^{\sigma_1}(\xi)cn^{\sigma_2}(\xi)dn^{\sigma_3}(\xi)(\sigma_1,\sigma_2,\sigma_3 = 0,\ 1,\ 2,\ \ldots)$ by means of reducing to a common denominator and setting the numerator to zero. Then, collect all terms with the same powers and put all the coefficients to zero leading to an over-determined system of nonlinear algebraic equations with respect to the unknown parameters $\rho,\ k,\ b_0,\ b_1,\ b_2,\ b_3,$ and $p_\hbar,\ r_\hbar, \hbar = 2\,,3,\ \ldots,\ L.$

Step 5. Solve the resulting algebraic system in Step 4 with the aid of Mathematica software to find out the values of $\rho,\ k,\ b_0,\ b_1,\ b_2,\ b_3,$ and $p_\hbar,\ r_\hbar,\ \hbar = 2\,,3,\ \ldots,\ L.$

Step 6. Substitute the obtained values in terms of $\rho,\ k,\ b_0,\ b_1,\ b_2,\ b_3,$ and $p_\hbar,\ r_\hbar$ for $\hbar = 2,\ 3,\ \ldots,\ L$ in the predicted solution (19); new types of abundant traveling wave solutions are provided to FPDEs (16) involving the Jacobi elliptic functions.

4. Solving the Space–Time Fractional MTM

This section is designed to perform the steps of the extended Jacobi elliptic function expansion algorithm to construct wave solutions for the space–time fractional MTM system (5). To perform this, we propose a complex wave transformation in the following form

$$F(x,t) \to \mathscr{F}(\xi)e^{i\hbar},\ g(x,t) \to \mathscr{G}(\xi)e^{i\hbar},\ \text{which } \xi = k_1x + k_2\frac{t^\alpha}{\Gamma(\alpha+1)},\ \hbar = r_1x + r_2\frac{t^\alpha}{\Gamma(\alpha+1)}, \tag{23}$$

where k_1, k_2, r_1 and r_2 are constants to be determined afterwards.

This transformation leads to the following results

$$D_t^\alpha F = \left(k_2\frac{d\mathscr{F}}{d\xi} + ir_2\mathscr{F}\right)e^{i\hbar},\ \frac{\partial F}{\partial x} = \left(k_1\frac{d\mathscr{F}}{d\xi} + ir_1\mathscr{F}\right)e^{i\hbar},\ |F|^2 = \mathscr{F}^2(\xi), \tag{24}$$

$$D_t^{\alpha}G = \left(k_2\frac{d\mathscr{G}}{d\xi} + ir_2\mathscr{G}\right)e^{i\hbar}, \frac{\partial G}{\partial x} = \left(k_1\frac{d\mathscr{G}}{d\xi} + ir_1\mathscr{G}\right)e^{i\hbar}, |G|^2 = \mathscr{G}^2(\xi). \tag{25}$$

By substituting assumption (23) with relations (24) and (25) together into the space–time fractional MTM system (5), we obtain the corresponding system of nonlinear ODEs in the form,

$$\begin{aligned} i(k_1+k_2)\tfrac{d\mathscr{F}}{d\xi} - (r_1+r_2)\mathscr{F} + \mathscr{G} - \mathscr{G}^2\mathscr{F} = 0, \\ i(k_2-k_1)\tfrac{d\mathscr{G}}{d\xi} - (r_2-r_1)\mathscr{G} + \mathscr{F} - \mathscr{F}^2\mathscr{G} = 0. \end{aligned} \tag{26}$$

Now, by balancing the highest order nonlinear term and highest order derivatives, we have $L = 1$. Then, the formal solutions of system (26) can be expressed as

$$\begin{aligned} \mathscr{F}(\xi) = p_0 + p_1Q_{\mathscr{J}}(\xi) + p_2R_{\mathscr{J}}(\xi) + p_3S_{\mathscr{J}}(\xi), \ \mathscr{J} = 1,2,\ldots,12, \\ \mathscr{G}(\xi) = q_0 + q_1Q_{\mathscr{J}}(\xi) + q_2R_{\mathscr{J}}(\xi) + q_3S_{\mathscr{J}}(\xi), \ \mathscr{J} = 1,2,\ldots,12. \end{aligned} \tag{27}$$

where $p_\hbar, q_\hbar, \hbar = 0,1,2,3$ are constants to be determined. Let $\mathscr{J} = 1$. Then, the formal solutions (27) becomes

$$\begin{aligned} \mathscr{F}(\xi) = p_0 + p_1\tfrac{1}{\rho+dn(\xi)} + p_2\tfrac{sn(\xi)}{\rho+dn(\xi)} + p_3\tfrac{cn(\xi)}{\rho+dn(\xi)}, \\ \mathscr{G}(\xi) = q_0 + q_1\tfrac{1}{\rho+dn(\xi)} + q_2\tfrac{sn(\xi)}{\rho+dn(\xi)} + q_3\tfrac{cn(\xi)}{\rho+dn(\xi)}. \end{aligned} \tag{28}$$

Substitute the solutions from (28) into the system from (26), and separate the real and imaginary parts so that the denominators are canceled in both parts. Then, collect the coefficients of $sn^{d_1}(\eta)cn^{d_2}(\eta)dn^{d_3}(\eta)(d_1,d_2,d_3 = 0,\ 1,\ 2,3)$, and set each coefficient to zero. Consequently, two sets of over-determined algebraic equations are constructed in terms of $\rho,\ k_1,\ k_2,\ r_1,\ r_2,\ p_{\mathscr{J}},\ q_{\mathscr{J}}, \mathscr{J} = 0,1,2,3$. The obtained sets of these algebraic equations are solved via the computer software of Mathematica, so that the resulting form of the imaginary part yields

$$k_1 = k_2 \text{ or } k_1 = -k_2. \tag{29}$$

and the resulting form of the real part yields the following solution families:

Family I: When $p_1 = q_1 = 0$, let $q_0,\ p_2,\ q_3,\ r_1$ and r_2 be arbitrary constants. Then, we get the following cases for and :

Case 1:

$$p_0 = \frac{-q_0}{q_0^2 - (r_1+r_2)}, \quad q_2 = \frac{p_2(q_0^2 - (r_1+r_2))}{q_0^2 + (r_1+r_2)}, \quad p_3 = \frac{-2q_3(r_1+r_2)}{\left(q_0^2 - (r_1+r_2)\right)^2}. \tag{30}$$

Case 2:

$$p_0 = \frac{-q_0}{q_0^2 - (r_1+r_2)}, \quad q_2 = 2p_2\left(q_0^2 - (r_1+r_2)\right), \quad p_3 = \frac{q_3}{\left(q_0^2 - (r_1+r_2)\right)}. \tag{31}$$

Case 3:

$$p_0 = \frac{-q_0}{q_0^2 - (r_1+r_2)}, \quad q_2 = -p_2\left(q_0^2 - (r_1+r_2)\right), \quad p_3 = \frac{-2q_3}{\left(q_0^2 - (r_1+r_2)\right)}. \tag{32}$$

Case 4:

$$p_0 = \frac{-q_0}{q_0^2 - (r_1+r_2)}, \quad q_2 = \frac{p_2\left(q_0^2 - (r_1+r_2)\right)^2}{2(r_1+r_2)}, \quad p_3 = \frac{q_3(q_0^2 + (r_1+r_2))}{\left(q_0^2 - (r_1+r_2)\right)^2}. \tag{33}$$

By substituting the results above into (28) and combining with (23), we can obtain four exact solutions $F_{\mathscr{J}}(x,t)$ and $G_{\mathscr{J}}(x,t)$, $\mathscr{J} = 1,2,3,4$, for the space–time fractional MTM system (5) in the forms of Jacobi elliptic functions. For example, some graphical representations of these solutions are presented in the following figures. Figure 1 shows the 3D plots of $|F_1(x,t)|^2$ and $|G_1(x,t)|^2$ at some parameters that were chosen randomly,

$r_1 = r_2 = 1, k_1 = k_2 = 1,\ q_0 = 0.6,\ p_2 = -2,\ q_3 = 0.8,\ \rho = 1$ and $\tau = 0$, in the intervals $0 \leq x \leq 20$ and $0 \leq t \leq 10$ at different values of the fractional derivative such that $\alpha = 1$ and $\alpha = 0.75$. While Figure 2 presents 3D plots of the real and imaginary parts of the periodic wave solutions $F_2(x,t)$ and $G_2(x,t)$ in $(x,t) \in [0,20] \times [0,10]$ with $r_1 = r_2 = 1, k_1 = k_2 = 1, q_0 = 0.2,\ p_2 = -1,\ q_3 = 0.5$ and $\rho = \tau = 1$ for the fractional order $\alpha = 0.85$. From these figures, it is observed that the propagation of the periodic wave forms propagation along the space direction over time by maintaining its shape and amplitude. The fractional order affects only the velocity of propagation.

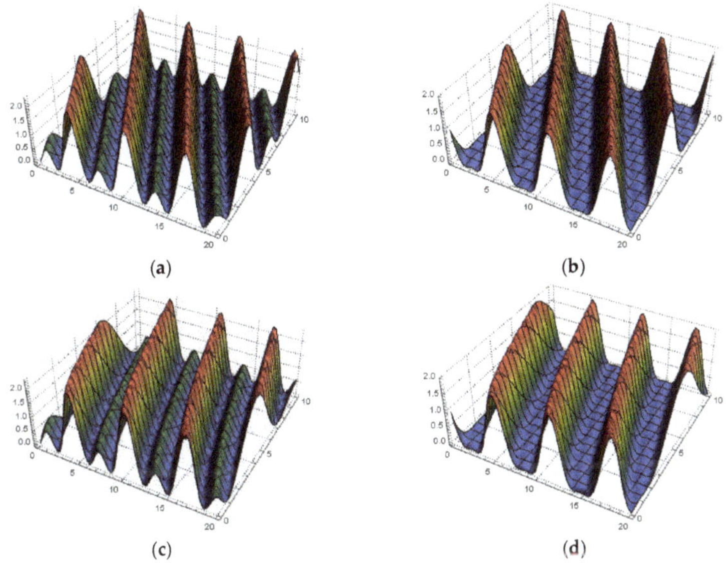

Figure 1. The 3D plots of $|F_1(x,t)|^2$ and $|G_1(x,t)|^2$ with the parameters $r_1 = r_2 = 1, k_1 = k_2 = 1$, $q_0 = 0.6,\ p_2 = -2,\ q_3 = 0.8, \rho = 1$ and $\tau = 0$ for various α values: (**a**) $|F_1|^2, \alpha = 1$, (**b**) $|G_1|^2, \alpha = 1$, (**c**) $|F_1|^2, \alpha = 0.75$ and (**d**) $|G_1|^2, \alpha = 0.75$.

Family II: When $p_2 = q_2 = 0$, let $q_0,\ p_3,\ q_1,\ r_1$ and r_2 be arbitrary constants. Then, we get the following cases for $p_0,\ p_1$ and q_3:

Case 1:

$$p_0 = \frac{-q_0}{q_0^2 - (r_1 + r_2)}, \quad p_1 = \frac{-q_1}{\left(q_0^2 - (r_1 + r_2)\right)}, \quad q_3 = 2p_3\left(q_0^2 - (r_1 + r_2)\right). \tag{34}$$

Case 2:

$$\begin{gathered} p_0 = \frac{-q_0}{q_0^2-(r_1+r_2)}, \quad p_1 = \frac{-2q_1\left(q_0^2+(r_1+r_2)\right)-\rho q_0\left(q_0^2+3(r_1+r_2)\right)}{\left(q_0^2-(r_1+r_2)\right)^2}, \\ q_3 = \frac{p_3\left(q_0^2-(r_1+r_2)\right)^2}{\left(q_0^2+(r_1+r_2)\right)}. \end{gathered} \tag{35}$$

Case 3:

$$\begin{gathered} p_0 = \frac{-q_0}{q_0^2-(r_1+r_2)}, \quad p_1 = \frac{\rho^2 q_0\left(q_0^2+3(r_1+r_2)\right)+2q_0q_1^2+\rho q_1\left(3q_0^2+2(r_1+r_2)\right)}{\left(q_0^2-(r_1+r_2)\right)\left(q_0q_1+\rho\left(q_0^2+(r_1+r_2)\right)\right)}, \\ q_3 = \frac{-p_3\left(q_0^2-(r_1+r_2)\right)\left(q_0q_1+\rho\left(q_0^2+(r_1+r_2)\right)\right)}{q_0q_1+\rho(r_1+r_2)}. \end{gathered} \tag{36}$$

Case 4:

$$
\begin{aligned}
p_0 &= \frac{-q_0}{q_0^2-(r_1+r_2)}, \\
p_1 &= \frac{-q_1\left(q_0q_1^2+\rho q_1\left(q_0^2+(r_1+r_2)\right)+2\rho^2 q_0(r_1+r_2)\right)}{\left(q_0^2-(r_1+r_2)\right)\left(q_0q_1^2+2\rho q_1\left(q_0^2-(r_1+r_2)\right)+\rho^2 q_0\left(q_0^2-(r_1+r_2)\right)\right)}, \\
q_3 &= \frac{p_3\left(q_0^2-(r_1+r_2)\right)\left(\mathrm{q0q1}^2+2q1\rho\left(\mathrm{q0}^2-(r1+r2)\right)\right)+\rho^2 q_0\left(q_0^2-(r_1+r_2)\right)}{2q_1\left(q_0q_1+\rho\left(q_0^2+(r_1+r_2)\right)\right)+\rho^2 q_0\left(q_0^2+(r_1+r_2)\right)}.
\end{aligned} \tag{37}
$$

Case 5:

$$
p_0 = \frac{-q_0}{q_0^2-(r_1+r_2)}, \quad p_1 = \frac{2q_1(r_1+r_2)}{\left(q_0^2-(r_1+r_2)\right)^2}, \quad q_3 = \frac{p_3\left(q_0^2-(r_1+r_2)\right)}{\left(q_0^2+(r_1+r_2)\right)}. \tag{38}
$$

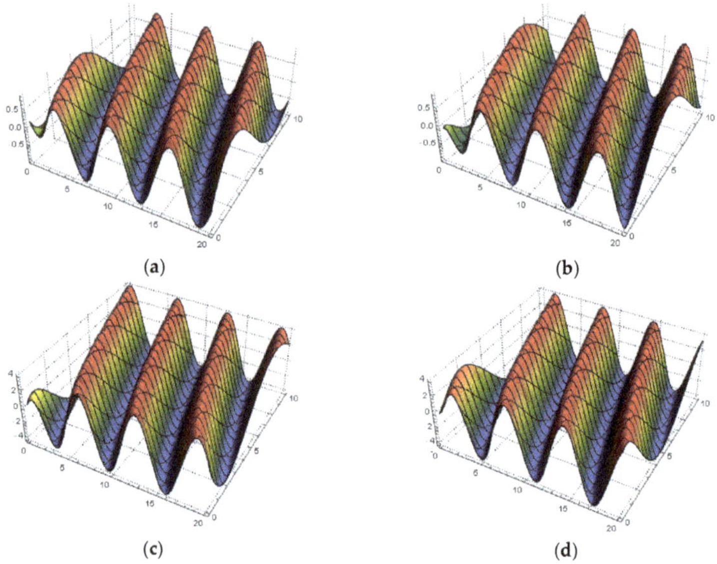

Figure 2. The 3D plots of the real and imaginary parts of $F_2(x,t)$ and with the parameters $r_1 = r_2 = 1$, $k_1 = k_2 = 1, q_0 = 0.2$, $p_2 = -1$, $q_3 = 0.5$ and $\rho = \tau = 1$ for the fractional order $\alpha = 0.85$: (**a**) $Re[F_2(x,t)]$, (**b**) $Im[F_2(x,t)]$, (**c**) $Re[G_2(x,t)]$ and (**d**) $Im[G_2(x,t)]$.

By substituting the results above into (28) and combining with (23), we can obtain five exact solutions $F_{\jmath}(x,t)$ and $G_{\jmath}(x,t)$, $\jmath = 5,6,7,8,9$, for the space–time fractional MTM system (5) in the forms of Jacobi elliptic functions. For physical illustration, some graphical representations of these solutions are drawn and introduced in the following figures. Figure 3 reveals the 3D plots of $|F_5(x,t)|^2$ and $|G_5(x,t)|^2$ with some selected parameters $r_1 = r_2 = -1$, $k_1 = k_2 = 1$, $q_0 = 0.05$, $p_3 = -0.3$, $q_1 = 2$, $\rho = 1$, and $\tau = 0$ over the intervals $0 \leq x \leq 20$ and $0 \leq t \leq 10$ for various values of $\alpha \in \{0.75, 1\}$.

Figures 4 and 5 show 3D plots of the real and imaginary parts of the periodic wave solutions $F_6(x,t), F_7(x,t), G_6(x,t)$, and $G_7(x,t)$ in $(x,t) \in [0,20] \times [0,10]$ with some selected physical free parameters and different fractional orders. The regularity, harmony and compatibility of the periodic wave solutions can be observed for different α values in all cases.

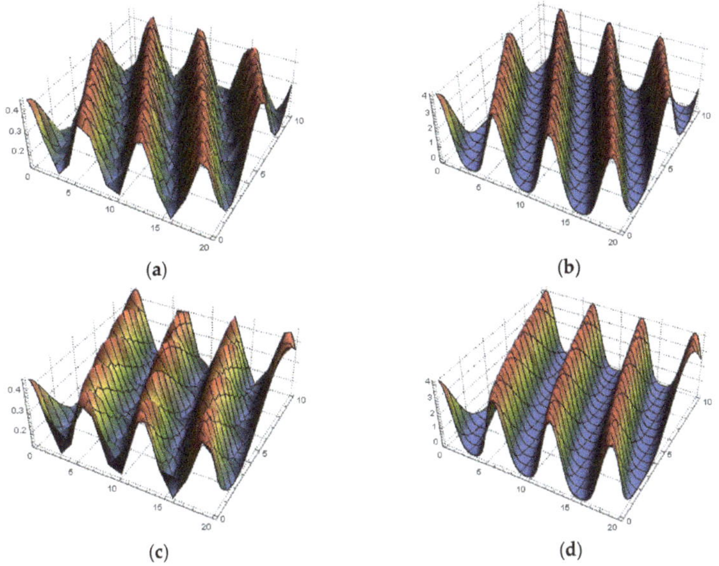

Figure 3. The 3D plots of $|F_5(x,t)|^2$ and $|G_5(x,t)|^2$ with the parameters $r_1 = r_2 = -1, k_1 = k_2 = 1$, $q_0 = 0.05$, $p_3 = -0.3$, $q_1 = 2, \rho = 1$ and $\tau = 0$ for various α values: (**a**) $|F_5|^2, \alpha = 1$, (**b**) $|G_5|^2, \alpha = 1$, (**c**) $|F_5|^2, \alpha = 0.75$ and (**d**) $|G_5|^2, \alpha = 0.75$.

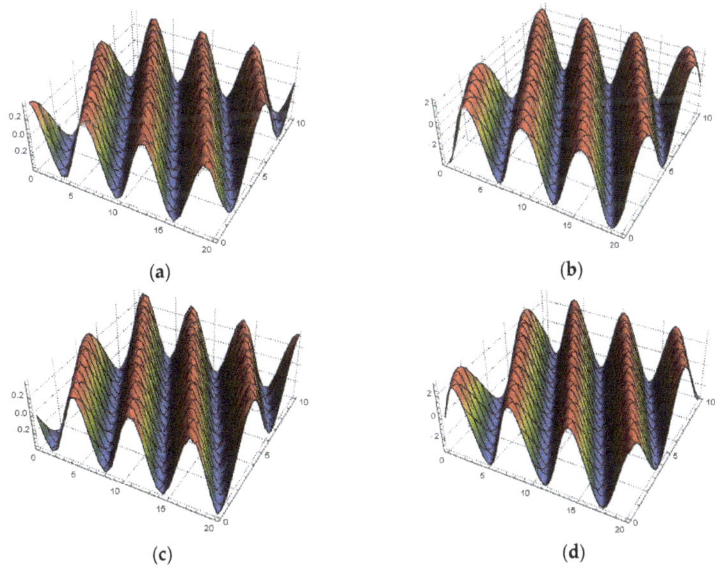

Figure 4. The 3D plots of the real and imaginary parts of $F_6(x,t)$ and $G_6(x,t)$ with the parameters $r_1 = r_2 = -1, k_1 = k_2 = 1, q_0 = -2.5$, $p_3 = 0$, $q_1 = -1, \rho = 1$ and $\tau = 0$ for the fractional order $\alpha = 1$: (**a**) $Re[F_6(x,t)]$, (**b**) $Re[G_6(x,t)]$, (**c**) $Im[F_6(x,t)]$ and (**d**) $Im[G_6(x,t)]$.

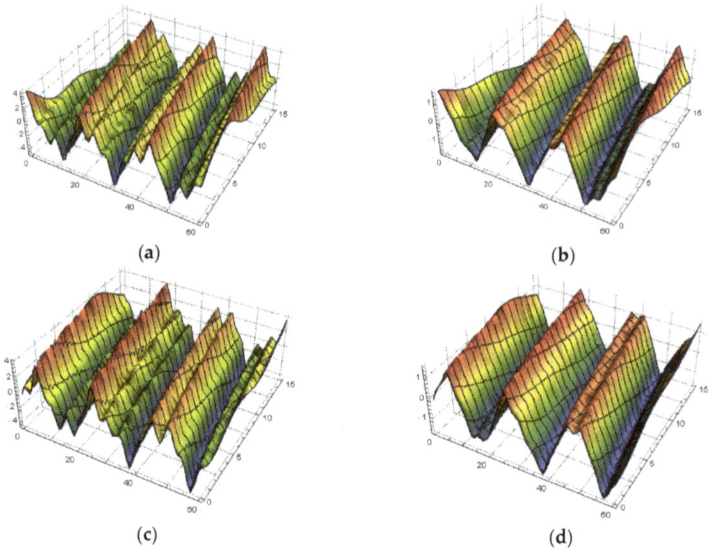

Figure 5. The 3D plots of the real and imaginary parts of $F_7(x,t)$ and $G_7(x,t)$ with the parameters $r_1 = r_2 = 0.3, k_1 = k_2 = 1, q_0 = 0.9,\ p_3 = 4,\ q_1 = 5/7, \rho = 1$ and $\tau = 0$ for the fractional order $\alpha = 0.65$: (**a**) $Re[F_7(x,t)]$, (**b**) $Re[G_7(x,t)]$, (**c**) $Im[F_7(x,t)]$ and (**d**) $Im[G_7(x,t)]$.

Family III: When $p_3 = q_3 = 0$, let $q_0,\ p_2,\ q_1,\ r_1$ and r_2 be arbitrary constants. Then, we get the following cases for p_0, p_1 and q_2:

Case 1:

$$\begin{aligned} p_0 &= \frac{-q_0}{q_0^2-(r_1+r_2)}, \\ p_1 &= \frac{2q_0q_1^2+\rho q_1\left(3q_0^2+2(r_1+r_2)\right)+\rho^2 q_0\left(q_0^2+3(r_1+r_2)\right)}{\left(q_0^2-(r_1+r_2)\right)\left(q_0q_1+\rho\left(q_0^2+(r_1+r_2)\right)\right)}, \\ q_2 &= \frac{-p_2\left(q_0^2-(r_1+r_2)\right)\left(q_0q_1+\rho\left(q_0^2+(r_1+r_2)\right)\right)}{q_0q_1+\rho(r1+r2)}. \end{aligned} \tag{39}$$

Case 2:

$$\begin{aligned} p_0 &= \frac{-q_0}{q_0^2-(r_1+r_2)}, \\ p_1 &= \frac{-q_1\left(q_0q_1^2+\rho q_1\left(q_0^2+(r_1+r_2)\right)+2\rho^2 q_0(r_1+r_2)\right)}{\left(q_0^2-(r_1+r_2)\right)\left(q_0q_1^2+2\rho q_1\left(q_0^2-(r_1+r_2)\right)+\rho^2 q_0\left(q_0^2-(r_1+r_2)\right)\right)}, \\ q_2 &= \frac{p_2\left(q_0^2-(r_1+r_2)\right)\left(q_0q_1^2+2\rho q_1\left(q_0^2-(r_1+r_2)\right)+\rho^2 q_0\left(q_0^2-(r_1+r_2)\right)\right)}{2q_0q_1^2+2\rho q_1\left(q_0^2+(r_1+r_2)\right)+\rho^2 q_0\left(q_0^2+(r_1+r_2)\right)} \end{aligned} \tag{40}$$

Case 3:

$$\begin{aligned} p_0 &= \frac{-q_0}{q_0^2-(r_1+r_2)}, \\ p_1 &= \frac{\rho\left(3q_0q_1^2+2\rho q_1\left(2q_0^2+(r_1+r_2)\right)+\rho^2 q_0\left(3q_0^2+(r_1+r_2)\right)\right)}{\left(q_0^2-(r_1+r_2)\right)\left(3q_1^2+6\rho q_0q_1+\rho^2\left(3q_0^2+(r_1+r_2)\right)\right)}, \\ q_2 &= \frac{p_2(3q_1^2+6q_0q_1\rho+\rho^2\left(3q_0^2+(r_1+r_2)\right)}{\rho^2}. \end{aligned} \tag{41}$$

Case 4:

$$p_0 = \frac{-q_0}{q_0^2-(r_1+r_2)}, \quad p_1 = \frac{-q_1}{\left(q_0^2-(r_1+r_2)\right)}, \quad q_2 = 2p_2\left(q_0^2-(r_1+r_2)\right). \tag{42}$$

Case 5:

$$p_0 = \frac{-q_0}{q_0^2-(r_1+r_2)}, \quad p_1 = \frac{-2q_1\left(q_0^2-(r_1+r_2)\right)-\rho q_0\left(q_0^2+3(r_1+r_2)\right)}{\left(q_0^2-(r_1+r_2)\right)^2}, \quad q_2 = \frac{q_1\left(q_0^2-(r_1+r_2)\right)^2}{\left(q_0^2+(r_1+r_2)\right)}. \tag{43}$$

By substituting the results above into (28) and combining with (23), we can obtain five exact solutions $F_{\jmath}(x,t)$ and $G_{\jmath}(x,t)$, $\jmath = 10,\ldots,14$, of the fractional MTM system (5) in the forms of Jacobi elliptic functions. The illustrations of these acquired solutions, for various values of α, are depicted in Figures 6–9.

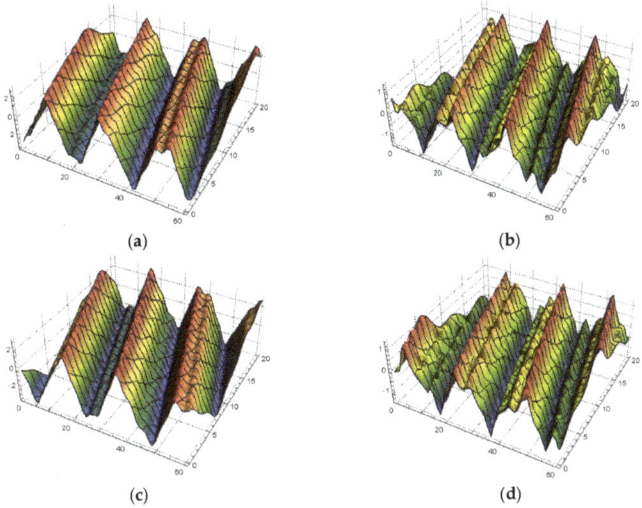

Figure 6. The 3D plots of the real and imaginary parts of $F_{10}(x,t)$ and $G_{10}(x,t)$ with the parameters $r_1 = r_2 = 0.3, k_1 = k_2 = 1, q_0 = 0.9,\ p_2 = 1,\ q_1 = -0.2, \rho = 0.5$ and $\tau = 0$ for the fractional order $\alpha = 0.9$: (**a**) $Re[F_{10}(x,t)]$, (**b**) $Re[G_{10}(x,t)]$, (**c**) $Im[F_{10}(x,t)]$ and (**d**) $Im[G_{10}(x,t)]$.

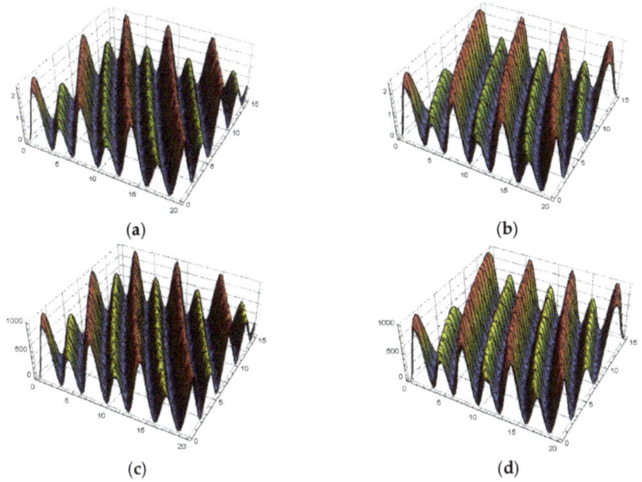

Figure 7. The 3D plots of $|F_{12}(x,t)|^2$ and $|G_{12}(x,t)|^2$ with the parameters $r_1 = r_2 = -3$, $k_1 = k_2 = 1, q_0 = 7,\ p_2 = 2,\ q_1 = -5, \rho = 0.5$ and $\tau = 0$ for various α values: (**a**) $|F_{12}|^2, \alpha = 0.95$, (**b**) $|G_{12}|^2, \alpha = 0.95$, (**c**) $|F_{12}|^2, \alpha = 0.75$ and (**d**) $|G_{12}|^2, \alpha = 0.75$.

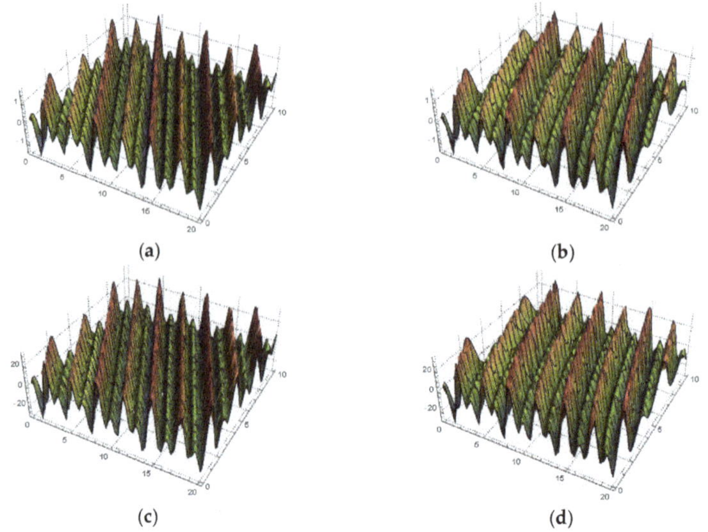

Figure 8. The 3D plots of the real and imaginary parts of $F_{13}(x,t)$ and $G_{13}(x,t)$ with the parameters $r_1 = r_2 = -3, k_1 = k_2 = 1, q_0 = 7,\ p_2 = 2,\ q_1 = -5, \rho = 0.5$, and $\tau = 0.1$ for the fractional order $\alpha = 0.8$: (**a**) $Re[F_{13}(x,t)]$, (**b**) $Re[G_{13}(x,t)]$, (**c**) $Im[F_{13}(x,t)]$, (**d**) $Im[G_{13}(x,t)]$.

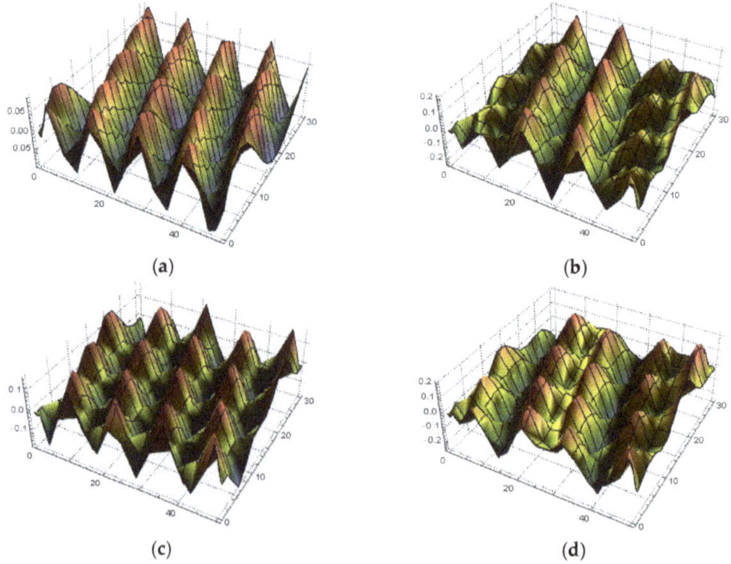

Figure 9. The 3D plots of the real and imaginary parts of $F_{14}(x,t)$ and $G_{14}(x,t)$ with the parameters $r_1 = r_2 = 0.5, k_1 = k_2 = 1, q_0 = 10,\ p_2 = 0.2,\ q_1 = 1, \rho = 1$ and $\tau = 0.1$ for the fractional order $\alpha = 0.75$: (**a**) $Re[F_{14}(x,t)]$, (**b**) $Re[G_{14}(x,t)]$, (**c**) $Im[F_{14}(x,t)]$ and (**d**) $Im[G_{14}(x,t)]$.

5. Conclusions

In this paper, the fractional massive Thirring model has been considered in the sense of the modified Riemann–Liouville fractional derivative. Based on the nonlinear fractional complex transformation, a series of exact traveling wave solutions for this model has been successfully obtained in terms of Jacobi elliptic functions. With the aid of the Mathematica wolfram computation package, the resulting algebraic system of free parameters was solved and graphical representations of some acquired solutions were performed in 3D plots. The proposed method provides a powerful and systematic tool for obtaining novel exact solutions and can be applied to deal with other governing nonlinear fractional evolution equations emerging in mathematical physics.

Author Contributions: Conceptualization, M.S.; methodology, M.A.-S.; software M.A.; validation, M.S., M.A., S.A.-O. and M.A.-S.; investigation, M.S.; writing—original draft preparation, M.A.; writing—review and editing, M.A. and S.A.-O.; visualization, M.A.-S.; supervision, S.A.-O.; project administration, M.A.; funding acquisition, M.A.-S. All authors have read and agreed to the published version of the manuscript.

Funding: This research was funded by the Deanship of Scientific Research at Prince Sattam Bin Abdulaziz University, grant number 2021/01/17993 and the APC was funded by the Deanship of Scientific Research at Prince Sattam Bin Abdulaziz University.

Acknowledgments: The authors extend their appreciation to the Deputyship for Research and innovations, Ministry of Education in Saudi Arabia for funding this research work through the project number (IF-PSAU/2021/01/17993).

Conflicts of Interest: The authors declare no conflict of interest. The funders had no role in the design of the study; in the collection, analyses, or interpretation of data; in the writing of the manuscript or in the decision to publish the results.

References

1. Beiser, A. *Concepts of Modern Physics*, 6th ed.; McGraw-Hill: New York, NY, USA, 1994; ISBN 978-0072448481.
2. Kiselev, V.; Shnir, Y.; Tregubovich, A. *Introduction to Quantum Field Theory*, 1st ed.; CRC Press: Boca Raton, FL, USA, 2000. [CrossRef]
3. Thirring, W. A soluble relativistic field theory. *Ann. Phys.* **1958**, *3*, 91–112. [CrossRef]
4. Kondo, K.-I. Bosonization and Duality of Massive Thirring Model. *Prog. Theor. Phys.* **1995**, *94*, 899–914. [CrossRef]
5. Kondo, K.-I. Thirring model as a gauge theory. *Nucl. Phys. B* **1995**, *450*, 251–266. [CrossRef]
6. Joshi, N.; Pelinovsky, D.E. Integrable semi-discretization of the massive Thirring system in laboratory coordinates. *J. Phys. A Math. Theor.* **2019**, *52*, 03LT01. [CrossRef]
7. Laskin, N. *Fractional Quantum Mechanics*; World Scientific Publishing Co. Pte., Ltd.: Singapore, 2018.
8. Lu, B. Bäcklund transformation of fractional Riccati equation and its applications to nonlinear fractional partial differential equations. *Phys. Lett. A* **2012**, *376*, 2045–2048. [CrossRef]
9. Zahran, E.H.M.; Khater, M.M.A. Modified extended tanh-function method and its applications to the Bogoyavlenskii equation. *Appl. Math. Model.* **2016**, *40*, 1769–1775. [CrossRef]
10. Dubey, V.P.; Kumar, R.; Kumar, D.; Khan, I.; Singh, J. An efficient computational scheme for nonlinear time fractional systems of partial differential equations arising in physical sciences. *Adv. Differ. Equat.* **2020**, *2020*, 46. [CrossRef]
11. Gaber, A.A.; Aljohani, A.F.; Ebaid, A.; Machado, J.T. The generalized Kudryashov method for nonlinear space–time fractional partial differential equations of Burgers type. *Nonlinear Dyn.* **2019**, *95*, 361–368. [CrossRef]
12. Benfatto, G.; Falco, P.; Mastropietro, V. Functional Integral Construction of the Massive Thirring model: Verification of Axioms and Massless Limit. *Commun. Math. Phys.* **2007**, *273*, 67–118. [CrossRef]
13. Bergknoff, H.; Thacker, H.B. Structure and solution of the massive Thirring model. *Phys. Rev. D* **1979**, *19*, 3666–3681. [CrossRef]
14. Fujita, T.; Sekiguchi, Y.; Yamamoto, K. A New Interpretation of Bethe Ansatz Solutions for Massive Thirring Model. *Ann. Phys.* **1997**, *255*, 204–227. [CrossRef]
15. Delépine, D.; Felipe, R.G.; Weyers, J. Equivalence of the sine-Gordon and massive Thirring models at finite temperature. *Phys. Lett. B* **1998**, *419*, 296–302. [CrossRef]
16. Aydogmus, F.; Tosyali, E. Numerical Analysis of Thirring Model under White Noise. *J. Phys. Conf. Ser.* **2015**, *633*, 012022. [CrossRef]
17. Bañuls, M.C.; Cichy, K.; Kao, Y.-J.; Lin, C.-J.D.; Lin, Y.-P.; Tan, D.T.-L. Phase structure of the (1+1)-dimensional massive Thirring model from matrix product states. *Phys. Rev. D* **2019**, *100*, 094504. [CrossRef]
18. Guo, L.; Wang, L.; Cheng, Y.; He, J. High-order rogue wave solutions of the classical massive Thirring model equations. *Commun. Nonlinear Sci. Numer. Simul.* **2017**, *52*, 11–23. [CrossRef]
19. Arafa, A.A.M.; Hagag, A.M.S. Q-homotopy analysis transform method applied to fractional Kundu–Eckhaus equation and fractional massive Thirring model arising in quantum field theory. *Asian Eur. J. Math.* **2019**, *12*, 1950045. [CrossRef]

20. Al-Smadi, M.; Abu Arqub, O.; Hadid, S. Approximate solutions of nonlinear fractional Kundu-Eckhaus and coupled fractional massive Thirring equations emerging in quantum field theory using conformable residual power series method. *Phys. Scr.* **2020**, *95*, 105205. [CrossRef]
21. Al-Smadi, M.; Freihat, A.; Khalil, H.; Momani, S.; Khan, R.A. Numerical multistep approach for solving fractional partial dif-ferential equations. *Int. J. Comput. Meth.* **2017**, *14*, 1750029. [CrossRef]
22. Hasan, S.; El-Ajou, A.; Hadid, S.; Al-Smadi, M.; Momani, S. Atangana-Baleanu fractional framework of reproducing kernel technique in solving fractional population dynamics system. *Chaos Solitons Fractals* **2020**, *133*, 109624. [CrossRef]
23. Al-Smadi, M.; Abu Arqub, O. Computational algorithm for solving fredholm time-fractional partial integrodifferential equations of dirichlet functions type with error estimates. *Appl. Math. Comput.* **2019**, *342*, 280–294. [CrossRef]
24. Al-Smadi, M.; Abu Arqub, O.; Momani, S. Numerical computations of coupled fractional resonant Schrödinger equations arising in quantum mechanics under conformable fractional derivative sense. *Phys. Scr.* **2020**, *95*, 075218. [CrossRef]
25. Al-Smadi, M.; Abu Arqub, O.; Hadid, S. An attractive analytical technique for coupled system of fractional partial differential equations in shallow water waves with conformable derivative. *Commun. Theor. Phys.* **2020**, *72*, 085001. [CrossRef]
26. Al-Smadi, M.; Abu Arqub, O.; Gaith, M. Numerical simulation of telegraph and Cattaneo fractional-type models using adaptive reproducing kernel framework. *Math. Methods Appl. Sci.* **2020**, *44*, 8472–8489. [CrossRef]
27. Nairat, M.; Shqair, M.; Alhalholy, T. Cylindrically Symmetric Fractional Helmholtz Equation. *Appl. Math.* **2019**, *19*, 708–717.
28. Shqair, M. Developing a new approaching technique of homotopy perturbation method to solve two-group reflected cy-lindrical reactor. *Results Phys.* **2019**, *12*, 1880–1887. [CrossRef]
29. Wazwaz, A.-M. A variety of multiple-soliton solutions for the integrable (4+1)-dimensional Fokas equation. *Waves Random Complex Media* **2021**, *31*, 46–56. [CrossRef]
30. Wen, X.; Feng, R.; Lin, J.; Liu, W.; Chen, F.; Yang, Q. Distorted light bullet in a tapered graded-index waveguide with PT symmetric potentials. *Optik* **2021**, *248*, 168092. [CrossRef]
31. Fang, J.J.; Mou, D.S.; Zhang, H.C.; Wang, Y.Y. Discrete fractional soliton dynamics of the fractional Ablowitz-Ladik model. *Optik* **2021**, *228*, 166186. [CrossRef]
32. Liu, C.-S. Counterexamples on Jumarie's two basic fractional calculus formulae. *Commun. Nonlinear Sci. Numer. Simul.* **2015**, *22*, 92–94. [CrossRef]
33. Liu, C.-S. Counterexamples on Jumarie's three basic fractional calculus formulae for non-differentiable continuous functions. *Chaos Solitons Fractals* **2018**, *109*, 219–222. [CrossRef]
34. Tarasov, V.E. No nonlocality. No fractional derivative. *Commun. Nonlinear Sci. Numer. Simulat.* **2018**, *62*, 157–163. [CrossRef]
35. Tarasov, V.E. No violation of the Leibniz rule. No fractional derivative. *Commun. Nonlinear. Sci. Numer. Simulat.* **2013**, *18*, 2945–2948. [CrossRef]
36. Yu, L.-J.; Wu, G.-Z.; Wang, Y.-Y.; Chen, Y.-X. Traveling wave solutions constructed by Mittag–Leffler function of a (2+1)-dimensional space-time fractional NLS equation. *Results Phys.* **2020**, *17*, 103156. [CrossRef]
37. Wu, G.-Z.; Yu, L.-J.; Wang, Y.-Y. Fractional optical solitons of the space-time fractional nonlinear Schrödinger equation. *Int. J. Light Electron Opt.* **2020**, *207*, 164405. [CrossRef]
38. Das, A.; Ghosh, N. Bifurcation of traveling waves and exact solutions of Kadomtsev–Petviashvili modified equal width equation with fractional temporal evolution. *Comput. Appl. Math.* **2019**, *38*, 9. [CrossRef]
39. Jiang, J.; Feng, Y.; Li, S. Improved Fractional Subequation Method and Exact Solutions to Fractional Partial Differential Equations. *J. Funct. Spaces* **2020**, *2020*, 5840920. [CrossRef]
40. Li, C.; Guo, Q.; Zhao, M. On the solutions of (2+1)-dimensional time-fractional Schrödinger equation. *Appl. Math. Lett.* **2019**, *94*, 238–243. [CrossRef]
41. Aksoy, E.; Bekir, A.; Çevikel, A.C. Study on Fractional Differential Equations with Modified Riemann–Liouville Derivative via Kudryashov Method. *Int. J. Nonlinear Sci. Numer. Simul.* **2019**, *20*, 511–516. [CrossRef]

symmetry MDPI

Article

Laplace Transform for Solving System of Integro-Fractional Differential Equations of Volterra Type with Variable Coefficients and Multi-Time Delay

Miran B. M. Amin [1,*] and Shazad Shawki Ahmad [2,*]

1 Technical College of Informatics, Sulaimani Polytechnic University, Sulaymaniyah 46001, Iraq
2 Department of Mathematics, College of Science, University of Sulaimani, Sulaymaniyah 46001, Iraq
* Correspondence: miran.bayan@spu.edu.iq (M.B.M.A.); shazad.ahmed@univsul.edu.iq (S.S.A.)

Abstract: This study is the first to use Laplace transform methods to solve a system of Caputo fractional Volterra integro-differential equations with variable coefficients and a constant multi-time delay. This technique is based on different types of kernels, which we will explain in this paper. Symmetry kernels, which have properties of difference kernels or simple degenerate kernels, are able to compute analytical work. These are demonstrated by solving certain examples and analyzing the effectiveness and precision of cause techniques.

Keywords: system fractional-integro differential equation; Laplace transform; Caputo fractional derivative; delay differential equations; difference and simple degenerate kernels

Citation: Amin, M.B.M.; Ahmad, S.S. Laplace Transform for Solving System of Integro-Fractional Differential Equations of Volterra Type with Variable Coefficients and Multi-Time Delay. *Symmetry* **2022**, *14*, 984. https://doi.org/10.3390/sym14050984

Academic Editor: António M. Lopes

Received: 18 April 2022
Accepted: 6 May 2022
Published: 11 May 2022

Publisher's Note: MDPI stays neutral with regard to jurisdictional claims in published maps and institutional affiliations.

1. Introduction

The purpose of this paper is to solve linear system integro-fractional differential equations of the Volterra type (LS-VIFDEs) with variable coefficients and multi-time delay of the retarded type (RD):

$$\begin{aligned} {}_a^C D_t^{\alpha} u_r(t) + \sum_{i=1}^{n-1} P_{ri}(t)\, {}_a^C D_t^{\alpha_{r(n-i)}} u_r(t) + P_{rn}(t) u_r(g(t,\tau_r)) \\ = f_r(t) + \sum_{j=0}^{m} \lambda_{rj} \int_a^t \mathcal{K}_{rj}\,(t,x) u_j(g(x,\tau_{rj}))dx,\ a \le t \le b. \end{aligned} \tag{1}$$

All $r = 0,1,2,\cdots,m$, as well as the fractional orders, have the basic ordering property $\alpha_{rn} > \alpha_{r(n-1)} > \alpha_{r(n-2)} > \ldots > \alpha_{r1} > \alpha_{r0} = 0$, and are given together with the initial conditions. For all $r = 0,1,\ldots,m$; $\left[u_r^{(k_r)}(t)\right]_{t=a} = u_{r,k_r}$ and historical functions, $u_r^{(k_r)}(t) = \varphi_r^{(k_r)}(t)$ for all $t \in [\overline{a}, a]$, as well as $\overline{a} = a - \max\{\tau_r, \tau_{rj} : j = 0,1,\ldots,m\}$, $k_r = 0,1,\ldots,\mu_r - 1$, $\mu_r = \max\{d_{r\ell} | \ \ell = 0,1,2,\ldots,n\}$, $d_{r\ell} = \lceil \alpha_{r\ell} \rceil$, where $u_r(t)$ are $(m+1)$. This function is unknown and is the solution of LS-VIFDE's multi-time RD, Equation (1), with conditions and functions: $\mathcal{K}_{rj} : S \times \mathbb{R} \to \mathbb{R}$. $(S = \{(t,x) : a \le x \le t \le b\})$, $r,j = 0,1,2,\ldots,m$ and $f_r; P_{ri} : [a,b] \to \mathbb{R}$ for all $i = 1,2,\ldots,n$; $r = 0,1,\ldots,m$ for all real bounded continuous functions. In addition, for all $r = 0,1,\ldots,m$, where $u_r(t) \in \mathbb{R}$, ${}_a^C D_t^{\alpha_{r\ell}} u_r(t)$ is the $\alpha_{r\ell}$-fractional Caputo-derivative order of the functions u_r on $[a,b]$ and all $\alpha_{r\ell}, \in \mathbb{R}^+$, $d_{r\ell} - 1 > \alpha_{r\ell} \le d_{r\ell}$, $d_{r\ell} = \lceil \alpha_{r\ell} \rceil$ for all $r = 0,1,\ldots,m$; $\ell = 1,2,\ldots,n$. Moreover, the value of $\tau_{rj}, \tau_r \in \mathbb{R}^+$ for all $j = 0,1,\ldots,m$ are called positive constant time lags or time delays. Because the problem of LS-delayed VIFDE's time delay is a relatively new topic in mathematics, there are only one or two ways of solving it, and since the specific analytic solution no longer exists, an approximation method must be used. In this paper, we use the Laplace transform to provide an explanation for how to solve Equation (1) with conditions.

The Laplace transform is a very useful method for solving various types of equations, such as integro-differential equations, integral equations, fractional equations, and delay differential equations. It can also be used to solve initial and boundary value problems related to differential equations and partial differentials with constant coefficients [1–6]. This transform method is also used for solving linear Caputo fractional-integro differential equations with multi-time retarded delays [7] and for solving linear system integro-fractional differential equation of Volterra-type equations [8]. When using this technique, it is important and necessary to explain and define several properties of the Laplace transform that are important for driving this transformation of delay functions and the Caputo fractional derivative, which is expressed in Equation (1).

This work is classified into these sections as follows: some definitions and important properties are shown in Section 2. In Section 3, a system of integro-fractional differential equations of the Volterra type with variable coefficients and multi-time delay technique is presented. In Section 4, the results are illustrated with all of the examples. Finally, a discussion of this method is included in Section 5.

2. Definitions with Important Properties

2.1. Fractional Calculus

In this subsection, we recall the most common definitions and results of fractional calculus that will be useful for this research. First, we start from the definition of function space $C_\gamma, \gamma \in \mathbb{R}$, which is the basic definition that operational calculus needs for the differential operator:

Definition 1. [4,7]. *A real valued function u defined on $[a,b]$ is in the space of γ-functions $C_\gamma[a,b]$, $\gamma \in \mathbb{R}$ if there exists a real number $r > \gamma$, such that $u(t) = (t-a)^r \hat{u}(t)$, where $\hat{u} \in C[a,b]$, and it is said to be in the space $C_\gamma^n[a,b]$ if and only if $u^{(n)} \in C_\gamma[a,b]$, $n \in \mathbb{N}_0$.*

Definition 2. [4,8]. *For a function $u \in C_\gamma[a,b]$, $\delta \geq -1$, the Reimann–Liouville fractional integral operator ${}_aJ_t^\alpha$ of fractional order $\alpha \in \mathbb{R}^+$ and origin point a is defined as:*

$$
\begin{gathered}
{}_aJ_t^\alpha u(t) = \tfrac{1}{\Gamma(\alpha)} \int_a^t (t-x)^{\alpha-1} u(x)dx. \\
{}_aJ_t^0 u(t) = u(t),\ a \leq t \leq b.
\end{gathered}
$$

where Γ is the gamma function. ${}_aJ_t^\alpha$ has an important (or semigroup) property, that is: ${}_aJ_t^\alpha\, {}_aJ_t^\beta u(t) = {}_aJ_t^\beta\, {}_aJ_t^\alpha u(t) = {}_aJ_t^{\alpha+\beta} u(t)$ for arbitrary $\alpha > 0$ and $\beta > 0$. Additionally, it has the following properties

$$
{}_aJ_t^\alpha (t-a)^{\delta} = \frac{\Gamma(\delta)}{\Gamma(\delta+\alpha+1)} (t-a)^{\delta+\alpha},\ \delta > -1.
$$

Definition 3. [7,8]. *Let $\alpha > 0$, $m = \alpha$ and $a \in \mathbb{R}$. The Reimann–Liouville fractional derivative of order α and starting point a of a function $u(t) \in C_{-1}^m[a,b]$ is given as:*

$$
\begin{gathered}
{}_a^R D_t^\alpha u(t) = D^m \left[{}_aJ_t^{m-\alpha} u(t) \right]. \\
{}_a^R D_t^0 u(t) = u(t),\ a \leq t \leq b.
\end{gathered}
$$

If $\alpha = m (\in \mathbb{Z}^+)$ and $u \in C^m[a,\ b]$, thus ${}_a^R D_t^m u(t) = \frac{d^m}{dt^m} u(t)$.

Definition 4. [8,9]. *Let $\alpha > 0$, $m = \alpha$,* then the *Caputo fractional derivative of order α and starting point a of a function $u(t) \in C_{-1}^m[a,b]$ is given as:*

$$
\begin{gathered}
{}_a^C D_t^\alpha u(t) = {}_aJ_t^{m-\alpha} u^{(m)}(t) = \tfrac{1}{\Gamma(m-\alpha)} \int_a^t (t-s)^{m-\alpha-1} u^{(m)}(s)ds. \\
{}_a^C D_t^0 u(t) = u(t),\ a \leq t \leq b.
\end{gathered}
$$

Additionally, if $\alpha = m (\in \mathbb{Z}^+)$ and *$u \in C^m[a,\ b]$, thus ${}_a^C D_t^m u(t) = \frac{d^m}{dt^m} u(t)$.*

2.2. Some Important Properties

In this subsection, we are interested some important properties which are used later on this paper [4,7–9].

i. ${}_a^R D_t^\alpha \mathcal{A} = \mathcal{A}\frac{(t-a)^{-\alpha}}{\Gamma(1-\alpha)}$; where $\mathcal{A}$ is any constant; ($\alpha \geq 0$, $\alpha \notin \mathbb{N}$).
ii. If the Caputo fractional derivative of a constant function is equal to zero, it means ${}_a^C D_t^\alpha \mathcal{A} = 0$, for any constant $\mathcal{A}$ and all $\alpha > 0$.
iii. The relationship between the R-L integral and Caputo derivatives are shown here: Let $\alpha \geq 0$, $m = \alpha$ and $u \in C^m[a,b]$, then:

$$ {}_a^C D_t^\alpha [{}_a J_t^\alpha u(t)] = u(t) \; ; \; a \leq t \leq b $$

$$ {}_a J_t^\alpha \left[{}_a^C D_t^\alpha u(t) \right] = u(t) - \sum_{k=0}^{m-1} \frac{u^{(k)}(a)}{k!}(t-a)^k . $$

iv. Let $T_{m-1}[\gamma; a]$ be the Taylor polynomial of degree $(m-1)$ for the function γ, then:

$$ {}_a^C D_t^\alpha \gamma(t) = {}_a^R D_t^\alpha [\gamma(t) - T_{m-1}[\gamma; a]], $$

where $(m - 1 < \alpha \leq m)$.
v. Let $u(t) = (t-a)^\beta$ and $\alpha > 0\,; m = \alpha$ for some $\beta \geq 0$, then:

$$ {}_a^C D_t^\alpha u(t) = \begin{cases} 0 & \text{if } \beta \in \{0,1,2,\cdots,m-1\} \\ \frac{\Gamma(\beta+1)}{\Gamma(\beta+1-\alpha)}(t-a)^{\beta-\alpha} & \text{if } \beta \in \mathbb{N} \text{ and } \beta \geq m \\ & \text{or } \beta \notin \mathbb{N} \text{ and } \beta > m-1 \end{cases} $$

Definition 5. [1,10]. *The Laplace transform (LT) for the suitable function, $u(t)$, of real variable $t \geq 0$, is the function $U(s)$, which is defined by the integral form:*

$$ U(s) = \mathcal{L}\{u(t)\} = \int_0^\infty e^{-st} u(t) dt \tag{2} $$

with $U(s)$ the LT of $u(t)$, and inverse Laplace transform of $U(s)$, denoted by $\mathcal{L}^{-1}\{U(s); t\}$, being the function u defined on $[0, \infty)$, which has the fewest number of discontinuities and satisfies $\mathcal{L}\{u(t); s\} = U(s)$. Laplace transform has various properties with some lemmas, which are the key for our work, as shown below [1,6,11–13]:

i. *If $u(t)$ and $q(t)$ have well-defined Laplace transforms, then $U(s) = \mathcal{L}\{u(t)\}$ and $Q(s) = \mathcal{L}\{q(t)\}$, respectively. Now, the Laplace transform of the convolution integral is defined by the form:*

$$ \mathcal{L}\{(u * q)(t)\} = \mathcal{L}\left\{ \int_0^t u(t-x)\, q(x) dx \right\} = U(s)Q(s) \tag{3} $$

If $u = 1$, then:

$$ \mathcal{L}\left\{ \int_0^t q(x) dx; s \right\} = \frac{1}{s}\, Q(s) \tag{4} $$

ii. *Put the power function t^m of order $m \in \mathbb{Z}^+$, then:*

$$ \mathcal{L}\{t^m u(t)\} = (-1)^m \frac{d^m}{ds^m} \mathcal{L}\{u(t)\} = (-1)^m \frac{d^m}{ds^m} U(s) \tag{5} $$

iii. *From (ii and iii), we obtain:*

$$ \mathcal{L}\left\{ \int_0^t t\, u(x) dx; s \right\} = -\frac{d}{ds}\left(\frac{1}{s} U(s) \right) \quad \text{and} \quad \mathcal{L}\left\{ \int_0^t x\, u(x) dx\,; s \right\} = -\frac{1}{s}\frac{d}{ds} U(s) \,. \tag{6} $$

The following shows the important lemma for the Laplace transform of a constant delay function:

Lemma 1. [7]. *Let $u(t)$be a continuous differentiable function on a closed bounded interval* $[0,b]$, $b \in \mathbb{R}^+$, *and let* τ *be a constant delay such that:*

$$u(t) = \varphi(t), \text{ for } -\tau \le t < 0. \tag{7}$$

Then, the Laplace transform of a $\tau -$ delay *function is given by:*

$$\mathcal{L}\{u(t-\tau); s\} = e^{-s\tau}\,[U(s) + Q(s,\tau)]. \tag{8}$$

where $Q(s,\tau) = \int_{-\tau}^{0} e^{-st}\varphi(t)dt$ *and* $\mathcal{L}\{u(t)\} = U(s)$. *If the historical function* $\varphi(t)$ *is defined by power function* $t^n (n \in \mathbb{Z}^+)$, *we obtain:*

$$\mathcal{L}\{u(t-\tau); s\} = e^{-s\tau}\, U(s) + \sum_{p=0}^{n}(-1)^{n-p}\, p! \begin{pmatrix} n \\ p \end{pmatrix} \frac{\tau^{n-p}}{s^{p+1}} - \frac{n!}{s^{n+1}}\, e^{-s\tau} \tag{9}$$

Lemma 2. [4,9]. *Laplace transform of Caputo fractional of order* α $(m-1 < \alpha \le m)$, $m = \alpha$ *can be obtained as:*

$$\begin{aligned} \mathcal{L}\{{}^{C}_{a}D^{\alpha}_{t}\, u(t); s\} &= \mathcal{L}\{J^{m-\alpha}_{t} D^{m}_{t} u(t); s\} = s^{-(m-\alpha)}\, \mathcal{L}\Big\{u^{(m)}(t); s\Big\} \\ &= s^{-(m-\alpha)} \left[s^{m}\, U(s) - \sum_{k=0}^{m-1} s^{m-k-1}\, u^{(k)}(0)\right] = s^{\alpha}\, U(s) - \sum_{k=0}^{m-1} s^{\alpha-k-1}\, u^{(k)}(0)\,. \end{aligned} \tag{10}$$

3. Solving LS-VIFDE's Multi-Time RD Using the Laplace Transform Technique

In this section, we try to find a general analytical solution to a linear system of integro-differential equations of the arbitrary orders with variable coefficients and multi-time delays using the Laplace transform method in various types of kernels.

3.1. First Type (Difference Kernel)

We use Equation (1) with different kernels and $a = 0$ as the starting point. Furthermore, we consider $P_{ri}(t)$ as a power function, with difference kernels form $\mathcal{K}_{rj}(t,x) = \mathcal{K}_{rj}(t-x)$, where $C_{ri}t^{\ell_{ri}}$, $C_{ri} \in \mathbb{R}$ are constants and ℓ_{ri} are arbitrary non-negative integers for all r and i, and the Laplace transformation is taken for all $r = 0,1,\ldots,m$, which is:

$$\begin{aligned} &\mathcal{L}\{{}^{C}_{a}D^{\alpha_{rn}}_{t} u_r(t); s\} + \mathcal{L}\left\{\sum_{i=1}^{n-1} P_{ri}(t)\, {}^{C}_{a}D^{\alpha_{r(n-i)}}_{t} u_r(t); s\right\} + \mathcal{L}\{P_{rn}(t) u_r(g(t,\tau_r)); s\} \\ &\quad = \mathcal{L}\{f_r(t); s\} + \sum_{j=0}^{m} \lambda_{rj} \mathcal{L}\Big\{ \int_0^t \mathcal{K}_{rj}(t-x) u_j(g(x,\tau_{rj}))dx; s\Big\}. \end{aligned} \tag{11}$$

After applying the Laplace transformation in Equation (11), using Lemma 2 with the initial condition for the first part, where $m_{\alpha_{rn}} - 1 < \alpha_{rn} \le m_{\alpha_{rn}}$ for all $r = 0,1,\ldots,m$, and also using Definition (5; part (ii)) and Lemma 2 for second parts, where $m_{\alpha_{r(n-i)}} - 1 < \alpha_{r(n-i)} \le m_{\alpha_{r(n-i)}}$, for all $r = 0,1,\ldots,m$, we obtain:

$$\begin{aligned} \mathcal{L}\{{}^{C}_{a}D^{\alpha_{rn}}_{t} u_r(t); s\} &= s^{\alpha_{rn}}\, U_r(s) - \sum_{k_r=0}^{m_{\alpha_{rn}}-1} s^{\alpha_{rn}-k_r-1}\, u_r^{(k_r)}(0) \\ &= s^{\alpha_{rn}}\, U_r(s) - \sum_{k_r=0}^{m_{\alpha_{rn}}-1} s^{\alpha_{rn}-k_r-1}\, u_{r,k_r}. \end{aligned} \tag{12}$$

where u_{r,k_r} are given for all r from the conditions. For all $r = 0, 1, \ldots, m$ using Equations (5) and (10) and conditions, for each $i = 1, 2, \ldots, n-1$, we obtain:

$$\begin{aligned} &\mathcal{L}\Big\{ P_{ri}(t)\, {}_a^C D_t^{\alpha_{r(n-i)}} u_r(t); s \Big\} \\ &= C_{ri}(-1)^{\ell_{ri}} \frac{d^{\ell_{ri}}}{ds^{\ell_{ri}}}\left[s^{\alpha_{r(n-i)}}\, U_r(s) \right] \\ &-C_{ri}(-1)^{\ell_{ri}} \frac{d^{\ell_{ri}}}{ds^{\ell_{ri}}}\left[\sum_{k_r=0}^{m_{\alpha_{r(n-i)}}-1} s^{\alpha_{r(n-i)}-k_r-1} u_{r,k_r} \right]. \end{aligned} \tag{13}$$

where ℓ_{ri} is the order of $P_{ri}(t)$ for each $i = 1, 2, \ldots, n-1$ and $r = 0, 1, \ldots, m$. Consequently, we use Equation (5) and then apply the Lemma (1, Equations (8) and (9)), respectively, with the defined $g(t, \tau_r) = t - \tau_r$, thus obtaining for each r:

$$\mathcal{L}\{P_{rn}(t) u_r(g(t, \tau_r)); s\} = C_{rn}(-1)^{\ell_{rn}} \frac{d^{\ell_{rn}}}{ds^{\ell_{rn}}}\left[e^{-s\tau_r}(U_r(s) + Q_r(s, \tau_r)) \right].$$

where:

$$Q_r(s, \tau_r) = \int_{-\tau_r}^{0} e^{-st} \varphi_r(t) dt.$$

If the historical function $\varphi_r(t)$ is t^{q_r}, $q_r \in \mathbb{Z}^+$ for all $r = 0, 1, \ldots, m$, in this special case, we obtain:

$$\begin{aligned} &\mathcal{L}\{P_{rn}(t) u_r(g(t, \tau_r)); s\} \\ &= C_{rn}\,(-1)^{\ell_{rn}} \left\{ \frac{d^{\ell_{rn}}}{ds^{\ell_{rn}}}\left[e^{-s\tau_r} U_r(s) \right] + \frac{d^{\ell_{rn}}}{ds^{\ell_{rn}}}\left[\sum_{p=0}^{q_r} (-1)^{q_r-p}\, p! \binom{q_r}{p} \frac{\tau_r{}^{q_r-p}}{s^{p+1}} \right] - \frac{d^{\ell_{rn}}}{ds^{\ell_{rn}}}\left[\frac{q_r!}{s^{q_r+1}} e^{-s\tau_r} \right] \right\}. \end{aligned} \tag{14}$$

the Laplace transform of the homogenous part is simply written as:

$$\mathcal{L}\{f_r(t); s\} = F_r(s),\ r = 0, 1, \ldots, m. \tag{15}$$

By applying Equation (3) from Definition 4 with Lemma (1, Equations (8) and (11)) with defined $g(x, \tau_{rj}) = x - \tau_{rj}$ for all $r; j = 0, 1, \ldots, m$, the last part of Equation (11) will become:

$$\mathcal{L}\left\{ \int_0^t \mathcal{K}_{rj}\,(t-x) u_j(g(x, \tau_{rj})) dx; s \right\} = \mathcal{K}_{rj}(s)\, e^{-s\tau_{rj}}\left[U_j(s) + Q_j(s, \tau_{rj}) \right].$$

where:

$$Q_j(s, \tau_{rj}) = \int_{-\tau_{rj}}^{0} e^{-st} \varphi_j(t) dt.$$

The symbolic $\mathcal{K}_{rj}(s)$ is the Laplace transform of the difference kernel $\mathcal{K}_{rj}\,(t-x)$ for each r and j. If the historical function $\varphi_j(t)$ is t^{q_r}, $q_r \in \mathbb{Z}^+$ for all $r = 0, 1, \ldots, m$, in this special case, we obtain:

$$\begin{aligned} &\mathcal{L}\left\{ \int_0^t \mathcal{K}_{rj}\,(t-x) u_j(g(x, \tau_{rj})) dx; s \right\} \\ &= \mathcal{K}_{rj}(s)\left[e^{-s\tau_{rj}}\, U_j(s) + \sum_{p=0}^{q_r} (-1)^{q_r-p}\, p! \binom{q_r}{p} \frac{\tau_{rj}{}^{q_r-p}}{s^{p+1}} - \frac{q_r!}{s^{q_r+1}} e^{-s\tau_{rj}} \right]. \end{aligned} \tag{16}$$

After putting Equations (12)–(16) into Equation (11), they become:

$$s^{\alpha_{rn}}U_r(s)-\sum_{k_r=0}^{m_{\alpha_{rn}}-1}s^{\alpha_{rn}-k_r-1}u_{r,k_r}+\sum_{i=1}^{n-1}C_{ri}(-1)^{\ell_{ri}}\frac{d^{\ell_{ri}}}{ds^{\ell_{ri}}}\left[s^{\alpha_{r(n-i)}}U_r(s)\right]$$
$$-\sum_{i=1}^{n-1}C_{ri}(-1)^{\ell_{ri}}\frac{d^{\ell_{ri}}}{ds^{\ell_{ri}}}\left[\sum_{k_r=0}^{m_{\alpha_{r(n-i)}}-1}s^{\alpha_{r(n-i)}-k_r-1}u_{r,k_r}\right]+C_{rn}(-1)^{\ell_{rn}}\left\{\frac{d^{\ell_{rn}}}{ds^{\ell_{rn}}}\left[e^{-s\tau_r}(U_r(s)+Q_r(s,\tau_r))\right]\right.$$
$$=F_r(s)+\sum_{j=0}^{m}\lambda_{rj}\mathcal{K}_{rj}(s)\,e^{-s\tau_{rj}}\left[U_j(s)+Q_j(s,\tau_{rj})\right].$$

If t^{q_r}, $q_r\in\mathbb{Z}^+$ for each $r=0,1,\ldots,m$ is a power function, which is also a historical function, using part two of Lemma 1 above the equation means it becomes:

$$\begin{aligned}&s^{\alpha_{rn}}U_r(s)-\sum_{k_r=0}^{m_{\alpha_{rn}}-1}s^{\alpha_{rn}-k_r-1}u_{r,k_r}\\&+\sum_{i=1}^{n-1}C_{ri}(-1)^{\ell_{ri}}\frac{d^{\ell_{ri}}}{ds^{\ell_{ri}}}\left[s^{\alpha_{r(n-i)}}U_r(s)\right]-\sum_{i=1}^{n-1}C_{ri}(-1)^{\ell_{ri}}\frac{d^{\ell_{ri}}}{ds^{\ell_{ri}}}\left[\sum_{k_r=0}^{m_{\alpha_{r(n-i)}}-1}s^{\alpha_{r(n-i)}-k_r-1}u_{r,k_r}\right]\\&+C_{rn}(-1)^{\ell_{rn}}\left\{\frac{d^{\ell_{rn}}}{ds^{\ell_{rn}}}\left[e^{-s\tau_r}U_r(s)\right]+\frac{d^{\ell_{rn}}}{ds^{\ell_{rn}}}\left[\sum_{p=0}^{q_r}(-1)^{q_r-p}p!\binom{q_r}{p}\frac{\tau_r{}^{q_r-p}}{s^{p+1}}\right]-\frac{d^{\ell_{rn}}}{ds^{\ell_{rn}}}\left[\frac{q_r!}{s^{q_r+1}}e^{-s\tau_r}\right]\right\}\\&=F_r(s)+\sum_{j=0}^{m}\lambda_{rj}\mathcal{K}_{rj}(s)\left[e^{-s\tau_{rj}}U_j(s)+\sum_{p=0}^{q_r}(-1)^{q_r-p}p!\binom{q_r}{p}\frac{\tau_{rj}{}^{q_r-p}}{s^{p+1}}-\frac{q_r!}{s^{q_r+1}}e^{-s\tau_{rj}}\right].\end{aligned}\tag{17}$$

Consequently, the system of ordinary differential equation of components $\{U_r(s):r=0,1,\ldots,m\}$ is solved to find $U_r(s)$. In the end, the inverse of the Laplace transform on $U_r(s)$ is used to obtain the solution $u_r(t)$ of LS-VIFDEs for multi-time RD (1). After some simple manipulations, from Equation (17), we obtain:

$$\begin{aligned}&\left[s^{\alpha_{rn}}+\sum_{i=1}^{n-1}C_{ri}(-1)^{\ell_{ri}}\frac{d^{\ell_{ri}}}{ds^{\ell_{ri}}}s^{\alpha_{r(n-i)}}+C_{rn}(-1)^{\ell_{rn}}\frac{d^{\ell_{rn}}}{ds^{\ell_{rn}}}e^{-s\tau_r}-\lambda_{rr}\mathcal{K}_{rr}(s)e^{-s\tau_{rr}}\right]U_r(s)\\&-\sum_{\substack{j=0\\j\neq r}}^{m}\lambda_{rj}\mathcal{K}_{rj}(s)e^{-s\tau_{rj}}U_j(s)+\sum_{i=1}^{n-1}C_{ri}(-1)^{\ell_{ri}}s^{\alpha_{r(n-i)}}\frac{d^{\ell_{ri}}}{ds^{\ell_{ri}}}U_r(s)\\&+C_{rn}(-1)^{\ell_{rn}}e^{-s\tau_r}\frac{d^{\ell_{rn}}}{ds^{\ell_{rn}}}U_r(s)=\overline{F}_r(s).\ r=0,1,\ldots,m\end{aligned}$$

where

$$\begin{aligned}\overline{F}_r(s)=F_r(s)&+\sum_{k_r=0}^{m_{\alpha_{rn}}-1}s^{\alpha_{rn}-k_r-1}u_{r,k_r}+\sum_{i=1}^{n-1}C_{ri}(-1)^{\ell_{ri}}\frac{d^{\ell_{ri}}}{ds^{\ell_{ri}}}\left[\sum_{k_r=0}^{m_{\alpha_{r(n-i)}}-1}s^{\alpha_{r(n-i)}-k_r-1}u_{r,k_r}\right]\\&-C_{rn}(-1)^{\ell_{rn}}\left\{\frac{d^{\ell_{rn}}}{ds^{\ell_{rn}}}\left[\sum_{p=0}^{q_r}(-1)^{q_r-p}p!\binom{q_r}{p}\frac{\tau_r{}^{q_r-p}}{s^{p+1}}\right]-\frac{d^{\ell_{rn}}}{ds^{\ell_{rn}}}\left[\frac{q_r!}{s^{q_r+1}}e^{-s\tau_r}\right]\right\}\\&+\sum_{j=0}^{m}\lambda_{rj}\mathcal{K}_{rj}(s)\left[\sum_{p=0}^{q_r}(-1)^{q_r-p}p!\binom{q_r}{p}\frac{\tau_{rj}{}^{q_r-p}}{s^{p+1}}-\frac{q_r!}{s^{q_r+1}}e^{-s\tau_{rj}}\right].\end{aligned}$$

As a special case, if the $P_{ri}(t)$ and $P_{rn}(t)$ are only constants, this means that ℓ_{ri} and ℓ_{rn} are equal to zero. Thus, after some simple manipulations, from Equation (17), we obtain the following system for all $r=0,1,\ldots,m$:

$$H_r(s)U_r(s)-\sum_{\substack{j=0\\j\neq r}}^{m}\lambda_{rj}\mathcal{K}_{rj}(s)e^{-s\tau_{rj}}U_j(s)=\overline{F}_r(s).\tag{18}$$

where:

$$H_r(s) = s^{\alpha_{rn}} + \sum_{i=1}^{n-1} C_{ri}(-1)^{\ell_{ri}} \frac{d^{\ell_{ri}}}{ds^{\ell_{ri}}} s^{\alpha_{r(n-i)}} + C_{rn}\,(-1)^{\ell_{rn}} \frac{d^{\ell_{rn}}}{ds^{\ell_{rn}}} e^{-s\tau_r} - \lambda_{rr}\,\mathcal{K}_{rr}(s)e^{-s\tau_{rr}}.$$

Finally, the system of ordinary differential equation of components $\{U_r(s) : r = 0, 1, \ldots, m\}$ is solved to find $U_r(s)$. In the end, the inverse of the Laplace transform on $U_r(s)$ is used to obtain the solution $u_r(t)$ of LS-VIFDEs for multi-time RD (1).

3.2. *Second Type (Simple Degenerate Kernel)*

Some types of linear-system VIFDEs of consistent multi-time can be solved using the Laplace transform approach. We take the same conditions as Equation (12) with all conditions by changing the kernel from difference kernel to a simple degenerate kernel. Define the kernel: $\mathcal{K}_{rj}\,(t,x) = c_{rj}t^{k^1_{rj}} + d_{rj}x^{k^2_{rj}}$, where $c_{rj},\ d_{rj} \in \mathbb{R}$ for all $r, j = 0, 1, \ldots, m$ and $k^1_{rj}, k^2_{rj} \in \mathbb{Z}^+$; then:

$$\begin{aligned} &\mathcal{L}\{{}^C_a D^{\alpha_{rn}}_t u_r(t); s\} + \mathcal{L}\left\{\sum_{i=1}^{n-1} P_{ri}(t)\ {}^C_a D^{\alpha_{r(n-i)}}_t u_r(t); s\right\} + \mathcal{L}\{P_{rn}(t)u_r(g(t,\tau_r)); s\} \\ &\quad = \mathcal{L}\{f_r(t); s\} + \sum_{j=0}^{m} \lambda_{rj}\mathcal{L}\left\{\ \int_0^t \left[c_{rj}t^{k^1_{rj}} + d_{rj}x^{k^2_{rj}}\right] u_j(g(x,\tau_{rj}))dx; s\right\}. \end{aligned} \tag{19}$$

The left hands in all parts of Equation (19) are the same as Equation (11) in Section 3.1, while for the integral part, it is different. We apply the important property of Equation (6) part (iii) in Section 2.2 using Equations (8) and (9), respectively, and for higher derivative of multiplication functions using Leibniz's formula [7,14], with the property $g(x, \tau_{rj}) = x - \tau_{rj}$; then, after some manipulating, we obtain:

$$\begin{aligned} &\mathcal{L}\left\{\ \int_0^t \left[c_{rj}t^{k^1_{rj}} + d_{rj}x^{k^2_{rj}}\right] u_j(g(x,\tau_{rj}))dx; s\right\} \\ &= \frac{e^{-s\tau_{rj}}}{s}\left\{\left[c_{rj}\left(\sum_{b=0}^{k^1_{rj}} b!\begin{pmatrix} k^1_{rj} \\ b \end{pmatrix}\frac{1}{s^b}{\tau_{rj}}^{k^1_{rj}-b}\right) + d_{rj}{\tau_{rj}}^{k^2_{rj}}\right] + \left[d_{rj}\sum_{b=0}^{k^2_{rj}-1}(-1)^{b+k^2_{rj}}{\tau_{rj}}^b\begin{pmatrix} k^2_{rj} \\ b \end{pmatrix}\frac{d^{k^2_{rj}-b}}{ds^{k^2_{rj}-b}}\right]\right. \\ &\quad \left. + \left[c_{rj}\sum_{b=0}^{k^1_{rj}-1}(-1)^{b+k^1_{rj}}b!\begin{pmatrix} k^1_{rj} \\ b \end{pmatrix}\frac{1}{s^b}\left(\sum_{p=0}^{k^1_{rj}-b-1}(-1)^p{\tau_{rj}}^p\begin{pmatrix} k^1_{rj}-b \\ p \end{pmatrix}\frac{d^{k^1_{rj}-b-p}}{ds^{k^1_{rj}-b-p}}\right)\right]\right\}U_j(s) \\ &\quad + \frac{1}{s}\left\{c_{rj}\left[\sum_{b=0}^{k^1_{rj}}(-1)^{b+k^1_{rj}}b!\begin{pmatrix} k^1_{rj} \\ b \end{pmatrix}\frac{1}{s^b}\ \frac{d^{k^1_{rj}-b}}{ds^{k^1_{rj}-b}}\right] + d_{rj}\left[(-1)^{k^2_{rj}}\frac{d^{k^2_{rj}}}{ds^{k^2_{rj}}}\right]\right\}H^q_{rj}(s). \end{aligned} \tag{20}$$

for all $r, j = 0, 1, \ldots, m$, where:

$$H^q_{rj}(s) = \begin{cases} e^{-s\tau_{rj}}Q_j(s,\tau_{rj})\ ;\ \text{if the historical function be any countinous differential function.} \\ \displaystyle\sum_{p=0}^{q_r}(-1)^{q_r-p}\ p!\begin{pmatrix} q_r \\ p \end{pmatrix}\frac{{\tau_{rj}}^{q_r-p}}{s^{p+1}} - \frac{q_r!}{s^{q_r+1}}e^{-s\tau_{rj}}\ ;\ if\ \varphi_r(t) = t^{q_r}. \end{cases}$$

and:

$$Q_j(s,\tau_{rj}) = \int_{-\tau_{rj}}^{0} e^{-st}\varphi_j(t)dt.$$

After some simple manipulations, and using Equation (20), we obtain the general solution for Equation (19):

$$\begin{gathered}
s^{\alpha_{rn}}\,U_r(s)-\sum_{k=0}^{m_{\alpha_{rn}}-1}s^{\alpha_{rn}-k-1}\,u_{r,k_r}\\
+\sum_{i=1}^{n-1}C_{ri}(-1)^{\ell_{ri}}\frac{d^{\ell_{ri}}}{ds^{\ell_{ri}}}\left[s^{\alpha_{r(n-i)}}\,U_r(s)\right]+\sum_{i=1}^{n-1}C_{ri}(-1)^{\ell_{ri}}\frac{d^{\ell_{ri}}}{ds^{\ell_{ri}}}\left[\sum_{k=0}^{m_{\alpha_{r(n-i)}}-1}s^{\alpha_{r(n-i)}-k-1}u_{r,k_r}\right]\\
+C_{rn}\,(-1)^{\ell_{rn}}\left\{\frac{d^{\ell_{rn}}}{ds^{\ell_{rn}}}\left[e^{-s\tau_r}U_r(s)\right]+\frac{d^{\ell_{rn}}}{ds^{\ell_{rn}}}\left[\sum_{p=0}^{q_r}(-1)^{q_r-p}\,p!\begin{pmatrix}q_r\\p\end{pmatrix}\frac{{\tau_r}^{q_r-p}}{s^{p+1}}\right]-\frac{d^{\ell_{rn}}}{ds^{\ell_{rn}}}\left[\frac{q_r!}{s^{q_r+1}}e^{-s\tau_r}\right]\right\}\\
=F_r(s)\\
+\sum_{j=0}^{m}\lambda_{rj}\frac{e^{-s\tau_{rj}}}{s}\left\{\begin{array}{l}
\left\{\begin{array}{l}\left[c_{rj}\left(\sum_{b=0}^{k^1_{rj}}b!\begin{pmatrix}k^1_{rj}\\b\end{pmatrix}\frac{1}{s^b}{\tau_{rj}}^{k^1_{rj}-b}\right)+d_{rj}{\tau_{rj}}^{k^2_{rj}}\right]+\left[d_{rj}\sum_{b=0}^{k^2_{rj}-1}(-1)^{b+k^2_{rj}}{\tau_{rj}}^{b}\begin{pmatrix}k^2_{rj}\\b\end{pmatrix}\frac{d^{k^2_{rj}-b}}{ds^{k^2_{rj}-b}}\right]\\
+\left[c_{rj}\sum_{b=0}^{k^2_{rj}-1}(-1)^{b+k^1_{rj}}b!\begin{pmatrix}k^1_{rj}\\b\end{pmatrix}\frac{1}{s^b}\left(\sum_{p=0}^{k^2_{rj}-b-1}(-1)p_{\tau_{rj}}p\begin{pmatrix}k^1_{rj}-b\\p\end{pmatrix}\frac{d^{k^1_{rj}-b-p}}{ds^{k^1_{rj}-b-p}}\right)\right]\end{array}\right\}U_j(s)\\
+\frac{1}{s}\left\{c_{rj}\left[\sum_{b=0}^{k^1_{rj}}(-1)^{b+k^1_{rj}}b!\begin{pmatrix}k^1_{rj}\\b\end{pmatrix}\frac{1}{s^b}\frac{d^{k^1_{rj}-b}}{ds^{k^1_{rj}-b}}\right]+d_{rj}\left[(-1)^{k^2_{rj}}\frac{d^{k^2_{rj}}}{ds^{k^2_{rj}}}\right]\right\}H^q_{rj}(s)
\end{array}\right\}.
\end{gathered}\tag{21}$$

Equation (21) becomes:

$$\begin{gathered}
\overline{F}_r(s)=F_r(s)+\sum_{k_r=0}^{m_{\alpha_{rn}}-1}s^{\alpha_{rn}-k_r-1}\,u_{r,k_r}+\sum_{i=1}^{n-1}C_{ri}(-1)^{\ell_{ri}}\frac{d^{\ell_{ri}}}{ds^{\ell_{ri}}}\left[\sum_{k_r=0}^{m_{\alpha_{r(n-i)}}-1}s^{\alpha_{r(n-i)}-k_r-1}u_{r,k_r}\right]\\
-C_{rn}(-1)^{\ell_{rn}}\left\{\frac{d^{\ell_{rn}}}{ds^{\ell_{rn}}}\left[\sum_{p=0}^{q_r}(-1)^{q_r-p}\,p!\begin{pmatrix}q_r\\p\end{pmatrix}\frac{{\tau_r}^{q_r-p}}{s^{p+1}}\right]-\frac{d^{\ell_{rn}}}{ds^{\ell_{rn}}}\left[\frac{q_r!}{s^{q_r+1}}e^{-s\tau_r}\right]\right\}\\
+\sum_{j=0}^{m}\lambda_{rj}\frac{1}{s}\left\{c_{rj}\left[\sum_{b=0}^{k^1_{rj}}(-1)^{b+k^1_{rj}}b!\begin{pmatrix}k^1_{rj}\\b\end{pmatrix}\frac{1}{s^b}\frac{d^{k^1_{rj}-b}}{ds^{k^1_{rj}-b}}\right]+d_{rj}\left[(-1)^{k^2_{rj}}\frac{d^{k^2_{rj}}}{ds^{k^2_{rj}}}\right]\right\}H^q_{rj}(s).
\end{gathered}$$

As a special case, if the $P_{ri}(t)$ and $P_{rn}(t)$ are the only constants, this means that ℓ_{ri} and ℓ_{rn} are equal to zero. Thus, after some simple manipulations, system Equation (21) was formed, and we obtained the following system, for all $r=0,1,\ldots,m$:

$$H_r(s)U_r(s)-\sum_{\substack{j=0\\ j\neq r}}^{m}\lambda_{rj}\,\overline{K}_{rj}(s)e^{-s\tau_{rj}}U_j(s)=\overline{F}_r(s).\tag{22}$$

where:

$$H_r(s)=s^{\alpha_{rn}}+\sum_{i=1}^{n-1}C_{ri}(-1)^{\ell_{ri}}\frac{d^{\ell_{ri}}}{ds^{\ell_{ri}}}s^{\alpha_{r(n-i)}}+C_{rn}\,(-1)^{\ell_{rn}}\frac{d^{\ell_{rn}}}{ds^{\ell_{rn}}}e^{-s\tau_r}-\lambda_{rr}\,\overline{K}_{rr}(s)e^{-s\tau_{rr}}.$$

and:

$$\begin{gathered}
\overline{K}_{rj}(s)=\left[c_{rj}\left(\sum_{b=0}^{k^1_{rj}}b!\begin{pmatrix}k^1_{rj}\\b\end{pmatrix}\frac{1}{s^b}{\tau_{rj}}^{k^1_{rj}-b}\right)+d_{rj}{\tau_{rj}}^{k^2_{rj}}\right]+\left[d_{rj}\sum_{b=0}^{k^2_{rj}-1}(-1)^{b+k^2_{rj}}{\tau_{rj}}^{b}\begin{pmatrix}k^2_{rj}\\b\end{pmatrix}\frac{d^{k^2_{rj}-b}}{ds^{k^2_{rj}-b}}\right]\\
+\left[c_{rj}\sum_{b=0}^{k^1_{rj}-1}(-1)^{b+k^1_{rj}}b!\begin{pmatrix}k^1_{rj}\\b\end{pmatrix}\frac{1}{s^b}\left(\sum_{p=0}^{k^1_{rj}-b-1}(-1)^p{\tau_{rj}}^p\begin{pmatrix}k^1_{rj}-b\\p\end{pmatrix}\frac{d^{k^1_{rj}-b-p}}{ds^{k^1_{rj}-b-p}}\right)\right].
\end{gathered}$$

If the (HF) is any continuously differentiable function $\varphi_r(t)$. Consequently, there is an ordinary differential equation in $U_r(s),U_j(s)$, which is solved to find $U_r(s),U_j(s)$. Finally, the inverse of the Laplace transform is used on $U_r(s),U_j(s)$ to obtain the solution $u_r(t),u_j(t)$ for the system of integro-fractional differential equations with variable coefficients and multi-delays.

4. Analytic Examples

Here are some examples of the system of integro-fractional differential equations with variable coefficients and multi-delays, which were solved by Laplace transform method:

Example 1. *Consider the linear SIFDEs of the Volterra type with the constant multi-time delay and variable coefficients of retarded delay on* $[0,\ 1]$:

$$\begin{aligned} {}_{0}^{C}D_{t}^{1.5}u_0(t) - t\,{}_{0}^{C}D_{t}^{0.5}u_0(t) - 3t\ u_0(t-1) \\ = f_0(t) + \textstyle\int_0^t \left[(t-x)u_0(x-2) - e^{t-x}u_1(x-1)\right]\,dx. \end{aligned} \tag{23}$$

$$\begin{aligned} {}_{0}^{C}D_{t}^{0.9}u_1(t) - \tfrac{1}{2}\,{}_{0}^{C}D_{t}^{0.5}u_1(t) + \tfrac{1}{2}\ u_1(t-0.2) \\ = f_1(t) + \textstyle\int_0^t \left[(t-x)u_0(x-0.3) + (t-x)^2u_1(x-0.5)\right]\,dx. \end{aligned} \tag{24}$$

where:

$$f_0(t) = \frac{2}{\Gamma(1.5)}t^{0.5} + \frac{2}{\Gamma(2.5)}t^{2.5} + e^t - \frac{1}{12}t^4 - \frac{7}{3}t^3 + 4t^2 - 5t - 1.$$

$$f_1(t) = \frac{2}{\Gamma(1.1)}t^{0.1} - \frac{1}{\Gamma(1.5)}t^{0.5} - \frac{1}{4}t^4 + 0.1\ t^3 - 0.045\ t^2 + t + 0.3.$$

with historical function (HF) and initial condition $u_0(0) = 0; u_0'(0) = 0; \varphi_0(t) = t^2; u_1(0) = 1;\ \ u_1'(0) = 2; \varphi_1(t) = 2t+1$, *so we have:* $\mathcal{K}_{0,1}(t,x) = (t-x)\ ; \mathcal{K}_{0,2}(t,x) = e^{t-x}, \mathcal{K}_{1,1}(t,x) = (t-x); \mathcal{K}_{1,2}(t,x) = (t-x)^2$ *and* $\tau_0 = 1, \tau_{0,1} = 2, \tau_{0,2} = 1, \tau_1 = 0.2,\ \tau_{1,1} = 0.3\ ; \tau_{1,2} = 0.5$, *which are constant different time delays, and* $P_{0,1}(t) = t,\ P_{0,2}(t) = -3t,\ P_{1,1}(t) = \frac{-1}{2}, P_{1,2}(t) = \frac{1}{2}$ *are variable coefficients.*

The Laplace transform is taken to the above equation and Equations (17) and (18) are used to obtain:

$$H_0(s)U_0(s) + \frac{e^{-s}}{(s-1)}U_1(s) = \overline{F}_0(s). \tag{25}$$

$$H_1(s)U_1(s) - \frac{e^{-0.3s}}{s^2}U_0(s) = \overline{F}_1(s). \tag{26}$$

where:

$$H_0(s) = s^{1.5} - \frac{d}{ds}s^{0.5} + 3\frac{d}{ds}e^{-s} - \frac{1}{s^2}e^{-2s}.$$

$$H_1(s) = s^{0.9} - \frac{1}{2}s^{0.5} + \frac{1}{2}e^{-0.2s} - \frac{2}{s^3}e^{-0.5s}.$$

and:

$$\overline{F}_0(s) = \frac{2}{s^{1.5}} + \frac{5}{s^{3.5}} - \frac{6\,e^{-s}}{s^3} - \frac{18\,e^{-s}}{s^4} - \frac{2\,e^{-2s}}{s^5} + \frac{2e^{-s}}{s^2(s-1)} + \frac{e^{-s}}{s(s-1)}.$$

$$\overline{F}_1(s) = \frac{2}{s^{1.1}} - \frac{1}{s^{1.5}} + \frac{1}{s^{0.1}} - \frac{1}{2s^{0.5}} + \frac{e^{-0.2s}}{s^2} + \frac{e^{-0.2s}}{2s} - \frac{2e^{-0.3s}}{s^5} - \frac{4e^{-0.5s}}{s^5} - \frac{2e^{-0.5s}}{s^4}.$$

After substituting Equation (25) into Equation (26) and solving this with $U(\infty) = 0$, which is ODE of the first order, the following is obtained: $U_0(s) = \frac{2}{s^3}$.

By substituting $U_0(s)$ into one of either Equation (25) or Equation (26), we obtain: $U_1(s) = \frac{2}{s^2} + \frac{1}{s}$.

By taking the inverse of the Laplace transform of $U_0(s)$ and $U_1(s)$, the exact solutions, $u_0(t)$ and $u_1(t)$, are obtained from Equations (22) and (23): $u_0(t) = \mathcal{L}^{-1}\left\{\frac{2}{s^3}\right\} = t^2; u_1(t) = \mathcal{L}^{-1}\left\{\frac{2}{s^2} + \frac{1}{s}\right\} = 2t+1$, which is the exact solution for our given system.

Example 2. *Consider linear SIFDEs of a constant multi-time retarded delay with variable coefficients on* $[0,\ 1]$:

$$ {}_0^C D_t^{1.3} u_0(t) + 2\, u_0(t-0.4) = f_0(t) + \int_0^t (t+x) u_1(x-1)\, dx. \tag{27} $$

$$ {}_0^C D_t^{0.8} u_1(t) - \frac{1}{2}\, {}_0^C D_t^{0.5} u_1(t) = f_1(t) + \int_0^t \left(2t + 2x^2\right) u_1(x-0.2)\, dx. \tag{28} $$

$$ \text{where}: \ f_0(t) = \frac{1}{\Gamma(1.7)} t^{0.7} - \frac{5t}{6} t^3 + t^2 - 0.8\, t + 0.16. $$

$$ f_1(t) = \frac{1}{\Gamma(1.2)} t^{0.2} - \frac{1}{2\,\Gamma(1.5)} t^{0.5} - \frac{1}{5} t^5 - \frac{0.7}{3}\, t^4 + \frac{0.64}{3}\, t^3 + 0.04\ t^2. $$

With initial conditions and historical functions:

$u_0(0) = 0; u_0'(0) = 0; \varphi_0(t) = \frac{1}{2} t^2$; $u_1(0) = 1; u_1'(0) = 2; \varphi_1(t) = t + 1$, *since here we have:* $\mathcal{K}_{0,1}(t,x) = (t+x)$; $\mathcal{K}_{1,1}(t,x) = \left(2t + 2x^2\right)$; $\tau_0 = 0.4,\ \tau_{0,1} = 1, \tau_{1,1} = 0.2$, *which are constant different time delays, and* $P_{0,2}(t) = 2,\ P_{1,1}(t) = \frac{-1}{2}$; *are variable coefficients.*

Taking the Laplace transform for the above equation and using Equations (21) and (22), we obtain:

$$ H_0(s) U_0(s) + \sum_{\substack{j=0 \\ j \neq r}}^{m} \lambda_{01}\, \overline{K}_{01}(s) e^{-s\tau_{01}} U_1(s) = \overline{F}_0(s). \tag{29} $$

$$ H_1(s) U_1(s) + \sum_{\substack{j=0 \\ j \neq r}}^{m} \lambda_{10}\, \overline{K}_{10}(s) e^{-s\tau_{10}} U_0(s) = \overline{F}_1(s). \tag{30} $$

where:

$$ \overline{K}_{01}(s) = \frac{1}{s}\left\{2 + \frac{1}{s} - 2\frac{d}{ds}\right\}. $$

$$ \overline{K}_{10}(s) = \frac{1}{s}\left\{0.48 + \frac{2}{s} + 2\frac{d^2}{ds^2} - 2.8\frac{d}{ds}\right\}. $$

$$ H_0(s) = s^{1.3} + 2e^{-0.4s}. $$

$$ H_1(s) = s^{0.8} - \frac{1}{2} s^{0.5}. $$

and:

$$ \overline{F}_0(s) = \frac{1}{s^{1.7}} + \frac{2e^{-0.4s}}{s^3} - \frac{5\, e^{-s}}{s^3} - \frac{5\, e^{-s}}{s^4} - \frac{2\, e^{-s}}{s^2}. $$

$$ \overline{F}_1(s) = \frac{1}{s^{1.2}} - \frac{1}{2s^{1.5}} + \frac{1}{s^{0.2}} - \frac{1}{2s^{0.5}} - \frac{10.4\, e^{-0.2s}}{s^5} - \frac{0.48\, e^{-0.2s}}{s^4} - \frac{24\, e^{-0.2s}}{s^6}. $$

After substituting Equation (29) into Equation (30) and with $U(\infty) = 0$, which is ODE of the first order, after solving it, the following is obtained:$U_0(s) = \frac{1}{s^3}$. Next, by substituting $U_0(s)$ in either one of Equation (29) or Equation (30), we obtain: $U_1(s) = \frac{2}{s} + \frac{1}{s}$. By taking the inverse of the Laplace transform of $U_0(s)$ and $U_1(s)$, the exact solutions, $u_0(t)$ and $u_1(t)$, are obtained from Equations (27) and (28): $u_0(t) = \mathcal{L}^{-1}\left\{\frac{2}{s^3}\right\} = \frac{1}{2} t^2$; $u_1(t) = \mathcal{L}^{-1}\left\{\frac{2}{s^2} + \frac{1}{s}\right\} = t + 1$, which are the exact solutions for our given system.

5. Discussion

In this work, after using the Laplace transform to solve a linear system of integro-fractional differential equations of the Volterra type with variable coefficients and multi-time retarded delay using some illustrating examples, we found the following:

1. Generally, this method which was amended here, provided good results and validation.
2. Here: we successfully applied the Laplace transform method for two different types of kernels, which were difference and simple degenerate kernels.

Author Contributions: Conceptualization, M.B.M.A. and S.S.A.; methodology, M.B.M.A.; validation, M.B.M.A. and S.S.A.; formal analysis, S.S.A.; investigation, M.B.M.A.; resources, S.S.A.; writing—original draft preparation, M.B.M.A.; writing—review, S.S.A.; editing, M.B.M.A.; visualization, M.B.M.A.; supervision, S.S.A.; project administration, M.B.M.A.; funding acquisition, S.S.A. All authors have read and agreed to the published version of the manuscript.

Funding: This research received no external funding.

Institutional Review Board Statement: The study was conducted according to the guidelines of the Declaration of Helsinki, and approved by the Institutional Ethics Committee of Technical college of Informatics, Sulaimani Polytechnic University, and Department of Mathematics, College of Science, University of Sulaimani Sulaymaniyah 46001, Kurdistan Region, Iraq.

Informed Consent Statement: Informed consent was obtained from all subjects involved in the study.

Data Availability Statement: The data used during the study are available from the corresponding author.

Conflicts of Interest: The authors declare no conflict of interest.

References

1. Jerri, A.J. *Introduction to Integral Equations with Applications*; Marcel Dekker, Inc.: New York, NY, USA, 1985.
2. Zwillinger, D. *Handbook of Differential Equations*, 3rd ed.; Academic Boston: Boston, MA, USA, 1997.
3. Mustafa, M. Numerical Solution of Volterra Integral Equations with Delay Using Block Methods. *AL-Fatih J.* **2008**, *36*, 89–90.
4. Podldubny, I. *Fractional Differential Equation*; Academic Press: San Diego, CA, USA, 1999.
5. Ahmed, S.S. Numerical Solution of Linear Volterra Integro-Differential Equations. Master's Thesis, Technology University, Baghdad, Iraq, 2002.
6. Hama Salih, S.A. Some Computational Methods for Solving Linear Volterra Integro-Fractional Differential Equations. Master's Thesis, University of Sulaimani, Sulaymaniyah, Iraq, 2011.
7. Ahamed, S.S.; Amin, M.B. Solving Linear Volterra Integro-Fractional Differential Equations in Caputo Sense with Constant Multi-Time Retarded Delay by Laplace Transform. *Zanco J. Pure Appl. Sci.* **2019**, *31*, 80–89.
8. Ahmed, S.S. On System of Linear Volterra Integro-Fractional Differential Equations. Ph.D. Thesis, Sulaimani University, Sulaymaniyah, Iraq, 2009.
9. Miller, K.S.; Ross, B. *An Introduction to the Fractional Calculus and Fractional Differential Equations*; John Wiley & Sons: New York, NY, USA, 1993.
10. Gorenflo, R.; Mainardi, F. *Fractional Calculus: Integral and Differential Equations of Fractional Order*; CIAM Lecture Notes; International Center for Mechanical Sciences (CIAM): Berlin, Germany, 2000; Volume 378, ISBN 3-211-82913-X.
11. Ahmad, M.R. Some Numerical Methods for Solving Non-Linear Integro-Fractional Differential Equations of the Volterra-Hammerstein Type. Master's Thesis, University of Sulaimani, Sulaymaniyah, Iraq, 2013.
12. Spiegel, M.R. *Theory and Problems of Laplace Transforms, Hartford Graduate Center*; Schaum's Outline Series; McGraw-Hill. Inc.: New York, NY, USA, 1965.
13. Brunner, H.; Linz, P. Analytical and Numerical Methods for Volterra Equations. *Math. Comput.* **1987**, *48*, 841. [CrossRef]
14. Weilbeer, M. *Efficient Numerical Methods for Fractional Differential Equations and their Analytical Background*; US Army Medical Research and Material Command, University of Braunschweig: Braunschweig, Germany, 2005.

fractal and fractional

MDPI

Article

Hadamard-Type Fractional Integro-Differential Problem: A Note on Some Asymptotic Behavior of Solutions

Ahmad Mugbil [1,*] and Nasser-Eddine Tatar [2]

[1] Prep Year Math Program, College of General Studies, King Fahd University of Petroleum and Minerals, Dhahran 31261, Saudi Arabia
[2] Department of Mathematics, IRC for Intelligent Manufacturing and Robotics, King Fahd University of Petroleum and Minerals, Dhahran 31261, Saudi Arabia; tatarn@kfupm.edu.sa
* Correspondence: mugbil@kfupm.edu.sa

Abstract: As a follow-up to the inherent nature of Hadamard-Type Fractional Integro-differential problem, little is known about some asymptotic behaviors of solutions. In this paper, an integro-differential problem involving Hadamard fractional derivatives is investigated. The leading derivative is of an order between one and two whereas the nonlinearities may contain fractional derivatives of an order between zero and one as well as some non-local terms. Under some reasonable conditions, we prove that solutions are asymptotic to logarithmic functions. Our approach is based on a generalized version of Bihari–LaSalle inequality, which we prove. In addition, several manipulations and crucial estimates have been used. An example supporting our findings is provided.

Keywords: asymptotic behavior; fractional differential equation; Hadamard fractional derivative

Citation: Mugbil, A.; Tatar, N.-E. Hadamard-Type Fractional Integro-Differential Problem: A Note on Some Asymptotic Behavior of Solutions. *Fractal Fract.* **2022**, *6*, 267. https://doi.org/10.3390/fractalfract6050267

Academic Editors: António M. Lopes, Alireza Alfi, Liping Chen and Sergio Adriani David

Received: 30 March 2022
Accepted: 13 May 2022
Published: 15 May 2022

1. Introduction

Of concern is the following general class of initial value problems modelled by:

$$\begin{cases} \left({}_H\mathcal{D}^{\alpha}_{t_0}u\right)'(t) = f\left(t, \left({}_H\mathcal{D}^{\alpha_1}_{t_0}u\right)(t), \int_{t_0}^{t} h\left(t,s,\left({}_H\mathcal{D}^{\alpha_2}_{t_0}u\right)(s)\right)ds\right),\ t > t_0 > 0, \\ \left({}_H\mathcal{I}^{1-\alpha}_{t_0}u\right)(t_0^+) = u_1,\ \left({}_H\mathcal{D}^{\alpha}_{t_0}u\right)(t_0^+) = u_2,\ u_1, u_2 \in \mathbb{R}, \end{cases} \tag{1}$$

where ${}_H\mathcal{D}^{\alpha}_{t_0}$, ${}_H\mathcal{D}^{\alpha_1}_{t_0}$ and ${}_H\mathcal{D}^{\alpha_2}_{t_0}$ are the Hadamard fractional derivatives of orders α, α_1 and α_2, respectively, $0 \leq \alpha_1 < \alpha < 1$ and $0 \leq \alpha_2 < \alpha < 1$. The operator ${}_H\mathcal{I}^{\rho}_{t_0}$ is the Hadamard fractional integral of order $\rho \geq 0$. The definitions of these operators are given in Section 2.

We shall investigate the asymptotic behavior of solutions for Problem (1). Sufficient conditions on the nonlinear source term guaranteeing the convergence of solutions to logarithmic functions, for large values of time, are established. The importance of using analytical techniques to study the asymptotic behavior of solutions for Problem (1) arises from the lack of explicit solutions.

It is known that solutions for many kinds of (integer-order) ordinary differential equations may approach a certain function as time goes to infinity; in particular they may decay to zero, oscillate, or blow up in finite time. Many results in this regard exist in the literature. For example, we refer the reader to the papers [1–6], in which various classes of linear and nonlinear ordinary differential equations have been studied. Generalizing the existing results from integer orders to non-integer fractional orders is of great importance due to their numerous applications; see for instance, [7–10]. Unfortunately, imitating the techniques verbatim is not straightforward. Many difficulties arise when trying to do so. Some of these difficulties are due to the nature of the fractional derivatives themselves as they involve by definition all the past memory of solutions as well as nonregular kernels. In addition, many fundamental properties of integer-order derivatives are not valid for fractional-order derivatives. The chain rule is an example of such invalid properties. We will go around these difficulties by utilizing some adequate estimations, like desingularization methods, to deal with singular terms and by modifying and/or generalizing some versions of Bihari–LaSalle inequality.

The study of the asymptotic behavior of solutions for fractional differential equations, with Riemann–Liouville or Caputo fractional derivatives, has been investigated by many researchers, see e.g., [11–20]. The authors of [15] considered the fractional differential equation:

$$\left(D_{0^+}^{\alpha} u'\right)(t) + f(t,u) = 0,\ t > 0,$$

under the condition

$$|f(t,u)| \le \phi\left(t, \frac{|u|}{(1+t)^{\alpha}}\right),\ t \ge 0,\ u \in \mathbb{R},$$

where $D_{0^+}^{\alpha}$ is the Riemann–Liouville fractional derivative of order α, $0 < \alpha < 1$. The function $f : [0,\infty) \times \mathbb{R} \to \mathbb{R}$ is continuous and the function $\phi : [0,\infty) \times [0,\infty) \to [0,\infty)$ is continuous in each argument and nondecreasing in the second one. They proved that the solutions can be represented asymptotically as $a_1 + a_2 t^{\alpha} + O(t^{\alpha-1})$, $a_1, a_2 \in \mathbb{R}$.

In [20], the case when the source function f depends on the solution and its sub-first-order fractional derivative has been considered, namely,

$$\begin{cases} \left({}^{C}D_{t_0^+}^{\alpha} u\right)(t) = f\left(t, u(t), \left({}^{C}D_{t_0^+}^{\alpha_1} u\right)(t)\right),\ t > t_0 > 0, \\ u(t_0) = u_0, \end{cases} \tag{2}$$

where ${}^{C}D_{t_0^+}^{\alpha}$ is the Caputo fractional derivative of order α, $0 < \alpha_1 < \alpha < 1$. The authors showed that any global solution of Problem (2) is asymptotic to ct^{α_1} for some real number c.

The present authors investigated the boundedness, power-type decay and asymptotic behavior of solutions for the initial value problems:

$$\begin{cases} \left({}^{C}D_{0^+}^{\alpha} u\right)(t) = f\left(t, u(t), \int_0^t h(t,s,u(s))ds\right),\ t > 0,\ 0 < \alpha \le 1 \\ u(0) = u_0,\ u_0 \in \mathbb{R}, \end{cases}$$

and

$$\begin{cases} \left(D_{0^+}^{\alpha+1} u\right)(t) = f\left(t, (D_{0^+}^{\alpha_1} u)(t), \int_0^t h(t,s,(D_{0^+}^{\alpha_2} u)(s))ds\right),\ t > 0, 0 \le \alpha_1, \alpha_2 \le \alpha < 1 \\ \left(I_{0^+}^{1-\alpha} u\right)(0^+) = u_0,\ \left(D_{0^+}^{\alpha} u\right)(0^+) = u_1,\ u_0, u_1 \in \mathbb{R}. \end{cases}$$

Several different classes of source functions f such as

$$\begin{aligned} |f(t,u,v)| &\le k(t)P(|u|) + l(t)Q(|v|),\ |f(t,u,v)| \le k(t)P(t^{\alpha_2}|u|)Q(|v|), \\ \text{or } |f(t,u,v)| &\le k(t)P\left(t^{1-\alpha+\alpha_1}|u|\right) + l(t)Q(|v|), \end{aligned}$$

and on the kernel h such as:

$$\begin{aligned} |h(t,s,u)| &\le w(s)K(|u|),\ |h(t,s,u)| \le w(s)K(s^{\alpha_2}|u|),\ |h(t,s,u)| \le w(t,s)K(|u|), \\ \text{or } |h(t,s,u)| &\le w(s)K\left(t^{1-\alpha+\alpha_2}|u|\right), \end{aligned}$$

for some functions k, l, P, Q, w and K have been treated, see [11,12,21–23].

For fractional differential equations with Hadamard-type fractional derivatives, we found relatively few results in the literature tackling the long-time behavior of solutions of fractional initial value problems, see, [24–28]. The authors of [28] studied the stability and decay rate of the zero solution of the fractional differential problem:

$$\begin{cases} \left({}_H\mathcal{D}^{\alpha}_{t_0}u\right)(t) = f(u(t)),\ t > t_0 > 0, 0 < \alpha < 1 \\ \left({}_H\mathcal{I}^{1-\alpha}_{t_0}u\right)(t_0^+) = u_0,\ u_0 \in \mathbb{R}. \end{cases} \tag{3}$$

They considered first the linear case, $f(u) = cu$, $c \in \mathbb{R}$, and established a criteria for the decay rate of solutions and the Lyapunov stability of the zero equilibrium. For the nonlinear case, they obtained the stability and decay rate of the hyperbolic zero equilibrium. They used a modified Laplace transform to express solutions by Mittag–Leffler functions and then used the asymptotic expansions of these functions to discuss the stability and logarithmic decay of the solutions. In [25], the authors discussed the stability of logarithmic type for the initial value problem:

$$\begin{cases} \left({}_H\mathcal{D}^{\alpha}_{t_0}u\right)(t) = f\left(t, u(t), \left({}_H\mathcal{D}^{\alpha_1}_{t_0}u\right)(t)\right),\ t > t_0 > 0,\ 0 < \alpha_1 < \alpha < 1, \\ \left({}_H\mathcal{D}^{\alpha-1}_{t_0}u\right)(t_0^+) = u_0,\ u_0 \in \mathbb{R}. \end{cases} \tag{4}$$

Under some sufficient growth conditions of f, it has been shown that the solutions decay to zero as the logarithmic function $\left(\ln \frac{t}{t_0}\right)^{\alpha-1}$. Recently, the same authors considered Problem (4) in [26] with $\frac{d}{dt}\left({}_H\mathcal{D}^{\alpha}_{t_0}u\right)(t)$ on the left hand side and the additional initial condition $\left({}_H\mathcal{D}^{\alpha}_{t_0}u\right)(t_0^+) = u_1 \in \mathbb{R}$. They showed that solutions approach a logarithmic function as time goes to infinity.

To the best of our knowledge, the long-time behavior of solutions for the class of fractional integrodifferential equations with Hadamard fractional derivatives (1) has not been investigated so far. In this paper, we prove that solutions of (1) are asymptotic to the logarithmic function $\left(\ln \frac{t}{t_0}\right)^{\alpha}$ where α is the order of the involved fractional derivative. Under sufficient growth conditions, we show that there exist a real number r such that any solution for (1) in the space $u \in C^{\alpha+1}_{1-\alpha,\ln}[t_0, \infty)$, see (16), has the following property $\lim_{t\to\infty} \frac{u(t)}{\left(\ln \frac{t}{t_0}\right)^{\alpha}} = r$.

The rest of this paper is organized as follows. In the next section, Section 2, we give some notations from fractional calculus and present some preliminary results. In Section 3, we introduce and prove our main results. Section 4 is devoted to an example that supports our results. A brief conclusion is presented at the end of the study in Section 5.

2. Preliminaries

This section is devoted to briefly introduce some basic definitions, notions, and properties from fractional calculus and fractional differential equations theory which will be used in further considerations.

Definition 1 ([7]). *We denote by $C_{\gamma,\ln}[t_0, T]$, $0 \le \gamma < 1$, the following weighted space of continuous functions:*

$$C_{\gamma,\ln}[t_0, T] = \left\{\xi : (t_0, T] \to \mathbb{R} : \left(\ln \frac{t}{t_0}\right)^{\gamma} \xi(t) \in C[t_0, T]\right\}, \tag{5}$$

with the norm

$$\|\xi\|_{C_{\gamma,\ln}} = \left\|\left(\ln \frac{t}{t_0}\right)^{\gamma} \xi(t)\right\|_{C_{0,\ln}},$$

where $C[t_0, T] = C_{0,\ln}[t_0, T]$ *is the space of continuous functions on* $[t_0, T]$.

Definition 2 ([7]). *Let* $\delta = t\frac{d}{dt}$ *be the* δ*-derivative. For* $n \in \mathbb{N}$ *and* $0 \leq \gamma < 1$, *the weighted space of continuously* δ*-differentiable functions up to order* $n-1$ *with* n*th* δ*-derivative in* $C_{\gamma,\ln}[t_0, T]$, *is denoted by* $C^n_{\delta,\gamma}[t_0, T]$ *and defined by:*

$$C^n_{\delta,\gamma}[t_0, T] = \left\{\xi : (t_0, T] \to \mathbb{R} \mid \delta^i\xi \in C[t_0, T],\ i = 0, 1, 2, \ldots, n-1,\ \delta^n\xi \in C_{\gamma,\ln}[t_0, T]\right\}, \tag{6}$$

with the norm

$$\|\xi\|_{C^n_{\delta,\gamma}} = \sum_{i=0}^{n-1} \left\|\delta^i\xi\right\|_C + \|\ \delta^n\xi\|_{C_{\gamma,\ln}}.$$

In particular, $C^0_{\delta,\gamma}[t_0, T] = C_{\gamma,\ln}[t_0, T]$.

A characterization of the space $C^n_{\delta,\gamma}[t_0, T]$ is given as follows [7]: The functions ξ in the space $C^n_{\delta,\gamma}[t_0, T]$, $n \in \mathbb{N}$ and $0 \leq \gamma < 1$, can be represented as:

$$\xi(t) = \frac{1}{(n-1)!}\int_{t_0}^{t}\left(\ln\frac{t}{s}\right)^{n-1}\frac{h(s)}{s}ds + \sum_{i=0}^{n-1} b_i\left(\ln\frac{t}{t_0}\right)^i,$$

where $h \in C_{\gamma,\ln}[t_0, T]$ and b_i , $i = 0, 1, 2, \ldots, n-1$, are arbitrary constants. In fact, $h(t) = (\delta^n\xi)(t)$ and $b_i = \frac{(\delta^i\xi)(t_0)}{i!}$.

Definition 3 ([7]). *The Hadamard left-sided fractional integral of order* $\alpha > 0$ *is defined by:*

$$\left({}_H\mathcal{I}^{\alpha}_{t_0}w\right)(t) = \frac{1}{\Gamma(\alpha)}\int_{t_0}^{t}\left(\ln\frac{t}{s}\right)^{\alpha-1}\frac{w(s)}{s}ds,\ t > t_0, \tag{7}$$

provided the right-hand side exists. We define ${}_H\mathcal{I}^0_{t_0}w = w$. *The function* Γ *is the Euler gamma function defined by* $\Gamma(\alpha) = \int_0^\infty t^{\alpha-1}e^{-t}dt$, $\alpha > 0$, *where* $t^{\alpha-1} = e^{(\alpha-1)\ln t}$.

Definition 4 ([7]). *The Hadamard left-sided fractional derivative of order* $\alpha > 0$, *is defined by:*

$$\left({}_H\mathcal{D}^{\alpha}_{t_0}w\right)(t) = \frac{1}{\Gamma(n-\alpha)}\delta^n\int_{t_0}^{t}\left(\ln\frac{t}{s}\right)^{n-\alpha-1}\frac{w(s)}{s}ds,\ t > t_0,$$

that is,

$$\left({}_H\mathcal{D}^{\alpha}_{t_0}w\right)(t) = \delta^n\left({}_H\mathcal{I}^{n-\alpha}_{t_0}w\right)(t),\ t > t_0, \tag{8}$$

where $\delta^n = \left(t\frac{d}{dt}\right)^n$, $n = -[-\alpha]$. *In particular, when* $\alpha = m \in \mathbb{N}_0$, *we have* ${}_H\mathcal{D}^m_{t_0}w = \delta^m w$.

The next lemma shows that the Hadamard fractional derivative (or integral) of a logarithmic function results in a multiple of the same logarithmic function with the order of the fractional derivative (or integral) subtracted from (or added to) its power.

Lemma 1 ([7]). *If* $\alpha > 0$, $\beta > 0$, *then:*

$$\left({}_H\mathcal{I}^{\alpha}_{t_0}\left(\ln\frac{s}{t_0}\right)^{\beta-1}\right)(t) = \frac{\Gamma(\beta)}{\Gamma(\beta+\alpha)}\left(\ln\frac{t}{t_0}\right)^{\beta+\alpha-1},\ t > t_0,$$

$$\left({}_H\mathcal{D}^{\alpha}_{t_0}\left(\ln\frac{s}{t_0}\right)^{\beta-1}\right)(t) = \frac{\Gamma(\beta)}{\Gamma(\beta-\alpha)}\left(\ln\frac{t}{t_0}\right)^{\beta-\alpha-1},\ t > t_0.$$

In particular, when $0 < \alpha < 1$, $\beta = 1$, then:

$$\left({}_H\mathcal{I}^{\alpha}_{t_0}1\right)(t) = \frac{1}{\Gamma(1+\alpha)}\left(\ln\frac{t}{t_0}\right)^{\alpha}, \ t > t_0,$$

$$\left({}_H\mathcal{D}^{\alpha}_{t_0}1\right)(t) = \frac{1}{\Gamma(1-\alpha)}\left(\ln\frac{t}{t_0}\right)^{-\alpha}, \ t > t_0.$$

The last property shows that the Hadamard-type derivative of a constant is not zero.

The composite of the Hadamard operators of fractional differentiation and integration with different orders is given next.

Lemma 2 ([7]). *Let $0 < \beta < \alpha$ and $0 \leq \gamma < 1$, then:*

$${}_H\mathcal{D}^{\beta}_{t_0}\,{}_H\mathcal{I}^{\alpha}_{t_0}w \;=\; {}_H\mathcal{I}^{\alpha-\beta}_{t_0}w$$

at every point in $(t_0, T]$ if $w \in C_{\gamma,\ln}[t_0, T]$ and at every point in $[t_0, T]$ if $w \in C[t_0, T]$. In particular, when $\alpha > \beta = m \in \mathbb{N}$, we obtain:

$${}_H\mathcal{D}^{m}_{t_0}\,{}_H\mathcal{I}^{\alpha}_{t_0}w \;=\; {}_H\mathcal{I}^{\alpha-m}_{t_0}w.$$

The Hadamard differentiation operator is the left inverse to the associated Hadamard integration operator [7]. That is, ${}_H\mathcal{D}^{\alpha}_{t_0}\,{}_H\mathcal{I}^{\alpha}_{t_0}w = w$ at every point in $(t_0, T]$ if $w \in C_{\gamma,\ln}[t_0, T]$. This property is not valid when the Hadamard fractional derivative and the Hadamard fractional integral are inverted as shown in the lemma below.

Lemma 3 ([7]). *Let $\alpha \geq 0$ and $n = -[-\alpha]$. If $w \in C_{\gamma,\ln}[t_0, T]$, $0 \leq \gamma < 1$ and ${}_H\mathcal{I}^{n-\alpha}_{t_0}w \in C^n_{\delta,\gamma}[t_0, T]$, then:*

$$\left({}_H\mathcal{I}^{\alpha}_{t_0}\,{}_H\mathcal{D}^{\alpha}_{t_0}w\right)(t) = w(t) - \sum_{i=1}^{n}\frac{\left(\delta^{n-i}\left({}_H\mathcal{I}^{n-\alpha}_{t_0}w\right)\right)(t_0^+)}{\Gamma(\alpha-i+1)}\left(\ln\frac{t}{t_0}\right)^{\alpha-i}, \tag{9}$$

for all $t \in (t_0, T]$. In particular, for $0 \leq \alpha < 1$, we have:

$$\left({}_H\mathcal{I}^{\alpha}_{t_0}\,{}_H\mathcal{D}^{\alpha}_{t_0}w\right)(t) = w(t) - \frac{\left({}_H\mathcal{I}^{1-\alpha}_{t_0}w\right)(t_0^+)}{\Gamma(\alpha)}\left(\ln\frac{t}{t_0}\right)^{\alpha-1} \tag{10}$$

at every point in $(t_0, T]$ if $w \in C_{\gamma,\ln}[t_0, T]$ and at every point in $[t_0, T]$ if $w \in C[t_0, T]$ and ${}_H\mathcal{I}^{1-\alpha}_{t_0}w \in C^1_{\delta,\gamma}[t_0, T]$.

For more about Hadamard fractional integral and derivative, we refer to the books [7,29,30].

The limit of the ratio of the Hadamard fractional integral $\left({}_H\mathcal{I}^{\alpha+1}_{t_0}sf(s,u(s),v(s))\right)(t)$ and the power function $\frac{1}{\Gamma(\alpha+1)}\left(\ln\frac{t}{t_0}\right)^{\alpha}$ as $t \to \infty$ is treated in the lemma below.

Lemma 4. *Let $f \in L^1(t_0, \infty)$, $t_0 > 0$. Suppose that u and v are real-valued functions defined on $[t_0, \infty)$, then:*

$$\begin{aligned}\lim_{t\to\infty}\frac{\left({}_H\mathcal{I}^{\alpha+1}_{t_0}sf(s,u(s),v(s))\right)(t)}{\frac{1}{\Gamma(\alpha+1)}\left(\ln\frac{t}{t_0}\right)^{\alpha}} &= \lim_{t\to\infty}\frac{1}{\left(\ln\frac{t}{t_0}\right)^{\alpha}}\int_{t_0}^{t}\left(\ln\frac{t}{s}\right)^{\alpha}f(s,u(s),v(s))ds \\ &= \int_{t_0}^{\infty}f(s,u(s),v(s))ds, \ \alpha > 0.\end{aligned}$$

Proof. It is easy to see that:

$$\begin{aligned}
&\left| \frac{\left({}_H\mathcal{I}_{t_0}^{\alpha+1} s f(s,u(s),v(s))\right)(t)}{\frac{1}{\Gamma(\alpha+1)}\left(\ln\frac{t}{t_0}\right)^{\alpha}} - \int_{t_0}^{\infty} f(s,u(s),v(s))ds \right| \\
&= \left| \frac{1}{\left(\ln\frac{t}{t_0}\right)^{\alpha}} \int_{t_0}^{t} \left(\ln\frac{t}{s}\right)^{\alpha} f(s,u(s),v(s))ds - \int_{t_0}^{\infty} f(s,u(s),v(s))ds \right| \\
&= \left| \int_{t_0}^{t} \left(\frac{\ln\frac{t}{t_0} - \ln\frac{s}{t_0}}{\ln\frac{t}{t_0}}\right)^{\alpha} f(s,u(s),v(s))ds - \int_{t_0}^{\infty} f(s,u(s),v(s))ds \right| \\
&= \left| \int_{t_0}^{\infty} \left[\left(1 - \frac{\ln\frac{s}{t_0}}{\ln\frac{t}{t_0}}\right)^{\alpha} \chi_{[t_0,t]}(s) - 1\right] f(s,u(s),v(s))ds \right| \\
&\leq \int_{t_0}^{\infty} \left| \left(1 - \frac{\ln\frac{s}{t_0}}{\ln\frac{t}{t_0}}\right)^{\alpha} \chi_{[t_0,t]}(s) - 1\right| |f(s,u(s),v(s))|ds,
\end{aligned}$$

where

$$\chi_{[t_0,t]}(s) = \begin{cases} 1 \text{ if } t_0 \leq s \leq t, \\ 0, \quad \text{otherwise.} \end{cases}.$$

As $f \in L^1(t_0,\infty)$ and

$$\lim_{t\to\infty} \left(1 - \frac{\ln\frac{s}{t_0}}{\ln\frac{t}{t_0}}\right)^{\alpha} \chi_{[t_0,t]}(s) = 1, \text{ for } s < t,$$

we get from the Dominated Convergence Theorem [31],

$$\begin{aligned}
&\lim_{t\to\infty} \left| \frac{\left({}_H\mathcal{I}_{t_0}^{\alpha+1} s f(s,u(s),v(s))\right)(t)}{\frac{1}{\Gamma(\alpha+1)}\left(\ln\frac{t}{t_0}\right)^{\alpha}} - \int_{t_0}^{\infty} f(s,u(s),v(s))ds \right| \\
&\leq \lim_{t\to\infty} \int_{t_0}^{\infty} \left| \left(1 - \frac{\ln\frac{s}{t_0}}{\ln\frac{t}{t_0}}\right)^{\alpha} \chi_{[t_0,t]}(s) - 1\right| |f(s,u(s),v(s))|ds \\
&= \int_{t_0}^{\infty} \lim_{t\to\infty} \left| \left(1 - \frac{\ln\frac{s}{t_0}}{\ln\frac{t}{t_0}}\right)^{\alpha} \chi_{[t_0,t]}(s) - 1\right| |f(s,u(s),v(s))|ds = 0.
\end{aligned}$$

This completes the proof. □

The next lemma can be considered as a Hadamard fractional version of L'Hôpital's rule when applied to the solution of problem (1).

Lemma 5. *Let u be a solution of problem* (1) *with* $f \in L^1(0,\infty)$. *Then,*

$$\begin{aligned}
\lim_{t\to\infty} \frac{u(t)}{\left(\ln\frac{t}{t_0}\right)^{\alpha}} &= \lim_{t\to\infty} \frac{\left({}_H\mathcal{D}_{t_0}^{\alpha} u\right)(t)}{\Gamma(\alpha+1)} \\
&= \frac{1}{\Gamma(\alpha+1)} \left(u_2 + \int_{t_0}^{\infty} f\left(s, \left({}_H\mathcal{D}_{t_0}^{\alpha_1} u\right)(s), \int_{t_0}^{s} h(s,\tau,\left({}_H\mathcal{D}_{t_0}^{\alpha_2} u\right)(\tau))d\tau\right)ds\right).
\end{aligned}$$

Proof. Integrating both sides of the equation in (1) over the interval $[t_0,t]$, we obtain:

$$\left({}_H\mathcal{D}_{t_0}^{\alpha} u\right)(t) = u_2 + \int_{t_0}^{t} f\left(s, \left({}_H\mathcal{D}_{t_0}^{\alpha_1} u\right)(s), \int_{t_0}^{s} h(s,\tau,\left({}_H\mathcal{D}_{t_0}^{\alpha_2} u\right)(\tau))d\tau\right)ds. \tag{11}$$

Apply ${}_H\mathcal{I}^{\alpha}_{t_0}$ to (11) and use Lemmas 1 and 3, to find that:

$$u(t)-\frac{u_1\left(\ln\frac{t}{t_0}\right)^{\alpha-1}}{\Gamma(\alpha)} = \frac{u_2\left(\ln\frac{t}{t_0}\right)^{\alpha}}{\Gamma(\alpha+1)}+\frac{1}{\Gamma(\alpha)}\int_{t_0}^{t}\left(\ln\frac{t}{s}\right)^{\alpha-1} \times\int_{t_0}^{s} f\left(\tau,\left({}_H\mathcal{D}^{\alpha_1}_{t_0}u\right)(\tau),\int_{t_0}^{\tau} h(\tau,\sigma,\left({}_H\mathcal{D}^{\alpha_2}_{t_0}u\right)(\sigma))d\sigma\right)d\tau\frac{ds}{s}, \tag{12}$$

for all $t>t_0>0$. Reorder the double integral on the right-hand side and integrate by substitution to have:

$$\begin{aligned} u(t) &= \frac{u_1\left(\ln\frac{t}{t_0}\right)^{\alpha-1}}{\Gamma(\alpha)}+\frac{u_2\left(\ln\frac{t}{t_0}\right)^{\alpha}}{\Gamma(\alpha+1)}+\frac{1}{\Gamma(\alpha)}\int_{t_0}^{t}\int_{\tau}^{t}\left(\ln\frac{t}{s}\right)^{\alpha-1} \\ &\quad\times f\left(\tau,\left({}_H\mathcal{D}^{\alpha_1}_{t_0}u\right)(\tau),\int_{t_0}^{\tau} h(\tau,\sigma,\left({}_H\mathcal{D}^{\alpha_2}_{t_0}u\right)(\sigma))d\sigma\right)\frac{ds}{s}d\tau \\ &= \frac{u_1\left(\ln\frac{t}{t_0}\right)^{\alpha-1}}{\Gamma(\alpha)}+\frac{u_2\left(\ln\frac{t}{t_0}\right)^{\alpha}}{\Gamma(\alpha+1)}+\frac{1}{\Gamma(\alpha+1)}\int_{t_0}^{t}\left(\ln\frac{t}{\tau}\right)^{\alpha} \\ &\quad\times f\left(\tau,\left({}_H\mathcal{D}^{\alpha_1}_{t_0}u\right)(\tau),\int_{t_0}^{\tau} h(\tau,\sigma,\left({}_H\mathcal{D}^{\alpha_2}_{t_0}u\right)(\sigma))d\sigma\right)d\tau. \end{aligned} \tag{13}$$

Dividing both sides of (13) by $\left(\ln\frac{t}{t_0}\right)^{\alpha}$ gives:

$$\begin{aligned} \frac{u(t)}{\left(\ln\frac{t}{t_0}\right)^{\alpha}} &= \frac{u_1}{\Gamma(\alpha)\ln\frac{t}{t_0}}+\frac{u_2}{\Gamma(\alpha+1)}+\frac{1}{\Gamma(\alpha+1)\left(\ln\frac{t}{t_0}\right)^{\alpha}}\int_{t_0}^{t}\left(\ln\frac{t}{\tau}\right)^{\alpha} \\ &\quad\times f\left(\tau,\left({}_H\mathcal{D}^{\alpha_1}_{t_0}u\right)(\tau),\int_{t_0}^{\tau} h(\tau,\sigma,\left({}_H\mathcal{D}^{\alpha_2}_{t_0}u\right)(\sigma))d\sigma\right)d\tau, \end{aligned} \tag{14}$$

for all $t>t_0>0$. Taking the limit of the resulting ratio at infinity and applying Lemma 4 leads to the desired result. □

In the next lemma, we recall Bihari–LaSalle inequality which is a nonlinear generalization of the well-known Grönwall–Bellman inequality.

Lemma 6 ([32,33])**.** *Suppose that w and g are nonnegative continuous functions on $[t_0,\infty)$ and φ is a positive function on $(0,\infty)$, continuous and nondecreasing on $[0,\infty)$. If*

$$w(t)\le c+\int_{t_0}^{t} g(\tau)\varphi(w(\tau))d\tau,\ t\in[t_0,\infty),$$

where $c>0$, then

$$w(t)\le\Phi^{-1}\left(\Phi(c)+\int_{t_0}^{t} g(\tau)d\tau\right),\ t\in[t_0,T_1],$$

where Φ^{-1} is the inverse function of Φ,

$$\Phi(x)=\int_{x_0}^{x}\frac{ds}{\varphi(s)},\ x>0,\ x_0>0,$$

and T_1 is chosen so that $\Phi(c)+\int_{t_0}^{t} g(\tau)d\tau$ is in the domain of Φ^{-1} for all $t\in[t_0,T_1]$.

The next nonlinear integral inequality can be considered a generalization of Bihari–LaSalle inequality that has been recalled in Lemma 6.

Lemma 7 ([34]). *Assume that w and η_j, $j = 1, \dots, n$ are nonnegative continuous functions on $[t_0, T]$ and φ_j, $j = 1, \dots, n$ are nonnegative, continuous and nondecreasing on $[0, \infty)$ such that $\varphi_1 \propto \varphi_2 \propto \cdots \propto \varphi_n$ (that is, $\varphi_n/\varphi_{n-1}, \dots, \varphi_2/\varphi_1$ are nondecreasing functions). Assume further that c is a positive constant and*

$$w(t) \leq c + \sum_{j=1}^{n} \int_{t_0}^{t} \eta_j(s)\varphi_j(w(s))ds, \ t \in [t_0, T],$$

then, for all $t \in [t_0, T_1]$,

$$w(t) \leq \Phi_n^{-1}\left(\Phi_n(c_{n-1}) + \int_{t_0}^{t} \eta_n(s)ds\right),$$

where

1. Φ_j^{-1} *is the inverse function of Φ_j and $\Phi_j(x) = \int_{x_j}^{x} \frac{ds}{\varphi_j(s)}, x > 0, x_j > 0, , j = 1, \dots, n$.*
2. *The constants c_j are given by $c_0 = c$ and $c_j = \Phi_j^{-1}\left(\Phi_j(c_{j-1}) + \int_{t_0}^{T_1} \eta_j(\tau)d\tau\right), j = 1, \dots, n - 1$.*
3. *The number $T_1 \in [t_0, T]$ is the largest number such that:*

$$\int_{t_0}^{T_1} \eta_j(\tau)d\tau \leq \int_{c_{j-1}}^{\infty} \frac{d\tau}{\varphi_j(\tau)}, \ j = 1, \dots, n.$$

Lemma 8 ([34]). *Suppose that w and η_j, $j = 1, 2, 3$ are nonnegative continuous functions on $[t_0, T]$ and φ_j, $j = 1, 2, 3$ are nonnegative, continuous and nondecreasing on $[0, \infty)$ such that $\varphi_1 \propto \varphi_2 \propto \varphi_3$, (that is, φ_3/φ_2 and φ_2/φ_1 are nondecreasing functions). Assume further that c is a positive constant. If*

$$w(t) \leq c + \int_{t_0}^{t} \eta_1(\tau)\varphi_1(w(\tau))d\tau + \int_{t_0}^{t} \eta_2(\tau)\varphi_2\left(\int_{t_0}^{\tau} \eta_3(s)\varphi_3(w(s))ds\right)d\tau,$$

then, for all $t \in [t_0, T_1]$,

$$w(t) \leq \Phi_3^{-1}\left(\Phi_3(c_2) + \int_{t_0}^{t} \eta_3(\tau)d\tau\right),$$

where the functions $\Phi_j^{-1}, \Phi_j, j = 1, 2, 3$ and the constants c_0, c_1, c_2 are the same as those given in Lemma 7.

Remark 1. *By considering the following functions,*

$$\begin{aligned} \varpi_1(t) &:= \max_{\tau \in [0,t]} \{\varphi_1(\tau)\}, \\ \varpi_j(t) &:= \max_{\tau \in [0,t]} \left\{\frac{\varphi_j(\tau)}{\varpi_{j-1}(\tau)}\right\}\varpi_{j-1}(t), \ j = 2, 3, \end{aligned} \tag{15}$$

we can drop the ordering and monotonicity requirements in Lemma 8. It is clear that $\varphi_j(t) \leq \varpi_j(t)$, ϖ_j are nonnegative and nondecreasing functions on $[0, \infty)$ for all $t \in [0, \infty)$, $j = 1, 2, 3$ and $\varpi_1 \propto \varpi_2 \propto \varpi_3$.

3. Main Results

In this section, we study the asymptotic behavior of continuable solutions for the problem (1) in the space $C^{\alpha+1}_{1-\alpha,\ln}[t_0, T]$, $0 < t_0 < T \leq \infty$, defined by:

$$C^{\alpha+1}_{1-\alpha,\ln}[t_0, T] = \left\{u : (0, T] \to \mathbb{R} \mid u \in C_{1-\alpha,\ln}[t_0, T], \ \frac{d\left({}_H\mathcal{D}^{\alpha}_{t_0} u(t)\right)}{dt} \in C_{1-\alpha,\ln}[t_0, T]\right\}, \tag{16}$$

where the space $C_{1-\alpha,\ln}[t_0, T]$ is defined in (5).

The following two types of functions are used repeatedly in the rest of this paper.

Definition 5. *A function g is said to be $\Omega_\varkappa$-type function if it is continuous, nonnegative on (t_0, ∞) and*

$$\int_{t_0}^{\infty} \left(\ln \frac{t}{t_0}\right)^{\varkappa} g(t)dt < \infty, \ \varkappa = 0 \text{ or } 1.$$

Definition 6. *A function ψ is said to be Ψ-type function if it is continuous, positive, nondecreasing on $(0, \infty)$,*

$$\psi(a) \le b\psi\left(\frac{a}{b}\right) \text{ for all } \ge 1, b \ge 1,$$

and

$$\int_{\rho}^{t} \frac{ds}{\psi(s)} \to \infty \text{ as } t \to \infty \text{ for any } \rho > 0.$$

The two classes of functions introduced above are not empty, see the example provided in Section 4.

Consider the following nonlinear inequality:

$$w(t) \le a_1 + \left(\ln \frac{t}{t_0}\right)\left(a_2 + a_3 \int_{t_0}^{t}\left[g_1(s)\varphi_1(w(s)) + g_2(s)\varphi_2\left(\int_{t_0}^{s} g_3(\tau)\varphi_3(w(\tau))d\tau\right)\right]ds\right), \tag{17}$$

for all $t > t_0$, where a_1, a_2 and a_3 are positive constants, g_1, g_3 are Ω_1-type functions, g_2 is Ω_0-type function and $\varphi_j, j = 1,2,3$ are Ψ-type functions with $\varphi_1 \propto \varphi_2 \propto \varphi_3$.

Let

$$K := \Phi_3(b_3) + \int_{t_0}^{t_0 e} g_3(s)ds, \tag{18}$$

and

$$K_1 := \Phi_3(c_2) + \int_{t_0 e}^{\infty}\left(\ln \frac{t}{t_0}\right)g_3(t)dt, \tag{19}$$

where

$$\begin{aligned}
b_3 &= \Phi_2^{-1}\left(\Phi_2(b_2) + a_3 \int_{t_0}^{t_0 e} g_2(s)ds\right), \ b_2 = \Phi_1^{-1}\left(\Phi_1(a_1 + a_2) + a_3 \int_{t_0}^{t_0 e} g_1(s)ds\right), \\
c_2 &= \Phi_2^{-1}\left(\Phi_2(c_1) + a_3 \int_{t_0 e}^{\infty} g_2(t)dt\right), \ c_1 = \Phi_1^{-1}\left(\Phi_1(K_2) + a_3 \int_{t_0 e}^{\infty}\left(\ln \frac{t}{t_0}\right)g_1(t)dt\right), \\
K_2 &= a_1 + a_2 + a_3\varphi_1\left(\Phi_3^{-1}(K)\right)\int_{t_0}^{t_0 e} g_1(s)ds + a_3\varphi_2\left(\varphi_3\left(\Phi_3^{-1}(K)\right)\int_{t_0}^{t_0 e} g_3(\tau)d\tau\right)\int_{t_0}^{t_0 e} g_2(s)ds,
\end{aligned} \tag{20}$$

and Φ_j^{-1} is the inverse functions of $\Phi_j(x) = \int_{\rho}^{x} \frac{ds}{\varphi_j(s)}, j = 1,2,3, x > \rho > 0$.

A generalized version of Lemma 8 is introduced below. We shall provide an estimate for an integral term that arises later in our present problem. Although this estimate is not the best possible, it ensures that such an integral is bounded, which is exactly what we will need to prove our results below.

Theorem 1. *Suppose that $w(t)$ is a continuous nonnegative function on (t_0, ∞) satisfying Inequality (17) for all $t > t_0$, a_1, a_2 and a_3 are positive constants, g_1, g_3 are Ω_1-type functions, g_2 is Ω_0-type function and $\varphi_j, j = 1,2,3$, are Ψ-type functions with $\varphi_1 \propto \varphi_2 \propto \varphi_3$. Then,*

$$w(t) \le \Phi_3^{-1}(K) \text{ for all } t_0 < t < t_0 e, \tag{21}$$

and

$$w(t) \le \Phi_3^{-1}(K_1)\left(\ln \frac{t}{t_0}\right) \text{ for all } t \ge t_0 e, \tag{22}$$

where K and K_1 are given in (18) and (19), respectively.

Proof. For $t_0 < t < t_0 e$, the inequality (17) becomes:

$$w(t) \leq a_1 + a_2 + a_3 \int_{t_0}^{t} \left[g_1(s)\varphi_1(w(s)) + g_2(s)\varphi_2\left(\int_{t_0}^{s} g_3(\tau)\varphi_3(w(\tau))d\tau \right) \right] ds, t_0 < t < t_0 e, \tag{23}$$

and Lemma 8 is applicable. The relation (21) follows immediately.

For the case $t \geq t_0 e$, we have $\ln \frac{t}{t_0} \geq 1$ and (17) may be rewritten as:

$$\begin{aligned} \frac{w(t)}{\ln \frac{t}{t_0}} &\leq a_1 + a_2 + a_3 \int_{t_0}^{t} \left[g_1(s)\varphi_1(w(s)) + g_2(s)\varphi_2\left(\int_{t_0}^{s} g_3(\tau)\varphi_3(w(\tau))d\tau \right) \right] ds \\ &\leq a_1 + a_2 + a_3 \int_{t_0}^{t_0 e} \left[g_1(s)\varphi_1(w(s)) + g_2(s)\varphi_2\left(\int_{t_0}^{s} g_3(\tau)\varphi_3(w(\tau))d\tau \right) \right] ds \\ &\quad + a_3 \int_{t_0 e}^{t} \left[g_1(s)\varphi_1(w(s)) + g_2(s)\varphi_2\left(\int_{t_0}^{s} g_3(\tau)\varphi_3(w(\tau))d\tau \right) \right] ds. \end{aligned} \tag{24}$$

In virtue of the estimate (21) together with the continuity and monotonicity of the functions $\varphi_i, i = 1,2,3$, we get:

$$\frac{w(t)}{\ln \frac{t}{t_0}} \leq K_2 + a_3 \int_{t_0 e}^{t} \left[g_1(s)\varphi_1(w(s)) + g_2(s)\varphi_2\left(\int_{t_0}^{s} g_3(\tau)\varphi_3(w(\tau))d\tau \right) \right] ds, \tag{25}$$

where K_2 is the constant given in (20).

Let

$$z := z_1 + z_2 + z_3, \tag{26}$$

where

$$\begin{aligned} z_1(t) &:= K_2 + a_3 \int_{t_0 e}^{t} g_1(s)\varphi_1(w(s))ds, \; t \geq t_0 e, \\ z_2(t) &:= a_3 \int_{t_0 e}^{t} g_2(s)\varphi_2(z_3(s))ds, \; t \geq t_0 e, \\ z_3(t) &:= \int_{t_0}^{t} g_3(s)\varphi_3(w(s))ds, \; t > t_0. \end{aligned} \tag{27}$$

It is clear that

$$\frac{w(t)}{\ln \frac{t}{t_0}} < z(t) \text{ for all } t \geq t_0 e. \tag{28}$$

In light of the types of the functions g_i, and $\varphi_i, i = 1,2,3$, see Definitions 5 and 6, differentiating z yields:

$$\begin{aligned} z'(t) &= a_3 g_1(t)\varphi_1(w(t)) + a_3 g_2(t)\varphi_2(z_3(t)) + g_3(t)\varphi_3(w(t)) \\ &\leq a_3 g_1(t)\left(\ln \frac{t}{t_0}\right)\varphi_1\left(\frac{w(t)}{\ln \frac{t}{t_0}}\right) + a_3 g_2(t)\varphi_2(z(t)) + g_3(t)\left(\ln \frac{t}{t_0}\right)\varphi_3\left(\frac{w(t)}{\ln \frac{t}{t_0}}\right) \\ &\leq a_3\left(\ln \frac{t}{t_0}\right) g_1(t)\varphi_1(z(t)) + a_3 g_2(t)\varphi_2(z(t)) + \left(\ln \frac{t}{t_0}\right) g_3(t)\varphi_3(z(t)), t \geq t_0 e. \end{aligned} \tag{29}$$

Now, we integrate both sides of (29) over the interval $[t_0 e, t]$ to find:

$$\begin{aligned} z(t) &\leq z(t_0 e) + a_3 \int_{t_0 e}^{t} \left(\ln \frac{s}{t_0}\right) g_1(s)\varphi_1(z(s))ds + a_3 \int_{t_0 e}^{t} g_2(s)\varphi_2(z(s))ds \\ &\quad + \int_{t_0 e}^{t} \left(\ln \frac{s}{t_0}\right) g_3(s)\varphi_3(z(s))ds. \end{aligned} \tag{30}$$

Applying Lemma 7 with $\eta_1(t) = a_3\left(\ln \frac{t}{t_0}\right)g_1(t)$, $\eta_2(t) = a_3 g_2(t)$, $\eta_3(t) = \left(\ln \frac{t}{t_0}\right)g_3(t)$ and $T_1 = \infty$ (by assumption $\int_\rho^\infty \frac{d\tau}{\varphi_i(\tau)} = \infty$, $i = 1,2,3$ for any $\rho > 0$), the inequality (30) leads to:

$$z(t) \leq \Phi_3^{-1}(K_1), \text{ for all } t \geq t_0 e,$$

as desired. □

From now on, we assume that the functions f and h on the right hand-side of (1), satisfy the conditions below:

(A$_1$) $f(t,u,v) : (t_0,\infty) \times \mathbb{R}^2 \to \mathbb{R}$ is a $C_{1-\alpha,\ln}[t_0,\infty)$ function in $E_1 = \{(t,u,v) : t > t_0 > 0, u, v \in C_{1-\alpha,\ln}[t_0,\infty)\}$.

(A$_2$) $h(t,s,u)$ is a continuous function in $E_2 = \{(t,s,u) : t_0 \leq s < t < \infty, u \in C_{1-\alpha,\ln}[t_0,\infty)\}$.

(A$_3$) There are Ω_1-type functions g_1, g_3, an Ω_0-type function g_2 and Ψ-type functions φ_i, $i = 1,2,3$ with $\varphi_1 \propto \varphi_2 \propto \varphi_3$ such that:

$$|f(t,u,v)| \leq g_1(t)\varphi_1\left(\left(\ln \frac{t}{t_0}\right)^{1-\alpha+\alpha_1}|u|\right) + g_2(t)\varphi_2(|v|),\ (t,u,v) \in E_1,$$

$$|h(t,s,u)| \leq g_3(s)\varphi_3\left(\left(\ln \frac{s}{t_0}\right)^{1-\alpha+\alpha_2}|u|\right),\ (t,s,u) \in E_2,$$

$$0 \leq \alpha_1 < \alpha < 1 \text{ and } 0 \leq \alpha_2 < \alpha < 1.$$

Functions satisfying the above hypotheses are given in Section 4.

In the next result, we shall show that the solution for Problem (1) satisfies the useful nonlinear inequality below.

Lemma 9. *Suppose that $u(t)$ is a $C^{\alpha+1}_{1-\alpha,\ln}[t_0,\infty)$-solution for Problem (1) and the functions f and h satisfy (A$_1$), (A$_2$) and (A$_3$). Then,*

$$\left(\ln \frac{t}{t_0}\right)^{1-\alpha}|u(t)| \leq v(t),\ t > t_0, \tag{31}$$

and

$$\left(\ln \frac{t}{t_0}\right)^{1-\alpha+\alpha_j}\left|\left({}_H\mathcal{D}^{\alpha_j}_{t_0}u\right)(t)\right| \leq v_j(t),\ t > t_0, \tag{32}$$

where

$$\begin{aligned} v(t) &= \frac{|u_1|}{\Gamma(\alpha)} + \frac{\ln \frac{t}{t_0}}{\Gamma(\alpha+1)}\left\{|u_2| + \int_{t_0}^t \left[g_1(s)\varphi_1\left(\left(\ln \frac{s}{t_0}\right)^{1-\alpha+\alpha_1}\left|\left({}_H\mathcal{D}^{\alpha_1}_{t_0}u\right)(s)\right|\right)\right.\right. \\ &\quad \left.\left. + g_2(s)\varphi_2\left(\int_{t_0}^\tau g_3(\tau)\varphi_3\left(\left(\ln \frac{\tau}{t_0}\right)^{1-\alpha+\alpha_2}\left|\left({}_H\mathcal{D}^{\alpha_2}_{t_0}u\right)(\tau)\right|\right)d\tau\right)\right]ds\right\}, \end{aligned} \tag{33}$$

and

$$\begin{aligned} v_j(t) &= \frac{|u_1|}{\Gamma(\alpha-\alpha_j)} + \frac{\ln \frac{t}{t_0}}{\Gamma(\alpha-\alpha_j+1)}\left\{|u_2| + \int_{t_0}^t \left[g_1(s)\varphi_1\left(\left(\ln \frac{s}{t_0}\right)^{1-\alpha+\alpha_1}\left|\left({}_H\mathcal{D}^{\alpha_1}_{t_0}u\right)(s)\right|\right)\right.\right. \\ &\quad \left.\left. + g_2(s)\varphi_2\left(\int_{t_0}^\tau g_3(\tau)\varphi_3\left(\left(\ln \frac{\tau}{t_0}\right)^{1-\alpha+\alpha_2}\left|\left({}_H\mathcal{D}^{\alpha_2}_{t_0}u\right)(\tau)\right|\right)d\tau\right)\right]ds\right\}, \end{aligned} \tag{34}$$

for all $t > t_0$ and $j = 1,2$.

Proof. Firstly, we recall the relations (12) and (13) from the proof of Lemma 5,

$$\begin{aligned} u(t) &= \frac{u_1\left(\ln\frac{t}{t_0}\right)^{\alpha-1}}{\Gamma(\alpha)} + \frac{u_2\left(\ln\frac{t}{t_0}\right)^{\alpha}}{\Gamma(\alpha+1)} + \frac{1}{\Gamma(\alpha)}\int_{t_0}^{t}\left(\ln\frac{t}{s}\right)^{\alpha-1} \\ &\times \int_{t_0}^{s} f\left(\tau, \left({}_H\mathcal{D}_{t_0}^{\alpha_1}u\right)(\tau), \int_{t_0}^{\tau} h(\tau,\sigma,\left({}_H\mathcal{D}_{t_0}^{\alpha_2}u\right)(\sigma))d\sigma\right)d\tau\frac{ds}{s},\ t>t_0, \end{aligned} \tag{35}$$

$$\begin{aligned} u(t) &= \frac{u_1\left(\ln\frac{t}{t_0}\right)^{\alpha-1}}{\Gamma(\alpha)} + \frac{u_2\left(\ln\frac{t}{t_0}\right)^{\alpha}}{\Gamma(\alpha+1)} + \frac{1}{\Gamma(\alpha+1)}\int_{t_0}^{t}\left(\ln\frac{t}{\tau}\right)^{\alpha} \\ &\times f\left(\tau, \left({}_H\mathcal{D}_{t_0}^{\alpha_1}u\right)(\tau), \int_{t_0}^{\tau} h(\tau,\sigma,\left({}_H\mathcal{D}_{t_0}^{\alpha_2}u\right)(\sigma))d\sigma\right)d\tau,\ t>t_0. \end{aligned} \tag{36}$$

Equation (36) leads to the following bound on $|u(t)|$,

$$\begin{aligned} |u(t)| &\le \frac{|u_1|\left(\ln\frac{t}{t_0}\right)^{\alpha-1}}{\Gamma(\alpha)} + \frac{|u_2|\left(\ln\frac{t}{t_0}\right)^{\alpha}}{\Gamma(\alpha+1)} + \frac{\left(\ln\frac{t}{t_0}\right)^{\alpha}}{\Gamma(\alpha+1)} \\ &\times \int_{t_0}^{t}\left|f\left(\tau, \left({}_H\mathcal{D}_{t_0}^{\alpha_1}u\right)(\tau), \int_{t_0}^{\tau} h(\tau,\sigma,\left({}_H\mathcal{D}_{t_0}^{\alpha_2}u\right)(\sigma))d\sigma\right)\right|d\tau, t>t_0, \end{aligned} \tag{37}$$

or

$$\begin{aligned} \left(\ln\frac{t}{t_0}\right)^{1-\alpha}|u(t)| &\le \frac{|u_1|}{\Gamma(\alpha)} + \frac{|u_2|\ln\frac{t}{t_0}}{\Gamma(\alpha+1)} + \frac{\ln\frac{t}{t_0}}{\Gamma(\alpha+1)} \\ &\times \int_{t_0}^{t}\left|f\left(\tau, \left({}_H\mathcal{D}_{t_0}^{\alpha_1}u\right)(\tau), \int_{t_0}^{\tau} h(\tau,\sigma,\left({}_H\mathcal{D}_{t_0}^{\alpha_2}u\right)(\sigma))d\sigma\right)\right|d\tau, \end{aligned} \tag{38}$$

for all $t > t_0$, which, in the light of the hypothesis ($\mathbf{A}_3$), leads to (31) as desired.

Now, apply the Hadamard differentiation operator ${}_H\mathcal{D}_{t_0}^{\alpha_j}$, $j = 1, 2$ to (35), then employ Lemmas 1 and 2 (with $\beta = \alpha_j$ and $\gamma = 1-\alpha$, see (16)) to get:

$$\begin{aligned} \left({}_H\mathcal{D}_{t_0}^{\alpha_j}u\right)(t) &= \frac{u_1\left(\ln\frac{t}{t_0}\right)^{\alpha-\alpha_j-1}}{\Gamma(\alpha-\alpha_j)} + \frac{u_2\left(\ln\frac{t}{t_0}\right)^{\alpha-\alpha_j}}{\Gamma(\alpha-\alpha_j+1)} + \frac{1}{\Gamma(\alpha-\alpha_j)}\int_{t_0}^{t}\left(\ln\frac{t}{s}\right)^{\alpha-\alpha_j-1} \\ &\times \int_{t_0}^{s} f\left(\tau, \left({}_H\mathcal{D}_{t_0}^{\alpha_1}u\right)(\tau), \int_{t_0}^{\tau} h(\tau,\sigma,\left({}_H\mathcal{D}_{t_0}^{\alpha_2}u\right)(\sigma))d\sigma\right)d\tau\frac{ds}{s},\ t>t_0. \end{aligned} \tag{39}$$

In a similar way to that used to obtain (36), the relation (39) reduces to:

$$\begin{aligned} \left({}_H\mathcal{D}_{t_0}^{\alpha_j}u\right)(t) &= \frac{u_1\left(\ln\frac{t}{t_0}\right)^{\alpha-\alpha_j-1}}{\Gamma(\alpha-\alpha_j)} + \frac{u_2\left(\ln\frac{t}{t_0}\right)^{\alpha-\alpha_j}}{\Gamma(\alpha-\alpha_j+1)} + \frac{1}{\Gamma(\alpha-\alpha_j+1)}\int_{t_0}^{t}\left(\ln\frac{t}{\tau}\right)^{\alpha-\alpha_j} \\ &\times f\left(\tau, \left({}_H\mathcal{D}_{t_0}^{\alpha_1}u\right)(\tau), \int_{t_0}^{\tau} h(\tau,\sigma,\left({}_H\mathcal{D}_{t_0}^{\alpha_2}u\right)(\sigma))d\sigma\right)d\tau,\ t>t_0, \end{aligned} \tag{40}$$

and consequently,

$$\begin{aligned}\left|\left({}_H\mathcal{D}^{\alpha_j}_{t_0}u\right)(t)\right| &\le \frac{|u_1|\left(\ln\frac{t}{t_0}\right)^{\alpha-\alpha_j-1}}{\Gamma(\alpha-\alpha_j)}+\frac{|u_2|\left(\ln\frac{t}{t_0}\right)^{\alpha-\alpha_j}}{\Gamma(\alpha-\alpha_j+1)}+\frac{1}{\Gamma(\alpha-\alpha_j+1)}\int_{t_0}^{t}\left(\ln\frac{t}{\tau}\right)^{\alpha-\alpha_j}\\ &\times\left|f\left(\tau,\left({}_H\mathcal{D}^{\alpha_1}_{t_0}u\right)(\tau),\int_{t_0}^{\tau}h(\tau,\sigma,\left({}_H\mathcal{D}^{\alpha_2}_{t_0}u\right)(\sigma))d\sigma\right)\right|d\tau\\ &\le \frac{|u_1|\left(\ln\frac{t}{t_0}\right)^{\alpha-\alpha_j-1}}{\Gamma(\alpha-\alpha_j)}+\frac{\left(\ln\frac{t}{t_0}\right)^{\alpha-\alpha_j}}{\Gamma(\alpha-\alpha_j+1)}\Big[\,|u_2|+\\ &\int_{t_0}^{t}\left|f\left(\tau,\left({}_H\mathcal{D}^{\alpha_1}_{t_0}u\right)(\tau),\int_{t_0}^{\tau}h(\tau,\sigma,\left({}_H\mathcal{D}^{\alpha_2}_{t_0}u\right)(\sigma))d\sigma\right)\right|d\tau\Big],\ t>t_0,\end{aligned} \tag{41}$$

which yields, in light of the hypothesis ($\mathbf{A}_3$), the desired result in (32) and completes the proof. □

The main result of this section is given below.

Theorem 2. *Suppose that the hypotheses (A_1), (A_2) and (A_3) are satisfied, then there exists a real number r such that any solution $u\in C^{\alpha+1}_{1-\alpha,\ln}[t_0,\infty)$ of Problem (1), has the following asymptotic property* $\lim\limits_{t\to\infty}\frac{u(t)}{\left(\ln\frac{t}{t_0}\right)^{\alpha}}=r$.

Proof. Let us start by recalling the relations (31) and (32) in Lemma 9,

$$\left(\ln\frac{t}{t_0}\right)^{1-\alpha}|u(t)|\le v(t),\ t>t_0, \tag{42}$$

and

$$\left(\ln\frac{t}{t_0}\right)^{1-\alpha+\alpha_j}\left|\left({}_H\mathcal{D}^{\alpha_j}_{t_0}u\right)(t)\right|\le v_j(t),\ t>t_0,\ j=1,2, \tag{43}$$

where u is a $C^{\alpha+1}_{1-\alpha,\ln}[t_0,\infty)$-solution for Problem (1), $v(t)$ and $v_j(t)$, $j=1,2$ are given in (33) and (34), respectively.

Let

$$\begin{aligned} a_1 &= |u_1|\max_{j=1,2}\left\{\frac{1}{\Gamma(\alpha)},\frac{1}{\Gamma(\alpha-\alpha_j)}\right\},\ a_2=|u_2|\max_{j=1,2}\left\{\frac{1}{\Gamma(\alpha+1)},\frac{1}{\Gamma(\alpha-\alpha_j+1)}\right\},\\ a_3 &= \max_{j=1,2}\left\{\frac{1}{\Gamma(\alpha+1)},\frac{1}{\Gamma(\alpha-\alpha_j+1)}\right\},\end{aligned} \tag{44}$$

and

$$\begin{aligned} w(t) &= a_1+\left(\ln\frac{t}{t_0}\right)\left\{a_2+a_3\int_{t_0}^{t}\left[g_1(s)\varphi_1\left(\left(\ln\frac{s}{t_0}\right)^{1-\alpha+\alpha_1}\left|\left({}_H\mathcal{D}^{\alpha_1}_{t_0}u\right)(s)\right|\right)\right.\right.\\ &\left.\left.+g_2(s)\varphi_2\left(\int_{t_0}^{\tau}g_3(\tau)\varphi_3\left(\left(\ln\frac{\tau}{t_0}\right)^{1-\alpha+\alpha_2}\left|\left({}_H\mathcal{D}^{\alpha_2}_{t_0}u\right)(\tau)\right|\right)d\tau\right)\right]ds\right\},\ t>t_0,\end{aligned} \tag{45}$$

then,

$$v(t)\le w(t)\text{ and }v_j(t)\le w(t)\text{ for all }t>t_0,\ j=1,2. \tag{46}$$

From the nondecreasingness property of the functions φ_i, $i=1,2,3$, we have:

$$\begin{aligned} w(t) &= a_1 + \left(\ln\frac{t}{t_0}\right)\left\{a_2 + a_3\int_{t_0}^{t}\left[g_1(s)\varphi_1(v_1(s)) + g_2(s)\varphi_2\left(\int_{t_0}^{\tau} g_3(\tau)\varphi_3(v_2(\tau))d\tau\right)\right]ds\right\} \\ &\le a_1 + \left(\ln\frac{t}{t_0}\right)\left\{a_2 + a_3\int_{t_0}^{t}\left[g_1(s)\varphi_1(w(s)) + g_2(s)\varphi_2\left(\int_{t_0}^{\tau} g_3(\tau)\varphi_3(w(\tau))d\tau\right)\right]ds\right\}, \end{aligned}$$

for all $t > t_0$, which is Inequality (17). Therefore, we get from Theorem 1 that:

$$w(t) \le \left(\ln\frac{t}{t_0}\right)\Phi_3^{-1}(K_1) \text{ for all } t \ge t_0 e, \tag{47}$$

and as a consequence of the estimates (42) and (46), we find:

$$\left(\ln\frac{t}{t_0}\right)^{1-\alpha}|u(t)| \le \left(\ln\frac{t}{t_0}\right)\Phi_3^{-1}(K_1) \text{ for all } t > t_0 e, \tag{48}$$

or

$$\frac{|u(t)|}{\left(\ln\frac{t}{t_0}\right)^{\alpha}} \le K_3 := \Phi_3^{-1}(K_1) \text{ for all } t > t_0 e, \tag{49}$$

where K_1 is as in (19).

Now, in the light of Hypothesis ($\mathbf{A}_3$), and the inequalities (43) and (46), we deduce that:

$$\begin{aligned} \mathcal{J} \;:&= \left|\int_{t_0}^{t} f\left(s, \left({}_H\mathcal{D}_{t_0}^{\alpha_1}u\right)(s), \int_{t_0}^{s} h(s,\tau,\left({}_H\mathcal{D}_{t_0}^{\alpha_2}u\right)(\tau))d\tau\right)ds\right| \\ &\le \int_{t_0}^{t}\left|f\left(s, \left({}_H\mathcal{D}_{t_0}^{\alpha_1}u\right)(s), \int_{t_0}^{s} h(s,\tau,\left({}_H\mathcal{D}_{t_0}^{\alpha_2}u\right)(\tau))d\tau\right)\right|ds \\ &\le \int_{t_0}^{t} g_1(s)\varphi_1\left(\left(\ln\frac{s}{t_0}\right)^{1-\alpha+\alpha_1}\left|\left({}_H\mathcal{D}_{t_0}^{\alpha_1}u\right)(s)\right|\right)ds + \int_{t_0}^{t} g_2(s) \\ &\quad\times\varphi_2\left(\int_{t_0}^{s} g_3(\tau)\varphi_3\left(\left(\ln\frac{\tau}{t_0}\right)^{1-\alpha+\alpha_2}\left|\left({}_H\mathcal{D}_{t_0}^{\alpha_2}u\right)(\tau)\right|\right)d\tau\right)ds \\ &\le \int_{t_0}^{t_0 e} g_1(s)\varphi_1(w(s))ds + \int_{t_0}^{t_0 e} g_2(s)\varphi_2\left(\int_{t_0}^{s} g_3(\tau)\varphi_3(w(\tau))d\tau\right)ds \\ &\quad+ \int_{t_0 e}^{t} g_1(s)\varphi_1(w(s))ds + \int_{t_0 e}^{t} g_2(s)\varphi_2\left(\int_{t_0}^{s} g_3(\tau)\varphi_3(w(\tau))d\tau\right)ds \\ &= \mathcal{J}_1 + \mathcal{J}_2. \end{aligned} \tag{50}$$

The first integral,

$$\begin{aligned} \mathcal{J}_1 \;:&= \int_{t_0}^{t_0 e} g_1(s)\varphi_1(w(s))ds + \int_{t_0}^{t_0 e} g_2(s)\varphi_2\left(\int_{t_0}^{s} g_3(\tau)\varphi_3(w(\tau))d\tau\right)ds \\ &\le \int_{t_0}^{t_0 e} g_1(s)\varphi_1\left(\Phi_3^{-1}(K)\right)ds + \int_{t_0}^{t_0 e} g_2(s)\varphi_2\left(\int_{t_0}^{s} g_3(\tau)\varphi_3\left(\Phi_3^{-1}(K)\right)d\tau\right)ds \\ &\le \varphi_1(K_4)\int_{t_0}^{t_0 e} g_1(s)ds + \int_{t_0}^{t_0 e} g_2(s)\varphi_2\left(\varphi_3(K_4)\int_{t_0}^{s} g_3(\tau)d\tau\right)ds \end{aligned} \tag{51}$$

is finite by (21) from Theorem 1, $K_4 := \Phi_3^{-1}(K)$ and K is given in (18).

The second integral,

$$\mathcal{J}_2 := \int_{t_0 e}^{t} g_1(s)\varphi_1(w(s))ds + \int_{t_0 e}^{t} g_2(s)\varphi_2\left(\int_{t_0}^{s} g_3(\tau)\varphi_3(w(\tau))d\tau\right)ds,\ t \ge t_0 e, \tag{52}$$

can be estimated in view of (47), Theorem 1 and the type of the functions $\varphi_i, i = 1,2,3$ as follows:

$$\begin{aligned}\mathcal{J}_2 &\leq \int_{t_0e}^{t}\left(\ln\frac{s}{t_0}\right)g_1(s)\varphi_1(K_3)ds + \int_{t_0e}^{t} g_2(s)\varphi_2\left(\int_{t_0}^{t_0e} g_3(\tau)\varphi_3(K_4)d\tau\right. \\ &\quad \left.+\int_{t_0e}^{s}\left(\ln\frac{\tau}{t_0}\right)g_3(\tau)\varphi_3(K_3)d\tau\right)ds \\ &\leq \varphi_1(K_3)\int_{t_0e}^{t}\left(\ln\frac{s}{t_0}\right)g_1(s)ds + \int_{t_0e}^{t} g_2(s)\varphi_2\left(\varphi_3(K_4)\int_{t_0}^{t_0e} g_3(\tau)d\tau\right. \\ &\quad \left.+\varphi_3(K_3)\int_{t_0e}^{s}\left(\ln\frac{\tau}{t_0}\right)g_3(\tau)d\tau\right)ds, \text{ for all } t \geq t_0e. \end{aligned} \tag{53}$$

Since g_1 and g_3 are Ω_1-type functions and g_2 is an Ω_0-type function, we see that the integral $\mathcal{J}_2$ is uniformly bounded and so is the integral $\mathcal{J}$.

Therefore, the integral $\int_{t_0}^{t} f\left(s, \left({}_H\mathcal{D}_{t_0}^{\alpha_1}u\right)(s), \int_{t_0}^{s} h(s,\tau,\left({}_H\mathcal{D}_{t_0}^{\alpha_2}u\right)(\tau))d\tau\right)ds$ absolutely convergent and, consequently,

$$\lim_{t\to\infty}\int_{t_0}^{t} f\left(s, \left({}_H\mathcal{D}_{t_0}^{\alpha_1}u\right)(s), \int_{t_0}^{s} h(s,\tau,\left({}_H\mathcal{D}_{t_0}^{\alpha_2}u\right)(\tau))d\tau\right)ds < \infty, \tag{54}$$

Using Lemma 5, there exits a finite real number r such that:

$$\lim_{t\to\infty}\frac{u(t)}{\left(\ln\frac{t}{t_0}\right)^{\alpha}} = \frac{1}{\Gamma(\alpha+1)}\left(u_2 + \lim_{t\to\infty}\int_{t_0}^{t} f\left(s, \left({}_H\mathcal{D}_{t_0}^{\alpha_1}u\right)(s), \int_{t_0}^{s} h(s,\tau,\left({}_H\mathcal{D}_{t_0}^{\alpha_2}u\right)(\tau))d\tau\right)ds\right) = r, \tag{55}$$

as wanted. □

Remark 2. *If the condition ($\mathbf{A}_3$) is replaced by the condition:*

($\mathbf{A}_4$) *There are Ω_1-type functions ξ_1, ξ_2 and Ψ-type functions ϕ_i, $i = 1,2,3$ with $\phi_1\phi_2 \propto \phi_3$ such that*

$$|f(t,u,v)| \leq \xi_1(t)\phi_1\left(\left(\ln\frac{t}{t_0}\right)^{1-\alpha+\alpha_1}|u|\right)\phi_2(|v|),\ (t,u,v) \in E_1,\ 0 \leq \alpha_1 < \alpha < 1,$$

and

$$|h(t,s,u)| \leq \xi_2(s)\phi_3\left(\left(\ln\frac{s}{t_0}\right)^{1-\alpha+\alpha_2}|u|\right),\ (t,s,u) \in E_2,\ 0 \leq \alpha_2 < \alpha < 1,$$

then the conclusion of Theorem 2 is still valid. We state this fact below.

Theorem 3. *Suppose that the functions f and h satisfy the conditions ($\mathbf{A}_1$), ($\mathbf{A}_2$) and ($\mathbf{A}_4$). Then, there exists a real number r such that any solution $u \in C_{1-\alpha,\ln}^{\alpha+1}[t_0,\infty)$ for Problem (1) satisfies $\lim_{t\to\infty}\frac{u(t)}{\left(\ln\frac{t}{t_0}\right)^{\alpha}} = r$.*

The proof is skipped as it can be shown in a similar manner to that used in the proof of Theorem 2.

Remark 3. *The problem,*

$$\begin{cases} \left({}_H\mathcal{D}^{\alpha}_{t_0}u\right)'(t) = f\left(t, u(t), \int_{t_0}^{t} h(t,s,u(s))ds\right),\ t > t_0 > 0,\ 0 < \alpha < 1, \\ \left({}_H\mathcal{I}^{1-\alpha}_{t_0}u\right)(t_0^+) = u_1,\ \left({}_H\mathcal{D}^{\alpha}_{t_0}u\right)(t_0^+) = u_2,\ u_1, u_2 \in \mathbb{R}. \end{cases} \tag{56}$$

is a special case of Problem (1) *when* $\alpha_1 = \alpha_2 = 0$*. Therefore, we can conclude that there exists a constant* $r \in \mathbb{R}$ *such that any solution* $u \in C^{\alpha+1}_{1-\alpha,\ln}[t_0, \infty)$ *for Problem* (56) *satisfies* $\lim_{t\to\infty} \frac{u(t)}{\left(\ln \frac{t}{t_0}\right)^{\alpha}} = r.$

4. Example

Consider the initial value problem:

$$\begin{cases} \left({}_H\mathcal{D}^{\alpha}_{t_0}u\right)'(t) = t^{-\sigma_1}\left(\ln \frac{t}{t_0}\right)^{\beta_1}\left({}_H\mathcal{D}^{\alpha_1}_{t_0}u(t)\right)^{\gamma_1} + t^{-\sigma_2}\left(\ln \frac{t}{t_0}\right)^{\beta_2}\left[\int_{t_0}^{t}(t+s)^{-\sigma_3}\right. \\ \qquad \left. \times \left(\ln \frac{s}{t_0}\right)^{\beta_3}\left({}_H\mathcal{D}^{\alpha_2}_{t_0}u(s)\right)^{\gamma_3}ds\right]^{\gamma_2},\ t > t_0 > 0, \\ \left({}_H\mathcal{I}^{1-\alpha}_{t_0}u\right)(t_0^+) = u_1,\ \left({}_H\mathcal{D}^{\alpha}_{t_0}u\right)(t_0^+) = u_2,\ u_1, u_2 \in \mathbb{R}, \end{cases} \tag{57}$$

where $0 \le \alpha_1 < \alpha < 1$, $0 \le \alpha_2 < \alpha < 1$, $\sigma_j > 1$, $j = 1,2,3$, $\beta_1 > (1-\alpha+\alpha_1)\gamma_1 - 1$, $\beta_2 > -1$, $\beta_3 > (1-\alpha+\alpha_2)\gamma_3 - 1$ and $0 < \gamma_1 \le \gamma_2 \le \gamma_3 < 1$.

The source function,

$$f(t,u,v) = t^{-\sigma_1}\left(\ln \frac{t}{t_0}\right)^{\beta_1} u^{\gamma_1} + t^{-\sigma_2}\left(\ln \frac{t}{t_0}\right)^{\beta_2} v^{\gamma_2},\ t > t_0 > 0, \tag{58}$$

satisfies

$$\begin{aligned} &\left| f\left(t, {}_H\mathcal{D}^{\alpha_1}_{t_0}u(t), \int_{t_0}^{t} h\left(t,s,{}_H\mathcal{D}^{\alpha_2}_{t_0}u(s)\right)ds\right)\right| \\ = &\left| t^{-\sigma_1}\left(\ln \frac{t}{t_0}\right)^{\beta_1}\left({}_H\mathcal{D}^{\alpha_1}_{t_0}u(t)\right)^{\gamma_1} + t^{-\sigma_2}\left(\ln \frac{t}{t_0}\right)^{\beta_2}\left(\int_{t_0}^{t}(t+s)^{-\sigma_3}\right.\right. \\ &\left.\left. \times\left(\ln \frac{s}{t_0}\right)^{\beta_3}\left({}_H\mathcal{D}^{\alpha_2}_{t_0}u(s)\right)^{\gamma_3}ds\right)^{\gamma_2}\right| \\ \le\ & g_1(t)\varphi_1\left(\left(\ln \frac{t}{t_0}\right)^{1-\alpha+\alpha_1}\left|{}_H\mathcal{D}^{\alpha_1}_{t_0}u(t)\right|\right) + g_2(t)\varphi_2\left(\int_{t_0}^{t} g_3(s)\right. \\ &\left. \times\varphi_3\left(\left(\ln \frac{s}{t_0}\right)^{1-\alpha+\alpha_2}\left|{}_H\mathcal{D}^{\alpha_2}_{t_0}u(s)\right|\right)ds\right), \end{aligned}$$

with

$$\begin{aligned} h(t,s,u) &= (t+s)^{-\sigma_3}\left(\ln \frac{s}{t_0}\right)^{\beta_3}u^{\gamma_3},\ g_1(t) = t^{-\sigma_1}\left(\ln \frac{t}{t_0}\right)^{\beta_1+(\alpha-\alpha_1-1)\gamma_1}, \\ g_2(t) &= t^{-\sigma_2}\left(\ln \frac{t}{t_0}\right)^{\beta_2},\ g_3(t) = t^{-\sigma_3}\left(\ln \frac{t}{t_0}\right)^{\beta_3+(\alpha-\alpha_2-1)\gamma_3},\ \varphi_j(t) = t^{\gamma_j},\ t > t_0 > 0, \end{aligned}$$

where $\beta_1 > (1-\alpha+\alpha_1)\gamma_1 - 1$, $\beta_2 > -1$, $\beta_3 > (1-\alpha+\alpha_2)\gamma_3 - 1$, $\sigma_j > 1$, $j = 1,2,3$ and $0 < \gamma_1 \le \gamma_2 \le \gamma_3 \le 1$.

The functions g_j, $j = 1, 2, 3$ are continuous, nonnegative on (t_0, ∞),

$$\begin{aligned}\int_{t_0}^{t_0 e} g_1(t)dt &= \int_{t_0}^{t_0 e} \left(\ln \frac{t}{t_0}\right)^{\beta_1+(\alpha-\alpha_1-1)\gamma_1} \frac{dt}{t^{\sigma_1}} \leq \frac{1}{t_0^{\sigma_1-1}} \int_{t_0}^{t_0 e} \left(\ln \frac{t}{t_0}\right)^{\beta_1+(\alpha-\alpha_1-1)\gamma_1} \frac{dt}{t} \\ &= \frac{1}{t_0^{\sigma_1-1}} \int_0^1 s^{\beta_1+(\alpha-\alpha_1-1)\gamma_1} ds = \frac{1}{(\beta_1+(\alpha-\alpha_1-1)\gamma_1+1)t_0^{\sigma_1-1}} < \infty,\end{aligned}$$

$$\int_{t_0}^{t_0 e} g_3(t)dt = \int_{t_0}^{t_0 e} \left(\ln \frac{t}{t_0}\right)^{\beta_3+(\alpha-\alpha_2-1)\gamma_1} \frac{dt}{t^{\sigma_3}} \leq \frac{1}{(\beta_3+(\alpha-\alpha_3-1)\gamma_3+1)t_0^{\sigma_3-1}} < \infty,$$

and

$$\int_{t_0}^{t_0 e} g_2(t)dt = \int_{t_0}^{t_0 e} \left(\ln \frac{t}{t_0}\right)^{\beta_2} \frac{dt}{t^{\sigma_2}} \leq \frac{1}{t_0^{\sigma_2-1}} \int_{t_0}^{t_0 e} \left(\ln \frac{t}{t_0}\right)^{\beta_2} \frac{dt}{t} = \frac{1}{(\beta_2+1)t_0^{\sigma_2-1}} < \infty.$$

The function g_2 is an Ω_0-type because:

$$\begin{aligned}\int_{t_0 e}^{\infty} g_2(t)dt &= \int_{t_0 e}^{\infty} \left(\ln \frac{t}{t_0}\right)^{\beta_2} \frac{dt}{t^{\sigma_2}} = \frac{1}{t_0^{\sigma_2-1}} \int_{t_0 e}^{\infty} \left(\ln \frac{t}{t_0}\right)^{\beta_2} \left(\frac{t_0}{t}\right)^{\sigma_2-1} \frac{dt}{t} \\ &\leq \frac{1}{t_0^{\sigma_2-1}} \int_{t_0}^{\infty} \left(\ln \frac{t}{t_0}\right)^{\beta_2} e^{-(\sigma_2-1)\ln\frac{t}{t_0}} \frac{dt}{t} = \frac{1}{t_0^{\sigma_2-1}} \int_0^{\infty} s^{\beta_2} e^{-(\sigma_2-1)s} ds \\ &= \frac{1}{(\sigma_2-1)^{\beta_2+1} t_0^{\sigma_2-1}} \int_0^{\infty} \tau^{\beta_2} e^{-\tau} d\tau = \frac{\Gamma(\beta_2+1)}{(\sigma_2-1)^{\beta_2+1} t_0^{\sigma_2-1}} < \infty,\end{aligned}$$

whereas the functions g_1 and g_3 are Ω_1-type functions since

$$\begin{aligned}\int_{t_0 e}^{\infty} \left(\ln \frac{t}{t_0}\right) g_1(t)dt &= \int_{t_0 e}^{\infty} \left(\ln \frac{t}{t_0}\right)^{\beta_1+(\alpha-\alpha_1-1)\gamma_1+1} \frac{dt}{t^{\sigma_1}} \\ &\leq \frac{1}{t_0^{\sigma_1-1}} \int_{t_0}^{\infty} \left(\ln \frac{t}{t_0}\right)^{\beta_1+(\alpha-\alpha_1-1)\gamma_1+1} e^{-(\sigma_1-1)\ln\frac{t}{t_0}} \frac{dt}{t} \\ &= \frac{1}{t_0^{\sigma_1-1}} \int_0^{\infty} s^{\beta_1+(\alpha-\alpha_1-1)\gamma_1+1} e^{-(\sigma_1-1)s} ds \\ &= \frac{\Gamma(\beta_1+(\alpha-\alpha_1-1)\gamma_1+2)}{(\sigma_1-1)^{\beta_1+(\alpha-\alpha_1-1)\gamma_1+2} t_0^{\sigma_1-1}} < \infty,\end{aligned}$$

and

$$\int_{t_0 e}^{\infty} \left(\ln \frac{t}{t_0}\right) g_3(t)dt = \int_{t_0 e}^{\infty} \left(\ln \frac{t}{t_0}\right)^{\beta_3+(\alpha-\alpha_2-1)\gamma_3+1} \frac{dt}{t^{\sigma_3}} \leq \frac{\Gamma(\beta_3+(\alpha-\alpha_2-1)\gamma_3+2)}{(\sigma_3-1)^{\beta_3+(\alpha-\alpha_2-1)\gamma_3+2} t_0^{\sigma_3-1}} < \infty.$$

The functions $\varphi_j(t) = t^{\gamma_j}$, $j = 1, 2, 3$, $0 < \gamma_1 \leq \gamma_2 \leq \gamma_3 \leq 1$, are Ψ-type functions with $\varphi_1 \propto \varphi_2 \propto \varphi_3$. These three functions are continuous, positive, nondecreasing on $(0, \infty)$,

$$\varphi_j(a) = a^{\gamma_j} \leq b\left(\frac{a}{b}\right)^{\gamma_j} = b\varphi_j\left(\frac{a}{b}\right) \text{ for all } a \geq 1,\ b \geq 1,\ 0 < \gamma_j \leq 1,$$

and

$$\int_{\rho}^{x} \frac{dt}{\varphi_j(t)} = \int_{\rho}^{x} \frac{dt}{t^{\gamma_j}} \to \infty \text{ as } x \to \infty \text{ for any } \rho > 0.$$

As $0 < \gamma_1 \leq \gamma_2 \leq \gamma_3 \leq 1$, then φ_3/φ_2 and φ_2/φ_1 are nondecreasing functions and so $\varphi_1 \propto \varphi_2 \propto \varphi_3$.

Obviously, Conditions ($\mathbf{A}_1$), ($\mathbf{A}_2$) and ($\mathbf{A}_3$) are fulfilled with these functions and the hypotheses of Theorem 2 as well. Therefore, there exists a real constant $r \in \mathbb{R}$ such that solutions of Problem (57) satisfy $\lim_{t\to\infty} \frac{u(t)}{\left(\ln \frac{t}{t_0}\right)^{\alpha}} = r$.

5. Conclusions

In this article, we considered a fractional integro-differential problem with Hadamard-Type fractional derivatives. The nonlinear source function depends on a lower-order Hadamard fractional derivative of the state and an integral involving another lower-order Hadamard fractional derivative of the state. We assumed the boundedness of the nonlinearities in question by some special kinds of functions in some appropriate spaces. Under these nonlinear growth conditions, we demonstrated that solutions of the initial value fractional problem under consideration are not only bounded by logarithmic functions but actually they converge asymptotically to logarithmic functions.

Author Contributions: Conceptualization, A.M. and N.-E.T.; methodology, A.M. and N.-E.T.; validation, A.M. and N.-E.T.; formal analysis, A.M. and N.-E.T.; investigation, A.M.; writing original draft preparation, A.M.; writing, review and editing, N.-E.T.; Funding acquisition, A.M.; project administration, A.M. All authors have read and agreed to the published version of the manuscript.

Funding: This research and the APC were funded by King Fahd University of Petroleum and Minerals through project number SB191023.

Institutional Review Board Statement: Not applicable.

Informed Consent Statement: Not applicable.

Data Availability Statement: Not applicable.

Acknowledgments: The authors would like to acknowledge the support provided by King Fahd University of Petroleum and Minerals (KFUPM) through project number SB191023.

Conflicts of Interest: The authors declare no conflict of interest.

References

1. Halanay, A. On the asymptotic behavior of the solutions of an integro-differential equation. *J. Math. Anal. Appl.* **1965**, *10*, 319–324. [CrossRef]
2. Cohen, D.S. The asymptotic behavior of a class of nonlinear differential equations. *Proc. Am. Math. Soc.* **1967**, *18*, 607–609. [CrossRef]
3. Dannan, F.M. Integral inequalities of Gronwall-Bellman-Bihari type and asymptotic behavior of certain second order nonlinear differential equations. *J. Math. Anal. Appl.* **1985**, *108*, 151–164. [CrossRef]
4. Constantin, A. On the asymptotic behavior of second order nonlinear differential equations. *Rendiconti di Matematica e delle sue Applicazioni* **1993**, *13*, 627–634.
5. Philos, C.G.; Tsamatos, P.C. Solutions approaching polynomials at infinity to nonlinear ordinary differential equations. *Electron. J. Differ. Equ.* **2005**, *2005*, 1–25.
6. Mustafa, O.G.; Rogovchenko, Y.V. Asymptotic integration of a class of nonlinear differential equations. *Appl. Math. Lett.* **2006**, *19*, 849–853. [CrossRef]
7. Kilbas, A.A.; Srivastava, H.M.; Trujillo, J.J. *Theory and Applications of Fractional Differential Equations*; Elsevier Science Limited: Amsterdam, The Netherlands, 2006; Volume 204.
8. Magin, R.L.; Abdullah, O.; Baleanu, D.; Zhou, X.J. Anomalous diffusion expressed through fractional order differential operators in the Bloch-Torrey equation. *J. Magn. Reson.* **2008**, *190*, 255–270. [CrossRef]
9. Sabatier, J.; Agrawal, O.P.; Machado, J.T. *Advances in Fractional Calculus: Theoretical Developments and Applications in Physics and Engineering*; Springer: Berlin/Heidelberg, Germany, 2007. [CrossRef]
10. Shah, N.A.; Elnaqeeb, T.; Animasaun, I.; Mahsud, Y. Insight into the natural convection flow through a vertical cylinder using caputo time-fractional derivatives. *Int. J. Appl. Comput. Math.* **2018**, *4*, 1–18. [CrossRef]
11. Ahmad, A.M.; Furati, K.M.; Tatar, N.E. Asymptotic power type behavior of solutions to a nonlinear fractional integro-differential equation. *Electron. J. Differ. Equ.* **2017**, *2017*, 1–16.
12. Ahmad, A.M.; Furati, K.M.; Tatar, N.E. Asymptotic Behavior of Solutions for a Class of Fractional Integro-differential Equations. *Mediterr. J. Math.* **2018**, *15*, 188. [CrossRef]

13. Băleanu, D.; Mustafa, O.G. On the asymptotic integration of a class of sublinear fractional differential equations. *J. Math. Phys.* **2009**, *50*, 123520. [CrossRef]
14. Băleanu, D.; Mustafa, O.G.; Agarwal, R.P. Asymptotic integration of (1+ α)-order fractional differential equations. *Comput. Math. Appl.* **2011**, *62*, 1492–1500. [CrossRef]
15. Băleanu, D.; Agarwal, R.P.; Mustafa, O.G.; Coşulschi, M. Asymptotic integration of some nonlinear differential equations with fractional time derivative. *J. Phys. A Math. Theor.* **2011**, *44*, 055203. [CrossRef]
16. Brestovanska, E.; Medved', M. Asymptotic behavior of solutions to second-order differential equations with fractional derivative perturbations. *Electron. J. Differ. Equ.* **2014**, *2014*, 1–10.
17. Grace, S.R. On the oscillatory behavior of solutions of nonlinear fractional differential equations. *Appl. Math. Comput.* **2015**, *266*, 259–266. [CrossRef]
18. Medved', M. On the asymptotic behavior of solutions of nonlinear differential equations of integer and also of non-integer order. *Electron. J. Qual. Theory Differ. Equ.* **2012**, *10*, 1–9.
19. Medved', M. Asymptotic integration of some classes of fractional differential equations. *Tatra Mt. Math. Publ.* **2013**, *54*, 119–132. [CrossRef]
20. M. Medved' and M. Pospíšil. Asymptotic Integration of Fractional Differential Equations with Integrodifferential Right-Hand Side. *Math. Model. Anal.* **2015**, *20*, 471–489. [CrossRef]
21. Ahmad, A.M.; Furati, K.M.; Tatar, N.E. Boundedness and power-type decay of solutions for a class of generalized fractional Langevin equations. *Arab. J. Math.* **2019**, *8*, 79–94. [CrossRef]
22. Ahmad, A.M. On the Asymptotic Behavior of Solutions for a Fractional Differential Equation with a Singular Kernel. In Proceedings of the 24th International Conference on Circuits, Systems, Communications and Computers (CSCC), Chania, Greece, 19–22 July 2020; pp. 130–134. [CrossRef]
23. Ahmad, A.M. The Asymptotic Behavior of Solutions of a Fractional Integro-differential Equation. *WSEAS Trans. Syst. Control* **2020**, *15*, 341–348. [CrossRef]
24. Graef, J.R.; Grace, S.R.; Tunç, E. Asymptotic behavior of solutions of nonlinear fractional differential equations with Caputo-Type Hadamard derivatives. *Fract. Calc. Appl. Anal.* **2017**, *20*, 71–87. [CrossRef]
25. Kassim, M.D.; Tatar, N.E. Stability of logarithmic type for a Hadamard fractional differential problem. *J. Pseudo-Differ. Oper. Appl.* **2020**, *11*, 447–466. [CrossRef]
26. Kassim, M.D.; eddine Tatar, N. Asymptotic behavior of solutions of fractional differential equations with Hadamard fractional derivatives. *Fract. Calc. Appl. Anal.* **2021**, *24*, 483–508. [CrossRef]
27. Li, M.; Wang, J. Analysis of nonlinear Hadamard fractional differential equations via properties of Mittag-Leffler functions. *J. Appl. Math. Comput.* **2016**, *51*, 487–508. doi: [CrossRef]
28. Li, C.; Li, Z. Stability and Logarithmic Decay of the Solution to Hadamard-Type Fractional Differential Equation. *J. Nonlinear Sci.* **2021**, *31*, 1–60. [CrossRef]
29. Ahmad, B.; Alsaedi, A.; Ntouyas, S.K.; Tariboon, J. *Hadamard-Type Fractional Differential Equations, Inclusions and Inequalities*; Springer: Cham, Switzerland, 2017. [CrossRef]
30. Băleanu, D.; Diethelm, K.; Scalas, E.; Trujillo, J.J. *Fractional Calculus: Models and Numerical Methods*; World Scientific: Singapore, 2012; Volume 3.
31. De Barra, G. *Measure Theory and Integration*; Elsevier: Amsterdam, The Netherlands, 2003.
32. Bihari, I. A generalization of a lemma of Bellman and its application to uniqueness problems of differential equations. *Acta Math. Hung.* **1956**, *7*, 81–94. [CrossRef]
33. LaSalle, J. Uniqueness theorems and successive approximations. *Ann. Math.* **1949**, *50*, 722–730. [CrossRef]
34. Pinto, M. Integral inequalities of Bihari-type and applications. *Funkc. Ekvacioj* **1990**, *33*, 387–403.

MDPI
St. Alban-Anlage 66
4052 Basel
Switzerland
www.mdpi.com

MDPI Books Editorial Office
E-mail: books@mdpi.com
www.mdpi.com/books

www.ingramcontent.com/pod-product-compliance
Lightning Source LLC
LaVergne TN
LVHW070234100526
838202LV00015B/2128